TALES OF
SAN FRANCISCO

Tales of
San Francisco

Samuel Dickson

Stanford University
Stanford, California

Stanford University Press
Stanford, California
© 1947, 1949, 1955 by the Board of Trustees of
the Leland Stanford Junior University
Copyright renewed 1975 and 1977 by Barbara Dickson Gulmon and 1983 by Barbara
Dickson Gulmon, Catherine Dickson Scholes, and Helen Dickson Nestor
First published in this edition in 1957
Printed in the United States of America
Cloth ISBN 0-8047-0488-0
Paper ISBN 0-8047-2097-5
Last figure below indicates year of this printing:
01   00   99   98

CONTENTS

BOOK I · San Francisco Is Your Home

BOOK II San Francisco Kaleidoscope

BOOK ONE

SAN FRANCISCO IS YOUR HOME

For My Wife
and
For Our Granddaughter

CATHERINE SCHOLES

with our love of
San Francisco

Prologue

If I had had my way this book would have been called *San Francisco Kaleidoscope*. But at a round-table discussion the point was made that this generation, addicted to toy stratosphere planes and toy atomic bombs, would not know what a kaleidoscope was. There was, however, one member of the round table who sided with me.

"Why," he said, "that's absurd. Everybody knows what a kaleidoscope is. There's probably one in every family. As a matter of fact, we took ours out only the other evening. Had a very amusing time, too, looking at the pictures of the children through it."

Well, that settled it. In simple words we explained that what he referred to was not a kaleidoscope but a stereoscope.

"Then," he said, "just what is a kaleidoscope?"

A kaleidoscope is a cylindrical toy holding in its chamber bits of broken, colored glass. One end of the cylinder has a small aperture, and when it is held to the eye and the cylinder is revolved, the bits of glass, reflected in a mirror, fall into exciting and exquisite and ever-varying patterns and designs—just like life in San Francisco. There are bits of broken glass, fragments—some precious, some without value—odds and ends and ragtag scraps that, as they tumble out, form thrilling and lovely patterns. And, as in the kaleidoscope, so in the story of San Francisco, the more the bits are shaken up, the lovelier the patterns become. . . .

Sunday morning on Van Ness Avenue, before St. Mary's Cathedral, and little girls in white dresses and long pigtails to their waists, walking primly to their first Communion . . .

The Viennese orchestra at the Hofbrau Café playing "Where Has My Little Dog Gone?" while the patrons lift their seidels of Münchener and sing with the band . . .

A stout little man waddling fast as his short legs can carry him up the Jackson Street hill above Steiner, a black flute case under his arm. He is Elias Hecht, founder and sponsor of the San Francisco Chamber Music Society, hurrying to a rehearsal with Louis Persinger . . .

The sulphur smell of bunched California matches, relics of mining days, as the lamplighter kindles his taper to light the gas lamps on Clay Street . . .

The Seven-Day Bicycle Races in Mechanics' Pavilion . . .

Little Egypt dancing the hootchy-kootchy at the Midway Plaisance . . .

Teddy Webb and Ferris Hartman singing *The Mikado* at Idora Park . . .

Pastori's across the Bay, where you had your lunch under the trees with French bread soaked in garlic, great bowls of green salad with the dressing mixed at your table, porterhouse steaks two inches thick—black outside and red inside— and bottles of red wine and Brie cheese . . .

Frank Norris, Gelett Burgess, and Will Irwin walking down Montgomery Street, pausing to borrow a dollar from a friend, which dollar they drop, a block farther along, into the hat of Blind Joe, the Sansome Street panhandler . . .

The Estudillo House in San Leandro, where Sunday bicyclists stop to lunch beneath a great spreading grapevine, and the nine-course Sunday dinner with wine costs fifty cents . . .

Newsboys crying, *"Call, Chronicle, Examiner!* Read about it! Terrible murder in church belfry! The police have arrested Durant! Read about it!" . . .

Buffalo Bill and his Wild West Show in a sand lot in the Mission, with the stupendous spectacle of the Johnstown

4

flood . . .

Rabbi Voorsanger marching down Sutter Street to his Saturday morning pulpit, coattails flying in the wind, black beard flying in the wind, smoke from his huge black cigar wreathing his face . . .

Fire drill at the Pacific Heights School, with small boys falling out of line to run across the street and buy candy "brownies" at "Ossie's," the stationer's . . .

Rosie Murdock, at Polytechnic High School, arguing with her most stubborn pupil: "Every time I ask you to draw a pretty picture you draw a funny picture. That's not art! I just don't know what to do with you, Rube Goldberg!" . . .

The organ-grinder in Alta Plaza Park playing "Sweet Rosie O'Grady" and "Santa Lucia" . . .

John Tait, standing in the entrance of his Van Ness Avenue restaurant after the earthquake and fire, beaming and offering California champagne to the two bitter rival French champagne merchants, Ned Greenway and Dick Hotaling . . .

Sunset softly glowing on the windows of Old St. Mary's Church, and the character on the steps whispering, "Just one dollar for a trip through the mysteries of Chinatown. You'll see the slave girls, the opium dens, and the underground gambling hells all for one dollar" . . .

Blue-painted fishing boats putting out from Fisherman's Wharf at three in the morning, while an Italian girl and an Italian boy sit on the wharf, legs dangling, and sing "Torna a Sorrento" . . .

Teddy Roosevelt grinning, displaying his teeth, addressing two hundred fifty thousand San Franciscans in the colonnade of the Court of Nations at the 1915 Exposition . . .

Teddy Roosevelt, Jr., living with his wife on Pacific Avenue and confiding to me that San Francisco is the greatest city in the world and, even if his father protests, he intends to stay here the rest of his life . . .

Lincoln Park when it was a nine-hole golf course and the ninth hole was a straight drop of five hundred feet to a green at the ocean's edge directly beneath the eighth hole . . .

In 1896, the sister of a famous artist riding down Market Street on a bicycle, scandalizing the city by riding into the Palm Court of the Palace Hotel—wearing bloomers! . . .

Mascagni conducting the *première* of *Cavalleria Rusticana* . . .

Carriages circling around the music stand in Golden Gate Park while the band plays the "Semiramide Overture" . . .

The fog pouring through the Golden Gate at daybreak . . .

Sunlight at sunset on the windows of Buena Vista Heights . . .

The dolorous call of the foghorn on Alcatraz Island at night . . .

Moonlight on Telegraph Hill, and children dancing a saraband of shadows with a hillside goat . . .

Rain pouring down the California Street hill and rushing in pools through Chinatown alleys, reflecting the lights of lanterns and torches hanging above fruit stands and raw-meat stands and racks of skinned chickens . . .

The white waves beating their endless din on the rocks of Land's End . . .

The perfume of lavender and heliotrope and lemon verbena and geraniums in a thousand gardens . . .

6

In the tumbling, dancing patterns of the kaleidoscope, time has no meaning, and the figures are figures of a hundred years.

Just yesterday it was John Charles Thomas, swinging down the steps of the Bohemian Club, whistling for a cab; and seventy years ago it was "White Hat" McCarthy, strutting through the courts of the Palace Hotel, bowing right and left to people who had no idea who he was . . .

Here was old John Newbegin, sitting at the iron stove in the back of his Sutter Street bookstore, grumbling, "There are only two books worth reading—Bobbie Burns and the Bible.". . . And there was heavy, old Mo Gunst, sitting in his upholstered chair in the lobby of the St. Francis Hotel, day after day, year after year, his gnarled hands resting on the handle of his cane. And if you were of the uninitiate and, finding the chair empty, started to sit in it, a discreet bellhop would come up and whisper, "Sorry, sir. That chair is reserved for Mr. Gunst." Mo Gunst, whose little cigar stand on Kearny Street was the political hub of the city where the men who made the city and ran the city gathered and became known as the Cigarette Boys. And that shop became the nucleus of a great national chain . . .

"Kanaka" Davis, sitting in the warm sunshine of Mission Dolores, drinking mellow red wine with the padres and telling them of his dreams when, in 1840, he saw a great metropolis spread across the sand dunes of Yerba Buena . . .

William Chapman Ralston—Bill Ralston—driving his coach-and-six out the old Mission Road and down the Peninsula to his fabulous mansion in Belmont. And on the box, his uniformed hornsman sounding the long, brass coach trumpet to the delight of pursuing little boys . . . Bret

Harte, clumping down the steps of his small flat, a manuscript under his arm, shouting at his wife that he would never write another word, that no one appreciated art! And his wife grimly shouting after him, "Very well, Frank. Never write another word. But remember, I've got to eat even if you don't!" The manuscript was *The Luck of Roaring Camp* . . .

And Herman Heller, plump, shining-faced, hair growing thin, mounting the podium before a Sunday morning moving-picture audience, announcing, "For the first time in history you will see your moving picture displayed before your eyes while a great symphony orchestra plays" . . . Ferdé Grofé playing a honkey-tonk piano on the Barbary Coast . . . George Mardikian, huge, red-faced, and most beloved of San Francisco's epicurean chefs, shouting down all bidders and buying tens of thousands of dollars of war bonds to possess a captured Japanese trophy . . . Little Gertrude Atherton, eighty-eight years old and pretty as an old-fashioned picture, bobbing into the Mechanics' Library and demanding, "Have you got my newest book, and if not why not?" . . .

Two little Italian boys and two little Chinese girls dancing the conga in Portsmouth Square where R.L.S. once dreamed . . . An aged, white-haired Negro, sitting on his heels in Union Square, feeding popcorn to hundreds of pigeons . . . Joseph Henry Jackson, author and literary critic, leading a barbershop quartet in "Sweet Molly Malone" . . . A Greek bootblack on Taylor Street quoting Shakespeare . . . Gump's windows on Post Street with precious carvings from the Temples of Ankhor Thom . . .

Dr. Margaret Chung, Chinese woman physician, playing

host to ten thousand aviators . . . A sailor, sitting on the edge of the Embarcadero wharf, playing César Franck's *D-Minor Symphony* on a harmonica . . . Diamond Jim Brady ordering six dozen oysters on the half-shell in the Palace Hotel . . . Tessie Wall drinking a double magnum of Cliquot at Marchand's . . . A blind, old Englishman selling sweet lavender on Geary Street . . . Heavenly-voiced choirboys from Grace Cathedral coming out on Sacramento Street in their vestments to play—one foot across the gutter . . . Doddering old men pitching horseshoes in Golden Gate Park . . .

A portly magnate from Montgomery Street and a tart from Pine Street playing "Keno" at the beach . . . Young boys and young girls, and middle-aged men and young girls, parked in cars above Land's End . . . A sign in a Telegraph Hill window: "Midwife." And in the window a stout Italian woman singing *"Caro Nome"* . . . Sailors rowing girls in tiny boats on Stow Lake . . . A thousand daffodils in the windows of Podesta and Baldocchi . . . Alfred Hertz playing bridge at the Argonaut Club and humming *Tristan and Isolde* . . .

It is gray and quiet in San Francisco at dawn. In summer the fogs billow through the Golden Gate, moisture-laden and cold, and in winter the sun comes red and swaggering over the Berkeley hills. It is a gray city, a city of gray houses and gray streets, and yet every hour brings new color, new choreography of lights and shadows to the gulches and valleys and steep ravines and towering cliffs that are the city's streets.

A gay, colorful, gray, eager city of men—this is the kaleidoscope of San Francisco.

9

PART ONE

THE DAYS OF GOLD

I

Sam Brannan

Historians disagree about him in almost every way, save for the choice of the qualifying word—"fabulous." They call him the most fabulous, the most fantastic, and, by the same favor, the most typical of San Francisco's pioneers. Thus far they agree, but from then on there is dissension. They call him a saint, they call him a scoundrel; they call him the man who made the city great, and the worst grafter the city has ever known. They call him a great mind, and an ignorant charlatan. They tell how he came West in the name of the Lord, and brought with him an army of servants of the Lord, and charged the servants a heavy tax in the name of the Lord. And, when some remonstrated and said, "But this money you are collecting is not really being given to the Lord," then he said, "Go and tell [Brigham] Young that I'll give up the money when he sends me a receipt signed by the Lord."

The young man was Sam Brannan.

He came to San Francisco—to Yerba Buena as it was then called—in 1846. He brought with him an antiquated printing press, and some two hundred fifty Latter-day Saints, and a complete flour mill. He traveled around the Horn to the Sandwich Islands, in the Islands armed his Saints with one hundred fifty rifles, and then set sail for the Golden Gate and Yerba Buena to create a great Mormon empire, on the shores of San Francisco Bay.

Now, at just about the time that Sam embarked on his pilgrimage, Brigham Young was leading a far greater army of Latter-day Saints across the Rockies and, coming upon beautiful Salt Lake Valley, uttered his immortal *"This* is the place!" And so Salt Lake City and not San Francisco became the heart of the Mormon empire.

Serenely unaware of the proclamation of Brigham Young, Sam Brannan and his followers—whom he had charged a handsome penny for the voyage—sailed through the Golden Gate. They saw, as they rounded into the Bay, a tiny cluster of frame houses and a hill—Telegraph Hill—with an American flag instead of the colors of Mexico flying atop it. And standing on the deck of his chartered ship, the *Brooklyn,* Brannan roundly cursed, cursed not because he did not love the American flag—for he was a true patriot—but because he had dreamed of being the first to raise the Stars and Stripes over Yerba Buena. Captain John B. Montgomery of the sloop-of-war *Portsmouth* had beaten him by twenty days.

The ship dropped anchor and Sam Brannan went ashore. He was greeted by the entire population, a population outnumbered by the two hundred fifty Mormon newcomers. They saw a huge, broad-shouldered man with heavy sideburns and beard, flashing black eyes, elegant garments, a swaggering walk—a man who did not at all look the elder of a church. But church elder or gambler—and Sam Brannan was both—they greeted him as they greeted all newcomers, by initiating him into their membership. They took him to the Plaza, blindfolded him, turned him around three times, and made bets as to how long it would take him to walk to a signpost in the middle of the Plaza.

Brannan commenced his blindfolded march. At the corner of Clay and Kearny streets there was a large pool of slime formed by the mixing of clay and water to make adobe bricks. Into the pool marched Elder Brannan and wallowed in the mud up to his ears. And out he came, laughing a great, jovial laugh, wiping the mud from his mouth and ears. And then and there he was accepted, not as a saint but, as one of the historians of his day aptly put it, as "one of the boys."

Climbing out of the mud puddle into which he had plunged, Brannan immediately plunged into the muddled affairs of the village. A young couple wanted to be married. Brannan arranged the wedding, the wedding feast and celebration, and performed the first non-Catholic wedding ceremony in California, the first wedding under the American flag in San Francisco.

Brannan swiftly achieved a reputation for "firsts." He delivered in California the first sermon in the English language and the first non-Catholic sermon and was also the first defendant in a court of law under the American flag. In this court case the Mormon association brought charges of misuse of funds. A hung jury resulted in Brannan's release. All that ended the power of the Mormons in San Francisco, and ended Brannan's standing in the Church of Latter-day Saints.

But, having collected a considerable amount of money,

Sam found new affairs to occupy his mind. He landed his flour mill, started its wheels turning, the first in California. He found a wooden house back of the Old Adobe in which he established his wife and children and his printing press, and almost immediately started the press rolling. So he founded San Francisco's first newspaper, *The California Star*.

Shortly after the Mormons' arrival there was an alarm in the village, one of the periodic alarms caused by imaginary attacks by the Spanish Californians. Brannan's Mormon Battalion sprang to attention, armed with the Sandwich Island rifles. A few shots were fired under cover of night. The next morning the valiant Mormons went out to pick up the dead bodies and found the bullets had all found their mark—in a clump of scrub oaks.

A short time later there was a loud explosion in the village. This time it was unquestionably the Spanish Californians, invasion bent. Out came the Mormons, guns primed for trouble. The explosion proved to be of a coffee-pot in the just-established City Hotel. That ended the martial adventures of the Mormon Battalion. San Francisco was occupied by Americans without interference from the dispossessed Spanish Californians, much to the disappointment of the Americans. And the Mormon Battalion went out of existence.

Brannan went ahead on his own. His paper proclaimed the need of a public school. The first public school was founded, and Sam made the first contribution to it. Then he extended his operations, made a journey to the fort of John Augustus Sutter on the Sacramento River, opened a store in the village of Sacramento, and became an intimate friend of John Augustus. That was in November of 1847.

In January of 1848 gold was discovered in Sutter's millrace and Sam, with the instincts of the true newspaperman, started out to tell the world of the discovery. Sutter pleaded against it; to tell of the discovery of gold would bring hordes of gold-hungry men to destroy the agricultural empire Sutter was building. But Brannan shook him off, shouting, "Gold! Gold!"

Nothing else was talked of. The little settlements of a few hundred men went gold-mad. And whenever the excitement threatened to calm down, Sam Brannan would beat the drums and the gold fever would rise again. Wearing a beaver hat, coattails flying behind him, he dashed through the muddy roadway of Montgomery Street, waving a bottle of gold dust over his head and shrieking at the top of his lungs, *"Gold!* Gold! Gold from the American River!"

He led a cavalcade out of the village and up the river to the gold fields. On the day that Sam Brannan left San Francisco, the population that stayed behind consisted of seven men. Overnight his store in Sacramento began to coin money. An advance guard began to pour into San Francisco, and there Sam sold them newspapers and calico and sugar and coffee and flour and beans—and sand lots. But so far the newcomers were only harbingers of what was to come. Gold was discovered in January; the word did not reach New York until August. Then the mad rush began, the rush that historians call the greatest pilgrimage in all the history of man. And Sam Brannan was its herald, its prophet, its spieler, its pitchman. As he shouted and beat tin pans and made money, so his fame spread until he was, beyond question of doubt, the best-known man in the new metropolis.

The best-known man! When strangers wanted advice

on the law, on property values, on the best place to buy a pair of boots, or the name of the firm in China to which they should send their laundry, they went to Sam Brannan. There used to be a vendor of pies who shouted his wares at the corner of Montgomery and Sacramento streets. His cry was "Mince pies, apple pies, cheese pies! Everybody buys 'em! *Sam Brannan* buys 'em!"

Wealth piled up as Brannan's fame increased. He made millions; he was San Francisco's first millionaire. And, with the grand gesture—because he always loved the grand gesture—he gave away money as easily as he made it. He gave one piece of property to the Odd Fellows for a cemetery that in comparatively recent years was appraised at a half-million dollars. He gave generously to individual widows and orphans, in some cases giving them monthly endowments throughout their lives—or at least the life of his fortune. (But that is another and a later story.) He gave parties at the new hotels springing up in the city, and thought nothing of spending a thousand dollars a night to entertain his friends. He counted his friends by the thousands, and as for his enemies—well, Sam Brannan, Mormon elder, gambler, profligate spender, real estate boomer, newspaper publisher, flour-mill master, and *bon vivant*—Sam Brannan had only one class of enemy—the lawless.

They had come to San Francisco, the lawbreakers, like rats on a spree. The first contingent called itself the Bowery Boys—renegades from Tammany Hall. Later-comers formed groups; one lot, the Hounds, was sworn to hound foreigners —especially Spanish Americans—away from the rich lands the true and noble Americans now owned. They paraded the streets in ragtag uniforms and made general nuisances of themselves. They robbed merchants, raped women, and smashed and burned property. The scandals and the stories were deplorable, and they reached their climax when the word was passed that marauding Hounds had murdered a mother who was trying to protect her daughter from them.

That was the act that set off the powder keg. The powder keg in this case was a barrel rolled to the corner of Clay and Montgomery streets. Sam Brannan mounted it, rage in his eyes and fire and profound emotion and fearless courage in his voice. He denounced the scoundrels and denounced the alcalde who had been afraid to take action against the Hounds. The crowds gathered and cheered and screamed for revenge, and Brannan led them, roaring, to the alcalde's office. And there, on the roof of the shack, in a brilliant declaration Sam Brannan denounced lawlessness and proclaimed that if there was no law adequate to combat lawlessness then the decent citizens would have to take the law into their own hands. So, the first Committee of Safety was born, and Sam Brannan was its sire.

But that was only the beginning. There were vigilantes, but this was 1849; the real vigilance committee was yet to come. The first organized Committee of Vigilance was established in June of 1851 in Sam Brannan's office. He was its first president, and he saw to it that its work was done—and well done.

Owing chiefly to Hounds-incited incendiaries out for plunder and spoil, San Francisco had been gutted by fire five times in the year before the vigilance committee was organized. It was burned a sixth time in that June of 1851, and that was the city's last great conflagration—until 1906. Sam Brannan and the vigilantes and the fire companies saw to that. Especially Sam Brannan. For, when the city burned, not only his patriotism but his pocketbook suffered. By 1851 he owned one-fourth of the city of Sacramento and one-fifth of the city of San Francisco. His revenue from rentals was almost unbelievable. From a single property he collected an annual rental of over one hundred thousand dollars.

And all the while he continued to be the inspiration and pioneer in every new civic activity. He helped found the Society of California Pioneers. He lent large sums of money to the government of Mexico; he spent a fortune to develop trade with China, and made a fortune out of it. His financial appetite and genius knew no bounds.

But his dreams and his imagination finally led to disaster. Hot springs were discovered at the foot of Mount St. Helena in Napa Valley. Sam visited the springs, was fascinated by them and the beautiful country that surrounded them. So he embarked on his greatest project. He bought a tremendous tract of land and announced that he would make it the fashionable rage of the West—the Saratoga of the West. He combined the names of California and Saratoga and created the town of Calistoga. Among other projects there he built a large distillery, and then, when the bubble of his land boom burst and most of his fortune vanished with it, he became one of his own best customers.

From a handsome, alert, clear-eyed city father Brannan became, almost overnight, a dispirited alcoholic. Trying to retrieve what he had lost, he threw fortune after fortune into his Calistoga dream, and saw all the fortunes evaporate. His friends drifted away. His wife divorced him and returned to Germany with their four children. There was still fight in him; he was a leader in the struggle to save California from swinging to the South in the Civil War. But now his fighting front was greeted with chuckles by the few friends he had left.

His fortune gone, his friends gone, he turned in bitterness from the city he loved, the city in which he had been first. He drifted to San Diego County, married a Mexican woman and set up housekeeping on a small ranch near the Mexican border. At first he would not work the ranch; he lay in the sun and drank his wine. Later he could not work; paralysis set in. Once, heart-hungry, he wandered back to San Francisco. He spent a night in a twenty-five-cent lodginghouse and, heartsick, the next day found his way back to his San Diego ranch.

And then a miracle happened. To Sam Brannan, San Francisco's first millionaire, the Mexican government paid forty-nine thousand dollars in interest on the huge sums of money he had lent it. He was sixty-nine years old. He swore he would never touch another drop of intoxicating liquor— and kept his oath. Strength returned to him; his paralysis disappeared. He took the forty-nine thousand dollars, paid all his debts in full, and died penniless.

He was seventy years old.

II

Biscaccianti

The "Four Hundred" is an American tradition. The Four Hundred occupied the Diamond Horseshoe at the "Met." In the old days the Four Hundred owned pretentious mansions on Fifth Avenue in New York. It had summer homes at Newport and Saratoga, and winter homes at Palm Beach, and its sires made millions in copper and steel and railroads and Alaska furs. But the old order changed, and income tax took the millions, and today music lovers pre-empt the Diamond Horseshoe. So much for New York and the Four Hundred.

The "Five Hundred" is a San Francisco tradition. The Five Hundred had homes on Nob Hill and Russian Hill, and the more daring built stone piles out on Pacific Heights in the sand lots. It pre-empted the Diamond Horseshoe in the Grand Opera House on Mission Street. It went to Del Monte in summer, or even to the Hotel Rafael over in San Rafael in its palmy days. It went to Paris in the winter, and unless its gowns were imported from Paris with Paquin labels, Mme Baer or Mme Labourdette made its wedding dresses. It drank French champagne prescribed by Ned Greenway or by his rival, Dick Hotaling; it dined at Marchand's or the Old Poodle Dog, and its gay blades were wicked at the Trocadero.

It was the Five Hundred, and why New York should have only had a Four Hundred and San Francisco a Five Hundred has long been an unexplained mystery. Certainly San Francisco Society was more exclusive than New York Society. But San Francisco Society was the *Five* Hundred, and I believe I've discovered the reason.

It all stems back to one basic fact in the building of great cities. Cities are built by commerce, by industry, by money-making. And after the money is made and the cities are built, they must turn to the business of culture to keep alive. After all, when you have made all the money you think you want, and have bought all the things you think you want to own, life demands a new outlet. The logical outlet is culture. Of course, I mean nice, polite culture, not the culture that trades in esoteric philosophies and profound sciences and such, but the culture that finds expression in poets' poems and painters' paintings and literature and music and statues. That is probably the reason why there are so many bad statues in San Francisco. However, to get back to the Five Hundred . . .

In June of 1851, the St. Francis Hotel of that day, at the corner of Clay and Dupont streets, announced the first of a series of "soirees" at which Society would assemble for polite conversation, music, and terpsichorean revelry. The soirees attained their *recherché* climax in September with a function of which the local press said, "Never did the St. Francis present such a brilliant scene as on the night set aside by our gentlemen to respond to the happy compliment paid them by the ladies of that elegant and fashionable hotel. The ladies of San Francisco never appeared to more charming advantage."

Certainly the ladies appeared to charming advantage.

But the affair was, in the vernacular of our current vulgarity, a "flop." Only forty ladies appeared, and the gentlemen came by the hundreds. They crowded the ladies from the banquet table. They stalked around in their high-heeled boots, curling their elegant mustaches and swinging their six-shooters, and the gentle ladies huddled in corners and whispered behind their fans. No, that soiree of the St. Francis was not in the true sense of the word a social triumph.

But there was in San Francisco an organization reputed to succeed in everything it undertook. It was the Monumental Engine Company—Big Six—the most popular volunteer fire company in the city. The Monumental answered the failure of the St. Francis soiree by announcing a Grand Ball. The music would be the finest obtainable. The decorations nonpareil. The refreshments would compare bravely with the heaped banquet tables of Europe.

And——*and* there would be ladies! Society would be represented by *five hundred* ladies! Yes, that was the true beginning of San Francisco's Five Hundred.

Just where five hundred ladies worthy of the name were found in San Francisco mystified everyone. Finally the truth leaked out; some of the ladies had been brought from as far away as St. Joseph, Missouri, by Pony Express. So says legend. The fact that the Pony Express did not begin to function till some nine years later need not spoil the story or the triumph of the Monumental.

But, with the soirees of the St. Francis and the Grand Ball of the Monumental, the hunger for culture was not appeased. Early in the spring of 1852, culture arrived without fanfare and in a single night lifted the city from the rank of a vulgar boom town to a center of artistic endeavor.

In February a steamer docked—or, rather, it was a sailing

ship. It was at the height of the rainy season. The streets were rivers of mud. One of the proud boasts of San Francisco that year was that it was the muddiest city in the world. From the gangplank of the sailing ship a young girl stepped ashore—and sank to her dainty knees in mud. She stood there, with mud all about, and threw kisses to the assembled multitude of miners and businessmen and gamblers. They cheered, and she smiled, and they threw their hats in the air, and she threw more kisses. Then one of the biggest of the rugged men strode through the mud, lifted the girl in his arms and, holding her high above his head, marched with her through mud and mire to the St. Francis Hotel. And the crowd followed and cheered.

She was a Boston girl, delicate as a bit of French porcelain, pretty as a miniature painted on ivory. Every man in San Francisco was in love with her before the procession had splashed its way into the St. Francis.

A Boston girl, her mother a cultured woman, her father a musician of some distinction, she had received a refined education in Boston's exclusive schools. She had traveled around the world; she was lovely, she was exquisite, she was adored—and *she was cultured.* Her name was Elisa Biscaccianti.

Biscaccianti! There are San Franciscans still living whose fathers grew mellow-eyed when they spoke of The Biscaccianti. She was the most popular coloratura soprano of her day. She had sung leading roles in London, in Paris, in Milan and Vienna and Florence and St. Petersburg. And San Francisco took Biscaccianti to its warm heart just as, a half-century later, it would take Tetrazzini. Biscaccianti became San Francisco's own.

She did not remain for a concert, or two, or three. She

remained for more than a year, singing night after night, week after week. At her first concert she sang an operatic aria; it was on the night of March 22, 1852. She sang, and when she was finished the crowd arose and shrieked. She was showered with flowers. They cheered and would not stop cheering. And finally—and now I quote what I believe to be one of the most precious pieces of Western criticism ever written—"For encore she seated herself at the piano and sang, beneath a garniture of brilliant and varied ornament of rich brocades covered with point lace, 'Home Sweet Home' with embellishments."

That first concert and not the Grand Ball of the Monumental was, in all seriousness, the real beginning of San Francisco's social consciousness and culture.

Society flocked to the Biscaccianti concerts. Agonized letters were dispatched to Paris for court gowns and décolletés suitable for Society's great nights. Carriages appeared on the muddy streets, splashing their diamond-sparkling fares through the mud to the American Theatre at Sansome and Leidesdorff streets where Biscaccianti was singing. Again, quoting the local press the day after her first concert: "The evening marked an era in the musical, social and fashionable progress of the city."

Biscaccianti moved from the St. Francis to the Oriental Hotel. Adoring ladies and infatuated men filled her rooms with flowers. She walked through the streets and crowds followed her, cheering. The fire companies paraded in her honor. A small, three-year-old son of a fire chief appeared before her in the Plaza, made a speech, and presented her with roses. And night after night she sang, not songs to appeal to the population of an unschooled boom town, but the great arias of opera and the great songs of the concert

23

stage. And one noble citizen with a prophetic soul proclaimed, "San Francisco shall be the musical soul of the West, and Biscaccianti is the soul's Columbus."

A year of triumphs passed swiftly and in February 1853, Biscaccianti sailed away to tour the world. The city went to the Embarcadero with her. Strong men wept as she climbed up the gangplank. They flung flowers after the ship as it drew away from the wooden wharf, flowers that drifted in the ship's wake until it had sailed through the Golden Gate. Crowds stood on the cliffs above old Fort Point and watched the ship disappear in the west, taking away the city's most beloved treasure. They stood there and wept, and then they returned to their homes—and forgot about her.

But she had left a mark that could not be erased; she had brought culture to the Western city and a love of beauty. And, moreover, she had brought a consciousness that made San Francisco call itself for a generation the most exclusive of the centers of Society.

They sought the theater avidly now, these San Franciscans. They sought music, they welcomed operatic troupes and concert singers. Their hunger for the arts, awakened by Biscaccianti, could not be appeased; they wanted more and more. And in the cities of South America and Europe, Elisa Biscaccianti went from triumph to triumph, winning acclaim after acclaim. She sang for royalty, she sang in the great opera houses, and the critics said there had never been a coloratura soprano to compare with her in charm, in loveliness, in beauty of voice, in perfection of *bel canto*, and in the rich culture of her art.

Now, that is the story of how culture and music came to San Francisco, the story all but for one closing chapter—and that chapter is tragedy.

Biscaccianti returned to the city she loved in 1859. She had left it a muddy village and returned to find it a cosmopolitan port. In six years the city had grown up. San Franciscans had heard many singers, great artists, pianists, violinists; they had seen the great actors of the land. Theaters had sprung up on every hand. Entertainment ranged from the greatest musicians on the Continent to the bawdy shows of the Barbary Coast. The city was saturated with entertainment and art and culture. And Biscaccianti had become, in a few short years, just another name.

Oh, the city came to see her and said she sang very beautifully. But they threw no flowers. You did not have to pay premiums of bags of gold dust to hear the Biscaccianti. In fact, you could arrive fashionably late and have your choice of seats. The city had grown fickle with amazing speed.

At first Biscaccianti was dazed, then chagrined, then infuriated. Overnight she forgot her polite training and the traditions of her Boston home. Very well! If they would not pay to hear her sing the great operas, then she would sing the songs they wanted to hear her sing, not in the Opera House but in the already disreputable Bella Union. She had been kind to San Francisco when San Francisco was starved; now she demanded that the city buy her bread and butter.

If you were one of the hundreds who went to the Bella Union, you would have seen Biscaccianti, night after night, seated at a small table. She was called "Biscaccianti of the Bella Union" now. She had grown stout; her features had grown coarse. She would sit with the young man for whom she had deserted her husband. She was habitually drunk. Some said she was most amusing and sang best when she was most drunk.

For three years, night after night, she sat at her table in

the Bella Union, singing for her drinks. And through the fog of those awful hours there would come at times a hopeful glint in her eyes, a proud toss of her head when she thought she saw recognition of her past glories in the eyes of an old-timer passing her table. But, no; it was just another sight-seer wondering what had been the origin of Biscaccianti of the Bella Union. For three years she sat there, and then, one day she went away and was never heard of in San Francisco again. But the indomitable Biscaccianti was not finished: in Peru she staged a comeback, then she went to Milan where she taught and remarried, and in 1896 she died in the Musicians' Home in Paris.

III

Fire

There is a story often told in San Francisco of a well-known local citizen who was to be married. His name was Charlie Schultz; he was a violinist and orchestra leader. And the one thing in life that kindled greater pride in his poetical soul than music was his being a volunteer fireman.

Now, on his wedding day, Charlie laid aside his fireman's helmet with the foxtail, dressed himself in tails and a broad Ascot tie, polished his silk hat, and walked leisurely downtown. One of the boys on his fire truck was to be his best man, and Charlie stopped at the firehouse to discuss details of the ceremony. The time was ten in the morning; the wedding was to be at high noon. The two men were discussing details when the fire bell rang in the tower. Charlie looked at his best man, the best man looked at Charlie. Carefully Charlie removed his silk hat, donned his helmet, and sprang to the fire truck. And the horses plunged down the street, firebound.

Late that afternoon the truck returned, the fire vanquished by the valiant men of San Francisco's volunteer fire brigade. Very tired and very dirty and soaking wet, Charlie sank into a chair and swallowed a tumbler of whiskey to fortify himself. In fact, he closed his eyes for forty winks to fortify himself further. After all, marriage was an undertaking to be approached carefully, and a man needed to be in good form. So Charlie closed his eyes for forty winks. When he awoke the morning sun was high in the sky—he had slept for sixteen hours. He hastened to the home of his bride-to-be. The door was slammed in his face.

Charlie Schultz did marry. But it was many years later and to a different girl.

Now, Charlie Schultz, not in his marriage but in his love of fires, was characteristic of male San Franciscans, thousands of whom could not resist chasing a fire wagon. Why, in 1906, it was the earthquake they spoke of in low, solemn voices, the earthquake that had done comparatively small damage. But the *fire* was another thing. . . .

What that it had laid half the city in ashes? What that the property loss ran into hundreds of millions? What that thousands were homeless? They spoke of that fire with bright eyes as one of the greatest fires of all times. They were proud of it; they loved to boast of it. Would you believe it, they would ask you, the sky was so bright with flames that out in the Presidio miles away you could read a newspaper at midnight by the glare! It was a grand fire, a great fire, a heroic fire, a—why, it was one of the finest fires you had ever seen. Yes, through all the suffering they endured, San Franciscans were proud of their fire.

There was a reason for all this—this complex—this dementia. Certainly no sane man could be thrilled by the destruction that lay in the path of leaping tongues of flame. And yet, in many ways San Franciscans were quite sane. There was fire in their veins. They had known fire down through the years in a city built of wood. Their fathers and grandfathers had seen the entire city wiped out in a series of fires of such frequent recurrence that the inhabitants took on the nature of salamanders. San Franciscans not only lived through fires, they thrived on them. And each devastating holocaust was followed by the building of a new city finer than the one that smouldered in the ashes.

The first fire took place in the year that the population of the city had grown from two thousand to twenty-five thousand. That was 1849, the year that turned the village into a roaring, hectic, delirious carnival of gold. Four-fifths of the twenty-five thousand were men who had come from all over the world, most of them leaving wives and children behind. So, they went through the hectic year and were able to put aside the longings for home while they were busy playing the greatest game they knew—the quest for gold. But now a time approached when it would not be so easy to forget their homes. The Christmas season was on them.

With the childlike quality of men who never grow up, they went about the business of preparing for Christmas. They hung festoons and wreaths in the five hundred saloons and brothels and gambling houses. They paid ten dollars for a chicken, six dollars for a dozen eggs, to prepare Christmas dinner. They took baths in fresh water at a dollar a barrel. They emptied the store of Jacob Leese and Nathan Spear and Hinckley of trifles and notions and junk for which they paid fabulous prices. They might be a thousand miles from civilization but they did not intend to be cheated of their Christmas.

And then, early on the morning of December twenty-fourth, the cry of "Fire!" rang through the streets. It started in Dennison's Exchange on the east side of the Plaza that lay in the quadrangle of Clay and Washington and Montgomery and Kearny streets. It roared up one side of the Square and down the other. Buildings, tents, and shacks in its path fell like kindling in a steel furnace. It burned throughout the day and into Christmas Day, and more than a million dollars' worth of property was consumed.

And then the city fathers established a precedent that was to be an inspiration fifty-eight years later when the great fire of 1906 was to threaten the entire, widespread city. They blew up, with gunpowder, the buildings that stood beyond the actual flames, and the fire licked a path to the crumbled and blasted frames and died out. And the city fathers said, "We must do something about it. There must never be another fire."

That was in 1849. The day after Christmas the work of rebuilding the city commenced, and the celebration of Christmas was forgotten. The city fathers stored up the story they would tell of the great San Francisco fire, a fire which, as far as they knew, had been excelled only by the burning of Rome and the Fire of London.

Just four months later, on May 4, 1850, a fire broke out that made the blaze of 1849 look like a bonfire. It started between midnight and dawn. The streets of dust were dark; lights glimmered through the doors of saloons and dance halls, but a wise man kept out of the shadows, and the shadows were every place. A man standing in front of the United States Exchange shouted, "Fire!" And out of the shack-hotels and halls and dives poured the populace. In an hour a driving wind had spread the flames over the four blocks bounding the Plaza and across to the newer buildings that lay between Kearny Street and Dupont— later, Grant Avenue. Eight square blocks were in flames. Bucket brigades toted buckets from the Montgomery Street water front and emptied them with futile splashes into the furnace that scorned anything less than a tidal wave.

And then scandal was added to the destruction by flames. For, while hundreds of citizens fought bravely and futilely to beat out the flames, as many more hundreds refused to fight the fire unless they were well paid for their labor. The result was street rioting, and rioting led to pillage and plundering of stores.

Added to the scandal, word spread that incendiaries had started the disaster. But the fight continued. Again gunpowder was brought out; all the buildings on the west side of Dupont were blown up. Again the flames were halted, again the ashes cooled, leaving ruins estimated at more than four million dollars. And within a week, and before all the embers had died out, the new city was being built. But this time the wiser few shook their heads, for this time the new structures were more ramshackle, less substantial, more inflammable than they had been before.

Within a month of that second fire of May 4, 1850, the city was completely rebuilt. And on the fourteenth of June the third and biggest of the fires swept all that had been rebuilt, and all the territory that had been protected by gunpowder right down to the Bay's edge. It started in a bakeshop chimney at the rear of the Merchants' Hotel. It was eight o'clock in the morning—breakfast time. The miners gathered to sniff the burning bread and pastry, and to laugh at the overcooked breakfast. But their laughter soon ended. These men of San Francisco had lost three fortunes in fire in six months, and there was little joy in gold easily won when it went with greater ease. To add to the disaster and distress, provisions, clothing, tools, necessities that took months to round Cape Horn had been destroyed with priceless food. This third fire was not so much a matter of boastful pride to the pioneers. But, with the stubbornness of the spider that repairs its web even when it has been broken time after time, the city was rebuilt.

And then it happened again. Down on the north side of Jackson Street stood the Washington Market where venison and bear meat and an occasional cut of beef might be purchased. At four o'clock on the morning of September 17, only three months after the third fire, the charred smell of burning flesh choked the city lanes. Flames poured out of the Washington Market; flames poured out of the Philadelphia House close to the Market. Flames spread through every structure from Pacific Street to Washington, and from Dupont to the Bay. The loss, in dollars and cents, was not as great is in the earlier conflagrations; the citizens found little of which to boast in this fourth fire. Fires were simply becoming a nuisance, something to be expected, to be challenged by the volunteer fire companies and then gunpowdered out of memory so that the rebuilding of the city might commence. It was a nuisance; but San Francisco was a stubborn young city.

That fourth fire was late in 1850. The town had grown to cover a wide, populated area. There were periodic small blazes from time to time, and they were taken in their stride. But then, close to midnight on the night of May 3, 1851, the horror broke out once more. This time it was no town but a city that was burning. Buildings were blown up with gunpowder; flames, driven by a fierce wind, leaped the gunpowdered gaps. Thin streams of water were poured into the flames and the water turned to steam that drifted away. Legends claim that the crimson of the burning city was seen reflected in the sky of Monterey a hundred miles away. The entire business area of the city was on fire. Close to two thousand buildings were completely in ruins; property loss was estimated at twelve million dollars. One warehouse—and one alone—was saved by the owners pouring eighty thousand gallons of vinegar into the flames. It was an overwhelming challenge to the city builders. But, in the tradition of the place, the ashes cooled and the rebuilding commenced. Except that now the city fathers planned a substantial city, a city of fine buildings, a city that would endure.

And just a month later, on June 22, holocaust rampaged again. This time the residences were the greatest sufferers. The flames spread from Powell Street to Sansome, and from Clay to Broadway. Sixteen square blocks were burned out. The old landmarks of Yerba Buena went with this sixth conflagration, and with them went the courage of some of the builders. There was Tom Maguire. He had built the Jenny Lind Theatre. It had burned and he had built a finer one, and it burned and again he rebuilt—and again and again and again—six Jenny Lind Theatres, each to go down in flames. But—the gunpowder was brought out, the flames were blasted, the fires burned down—and the rebuilding of the city recommenced over hot ashes.

So, there was fire in the blood of San Franciscans. And when, in 1906, the greatest fire of all time swept up and down the city, the sons of pioneers brought out dynamite and blasted great city blocks, and the flames died and the ashes cooled. And San Franciscans said it was the greatest fire that ever was——and started to build a new and stronger and more beautiful city.

Yes, it is a strange dementia that makes men boast of disaster. And it is a strange urge that makes a city crumble before disaster on disaster and never know defeat. But then, San Francisco is a strange place.

33

IV

The Fire Companies

Up on the highest point of Telegraph Hill there is a monument familiar to every San Franciscan—the Coit Tower. The shaft was erected in memory of Howard Coit by his widow, but the truth is that Lillie Coit, who gave the tower to San Francisco, was separated from her husband after a short and hectic marriage. When Lillie built the tower in her husband's memory it may be that she did it with her charming tongue in her cheek. She was given to little idiosyncracies.

One of those idiosyncracies was that she always signed herself "Lillie Hitchcock Coit 5." "Lillie" was her given name, "Hitchcock" was her maiden name, "Coit" was her husband's name—and "5" was the number of her favorite fire company's engine. Knickerbocker Engine No. 5! For Lillie, as a young girl and through her maturing years, loved to chase fires in a San Francisco that was raised on and periodically razed by fires.

When Lillie was seventeen years old she acted as bridesmaid at a friend's wedding. This was in the early 'sixties. During the ceremony the fire engines raced by. Lillie deserted the festivities and chased down the street in her bridesmaid dress after her favorite engine, Knickerbocker No. 5—and later was made an honorary member of the Knickerbocker Company.

34

Now, the San Francisco fire companies were to the city what the Guard is to Buckingham Palace and Cossacks are to Russia. They were indispensable in the work they did. But, more than that, they were the social life and the entertainment entrepreneurs of the pioneer city. Their uniforms colored every parade; their meetings in the 'fifties and the 'sixties had the nature of lodge meetings of today. In fact, it is a matter of record that many wives wept for loneliness when their husbands went, or even said they were going, to a meeting of the fire company.

There were many companies and the rivalry between them was tense. The members served gratuitously; they were all volunteers. And the city loved them with sentimental emotion. When Lillie Coit died in 1929 at the age of eighty-six, she left to the city, erected in Columbus Square, a touching statue of heart-throbbing beauty—two noble firemen and a rescued child.

In the beginning the fire wagons were drawn by hand; four, six, or twenty men seized the ropes and dragged the lumbering engines through the streets. And before them raced important members of the company—the torch boys, holding their torches high as they ran, so that the way could be seen through the unlighted streets.

One of the most famous companies was founded by W. D. M. Howard. Mr. Howard ordered a shining engine made in Boston and had it brought around the Horn. Now, in the company, Howard had a rival—the well-known Sam Brannan. At first the company was called the Brannan Company, then, when the new engine arrived, the name was changed to the Howard Company. The Brannan faction, in the darkness of night, dragged the beautiful engine from its firehouse and dumped it into the Bay. The Howard

35

clan promptly raised it from the mud bed of the Bay, polished it, and returned it in glory.

That sort of thing could have gone on indefinitely. But, for the peace of mind of all the city, the organization decided to stop such antics, and even changed its name. It became known as the Social Company, and the name was well chosen. The members were social to a nice degree—so social, in fact, that the engine was always stocked with cases of champagne to bolster the endurance of the men during a fire. They did not bother to pull the corks in the accepted manner; they knocked the necks off the bottles and drank while they fought. Later, the Social Company redeemed itself by organizing the city's first temperance organization —The Dashaway Society. They "dashed away" all intoxicating temptation by smashing the bottles on the street, and Social Engine 3 became San Francisco's model of fiery propriety.

Wonderful progress in science and invention marked the era of Social 3. The world was entering the day of speed; anything could happen. Word came West of an invention that was too fantastic to be practical; it was a fire engine that pumped its water, not by hand pump, but by a steam engine. Social 3 invested in one of the contraptions. A rival company, High-Toned 12, sent a message by Pony Express to St. Joseph, Missouri, and thence by train to New York to order another. A third rival, Big 6, ordered a "steamer." The citizens became accustomed to the snorting monsters charging through the streets. Rivalry became hectic, each company trying to get up steam faster than the other.

The last member of Social 3 passed away recently—Godfrey Fisher, a beloved San Franciscan. Fisher in his youth had been stoker on the steam engine of Social 3. One night

36

a grocery store in the wholesale district burst into flames. Fisher confiscated and crashed packing crates to stoke his fire-box, and then fed sizzling hams into the flames, whispering a Jewish prayer as he did so. He soon had the fire so hot with roasting hams that the engine threw four powerful streams of water where the rival hand engine could only throw two. By the grace of a kindly Providence the engine did not explode, and Social 3 won new and enduring fame.

No athletic contest from the days of Marathon to a Big Ten track meet exceeded in rivalry the competition of Social 3 and Knickerbocker 5 and Manhattan 2 and Tiger 14 and the score of other companies in their endeavors to be first at a fire. The winner in each race was awarded a tail from a fox pelt. The foxtail became the treasured emblem of the San Francisco companies; foxtails were worn on the helmets, foxtails hung from engine smokestacks—and little boys pinned foxtails to their caps when they played "fireman." Just a few short years ago Godfrey Fisher—that same Godfrey Fisher who had stoked Social 3 with ham—found, hanging in a furrier's window, a moth-eaten, aged foxtail. He bought it in nostalgic memory of the days of the San Francisco fires, had it mounted on mahogany, and presented it on Admission Day to the Native Sons of the Golden West.

The competitions for the foxtail—the rivalry to see which company could get to a fire first, which company could throw the longest stream of water, and, later, which company could excel at tug of war—these were the tournaments of San Francisco prowess. And long years after the fire companies had been domesticated by city charter, one institution remained: at butchers' picnics and marksmen's picnics and picnics where the beer barrel had replaced the broken bottle of champagne, the Fireman's Tug of War was always the feature of the day.

Reading the roster of the companies was like reading the roster of the Five Hundred. Peter Donahue, one of the founders of the Pacific Gas and Electric Company, was a member of California 4; O'Brien, the partner of James Flood, was a fireman of California 4; Claus Spreckels belonged to Tiger 14; William T. Coleman, the moderator of the first Vigilance Committee, belonged to California 4; Robert Tobin of the Hibernian Bank belonged to Engine 10. And the company called Liberty Hose had a young adventurer—a sailor and master fire fighter—whose name, Tom Sawyer, is said to have given Mark Twain the name for his masterpiece. But the most famous and most feared of all the fire fighters was San Francisco's sheriff, David Scannell.

Scannell was famous as a fire fighter and famous as a gourmet and connoisseur of wine. It was said that he would eat two or three dozen Eastern oysters for lunch; it was claimed that he started each day by drinking a full tumbler of half-whiskey and half-absinthe before breakfast. Scannell, Tobin, O'Brien, Spreckels—these were only a few. Every merchant, every banker, every gambler, and every minister of the gospel was a member of San Francisco's proudest aristocracy—the firemen.

That was all long ago, the days of the fire companies. The end of the 'sixties saw the community become a prosperous and cosmopolitan city, and little remained but the glory of the firemen. Then forty years passed, and once again, in 1906, the flames raced through the city streets. The water mains were broken; debris piled the streets so that the engines could not get through. And out of the hotels and

38

the mansions and the shacks came the men of San Francisco
—sons of the men of the old fire companies!

Again they fought—fought with wet sacks, with sand,
with shovels, and brooms, and with dynamite. The flames
became one of the most terrible conflagrations in the history
of mankind, and the fire fighters mastered the flames, leaving
one-half the city in smoldering ruins. Little remains of those
ruins today. Out in Golden Gate Park at the edge of a lake
there is a stone archway that was once the doorway of the
Towne mansion on Nob Hill. Portals of the Past! It stands
there, mute, beautiful relic of the great fire, relic of the traditions of San Francisco's fire fighters.

V

The Bella Union

Two of San Francisco's traditional prides are in its theaters and in the strange characters seen on its streets. And once, one of its least important street characters and one of its most famous theaters came together in strange association. The unimportant street character was a disreputable creature called, Oofty Goofty. As for the place, "theater" is a misnomer; it was called a "melodeon." In those days melodeons claimed the popularity of theaters without having their dignity, and this most famous of them all was the Bella Union.

The Bella Union was built in 1849 as a gambling palace. Little by little the gambling fell off and the palace was devoted to convivial spectators who sat at tables, drinking their conviviality, and watching the performance on the small stage. Its manager was Sam Tetlow. Sam put on the forerunner of burlesque shows, and Sam put on legitimate drama, notably a dramatization of a new best-selling novel called *Dombey and Son* by young Mr. Dickens of London. The full-bearded miners drank their libations and sobbed great tears into their cups as they listened to the trials and heart-rending tribulations of Paul Dombey.

So, it was *Dombey and Son* one night at the Bella Union, and from the playbill of another night we quote: "Full-grown People Are Invited to Visit the *Bella Union* if You Want to 'Make a Night of It.' The Show Is Not of the Kindergarten Class, but Just Your Size, if You Are Inclined to Be Frisky and Sporty."

In the list of attractions at the Bella Union was found James A. Hearne who later became David Belasco's partner. The great minstrel, Charlie Reed, played there. And Ned Harrigan of Harrigan and Hart, the famous "Mulligan Guards." On a night in 1862 it featured between dramatic acts the great Mlle Ella Cadez. Ella, according to the bill of fare, would essay a "terrific ascension from the stage to the gallery, without a balancing pole, on a single wire."

Lotta Crabtree played the Bella Union; Eddie Foy played there, as did James O'Neill of Monte Cristo fame who was the father of Eugene O'Neill. Jeff de Angelis played there as had his father before him, and there was Lola Montez, also.

Lola had come to San Francisco by steamer. The vessel docked at the Howard Street wharf where the Telephone Building now stands. Five hundred San Franciscans detached horses from the carriage that was to carry La Montez through the streets. A thousand hands grasped the ropes and dragged the carriage, everyone cheering as they went. And in the carriage, bowing and smiling and tossing kisses to right and left, rode Lola.

They dragged the carriage to the Bella Union. They lifted Lola in their arms and carried her into the theater and placed her on the stage. They roared, "Dance, Lola! Sing, Lola!" And Lola, who could not dance very well and could not sing at all, danced and sang. And when she had finished they threw gold—bags of gold dust, nuggets of gold—on the stage, and the stagehands heaped the gold around her till she was completely hidden from sight . . . so the story is told.

In the 'eighties a lady arrived in San Francisco, claiming to be a wealthy widow. She was looking for a kind-hearted gentleman who would protect her fortune for her. She weighed two hundred eighty pounds; she was called by the only name she was ever known to have—Big Bertha. There were many kind-hearted gentlemen in San Francisco willing to guard Bertha's fortune. But, as a token of good faith, she demanded that they put up a sum of money for an investment the nature of which she would not divulge. The kind-hearted put up the money and never saw it again.

Bertha—Big Bertha—was finally arrested, but none of her victims was willing to face ridicule, and the charges were dismissed. And then the manager of the Bella Union hired an empty store on Market Street and exhibited her as "Big Bertha, the Queen of the Confidence Women, Admission Ten Cents." According to old-timers, Bertha would relate harrowing crimes she had never committed, and then she would sing "A Flower from My Angel Mother's Grave." She was a success; her popularity was unbounded. And, having earned a larger audience, she moved to the Bella Union.

At the time that Big Bertha was shaking the stage of the Bella Union with her song and her dance, another popular act was appearing in a Market Street sideshow. The actor was a very small man, very thin, and very hungry. He was bathed in tar, horsehair was applied to the tar, and the little man who wanted to be a great dramatic actor was billed as "The Wild Man from Borneo, Recently Captured in the Jungles and Brought to the Golden Gate at Great Expense."

San Francisco showered its dimes to see the "Wild Man."

42

When the place was crowded to the door, the Wild Man was revealed chained in his cage, and great hunks of raw meat would be thrust between the bars. The Wild Man would seize the meat and swallow hunks of it and then shake the bars of his cage and roar "Oofty Goofty!—Oofty Goofty!" And that was the only name by which he was ever known in San Francisco. Any old-timer will tell you that he remembers Oofty Goofty, or that his father remembered him. No character in the city had greater fame as a performer. But his real fame was to come later.

Over at the Bella Union, Big Bertha was playing to packed houses. Even so, the management felt that the show could not stand still; something needed to be added to sustain the popularity. Consequently, the management announced a colossal performance of the romantic drama, *Romeo and Juliet*, by William Shakespeare. And, announced the management, Juliet would be played by Big Bertha, and Romeo—Romeo would be played by Oofty Goofty!

And they played it! Of course, there had to be one innovation that Mr. Shakespeare had not planned: Big Bertha was too heavy to be hoisted to the balcony, and the balcony was too frail to support her. So, in the balcony scene, Big Bertha read Juliet's lines from the ground and little Oofty Goofty played Romeo in the balcony. But, small as he was, Oofty could not forget his training as the Wild Man of Borneo. He made of Romeo a roaring wild man, a brutal cave man. And Big Bertha emerged from each performance covered with black-and-blue bruises. She swore she would never play the part again. The Wild Man was given his notice. And Big Bertha traveled on alone from success to success until eventually she became the manager and owner of the Bella Union.

But Oofty Goofty's story was not ended. He went from theater to theater and melodeon to melodeon doing a song-and-dance act. He was broke; his dancing was bad, his singing was worse. He was booked at Bottle Koenig's, a disreputable dive on the Barbary Coast. One night, in a rage, the management of Bottle Koenig's lifted the little man bodily and flung him through the open door to the sidewalk. He landed with a crash that would have broken the backs of most men. But, to his surprise, Oofty Goofty found that he felt no pain. And out of that misadventure came his path to fortune. For years Oofty Goofty haunted the saloons and clubs of San Francisco; every San Franciscan knew him and his reputation. For a dime you could kick him as hard as you pleased; for fifty cents you could hit him across the haunches with a baseball bat. He was known in every disreputable and every respectable corner of the city. Every citizen of prominence kicked or hit Oofty Goofty—it was a San Francisco tradition. But none could hurt him. He was proud of his art, even prouder than he had been of his achievement as a Shakespearean Thespian.

And then, one day—one dismal day—the world's heavyweight champion boxer, John L. Sullivan, came to San Francisco. In his cups John L. was led to Oofty Goofty. The scene was a billiard parlor. They shook hands, the giant and the little wild man, and Oofty received his fee. Then John L. hit him with a billiard cue. It was a blow under which the average man would have died. But not Oofty! He limped away, his spine fractured, and disappeared from the city streets. He died a few years later, a pauper, ending the story of one of San Francisco's most famous and most unimportant characters.

44

VI

Jim Savage

This is the story of one of the most adventurous individuals ever to lend color to the story of California and San Francisco, and of his greatest adventure, one that will never be forgotten. But his name is forgotten save to a very few.

James Savage, or "Jim" as he was always called, was born somewhere in the Middle West sometime between 1815 and 1820. That is all very indefinite and equally unimportant. When he was about sixteen years old his family moved to Princeton, Illinois. He was one of six children, and if his history up to that time was indefinite, there was nothing indefinite about the mark the six young Savages made on Princeton. They were a lively brood, constantly in trouble, and constantly looking for and managing to find adventure. And Jim was the most adventurous of the brood, and his nose for trouble was proverbial. He was a straight-shouldered, good-looking lad, very tall, very strong, very good-natured, and thoroughly likable, and when his escapades became too serious his charm could always talk him out of trouble.

Jim fell in love with a girl named Eliza. Jim was wild, gay, reckless; Eliza was serious, quiet, and deeply religious. And because he was so much in love with her, he agreed to go to church with her one Sunday morning in Princeton.

The two of them, boy and girl, rode down the turnpike on their horses and into the churchyard. Services had already commenced. But it was a warm, sultry morning, and at the last moment Jim revolted. He would rather stay out in the sunshine than go into the crowded little church. Eliza insisted; she said it was unnatural for a man to have no religion. Jim said he was flooded with religion, but that he could pray just as well in the open air under God's sky as he could behind four walls. Patiently the good Eliza explained that every man needed at some time to kneel in prayer and give thanks to his Creator—and in church a body could kneel.

Jim shook his head and said, "No. When I want to kneel and pray I'll do it out in the open, under the Lord's heaven. Like this!"

And suiting the action to the word, he flicked the foreleg of his horse with a willow branch, and the horse, trained to do just that, settled to its knees, and Jim bowed his head in prayer. At that moment, to the mortified horror of Eliza, the doors of the church opened and out came the congregation led by the minister. With a great laugh the minister pointed to Jim astride his kneeling horse, and said, "There, my children, is a truly virtuous man."

A month after the alfresco prayer in the churchyard, Eliza and Jim Savage were married in that small church, and after they had been married a short time and Eliza had become imbued with Jim's love of adventure, the two started West to seek their fortune. Theirs was one of the first wagon trains to cross the plains headed for California. The year was 1846. The journey was hard and cruel; there were months of hunger and blistering heat and biting cold, there were the traditional attacks by hostile Indians. Jim and

Eliza and Jim's brother, Morgan, who accompanied them, took dangers and hardships in their stride.

But there came a day on the Great Plateau when Eliza's baby was born—dead. Eliza, strong under danger and privation, could find no strength to support her in the loss of her baby. Day after day, night after night, she lay weak and listless on her straw mattress in the wagon. Morgan Savage tried to cheer Jim with the promise of good things ahead. But one night, as the two men sat at the side of a campfire listening to the mournful howling of coyotes and speaking in low voices of their stupidity in bringing a young girl on such a hopeless journey, Eliza called Jim. He kneeled at her side and she held his hands and told him how happy they would be in the sunshine of California; in California she would find strength again, she would love the flowers that grew in California and the singing birds and the sunshine.

Eliza died that night peacefully in her sleep, her hands in Jim's. Savage buried her out there in the plains and then, heartbroken, lonely, all spirit of adventure, all ambition gone, he plodded on with the wagon train to the slopes of the Pacific. And just as darkness had come into his life, so for a long period the pages of his life were unrecorded history; no one knew what had become of him.

Of course, there were rumors, many rumors, many of them unfounded, some of them possibly true. Some say he fought in the Bear Flag Rebellion, fought with California against Mexico, and it is pretty certain that he did. You will find his name coupled with the adventures of Frémont and Kit Carson. He was seen walking along the dusty road in the village of Yerba Buena, a silent, morose man, unfriendly and uncivil. Yerba Buena was a quiet sleepy place

47

then—this was late in 1847—and Savage was marked because of his unfriendliness and his aloneness.

Then, with the coming of 1848 and the discovery of gold, and 1849 with the Gold Rush, the quiet, sleepy village of Yerba Buena became a hectic, wild, noisy city of thirty-five thousand men, men intent on finding gold and with nothing else to interest them. In the fighting, shouting, carousing crowd Jim Savage was ignored and then forgotten; when he again disappeared he was not missed. No man who disappeared was missed in the hectic and chaotic San Francisco of 1849.

But suddenly, just as swiftly as he had disappeared, his name began to be spoken of again. Only now fantastic tales were told about him, and his deeds became famous in every camp and digging of the Southern Mines. Men said he had surrounded himself with a tribe of Indians and had become more than their chieftain—he had become their king! It was a tribe unknown and nameless. Then they said he had become chief of the Mariposa tribe, and that five other Indian tribes had joined him, and that he had become the great power among all the Indian tribes of the Sierra.

His name traveled from mouth to mouth, and few white men knew him but all knew of him. It was reported first that he had taken an Indian wife and later that he had *five* Indian wives, one from each of the tribes he controlled. The wedding of a wife from each of the powerful tribes was said to have given him complete control over the tribesmen.

The stories claimed that he lived the life of a Persian potentate, his subjects bringing him fabulous treasures of gold, so that soon he was said to be the richest man in California. But, strangest of all the tales told about him was the one that told how at his order thousands of Indians were

48

carrying gold to him from secret pockets and veins unknown to white men.

Much of the fantastic story must have been true, for Jim Savage did accumulate great hills of gold dust and gold nuggets, and no white man knew their source, nor would the Indians reveal their secret. He established trading posts on the Mariposa River and the Fresno River and the south fork of the Merced. He brought from San Francisco calicoes and beads and cartridges, and traded them for more gold dust.

But he had enemies. There was one tribe of Indians high in the Sierra that continually attacked and plundered the trading posts. And these Sierra Indians were influencing his loyal followers, and there was civil war in the camps. So, Jim Savage called a council meeting and, speaking to his tribes, told them of a great city by a great water where there were tens of thousands of white men, a hundred white men for every Indian. And if the tribes did not mend their ways, he said, he would bring a great army of white men from that city by the great water and punish the Indian tribes.

The Indians were impressed but not convinced. A spokesman for the tribes said, "How shall we know that there is this great city by the Great Water?"

And, to convince them, Jim Savage organized one of the most amazing expeditions ever to visit San Francisco.

At that time the city was draped with flags and buntings. It was October 25, 1850. On the twenty-ninth the city would celebrate the admission of California into the Union. Bands played in the streets, men marched and countermarched and cheered and fought and drank—the roof was off. And into the celebration came Jim Savage and his band of Indians.

They straggled to the doors of the Revere House, a dozen painted and almost naked Indian braves. After them came three Indian squaws carrying a huge barrel of gold dust. As they went, the braves dipped their hands into the barrel and scattered gold dust to right and left. The streets of San Francisco were paved with gold that day. But while the Indians were scattering gold, Savage was spending gold, buying bolts of calico and muslin, buying guns and beads and coffee and sugar and brass collar buttons and gold chains and silk ribbons to take back to his trading posts to buy the good will of the rebel tribesmen.

On the twenty-ninth of October, when the celebration was at its height, Savage marched out of the city again, followed by his handful of Indians, whiskey-soaked, and the squaws soberly laden with merchandise for the trading posts. The expedition reached the Fresno River post to find it depleted by marauding tribes. White traders traveling through the valley of the San Joaquin had been killed by Indians. The Mariposa tribe was on the warpath. All the tribes were out of control.

But now California was a state of the United States and its Governor, John McDougal, was appealed to. He created a battalion of several hundred men and ordered them to put an end to Indian warfare. He named them the Mariposa Battalion and put Jim Savage at their head with the rank of Major. They came from all corners of Mariposa County, and in those days the county reached south to the Tehachapi. They came with squirrel rifles, with blunderbusses, with any kind of weapon they could lay their hands on, and went into encampment near the mining town of Mariposa. Hostile tribes, unimpressed, sallied into the village, plundering the stores, killing peaceful citizens, raping women, and causing general havoc. And strange and mysterious stories began to circulate; it was said that these Indians came from an inaccessible hiding place high in the Sierra, and that it was in this place, called by Indians the Home of the Gods, that the great and endless fortune of gold was hidden, the fortune that had supplied Jim Savage.

On March 25, 1851, Major Jim Savage marched at the head of his battalion. His aides were Captain Boling and a Dr. Lafayette H. Bunnell. They marched due east up the banks of the Merced River into a country no white man had ever before traversed, marched to Jim Savage's great adventure. The going was rough. Great trees bound together by a jungle of undergrowth blocked the way. They came to cliffs that were insurmountable, and miles of terrain had to be traversed to circle them. When the walls of the canyons were too sheer, they scrambled from rock to rock in the bed of the river, more than five hundred men fighting their way up that river through miles that had known no white man before.

Finally they came into a clearing on a rise of land. Through the trees they could see what appeared to be the edge of a precipice; it was the highest point of land in any direction. Savage ordered Boling to break the march there and rest with the men. He, Savage, would go ahead with Lafayette Bunnell to reconnoiter.

Slowly the two men, Savage and Bunnell, together with a reluctant Indian scout, worked their way, slashing shrubs and undergrowth with their axes. Savage was in the lead, Bunnell a dozen feet behind. Suddenly Savage cried out; he had reached the crest of the precipice. He stood there as though frozen, one arm extended at full length, his hand tense, his finger pointing straight ahead.

51

"Look, Bunnell!" he shouted. "Look! It's an inspiration!"

There, rising before them, rising from the floor of the valley below, were cliffs a mile high. There, at their left, like a great sentinel guarding the entrance to the valley, was a rock thousands of feet high. Falling from the crest of the cliff beyond, a ribbon-like waterfall plunged thousands of feet in two gigantic drops to the valley's floor. And on their right were three great rocks like three guardsmen, and down their side another waterfall, this one spreading like a veil—a bridal veil, and the sun falling on it, painting it with rainbow hues. And there, directly ahead of them, miles away and yet so close it seemed as though they could touch it with their outstretched hands, loomed a monstrous boulder, miles high, and cleft in half as though a giant had split a gigantic dome with a bolt of lightning.

"It's an inspiration!" Savage shouted again. "This is Inspiration Point!"

Jim Savage and Lafayette Bunnell stood in awed silence and watched the shadows lengthen—the first white men to look on the wonders of the Yosemite Valley. The point where they stood is called Inspiration Point today.

The men were inspired, but Savage had come on stern business. He called Captain Boling, assembled the battalion, and the men wound their way down the walls to the floor of the valley of the Yosemite. The Indian tribes had fled, leaving one toothless old squaw, too aged to travel.

Scouting parties were sent up beyond the huge Half Dome into the canyon of the Tenaya and into Merced Canyon beyond Merced Falls, but the camp of the Indians was never discovered nor was the source and the hiding place of their wealth of gold. Later they did capture Chief Tenaya

52

and a small group of his followers without bloodshed. With the discovery of the Yosemite the Mariposa Indian War ended and the Mariposa Battalion was disbanded.

And Jim Savage, the discoverer of the Yosemite, returned to his trading posts and his Indian tribes. New and glowing stories of his prowess began filtering up and down the San Joaquin Valley. He had won the good will of the Indians of the Tuolumne; he had won the favor of the Indians of the King's River tribes. His followers were increasing and his wealth was increasing. And in the wake of these reports came new rumors: the white traders of the King's River resented the business he was taking from them. They declared open warfare on him; under the leadership of Captain Walter Harvey they dared Jim Savage under penalty of death ever to set foot in King's River territory.

One day—it was in August of 1852—Jim Savage crossed King's River, rode up to the door of the trading post and jumped from his saddle. Out strode Captain Harvey.

"I'm James D. Savage," said Jim. "I understand, Captain, that you say I am no gentleman."

"I have frequently made that statement," the Captain answered.

In carefully chosen, polite, and deliberate phrases, Savage invited the Captain to leave the country. The Captain rejected the invitation.

"Then," said Savage, "maybe this will help you change your mind."

His fist caught Harvey on the chin and the Captain dropped to the ground. Slowly he pulled himself to his elbow and fired from his hip. And Jim Savage, friend of the Indians and discoverer of the Yosemite, lay dead, his body torn from four bullets from Captain Harvey's gun.

53

VII

"Lord" Charlie Fairfax

Down on Sacramento Street near Kearny many years ago, a group of men stood and stared at a spot that had stained the wooden sidewalk. A brown spot, it might have been mud or a pot of stew spilled from the head-tray of a Chinese cook— it might have been almost anything. But the men standing there knew that it was blood. They stared and shook their heads, and one said, "We ought to have it washed off. It will remind us too much of sorrow." But another of the group said, "No, that's the blood of the man who loves San Francisco more than any other of us, and is loved better than any other man in San Francisco. Let it stay there, a part of the city we're building. Strangers'll not know it's blood; they'll not even notice it. But we'll always know. Let it stay."

The men walked away, shaking their heads, and the rains came teeming down the Sacramento Street hill and dimmed and washed away the brown spot. The years came and went and erased all memory of the spot. The wooden sidewalk gave way to cement pavements, and the sleepy hill-street became a roadway of progress. But neither rains nor cement pavements nor progress could erase the joy of living in the city of the pioneers, the city where men loved living and loved excitement and above all else loved laughter. And no other monument in San Francisco to the love of life and excitement and laughter could have greater significance than that brown stain of blood on Sacramento Street—the blood of "Lord" Charlie Fairfax.

Charlie Fairfax was instinctively a nobleman and innately a gentleman. He was the popular Beau Brummell of San Francisco's golden dawn. He wore a brown velvet coat and lace ruffles on his shirt in the days when linens were white and stiffly starched and gentlemen wore frock coats and silk hats and high boots and carried heavy guns in their belts. Fairfax had a mild, pleasant voice, his eyes were kind and always laughing; he was courteous, gallant, debonair, a charming gentleman when ladies were present, and a heavy drinker always. Of course, in those days tradition and etiquette demanded that a gentleman never refuse a drink and should always carry his liquor like a gentleman. Charlie Fairfax was always a gentleman.

He was born in Virginia. The Fairfax estate was great; the Fairfax family was of the First Families of Virginia. Hundreds of slaves toiled on the broad Fairfax acres (that once George Washington surveyed), and the gentlemen of the family toiled not at all.

Charlie was a gentleman in his family's accepted tradition, and yet he distressed his parents at times, not by a propensity for physical labor but by his avid hunger for knowledge. He was a scholar in the days when to be a student was too much effort for most aristocratic Virginians; he was a great reader in a day when Virginia gentlemen were men of action and their inclination to read was rare. Yes, young Charlie was constantly a confusing problem to his fond parents. He even had a democratic philosophy, and he enjoyed the friendship of his Negro slaves more than he enjoyed the fox-hunting gentlemen of the First Families.

55

Later on, in San Francisco, they would call him "Lord" Charlie always. And certainly he was in line of succession to the ancient Fairfax barony in England. Another American Fairfax of Virginia, long after Charlie had passed away, returned to England and claimed the title. But Charlie had no interest in such trappings. Though a dutiful son at heart and distressed to see his father infuriated and his mother dissolved in tears, he decided one day to leave it to them to be of the First Families of Virginia. As for him, he was heading for a land where titles meant nothing and the only nobility recognized was nobility of the soul. Charlie Fairfax took steamer for California.

Sailing through the Golden Gate, he saw the green, mellow hills of Marin and loved them. At the foot of Mount Tamalpais, standing across the Golden Gate from San Francisco, he found a hidden valley that he loved and that is named in his memory to this day—Fairfax Manor. But San Francisco and its excitement was a lodestone. And it was there that he traveled the road of laughter; he was San Francisco's court jester. He never achieved wealth; or, rather, he never kept wealth, because every dollar that came to his hand burned his fingers. He never achieved greatness, nor did he ever achieve despair. But he traveled a gay, laughing, middle course, a gallant gentleman, loved by all who met him.

Because they loved him, his friends elected him clerk of the Supreme Court of California. He drew a salary of thirty thousand dollars a year. He always spent a little more than thirty thousand dollars a year. He was always in debt, but he carried his debts with proud dignity. He won a beautiful and wealthy wife—a niece of the fiery statesman, John C. Calhoun—and celebrated by buying drinks for most of the city's population. It almost broke his wife's heart; he was constantly breaking her heart and he adored her and she adored him to the end. She scolded him when he was sober, scolded him when he was drunk, and then would shake her head and sigh and say, "What can a person do with Charlie? He's charming when sober, magnificent when drunk. And he's always laughing."

There was the day he met a friend who lamented the long, dry season. It had not rained in months. The heat and the dust were insufferable. All day Charlie pondered the problem. Certainly rain would end the heat and dust. At two o'clock in the morning he pounded on the door of the general merchandise store, awoke the clerk asleep in his bed in the back room, and purchased a large silk umbrella. Then, with consummate dignity, he strode home, silently opened his front door, entered his wife's room, and bowed with gallant grace.

It was three o'clock in the morning. Charlie's gallantry was exasperating.

"Charlie," moaned Mrs. Fairfax, "what are you doing with that umbrella?"

"Waiting for the rain," said "Lord" Charlie and, seating himself in an armchair, he opened the umbrella over his head and went to sleep.

An hour later the rain fell in torrents on the Fairfax roof.

Today he might be on top of the world, tomorrow he might not have the price of a drink and a lunch. For example, there was the day he walked down Montgomery Street; he was hungry and he did not have a dollar in his pocket. He met a friend who said, "Charlie, I've been cleaned at the faro table. Stake me to a breakfast." Charlie looked up and down Montgomery Street and spotted a third friend, a *bon vivant* of parts, and invited the newcomer to buy breakfast. The newcomer agreed. The three entered a fashionable French restaurant and ordered a huge meal during which the third man excused himself to go out on the sidewalk to speak to an acquaintance—and did not return!

And so "Lord" Charlie and the first friend sat. The check for the huge meal lay on the table, ominous. The friend was worried; "Lord" Charlie laughed. He called the waiter and reordered—two roast chickens and a bottle of French wine this time—and ordered that the chickens be cooked slowly and carefully.

The two men were served. They sat for two hours, eating, smoking rich Havana cigars. Then a fourth friend entered the restaurant and Fairfax told him of their predicament. The newcomer joined in the laughter and handed Fairfax fifty dollars and walked out, still laughing.

Fairfax paid the check, and the two companions went out to the street and met the third friend—the one who had left them in the lurch. He explained that he, too, had been hungry and penniless and knew no other way to get a square meal. So Charlie gave him the balance of the fifty dollars and went home.

Up one day, down the next, he spent years in the gay, laughing, carefree life of San Francisco, loving it always. But there came a longing to see his home in Virginia and his parents.

He made the journey in style. He was greeted and folded in his mother's arms. She took him to her boudoir and whispered confidentially, "Charlie, you know father is a stern prohibitionist and frowns on strong liquor. But I know you must have become accustomed to the evil in the wild West. So, I have a bottle for you. But don't tell Father."

Charlie kissed his mother, drank a toast to her, hid the bottle in his room, and went to his father's study. His father solemnly closed the study door and spoke.

"Charles," he said, "you know my sentiments about whiskey. But I feel sure your system must have become accustomed to the foul habit in the wicked West. Here, my boy, is a bottle. But don't tell your mother."

"Lord" Charlie embraced his father, drank his health in a toast—and hid the bottle. Then he went to the stable to greet an old Negro-slave friend, named Jeff.

With mysterious gestures and whispers, Jeff closed the stable door and said, "Massa Charlie, ah jes' knows how powerful they drink in that wild California. Ah's got a bottle of whiskey for you, but don' tell yo' mammy and don' tell yo' pappy."

"Lord" Charlie Fairfax had a thoroughly enjoyable time during his short visit to the old homestead.

He returned to San Francisco to drive his devoted wife to distraction with his pranks. His old friends hailed him; San Francisco had not been the same without him. The city celebrated; it was a fine, a merry, and an alcoholic celebration.

Then, one day, he was walking down Sacramento Street. He was stopped by an individual who had been a deputy under him in the Supreme Court. The man called him to account for alleged injustices, challenging him in foul terms that no gentleman could countenance. Fairfax grasped him by the throat and shook him like a rat and flung him from him. And as Fairfax, disgusted, turned away, the deputy brandished his cane, whipped a sword from it, and attacked. Fairfax swung and countered the sword thrusts with his bare fists. But his assailant lunged and thrust him through the shoulder.

Charlie Fairfax sank to his knees, drew a derringer from his vest pocket and aimed it at his assailant. Then he shook his head, dropped the gun, and said, "No. What's the use? You are a cowardly murderer. You have killed me. But you have a wife and small children. On this account I will spare your life."

With that he sighed and fainted, and his blood streamed on the wooden pavement of Sacramento Street. Friends gathered, and careful hands lifted him and carried him away. He lay in his bed, dying, and scores clustered about his door and wept. It did not seem possible that Charlie Fairfax was going to die. He had been the life of the city, San Francisco's court jester, its Beau Brummell. It was not right that he should die this way, murdered in cold, treacherous blood. The brown stains on Sacramento Street were mute witness to the infamy. But it was hopeless. The blade of the sword had grazed his heart; the doctors knew that he could not live.

They tried to comfort the weeping wife who had stood by him through all his folly. And then suddenly Charlie Fairfax realized that his world was become a world of tears, and he hated tears. He began to laugh, to laugh aloud. Weakly he struggled up from his pillow, weakly he waved the remonstrating doctors away. And in a voice struggling for breath, he said, "I can't die yet. There's too much I still want to do. Too much fun I still want to have. I guess I'll not die this time."

Now, these have just been passing incidents of nonsense in the life of "Lord" Charlie Fairfax. He had been and he continued to be a leader in the city's civic life. He even helped to build the city's first fashionable residential park, South Park. The town of Fairfax in Marin County was named after him.

He lived for eleven years after the day of the attack on Sacramento Street, fully enjoying the ups and downs of fortune. He saw the golden dawn spread to the full brilliance of California maturity. He saw the gentlemen-vagabonds discard their high boots and don dancing pumps of patent leather; he saw men about town mix water with their whiskey; he saw them turn from rich, fifty-cent cigars to cigarettes. Cobblestones replaced the wooden sidewalks and streets of mud; cable cars clanged up the hills where goats had grazed; roistering gamblers and bearded vigilantes were crowded out by tea parties and college boys.

And "Lord" Charlie Fairfax, watching the changes, looked at the new city of San Francisco and chuckled, bowed his head and said, "What's the use?"—and died.

VIII

James Lick

The year was 1847. A three-master, with all canvas spread, bent her head to a driving gale and slid through the Golden Gate. She was the good ship *Lady Adam* out of South America with a precious cargo of coffee and rough mahogany and cowhide. She slid down the Bay and dropped anchor in the waters that washed the northern slope of Telegraph Hill. The little village of Yerba Buena—a half-dozen shacks, a few tents—spread there, as yet unawakened by gold.

A small boat put out to greet the *Lady Adam,* received a consignment of coffee and hides. And, said the skipper, a supercargo was to be put ashore too. The skipper of the *Lady Adam* was a swaggering, contemptuous figure. A supercargo to be put ashore, he said; a crazy individual—absolutely mad—come all the way from South America to make his fortune in the barren, fog-blanketed sand dunes of Yerba Buena! It was plain lunacy! There was no fortune to be made in a sleepy, Spanish-Californian village. But, concluded the skipper, that was what the creature had come for, and who was he, the skipper, to argue? Anyway, he was crazy and there was no arguing with him; let him go ashore and more power to him in his madness. His name was Lick.

James Lick had been born in Fredericksburg, Pennsylvania, in 1796. From early youth he craved wealth, not for the comforts it afforded, but for the pleasure of possession. He had been apprenticed to a manufacturer of pipe and reed organs, and from his apprenticeship had drifted into the manufacturing of pianos. Not that he had the soul or the instincts of an artist; he did not care for art and he did not care for music. There was money to be made in the piano business, and that was all that interested him. Literally that was all; life offered little else. He had no friends; he disliked people. He just wanted to make money and be left alone.

Being daft, he went from Pennsylvania to the Argentine, the last place in the world a man of reason would choose for profit in pianos. For ten years he sold pianos and bought hides, and with the profit made by trading in hides he sailed for Yerba Buena. Sewed in his pocket were his profits, forty thousand dollars, the beginning of his fortune.

The village of Yerba Buena, soon to be called San Francisco, was a village of a thousand people. They lived in shacks clustered at the foot of Telegraph Hill; they were explorers, adventurers, opportunists. The opportunists, in particular, were happy to greet James Lick and his forty thousand dollars. They would show him how to invest his money. Someday the village would probably double in size, and he would double his fortune. But, no! James Lick was not asking for advice. Advice freely given was advice to be approached with suspicion.

For days and weeks he plodded to and fro, through the sand dunes, morose, silent, speaking to no man. He was a strange-appearing creature, a scarecrow of a man. People said the skipper of the *Lady Adam* was right—he was a madman. But when he ignored all advice and invested his fortune in sand lots, then indeed the good folk of Yerba Buena called him a stark, raving maniac. Who, with a vestige of that intelligence with which every man is supposed to be born, could conceivably expect to make money by sinking forty thousand dollars in a cow path that cut through the sand dunes? That cow path was later named Montgomery Street.

Two years passed, and gold was discovered at John Sutter's millrace. The village of a thousand became a mad, hysterical city. One night a man in a saloon laughed and spat his tobacco at the wall and said, "James Lick is the sanest individual in this city of madmen." Lick sold his cow-path lots and bought twice as many cow-path lots with his profits. He began to reach out in his operations; he reached the heights of folly by buying a large tract of arid land near the Mission San José, fifty miles to the south.

After that, in the night a strange, disheveled creature was to be seen slinking through the streets and alleys of San Francisco. Over his back he carried a filthy gunny sack, a sack as filthy as the garments he wore. He would go to the back doors of the hotels and restaurants and beg for scraped bones, old bones that were, after all, no good to anybody. Each night he would slink away, no one knew where, with his heavy bag of bones. Unquestionably he was mad.

But, suddenly one day his name was on every lip. He was building a flour mill on his land at Mission San José. It would cost a quarter-million dollars. It was to be finished in the finest of Argentine mahogany. And to his mill he was bringing the sacks of bones that had cost him nothing, and he was grinding them into dust—bone dust.

He dug the dust into the ground and planted an orchard of fruit trees. That proved conclusively that he was mad;

64

everyone knew that fruit trees would not grow in California. But James Lick's fruit trees, fertilized with the dust of the bones he had begged, grew and flourished. They were the beginning of the richest fruit-growing region in the world, Santa Clara Valley, where today in the spring hundreds of thousands of acres of blossoms are a floral monument to James Lick—blossoms of prune and apricot and peach and cherry and pear and walnut.

The cow path had become Montgomery Street; the sand lots had turned Lick's forty thousand dollars into millions. But still James Lick had no friends, nor wanted friends. Men pointed at him when he walked down Montgomery Street clad in his one dirty and disreputable suit of clothes.

He had become a familiar sight in the city, one of the strange freaks of a city of freaks. Men called him the miser-millionaire. He gave nothing, spent almost nothing, not even for sustenance. His gaunt, skeleton-like frame gave witness to his starvation diet. It did not seem possible to live on the little he fed to his body. The restaurants that had given him free bones made little profit on the meals he bought.

And then, one day he walked down Montgomery Street and stopped at a crossing, a crossing that later was to be called the corner of Sutter and Montgomery streets. He stopped and he gave orders. A few days later the crossing was a beehive of activity. Men came by the score to excavate the sand lot, teams of horses hauled huge redwood piles that were driven into the shifting base of sand to make a firm foundation. And there James Lick built what was in that day the greatest hotel in the world.

The fame of the Lick House spread throughout the world and brought fame to San Francisco. No money had been spared to make it sensationally perfect. Into the great dining room the miser-millionaire poured a fortune. Here men could dine, could eat like kings. It was an exact replica of the dining hall of the Palace of Versailles. The floor of the salon was a beautiful masterpiece of wood laid in a mosaic of rich design; the walls were painted by America's greatest mural painters; between the murals hung great mirrors in exquisite frames of carved rosewood.

The Lick House opened, and Montgomery Street became a fashionable thoroughfare. And with the arrival of fashion, Lick's cow-path lots doubled and redoubled in value, again and again, till the miser-millionaire no longer knew how vast his fortune was.

At last the day came when James Lick faced the need of taking stock. He had been in California thirty years. In a city of vast fortunes, he was San Francisco's richest man. He was seventy-seven years old, his health was failing, he was tired and lonely—miserably, tragically lonely. He had no friends, no family, nothing in the world but countless millions of dollars. He sat in his dingy, dilapidated office and sent for an acquaintance, George Davidson, president of the California Academy of Sciences. George Davidson was a quiet man, a wise and kindly scholar. He listened quietly while Lick spoke, listened to the most amazing statement his scientific mind had ever grappled with. This was James Lick's summing up of his life. . . . '

He had, Lick said, devoted his years to the making of a fortune; he had labored harder than any laborer to make his fortune, and hard work had brought success. But now he was an old man. He could not live much longer, his health was bad and he was tired. All he had in the world was wealth; he was a pauper with a vast fortune of many millions, and he could not take a red penny of that fortune with him to the place he was going when he died. So—and this was to be his last great project—he would devote his remaining days or weeks or years, with the help of Davidson, to giving away his entire fortune before his death.

First, he would give the California Academy of Sciences a valuable piece of property on Market Street. Davidson thanked him and accepted the gift.

Then he would build, for humanity in general and California in particular, the world's greatest telescope. "It shall be the most powerful glass in the world," Lick said, "and I shall house it in the world's greatest and largest observatory. I shall build the observatory at the corner of Fourth and Market streets."

Davidson pointed out that an observatory at Fourth and Market would not be practical; the visibility and atmospheric conditions would be poor. He recommended that the observatory be built close to Lick's mahogany mill on the summit of Mount Hamilton. Lick, too tired to argue, accepted the advice. A hundred thousand dollars were spent to build a wagon road up the side of the mountain; a million and a quarter dollars were spent building the observatory.

And then Lick handed the balance of his fortune to George Davidson and said, "Give it to the poor. Tell them to wash and be clean." He had been a dirty, ill-kept man, but that became his favorite phrase—"Wash and be clean." A large portion of his fortune went to build the Lick Baths where not only free baths were at the disposal of the needy, but free laundry facilities as well.

He gave monies to erect an old ladies' home; he gave monies to the Society for the Prevention of Cruelty to Animals, and to various orphan asylums. And there was one more project conceived on the simple theory that a little learning helped a man to cope with the business of living, and that it was as important for the man who worked with his hands to understand his working tools as it was for the artist who designed the Palace of Versailles to understand the mechanics of his art. A school should be created, a school of manual arts and sciences. No, he did not want the school to bear his name; it should be called the California School of Mechanical Arts. With the remainder of his fortune he created that school which was to become, years after his death, the Lick-Wilmerding Polytechnic School.

James Lick's last days became a frenzy of giving, a desperate race to give away all his fortune before death should cheat him of his last triumph. Wealth had been easy to accumulate. He found it more difficult to give it away, at least with the speed that he demanded.

Finally, James Lick died, and San Francisco took stock of him. He had been the city's greatest miser. He had begged bones so that he would not have to buy fertilizer. He had starved his body to save pennies. He had ruthlessly refused to give a dime when a dime was begged of him; he had given to no man. He had no friends, no family, and, by the accepted standards of men, no happiness in life.

He had lived, the city's greatest miser.

He died, the city's greatest benefactor.

IX

Adah Isaacs Menken

Johnnie Heenan was a prize fighter. He had thick, black
hair; heavy, black eyebrows; a thick, black mustache, and a
brutal punch. He was born in the small California town of
Benicia and was known around the world as the Benicia
Boy. He fought, as was the custom of his times, with bare
fists. He was the boxing champion of America. He met
Tom Sayers, the international champion, in London, and
after they had fought for more than two hours and thirty-
seven rounds—during which Johnnie knocked Sayers down
twenty times—the British fight promoters, afraid that Johnnie would kill Sayers, called the fight off and naïvely called
it a draw.

Now, this is not to be the story of the Benicia Boy. But
he is important here because he married the lady who was
destined to be the most sensational actress—not the greatest
but the most sensational actress—San Francisco had ever
seen. She was Mrs. John C. Heenan. She was also Mrs.
Robert Henry Newell. She was also Mrs. James Barkley.
And she was Mrs. Alexander Isaac Menken. At birth she
was named Adah Bertha Theodore. To the world she was
the notorious, glamorous, beautiful, and infamous "Mazeppa"—Adah Isaacs Menken.

Adah Menken was to the San Francisco of Civil War

days what Tetrazzini was to the city in the early years of the twentieth century. She achieved her success and fame in San Francisco; she was a part of San Francisco life. From San Francisco her sensational fame as Mazeppa traveled around the world and, during the years she lived in the city and played Mazeppa (and her other forgotten roles), she belonged to the city. She was adored by its gay blades, and even to this day you may find very old gentlemen who, when you praise this or that actress, will look at you with pained surprise and say, "Young man, you and your generation have not lived. You should have known Adah Menken; you should have seen her in *Mazeppa*."

Not until 1938 were the probable facts of her birthplace and paternity established. Prior to that time she was variously reported to have been born in New York, Havana, and a half-dozen other places. She was said to have been born of a distinguished, old Southern family; another account claimed she was born in Arkansas of a French mother and an American-Indian father. Throughout the years of her life she consistently confused the issue by telling conflicting and varying stories, partly because she was ashamed of her parentage and partly because she was an actress always playing a role. The likeliest facts seem to be that Menken was born in New Orleans on June 15, 1835, that her mother was a very beautiful French Creole, that her father was Auguste Theodore, a highly respected "free" Negro of Louisiana.

She danced, when a child, in the ballet of the French Opera House in New Orleans. She was exceedingly bright; an exceptional scholar. She spoke French and Spanish fluently; she painted, wrote poetry that was of good quality and brought her early recognition. From New Orleans she went, while still a child, to Havana, danced there, and was

70

crowned queen of the Plaza. Then she forsook the ballet and turned to the stage and, on tour, landed in Texas. And in Texas, at the age of twenty-one, she married a very handsome and distinguished musician, Alexander Isaac Menken.

She adored Menken, and Menken worshiped her. But with the characteristics and traditions of his Jewish forebears, Menken wanted a wife, a home, a family. Adah was not at all interested in home or family; in fact, the only thing she shared sincerely with him was his religion—she adopted the Jewish faith and remained steadfast in it until her death. But as for home life—no. Adah preferred the adulations of her audience and the adoration of the young men who gathered at the stage door, arms heavy with roses. Menken swallowed his jealous pride as long as he could, but when Adah insisted on smoking cigarettes in public, that was the last straw. Ladies did not smoke! Menken left her.

So Adah Menken went her exciting way from town to town, and men fell in love with her and her poetry, with her intellect and her lovely face and her exquisite figure. And rather than see them unhappy, she was generous in her love.

In New York she met the Benicia Boy. He was a strong, a brutal man, not unattractive in his strength. His fame as a pugilist had traveled ahead of him, and Adah was fascinated. She married him. On their honeymoon the Benicia Boy taught her to box; she soon learned to hold her own when they sparred good-humoredly. But after a month of marriage the good humor went out of it, and Heenan made a practice of beating Adah every night after dinner. So she divorced him.

But then scandal broke. Search of the records showed that before marrying the Benicia Boy she had neglected to divorce Menken. She was quite innocent about it all; she had assumed it was the duty of the man of the family to attend to legal matters, including such details as divorce. But now the scandalmongers declared her a bigamist. Menken heard of the scandal, did the gentlemanly thing and divorced her, and everybody was happy.

Then Adah Menken gave birth to the Benicia Boy's son, and the baby died at birth. She had wanted, longed for, adored that baby. Its death, and the scandals, and her two marriages and divorces—all these coming swiftly one upon the other—were forerunners of a long period of tragic sorrow and failure. But never discouragement; she would never give up. She starved in New York. She gave readings from Shakespeare. She gave lectures on the life of the times. She had a boyish figure and she always wore her hair short—so, suddenly she appeared as Mr. Bones, blackface, in a minstrel show. Then, on the variety stage, she created a sensation by impersonations of Edwin Booth as Hamlet and Richelieu. But something—something truly sensational had to be done to make the public fully aware of her.

She met Blondin. Blondin was the brave gentleman who crossed the whirlpools of Niagara Falls on a tightrope. Blondin was enraptured by the beauty of the Menken. He wooed her, and she said perhaps—*perhaps* she would marry him if he would let her dance on the tightrope above Niagara with him—a husband-and-wife act.

Blondin said, "No." He was afraid Adah's beauty would distract him when he was above the whirlpool and he would fall to his death. No, he would do no tightrope act with the Menken. So they went on a vaudeville tour together.

That tour ended and Blondin went his way and Adah

went hers, and hers led to the door of her business manager, Jimmie Murdock. Adah told Jimmie, who adored her, that she wanted to be a great tragedienne—or a great comedienne —or both. She wanted to play Lady Macbeth and—or— Lady Teazle. Jimmie Murdock, something of a diplomat, told her she was too great to play Lady Teazle and not great enough to play Lady Macbeth, but that, because her boyish figure was so lovely and there was such fire in her voice and eyes, she should play in *Mazeppa*, the drama that was attracting some attention on Broadway. The story was based on the poem of Lord Byron. At the thrilling climax of the play, the noble Tartar lad, stripped of his clothes by his captors and bound to the back of a wild horse, dashed out of the wings up to the papier-mâché cliffs and disappeared in the clouds, while the audience grew hysterical with apoplectic applause.

It had been a tradition that during the ride of the barebacked horse, a stuffed dummy, naked and resembling Mazeppa, would be used. Menken would have no stuffed dummy. She would ride the horse herself. She would wear skin-tights. No matter how it shocked the audience that had never seen an actress in tights, she would play the role with dramatic realism; she would wear tights. So she wore tights. The audience was shocked——scandalized—horrified—*and* delighted! But New York was too stilted, too smug, too proper truly to appreciate great art. And Adah Menken said, "I'll go to the one place where the audience demands real art; I'll go to San Francisco."

On August 24, 1863, that supreme master of San Francisco's theatrical history, Tom Maguire, announced and presented at Maguire's Opera House the great Menken in the daring, the sensational, the unprecedented *Mazeppa* in which

"Miss Menken, stripped by her captors, will ride a fiery steed at furious gallop onto and across the stage and into the distance."

According to the San Francisco papers of the next day, that night all the streets leading to Maguire's Opera House were thronged with the most elegant of the city's elite. Ladies in diamonds and furs rode up in handsome carriages; gentlemen in opera capes and silk hats were their attendants. It was a first night such as the city had never before seen. And when (again quoting the San Francisco papers), at the sensational climax of the play, the Menken vaulted to the back of her full-blooded California mustang and, clad in flesh-colored tights with hair streaming down her back, galloped her steed at mad pace across the mountains of Tartary, the enthusiasm of the audience was a mad frenzy never to be forgotten. So thrilling was the performance that it is said that on the opening night the leading man, Junius Booth—brother of Edwin—stood in the wings and completely forgot his lines.

Among the young men in the audience that night, and night after night that followed, were the three friends—Bret Harte, Joaquin Miller, and Charles Warren Stoddard. And these three, and scores of others, fell in love with Adah Menken, and it was even whispered that she was lavish with her love in return. But of all her admirers, she smiled on the young American humorist, Robert Henry Newell, and he became her third husband.

Bohemian San Francisco took Adah Menken to its gay and ample bosom. She was an actress, and it loved actresses; she was a painter, and it loved artists; and, above all, she was a poetess, and it adored poets and poetesses. Wherever you went, to whomever you talked, the two favorite topics

74

of conversation in San Francisco—topics of equal importance —were the progress of the Civil War and the success of Adah Isaacs Menken.

Her fame increased. Imitators sprang up. In fact, one of these was Big Bertha, the circus fat lady who had played Juliet opposite Oofty Goofty's Romeo at the Bella Union. Big Bertha played Mazeppa in pink tights, strapped to the back of a donkey. But one night the donkey, with huge Bertha astride him, fell over the footlights into the theater pit, and the career of Bertha as Mazeppa ended.

Adah Menken's marriage to Robert Newell lasted two years. Then she divorced him and married Mr. James Barkley about whom little is known. After all, none of her husbands was important in the life of Adah Menken.

And San Francisco went on adoring her, the San Francisco that had adopted her as its favorite daughter. The St. Francis Hook and Ladder Company made her a member of its fire-fighting brigade; she was presented with a beautiful fire belt, and the entire brigade, accompanied by a brass band, serenaded her. Her world was at her feet.

And then, quite suddenly the Menken decided she wanted new worlds to conquer. She took *Mazeppa* to Paris and London. During the tour she fell in love with, and was adored by, Alexandre Dumas, *père*. Dumas, *fils,* threatened to horsewhip his father for being a senile Romeo. So Menken left Dumas and went to London.

She played Mazeppa, and London went wild. Charles Dickens fell in love with her; Charles Reade fell in love with her; Dante Gabriel Rossetti, Tom Hood, and a score of others wooed her. And, as always, the Menken was generous with her love. Life was full and rich and exciting.

But the tide turned. Ill health, the fruit of dissipation,

75

wasted her away. She had made a fortune; her great wealth disappeared, and she lived in comparative poverty. In London, desperately in need of funds, she published her volume of Victorian poems and realized a few dollars.

London was cold, unfriendly. She returned to Paris—and Paris had found new loves.

Faithful to her adopted religion, she spent her last hours speaking of life and faith and hope to a friendly rabbi. Then she wrote a brief note to an acquaintance. It was her hail and her farewell. She wrote, "I am lost to art and life. Yet, when all is said and done, have I not at my age tasted more of life than most women who live to be a hundred? It is fair, then, that I should go where old people go."

Then she died. She was thirty-three years old. Her passing was unmarked, save for a brief eulogy in verse that appeared in a Paris paper:

> Ungrateful animals, mankind;
> Walking his rider's hearse behind,
> Mourner-in-chief her horse appears,
> But where are all her cavaliers?

X

The Tragic Tragedian

This is the story of a tragic tragedian. He was a great man, and San Francisco discovered him. There will be many who will say he was discovered in Baltimore, in Sydney, Australia, in Sacramento, or in a half-dozen other cities. But he lived for many years in San Francisco, he first found expression in San Francisco, he was patted on the head by San Franciscans with a patronizing smile of approval, and later he was acclaimed by San Francisco as the greatest actor of his day.

He first attracted attention when he sat in the wings of a small theater off Sansome Street and strummed on a banjo and sang English ballads under his breath, while his father, slightly intoxicated, ranted and raved and chewed the scenery. The production was *King Lear*; his father was Junius Brutus Booth.

Junius had sired twelve children, some of whom, by the kindness of Providence, died in early youth, easing the household budget. The banjo-playing lad was the youngest of the lot. By the time he arrived, details of education had become unimportant in the busy life of Junius. His youngest son, Edwin, could get along without an education; he'd take him along to play the banjo for him.

So Edwin Booth, tragedian, was doomed to a life of

tragedy. He knew sorrow and disillusionment and hunger. But the greatest tragedy, fully recognized by him, was that he had been refused an education. In the years when he read the classics, he hungered for the background of Greek and Latin that would have spiced the fare. He said of his reading, "I find myself groping in shadows through a brilliant realm of treasure."

His brother, Junius, Jr., had come to California, lived in San Francisco two years, and found the boom town avid for entertainment. It was literally a gold mine for nomad Thespians. So Junius, Jr., sent for Junius, Sr., and the middle-aged and quite successful tragedian set out for California with his banjo-playing son.

They played to the miners of San Francisco. Junius, Sr., ranted and spouted and raved and fumed—and the crowds cheered. And one night young Edwin was given a small part to play and the crowd didn't cheer. After the final curtain, his kind, old, intoxicated, and sentimental father told the boy that he would never be a great actor. He didn't sound like an actor; didn't speak like an actor. He just spoke like everyday people.

That was the key to Edwin Booth's greatness, and the reason that it took so long for him to be acclaimed. He wanted to sound like an everyday being, to act as men acted in real life. He played the great scenes of Shakespeare in a "conversational, colloquial" manner, and the effect on his audience was similar to the effect music would have had on an audience if a composition of Stravinsky had been played in the days of Johann Sebastian Bach.

It was July 28, 1852. The steamship *California,* out of Panama, docked at the foot of Telegraph Hill. Junius Booth stalked ashore, a magnificent, a noble and impressive gentleman, every inch an actor. With a broad gesture he lifted his hand in mute salute to the boom town. And the boom town cheered. He pressed his hand to his heart, lifted his eyes to the seven hills, and slowly lowered his eyelids. And the crowd cheered. With a noble sweep of his hand he presented it to the boy who trailed him, and the boy, slightly dazed, stared at the crowd, frightened and fascinated. And the crowd, looking back at the boy, saw a lad of some say sixteen, some say nineteen, thin of body but of amazing grace and litheness, with a face of arresting beauty, jet-black hair, and deep and large black eyes. The crowd laughed; he looked like a pretty clown, a comedian. But they cheered his illustrious father. They cheered him into the most immediate emporium of liquid refreshment, and Junius, atop the bar, shouted Hamlet's first soliloquy while the boy, Edwin, fell asleep.

Two days later, on July 30, 1852, the three Booths appeared at the Jenny Lind Theatre in the melodrama *The Iron Chest*. The names of only Junius, Sr., and Junius, Jr., appeared in the announcements and on the program. And once again Junius, Sr., frankly told the young Edwin that he was not destined to be a great actor; it would be enough if he played his banjo with greatness. But—and here the shrewd wisdom of the old trouper came to the fore—but said Junius, "If you are determined to tread the boards as immortals have trod them, lo, these two hundred years, then bear in mind the greatness of the bullfrog who lived in the swamp pool of our family estate near Baltimore. He was a great bullfrog and he achieved immortality because he knew that what he said did not matter. All that mattered was that he said it perfectly, always entertaining, never faltering, every sound clearly articulate although meaningless."

79

"But," said Edwin, "I want to play Hamlet, and you can't play Hamlet like an articulate bullfrog."

"Bah," said Junius, "don't argue!" And he strode into the street in quest of refreshment, and the crowd followed him from bar to bar, cheering. Junius never walked; he always strode.

It was only a few days later that Edwin did play a small part opposite his father's Hamlet at the Jenny Lind. And Tom Maguire, the owner, and Junius agreed it was a pity Edwin did not have the makings of a great actor in him—he looked so impressive and melancholy in his black tights.

The three Booths played San Francisco for a season and then toured the Mother Lode. The tour was a failure. The one-night stands wrecked the health of Junius, Sr., aided by the liquor he absorbed. They returned to San Francisco in September, penniless and discouraged. Junius, Sr., gave a benefit performance for himself and raised sufficient money to buy passage East. Edwin refused to go; Junius, Jr., remained too.

But Edwin did go to the dock to see his father climb on the steamship *Brother Jonathan.* "Climb" is an undignified word. Notwithstanding his shattered health, he strode on board, clasped Edwin's hand and said, "My son, I give you the greatest gift in the power of man—opportunity."

And while Edwin stood on the dock, tears pouring down his cheeks, Junius, Sr., blew his nose and wiped his eyes and thrust his hand into his bosom. And the *Brother Jonathan* pulled out into the stream.

Then young Booth, on his own, joined a small company of itinerant troupers and started into the hills. They played Shakespeare in tents. They spent weeks in Grass Valley and Nevada City, playing their roles but never making quite enough to pay expenses. And finally, destitute, the troupe started to walk through the snow of the Sierra foothills, from Nevada City to San Francisco, planning to stop on the way for a one-night engagement in Marysville.

They had little food, inadequate clothing. They slogged through snow and slush, Edwin playing his banjo as they went. They forced their way mile after mile. A rider overtook them. Mail had come through from the Atlantic seaboard. There was a letter for Edwin. His friend, George Spear, handed it to him. His other good friend, Old Spudge, watched him with worry as he opened the envelope—watched him as he faltered, as tears welled into his eyes.

Edwin stood there in the snow, shoulders slumped.

"He looks like the Melancholy Dane," whispered Spudge.

"Hold your tongue," whispered Spear.

And then Edwin lifted his chin. "My father is dead," he said. "He was a great man and he is dead."

The troupers clustered close about the boy, tried to console him. He brushed them off. He frowned when Old Spudge muttered, "Now, I suppose you'll desert the travelers."

"Desert the travelers?" the boy echoed. "No! We have an engagement in Marysville. Lead on, Old Spudge, and I'll play my banjo."

They played Marysville, and left there, broke. The company disbanded. Edwin Booth borrowed ten dollars, traveled to San Francisco, and eventually found his way to Australia. But California was in his blood. He had discovered the San Francisco that was yet to discover him. Returning from Australia, he returned to the Golden Gate, found no chance for acting, and worked his way up the river to Sacramento.

As usual he was broke. But he sat one night in the New Orleans Hotel in Sacramento and fell into conversation with an architect named Butler, a cultured man of broad vision. Butler knew the work of Junius Booth; he had watched the debut of young Booth with keen eyes. Now he took matters into his own hands. He planned a benefit performance. He publicized it the length and width of Sutter County. The house was sold out. Tickets went for as high as twenty dollars. The mayor of Sacramento made a speech in honor of the dead Junius. He presented Edwin with a pin of pure California gold—a hand clasping a diamond. The play was presented, and at its ending Edwin Booth took curtain call after curtain call. After the final curtain fell, a bag, heavy with gold dust, was dumped into his lap. And he shelled out the gold dust right and left, paying every debt he owed, till there was not a pennyweight left inside the bag. He was out of debt; but he was broke again.

Mr. Butler refused to be defeated. He announced a second benefit. He sent to San Francisco for a troupe of its finest actors and actresses to support the young Thespian.

Then he said, "What will you play, son of Junius Booth?"

And Edwin said, "Once in my life—just once—I must play Hamlet."

He played Hamlet. Even to the unschooled miners, it was a performance transcending in its greatness anything they had conceived possible. The triumph was complete; the applause was shattering. And white, pale, sad-eyed, and frightened, the slender youngster made his way to the dock of the steamship that would take him to San Francisco.

But there was a delay. Something was holding up the sailing of the steamer. A whispered rumor ran through the crowd. Butler, the philanthropist, had the money taken at the benefit and had not put in an appearance. The whispered rumor became angry shouts, cries to "Lynch the thief!" The shouts became a roar. And on the deck of the little river boat, Edwin Booth raised his hand for silence. The roar subsided.

Then Booth spoke: "My friends, 'there comes a tide in the affairs of men, which, taken at the flood, leads on to fortune.' It is time for the steamer to leave; we take the tide at the flood. And if I leave behind the gold you've gathered for me, then, still, you will have paid me more than my talents deserve."

Solemn-eyed, the mob stood. And suddenly Butler came striding through the crowd, the bag of gold under his arm. Whether he had emulated old Junius and imbibed too freely, or just overslept, history doesn't say. The steamer sailed, and Edwin Booth went on to San Francisco to play Hamlet and Lear and Romeo. And the distinguished critics of that season wrote, "This young man gives promise of being a very fine actor someday."

Out of San Francisco, Booth set sail on his tour of the world. It would be twenty years, almost to the day, before he played San Francisco again, and then it would be in the historical California Theatre built by Bill Ralston. When he returned, it was to be acclaimed the greatest actor of the century. Today critics say he was more than that; some call him the greatest actor of all times. But those twenty years away from San Francisco were years of tragedy; years during which he doubted his art, when he was tormented by loneliness, when he fought the doom of his heritage of intemperance, and hungered for love and found only grief with the women he loved and married.

There were those years, and that one terrible, bleak, and

devastating year when the madness of his brother fired the shot at Ford's Theatre. And a broken Edwin Booth went to his manager and said, "A good man and a most justly honored and patriotic ruler has fallen in an hour of national joy by the hand of an assassin."

He went into seclusion. He swore he would never appear in public again. The public demanded him. When he finally agreed to perform, they came to stone him—and stayed to overwhelm him with cheers.

Edwin Booth, who had his beginnings in San Francisco, was a tragic tragedian. But he, more than any other man in history, raised the theater from a place of ranting caricature to a mirror of mankind.

PART TWO

THE COMSTOCK, THE RAILROAD, AND CHAMPAGNE

XI

Adolph Sutro

This is a story of a single adventure in the life of one of the most amazing, forceful men in the gallery of fighting men who built San Francisco.

I saw him once when I was a small boy, almost fifty years ago. We were walking up Sutter Street one Saturday morning, my grandmother and I, and he came toward us. He lifted his silk hat, and Grandma bowed. He was a handsome old man with a high forehead; he was a large old man, with a heavy mustache and white hair and a very full white beard that looked like cotton glued to his face. He patted me on the head and told Grandma that someday she should bring me to see the pretty ladies in his garden.

He went on his way. And some weeks later Grandma did take me on the steamcar out to his garden, and to my disappointment, shattering to a minor degree my faith in humanity, I discovered that the ladies—the pretty ladies in the garden—were plaster statues. The old gentleman was Adolph Sutro.

He was born in 1830, in Prussia, of German-Jewish parents. He had a good education and he had ambition. His chosen career was that of a mining engineer, and, characteristic of mining engineers, when he was twenty years old he decided to go to a foreign country to practice. The obvious field was America. Seventy-five years had passed since the Revolution, and the New World was in the heyday of its prosperity.

Sutro came to America in 1850, and in 1851 joined the cavalcade headed for California and the gold fields. It was a utopia made to order for a young mining engineer. San Francisco was crude, unshaped. Every activity was related directly or indirectly to the quest for raw gold. So, Adolph Sutro found plenty of room for activity in his chosen field, and was successful. And he came to love San Francisco with a deep love that was to continue throughout the years of his life.

As the gold furor waned in California, a new bonanza fired the West. It was a dozen years after the discovery of California gold, and now the eyes of the world turned to Virginia City in Nevada. Comstock Hill had revealed pockets of gold of inconceivable worth.

When the first flurry subsided, two men became the brains of the bonanza. One of them was William Ralston, a generous, well-loved man who lived life with a zest, a kindly individual always ready to help those who needed help. To him, one day, came a shrewd real estate operator who had lost his fortune in a stock-market swindle. He was William Sharon. He needed help. Listening to his story, Ralston learned incidentally that Sharon was a good poker player—and Ralston dearly loved a good poker game. So he agreed to help Sharon. The two men formed a partnership, centering their activities in the Comstock.

The mines of Comstock Hill were rich with gold. But for every ounce of gold that was taken out, tons of water rushed through the shafts and passages of the hill, drowning miners, flooding the works. What was worse, some of the streams of water were boiling hot. Miners had been scalded to death. Evil gases rose from the shafts, endangering lives. The constant flood of water resulted in pneumonia and tuberculosis for the drenched miners. There were millions in gold to be had but, unless the waters could be turned away, every ounce of gold would take a man's life.

One day Bill Ralston was seated in his office in the Bank of California when a huge, handsome, dark-haired man was introduced. He had the eyes of a prophet, the enthusiasm of an evangelist, the determination of a Caesar. He wanted money from Ralston, money to perfect an idea he had worked on for five years. Ralston listened patiently to the visitor's fantastic scheme. He covered his amusement by tearing paper into bits and trickling them on the floor while he listened. The huge man was the thirty-five-year-old dreamer, Adolph Sutro. His plan—he would dig a tunnel four miles long beneath Virginia City, from the Comstock Lode to the Carson River, drive his tunnel right through Mount Davidson and drain the water out of the Comstock.

Of course, it was an absurd, fantastic scheme; it could never be done! Mining engineers had all agreed that there was no way to drain the mines. But, on the other hand, Ralston was desperate. The constant flood in the Comstock was threatening his holdings, threatening even the stability of his Bank of California. A fantastic idea; it couldn't be done! But again, on the other hand, if practical plans failed, the only hope was in fantastic dreams. After all, Ralston was a gambler, and he liked the enthusiasm and the flaming eyes of young Sutro. Yes, he would give him the money to dig his fantastic tunnel.

Weighing against the impractical elements of the scheme were the profits to be gained. Ralston was a shrewd banker as well as a gambler, and he could understand profits. The tunnel, if it could be built, would be a cheap method of draining water from the mine shafts. Moreover, in the digging of the tunnel, many previously undiscovered veins of gold would be uncovered that alone could well pay the cost of the project. And, most important, the tunnel would provide a passageway from the base of the shaft to the level country. No more expensive and difficult hauling of machinery and supplies up over the mountain. Machinery and supplies could all go in through the tunnel—and out of the tunnel, without aid of hoists, would travel the gold-bearing ore.

So, Ralston agreed to finance the project. But Sutro was equally shrewd. He had gone ahead with plans before he had approached the banker. He had had the path of the tunnel surveyed; he had consulted with famous mining engineers from Europe. He had brought engineers from Central Europe to study the plan, and he had organized the Sutro Tunnel Company and incorporated it. The project was to be engineered on sound business principles. The money promised by Ralston was to be only half of the funds required. Sutro agreed to raise by popular subscription $3,000,000 in cash. Interest rates were lower in the East than in San Francisco. Sutro would go to New York to fulfill his part of the bargain.

88

He went, and Eastern financiers were interested. They agreed to supply $3,000,000 for the project just as soon as Western endorsements could be produced. Well, that would be a simple matter. Ralston, Sharon, and their associates would back their promise with endorsements.

It was all *too* simple. Sutro returned to California to find himself stalemated at every move. The waters in the mines had receded to a lower level. Why should the bankers invest great sums of money to control floods that were apparently controlling themselves? And even more significant, why should they finance a project that would make the movement of supplies and machinery and ore inexpensive, when they owned the express and drayage companies that were making a fortune in the transportation? And finally—and this was the clinching argument—why should they make Adolph Sutro a power, a great man? Why should they help him complete a project that would make him a financial rival? Every bit of strength that Sutro accumulated would weaken the strength of the giants of the Comstock. They summed it all up in mutual agreement— Adolph Sutro had to be crushed.

He faced the cold, dismal fact; he had been discarded because he was too strong. He was to be an outcast, driven back and back till he had nothing left. But Adolph Sutro was a fighter, and, as he saw the avalanche of opposition growing and growing against him, he took a solemn vow— he would drive the Sutro Tunnel under Mount Davidson if it took the balance of his life, and finally his life itself.

He returned to New York, called on J. P. Morgan, August Belmont, Commodore Vanderbilt, pleaded with them for funds to complete his task. They said, as they had said on their previous meeting, that they would finance the project when Sutro could show cash endorsements from the West. Very well! They should have their endorsements!

On the morning of April 7, 1869, an alarm burst on Virginia City. The Yellow Jacket Mine was on fire; forty-two miners were trapped and burned to death. Stories circulated that the fire had been caused by incendiaries as a protest against the ruthless exploitation of the miners by the Comstock millionaires. The country was in an uproar.

It was Sutro's great opportunity. Posters appeared suddenly on the walls of every building in Virginia City. Posters were handed to every miner in every mine in Mount Davidson, inviting the miners to a mass meeting at Maguire's Opera House.

They mobbed the Opera House, thousands of men, working men, not knowing what to expect. And Adolph Sutro stood before them, frock coat flung open, eyes blazing, fists clenched. For an hour and more he exposed the operations of the Comstock tycoons. He told how his efforts to build the tunnel had been frustrated; he bared the political machinations of the powers; he concluded, in a brilliant flow of oratory, with a plea that the miners themselves supply the funds to endorse the building of the tunnel.

One week later a delegation of miners came to Sutro. They brought a guaranty of $50,000 to be raised immediately to start the work, the first installment on the funds they would raise to carry on the work. Adolph Sutro had his endorsement, and the first battle was won.

Two months later, in a pouring rain, the miners and their families came marching down the hills and out of the streets of Virginia City to the point where the work on the tunnel was to commence. Before them, in a three-seater buggy, clad in a Prince Albert and a white beaver hat, rode Sutro.

Bands played and, under the drizzling rain, great tables were heaped with barbecued pork and beef, and loaves of bread, and twenty kegs of beer.

The band played "The Star-Spangled Banner." A cannon fired a salute. Sutro flung aside his black coat, rolled up his sleeves, tossed his white hat into the road, and shouldered a pick. He stood there, a giant of a man, and the crowd roared. He raised his hand, and there was silence. In a few, well-rounded sentences, he flung his challenge at the giants of the Comstock, then plunged his pick into the ground and tore away a mass of rock and dirt and mud. The digging of the Sutro Tunnel had commenced, a work that was to change the destiny of the West. The work had begun, but millions had still to be raised.

The Comstock millionaires had pressed their lobbying in New York, and the Eastern millionaires had lost interest in the project. Very well, if the funds could not be raised in New York, Sutro would go to Europe for the money he needed. He commenced negotiations with a Parisian banking house. It was interested. He planned to sail for Paris in the middle of July 1870. On July 15, 1870, the Franco-Prussian War commenced. The little project of a tunnel 'way out in western America was forgotten.

More setbacks, more obstacles were thrust in the tunnel's path by the Comstock men. And then, out of a clear, blue sky, came an offer from a London bank headed by a Scot, McClamont. The London bankers knew that the Comstock was producing $15,000,000 in gold every year. They were interested. They would finance the Sutro Tunnel, and, as a first installment, $650,000 were at the disposal of Adolph Sutro. A year later another $750,000 were handed to him. And the Ralston dynasty was beaten and on the downgrade.

The rest of the story is a story of work. Sutro was the driving force, himself setting off blasts of dynamite, leading the tunnel diggers, his own pick swinging ahead of theirs. He had to fight the floods that filled the shafts and threatened the lives of his workers. He had to fight avalanches, and mud slides and the more treacherous slides of clay, and the poisonous gases that made the underground work unbearable. He dug air shafts to relieve the danger; the shafts filled with water, one of them to a depth of nine hundred feet. He had to fight cave-ins and solid rock. Through the gruelling months, day after day and month after month, he marched ahead of his men, stripped to the waist, laboring with them, sweating with them, facing death with them, and, in the end, winning through with them to victory.

The last wall was crashed, the last obstacle crumbled—the Sutro Tunnel was an accomplished fact. Now Adolph Sutro had a new title; he was called the King of the Comstock. The Comstock millionaires came to him with their hats in their hands. Directors of mines, who had scorned his fantastic scheme, now bowed and begged for the privilege of tunnel rental. Every day in the year he drained between three and four million gallons of water from the mines. The rental of the tunnel averaged $10,000 a day for the Sutro Tunnel stockholders.

Adolph Sutro's great adventure was ended. But he wasn't yet ready to retire. Back he came to San Francisco, a giant of a man in a city that had known many giants. They made him mayor of the city; that was in 1894. He built the world's largest indoor swimming tank out near the Cliff House and called it Sutro's Baths. He was a familiar figure on the city streets in his frock coat and with his black cane and silk hat and white cotton beard. He collected a great library of rare books. He built a mansion in a wonderful garden on the cliffs that overlooked the ocean, and he filled the wonderful gardens of his mansion with a mystic maze of statues.

And of a morning he would be likely to stop a small boy on the street and pat him on the head and say, "Someday you must come to see the pretty ladies in my garden."

XII

Black Bart

One day, in 1883, a dapper little man walked down Bush Street in San Francisco, a Beau Brummell of a little man, faultlessly dressed. He wore a stylish derby hat, cocked at a rakish angle—rakish, but in good taste. He carried a natty, little walking stick. There was a diamond pin in his scarf, and a handsome diamond ring on his finger—well-dressed gentlemen affected diamonds in those days. Across his vest he wore a heavy, gold watch chain. He was slender; he walked with shoulders straight, walked briskly. He had deep, bright-blue eyes and high cheekbones; he wore a large, gray mustache, neatly trimmed and handsomely waxed, and a meticulously trimmed imperial beard. He might have been a model for a fashion plate in *Harper's Bazaar* or any of the magazines of the 'eighties that featured what the well-dressed gentleman, the man of the world, should wear. He looked just that—a dignified, cultured, cosmopolitan man of the world.

He smiled as he walked, a good-natured, benign smile, as though he found the world very much to his liking, a world that met with his aristocratic approval. He walked down Bush Street and met two gentlemen; one of them was a friend of his named Thomas Ware. Mr. Ware was the proprietor of a tobacco shop, and well-esteemed in San Francisco. The older gentleman was a stranger.

The dapper little gentleman greeted Mr. Ware and said, "It's a fine day!"

And Mr. Ware said, "Yes, it is, Mr. Bolton."

But when Mr. Ware, the tobacconist, wanted to introduce Mr. Bolton to the stranger who was accompanying him, he was embarrassed. He didn't know the stranger's name.

"I'm sorry, sir," he said. "I don't know your name."

The stranger said his name was Hamilton, and Mr. Ware said, "Mr. Bolton, this is Mr. Hamilton. I have been telling him about the mines you own in the Sierra, and he is interested in hearing more about them. As a matter of fact, he is very much interested in mining."

Mr. Bolton twisted his mustache neatly, and acknowledged that he was an authority on California mining operations and would be glad to give Mr. Hamilton any information he could. And Mr. Hamilton said he appreciated Mr. Bolton's courtesy, and would take it kindly if Mr. Bolton would accompany him to his office where they could talk without interruption. Mr. Bolton cleared his throat, and bowed, and said he was happy to oblige.

So the three men went to Mr. Hamilton's office in the Wells Fargo Bank Building. There they talked for many hours, and it became apparent that Mr. Bolton really did not know as much about California mines as he claimed. In fact, as time progressed, it became increasingly apparent that he did not even know for sure where the mines in which he was interested were located. And before the discussion ended, it was revealed that Mr. Hamilton was, in fact, the private detective, Harry Morse, and the dapper little gentleman with the well-waxed mustache was actually Black

Bart, the most notorious stagecoach bandit in the history of the West. . . .

On the third of August in the year 1877, a stagecoach rolled along the rough road between Point Arenas and Duncan Mills on the Russian River in northern California. The driver sat on his box, urging his horses along. There were no passengers on the stage; just the driver and his freight—a Wells Fargo strongbox containing a few hundred dollars in gold coin and a check.

The horses came to a sudden stop as a figure appeared before them in the roadway to take its stand between the lead horses' noses. The figure wore a long, linen duster, and over its head it wore a flour sack with eyeholes cut in. Between the horses' heads, it aimed a double-barreled shotgun at the stagecoach driver and, in a quiet and refined and polite voice, said, "Throw down the box."

That command was to be heard often in the years to come, and was to become famous. It was always gently spoken—"Throw down the box."

The stage driver did not hesitate. The voice had spoken from under the flour sack with gentle insistence, but it was the double-barreled shotgun that clinched the order.

The stage driver dropped the Wells Fargo box to the ground. And the gentle-voiced stranger, in a deep, hollow, assumed voice said, "Thank you. Now you may drive on."

So the stage driver drove on and reported the robbery. But he could not give much help in describing the bandit; after all, it is difficult to describe a man whose head is hidden beneath a flour sack. There was one peculiar thing about that flour sack, however. The eyes were an unreasonably long distance below the top of the head. Amateur detectives later deduced that the bandit wore a derby hat under the sack, and probably wore it because he was such a little man and felt his shortness did not measure up to his dignity as a bandit.

Yes, that was just about all the stagecoach driver could offer as a clue. So, a posse was dispatched to the scene of the robbery. They found the Wells Fargo box forced open and relieved of its contents. And they found a clue. A most amazing, a most unusual clue! The bandit had left a poem. It read:

> I've labored long and hard for bread,
> For honor and for riches,
> But on my corns too long you've tread,
> You fine-haired sons of bitches.

And he signed himself "Black Bart, the PO 8."

There have been more absurd legends and untrue stories told down through the years about Black Bart than all the lies he personally told during his nefarious career. The pseudo-historians have made him a chivalrous Robin Hood, robbing the rich to feed the poor. It was claimed that he left a different poem every time he robbed a stage—and he robbed twenty-eight stages. But only two poems have been accounted for. It was said that his fame as a poet was as great as his fame as a bandit. All the claims were absurd; his poetry was bad, but he was a highly successful stage robber.

At that first robbery on the Point Arena–Duncan Mills road, Black Bart did leave his poem. And he left a postscript; Bart was a great one for postscripts. This one read, "Driver, give my respects to our friend, the other driver. I really had a notion to hang my old disguise hat on his weather eye." That was in August 1877.

97

On July 28, 1878, high in the beautiful, green Feather River country, on the road between Quincy and Oroville, the Wells Fargo stage was rolling along at a lively pace. The driver, an accomplished whipman, slowed his horses as they approached a difficult turn in the road. As they slowed, a lone figure stepped out from behind bushes. A double-barreled shotgun in hand, it took a stand between the heads of the lead horses, leveled the gun at the driver, and said in a low, hollow, cultured voice, "Throw down the box!"

There are few arguments more convincing than the business end of a double-barreled shotgun. The driver didn't argue. He saw the lone stranger, head hidden in a flour sack with holes for eyes; he saw the gun, and he threw down the box. The highwayman thanked the driver courteously and told him to drive on. He drove on. Later, returning to the scene of the holdup, a posse found the rifled Wells Fargo box, a mail sack split at the top with a cut made in the shape of a letter T, and a poem, the second of Black Bart's lyric effusions. It read:

> Here I lay me down to sleep
> To wait the coming morrow,
> Perhaps success, perhaps defeat,
> And everlasting sorrow.
> Let come what will I'll try it on,
> My condition can't be worse;
> And if there's money in that box,
> 'Tis money in my purse.

Each line of the jingle was written in a different handwriting; Black Bart had a penchant for disguising his handwriting. By amazing deduction, strong minds figured that both robberies had been committed by the same individual.

William Irwin, Governor of California, offered a reward of three hundred dollars for the arrest and conviction of the bandit. Wells Fargo added three hundred, and the postal authorities two hundred. There were eight hundred dollars on the head of Black Bart.

And now the bandit had hit his stride. A week later he held up the stage between La Porte and Oroville; his low, hollow voice commanded, "Throw down the box," and the box was thrown down. In October, the man in the flour sack held up two stages in northern California. And Mr. J. B. Hume, Wells Fargo detective, was put on the trail.

Hume, enlisting all the art and science of storybook detectives, finally found a clue. A stranger, a tourist with a low, hollow voice, had stopped for dinner at a farmhouse owned by a Mrs. McCreary on the Eel River. Mrs. McCreary was glad to tell what she knew, and what she didn't know, her sixteen-year-old daughter supplied. . . .

Goodness no, the gentleman didn't seem one bit like a robber. He was so polite; he had such a handsome mustache and beautifully trimmed beard—and those deep-blue eyes! And he wouldn't smoke and he wouldn't touch liquor; he wouldn't drink anything but coffee. He talked very intellectual talk; he was more like a preacher than a robber, he certainly was.

That was all Mr. Hume could learn; the trail was lost. That was in October 1878. Every few months for five years after that, the lone stranger in the flour sack would turn up on some lonely road, stop the Wells Fargo stage, level his shotgun, and give the command, "Throw down the box." Black Bart never harmed a driver, never harmed a passenger, never robbed anyone or anything but the Wells Fargo box. Long afterward, he told of the time a terrified passenger voluntarily tossed him her purse. And he bowed politely and handed it back to her saying, "Madam, I am interested only in the Wells Fargo box and the United States mail."

Six years passed, and Black Bart had held up and robbed twenty-seven Wells Fargo stages. Then, on November 3, 1883, he stopped a stage out of Sonora, via Copperopolis, driven by Mr. Reason E. McConnell of Sonora. And in his low, hollow voice, he commanded, "Throw down the box."

Now, by chance, Mr. McConnell had had a passenger, a young friend named Jimmie Rolleri, whose mother, Grandma Rolleri, ran the famous Calaveras Hotel in Angels Camp. Jimmie had just come along for the ride and, after riding some miles, he had jumped off the stage and taken a short cut across country, figuring to catch up with the stage again. So McConnell was driving along, alone, when the command, "Throw down the box," was given.

But this time the box was not thrown down. The Nevada Stage Coach Company had riveted the box to the floor of the stage. Black Bart ordered McConnell to climb down while he, Bart, entered the stage and broke open the box. McConnell, at the point of the gun, obeyed orders. And while Bart was busy at his task, McConnell saw young Jimmie Rolleri approaching.

He signaled Jimmie to come up quietly. Jimmie had a gun. Either he fired at Black Bart, or McConnell fired. At any rate, the gun changed hands, and several shots were fired. Black Bart plunged into the chaparral and disappeared, leaving a trail of blood. A short time later, a posse from Copperopolis was at the scene. They found a mass of clues. Paper bags containing granulated sugar and crackers— a belt—a magnifying glass—a razor—two flour sacks with the name "Sperry and Company, Stockton"—a. leather case— three dirty linen cuffs—and——a handkerchief! All were the property of Black Bart, hidden in the rocks before he had held up the stage.

Now, these were, of course, all important clues. But only one of them was to prove of real significance—the pocket handkerchief. When Ben Thorn, sheriff of Calaveras County, examined the handkerchief he found a laundry mark in the corner of it: F.X.o.7.

Mr. Thorn told Mr. Hume about it, and Mr. Hume told the private detective, Harry Morse, and Harry Morse went to work. In a laundry agency in San Francisco he found that mark, F.X.o.7, on the customers' book.

The laundry agency was run by a tobacconist named Ware, the same Thomas Ware who, walking along Bush Street with a stranger, met Charles Bolton. And the stranger was Harry Morse. Yes, by strange coincidence, the courteous, dapper gentleman, the Beau Brummell of Bush Street, had the same laundry mark as Black Bart. So Mr. Morse invited him to accompany him to offices in the Wells Fargo Building to discuss gold mines.

That discussion lasted for many hours, and finally Charles Bolton—or maybe his name was Boles, for he had many names—confessed. He claimed his name wasn't Bolton, but Boles. He claimed he had been a captain in Company B, 116th Illinois Volunteer Infantry, during the Civil War; and then he demoted himself to lieutenant, and then to sergeant. He had a Bible inscribed, "To Charles E. Boles, by his wife as a New Year's gift."

Yes, he had a wife and children, and he adored them and they adored him, and he wrote beautiful letters to them while he was in prison. For he went to prison, sentenced to the penitentiary for six years. The six years were cut to four and a half, a modest-enough sentence in all reason for a cultured gentleman who had attempted twenty-eight stage robberies and succeeded in twenty-seven.

He was released; and that, to be very exact, is the end of his story. Of course, there were legends, plenty of legends, after he was released. Stagecoaches were held up, and people said, "My goodness, it's Black Bart." But such rumors were never proved.

There is one more detail—the name, "Black Bart." He confessed that he had borrowed it from a character in a famous book of California, *The Caxton Book,* and the story of "The Case of Summerfield." In that story there was an individual named "Black Bart," which proves that the real-life bandit, Black Bart, was a literary gentleman. Certainly he was a charming gentleman, but a very bad PO 8. One more poem does appear to prove that point, although it has not been definitely established that he wrote it:

> I rob the rich to feed the poor,
> Which hardly is a sin;
> A widow ne'er knocked at my door
> But what I let her in.
> So blame me not for what I've done,
> I don't deserve your curses,
> And if for any cause I'm hung,
> Let it be for my verses!

XIII

Nob Hill

With the coming of reasonable security and success, men have a tendency to move away from the crowd, to dig their caves high on the side of a cliff, or to build their homes high on a hilltop or away in a remote valley. That is what makes suburbs.

Now, in the early days of San Francisco's transformation from a village of miners to a city, there was a doctor in the village who cared for the population's ailments. His name was Hayne—Dr. Hayne. He was a good doctor, and doctors were rare and sickness was rampant. So the doctor's practice grew; he became eminently successful and a highly respected citizen.

But his successful practice was interfering with his sleep. At all hours of the day and night, fists pounding on his door called him to sickbeds or to the aid of the injured. There is a limit to human endurance, and Dr. Hayne reached it. He had to have sleep. He had to have hours of quiet so that he could read the medical books that came to him by sailing ship around the Horn. And there was no quiet for him and little sleep in his hotel room on Montgomery Street. So he looked to the west, up the hill.

It was a high hill, so steep that to climb the trail that led to the top of it was to tax the endurance of the climber. It was covered with green grass in the spring; it was a tempting escape from the mud and noise and turmoil of Montgomery Street. And there, on top of it, Dr. Hayne decided to build his house, a home where he could have quiet and privacy—and sleep.

Men called it "The Hill of Golden Promise." The sun, setting behind it each night, placed a crown of gold upon its brow. On its very crest Dr. Hayne built his home, a simple house of wood and stone. It was located exactly where the Fairmont Hotel now stands. That was the beginning of Nob Hill.

A score of years passed before Nob Hill really came into its own. Men of wealth built their ornate wooden houses along Mason and Taylor and Jones and O'Farrell and Geary and Post streets. But the steep trail leading to the crest of the Hill of Golden Promise discouraged even the most hardy and venturesome.

Then, in the 'seventies—the decade that was the fullness of San Francisco's golden era—millionaires sought the high hills. It was the decade of the bonanzas, of the Comstock, of the building of the Central Pacific Railroad. It was the decade during which millionaires were made, and their fortunes found their way from the Comstock and the railroads, and from San Francisco to New York—the fortunes of John W. Mackay, of George Hearst, the father of William Randolph Hearst, and the millions of Flood and Fair and O'Brien.

The first to build a mansion on the Hill of Golden Promise was Richard Tobin, the father of the ambassador to the Netherlands. The home stood at the corner of Taylor and California streets, the present site of the Huntington Apartments. On the top of his pioneer mansion Tobin built a tower, and from the tower the view stretched in all directions far beyond any dream of the city's growth. But the true romance of Nob Hill came with the fortunes of the Big Four, the nabobs who gave the hill its name—the builders of the railroad that connected the Atlantic and the Pacific.

Today the cable car that the eccentric millionaire, Andrew Hallidie, built in 1873, still grinds and grumbles its way up the hill. At the crest are the Mark Hopkins Hotel, the Stanford Court Apartments, Grace Cathedral, and Huntington Park with its green lawns in front of the Cathedral. These are the sites of the mansions of the Big Four—Crocker, Huntington, Hopkins, and Stanford.

The Stanfords were the first to build. Leland Stanford had become Governor of California. He had made a great fortune. But he and Mrs. Stanford were plain, quiet people, not given to ostentation. Their son, Leland, Jr., was a quiet, serious-minded, not overstrong youngster. The Stanfords wanted a quiet, simple life. They built their home on straight lines, a large, many-roomed house in dignified good taste, and in it they lived their quiet, simple life.

Now, before the building of their railroad under the inspiration of their silent partner, Theodore Judah, Stanford had been a grocer in Sacramento, Charlie Crocker had been a dry-goods clerk, Huntington and Hopkins had dealt in hardware. They were men who had lived plainly and frugally.

So, Mark Hopkins, even more than the Stanfords, wanted a simple residence. And he found it—a modest cottage that he rented for thirty-five dollars a month—and in it he lived till the day of his death.

But Mark Hopkins' wife had other ideas. She was twenty

years younger than he. She was a pleasantly quiet victorian lady, busy with housekeeping and embroidery. But the Crockers and the Huntingtons and the Stanfords were building mansions, and the Hopkinses were just as wealthy. Mrs. Hopkins did not intend to be outdone by her husband's partners. So, because she was so much younger than her husband, and because Victorian wives teased and wheedled till they got what they wanted, she finally talked Mark Hopkins into buying half the lot owned by Leland Stanford. The purchase price of the land was something over $30,000. Then came the matter of plans for the building. Hopkins was too busy with his railroad crises to worry about housebuilding. He told Mary to go ahead and please her lovely little heart. And Mary went ahead!

She built what was probably the most amazing house ever built in San Francisco. It was of wood painted in imitation of stone It had towers and turrets and verandas and porticos and a Gothic, glass conservatory. It had wings with towers of bay windows; it was a lurid imitation of a French castle, combining Gothic and Greek and Arabic and Provençal architecture. It had various roofs, ranging from mansard to a peak that looked like the apex of a Turkish mosque. With dismay, Mark Hopkins watched it being built and called it the "Hotel de Hopkins."

There was a baronial dining room to seat sixty guests. There were great halls that later served as rich art galleries. But the chef-d'œuvre was the master bedroom. It imitated the master's room of a Venetian palace. Its walls were of ebony inlaid with precious stones and with intricate designs of ivory. The doors to this, the master's room, were double, and the inner doors were padded with rich, blue velvet. Amorous cupids were painted on the ceiling.

106

And then, before the house was completed, Mark Hopkins died, and his widow, one of the richest women in the United States, moved East. Housebuilding had become a mania with her; she hired a prominent young architect, Edward Searles, and ordered a half-dozen mansions on the East coast. And during their building, she married Searles.

When Mary Hopkins Searles died in the early 'nineties, she disinherited her son, Timothy Hopkins, and left her entire fortune to Searles. There were scandals and lawsuits and settlements, and Searles gave the huge house—Hopkins' Folly—to the University of California, and it, with the nucleus of paintings in its art gallery, became the home of the San Francisco Art School, later the California School of Fine Arts.

Now, Charlie Crocker was unwilling to be outdone by the young wife of Mark Hopkins. So he bought the square block of land where Grace Cathedral now stands, bought all but twenty-five feet of it. The modest home of a Mr. Yung stood on those twenty-five feet.

The former dry-goods clerk had as much of a taste for art as had Mrs. Hopkins. His house was ornate; in many ways it had even more gingerbread ornamentation than the "Hotel de Hopkins." It was just plain fancy. But Crocker went abroad for his art. He bought paintings as some men are said to buy libraries. He said, "Give me a million dollars' worth of paintings." And he was given an amazing amount of junk and a few immortal masterpieces; among the masterpieces, the famous Millet canvas, "The Sower," hung in his gallery. It was saved when the mansion burned in the disaster of 1906.

Charlie Crocker was exceedingly proud of the road he had journeyed from the dry-goods store to the mansion on the Hill of Golden Promise. He wanted perfection in the mansion; he wanted that twenty-five feet of ground occupied by the modest home of Mr. Yung. But there was a fly in the ointment; Yung demanded an exorbitant price. Crocker would not pay. A feud developed, a feud that reached its climax when Crocker built a fence forty feet high, around three sides of Yung's house and lot, completely shutting off all light.

The Crocker-Yung spite fence became famous. San Franciscans came from all parts of the city to gaze at it, to conjecture who would win the fight. They had forgotten that Charlie Crocker had tackled bigger, more insurmountable obstacles along his railroad road to fame. He had built the most important railroad in the world when he had no money; he had won that fight and opened the highway from East to West. He won the fight with Mr. Yung by condemning him to darkness behind the forty-foot wall. Yung sold out at a reasonable figure, and the wall came tumbling down.

Of all the great mansions on the hill, only one stood after the fire of 1906. It was built by James Flood whose fortune had come out of the Comstock Lode after the building of the railroad. The Flood mansion, a dignified and imposing brownstone edifice, still stands, the home today of the Pacific Union Club. And it has its legends. When you stand before it, you will see the iron grille fence that circles the square block—dirty, black iron it appears to be. But it is not iron; it is solid brass put up, some claim, at a cost of $50,000, and painted to look like black iron to discourage thieves.

The great lawns of the clubhouse that was once the Flood mansion knew their day of adventure, too. For, while the great fire raged, art students fought their way into the Mark Hopkins Art Galleries, cut the world's masterpieces from their frames, and rolled the canvases and stacked them against the stone of the Flood mansion. They did not burn, but many of them were completely ruined by the intense heat of the flames that swept Nob Hill.

Across the street from the Flood home, Jim Flood's partner, James G. Fair, built a beautiful house on the edge of the hill where, many years before, Dr. Hayne had built his hideaway. Fair had two daughters, Mrs. Herman Oelrichs and Mrs. William K. Vanderbilt. Mrs. Oelrichs had a dream; she wanted to build the most beautifully located hotel in the land right there on the Fair estate. Plans were drawn, contracts were given, no expense was spared—it was to be a noble hotel. And then, a few short weeks before it was to have opened to the public, the flames of April 18, 1906, swept through it, and all that remained was the beautiful shell. But, one year later to the day, on April 18, 1907, the present Fairmont Hotel was opened.

These were only a few of the mansions of Nob Hill. There was the home where George and Phoebe, parents of William Randolph Hearst, entertained. There was the lovely Towne residence at Taylor and California, with its beautiful entrance portico of marble columns that now are the nostalgic Portals of the Past in Golden Gate Park. There was the imposing Huntington mansion where now there are the lawns of Huntington Park.

And—there is the Cathedral. It stands where the Crocker home once stood. Within a few months of the mansion's burning in the great fire, the land was given to the Episcopal diocese by the Crocker heirs. Plans for Grace Cathedral were drawn and work commenced. The cornerstone was laid in 1910, and for thirty-five years the builders have labored in creating the city's enduring affirmation of man's faith in God.

Work still continues, year after year, on this most beautiful of the houses of God. It looks out over the city and to the Bay and the hills beyond. Its steeples, when they are completed, will be seen from every corner of the city of hills that has grown so far since Dr. Hayne built his home on the Hill of Golden Promise.

This is that hill where, out of the fortunes made in mines and railroads and saloons and wild adventure and outrageous gambles, glittering palaces of pomp and circumstance stood in the days when champagne flowed as water in San Francisco, and the city was a backdrop for an Arabian Nights' dream. Pomp and circumstance, diamond tiaras and silks and satins, four-horse carriages—a world of gold!

The world changes; pomp and circumstance find their way to the discard. But Nob Hill remains, a land of great hotels, a land where debutantes and college boys go laughing along California Street in the small hours. To them, the names Crocker, Huntington, Stanford, Hopkins, Fair—these and the others are only names of hotels.

It's a new and a changing world. And of it all, the Cathedral, building now for more than thirty-five years, facing many years before it will be completed, stands squarely on the Hill of Golden Promise, spanning the years from yesterday to tomorrow.

XIV

"Filibuster" Walker

This is the story of a little man. He was an odd-appearing little fellow with blond hair. He was not much more than five feet tall. He weighed just about one hundred pounds. He had a little, high-pitched, squeaking voice. He was unquestionably the most amazing concentrated package of adventure ever to make history in San Francisco. Concentrated! He was a concentrated package of dynamite! There was not a man or animal or situation on earth of which he was afraid. His name was Walker—William Walker. History has labeled him "Filibuster" Walker.

He was born in Nashville, Tennessee, in 1824. His parents were Scotch—diligent, thrifty, industrious Scotsmen with a great capacity for learning. And little William Walker's blood ran rich with the rugged heritage. He graduated from the University of Nashville at the age of fourteen. He took his Doctor's degree in medicine at the University of Pennsylvania at the age of nineteen. He went to Paris for a postgraduate course in medicine and spent another year in Europe, learning as many foreign languages as possible. Then he returned to America, tossed his medical training out of the window, spent a year studying law, and, at the age of twenty-one, was admitted to the bar. He hung out his shingle in New Orleans—"William Walker, Attorney at Law."

Tragedy came to him in New Orleans, shattering all his youthful idealism and turning him into a ruthless man—ruthless, and yet a man of intense, almost fanatical philosophies. He fell in love with a beautiful Louisiana deaf-mute named Helen Martin. He adored and worshiped her, and she idolized him. She couldn't hear his speech; she couldn't speak to him. So, with the same easy rapidity with which he had mastered medicine and law, he mastered the sign language and soon was able to communicate with her as easily as though she were articulate. But, at the gates of their seventh heaven, just before they were to be married, yellow fever swept New Orleans and Helen Martin died.

Broken in spirit, a ship without a rudder, William Walker drifted to California, arriving in San Francisco in 1850 at the height of the Gold Rush.

Already a doctor and a lawyer, young Walker had, for a time, edited a newspaper in New Orleans. Now, in San Francisco, he became editor of the *Daily Herald*. Life in the boom town was centered in the saloons and gambling houses, so to the gambling halls and saloons he went for his city news. He seldom drank, and never gambled—that is, with cards or dice. With life he was always willing to gamble.

One night he was sitting in a melodeon. A maudlin troubadour was singing a sentimental heart-ballad, the kind that brought ready tears to sentimental eyes. And the lonely pioneers loved to weep when their heartstrings were tugged. It is claimed that there was not a dry eye in the saloon that night while the singer sang his song, not a dry eye save that of the young editor, Bill Walker. He sat, a cynical smile on his face, a smile that broadened to a grin as the sheriff approached him, demanded his gun, and told him he was under arrest. When he wanted to know on what grounds he had been arrested, the sheriff said he didn't know—the judge would answer the questions.

So, Walker was haled before Judge Levi Parsons, one of the most fantastic individuals ever to occupy the seat of dignity in a court of law. The judge asked Walker his name, his age, his color, and, finally, where he had been born. Walker told him. The judge asked him why he had left Tennessee. Walker answered by asking the judge why he had come to San Francisco. Infuriated, the judge charged him with writing and publishing scurrilous articles in the *Herald*, criticizing the way the San Francisco courts of law conducted themselves. Walker said that he wasn't aware that the courts conducted themselves at all. The judge warned him not to insult the dignity of the court. Walker said the dignity wasn't apparent.

The judge shouted, "The courts are the most honorable institution in American politics!"

Walker, unsmiling, answered, "The courts are a disgrace to American politics."

The judge sentenced him to a fine of five hundred dollars for contempt of court. Walker refused to pay the fine, and the judge ordered him to jail.

But William Walker did not stay in jail. He had a strange genius for making friends, and now his friends rallied and demanded his release. Indignation meetings and torchlight processions were held. A huge delegation called on him in jail and tendered him the sympathy of the city. Then a committee appeared before the new state Legislature at Monterey, presented the case, and the Legislature passed a resolution justifying the actions of Walker and demanding the

113

impeachment of Judge Levi Parsons. Walker was released; he packed his carpetbag and went to Marysville to practice law.

It was in Marysville that he conceived and promoted his first big project, the project that was to label him "Filibuster" Walker. Those were the days when expansion southward was looked on with favor by the American public. So, Walker decided to "colonize" the Mexican state of Sonora and Lower California with Americans. He raised money to equip an army to march on Sonora, to seize it and make it a part of the United States of America. Later, he was to expand his scheme to something more grandiose; he was to plan a military empire made up of all the small Central American republics. Later, he was even to plan building an interoceanic canal across Central America and introducing African slavery throughout Mexico and Central America for labor.

But now he went back to San Francisco, chartered a small vessel, the *Arrow*, collected a group of forty-six men, and prepared to set sail. But, before he could lift anchor and go out through the Golden Gate, the United States Army seized the ship as a violator of American neutrality. And, strutting in his full five feet four of dignity, Walker wrote to Franklin Pierce, President of the United States, demanding that he be permitted to sail.

A short time later he received a visit from General John Wool, commander of United States troops on the Pacific Coast. General Wool told Walker he had been informed that Mr. Walker planned to lead an expedition against Mexico, that this constituted a violation of international law, that, if the Army authorities stationed on Alcatraz Island in San Francisco Bay saw a vessel outfitting itself with any such

114

plan in mind, the Army authorities would have to take drastic action.

Walker said that was unfortunate.

General Wool agreed. Yes, it was unfortunate. But, he hastened to add, it had been arranged to move Army headquarters from Alcatraz Island to Benicia where it would be impossible to observe the movements of any ships in the Bay. And then the general said that it had been a pleasure to meet Mr. Walker, and Mr. Walker said the pleasure had been all his.

He gave up the small craft, the *Arrow*, chartered a larger bark, the *Caroline*, and, on October 16, 1853, sailed through the Golden Gate with his army.

Landing at La Paz on the peninsula of Lower California, he proclaimed the Republic of Lower California, kidnaped the governor, and named himself president under the flag of the United States of America.

San Francisco went wild with enthusiasm. A new army formed, another ship was chartered and sailed south to join the filibustering expedition. It was generally agreed that William Walker was destined to become the greatest man in the world.

Then, suddenly, as the reports had come of Walker's Napoleonic march, so reports came of disaster. His army was starving; the filibustering troops were in revolt; dozens of his men were deserting. The federal authorities in San Francisco had blocked the sending of needed supplies and reinforcements to him.

In desperate straits, the little expedition retraced its steps to the Colorado River and surrendered to troops of the United States. Some were jailed; some were fined and paroled. With that unbeatable assurance that saw him through every emergency, Walker appeared before the court-martial, pleaded his own case, and was acquitted.

A short time later a shingle was hung before a building in Stockton, California—"William Walker, Attorney at Law." But the four walls of a law office were too confining for a firebrand of Walker's measure. The year was 1855; revolution had broken out in Nicaragua. The revolutionists sent a delegation to the filibusterer to request his aid. Here was business to whet his appetite. He formed a new "army" of fifty-seven men, chartered the brig, *Vesta*, sailed for Nicaragua, joined the revolutionists, and stormed and captured the capital city of Granada. After that he proclaimed himself first dictator and president of Nicaragua.

Then followed the most amazing experience of William Walker's fantastic life. William Ralston, San Francisco financier, with a group of associates, planned to run a line of sailing ships between the Golden Gate and Nicaragua, then to transport the passengers across the Nicaraguan isthmus and up the Atlantic Coast to New York. Thus, the long and treacherous journey around Cape Horn would be eliminated.

The journey across the isthmus included a boat trip across large Lake Nicaragua. But the multimillionaire, Cornelius Vanderbilt, held a charter controlling boat travel on the lake. Walker, throwing in with the San Francisco interests, revoked the charter. Vanderbilt brought his millions into the fight to beat the Nicaraguan dictator. Walker stood pat and gave a twenty-five-year charter to Ralston of San Francisco and his associates. And the Nicaraguans, thoroughly enjoying a good fight—especially when the laurels went to the little man—rallied to the cause of Walker. He was man of the hour and idol of the nation.

But new disasters closed in on him. Cholera and yellow fever took toll of his soldiers. With Vanderbilt agents pulling the strings, millions were raised to finance the governments of Honduras, Guatemala, Salvador, and Costa Rica, so that they could send armies against the Nicaraguan revolutionists. They fought for two years. Every native of Nicaragua was with Walker, but the armies of the other nations outnumbered them. And one night, in his headquarters, Walker confessed to one of his lieutenants that so many of his men had deserted he could not continue to fight. He was beaten.

Beaten at last! But Bill Walker had no idea of surrendering—at least, not to his enemy. Nor did he intend to face a Central American firing squad. Instead, he surrendered to Commander Charles Henry Davis of the United States corvette *St. Mary*, lying in San Juan Harbor.

He was taken to New Orleans and placed under bond to keep the peace. They might as well have put a caged lion under bond and commanded him not to roar. Buchanan, President of the United States, issued a solemn proclamation condemning American citizens who led armies against nations with whom the United States was at peace. Walker was in disgrace with the President—and was the lionized hero of the nation.

But that role did not satisfy the little fighting man. He wanted action, and action was made to order for him. A new war broke out between Nicaragua and Costa Rica. Walker sailed south, mustered an army in Honduras, and started a march against the fighting factions in Nicaragua. Men were always glad to serve under him; his dynamic personality won him followers in every undertaking. And so, he marched out of Honduras and on Nicaragua, followed by the largest army he had ever led. It was a triumphant march, a march of adventure-drunk, cheering men; and always, striding at their head, was the little five-foot-four, towheaded, squeaky-voiced man. His men adored and worshiped him.

On and on the marching men pressed. But war differed then from war today. There were no well-established supply lines to bring up provisions and munitions for the marchers. The army of Filibuster Walker began to starve, and men cannot fight on empty stomachs.

Still the raggle-taggle army marched on across the Nica-raguan border. The battle was joined. Walker fell and, with his hand pressed to his bleeding wound, struggled to his knees and cheered his men on. The wound, however, was not serious. The battle continued, and now there was not a man in the filibuster army who would not have died for the valiant, wounded hero.

But, again, the odds of battle were against Walker and his men. Their stomachs were empty, their clothes were in tatters, their numbers were depleted, and the enemy was gaining by the hour in size and strength.

It was a hopeless cause, and Walker knew it and sur-rendered, again not to the enemy, but to the captain of the British warship, _Icarus,_ at anchor in the Bay of Trujillo. Now, the British men of uniform admired the little fighting man as much as the American officers had. But a British officer could not afford to be involved in a highly compli-cated international fiasco; Walker was turned over to Gen-eral Alvarez, commanding the army of Honduras.

The court-martial was brief. Walker was found guilty of spreading insurrection and marching against the armies of the neighboring—and for the time being—friendly state of Nicaragua. He was asked what he had to say. He said he had nothing to say.

The General drew himself up to his full, gold-braided dignity and demanded, "Are you ready to hear your sentence?"

Walker said, "I am."

"Then," proclaimed General Alvarez, "for the crimes of insurrection, revolution, and murder you are condemned to die. May God have mercy on your soul."

Into the yard of the Honduran palace marched the comic-opera firing squad, William Walker in its midst. A sharp order was given. Walker stepped out of the ranks and stood with his back to the wall. A soldier approached to blindfold him. Walker brushed him aside. There was the roll of muffled drums, a brisk command in Spanish—"Ready!"

The beat of the drums accelerated.

"Aim!"

The drum roll was louder.

"Fire!"

The guns roared and echoed through the palace yard. And William Walker, filibusterer, lay crumpled at the foot of the adobe-brick wall.

Lotta Crabtree

The statues and monuments that grace most city streets and parks are clumsy, ugly things, and San Francisco's statues and monuments are worse than many. So ugly are many of its three-dimensional still lifes that it has become a pastime of self-appointed critics to condemn all outdoor art; the critics confess that they would not like the marbles and the bronzes even if they were good.

Most of the statuary is of the genus of the small boy pulling a thorn out of the sole of his foot; he has sat on our mantel and pulled for countless years, but the thorn persists. In the parks valiant, bronze riders are perched on great, noble horses, and the horses invariably have one leg raised as if they were just about to take off. But nothing ever happens.

Of course, according to one's personal taste, there is beauty in some of the city's statuary. There is the lovely metal statue of Dr. Sun Yat-sen in Chinatown in the square off California Street; it is beautiful by day in the sun or rain or fog, and it is loveliest at night when the moon and neon lights are reflected on it. And we have a warm and sentimental love for the little bronze ship that is the memorial of Robert Louis Stevenson in Portsmouth Square.

But there is one monument in San Francisco so ugly that

the public is single-minded about it, agreeing that it is not only an unaesthetic monstrosity but the ugliest monument in the city. Indignation meetings have been held about it. Artists, with varying tastes, have painted it and gilded it and bronzed it and cut pieces off of it and added pieces to it— and it still remains, ugly and unashamed. But let some daring critic suggest its removal, and the city will rise in hysterical wrath.

It is a pile of painted bronze, without beauty or charm, an ungraceful thing with scraps of newspaper and street sweepings usually heaped at its base, and pigeons or gulls perched on its uninspiring cap. Perhaps it would not have been so bad if it had been hidden in shrubbery in an unfrequented park, or even perched at the end of an untraveled alley. But, with shameless pride, it stands and has stood, year in and year out, at the junction of the most important cross streets in San Francisco—the corners of Kearny, Market, and Geary streets.

It is called Lotta's Fountain, but it is no longer a fountain; the drinking pools and the horse trough were some of the appendages removed by renovating artists. It stands there today, a poor, libeled thing, and we hope it will stand there for another hundred years and more.

There are so many sentimental traditions about it. Once it was in the triangle bounded by the offices of the three city newspapers. On a platform before it, Tetrazzini sang on Christmas Eve. Generations have grown up and taken Lotta's Fountain for granted. There are even a few living today who still remember Lotta. But, when another generation has passed, probably Lotta—Lotta Crabtree—will only be a name found in books of old San Francisco memories, a name without charm, and meaningless. And then, in the name of art, Lotta's (waterless) Fountain will probably be dragged away.

And this is the monument of the girl who was the very quintessence of San Francisco's love of life, a vivacious, an irresistible minx of a girl, winsome as a Kate Greenaway drawing, whimsical as a character in *Alice in Wonderland* —pretty as a canary bird set free.

It was in 1853 that Mary Ann Crabtree came West in search of her errant husband, John. John Crabtree was not a bad man; he was simply a cheerful failure. He came West to find gold and never found any. He was a careless sort with money, with his family, with life itself. So, when he came West, it was only innocent carelessness that kept him from notifying Mary Ann in just what part of California he was pursuing his elusive fortunes. His letters said something vaguely about being in the hills, and that was all.

In 1853, Mary Ann, with her tiny, six-year-old daughter, Lotta, came to San Francisco by steamship. They landed on the docks; they were greeted by friends from home who confessed that they did not know John's whereabouts, but would gladly take John's wife and daughter under their wing.

The friendly little cavalcade started a tour of the embryonic city, and then and there destiny wrote its prophecy. There were very few children in San Francisco in 1853, and practically no pretty children. As Mary Ann and small, black-eyed Lotta drove through the streets, crude, rough-garbed, heavy-bearded, rum-soaked miners stopped and stared—and waved their hands to the child, and cheered. And Lotta played to her gallery. She reached out her tiny hands to the rough miners and laughed loud peals of childish laughter; throughout her long and eventful life Lotta was to be famed for her beauty, her singing, her dancing, her acting—but above all for her laughter.

San Francisco was teeming with theatrical folk come to entertain the miners. In the streets one saw George and Mary Chapman; one saw the distinguished Mrs. Judah, and Junius Booth and his son, Edwin. But no John Crabtree.

And then word did come from John. He was in Grass Valley, about to make a fortune. A great and famous lady had made Grass Valley her home, had created in the mining town a salon to which came the great men of the world. Grass Valley was destined to be, according to John, the cultural center of the West, and the lady was to be its queen. Her name was Lola Montez. Two charming gentlemen, two of Lola's countless admirers, could find no dwelling place in crowded Grass Valley. So, Crabtree planned to open a lodginghouse and make his fortune; Mary Ann was to come at once with Lotta, and, of course, manage the enterprise, while John dreamed of the fortune to be made.

Up the Sacramento River by river boat went Mary Ann and Lotta. Then, by stage, they traveled to Grass Valley. And John, who had no actor's blood in his happy veins, greeted them with a bow and a huzzah that would have done credit to Mr. Booth himself. And, having established his family, John went seeking ephemeral fortunes, while Mary Ann ran the boardinghouse and Lotta went out to play.

Now, the streets of Grass Valley were a sorry playground for children in the early 'fifties. There were rough miners, gamblers, ne'er-do-wells, and prostitutes. And of all of them, with the strange perversity of children, Lotta chose for a companion one who had brought on her head the wrath of all the good ladies of California. Lotta strolled into her garden one day, and the beautiful lady and the beautiful child became bosom friends. They sang together, they danced together, they laughed together, they played fantastic games together, they adored each other.

Of course, the child could not know that the beautiful lady had been the mistress of kings and poets and vagabonds, nor that she had so enraged self-respecting California ladies that she had to hide under an assumed name. True, it was not actually an assumed name; she had been given it by a king. But she had discarded it, then taken it again. So, Lola Montez was known in Grass Valley and to small Lotta Crabtrèe as the Countess Landsfeld.

The ladies of Grass Valley whispered. Mary Ann Crabtree investigated and discovered that she liked the Lola of the Sierra, Lola in calico singing her songs, teaching ballet steps to tiny Lotta, teaching Lotta to ride horseback, and finally, one day, delighting the men in the streets by placing the small Lotta on an anvil in the blacksmith shop and clapping her hands in rhythm while Lotta danced the fandango she had taught her.

Then, Papa Crabtree announced a new utopia. The town of Rabbit Creek, high in the Feather River country was, according to no less a prophet than himself, destined to be the greatest city in California. The Crabtrees gave up their boardinghouse and moved to Rabbit Creek. The move had significant reverberations. In the town of Rabbit Creek there was a young Italian named Mart Taylor. He was a shoemaker, a musician, a dancer, and a saloonkeeper. He also had a tiny, log-cabin theater where traveling companies appeared, and between shows he maintained a dancing school for the few children of the village.

Mart fell in love with little eight-year-old Lotta. She danced for him, and he announced that he would present her professionally to the entertainment-hungry mining camp. Mary Ann made the child a long-tailed, green coat and a tall, green hat! Lotta carried a miniature shillelagh, and she danced for the miners. She danced well; they loved her dancing of the Irish jig. They loved her mop of red hair and her bright, black eyes. But the thing they could not forget was her laughter. All the time she danced and all the time she sang, she laughed. She laughed, and the chorus of miners roared back with laughter.

So, in Taylor's log-cabin saloon-theater in Rabbit Creek, Lotta sang and danced and laughed for the miners, and they rained gold nuggets and bags of gold dust and silver Mexican dollars about her feet. Mary Ann found herself with more wealth than she had ever possessed in her life—found herself with wealth and a prodigy of a daughter and a husband who had chosen an untimely moment to disappear again in quest of fortune. Taking a page out of John Crabtree's own book, Mary Ann also disappeared, leaving a polite note for John with a loaf of bread and a pot of beans. She started out on a theatrical tour with Lotta, Taylor, and a violinist.

They played in saloons and gambling halls and dives in town after town, up and down the Mother Lode; they played in the light of candles thrust into bottle necks. And only once did Lotta fail to laugh. That was when, in one of the camps, Mary Ann, worried by the child's habit of striking an unladylike pose by thrusting her small hands in her pockets, sewed up the pockets. Lotta, reaching for them, found them gone. In the middle of the dance she burst into tears and rushed off the stage. Thereafter the pockets were unsewn, and Lotta danced untrammeled by refinement.

That was in 1855. Lotta was eight years old. For almost

ten years Lotta and Mary Ann—and from time to time the bad penny, John—toured from San Francisco into the hills, up and down California, adored by all the West, idolized in San Francisco. She added drama and broad comedy to her dancing and her singing; she was California's most popular and most beloved star.

Then she went to New York, to Philadelphia, to Boston. Wherever she went she was the star, but a strange star, a generation ahead of her time. She ignored stage etiquette. She ad-libbed through her lines, rollicked through her lines, laughed and talked to the audience, and, with every rule of the theater that she broke, she made thousands of new friends. Mary Ann Crabtree was the staid, wise, stage mother; Lotta was an adorable hoyden—refined, but a hoyden.

She appeared in Philadelphia under the management of Mrs. John Drew and shocked that traditional lady of the theater by her disregard for etiquette. She returned to California in time for the opening season of the famous California Theatre built by William Ralston. She was surrounded by the great names of The California—Barrett, McCullough, Raymond, and lovely little Emilie Melville.

She went to London with her greatest success, *Heartsease*. She returned to America to appear with Mrs. John Drew and E. H. Sothern. She played with the famous vaudeville team of Harrigan and Hart; her repertoire ranged from Irish jigs and the "Mulligan Guard" to blackface impersonations and Desdemona in *Othello*.

She came back to San Francisco to play opposite David Belasco at the Baldwin Theatre. And now, the elfin, laughing child was a thing of the past. Lotta had become a beautiful, vivacious, laughing woman, a woman who knew no life of her own save that of life backstage. She was highly strung. She obeyed no laws of society. She calmed her nerves by constantly smoking large black cigars. She never married; she had no time for marriage. She belonged to the crowd, and the crowd loved her, and men said of her that she brought more laughter into their time than any other living creature.

Lotta Crabtree, born in 1847 of an improvident father and a wise mother, died at the age of seventy-seven. The year was 1924. She left a fortune of nearly four million dollars. She willed one-half of her fortune to a foundation for the relief of needy veterans of World War I; she gave bequests to hospitals, to actors' funds, to funds for music students; she left a fortune to care for stray dogs and old horses—to the world she left a heritage of laughter.

And to San Francisco, the city that she loved above all others, she left a world of cherished memories——and Lotta's Fountain.

XVI

Minstrels

It must be very annoying to other self-respecting cities to hear the often-quoted words, "There are only three real theater towns in America—New York, Boston, and San Francisco—and of them, the troupers love San Francisco the most." So, I am not going to quote the line. But I insist that in few places in the world is there so deeply rooted a love of the theater as there is in the sentimental heart of San Francisco.

In the very beginning, in the days when the village was shedding its Argonaut dress and becoming a city, the citizens had nothing to do but drink and fight and gamble and work, and their craving for entertainment, good or bad, was almost unbearable at times. Then along came Stephen Massett with a one-man minstrel show, and then came the others, and for years there was another phrase used, perhaps too freely—"San Francisco is the traditional home of minstrels." Of course, San Francisco was not the birthplace of minstrels, and whether that birthplace was in Ireland or Dixie is a question you may argue at leisure. But for decades the minstrels found a perennial home in San Francisco, right down to the days of George Primrose and Billy West and Lew Dockstader, Eddie Leonard, "Honey Boy" Evans, McIntyre and Heath, and the two most beloved of all minstrels in every song-loving land in which they appeared—Bert Williams and Billy Emerson. Many will argue and say, "But you've forgotten my favorite, Jack So-and-so." Or, "You've forgotten my friend, Charlie Backus, and his singing of 'O Susanna!'"

So we have. Charlie Backus came to San Francisco with the Gold Rush. The miners and the gamblers and the lonely derelicts who drifted through the mining camps were starving for entertainment. They were rough men and at the same time sentimental. They would steal and fight and get drunk, and they would murder, and they would sit in the dance halls and saloons, and a wandering minstrel would come to town and sing "The Last Rose of Summer," and sentimental tears would gush like spring freshets down their cheeks. They loved songs that made them cry. So, Charlie Backus came to town.

With Charlie was Billy Birch. The two, little by little, surrounded themselves with a company that achieved fame throughout the entertainment world; they were called the San Francisco Minstrels. There were singers and there were dancers and there were funny men; they appeared at the San Francisco Hall in burnt cork. Charlie had false teeth, removable at will, and when he appeared before his audience, toothless, the crowd thought it was the funniest thing it had ever seen. Billy, on the other hand, did not have false teeth; he had a head as bald as the bromidic billiard ball. And it was hard to say which was funnier, Billy's bald head or Charlie's toothless mouth. It did not matter very much; the crowd loved them and howled with delight at their entertainment. They were the sensations of San Francisco's night life. That was in 1855.

They were under the management of Tom Maguire, the

first great San Francisco impresario and producer. Now, a year earlier, Christy's famous minstrels had come to town. The city loved them, and they stayed a long time. With the coming of Backus and Birch, the two organizations joined forces under the banner of Tom Maguire; he built the San Francisco Hall of Minstrelsy for them, and the San Francisco Minstrels made history. To the troupe came Sam Wells and Ephraim Horn. Eph was a singer and dancer, but he was famed for his imitation of a steamcar and a steamer whistle. And, dressed in feminine garb, he caused a sensation and was almost mobbed for delivering a speech on Women's Rights.

The great hit of the San Francisco Minstrels was the Shakespeare revivals. Night after night in burnt cork the cast gave parodies of *Macbeth, Hamlet, Romeo and Juliet,* and, above all, *Othello.* In the *Othello* production all the cast was blackface except Othello himself; he played his part white face. Sam Wells excelled as a punster and end-man propounder of conundrums. Unfortunately, Sam had a taste for the vulgar bordering on the obscene in his choice of conundrums, and this brought the wrath of the community on his head. The gentlemen miners, the press announced, and the gentlemen gamblers could not endure the filth. But, on the other hand, the press confessed, the more vulgar the conundrum the greater the applause seemed to be. To which poor Sam replied, "I only read conundrums as a favor, and I have no time to look them over first to see that they are proper material for our select and genteel audience."

So, the minstrels became San Francisco's most popular form of entertainment, and the professionals were augmented by amateurs. During the days of the California wars, the

New York Volunteers—Colonel Stevenson's famous regiment—came to town and moved from encampment to encampment up and down the northern stretches of the state. Wherever they went they found time between skirmishes and drills to give minstrel shows. Every town in the Mother Lode developed its minstrel troupe. The most famous held forth in Grass Valley.

That was in 1851. The program, written in longhand, announced, "Grand Vocal and Instrumental Concert by the Grass Valley Minstrels. Cards of Admission only Fifty Cents. Ladies Accompanied by Gentlemen Admitted Free." The performers all were in blackface; the ushers achieved elegance by wearing white gloves and brilliant neckties. According to the record, the first performance of the Grass Valley Minstrels got off to a flying start. As the interlocutor entered, he accidentally tripped and fell flat on his face, and the entertainers, following quickly on his heels, piled on top of him till four or five were prone upon the stage. From then on to the end of the season the Grass Valley Minstrels were a success. The fall that was accidental in the first performance became the high spot of every show.

Now, all of these memories of San Francisco minstrel days take us back to the early 'fifties. It was not until the 'eighties that the most popular minstrel show the West and, for that matter, the entire nation had ever known—Billy Emerson's Minstrels, began to lose its popularity. Billy was a grand entertainer; everybody loved him. Everybody talked about his show; he had more friends than any other individual in the show business. For many years he had entertained and he was growing tired, tired and a little old. So, one day he turned over his show, lock, stock, and barrel, to Charlie Reed. Charlie was a good showman, but he was not

Billy Emerson. He booked his minstrels in San Francisco, and a few people came to see them. But they missed Billy Emerson. Reed had not paid much for the show, but even so the receipts were not big enough to pay expenses. Perhaps San Francisco was growing blasé. Charlie booked the show for two weeks in Sacramento. Sacramento was even worse. It was a hot summer as any summer is hot in Sacramento. The audience would not sit through the heat and listen to the same jokes they had heard for years.

The talent was good, but it was all talent that had been seen year after year in Billy Emerson's company. In the old days the audience had sung the songs along with the entertainers. Now it just sat glumly and smoked cigars. Charlie Reed closed his eyes to the dismal failure as long as he could, but closing his eyes would not pay expenses. So, one afternoon after the matinee, he went backstage to post the two-week closing notice. And there he found his old friend, Barnett. Barnett was something of a talent scout. Barnett knew show business as few others knew it.

He watched Reed post the closing notice, took it from the bulletin board, tore it into shreds, and scattered it like stage snow. And then he gave Reed a friendly, fatherly lecture, straight from the heart.

"Charlie," he said, "you've got a fine show and fine talent, but no show can keep on forever without new blood and young blood. And I've found your young blood. A sixteen-year-old kid down in Reno, Nevada. He's a blacksmith, and an amateur prize fighter. A husky little fellow. Fights like a whirlwind."

Reed grunted. A prize fighter and blacksmith! Did Barnett expect him to introduce prize fights in his minstrel show?

132

And Barnett repeated, "He's a prize fighter and a black-smith—and he sings like an angel."

A few days later, during a dismal performance of the Reed Minstrels, the sixteen-year-old boy from Reno arrived. He sat backstage, tearing his straw hat into shreds. Out front Tambo and Bones were roaring at their own jokes—and the audience was sitting glumly. Then it became restless; then it began to grumble. Reed saw trouble coming. He walked into the wings and found the boy sitting there.

"Can you sing?" demanded Reed.

"Yes, sir," said the boy. "I sing all the time in saloons and parlor houses down in Reno."

"What's your name?" yelled Reed.

"Dick Jos," the boy whispered.

"How do you spell it?" Reed groaned.

"J-O-S," said the boy.

"That's a terrible name," said Reed. "We'll have to change it. We'll add an *e* to it and give you a Spanish-California name. Come along with me."

He led the boy to the middle of the stage. Tambo was doing a buck and wing. Reed raised his hand, and the dance stopped.

"Ladies and gentlemen," said Charlie Reed, "we interrupt our show to bring you the most sensational voice the theater has ever known. Presenting the young Spanish-California boy soprano, Mr. Richard José, singing—what are you going to sing, boy?"

And Dick José said, " 'Silver Threads Among the Gold.' "

For fifty years Dick José sang "Silver Threads Among the Gold," but never with a greater triumph than that night in Sacramento early in 1887. The audience cheered and shrieked and sobbed, and Charlie Reed and Billy Barnett stood in the wings, tears cascading down their cheeks. The boy sang again and again, and the rest of the Reed Minstrel Show was never finished. But the next night the theater was mobbed; Dick José's fame had been achieved in a single night.

The rest of the engagement was a sensation. The troupe rushed back to San Francisco, and San Francisco went mad. The first week Charlie Reed handed Dick José his pay—a check for twelve dollars. The boy did not know what to do with so much money. Four weeks later a telegram arrived from New York, addressed to Dick José: "Leave for New York immediately. Come at your own terms." It was signed, "Lew Dockstader."

Dick José went to New York and became the star of the Dockstader Minstrels. Then he joined Denman Thompson in the original production of *The Old Homestead,* and in it he sang "Silver Threads Among the Gold" every night for three years.

Now, that is the story of Dick José's triumph. The rest of the story he told me personally, for Dick José traveled all over the world and was a favorite for many years. But, as he grew older, he longed for San Francisco, the scene of his first fame. He lived in San Francisco for many years. He retired from show business, but at clubs and private parties, or in a café at night, or at picnics or lodge meetings you were sure to hear Dick José sing, and no matter what other songs he sang in his high soprano-tenor, he always ended with "Silver Threads Among the Gold."

So, I knew Dick José well. One night I sat with him, reminiscing about the old days of the San Francisco theater. I asked him, "Dick, you came to California from Reno. Were you born there?"

And Dick said, "No, I was born in Cornwall in England."

And I asked him if he had ever gone back to Cornwall after fame had come to him.

Dick said, "Yes, I went back to Cornwall. I had left there a poor boy, left because I didn't want to spend a lifetime in the coal mines. It was a little village I had come from, and I'd always wanted to see it again. So, after the world had been so good to me, and life had been so fine, and I was growing old, I was touring Europe with my wife. Oh, we were both sentimental old folk, but we had a longing to see my childhood home; just wanted to see if I'd still recognize any of the old places.

"So, we sneaked into the little village one night, didn't let anyone know we were coming, didn't intend to let anyone know who we were. But they found out some way or other.

"We walked into the village at night, down one little street and up another. And we saw something we couldn't explain. In the window of every little house in that Cornish village there was a candle burning. We met a stranger and we said to him, 'Can you tell us what the candles are burning for?' And he said, 'Yes sir, I can. The greatest man ever to go out of this village is coming home; he went away a poor blacksmith and he's coming home a famous man. We're burning these candles to welcome our wandering boy, Dick Jos.'" . . .

Dick José was a San Francisco minstrel, and the minstrels and their songs were a part of the pageant that made San Francisco a "theater town."

XVII

Emperor Norton

He came to San Francisco in 1849. His father had been an industrious Jewish merchant in London. He sailed away to make his fortune, and by devious routes landed in the boom town of San Francisco, where he registered at the William Tell House and started out to see the city.

It was a little place then, a sprawling, clumsy village along the water front, muddy, ramshackle, and hectic—the picture that greeted the eye was dismal. But there was the majesty of the hills that rose above the village, and the serene beauty of the Bay that spilled at its feet. And Joshua Norton looked at it and said, "I shall stay here till I have seen this village grow to be one of the world's greatest and most beautiful cities."

Men were rushing out of the village, away to the hills and the gold mines to find their fortunes. Norton said, "I'll stay here and find my fortune here, and someday the men will come back from the hills, multiplied a thousand times."

He hung out his shingle—"J. A. Norton, Merchant." He was financially successful from the beginning. He won the immediate respect of the San Francisco citizens. He purchased empty lots, sand lots, and lots flooded by the high tides of the Bay; he built stores and warehouses, and sold them, and his fortune increased. Men called him the merchant with the Midas touch. The city bankers came to him for advice; his judgment was called infallible. He worked arduously to turn the village into a metropolis. Men of affairs called him into consultation before they embarked on new undertakings. When a man was in doubt about the value of an investment, friends would advise him to consult Joshua Norton. They called him a genius; they said he was destined for great things; they said he had the potentialities of an empire builder, the qualities of an emperor. That was the word—an *emperor*.

They used the word freely, half in joke, half seriously. They would meet him on the street and grin and say, "How are you, Emperor?"

And Joshua Norton would grin and say, "Fine. Making money as usual. But don't call me an emperor! This is a great country and its strength is in its democracy."

He was a very wise man, was Joshua Norton. He knew the strength inherent in democracy. But still they grinned and called him—emperor.

In four years' time Joshua Norton had accumulated a modest fortune; some say it amounted to more than a quarter-million dollars. And, with the wealth in hand, he embarked on a project to corner the rice market of the world. In good faith he induced friends to invest their fortunes in the project. He had entree to all the banks; investors were easily found. The Norton rice market was famous. Approximately three hundred thousand dollars were poured into it before the bubble burst. The investors lost their investments, and Joshua Norton threw every dollar of his fortune into the pool to pay as many losses as possible.

Now he was penniless; he walked through the village streets, tragically alone, a pauper. Then he disappeared. For several months San Francisco heard nothing of him, and San Francisco said, "It is just as well. He was an emperor for a day; he has no place in the city of his past glories." They smiled a patronizing smile, remembering the dignified little gentleman, and then forgot all about him.

And then, one day, the man whom businessmen had called "emperor," strode majestically down Montgomery Street. He wore a uniform that was a combination of Army and Navy regalia. He wore extremely high epaulets on his shoulders; he carried a gnarled cane of grapevine wood; he wore a high beaver hat with a brass clasp holding three brightly colored feathers on the front of it. He strode to the office of the *Bulletin* and inserted an announcement proclaiming himself *Norton I, Emperor of the United States and Protector of Mexico*.

It was in 1854 that Joshua Abraham Norton disappeared to reappear as the Emperor Norton. For twenty-six years after that he was a familiar sight on the city streets, a grotesque, comic-opera figure of a man, a madman—full-bearded, sharp-eyed—wearing his absurd uniform and busily ruling his imaginary empire. He sent cablegrams to Queen Victoria and to the Czar of Russia and to the Kaiser, telling them how to run their business—a megalomaniac in the days before that word had become popular. Yet, Norton's every undertaking in his empire of fantasy was constructive, an act of kindness, an act of friendliness, or for the good of mankind in general.

Certainly, to be a successful emperor one had to have a royal exchequer. So, Norton went to a friendly printer on Leidesdorf Street and ordered royal currency printed. The printer, humoring the kindly little madman, ran off a mass of cash certificates in ten-, twenty-five-, and fifty-cent denominations. He printed them as a joke, but the Emperor saw no humor in it. He used the certificates whenever he needed cash, and through all his years in the city any San Francisco merchant would accept and honor a cash certificate of Norton I, Emperor of the United States.

As a matter of fact, there was one occasion—and only one that we have been able to discover—when his royal currency was turned down. He was journeying to the state capital at Sacramento to attend, as he regularly attended, the session of the Legislature, and to advise the legislators. The colored dining-car waiter did not know the traditions of the Emperor's currency and refused to honor it. It was one of the few times in his life on which Norton flew into a rage. He pounded the table and shouted for all to hear, declaring that he would revoke the railroad's franchise. The commotion spread the length of the train. The train conductor rushed in, recognized Norton, apologized to the Emperor in the name of the Central Railroad and the Empire in general. And the next day the Central Pacific sent Emperor Norton a pass good on all trains, with free service in its dining cars for life.

His Imperial Palace was a lodginghouse on Commercial Street. Each night he paid fifty cents for his room; he refused to rent it by the week or month, although he lived in it for seventeen years. It is generally believed that the money was contributed regularly by the Occidental Lodge of Masons of which Norton was a respected member.

He was a man of profound religious faith. The precept of his Jewish tradition was that there was only one God. Each Saturday morning he went to the Synagogue Emanu-El and, seated in the first row of the balcony, with his nondescript mongrel dogs, Bummer and Lazarus, asleep at his feet, he devoutly followed the ancient ritual. But, because he knew that there was only one God, he reasoned that his God must serve all mankind and all faiths. So, each Sunday morning, accompanied by Bummer and Lazarus, he went to mass at the Catholic Old St. Mary's Church.

Bummer and Lazarus went everywhere with him. No theatrical performance opened in San Francisco from 1855 to 1880 that three complimentary tickets for the first row of the balcony were not put aside for Bummer and Lazarus and Norton I, Emperor of the United States. It was a custom that held until that tragic day when his beloved mongrel, Lazarus, died, and thousands of San Franciscans followed it to its grave where it was buried as a ward of the city.

Norton's opinions were decided. He was a fervent opponent of woman suffrage. He almost broke up a meeting of the National Woman Suffrage Association by telling the lady speaker to go home and clean house and have children and leave lawmaking to the men who understood the making of laws.

There was another meeting attended by Norton. Hoodlums and ruffians were making the life of the city's Chinese population miserable. A mass meeting of indignant citizens was held. During the speeches the hoodlums commenced booing. A fight, started between two hoodlums, spread throughout the floor of the assemblage and developed into a free-for-all. At the height of the melee, a funny little man in a blue-and-red uniform mounted the platform and pounded with his grapevine cane. The rioters paused long enough to laugh at the absurd figure, and—and then became quiet. Slowly, deliberately, in a quiet but compelling voice, Joshua Norton was reading the Lord's Prayer. The meeting ended in solemn silence.

A madman. But there was the strength of wisdom in all of Norton's madness, and men recognized it. In Sacramento, a seat was reserved for him in the visitors' gallery of the Senate. He was an honored guest and when, on occasion, he was permitted to take the floor, his remarks, although listened to with suppressed chuckles, were heard nonetheless with respect.

A case in point of the wisdom of his madness was his obsession that there was need of mutual understanding between England and the United States if this civilization were to endure. So, to cement the friendship of the two nations, he sent a telegram to Abraham Lincoln ordering him to marry the widowed Victoria, Queen of England. The telegram was received, and the President's secretary promptly dispatched an answer promising that Mr. Lincoln would give careful consideration to the command.

Norton sent telegrams to the Kaiser and the Czar also, telling them how best to manage their empires, and practical jokers sent telegrams to Norton from the Czar and the Kaiser, promising to obey his edicts. Norton saved and cherished these spurious telegrams, and they were found among his effects after his death.

Then there was the day he appeared at the desk of the president of the city's most representative bank, and handed over a check for three million dollars with the command that the money be used to bridge San Francisco Bay. The dignified president listened with concealed amusement to the preposterous suggestion of the madman. It was utterly absurd; everyone knew that the Bay could never be bridged.

And there was that other day when Norton evolved the fantastic idea that Christmas was a day for children, and that a public Christmas tree should be lighted in Union

Square. A mad, crazy idea, but the city approved, and the first outdoor Christmas tree was lighted at the command of the little London Jew.

Such was the wisdom of Norton's madness. But, meanwhile, he faced personal problems, too. His imperial uniform wore out. So, appearing before the San Francisco Board of Supervisors, he said that it was a disgrace that the city should permit its Emperor to appear in such unseemly garb. And, without a smile, the supervisors went into executive session and wrote into the city charter an act whereby Norton I, Emperor of the United States and Protector of Mexico, would receive thirty dollars a year with which to buy uniforms as long as he lived. For a dozen years after that, each spring Norton appeared before the Board and collected thirty dollars for a new uniform, and it was assessed against the taxpayers.

On a January day in 1880, Joshua Norton was walking slowly along Kearny Street toward California Street. He was tired and he was lonely; his companions, Bummer and Lazarus, were dead. Slowly he turned up California Street and paused in front of Old St. Mary's Church where Sunday after Sunday he had attended mass—he paused and stumbled and fell. And before a hack could speed him across the cobblestoned streets to the receiving hospital, he was dead.

The city he loved went into mourning for the mad emperor. Flags were flown at half-mast. Thirty thousand people followed the funeral cortege to the grave that had been dug for him in the family plot of the wealthy San Francisco pioneer, Joseph G. Eastland. And the funeral expenses were defrayed by Eastland's club, The Pacific Club, later to become the Pacific Union.

That was in 1880. Fifty-four years later, in 1934, members

of the Pacific Union Club moved the mortal remains of Joshua Norton to Woodlawn Cemetery. The mayor spoke, the municipal band played, a military salute was fired, and taps were sounded from the hilltop.

And newcomers to the city said, "What a fantastic city— what a mad, outrageous city! All that fuss for a man who thought himself an emperor! A poor, crazy, little man in a red-and-blue uniform with feathers in his hat." . . .

XVIII

Lucky Baldwin

This is the story of a man who did not believe in luck. He spent an exceedingly busy life; he had more ramified details to take care of in a day than the average man faces in a month. His was a story of fabulous success. He started with nothing and, surpassing any success story Horatio Alger ever conceived, he became an industrial giant.

Luck? No, there was no luck to it. He stated bluntly that everything he ever had, everything he ever accomplished was the fruit of his own labor and brain. He said that you never got anything in life that you did not go after. Sometimes it meant hard work; sometimes it meant being smarter than the other fellow. But it never depended on luck. There was no such thing as luck. He did not believe in luck—and men called him "Lucky" Baldwin.

Elias Jackson Baldwin—Lucky Baldwin—came to San Francisco in 1853. He was twenty-five years old. Most of those twenty-five years had been spent in the journey across the continent from Ohio. The senior Baldwin, with the enthusiasm of thousands of other pioneer Americans, saw promise in the West. From city to city and town to town the Baldwin cavalcade moved, stopping in places for years at a time on the westward trek.

The journey was too slow for young Elias; leaving his parents, he moved on alone. He managed a hotel. He married and was a father before he was twenty. He traded horses, sold horses, and made a few thousand dollars. In 1853, with a few horses to sell and seven thousand dollars in his pocket, he landed in San Francisco.

His coming to San Francisco was not a matter of chance —or luck. He understood and loved horses; the boom town of San Francisco was wealthy and its prosperous citizens found infinite delight in displaying their wealth in the costly and dashing horses they rode or drove. With a population of twenty-five thousand, Baldwin saw possibilities in a livery stable.

The town was lacking in adequate living accommodations for men as well as for beasts. The most remarkable and perhaps the most popular place of lodging was the Niantic Hotel, built on the hull of the sailing ship, *Niantic*, which had gone aground at Sansome and Clay streets. Then there was the Pacific Temperance Hotel; that was the establishment where Baldwin found lodging. After a few days in that badly run hostelry, Elias decided he could do a better job of running it and make money in the bargain. He offered to buy. The proprietor asked six thousand dollars. Baldwin offered five thousand.

The proprietor said, "Supposing I had asked five thousand?"

Baldwin answered, "Then I would have offered you four."

145

For three days the two men, the horse trader and the hotel man, dickered. At the end of three days Baldwin wrote a check for five thousand dollars, and the hotel was his. Then Baldwin made a suggestion, a very simple suggestion, that the check and bill of sale be dated three days earlier so that he could show folks back East what a fast operator he was. The ex-hotel man agreed. The lease and the check changed hands.

"And now," said Lucky Baldwin, "there is a little matter of three days' board and lodging."

"Oh, yes," said the hotel man, "you do owe me for three days."

"On the contrary," said Baldwin. "*You* owe *me*. According to this check and agreement, I have owned the hotel for three days."

No, Lucky Baldwin's success was not based on luck. A month after he bought the hotel, he sold it, doubling his money for a profit of five thousand dollars.

After that, he turned to his favorite diversion, horses, and opened a livery stable. The stable was to be unimportant in his building of a fortune, but it was his favorite enterprise nonetheless, an enterprise with which his name was to be associated long after his death.

Some years later, when he was running two stables, he decided to sell one. He found a prospective buyer and gave him a thirty-day option, agreeing that the prospective buyer could run the stable for the thirty days and then, if he were satisfied, could buy it for ten thousand dollars. The buyer agreed and assumed management. And Baldwin deflected all the business from the stable he was retaining to the stable in the hands of the buyer. The purchaser, finding that business exceeded his most optimistic hopes, paid the ten thousand dollars, received his bill of sale—and the next day business fell off.

Of course, these stories of Lucky Baldwin are considered examples of sharp and unethical practice today. But, if we can believe the critics of his day, such promotion in the 'sixties and 'seventies was simply called "shrewd business." Horse traders were admired, and the sharper the trade, the more admiration it won. All this, of course, before humanity mended its ways and business became ethical.

But livery stables and hotels were small business. Baldwin had made profits and now he sought a game with greater glory. The game was ready at hand. The first Comstock Bonanza in the hills back of Virginia City, Nevada, was at its height. Baldwin invested, sold when stocks were high, bought when they were low. By the time the ebb tide came and the Bonanza kings were counting their losses, Baldwin was a millionaire.

And then he decided to travel. He went to India hunting big game; he went to the Orient and there he saw a troupe of entertainers that amazed him, peculiar little men who did amazing feats of juggling and wrestling. With the instinct of a showman, he realized that such an act would be a sensation in sensation-loving America; no Oriental acrobats had ever crossed the Pacific. He brought the troupe home with him, toured the United States with it, made another fortune out of it, and then sold it to a young Englishman who wanted to take a novelty act to London.

And so, the young Englishman returned to Piccadilly with his Japanese jugglers, and they inspired him and his partner to write an opera. The young man was W. G. Gilbert and his partner was Arthur Sullivan. The opera was *The Mikado*.

Baldwin's venture in the vaudeville business was at an end, but his love of the theater was intensified. He used to sit in his livery stable and talk about it. He liked to talk to a young street urchin who sold newspapers, a youngster who spent most of his time in Baldwin's stable.

"Davey," Baldwin would say to the boy, "someday I'll build you a fine theater and you shall be my star actor."

The newspaper boy was David Belasco.

Baldwin built that theater for David Belasco, incorporating it in the Baldwin Hotel at the corner of Powell and Market streets in San Francisco. But, meanwhile, fate or luck—that luck he had always scorned—took a hand in his affairs. Before sailing for India, he had told his broker to sell some of his Comstock investments. Now, on his return, he learned that he had sailed carrying the key to his safe in his pocket. The stocks, locked in the safe, could not be sold. And during his absence they had increased in value to such a degree that they were worth from four to five million dollars. The story was told on Bush Street and spread through the city, and overnight Elias Baldwin became "Lucky" Baldwin.

In 1875 Baldwin was instrumental in developing the Pacific Stock Exchange, later to be the San Francisco Stock Exchange. He was elected its first president. He was forty-seven years old. His fortune was estimated at seven million dollars, and now, with the zest for money-making less important, he turned to the furnishing of his dream-hotel.

The hotel was completed and opened a year before the Palace Hotel. He purchased a clock for twenty-five thousand dollars and had it placed at the entrance. He had the great mural painters of the day decorate walls and ceilings and he lined other walls with rich mahogany; he hung crystal chandeliers more dazzling than those in the Palace of Versailles; he ordered his architects to pile the edifice with cornices and carved turrets and balconies.

Finally, the Baldwin Hotel opened. And on a night late in the fall of 1875, the Baldwin Theatre—originally called Baldwin Academy of Music—opened with Shakespeare's *Othello*. The part of the Moor was played by Louis James, and Iago was played by James O'Neill, the father of Eugene. It was San Francisco's first great theater; the opening night was a scene of splendor that has not been forgotten to this day.

Then Lucky Baldwin turned to new fields. He was not a dabbler tiring of a toy as soon as he had acquired it. But, for his appetite, he had to have a score of interests and activities all at the boiling point at one time. He had heard of the beauty of southern California. He toured the south and fell in love with the richness of the San Gabriel Valley. Here was the opportunity he had dreamed of; he loved horses, knew, and understood horses. He would build the greatest racing stable in the world.

He bought tens of thousands of acres of land at a cost in the neighborhood of a half-million dollars. And he built a race track to show and race his horses, a track that he named Santa Anita—that same track that was closed for many years and in our day was reopened by his favorite daughter, Anita.

Yes, the interests of Lucky Baldwin were pyramiding. A great hotel and a great theater in San Francisco; a vast ranch and race track in southern California. And next he visited Lake Tahoe, fell in love with its beauty, and built another great hotel—the Tallac. In all, his lands covered some seventy thousand acres, his racing stables became the greatest in the world, his theater was the most beautiful west of Chicago, and—amazingly, due to lawsuits, due to national panics, due to a score of reasons—Elias Baldwin found himself a man of mighty wealth but devoid of cash. He refused to pay bills. New lawsuits were instituted. Judgments piled up against him, and he evaded the judgments. Elias Baldwin had scorned luck, and Lady Luck was turning against him.

"But no," he persisted. "There's no such thing as luck. A man gets what he pays for."

And so, he staged the first of his many comebacks. An incident illustrates his methods. The gas bill for the Baldwin Hotel was two thousand dollars a month. He could not pay the bill, and the utility company threatened to turn off the gas. So he built his own gasworks and sold the surplus not required for the hotel, making a profit that made the lighting of the hotel cost him less than nothing.

But he had to have cash. He commenced subdividing and selling some of his vast holdings in southern California. He was the south's first land promoter. And he achieved new fame by a statement he made in 1881 when a prospective purchaser objected to paying Baldwin's price for unimproved land.

"Hell," said Lucky Baldwin, "we're giving away the land. We're *selling* the climate."

And, finally, with the coming of the 'nineties and the national panic of 1894, the Baldwin Hotel and Theatre were not paying. The Tallac was not paying. New lawsuits were piling up against his name, and his lands in the south were being eaten by taxes. Of these holdings he loved best La Merced Ranch. In fact, he loved it so much that, when he was in dire need of money, he found feeble excuses to prevent his selling it. Why, he even made up a fantastic story that there was oil on La Merced, so, of course, he would not sell it.

The 'nineties neared their end. He still owned his hotel and theater; he still owned La Merced Ranch and Santa Anita; he still owned Tallac on Lake Tahoe. He owned thousands of acres in Bear Valley. And then, in 1898, in one of the most disastrous hotel and theater fires in history, the Baldwin Hotel and Theatre burned to the ground. Many lives were lost in the blaze. The value of the hotel and theater was three million dollars, all uninsured. Baldwin sold the land to James Flood, and the Flood Building stands on the site today at Powell and Market. And at the age of seventy-two, Lucky Baldwin started out to make a new fortune.

His adventures took him to the gold fields of the Klondike. He did make a fortune in Nome, and again he found himself possessing vast holdings—but still with no money.

And so, he came home to the city he loved, but not to die. He would end his days in San Francisco, but first he would prove he was not beaten. He was only in his seventies and he figured he had time to make several more fortunes—yes, and perhaps to lose them, too. But it would not be luck; if he lost, it would be because he had not been shrewd enough, or wise enough, or perhaps he had been too sentimental. To succeed, a man could not be sentimental as he had been sentimental about Santa Anita and La Merced Ranch and San Francisco. No, a man could not be so sentimental about his land that he would claim there was oil on it, just so he would not have to sell it.

Elias Baldwin—Lucky Baldwin—died in 1909. He was eighty-one years old. He had no cash. But, shortly after his death, oil was discovered on La Merced Ranch. When his estate was appraised, it was found that the most fantastic, the most colorful, in some ways the most unscrupulous and in other ways the most trusted, the most sentimental and picturesque of San Francisco's giants had died leaving a fortune of thirty-five million dollars.

XIX

David Belasco

San Francisco loves its traditions—every San Franciscan knows that—and one of the city's favorite traditions is the Lincoln Grammar School Association. The old Lincoln School on Fifth Street near Mission had more famous graduates than the average university. The Lincoln boys meet every year to tell themselves what a wonderful bunch of kids they were. This is the story of one of the school's favorite sons.

The story really does not start with Lincoln School or in San Francisco; it starts in Vancouver, British Columbia, in the hotel room of a circus clown. His name was Ledo. He was a kindly, whimsical, lonely man. One day he was sitting in his dingy room when a police officer visited him. The officer had been informed that Ledo was nursing a sick boy. Yes, Ledo acknowledged, the boy was very sick. He would probably die. Where were his parents? Ledo was not sure. The boy had been born in San Francisco; his parents had moved to Victoria. The lad had run away to sea, reached Vancouver, had been given shelter in a monastery, and had again run away, this time to join the circus. He was a wonderful boy, Ledo said. He was a daring bareback rider. He rode a white horse around the ring and leaped through burning hoops, a feat that had never before been done.

"But," said Ledo, "he'll probably never do it again; he'll probably die."

The officer asked the boy's name, and Ledo said, "Davey."

Davey? But what was his full name?

Ledo answered, "Davey Belasco."

With the officer's aid, Ledo located Davey Belasco's parents—who had returned to San Francisco—and he set sail for California with the sick boy. They reached the Golden Gate. Davey recovered, but Ledo caught the fever from him and died.

The Belascos were poor. Davey wanted to go to work at once to make a fortune for the family; this was when he was ten years old. But Humphrey Abraham Belasco had the deep love of learning characteristic of his race; he ordered young David to school—there would be plenty of time later to make a fortune.

Davey entered the Lincoln School. He drove the teachers to desperation. He would not study. He balked at grinding through Greek tragedies and Shakespeare. He preferred to recite inane, melodramatic poems, one in particular—"The Maniac." His English teacher pleaded with him to "choose the fine things, Davey, the beautiful things!" And David said he would, and continued to recite—"The Maniac." Yet, years later, David Belasco said, "My first love of the classics was inspired by that teacher, Nellie Holbrook." Nellie Holbrook. Later she gave up schoolteaching, married a gentleman named Blinn, and had a son who was Holbrook Blinn.

Now, the one thing that Davey Belasco liked, even more than ranting melodramatic poetry, was to play hooky from

154

school and visit a tobacco-chewing friend who owned a livery stable. They both wanted money—the stable owner so that he could buy horses, the boy so that he could be an actor and own his own theater. They made a bargain. The stable owner would make a fortune and build a theater for the boy. And then Dave could act and the stable owner could come to see the performances free. The stable owner's name was Lucky Baldwin.

Baldwin made his fortune. He built the Baldwin Hotel and Theatre—the Baldwin Academy of Music—on Market Street near Powell, and young David Belasco played there, played one hundred seventy-five different roles in all.

One of the actors in the Baldwin cast was James A. Hearne. Hearne and young Belasco wrote a play, *Hearts of Oak*. Belasco formed a company and started a tour across the continent with the *Hearts of Oak* cast. He landed in New York, penniless. He gave recitations on street corners for the coins of passers-by. He washed dishes for his meals. He cleaned out a stable for the price of a bed. And then he shook the dust of New York streets from his worn-out boots and started to walk to California. A friendly brakeman let him ride free a part of the way; farmers gave him lifts in their wagons.

"I wanted," he said later, "only one thing in the world. I wanted to be back in the city I loved more than any other place in the world—San Francisco."

But David Belasco did not stay in San Francisco. Playing the Baldwin Theatre one night, he met two young men who were with the Haverly Minstrels. He sat with them all night in the Rathskeller at the corner of Kearny and Sutter streets. All night long they talked until one of the young men fell asleep just as the sun came through the swinging doors— and David Belasco signed an agreement with the other young man. He would go to New York as his stage director. The other young man was Charlie Frohman.

So, David Belasco became a stage director and then a producer, and finally he built his own theaters and presented his own great stars. Among his possessions was a book in which he wrote the names of the actors and actresses he discovered, and to whom he gave their start.

There was Mary Pickford. She was fifteen years old at the time Belasco first saw her. There were Frances Starr and her sensational success in *The Easiest Way*, and Leslie Carter, Blanche Bates of San Francisco in *The Darling of the Gods,* Lenore Ulric, David Warfield, Ina Claire, Henrietta Crossman, Madame Modjeska, Nance O'Neill! And there was one other whose name means little to the generation of today—Adelaide Neilson, the loveliest Juliet of all time.

Belasco came to Adelaide's dressing room one night after the final curtain had fallen on *Romeo and Juliet.* In his hand he held Juliet's slipper; she had lost it in the tomb scene.

"I want to keep the slipper," he said, "in memory of the most wonderful night the theater has ever known."

Adelaide gave him the slipper, and he nailed it on the star's dressing-room door of the Baldwin Theatre, to hang there till the theater burned down, in 1898, in one of the most terrible theater disasters of all time.

"And because I love you so," Adelaide Nielson said, "I want you to have a memory of me that you can carry in your pocket."

She emptied on the table a bag of precious jewels and insisted that Belasco choose one of them. He selected a black pearl. Adelaide shook her head. Not that; anything but the black pearl. She was very superstitious. She had a premonition that when the pearl left her possession her life would end. She took the pearl out of Belasco's hand, and in its place handed him a beautiful, flawless emerald. The following day she left on her Eastern tour.

A month later, David Belasco received a package from Adelaide Nielson containing the black pearl and a card on which she had written "Davey, I can't get your voice out of my mind." She died that day. . . .

In 1909, the boys of the Lincoln Grammar School held a reunion to honor one of their favorite sons. A committee was formed to greet him. Discussing the banquet to be held, the committee said, "Let's make it an annual affair. We'll form the Lincoln School Association and meet once a year."

The banquet was held in the Hofbrau Café. The Lincoln School boys stood and cheered as the honored guest walked in, walked in with sentimental tears cascading down his cheeks. He stood at the banquet table, America's most spectacular producer, David Belasco. And when the cheers had subsided, someone shouted, "Now act for us, Davey. Give us some Shakespeare."

David Belasco shook his head. "No," he said, "I'm not an actor. I'm just one of the Lincoln School boys come home. I'll not act for you, I'll recite for you."

And he recited the poem that had driven Nellie Holbrook Blinn desperate almost fifty years before——"*The Maniac!*"

XX

R.L.S.

For several years a small group of San Franciscans have met together on November thirteenth to celebrate a birthday— the birthday of a king. They celebrate, and they sit and talk of their memories of the king, and a favorite chapter of their memories has to do with the royal expedition of the King, the Queen, the Crown Prince, and the Grand Duke into a little-known valley of California a generation ago.

The story has something of the quality of a fairy tale, for, after all, there have not been many kings and queens and crown princes in San Francisco. There was old Emperor Norton, but he was mad. There was Queen Liliuokalani of the Sandwich Islands—she stayed at the Palace Hotel for a brief visit—and there was the visit of the beloved Albert of Belgium, and there may have been one or two others. But they all, with the exception of Norton I, were royal by divine decree. Our King and his Queen and the Crown Prince had assumed their titles just because they liked them, and because, confidentially, the King had a penchant for making believe. As for the Grand Duke, he was not even of pure blood: he was a dog, half-setter and half-spaniel.

The journey made by the King and the Queen and the Crown Prince and the Grand Duke who was a dog was in the nature of a honeymoon. Which, of course, makes the story more confusing because one does not usually take a crown prince on a honeymoon, to say nothing of a dog of questionable parentage. So let us begin at the beginning.

The young man who was king lived in a poor and modest lodginghouse on Bush Street run by a Mr. and Mrs. Carson. He was not a very well-fed young man; he was usually hungry, and unfortunately his stomach was weak. As a matter of record, he always looked hungry and he always appeared pale. So, looking pale and hungry, he walked from Carson's lodginghouse on Bush Street to the home of a minister friend on Sutter Street. And he stood, the hungry, pale young man, at the side of his bride-to-be. And the minister, Dr. Scott, spoke the words that made them man and wife. . . .

"Do you, Fanny Osbourne, take this man——" And, "Do you, Robert Louis Stevenson, take this woman for your lawful, wedded wife?"

Then the king who was Robert Louis Stevenson, and the bride who had been Fanny Osbourne, and the crown prince who was her son, Lloyd, by an earlier marriage, and the illegitimate Grand Duke who had adopted the family, started out on their honeymoon.

They walked down the front steps of Dr. Scott's house and then down Sutter Street to Market, walking on the north side of the street because that was the sunnier side and the king hungered for sunshine. They came to the Ferry Building which was a somber, small, gray wooden shack in those days, and they took a ferryboat that worked its way, panting and wheezing, between Alcatraz Island and Goat Island to the town of Vallejo. Stevenson hated the journey. He found the muddy waterway to the wooden docks of Vallejo a dismal passage; he sat up forward on the boat and looked hopefully into the north. He coughed as the Bay fogs closed about the boat, and his wife pinned a brown-plaid shawl about his shoulders.

She said, "Robbie, the fog is bad for your lungs."

And he said, "Nonsense! My royal lungs scorn wind and fog. Do they not, Your Highness?"

And young Lloyd Osbourne whom they called "Sam," said, "Yes, Your Majesty. Wh-huh!" And he scratched the Grand Duke's ears.

Mrs. Stevenson was worried; she knew her husband to be physically weak. She had seen the threatening hand of Death in his cough. But when she pleaded with him, saying that perhaps the journey they were making was ill-advised, he said, "Nonsense!" He laughed, and repeated it: "Nonsense. I'm taking you to a world of silver. We're going to make a fortune that will build our kingdom. There's prosperity ahead for this royal family."

Now, Stevenson, the writer, the poet, the man who delighted to make believe, was not entirely making believe in his promise of a fortune of silver. Rumors had circulated years before of a silver mine that lay on the side of Mount Saint Helena at a settlement called Silverado. The silver had never been found, but neither had the end of the rainbow, and if there was gold at the end of the rainbow, why should there not be silver on Mount Saint Helena? So, Stevenson and his royal family started their quest for hidden treasure. They traveled through the Napa Valley, and Stevenson found virtue in the wine of the Napa Valley vineyards. They came to Calistoga and traveled out of Calistoga, as strange a royal cortege as ever journeyed to Cathay. But Calistoga was only fifty or sixty miles from San Francisco.

First, according to Stevenson's own narrative of the journey, the Crown Prince rode like an outrider on horseback. Then came King Robert and Queen Fanny and the Grand Duke in a double buggy. Later, another wagon would follow with family clothing and a second-hand stove.

Young Lloyd, cantering on ahead, suddenly shouted triumphantly.

Stevenson, driving up to him, said, "Have you found silver?"

And Lloyd said, "No, I've found a sign!"

There, nailed to a tree, was a sign that read "Toll Road. One-horse Rig—Fifty Cents. Two-horse Team and Wagon —Seventy-five Cents. Hogs, Sheep, and Goats—Three Cents."

Just beyond the sign the Stevenson family took squatter's claim in a cabin within stone's throw of the old Toll Road Inn above Silverado.

Telling of it years later, Stevenson said to a friend, "In all my travels, from Scotland to Italy and Switzerland and across the Atlantic and the Pacific and to Samoa, no country was lovelier, no country richer, than were those Silverado hills above the Napa Valley."

He had been sick. He forgot his sickness and said, "I came out of all that and got my feet once more on a little hilltop with a fair prospect of life and a new desire for living."

And when Mrs. Stevenson said, "Robbie, it's time for supper," he waved away the thought of food, and said, "It's enough that it is a beautiful day, that the sky is one field of azure; there's the fragrance of the buckeye that puts forth its twisted horn of blossom. Not a leaf moves. Not a speck appears in the heaven. Here, on the one hand, we have a little stream tinkling by, big enough perhaps after the rains, but already yielding up its life; overhead, and on all sides, a bower of green and tangled thicket, still fragrant and still flower-bespangled by the early season."

Then he sighed and said, "You've married a wreck of a man, Fanny, a mere complement of cough and bones. But a new life is flowing in my veins."

And Fanny Osbourne Stevenson told him to go take a walk and she would fix supper.

So Robert Louis Stevenson took his walk, up the hillside to the point just below the summit of Saint Helena and there, in the Toll House cottage that stood where the Inn had been before fire leveled it, he heard the story of the silver mines of Silverado. . . .

It had been in the 'fifties of the nineteenth century that the first story, the first rumor of a vast fortune in silver, came down the mountainside. Men had found deposits, deposits that promised unlimited pockets beneath them. The stories spread and pyramided; stories without foundation. More than a half-million dollars in silver taken out of the mine below the Toll House! Fifty million dollars in silver still waiting to be taken out! The mountainside became a bedlam of excitement. In a day's time Jonestown became a roaring city. All night and all day the sound of picks and axes crashed through the trees. At night the whole mountain was ablaze with flickering oil lamps and candlelight. Finally, an old shepherd named Bennie posted his son at the side of his claim with a shotgun and then went down to the town of Napa with a heavy sack over his shoulder. He dumped the sack onto the desk of the editor of the *Napa Reporter* and said, "There you are, Mr. Editor. Ten pounds of solid silver taken out of just one crack in our claim."

The editor opened the sack, ran a handful of the glittering ore through his fingers, and shook his head. Bennie eyed him anxiously. It was his, all right, wasn't it? He was entitled to it, wasn't he? It had come out of his land all right, hadn't it? The editor said, yes, it was his. But it wasn't silver; it was worthless iron pyrites.

Worthless iron pyrites! But that did not stop the rush. People would not believe the whole thing was a hoax. They continued to pour in from a radius of hundreds of miles— prospectors, claim jumpers, gamblers, camp followers— Mount Saint Helena lived through a nightmare of hectic madness and lawlessness. Squatters seized claims, claim jumpers were killed, claim holders were murdered. There may have been a little silver on Saint Helena; there may have been swindlers, as some said, who came in from the East and salted the hill with silver. For a passing moment Mount Saint Helena was a hub of excitement, and just as swiftly as the moment came, so it went. The towns that had sprung up overnight disappeared overnight. The gamblers and the grubstakers and the squatters and the claim jumpers drifted away, and all that was left was the Toll House and the sign "Hogs, Sheep, and Goats—Three Cents."

That was the story as it was told to Robert Louis Stevenson, and he listened and said, "I still think there's silver here," and returned to the cabin and his wife and his stepson—and supper.

Those days on the side of Mount Saint Helena where Robert Louis Stevenson prepared to write *The Silverado Squatters* were probably the happiest in all his life. He continued to make believe. He was King, his wife was Queen, the small boy, Lloyd, was Crown Prince, and when his lungs were torn by wracking coughs he would draw himself up and frown at Fanny and say, "Madam, you forget yourself. I am King, and if I wish to cough, that is my kingly prerogative."

Strangely, for the first time since he had come to America, he put on flesh; there was natural color in his cheeks instead of the unhealthy flush that came at times to his pallid complexion. And when his wife worried about the fog, he said, "It was strangely beautiful this morning when I arose, Fanny. Away in the extreme south, a little hill of fog arose against the sky above the general surface, and as it had already caught the sun, it shone on the horizon like the topsail of some giant ship. In every cove along the line of mountains the fog was being piled higher and higher, as though by some wind that was inaudible to me.

"It was to flee these poisonous fogs that I left the seaboard and climbed so high among these mountains. And now, behold, here came the fog to besiege me in my chosen altitudes, and yet came so beautifully that my first thought was of welcome."

And so he wrote his book, and grew strong, and went down the hill with his Queen and Crown Prince and the Grand Duke who was a dog of strange parentage.

And, sitting at his window on a hill in San Francisco, looking out to the silver ocean of fog that flowed below him through the Golden Gate, he was wont to tell friends of the silver he had found on the sides of Mount Saint Helena—silver that came in with the fog from the valley, silver that was more beautiful than all the mineral wealth beneath the surface of the earth.

And friends who knew him and loved him shook their heads and said, "Yes, R.L.S. always loves to make believe!"

XXI

Ina Coolbrith

The San Francisco newspapers in 1928 recorded the death of a lady. Some people said, "What an odd name." Most people—people in the habit of reading vital statistics in the morning papers—did not even pause to note the name; it meant nothing. But to a few that brief death notice and even briefer obituary brought a catch to the breath and a sense of great loss. It was not because a lady had died—all must die and she was very old; she had passed her eighty-seventh birthday—it was because in her death an era ended.

She was born on March 10, 1842. Her father was Don Carlos Smith, brother of Joseph Smith, the patriarch of the Mormon church. Her mother was an orphan raised by Joseph Smith's mother in the Smith home in Ohio. And to this couple was born the lady of our story. She was christened Josephine D. Smith. Four months after her birth, Don Carlos died at the age of twenty-five, leaving his widow with three children of whom Josephine was the youngest.

The widow, hating the doctrine of polygamy as her husband had hated it, abjured the Mormon faith and started West, caring as best she could for her three children. In St. Louis she married a newspaperman, William Pickett. And then, in 1849, she and Pickett, her three daughters and two sons by Pickett started overland for California.

It was an epic journey. In a chronicle of it we read that when the wagon train hove in sight at the crossing of the Truckee River under a pelting rain, the Pickett wagon looked like a relic of a revolution. Its cover had holes burned in it and was torn to tatters, its strong axles had been replaced by branches roughhewn by the wayside, the iron tires were bound on with ropes, the iron linchpins were gone and chips of hickory substituted, and rags—kept continually wetted—were wound around the hubs to prevent their falling to pieces.

The immigrants, continues the chronicle, had been in constant danger of attack from the Indians in Utah Territory; they had suffered terribly from thirst and fatigue. They were half-starved now when they came in sight of the Truckee, and the oxen could hardly drag the wagon.

But, said the historian, in the dismal picture, there was a child, a dark-haired, gray-eyed child, ten years old and the prettiest thing that had ever come into the Sierra. Her name was Josephine D. Smith, and she had been the first white child to enter California over the Beckwourth Pass. Jim Beckwourth himself, the famous scout and White Chief of the Crow Indians, had placed her before him on his saddle to make sure she would really be first.

The Pickett family moved down the foothills of the Sierra, stopping at times for William Pickett to seek unsuccessfully for a fortune in gold. They came to Marysville and suffered new hardships and hunger and loneliness, and disaster by fire and flood.

They came to San Francisco and found it a maelstrom of riffraff; they traveled by slow stages down through the California valleys to the village that was called wickedest and toughest in all the West—the pueblo of Los Angeles.

166

In Los Angeles, Josephine attended the first school established there and astounded the teacher by writing highly dramatic and amazingly good poetry. At the age of eleven she had her poems published in the *Los Angeles Star*. She became a personage in the village that knew so few personages. She was chosen to lead the grand march at a great Ball and Fiesta on the arm of the former governor, Pío Pico.

She sent her poems far afield; they were printed even in papers as far north as San Francisco. And, at the age of seventeen, she married a former Bones in a minstrel show, Robert B. Carsley. The marriage lasted for three years of cruel disillusionment and brutality at the hands of an insanely jealous husband. At the end of three years, Josephine divorced him and moved to San Francisco.

Thus she ended the first chapter in her amazing life; she ended, in fact, the story of Josephine D. Smith. In San Francisco she took the name under which she had written her poems, the name that combined a nickname and her mother's maiden name—she became Ina Donna Coolbrith.

And so our story of the lady who died in 1928 is the story of California's greatest poetess. But Ina Coolbrith was far more than that. She, more than any other one person, was the inspiration for the circle of writers, poets, essayists, artists, and philosophers who brought fame to San Francisco in its formative years. She inspired them, held them together, was the living prophet of the Victorian era in the West— and she was beloved. Beloved! And yet, strangely enough, the great men who loved her knew nothing of her past, neither that she was a niece of the patriarch, Joseph Smith, nor that she had been married and divorced. They called her the Virgin Poetess.

Who were these men who loved her? Perhaps that can

best be told when we tell you of the disaster that befell her during the earthquake and fire of 1906.

Those dark days in San Francisco destroyed many things that money could replace. But not all the wealth in the world could bring back the treasures that Ina Coolbrith lost in her home high on Russian Hill. There were the letters her friends had written her, her friends, Alfred, Lord Tennyson, George Meredith, Dante Gabriel Rossetti, John Whittier, Henry Wadsworth Longfellow, Marie, Queen of Roumania. Those were the poets of Europe and New England who adored the little San Francisco poetess and her dreams and wrote her priceless letters. And there were more names, those of her intimates, her close, everyday friends—Mark Twain, Bret Harte, Joaquin Miller, and Charles Warren Stoddard.

Ina met Mark Twain, as she met Stoddard and Bret Harte, in the offices of the *Overland Monthly*. During the days that Bret Harte edited the magazine, Ina was his unofficial advisory board and ex-officio editor. Mark Twain worshiped her. Bret Harte, although married, wanted to divorce his wife to wed Ina. Charles Stoddard, perhaps the least famous and least strong of the three, threatened to kill himself if she would not marry him. But Ina had known marriage and would have no more of it.

And here, from putting bits picked up here and there together, there is a temptation to re-create the picture of the friendship of Ina Coolbrith and Bret Harte and Stoddard; but it would be a temptation to delve into fiction, and Ina Coolbrith's life was more fascinating than fiction.

We do know that at almost any hour of the day or night you were likely to find the three of them seated on the floor of Ina's little Russian Hill house, drinking coffee and reading poetry, especially the poetry of the one poet Ina adored above all others—Lord Byron.

We know that day after day they were seen hiking the trails of Mount Tamalpais and Muir Woods, or drinking wine in little shops in Sausalito.

We know that at unexpected and unreasonable hours, they were to be seen wandering through Chinatown or the Latin Quarter or in the Presidio Hills, and that on their walks they were joined at times by a fourth who adored Ina as the others did—he was Ambrose Bierce. And, with a Bohemian contempt for convention, when the men were not at Ina's home drinking her coffee, she went to theirs.

Years passed and Ina Coolbrith's poetry was known around the world. But poet's gold does not buy bread and butter, and not only did Ina have a good appetite and the need of bread and butter, but, in addition, she assumed the support of her ailing mother, her sister's two orphaned children, and Joaquin Miller's daughter, Cali-Shasta, whom he had placed in Ina's hands.

Yes, something more than poet's gold was needed. So, Ina Coolbrith took a job. She became librarian of the Oakland Public Library. It is a grave responsibility, that of being a librarian. A librarian can so easily shape human destinies for evil—or for good.

One day, a small boy came to the librarian, Miss Coolbrith. He was twelve years old, a dirty, small boy. He had a bundle of newspapers under his arm; he was poor, shabby, uncared-for. And he said, please, Miss, could he have something to read? Something to read! That small boy was Jack London, and Ina Coolbrith gave him something to read. For months and years she gave him something to read; she guided him, inspired him, and won his undying adoration.

He was a small, twelve-year-old boy; she was a middle-aged, lovely woman. And Jack London said long years later, "I loved Ina Coolbrith above all womankind, and what I am and what I have done that is good I owe to her."

There was Jack London, and there was the little bright-eyed, dancing-eyed girl who came to Ina Coolbrith and said, please, Miss, could she have something to read? And Ina Coolbrith gave the small girl books, and led her and guided her, and, in later years, the small girl, when she had become a famous woman, said, "All that I am that is good I owe to Ina Coolbrith." The small girl was Isadora Duncan.

For years Ina Coolbrith was librarian of the Oakland Public Library, and for additional years she was librarian of San Francisco's Bohemian Club. They were years of rich treasures and fullness of life—and Ina Coolbrith grew old.

She was seventy-three years old when, in 1915, she was called before the Regents of the University of California. We saw her that day, standing there before the black-robed men of learning, a slender, little, white-haired woman. Slender and little. We think of her as that because she had shrunk with age; the truth is she was large and strong-framed. At seventy-three, her handclasp was still firm, her eyes still danced with light, and the beauty that had been hers in her youth still remained. She stood before the Regents and bowed her head, and there were tears in her eyes as a laurel wreath was placed in her hand in the tradition of the ancient Greek worship of the Muses. With the laurel wreath, Ina Coolbrith was proclaimed California's poet laureate.

There was to be another event in her life to add riches to her contentment, an event that stemmed from a controversy that had raged through many years of the Victorian era. Factions had condemned Lord Byron; his grave was a nondescript slab in a small churchyard. Lord Byron had offended the conventions of Victorian society, and the Victorians had ostracized him in death.

Ina Coolbrith, the last of the Victorians, had nothing but contempt for conventions. One day she sat down and wrote letters in plain words of one syllable to distinguished leaders in London, told them in language that could not be misunderstood just what she thought of them. And then she made a pilgrimage to Muir Woods; she was growing old and there were tasks still to be done. She tramped through the woods from tree to tree till she found the tree worthy of her mission, a full-blown laurel with its leaves rich-green and vital. And she made a laurel wreath and wrote a poem and sent the wreath and the poem to London in the keeping of her emissary, white-haired old Joaquin Miller, and gave Miller clear instructions for his subsequent actions. Miller arrived in London, presented the poem and Ina Coolbrith's demands, and the controversy that had died down flared again and became a celebrated case.

Up and down Mayfair and on Fleet Street and into the sacrosanct halls of Buckingham Palace the controversy traveled, and the result was that the remains of Lord Byron were removed from their nondescript grave and buried with pomp and ceremony in Westminster Abbey. And the laurel wreath that Ina Coolbrith had woven was placed upon his bier.

We last saw Ina Coolbrith in 1927, just a few months before her death. It was at a party in her honor. She sat in a deep chair in the center of the room out on Pacific Heights. Her hands were clasped in her lap, the white-lace mantilla she always wore was draped over her white hair. And strange people came and courted her favor and pressed flowers in her hands and kissed her hands and sighed and looked solemn—strange people, lesser poets and artists, foreign diplomats and hero-worshipers, and little people who wanted to be heroes. And she smiled and probably did not hear a word of the effusions that were poured before her. She was very old, and if she was a little forgetful, a little inattentive, a little vague, then that all could be forgiven, for she was living in a day sixty years earlier.

When someone said, "Miss Coolbrith, do you remember ——" she answered, without waiting for the question to be finished, "Yes, I remember them all—all my friends. Alfred Tennyson—John Whittier—Mark Twain—hmmm, and Bret Harte—Charlie Stoddard—and little Jack London——he asked me for something to read."

And the crowd milled around her and gushed about her, the lady who was the last of the Victorians.

XXII

Ambrose Bierce

At the very beginning artists and musicians, actors and writers, poets and singers joined the overland cavalcade to the Western frontier. Mark Twain, Bret Harte, Joaquin Miller, and the economist, Henry George, in the 'fifties and 'sixties, and, later, Robert Louis Stevenson and Rudyard Kipling, and scores of others found their way to the Golden Gate.

Rudyard Kipling. With empty pockets, armed only with a stout manuscript, he came to the editorial rooms of the foremost Western newspaper. The editor-in-chief lent a sympathetic ear, even agreed to read the manuscript of the strange, cynical young unknown. He read it and saw some virtuous seed in it, but he was afraid it did not quite merit the space it would require. Furious, the strange young man left the manuscript but returned some days later to pick it up. This time the editor had no time for him; the manuscript was handed to him by the editor's Negro doorman and factotum. And as the Negro boy handed the young man the manuscript, he said, "Ah sho' is sorry we cain't buy this, Mr. Kiplin', suh. It sho' is a pow'ful fine story." The story was *The Light That Failed*.

But this is not a chronicle of Rudyard Kipling; it is a sketch, briefly drawn, of a young man who came to San

Francisco in 1866 when Rudyard Kipling was but one year old. The reason for his coming has been explained in a dozen different ways by a dozen different biographers. Perhaps as good a reason as any was the fact that his parents were poor and he was the youngest of ten children. Not only that, but he had to live down the ridicule of the family names. With meticulous care that the name of each child commence with the letter "A," the brood was called Abigail, Addison, Aurelius, Almeda, Ann, Amelia, Augustus, Andrew, and Albert. And the tenth and youngest was Ambrose.

At the age of nineteen Ambrose Bierce joined the Union forces. He fought through the major battles of the Civil War. He was given the rank of first lieutenant. He saw horrors of war that forever embittered him, not only against war itself, but against the cruel stupidities of mankind. He was made prisoner, escaped, and in the battle of Kenesaw Mountain he received severe wounds that caused him suffering as long as he lived.

The horrors of war and the pain of wounds and the stupidities of men and the poverty of a large family, all of these things sent Ambrose Bierce out West at the age of twenty-four, a bitter, cynical, vitriol-tongued misanthrope. He scorned books, he scorned mankind, above all he scorned women. His opinions of womankind, freely expressed wherever he chanced to be, became a tradition—and women adored him. For Fate or Providence or Nature, all three were constantly playing tricks on Bierce, and one of those tricks made him one of the handsomest men of his day in San Francisco. Tall, broad-shouldered, with a fine, strong face and a heavy mane of hair that was snow-white in his later years, Bierce was a splendid figure of a heartbreaker. Women worshiped him, fought for him, and the woman hater was constantly falling in love and out of love. He hated women and couldn't resist them. Finally he married and lived a stormy married life.

In San Francisco he worked for the United States Sub-Treasury. But, among other things that he disliked he included business and money. To relieve his hatred of anything and everything, he wrote, during his first two years in San Francisco, sundry satirical poems. As poetry they were not very good, as satire they were cruel and powerful. They were published in *The Californian* and the *Overland Monthly*. In them he cried out against social activities, against men and women—and especially against dogs. He said of womankind, "Her babies and her visitors are about her only society. And though the former are usually a source of delight, and the latter of annoyance, neither is particularly well calculated to give her broad views or mental culture." Yes, Ambrose Bierce cried out against everything, and soon became known as San Francisco's Town Crier.

Thus far the picture is a dismal one. But Ambrose Bierce was a man of strange contradictions. He hated living—and loved life. He hated women—and fell in and out of love with the greatest of ease. He hated war—and was a brave soldier. He said nothing was worth while, and labored steadily to produce voluminous volumes of perhaps some of the most beautiful writing to come out of the West.

From the *Overland Monthly* he turned to writing for the San Francisco *News-Letter*. In the *News-Letter* and other weekly and monthly periodicals on which he was both editor and contributor, he published a column of prattle which he called just that—"Prattle." And Bierce's "Prattle" column—later transferred to William Randolph Hearst's Sunday *Examiner*—established him as America's first columnist. He wrote books, he wrote poems, brilliant essays, and thrilling war and ghost stories; he wrote stories of profound philosophical meditation, vitriolic lampoons, and stories of satirical humor that established him as one of America's great wits.

The fame of that first column spread, spread to London. His fame in London was greater than it was in San Francisco, the city of his residence. "Prattle" brought him fame and brought him enemies; he made as many enemies as friends with every column. One resentful gentleman pummelled in "Prattle," called Bierce a drunken scoundrel and said that he would kill him on sight. Bierce disclaimed the "scoundrel" but accepted the "drunken." In his next column he announced that on such and such an hour on such and such a day he would walk up Montgomery Street past the door of his enemy. He kept his word. But the resentful gentleman left town and was never heard from again.

Bierce loved good food; in the company of writers and artists he was continually in the San Francisco restaurants that were becoming world-famous. Even better than food, Bierce loved drink. It was said on Montgomery Street that no man in San Francisco could buy Ambrose Bierce the last drink. When his companions at the convivial board went to sleep, Bierce would sit, bright-eyed, quiet, handsome, and immaculate, keenly awake and scorning the weak flesh of his companions. So, Ambrose Bierce became a familiar figure on the streets of the city in the years that it was coming of age.

But he was a sick man, and the torment of his sick body added torture to his unhappy mind. Severe attacks of asthma followed one on the other. He fled from San Francisco, went to London. London acclaimed him, lionized him. He was a friend of Tom Hood, of W. S. Gilbert, of a host of great and famous men. And when his friends were asked about him, they looked puzzled and said, "frankly we don't know anything about his life."

Bierce returned to San Francisco. His friends and disciples were George Sterling, Joaquin Miller, Gertrude Atherton, and hundreds of others. And, as his London friends had, so his San Francisco friends said, "Really, we don't know anything about him."

The stories of his activities became less savory as his vitriolic pen increased in strength. It was said that time and time again he was found sprawled in a gutter, drunk and asleep. And friends would take him home and clean the dirt of the streets from him, and he would amble off to his rooms to write—to write such works as the *Devil's Dictionary,* sardonic comments on a world he knew too well.

Ambrose Bierce was the strangest enigma the West had ever known. People read mystery into his life, and when the mystery was sought none could be found. There was none. Bierce was simply a great mind bruised by life, a dreamer starving for the beauty of life, longing for human companionship and standing alone, horrified by humanity's frailty.

And so the struggle went on, year after year, until finally, a straight-shouldered, white-haired old man, Ambrose grew tired of the struggle. The zest had gone out of the conflict.

One day he disappeared. He has never been seen or heard of since that day. Collectors have collected his books, critics have acclaimed him one of the greatest minds of the nineteenth century. But the book of the life of Ambrose Bierce was closed with the last chapter forever unwritten.

There has been plenty of conjecture; there have been allegations and disclaimers. Of all the stories of Bierce's disappearance the one that received greatest credence was that he died in Mexico. Perhaps the story is true; true or untrue it cannot diminish his art or the stature of the man. And it is certain that he did disappear into warring Mexico and that he wrote from there in one of his last letters, "Goodbye. If you hear of my being stood up against a Mexican stone wall and shot to rags please know that I think it a pretty good way to depart this life. It beats old age, disease, or falling down the cellar stairs. To be a Gringo in Mexico— ah, that is euthanasia!"

According to the most accepted legend of Bierce's death, he traveled alone into Mexico. Then, the storyteller says, one night in 1914, General Pancho Villa was sitting before his shack, smoking. Suddenly he was brought to his feet by the presence before him of a huge, handsome, white-haired man with piercing eyes. He stood there, this leonine figure, prisoner in the hands of two grinning little peons. The prisoner, according to the storyteller, was Ambrose Bierce. Bierce demanded that his chains be struck from him. Villa ordered him set free. And the two men sat down to talk.

I do not know by what strange power the storyteller projected his own astral being into the precious company to record the conversation. But this is the legend.

As the two men talked together, Bierce asked why he had been made prisoner. Pancha Villa answered that stories had been circulated that Bierce was a friend of the political opposition. To show his adherence to the revolutionist cause, Bierce demanded an opportunity to fight for Villa. A gun was placed in his hands, and he went out and killed a few opposition soldiers.

Upon his return Pancha Villa smiled and squeezed his hands together and said, "My friend, you are a good man.

But Mexico is not big enough for two such good men as you and I. I recommend that you return to the United States of America."

"With pleasure," said Ambrose Bierce.

And so—still following the tale of the storyteller—Bierce set out at sunset, unarmed and accompanied by two rebel soldiers with leveled guns. Some hours later the soldiers returned to Villa's camp—alone.

Ambrose Bierce was never heard of again. But on a Mexican mesa a body was found and buried with Christian simplicity.

Yes, after all, the story of Ambrose Bierce is San Francisco's strangest enigma.

XXIII

George Sterling

He was a strange man. He was a lonely man, and yet he had more friends than most men. He loved life, and he was an unhappy man. He had a great mind, and he was irresponsible. From the very beginning his life was a confusion of contradictions. Loving life, he died by his own hand. His name was George Sterling.

Sterling spent most of his adult years on the shores of San Francisco Bay. He was a businessman through force of circumstance, a poet by instinct. He loved San Francisco, the hills, and the Bay; he liked to come to my office because it was on the sixteenth floor of a downtown building with a window that looked east to the Berkeley hills. He loved the view.

He sat at that window one morning. He had come by appointment to meet a fifteen-year-old girl who wanted to be a poet. Sterling did not have much patience with adolescent geniuses. But this child had something. She was Audrey Wurdemann, later winner of the Pulitzer Prize for American poetry. But that spring morning in 1926 she was very young and very excited in the presence of George Sterling who had been called California's greatest poet.

Sterling sat in a straight chair, looking out of the window, the physical reincarnation of Dante. His hair was tousled under his tweed cap, his Grecian nose was long and straight, his warm, kind eyes looked through you and past you.

He looked at Audrey and said, "Now, what do you want to do?"

"I want to learn to write great poetry," she said. "Someday I want to be able to describe all nature in my poems—the sky, the earth, the sunrise, and the sunset—everything!"

"Well," Sterling said, "that's very nice. God created the earth and the forests and the trees, and you want to do as fine a thing as God has done. I wish that someday I could write a perfect poem about a single leaf of a tree, with all its wonderful mystery and beauty. But I haven't the courage to undertake the task."

"Then," the child said, "I'd like to write great music. I'd like to sit at this window and describe what I see in music, and make it sound like a great symphony orchestra of a thousand musicians."

"That would be nice, too," he said. "But I'd rather make it a simple song. The kind anybody could sing."

He reached over to my desk and took a sheet of paper and a pencil and scribbled for her four lines that he had written many months before. I wish I had that page of scribbled paper now, but I remember the lines:

> At the end of our streets is sunrise;
> At the end of our streets are spars;
> At the end of our streets is sunset;
> At the end of our streets are stars.

George Sterling was a confusion of contradictions, a mixture of clown and philosopher, realist and dreamer—of laughter and despondency. A strange blood mixture accounted for his love of laughter and the neuroses of his tragic hours. His father was a neurotic physician; his maternal grandfather was a two-fisted whaling-ship captain of Sag Harbor, New York.

Sterling was born in Sag Harbor in 1869. He had six sisters and two brothers. Their childhood was as normal as might be expected under the domination of an emotionally unstable parent of nine children. Sterling Senior was a religious man, stumbling from faith to faith in quest of verity. He had been an Episcopalian; he was converted to Catholicism. He determined to make a priest of one of his sons. George, being the eldest, was selected. He was sent to St. Charles' College in Maryland for three years. But he was poor material for the Church. A broad puritanical vein was in him, to remain with him throughout his life, but it was in constant conflict with his raffish humor. No, he was not material for the Church.

On the other hand, those three years at St. Charles' were to be the inspiration for his future life, although he did not realize it till long afterward. His English instructor was John Banister Tabb. Father Tabb did not like George; George did not like Father Tabb. But Father Tabb was a poet, a great poet, although he never achieved fame. He was an adventurous spirit; he had fought through the War of the Rebellion, had been prisoner in a Northern camp, had faced hardships and stood up under the brutalities of rugged living. And the few critics who knew him called him the great American classicist and a lyric poet with art to equal the Greek dramatists. His writing, reflected so often in later years by George Sterling, was a powerful intermingling of satire and lyric beauty, earthy realism and ephemeral aestheticisim. He was an inspiration to those he liked, but he did not like and, for that matter, did not keenly dislike George

182

Sterling. George was simply an average American boy with a fairly good mind and a hatred of study.

The lives of the two men ran in parallel lines for those three years at St. Charles' College, and met only in accidental collision. Although I do not know the story behind it, I read once that the only thing George Sterling learned from Father Tabb was to eat nasturtiums. And yet, in the years to come, the poetry, the realism, the satirical scorn, the love of beauty inherent in Father Tabb were to dominate all of Sterling's writings. But the priest failed utterly in imparting religious fervor to the boy. The neophyte, Sterling, was by nature a pagan.

He left St. Charles' College when he was twenty years old. He went home, and his physician-father squarely faced the knowledge that at least this one of his sons would never be a priest. He accused George of a lack of ambition, of a lack of interest in anything. He told George he had eight other children to support and that he would no longer support him. And finally he thundered, "Go West and be a businessman!" He might as well have said to a businessman of the 'eighties, "Go West and be a poet!"

So, George Sterling came West to take up the labors of a businessman in the office of his mother's brother, Frank C. Havens, in Oakland. Havens was a prominent realtor. Sterling became a real estate salesman; he was a salesman for eighteen years, years of bitterness, frustration, and a crying need for that song in his soul to be released from bondage to the workaday world.

The real estate business took him daily from Oakland to San Francisco by ferryboat. From the start the twenty-one-year-old boy, always an introvert, found no companionship in his fellow travelers. But two influences began to register.

183

From his whaling-ship grandfather he had inherited a love of the sea, and San Francisco Bay under sunshine and fog, and the glamour and mystery and beauty of the ships that plied in and out of the Golden Gate were poetry to him. Less apparent but more insidious, the influence of Father Tabb guided Sterling's hand. On his daily journeys he began to write jingles and quatrains and poems. He spelled the word "p-o-m-e."

There was no thought of selling the "pomes" then; for that matter, at first there was no thought of showing them to anybody. Sterling wrote to relieve his growing pains. Sell them? That was absurd! In the twenty-five years that followed he gained fame, artistic stature, and his poems were widely published. But he would always give his poems away freely as a child; he liked to give them away. He did not care; one did not sing just to buy bread and butter and red wine.

After the first two years of voyaging by ferryboat, with its narcotic relief of poetry writing, a new influence came into Sterling's life, one that was to have even more far-reaching results than had Father Tabb's.

Father Tabb had been a satirical classicist. Ambrose Bierce was a misanthropic satirist, bitter and bigoted. Sick in body, sick in soul, he was bad medicine for impressionable youth. And yet, as Sterling was to become the West's greatest poet, so Bierce was probably the West's greatest writer of prose-poetry. Sterling was twenty-two; Bierce was close to fifty. And Ambrose Bierce guided George Sterling through his formative years as a poet. He was a hard taskmaster. Often careless in his own creative work, he would brook no carelessness in his disciples. For, underlying Bierce's bitter scorns, hatreds, and pessimisms, there was an all-prevailing

184

love of beauty and an enduring though struggling faith in ultimate divinity. Such was the teacher set to guide the hand of the twenty-two-year-old real estate salesman and embryonic poet.

Bierce, having an intensely jealous nature, resented Sterling's contacts with life, resented the associates who crossed Sterling's path. And, introvert though he was, Sterling drew people to him. His best friend was the uncouth lad recently out of Oakland High School, Jack London. The two boys had in common a love of strength, a love of the outdoors and of sports, .boxing and swimming in particular. Both were jugglers of words. And in their youthful cynicism, both leaned to the left—Sterling vaguely antisocial, London an avowed Socialist. Sterling was to persist in his antisocial unhappiness but, with the coming of prosperity, London's socialism faded to a pleasant pink hue. The two men were friends for years. Bierce met London once, resented him, labeled him an upstart and would have nothing to do with him. Their only meeting was not a pleasant one.

So, George Sterling went from Ambrose Bierce to Jack London, and from London to Bierce, and in the five years after the meeting with the older man he wrote continually. But not for publication, not for sale! He wrote because he had to write.

In 1903, Bierce acclaimed Sterling's first major work, *The Testimony of the Suns*. In 1905, Sterling's greatest poem, *A Wine of Wizardry*, was published, and Bierce wrote to him, "I hardly know how to speak of it. No poem in English of equal length has so bewildering a wealth of imagination. Not Spenser himself has flung such a profusion of jewels into so small a casket."

Yes, the poem was rich in the jewels of imagination,

and it had lines that were music, lines as simple and pure as pearls, such lines as

> Where dawn upon a pansy's breast has laid
> A single tear, and whence the wind has flown
> And left a silence.

And this was the same Sterling who went to Carmel and wrote:

> In Carmel Bay the people say,
> We feed the Lazaroni
> On caramels and cockle shells
> And hunks of abalone.
>
> O some folks boast of quail on toast
> Because they think it's tony,
> But my tomcat gets nice and fat
> On hunks of abalone.

There were about a hundred more quatrains, most of them unprintable and never printed.

By 1908 the circle of Sterling's friends was wide, and among them was the artist, Charles Rollo Peters. Peters was to a degree responsible for the poet's move to Carmel. The sleepy hamlet behind the cypress of Monterey Bay had been discovered by Charles Warren Stoddard and a few others, but it remained for Sterling to spread its fame around the world. His aunt, Mrs. Havens, realizing the suffering of her nephew as a real estate salesman, financed a house for him in the Carmel pines. And for six years he lived there in the days before Carmel had assumed its rococo dress of gift shoppes, antique shops, and tea rooms, and girls in slacks and boys with long hair. Sterling lived a completely uninhibited life there, and his friends were Jimmie Hopper, Mary Austin, Albert Bender, Jack London, Lincoln Steffens, Upton Sinclair, Xavier Martinez, and many others.

186

The six years in Carmel were fruitful years. The beauty of the rugged coast and the gray sea and the pines and the cypress, and the natives Sterling met in the valleys and hills that lay between Carmel and the Big Sur were to influence all his writings. But the frustrations and bitterness that had pervaded so much of his life were beginning to take toll. He had always been a steady drinker; now he became a slave to drink. His wife left him. He could no longer endure even Carmel.

When he came back to San Francisco it was under the aegis of Alex Robertson, the beloved Scotch bookseller of Union Square. Robertson, canny, careful, had thrown his instinctive shrewdness to the winds and invested hard cash in the publication of volume after volume of the poetry of California's greatest poet. Of course, he made no money in the enterprise; of course, Sterling made no money out of the books. He never made money; money was valueless and, after all, if one had to work to live then what was the use of living?

He came to my office one day. I was publishing a children's magazine at the time.

"Here," he said. "I've written some jingles for your children."

He handed me not a few lines, but forty quatrains—*The Saga of the Pony Express*. It was a gift from the gods, but I was in a predicament: how was I to pay for so rich a gift? I hunted for words and eventually blurted out the truth:

"Sterling, I haven't the money to pay for such a poem as this."

He froze me with a glassy stare.

"Do you think I'd take money?" he demanded. "I like children and I like your magazine."

"But," I persisted, "we have a definite rule never to publish anything we haven't paid for."

"Very well," he said, "send me a couple of bottles of whiskey."

Well, one could not help but laugh at the idea of paying for poetry for an idealistic children's magazine with whiskey. I laughed and told him why I was laughing, and he laughed too.

"Send it to me," he said. "I don't want it for myself. I'm going to entertain the one man I admire more than any other in America. He's coming to San Francisco to visit me; he's H. L. Mencken. I'm planning a huge party for him."

And so the stage was set for Destiny to play a diabolical trick on George Sterling. Mencken was traveling to San Francisco via Los Angeles with Joseph Hergesheimer. And in Los Angeles, Hergesheimer became involved in a chess game with a delightful young woman. Hergesheimer was almost unbeatable at chess; he had never been beaten by a woman. But this young girl beat him game after game and day after day. Mencken and Hergesheimer stayed in Los Angeles while the author traded knights and pawns and bishops with his feminine opponent.

Sterling grew impatient. He sent letters, sent telegrams. The day of the party arrived; many guests had been invited. But Mencken had not arrived. The party was postponed. There were more letters, more wires! George Sterling sat in his Bohemian Club room and brooded. The bitterness of years became an unendurable melancholia. He waited and waited—and his room became a shamble of empty bottles. And when Henry Mencken did arrive, George Sterling was in such a state he could not preside at that long-anticipated party. He lay upstairs abed while another writer substituted for him—a writer he particularly disliked. And the next morning, when Henry Mencken went to his room, he found that George Sterling had drunk his last libation—a vial of poison.

At noon on June 25, 1928, a small group of men made a pilgrimage to the crest of the Hyde Street hill in San Francisco. There, before the Spring Valley Reservoir, a stone bench was set where George Sterling had loved to watch laughing children at play on the green grass. Sterling's friends stood and dedicated the bench to his memory. Then they sang songs that Sterling loved, and the lines of a song Sterling had written but never published:

> Give, O gods, a laughing lass,
> Give, O gods, a brimming glass—
> But to crown the blessing, send,
> Kindly gods, a faithful friend.

George Sterling had been an introvert, an antisocial in his bearing and unapproachable in his hours of solitude. He died, and his friends were legion, friends who loved the human, sympathetic, generous, life-loving Puck; friends who loved the poetry of his brain and the profound beauty of his dreams.

I think, in many ways the most beautiful though not the greatest poem George Sterling wrote was the one in which he told of his adoration of San Francisco: "The Cool, Grey City of Love, the City of Saint Francis." And up there on Russian Hill, that bench around which children play, stands a memorial to his gentle hand; it stands looking out at the hills and the Bay that he loved, and at the city with its laughing sunshine and its cool, gray fogs.

XXIV

Jane Lathrop Stanford

The story of San Francisco is a story of colorful men; in pioneer days the women who came West with their men did not have much time to be colorful. No streets have been named after them, no statues raised to their memories. For instance, there was Jane Lathrop. Going through the many pages of a thick book of San Francisco personalities and events, I found three lines devoted to Jane Lathrop. She was, it said, "a plain, gentle little body who liked beautiful things. Her collection of rubies was said to be the finest in the world, and her laces were as exquisite as Marie Antoinette's."

And so there, in print, were Jane Lathrop's claims to immortality. She was the daughter of a shopkeeper in Albany, New York. She was a Victorian girl. That has become a label of dull futility—a Victorian girl! Victorian girls were colorless creatures who practiced the gentle art of fainting frequently and with the greatest of ease. They were genteel and subdued and priggish and prim; they were tiresome and their culture consisted of lessons on the pianoforte and in china painting; they were not expected to think, and if inadvertently they did chance to think, then, under no circumstances were they to express their thoughts—men were the thinkers!

Of course, the picture is unfair, inaccurate, and absurd. After all, the era was named for good Queen Victoria and she did not hesitate to think, and when she wanted a thing she went after it, whether it was an empire or a husband. And having picked her man, she stood behind him with a spiritual pitchfork, prodding him on to greater achievements. That was Queen Victoria, and that is a fairly comprehensive picture of Jane Lathrop as a girl. As she grew older, people said that she looked like Queen Victoria. When she was quite old she dressed like Queen Victoria and loved to have people say, "Doesn't she remind you of the British Queen?" She was born just a few years after the birth of Victoria; she died within three years of her passing.

Storekeeper Lathrop had a pleasant home on tree-shaded Washington Avenue in Albany. And one day, near her home, Jane surprised a lad, mouth agape, staring at her. Dressed in rough working clothes, he was perched on top of a load of firewood in a rustic wagon drawn by an unprepossessing steed. The eyes of the boy and girl met; the boy looked quickly away, clucked to his horse and drove off. But after that first ephemeral encounter, the boy—he was then fifteen or sixteen—must have been conscious of young Jane, for he seems to have avoided passing the Lathrop home on his rounds of delivering firewood. Conscious of his rough work clothes, he was shy and withdrawn. What was more, he was busy helping his father in the carrying out of a large contract to deliver wood cut on his father's property, and so was earning his own future school expenses.

At seventeen he went away to a school in Clinton, New York, and later to another school in Cazenovia, and then returned to read law in an Albany law office. It was then that Victorian Jane would have no more of his timid modesty. Introduced by her elder brother, the two became good friends, so good that when, in 1848, he was admitted to the bar, he and Jane became engaged. Two years later they were married and headed West to make their fortune, first in Wisconsin and then in California. Long afterward he said, "No, Jane did not advise me to go West; she simply said the future of the country was West, and wherever I wanted to go she would go." The young man's name was Leland Stanford.

Now, during the years that Leland Stanford lived, his wife was a good and gentle wife, devoted to him, giving him renewed courage and strength when the going was hard. But it was after his death that Jane Lathrop Stanford became a personage. They had worked together; they had been happy together. She had seen him correlate the forces that laid the rails of the Central Pacific Railroad; she had seen wealth come. They had traveled to Europe and tragedy had struck—their son lay dead in Italy. They had returned, brokenhearted, and then with the indomitable will and courage that was so characteristic of early San Francisco pioneers, they had made a business of filling their life with work that would partially fill the void left by the death of their son.

"The children of California shall be our children," Leland Stanford had told his wife after their great loss. So, together, they founded Leland Stanford Junior University and endowed it richly. But litigation, conflict, and a growing national panic shook their endowment, and it was during his great effort to keep his university alive that Leland Stanford died—died leaving many and various monuments, some of them almost forgotten, some that never bore his name.

One of these was the California Street Cable Railroad

Company. When Leland Stanford built his great mansion at Powell and California streets, it was so difficult for his wife's horses and carriage to mount the hill that he had the cable-car line built to make it easy to get home. Yes, the anti-quated old California Street Line, condemned by this realistic jet-propelled day, is one of Leland Stanford's monuments.

The University was operating in 1891. Leland Stanford died in 1893, and Jane Stanford took up his work. The Victorian old lady who looked like Queen Victoria was tremendously active. She had known great wealth; now she was still able to live in comparative luxury, but her days were a continual struggle to meet her obligations, par-ticularly the obligations of the University. She became ex-ceedingly frugal; she prided herself on her economy and her shrewd management. She was to be seen, a tiny, elderly woman in flowing, black widow's veils, climbing the steep Powell Street hill on foot. And when she was scolded by friends who said she must not tax her strength, she said, "But you know I can't afford a carriage."

Leland Stanford had maintained several homes—one in Sacramento when he was Governor of California, one in Washington, D.C., when he was a Senator, one in Palo Alto, and the mansion on Nob Hill. Mrs. Stanford decided to close the place in Washington. Now, one honorarium of her husband's association with the railroad builders had been a perpetual pass over every railroad in the nation and a right of way without cost for her private car. So, the year follow-ing the death of her husband, she started for the national capital to close the house there.

She made the journey by private car. She carried five hundred dollars in her purse, determined that that amount should cover the entire journey. She took her own cook with her and food for the journey. She slept in the car during her entire stay in Washington to obviate the cost of hotel rooms. She closed the Washington house, attended to the disposition of furniture and other details, and returned to California. And she had three hundred forty dollars in her purse; the trip had cost one hundred sixty dollars.

She felt no sacrifice in depriving herself to save the young University. But she suffered to see the University suffer as it did financially during those years of nation-wide depression. Each week she traveled down the Peninsula by train to Palo Alto. And as the train pulled out of Menlo Park, the little old lady in black would press her cheek to the train window and stare straight ahead, waiting for that first reassuring glimpse of smoke pouring from the stack of the University heating plant. Then she would sigh and relax, hands folded in her lap—the supply of coal had not run out, classes were in session, the University was still functioning.

People would see her, sitting silently in the train, and they would say, "She looks like Queen Victoria; doesn't she?" At times she would hear the comment and smile to herself. She liked the comparison. She was not beautiful, but neither was Queen Victoria beautiful. She had a short, dumpy figure, and Victoria was so short and dumpy that cartoonists pictured her as an animated pyramid. She would follow the stories of Victoria in the press, collect pictures of Victoria, and imitate the Queen's dress and carriage.

And one day Jane Stanford decided to go and visit the Queen. Oh, not actually to go to court and be presented, but just to see the Queen at close range. So, she made her famous "jewel journey." Ostensibly, she was going to London to try to dispose of her collection of jewels for a half-million dollars, to pour new gold into the University's purse.

She packed the jewels, including the wonderful collection of rubies, and she started out.

It was 1897, the year of the Diamond Jubilee. Victoria had been queen for sixty years. Mrs. Stanford's journey, her pilgrimage, was a failure as far as disposing of the jewels was concerned. People were polite; they agreed that the collection was beautiful and impressive. But they had more important things on their minds that June of 1897. They were honoring the Widow of Windsor and had no time for the California widow. Jewels clutched in her small black bag, she carried them everywhere. She objected to the high fees charged for safe-deposit box rental or even for insurance. No, she would guard the jewels herself. But she could not sell them; the business side of the trip was a failure.

On the other hand, an eager, excited little old lady was up before daylight on the morning of June 22, 1897. At seven, quoting the colorful account written by Oscar Lewis, she was driving through London's brilliantly decorated streets. She had leased a window in a Fleet Street house, and down Fleet Street would come the carriage of Victoria. Long hours of waiting were ahead, but Jane Stanford sat patiently in her window, hands in their black-lace mittens folded in her lap.

And now, far in the distance, the head of the parade appeared. Slowly it passed down Fleet Street to Ludgate Circus, then to St. Paul's. As the head of the procession reached the Cathedral, hundreds of thousands of cheering, ecstatic Britishers surged into the open way, forcing the parade to stop. And before the window of Jane Stanford, the carriage of Victoria stopped.

The Queen lowered her parasol. She turned and smiled to the cheering crowd. And then she looked up, up to Jane

Stanford's window. The eyes of the two women met. Victoria bowed! Jane Stanford bowed low, and pressed her hand to her heart. And the parade moved on again, and Jane touched her fingers to her lips and tossed a kiss after the disappearing carriage.

It had been a wonderful, wonderful day, and Jane Stanford was ready to go home. She returned to California, to take up her work for the University. She gave it her time and energy and personal wealth. But whenever the restless urge for travel would sweep over her again, out would come the old private car, thirty years old, its upholstery faded and worn—the old car and the old lady, symbols of a faded gentility. She would travel, and friends, countless friends in every place, would greet her. In every place save one. . . .

During his lifetime Leland Stanford had made enemies. And there was always this one enemy, this man who had worked with him to build the Central Pacific Railroad, his partner who had become an avowed enemy a few years before his death. According to the story told, this man, Collis P. Huntington, had caused the financial difficulties that troubled Senator Stanford's last days. So Collis P. Huntington's enmity could not be forgotten; he was an enemy of the widow, Jane.

One day, a little old lady in black came to Huntington's office in New York City. There was no color in her cheeks, her eyes were dim. But her hands were quiet, folded in her lap as she sat before him.

"Mr. Huntington," she said, "I have come to make my peace with you."

Huntington was almost eighty years old, an old man. He stood a moment, as though bewildered, muttered, "Well, I declare—" He sat down before her and his hand shook.

Jane Stanford told him that they were both old people, the time was past for grievance and unkind thoughts. And Huntington nodded, "Of course, of course—"

There were tears in Jane Stanford's eyes and there were tears in Huntington's eyes and Huntington had been a hard and a cold man all his life.

It was not long after that, that, obsessed by a fear of vague enemies, Jane Stanford made a trip to the Hawaiian Islands. And it was shortly after her arrival in Honolulu that a cable came to the mainland telling of her death.

Her jewels were left to the University she and her husband had created and loved. They were sold, and the gold they brought became a fund to supply needed books to University students.

In a mausoleum on the campus of now-famous Stanford University, Jane Stanford lies by the side of her husband and her son. And the few living today who remember speak quietly of the three—of the plain, gentle, little boy who liked beautiful things, and of the man who built a highroad to the empire of the West, and of the gentle little old lady, the little old Victorian lady with the fighting spirit of Queen Victoria herself. . . .

The Color of the City

The color of a city is an intangible thing. It is much more than the glint of the setting sun on the western windows of the city's houses. The color of a city—of San Francisco—is much more than the lights that "sparkle" like a queen's necklace when they are seen from Twin Peaks, more than the gray, wooden, narrow houses out on Pine Street near Fillmore, more than the red of the neon lights reflected in fog along Powell Street, more than the contrast of stone palaces against pine wood hovels. The color of the city is lights and shadows and sounds and smells and memories.

For example, when I was a small boy more than fifty years ago, I went to the Grant Primary School up on Pacific Avenue near Broderick Street. I can walk up Pacific Avenue today—any day—and smell the same odor, a clean, inoffensive odor but a definite odor that was familiar to my nostrils fifty years ago. And inevitably I will forget the intervening years. I will be back in the day when I was called into the office of the principal, Mrs. Shaw, and stood shaking in my buttoned shoes while Mrs. Shaw, with sorrow in her voice and Macbethian menace in her eyes demanded, "Did your mother really write this note to say you had to stay home from school yesterday, or did you write it yourself?"

I have wondered at times just where I would start to show the color of the city to a visitor from far away. There could be so many points of departure. The Civic Center that is like every big and every little civic center across the land —the Coit Memorial Tower high on Telegraph Hill— Fleishhacker Zoo—Chinatown? No, I think I would take my visitor to a little restaurant in an alley behind the Hall of Justice.

That restaurant has changed hands many times since its heyday. But in its prime—and its prime was during the great folly called the Prohibition Experiment—the restaurant was called The Philosophers' Inn. Its cuisine and wine cellar were presided over by a charming, intelligent woman— legend had it that she had once been an opera singer. You walked down the alley that faced the back door of the city prison and the morgue. You entered through an iron-grilled gate into the tiny entrance courtyard with its flowers and fountain and philosopher's stone. You mounted the narrow flight of steps and were greeted by the hostess; she led you to a table dimly lighted by a candle thrust into the neck of a Benedictine bottle. You ate rare dishes, dishes to delight the soul of an epicure; you drank Rhine wines and Moselle wines and California vintages that had been selected by a *bon vivant*. And while you dined and drank, the hostess would stand, looking out of the grilled window to the entrance of the morgue, and she would sing "Water Boy," or "Foggy, Foggy Dew." Inevitably, if she liked you, she would come to your table and sit down and discuss Herbert Hoover's administration, or the newest play of Sacha Guitry, or the philosophy of Spinoza and Socrates versus the philosophy of Kathleen Norris. And she would drift back to the window and gaze at the morgue and sing in her rich contralto a subdued bawdy song with suave gentility. Yes, I would take my guest to The Philosophers' Inn.

I would take him, too, down Sansome Street and show him a great industrial building. I would tell him the story of the boy who came to San Francisco in the late 'fifties or early 'sixties. He had a family to support and practically no money. So he bought himself a wheelbarrow, filled it with business stationery, and trundled it from door to door, taking orders for stationery and wrapping paper. And, as though that were an everyday occurrence, I would explain that the barrow-trundling boy prospered till he had founded the great firm that bears his name—Zellerbach—and occupies that great industrial building of the Crown Zellerbach Paper Company.

Then I would take my guest up Van Ness Avenue and show him the Richelieu Hotel on the corner of Van Ness Avenue and Geary Street. In the 'eighties and 'nineties of the last century it was the only uptown family hotel of quality in the city. And I used to play in its halls with two small boys some years older than myself. One was Holbrook Blinn, one of the greatest actors San Francisco gave to the American stage—Blinn, for so many years the leading man of Minnie Maddern Fiske. And the other small boy, Frank Norris, was to become California's greatest novelist.

I would take my friend up Rincon Hill, up to where the western pillars of the Bay Bridge stand, and I would show him South Park below us. South Park, a tiny square surrounded by dilapidated shacks and tenements; South Park, where carriages in days gone by rolled along behind spanking horses (I have always wondered what a "spanking" horse was). In the golden days South Park was the Mayfair of the city.

With my guest I would walk up Market Street to Grant Avenue, the street called the "Avenue of the Best-Dressed Women in America." We would stop before a flower stand and then travel from sidewalk stand to flower stand heaped twelve months in the year with gay color—the living color of the city. There are not as many flower stands as there used to be. You can rarely buy violets as you formerly bought them, for five cents a bunch, and the flower-stand man charges you for your lapel carnation instead of giving it to you as he did in the past when you were a customer. A little of the glory has gone out of the flower stands. But when a new coat of arms is designed for San Francisco it should be a multicolored flower stand upon a field of gold.

We would go out to Green Street next, and I would show my friend the depressing hall called the Green Street Theatre. I would tell him of the time, sixteen years ago, when a play ran there for twenty-one months, the longest run of any play in San Francisco's theatrical history. I wrote the play; it was a disreputable affair built on the lines of the naughty French farces of years ago. It was called *Easy for Zee Zee*. The disreputable stories of that disreputable play are many. There are records of weekly raids by the police, most of them organized by the management for publicity. There were murders and suicides and scandals, and the names of the cast's principals made newspaper headlines periodically.

There was an Italian restaurant in the basement of the theater, and if your theater ticket was for an orchestra seat it entitled you to a seven-course dinner with wine before the performance. And, hovering about the premises, was the impresario. He was a stout, short gentleman, very proud of his false teeth; he had acquired them at considerable cost and always carried them in his vest pocket—he never wore them.

An amazing event took place one day at the Green Street Theatre. It was before the Wednesday matinee. The theater was crowded. Close to curtain time, horrible groans were heard coming from backstage. The manager rushed into the wings to find the leading man stretched on the stage, unconscious and groaning. A doctor was called, and after a brief examination he said the actor would be dead within an hour. An ambulance came, the leading man was rushed to the hospital, and the money was refunded to the audience. Now, to go ahead a bit, I should say at once that the leading man did not die. He had suffered an attack of acute indigestion possibly inspired by the basement restaurant; he was back in his part in two weeks.

But the manager, having refunded the money for the matinee, took stock of his false teeth in his pocket and could not face refunding the money for the night performance. He rushed out of the theater and at four o'clock returned with a down-at-heel "at liberty" actor. He sat him in a tiny chair facing the footlights. He put a copy of the book of the play in his hand and told him to read his part, by far the longest part, consisting of sixty sides—a huge part in any man's theater. He ordered the cast to walk through their lines while the down-at-heel read his lines once through; then the manager told him to go home, study his part for three hours, and return to play it that night.

But the actor, who had not acted for countless inconstant

moons and was reasonably hungry and thirsty, went instead to the basement Italian restaurant, ate a huge meal, drank a bottle of red wine, and went home and to sleep. He was awakened by the desperate manager at eight-thirty, rushed back to the theater, thrown into his costume, and without a single rehearsal and with but one reading of the book, gave what the critics declared in the papers the next morning was practically a perfect performance. Unfortunately, I have forgotten, and the city has forgotten, the name of that actor.

From the Green Street Theatre I would take my visiting friend down dignified Post Street to the dignified Mechanics' Library, one of the oldest and most respected of the city's institutions. We would by-pass the Library itself and go to the floor above where, in a small room, congregate the addicts of the Mechanics' Chess Club. Day after day and night after night, year in and year out, the same characters gather there; there are more personalities, more rare and precious characters to be found in the Chess Room of the Mechanics' Library than in a novel of Dickens. They are all silently intent on the business of shoving the small pieces up and down the board, and around them stand others, silently intent, watching. To this room of grim purpose have come the world's great champions; it has been called the most famous chess club in the world.

Then my friend and I would go out Broadway to a house that faces the entrance of the Dante Hospital. It is the home of a distinguished dentist, a genius of rare attributes, a man who has filled his home with more weird contrivances than were ever thought of in a chamber of horrors. Here is a mechanical doll reclining on a couch. No buttons are pressed, the doll is not touched, but at your command she will play your choice of a thousand tunes on a zither. At specified times toy trumpeters come out of niches in the walls and play fanfares, and a great organ in the basement plays while its reverberations shake the house to its foundations. But, most unusual about this unusual dwelling, are the windows that look in from the street. The words "look *in*" are poorly chosen. The windows have not been washed for thirty years because the owner does not wish anyone to look in from the street.

He is a royal entertainer, my dentist friend. He gives great and crowded and lavish parties. At one such, with some two hundred oddly assorted people crowded into two modest rooms, I saw Gertrude Lawrence, the guest of honor, submit to the art of a professional hypnotist. Gertie, beautiful actress even under hypnosis, closed her eyes, sighed, and to all intents and purposes was asleep. But I saw the grace with which her relaxed hand rested at her side, and I unfortunately laughed aloud. And Gertie opened her eyes and winked—and went to sleep again.

I would take my friend up Russian Hill to a small street that rounds the crest of the hill. There is nothing very unusual about the street; I don't even know its given name. It ends against a stone wall. It is a rounded lane, like the street in Louis N. Parker's beautiful old play *Pomander Walk*. So we call it Pomander Walk. And Pomander Walk is San Francisco of yesterday, Victorian San Francisco. Soft lights of oil lamps gleam in windows of rose-covered cottages; old ladies in black-silk dresses and with white-lace shawls about their heads sit in the windows and nod and smile at the sparrows on the wires. And Martha Washington geraniums spill from the window boxes.

I would walk with my friend down Third Street, the

street called Skid Row, the street of the derelicts, of blind beggars and legless panhandlers, the street of hard-working men and men out of work, the street of flophouses and mass employment agencies and revival halls and saloons and hamburger-and-onion joints and Greek coffeehouses. We would turn out of Third Street into colorless lower Mission Street, the street of very industrious and dull houses of industry. And just off Third Street, next to the little Catholic church, I would show him where the Grand Opera House stood. There Eugene O'Neill's father, James O'Neill, was arrested for appearing as the Christus in a Passion play; there the ladies of the chorus shocked the audience by appearing in tights in *The Black Crook*. This was the Grand Opera House where *East Lynne* played, and *The Two Orphans*, and *Quo Vadis*, and *Ben Hur*, and *Nellie the Sewing Machine Girl*, and *The Count of Monte Cristo*; the Opera House where Melba sang, and Jean de Reszke and Nordica and Sembrich and Scotti and Calvé and Gadski and Schumann-Heink—and where Caruso sang on the night before the earthquake of 1906. And now, before the Grand Opera House site, a Salvation Army band plays "Onward Christian Soldiers"—syncopated. . . .

The gay array of flower stands, and the mystery of ominous alleys; smart women and disreputable waifs; strong men, and beggars and dreamers and thieves—these are the color of the city that is San Francisco.

XXVI

John McLaren

There was a young Scotsman came to California in 1870. John McLaren he was called, as though it were a single word —JohnMcLaren. Throughout his life friends would meet him and greet him with, "How are you, JohnMcLaren, and how are your trees?"

He came to California in 1870 and saw a new and young country, a country of young men who were enthusiastic builders. Everything was new and young; the fortunes that were being made; the cities that were being built. Young and new! But he saw one other thing that meant more to him than all the other amazing wonders of the young West. In the hills behind San Mateo he saw the *Sequoia sempervirens*—the "evergreen" redwoods. They were the oldest living things on earth. Their seeds had fallen and the earth had taken them and new trees had grown before Christ was born. They had stood for more than two thousand years, the everlasting trees. They would stand through untold generations ahead unless—unless the avarice of man and the folly of man should spread destruction and fire through the glorious avenues of the groves.

John McLaren looked at the redwoods and said, "I, too, would like to grow redwoods."

Men who knew the young Scotsman laughed and told

him to stick to his gardens. It took thousands of years to grow a redwood.

Now, that dream of growing redwoods was only a phase, an incident, in the life of John McLaren. But because I believe it led to the most beautiful pages of the story of his life, I will return to it presently.

John McLaren had been a dairyman in his native land and had driven his cattle along the banks of the Bannock. Before he was twenty he deserted the dairy lands and went to Edinburgh to study horticulture in the Royal Botanical Gardens. His curriculum was a practical one; he was hired as gardener's helper in the gardens. After he had served his apprenticeship he followed the path of dreams to California, to the fields of gold, to the land that was said to have the climate of Italy and the beauty of an English country garden. He came to San Francisco in 1870—and saw the redwoods. And he remembered his father's frequently reiterated admonition: "Me boy, if ye have nothing to do, go plant a tree and it'll grow while ye sleep."

So, young McLaren planted trees, planted them on the huge estate of George Howard that was sprawled across the San Mateo foothills; he planted trees on the ranch of Leland Stanford at Palo Alto, and turned grainfields into a botanical garden. On a small peninsula called Coyote Point that juts into the Bay, he planted at one time seventy thousand trees. And in the days that were still the days of his youth, he said, "I hope to plant a million trees before I die. Firs—pines—redwoods—eucalyptus——a million trees!"

So, McLaren planted trees for fifteen years, and during those years the village that was sprawled along the water front of San Francisco Bay became a city. It was no longer a boom town, no longer a hectic mushroom town. Its dwellings had reached westward, past the elegant, rococo mansions of Mason and Taylor and O'Farrell streets; its homes were reaching out across Van Ness Avenue, out toward the Presidio and the hundreds of thousands of acres of sand dunes that lay between it and the ocean.

And in those sand dunes an idea was conceived, so fantastic that even the men who dreamed the dream said, "It's only a utopian fantasy that never can come true, but it would be a fine thing if some day, some way, those acres of sand could be turned into a great park."

Then someone thought of John McLaren. He had been successful in his first big enterprise in Scotland; he had planted the grass called "sea bent" in the shifting sands that were swept by the winds of the North Sea and had fastened down the sands along the Firth of Forth. Perhaps he could plant sea bent in the hundred thousand acres of city-owned dunes that ran down to the waters of Golden Gate. Yes, McLaren said he could do it. Yes, and he would take on the job of building a Golden Gate Park. But first he had certain demands to make. These were his demands:

He was to have thirty thousand dollars a year for grading and planting.

He was to have all the water he wanted and needed.

He was to have the sweepings of San Francisco streets to fertilize his ground.

And above all, he insisted that never in this park of his should a sign read "Keep Off the Grass." The parks and the green lawns were to be places where men could sleep in the sun, where children could play, where the city could enjoy green grass and shade trees and beds of flowers unhampered by "No Trespass" signs.

Well, of course, that last demand was a whim; they

would humor the young Scotsman and there would be no "Keep Off the Grass" signs. As for water, he could have as much as he wanted—if he could find it. So John McLaren built two Dutch windmills out near the ocean and pumped water. And the city smiled a kindly smile and said, "He'll pump salt water. Nothing will grow." But there was no salt in the water McLaren pumped. As for the sweepings of the city streets, obviously he was welcome to them. Welcome? It almost broke John McLaren's heart when the horse and buggy gave way to the automobile.

But, about the first demand—thirty thousand dollars a year—people said the city fathers were crazy. Editorials appeared in the papers. San Francisco was reverting to the madness of forty-niner days; it figured to turn sand dunes into flower gardens and that could not be done. And John McLaren planted his sea bent and his seedlings. They said there was no excuse for a hundred-thousand-acre park in San Francisco. And John McLaren planted rhododendrons. They said, "Well, if there's going to be a park there'll have to be statues." So they built statues of every great and near-great man of whom they could think.

John McLaren hated statues. "Stookies!" he called them. So, every time the city fathers planted a "stookie" John planted trees to hide it. Some of the most beautiful groves planted by McLaren are there to hide the "stookie" of a famous man.

For almost ten years he emptied the sweepings of the city streets into his hundred thousand acres of sand dune. And Golden Gate Park became a beautiful reality. The trees were growing, the flowers were growing, bridle paths ran along the broad driveways, an artificial lake was created in a plateau of sand—a lake called Strawberry where, with the instinct of the busman on holiday, sailors take their girls rowing in little boats. The park almost reached to the ocean's edge; almost, but not quite.

John McLaren had tied down the sand dunes, but he had not yet controlled the ocean waves that swept new sands over the man-made garden. Something had to be done about the ocean waves and McLaren was the man to do it. He put the waves to work. Along the ocean beach he put down a row of thousands of bundles of laths. In front of the laths, facing the ocean, he dumped twigs and branches that had been pruned from the park trees. The ocean piled sand into this simple barricade. A nice ridge ran the length of the beach. McLaren planted more laths atop the ridge. Again the ocean piled sand around them. There were more laths, higher still, more twigs and branches piled up, more sand sweeping it from the ocean. That was a job that took forty years, and when it was finished the ocean had built an esplanade twenty feet high and three hundred yards wide. That is the story of the Esplanade with its double highway that runs from the Cliff House along the ocean's edge, mile after mile. It was a task that took John McLaren and the Pacific Ocean forty years. But McLaren never bothered about time. He still wanted to plant a million trees and grow redwoods.

In the early 'nineties there was an exposition in Chicago, a world's fair. A San Francisco delegation visited it, led by Michel de Young, a newspaper publisher of San Francisco. De Young, inspired by the Chicago Fair, said he would build a finer one in San Francisco's Golden Gate Park. He headed a subscription list, raised funds, and, as the country was just emerging from a national panic, the Midwinter Fair opened.

It was not much of a fair as world's fairs go. Little is

remembered of it. Old-timers will tell of the Midway, of the Ferris Wheel, of the Streets of Cairo where Little Egypt danced. They will tell of Chiquita, the smallest woman in the world, of the Indian Village and of the Music Stand. The Fair went the dilapidated way of all discarded fairs, and all that remained was a museum and the Music Stand.

The museum was the depository for all the old junk San Franciscans did not want in their parlors. It took years to clear the junk away, but today, according to established records, more people pass through the turnstile of the beautiful De Young Museum than visit the Metropolitan Museum in New York in a year's time. As for the bandstand, it remained, and in the days when society still traveled in victorias and phaetons and buckboards, each Sunday everyone who counted drove his or her horses around it and listened to the melodies of Victor Herbert and the "Chimes of Normandy," and the "Fledermaus." Children found their haven just east of the bandstand in the playground where donkey rides were a thrilling delight and the most delicious spongecake in the world was to be had. All of which has little to do with John McLaren. Little—and yet McLaren loved children, and his park was their park.

With the passing of the Midwinter Fair a new and dangerous craze swept the land—the bicycle age. Tricycles, bicycles, tandems, and family affairs with four, five, or six seats spun along the path to the Cyclers' Rest. There the gay blades smoked Sweet Caporals and bought Queen Charlottes for their bloomered girl friends. And John snorted and went right ahead planting his flowers and his trees.

That was all more than forty years ago. Today tens of thousands find their way to the De Young Museum, the Steinhart Aquarium, the Fleishhaker Zoo, or to the Conservatories where exotic flowers bloom. They listen to the music from the bandstand. They please the soul of John McLaren by walking on the grass. They walk in quiet awe through the tens of thousands of blooming rhododendrons or row their boats on Strawberry Lake—Stow Lake, some call it. They steer their model yachts across the yacht lake in front of the Portals of the Past, and walk through Lovers' Lane, and shriek from the bleachers at Kezar Stadium where the East-West Game is an annual event.

And, hovering over it all—this most beautiful of parks grown in shifting sands—is the spirit of John McLaren. He died in 1943; he was ninety-seven years old. For eighty years he had lived by his father's admonition: "Me boy, if ye have nothing to do, go plant a tree and it'll grow while ye sleep." John McLaren planted more than two million trees.

The *Sequoia sempervirens*. The oldest living things on earth, trees that took thousands of years to attain their full stature! John McLaren wanted to grow redwoods, and wise men laughed at his folly. So, from seeds McLaren planted the grove of *Sequoia sempervirens,* the evergreen redwoods, in Golden Gate Park. He was eighty years when he planted them. He lived to be ninety-seven, a clear-eyed little Scotsman working almost to the day of his death. And when he died, his grove of redwoods stood in Golden Gate Park—trees thirty feet high!

No, John McLaren did not like statues—"Stookies." But he loved trees.

XXVII

Mardikian and Food

Almost all San Franciscans like food at any time of the day or night. We mean that literally. Why, one of San Francisco's most famous dishes was invented to appease the wives of husbands who came home from the club at two or three in the morning. That dish was the "oyster loaf," invented in San Francisco and originally famous at the California Market.

You would go to your club and play "table stake" poker, and you would stay for just another round and another roodle, and then it was late. So, you would stop at the Market on your way home, and they would fix you up an oyster loaf. They would wrap it in pages and pages of newspaper to keep in the heat, and you would tuck it under your arm and either climb into your hack from Kelly's Stables or catch an Owl cable car and, arriving home, you would awaken your suffering, sleepless wife and say "Look, dear, an oyster loaf!" Whereupon she would sit up in bed and smile mournfully and eat the oyster loaf and forgive you all your sins and shortcomings—and late comings.

Now, in case you are a foreigner—and anyone who does not live in San Francisco is a foreigner—and you are uninitiated into the delectable mysteries of an oyster loaf, it is only fair to explain that an oyster loaf is just what the name implies—a half-loaf of bread with most of the insides dug out, making a sort of cradle of the remainder. In the cradle are deposited a dozen fried oysters, well-seasoned and garnished with parsley, a slice or two of lemon, a slab of butter (and plenty of butter saturating the lining of the loaf). Then it is all tenderly placed in the oven, toasted, wrapped in the pages and pages of newspaper—and there you are.

George Mardikian, the most colorful restaurateur in San Francisco today, wrote a colorful book which he called *Dinner at Omar Khayyam's*. And the distinguished book reviewer, Joseph Henry Jackson, wrote an introduction to the book in which he said, "The truth is, San Franciscans have always been sympathetic to the great art of eating and drinking."

It is just like the traditions of the theater. When you have an audience-population that appreciates theater you will find a good theater town. San Francisco was always that and a good town for good food, too. In the lamented good old days there were more interesting eating places in San Francisco and more interesting dishes to be eaten than a dyspeptic epicure could shake a fork at. They still are here, many of them, but many of them have lost the glamour that was theirs when the big city was a pleasant cosmopolitan outpost.

The main difference, today and yesterday, between San Francisco and most other cities, is that in the other cities people eat to fuel their bodies and revive their energy. But the dyed-in-the-linen San Franciscan says, "Let's go out for dinner and enjoy ourselves."

Now, all of us have personal preferences, and our most cherished memory is of dinner at Papa Coppa's. In the old days when Papa Coppa was the friend of every painter, every

214

poet, every musician, and every Bohemian who spent his life doing nothing but talk about art, his restaurant was down in the old Montgomery Block, the oldest building still standing in San Francisco. Papa Coppa is gone on his long journey, but the Montgomery Block is still there, and if you will walk past it in the small hours you are likely to capture the ghost of the perfume of one of his dinners. And other ghosts walk there, too. There was one table where, night after night, you could find George Sterling and Jimmie Hopper and Gelett Burgess and Porter Garnett—Burgess and Garnett wrote for the *Lark* in the gay 'nineties. And you would find the artists Charles Rollo Peters and Xavier Martinez, and, frequently, the writer, Mary Austin. And around them drifted the lesser Bohemians. But that was before our salad days. Our first memory of Papa Coppa's was when it had moved into the alley just off California Street.

Memories! There was toasted French bread dripping with butter and rubbed with chopped garlic. There was Chateaubriand—and you could not possibly be old enough to know that a Chateaubriand is a double filet mignon about six inches thick and six inches in diameter, broiled with a black crust a quarter-inch thick to keep in the juice, and red inside as a schoolgirl's lipstick. It was garnished with lemon sprinkled with paprika! Then, there were black coffee and Roquefort cheese. You mixed the cheese yourself, mixed it with a fork, blending in paprika and butter and Worcestershire sauce and a clove of garlic. That was all. That was dinner.

But before the days when we could afford the luxury of Coppa's, in the days when we had recently left high school gladly behind us, we had our first job in the business world. We did not like the job; we emphatically disliked the job.

215

So, we would start out reasonably early in the morning, dragging our sample case of jewelry. And five times a week we would go to Buon Gusto for lunch. Of course, this was almost forty years ago in the days of the old Buon Gusto, the days when there would be a sign in the window—"Ravioli on Thursday." But ravioli was not our dish.

We would go into Buon Gusto at about eleven in the morning. There would be perhaps an Italian family at a table, with the children eating *pasta* and drinking red wine. We would walk to the rear and sit down at our favorite table in the most isolated corner. The waiter would salute us from across the floor: *"Buon giorno, Signor."* There was something very pleasant in that *"Signor"* when we were eighteen years old. He would never bother to ask us for our order; he would bring us a quart of red wine and a platter of *taglierini*. Now, the true epicure never cuts his *taglierini*; it is as important to eat the yard-long strings wound around the fork (and the fork grasped, not between the fingers but in the palm of the hand) as it is to drink wine out of the proper glass. The *taglierini* was heaped high, overflowing the sides of a platter large enough to accommodate a sixteen-pound turkey. And it was mixed, most pleasantly, with a sauce of very rich meat stock, slightly thickened, well developed with chopped garlic, with fresh mushrooms in season or dried mushrooms out of season and bits of crisp bacon and ground beef. And with it there was a loaf of French bread and a hunk of dry cheese.

We would prop a book against the wine bottle and read while we ate. We became ambidextrous in the art of holding our wine glass in our left hand, twisting our *taglierini* with our right hand the while we ate. We read Rabelais and Nietzsche and Joseph Conrad and George Barr McCutcheon.

216

We usually took from four to five hours over our lunch and our book and our bottle of wine, and late in the afternoon we would return to the world of business and, with an unhappy, slightly flushed face, we would explain to our employer that business had been very bad that day, we had not sold a thing.

It was in San Francisco, at Pete Sanguinetti's, that one learned to put red wine in one's soup and black coffee on one's ice cream and brandy in one's black coffee. It was in San Francisco that the small Olympia oysters, a half-inch in diameter, inspired a chef to serve them in a small glass with tomato sauce and lemon and horse-radish. So, oyster cocktails were a San Francisco invention. It was in San Francisco that the large crab legs were fried in butter highly and copiously seasoned with garlic, and Crab Legs *Meuniere* became a San Francisco creation. It was in San Francisco that John C. Kirkpatrick, manager of the Palace Hotel, first thought of baking oysters in their shells, with a highly seasoned tomato sauce, garnished with lemon and parsley, and that delectable delight of gourmets, Oysters Kirkpatrick, was born.

It was in San Francisco, too, that a misguided Oriental gentleman heaped a dish with everything he could find in the larder—including fried noodles and shredded pork and shredded chicken and sliced onions—and called it Chop Suey, declaring it to be the national dish of China. Of course, the fact that it had never been heard of in China did not destroy its popularity, first in San Francisco, then in New York, and ultimately in every village that boasted a railroad café.

And it was at John Tait's down on O'Farrell Street in the Old Rainbow Lane that a waiter, who merits a special place in the epicure's Elysian fields, declared that there was only one thing fit to eat when one drank good French champagne:

217

by-passing the dishes of the exemplary Tait kitchen, he would go out into Powell Street and buy you a paper bag of hot, roasted chestnuts to eat with your sparkling wine.

Now, of the more famous San Francisco dishes we can claim to be only an appreciative patron, ignorant of the recipe. For example, it was a great day at the Bohemian Club whenever Raphael Weill would don a white apron and prepare a chicken casserole, served with a beautiful sauce of this and that and other titillating secrets, combined with chopped mushrooms. That was the genesis of Chicken Raphael Weill.

In the old days, long before the popularity of Julius' Castle on the edge of Telegraph Hill overlooking the Bay, Julius was the proprietor and cook and waiter of a modest little place on Green Street just off Columbus. He had only eight tables; that was all he could take care of. It did not concern him much whether or not you patronized him; as a matter of fact, unless he found you sympathetic he preferred not to have your patronage. But Julius had, in that little hole in the wall, the finest cellar of imported wines in the city. And after your dinner of veal, or a broiled chop, Julius would say, "And now I bring you—oh, my, what I bring you!" And he would bring you fritters—banana fritters, light as spring clouds—and he would heap them and completely submerge them beneath whipped cream, deliciously flavored and seasoned with ground cloves. It was such a simple thing and such an indescribably exciting thing!

Then there was the cocktail route. That was the road traveled by all self-respecting businessmen on their way home at five o'clock. Into quiet, dignified taverns of refreshment the road led, taverns where the voice of woman was never heard; it was a man's world, sacred to men. On that Cocktail Route of blessed memory, few places were more popular than the Waldorf across the street from the Palace Hotel. As you entered the large room there would be George, a huge, laughing, good-natured Negro in his high white chef's hat and his immaculate white suit and white apron—George, behind his tall, little table with a Gargantuan baked ham on it, and the syrup of a clove-spiced white-wine sauce oozing out of the ham and perfuming the night. And George would say, "Good evenin' suh. How ah yo', suh? Ah hopes you'ah fit, suh"—and hand you a plate with a split biscuit and a hunk of that melting, tantalizing baked ham. That was the prologue to the evening in San Francisco.

And, finally, we come to George Mardikian, genius of American chefs, a huge, smiling, kindly person who can never forget and never stops remembering the kindness of America after his struggle and hardships in Armenia.

George serves spinach, raw spinach in a salad, and makes it taste like ambrosia. We do not know how he does it, for it is his secret. George just laughs and says, "It's simple, very simple." He serves you a delectable fantasy called Chicken Tchakhokhbelli with its flavor of sherry wine; it is simple to prepare but it cannot be prepared without the magic touch of George Mardikian. Then, there is his Shish Kebab with its flavor of gypsy campfires. You draw the bits of lamb from the skewer and savor the delightful flavor, and George stands and beams and says, "Are you enjoying yourself?"

So, we are back where we started: The main difference between San Francisco and most other cities is that in other cities people eat to fuel their bodies and revive their energy. But in San Francisco they say, "Let's go out and have dinner and enjoy ourselves." . . .

XXVIII

The Earthquake

For many years San Franciscans were willing to tell—they were even boastfully proud to tell of the fire that devastated the city in 1906. They would not mention the earthquake; earthquakes were things of fearful mystery. But fires—well, every city has fires. So, they spoke of the fire and closed their minds to the earthquake until, with the passing of years, the trembling of the earth became a rather vague memory out of which a beautiful city had grown.

I was seventeen years old in April of 1906. But years before that, when I was a very small boy, I had read a book that made a deep impression on my youthful susceptibilities—*The Earth Trembled,* by E. P. Roe—a story of the Baltimore earthquake. One line had made a lasting impression on me: when the boy in the story came running to his father after the earth had trembled, the senior said with emotion, "My boy, terrible things are happening downtown in the city." On the morning of the San Francisco earthquake, when I broke down the jammed door of my room and stumbled down the still trembling stairs to my father, he greeted me with, "My boy, terrible things are happening downtown in the city." That was a fascinating experience. With a phrase I had been raised to the level of a character in fiction. It made a deeper impression on me than did the disaster itself. But memories in detail come back after forty years.

We had gone, a friend and I, to the opera the night before. We had stood in the gallery of the Grand Opera House on Mission Street and heard Caruso sing Don José in *Carmen*. That in itself was a shaking experience when you were seventeen. After the final curtain we were so deeply stirred by the emotional earthquake we had experienced that, instead of going to Zinkand's for a Swiss cheese sandwich and a glass of Münchener, we walked up Telegraph Hill and stood leaning against the eucalyptus trees that swayed in the breeze where now the Coit Tower rises serenely indifferent to breezes.

We looked at the city. We stayed up there till one-thirty in the morning, looking. And my friend, who was only sixteen but mature of mind, looked out to the south, across the arc lights of the Barbary Coast, across the steeples of Old St. Mary's Church and the rounded Oriental domes of the Temple Emanu-El and the alleys of Chinatown and the distant gilded dome on the City Hall with Liberty perched atop it, and he said, "It's the most beautiful city in the world. It's going to grow and grow. I hope it doesn't lose its beauty as it grows."

Then we walked home. I lived in a house out near the Presidio wall. My room was on the top floor, the fourth floor. It was what we would call a rumpus room today, a large room with a billiard table in it, school pennants on the walls, hanging bookshelves, a Holbein "Erasmus," and a monstrosity of a combination gas-and-electric chandelier.

Excited by *Carmen* and the voice of Caruso, excited by the walk up Telegraph Hill, I climbed into my pajamas and then sat at the window and looked out across the Presidio to the Golden Gate. It was a foggy night; the red and green lights of the boats in the Bay were dim-colored sparks in an aura of green-and-red fog. I sat there and thought of my friend's comment. Why should not a thing that was beautiful, as beautiful as all this, remain beautiful always?

It was a profound thought and I was pleased with myself for having conceived it. I went to bed and was instantly asleep, my profound thought and Carmen singing the "Habañera" and the red and green lights of the Bay all jumbled in fog.

I was awakened a half-hour later. It was five-fifteen. I did not know what had awakened me. There was noise and there was a swaying sensation and there was a tense vibration like a strong fist closed tight, grimly shaking. Then the chimney came through the roof and landed in a pile of bricks on the billiard table, and I climbed out of bed.

It was difficult to walk across the room to the door. The floor was still swaying like a slowly rolling ship; it was littered with fallen bricks and the remains of the combination gas-and-electric chandelier and "Erasmus." The door was jammed; I crashed it open with the aid of an iron dumbbell. I stumbled down the stairs and my father solemnly held my arm and said, "My boy, terrible things are happening downtown in the city."

He was grim with excitement. He wore a long flannel nightgown and flopping slippers. He gave military orders: we were all to march quietly out of the house and into the street.

But my mother stood there, laughing at him, and said, "Don't be silly. Put some clothes on first and brush your hair."

222

And my father groaned and said, "Women just can't understand the seriousness of things."

We got dressed, and he brushed his hair, and we went out on the sidewalk.

We lived on the Jackson Street hill below Presidio Avenue. Neighbors from up and down the block were gathered on the sidewalk, just standing there, not quite knowing what to do. It was cold; the fog was almost a drizzle. People whispered to each other. I don't know why, but they all spoke in low voices as though they were afraid that any loud noise might suddenly start the earth to careening again.

So, while we stood there and we men wondered what we ought to do, my mother went into the house and filled all the basins and tubs and pots and pans in the kitchen with water. We were one of the few families that had a supply of water for the next few days. Of course, we were careful with it. We would use what we needed for cooking, and then we would save the cooking water to bathe ourselves; we gave no thought to washing pots and pans.

By about seven o'clock we all were relaxed. The terror was gone; my father was telling us that we should be calm and collected, that there was really no reason for excitement. And then a man rode out Jackson Street on a bicycle and told us that the city was burning.

My father insisted that the family should remain together; there were four of us children and our father and mother, and none of us was to move a foot from the house.

But our grandmother lived in lonely splendor in the Marie Antoinette Apartments on Van Ness Avenue some dozen blocks away, and I volunteered and was given permission to walk down there and give what help I could. She was an old lady but she didn't need help. I found her seated on a Pear's Soap box on the sidewalk; she assumed that someone would be along for her. She sat there in a dress of black alpaca, a white-lace collar, a little black bonnet on her head, and her white hair perfectly dressed.

She had collected many rare things—cameos and laces and carvings—during her annual European tours, and I said I would go up into the apartment and save what I could. Of course, the elevators were out of commission. I climbed flights of stairs, stopping on the third floor to lean against a door that had always been the door of a shrine to me—the rooms Tetrazzini occupied. Through these walls I had heard her, time and time again, humming to herself, or practicing or vocalizing.

I started to climb to the fourth floor but was stopped by a soldier. He peremptorily ordered me out of the building; he said it was likely to burn at any minute. Of course, it never did burn; it was dynamited three days later. But then, the zealous soldier would not let me enter my grandmother's room. All her treasure collection, her famous collection of cameos, her chests of French and Italian lace, her jewels, and her miniatures were doomed.

So, I returned to Grandma, hailed a passing express wagon, hoisted her on to it, and gave the black-market expressman twenty dollars to deliver her to Jackson Street and Presidio Avenue.

Reaching home, I found the family preparing for an exodus. We were going to anticipate the flames that might eventually reach the Western Addition and head for the Presidio hills. Each member of the family had something to carry; with the wisdom displayed by most of the women, my mother prepared a roll of blankets for each of us. I mounted a laundry basket on the seat of my bicycle, strapped it so that it would not wobble more than could be helped, and filled it with a set of my favorite books and a case of my father's finest Moselle wine. The books came back to their shelves a couple of days later but the wine did not.

Soldiers on the Presidio hills were helping fathers of families to construct temporary tents of bed sheets and blankets; social barriers were broken down, discarded, and everybody was friendly with everybody else. Before night-fall truckloads of food arrived from neighboring towns, and the first bread lines were formed.

As day turned to night the blanket of smoke that had hung in the sky all day turned to crimson, turned to more than crimson. As the flames of the fire spread up one side of Market Street and down the other, they became a glare almost as bright as the sun, and people clustered around the owner of an evening paper of the day before and convinced each other that they could read by the glare of the flames a couple of miles away.

An ominous scene! A terrible scene! And yet, withal, it was a scene of unreasonable beauty, of brave fortitude and stubborn courage, of men and women who were the sons and daughters of the men and women who had built the city in days of rough labor and primitive struggle and now were standing straight-shouldered to keep the pioneer spirit alive in the time of the city's most terrible disaster. But this is not to be the eulogy so often sung of the city's courage. It is simply the memory of the incidents that made the deepest impression on a boy of seventeen.

One impression persists and will not be put aside, the feeling that all those San Franciscans on the Presidio hills, on the heights of Buena Vista and Twin Peaks—all those people were participating in a gigantic picnic. The children laughed and played games, the men and women laughed and sang songs, ragtime songs mingled with hymns. And when men looked at the burning city and could see no hope for a tomorrow, the women laughed at them and sent them to fetch buckets of water or to stand in line for a can of pressed corned beef.

That was forty years ago, and for forty years I have been allergic to pressed corned beef. We had it for supper, for lunch, and for breakfast. No one, at least none we knew of, went hungry. From all over the United States trains were rushing with cars of food; from all over the world aid was coming. Whether you were a ditchdigger or a millionaire, you stood in line and were given your allotment of food, including pressed corned beef, the same amount to millionaire and ditchdigger alike.

While the city burned, babies were born, and there were deaths from natural causes. Life went on out of doors. And on Thursday morning, April 19—the day after the earthquake—the three rival, unfriendly city newspapers joined hands in a combined edition that told little because little as yet could be told, but that did a great service. The Thursday and Friday papers appeared listing thousands of names of families to whom help was being offered by relatives and friends in the East Bay and Peninsula suburbs. An uncle of mine advertised our family name. He had started for New York the day before the disaster but turned back at Reno when the first news of the shake reached there. His printed message was brief: "Send the children and Grandma to Oakland. I'll take them East."

So, Grandma and my sisters and brother crossed the Bay. (Of course, there were no fares to pay either there or on transcontinental trains.) The next day they were on their way to New York and a European tour. I remained behind with my parents to see the rebuilding of the city, an experience far more thrilling than any decadent Europe could offer.

As the fire swept on, into the confusion of flames and smoke came a new element, deep reverberations like the firing of huge cannon. Soldiers were dynamiting twelve city blocks of buildings between Van Ness Avenue and Polk Street. Twelve blocks of buildings crumbled before the dynamite to make a barrier across which the flames would not leap. The fire stopped at Van Ness Avenue, and we left the picnic on the Presidio hills and went home.

We went home to a primitive manner of life. That April was cold. There could be no artificial heat of any kind in any house; there was no light, no water, no means of cooking. Most chimneys had fallen; those that had not could not be used until they had been inspected by the authorities, and in many cases the inspectors took weeks to reach a neighborhood.

So, we collected fallen bricks and built ovens on the edge of the sidewalks—sometimes I think those sidewalk ovens must have been the initial impetus for the great popularity of barbecue pits today. We cooked out there on our curb grills. We saved the hot water to wash ourselves and our dishes and utensils. There were no telephones, no street cars —we walked down town. Within a week we saw the sleepy street of family markets, Fillmore Street, become the center of a huge shopping district. And quite suddenly we found we had need of such a shopping district—the city was flooded with gold.

Families who had lived comfortably but had kept little cash in their homes now found their coffers filled. Friends and relatives sent gold—not checks, but *gold* by express.

Insurance companies began paying losses. Merchants found stocks of merchandise and a great market for them in the replacing of possessions lost in the flames. And people who had money said, "What's the use of saving it? We have seen what disaster can do in the passing of a moment." So they spent.

The great fire was out, but blazes sprang up here and there and smoldered for weeks. One wholesale coffee concern on Howard Street was buried beneath collapsing walls of brick; hundreds of sacks of unroasted coffee were buried. The fire wormed its way into the debris, and for six months smoke curled and an exquisite odor of roasting coffee drifted through the district.

I had had two cherished haunts in the city that was gone. One had been the art room of Polytechnic High School, a drab, red-brick structure at the corner of Bush and Stockton streets. I went down there a week after the fire had burned itself out, and from the debris I salvaged schoolday cartoons of two of the boys who had gone to Poly—Rube Goldberg and Tad (Tom Dorgan).

My other haunt had been the Grand Opera House on Mission Street where Caruso sang Don José on the night before the shake. The building was gone after the fire; nothing remained but the ghost of ten thousand wonderful hours. And in the ashes I knew were the crumbled remains of one of the world's greatest theatrical libraries, the library of Charles and Sigmund Ackerman, the managers of the house. In those ashes were David Garrick's promptbooks, especially his *Hamlet*; once I had held it in my hand. There were rare folio Shakespeares, rare old copies of *The Rivals* and *The School for Scandal*, books from which Salvini and Henry Irving and Joe Jefferson and Sarah Bernhardt had

228

read their lines. Oh, there were vastly greater treasures destroyed in the fire of 1906, but some of us cherish one thing and some another.

I have tried from time to time to put into words a reason why San Franciscans—why *I* love San Francisco. And all the reasons I have ever given are all still true. But added to them, I think, is the fact that I really learned to know and love San Francisco when I saw it go through disaster and fire, and then laugh and make a picnic, and only stop the picnic and the laughter to begin the task of rebuilding anew.

XXIX

Sadakichi Hartmann

We were having dinner at Bigin's. It was in 1917. Bigin's was a restaurant on Columbus Avenue between Pacific Avenue and Broadway. To be exact, Bigin's was a long, narrow restaurant with an entrance on Columbus Avenue and an entrance at the rear on Kearny Street. It was like a long hallway; there were tables along the two sides and a long aisle that ran from door to door.

Now there was nothing particularly distinguished about Bigin's; it was like a hundred other Italian restaurants in San Francisco. It served a good, six-course dinner with red wine for sixty cents. But Bigin himself was distinguished. He was a dignified, fairly heavy, smooth-faced Italian, with a pleasant habit of wandering from table to table to sit down and talk with his friends. Bigin's great interest in life, even beyond his restaurant, was art. He was the patron saint, the good Samaritan of the artist colony. A hungry artist could always depend on a free dinner at Bigin's, and a few coins in his pocket when he needed them. Bigin was concerned with the lives of the artists, and with their loves, and above all with their art. Bigin worshiped art.

So, we were having dinner at Bigin's that rainy night in 1917, my wife and I. We were eating *taglierini* with mushrooms when the Kearny Street door opened and a strange figure of a man came in out of the rain. He wore a long, black opera cape and a crushed black fedora; he clutched a portfolio under his arm. He had an unhealthy, haggard look and deep pouches under his eyes; he wore a thin, scraggly mustache of long black hairs, and a few unrelated black hairs on his chin like the beard of a Chinaman. He stood there, and Bigin saw and approached him.

"Good evening," said the visitor.

"Good evening," said Bigin. "You want something?"

"Yes," said the visitor, "I wish dinner."

"Oh, it is dinner you wish," said Bigin. Whereupon he quickly stepped behind the visitor, seized him by the collar of his cape and the seat of his pants and ran him the length of the hallway restaurant to the Columbus Avenue door. He kicked the door open with his foot and flung the strange figure of a man out onto the sidewalk to sprawl in the pouring rain. Then Bigin closed the door, wiped his hands as though brushing off something unpleasant to the touch, and stalked the length of his restaurant, scowling at his patrons.

Later, Bigin came to our table and sat down, and we sipped our wine and commented on the long season of rain. He crumbled stalks of French bread between his fingers and shook his head and growled, and we continued to talk about the rainy season.

"That man, he is bad," said Bigin. "He make me too angry. He criticize the artist, the painter of San Francisco. In the newspaper he say the artist of San Francisco is lazy and bad and not a good artist at all. He say nobody but him know real art. He say San Francisco artist pretend to be something he is not. He make me very angry. I will not have him to eat in my restaurant."

Then Bigin grinned at me and winked at my wife and

said, "There are lots of plenty of good people; why must we have bad people?"

And he brushed the French-bread crumbs from his hands and strolled to another table.

The strange individual who was tossed into the rain that night by Bigin was Sadakichi Hartmann. Hartmann was born in Japan. His mother was a Japanese, his father, a German scientist. And in art circles throughout the world Sadakichi Hartmann in his day was called the world's foremost art critic. He had written many books on art in flawless style. His *History of American Art* was an accepted standard. He wrote strange and beautiful exotic poetry; he wrote plays that were banned for their frank daring and were acclaimed by the critics. He painted with consummate skill. He was an actor of remarkable ability; strangely clumsy, his interpretive dancing was a beautiful expression of aesthetic genius. Sadakichi Hartmann was a great artist —and a poor figure of a man.

He was born in Nagasaki in 1869. At the age of thirteen he was brought to America by his father, and ten years later he wrote and produced his first play. It was a life of Christ, depicting the Saviour as an average man of the people. Boston saw the production; Boston was shocked. The police came and saw the production and were shocked. They closed the theater. Critics praised the writing as a scholarly achievement. Hartmann was arrested, and released.

The following year, when he was twenty-five years old, he became an American citizen. He traveled, wrote, danced, sang, acted, and painted. He drifted to Paris and became an intimate friend of the trilogy of French decadents—Verlaine, Baudelaire, and Debussy. He visited his father's home in

232

Germany and hated everything German. He hated his parentage. "Germans and Japanese," he said, "make me tired."

And years later in San Francisco, in 1918, during one of the many periods in which he was in the hands of the law, he was accused of being pro-German. His answer to the judge was, "I hate Germany. I was arrested in Berlin for calling the Kaiser names." And then he added, irrelevantly, "I am a genius. At nineteen I had read all the literature in the world."

In America critics said, "Yes, he's a genius. A mad genius."

He drifted to San Francisco in the early years of World War I. He loved the city, loved its color and its traditions and its beautiful hills and the waters of the Bay. And he grumbled, "These people are savages. They have all the world can provide to make life beautiful, and they live like savages."

But he threw himself into the artistic and aesthetic life of the city, maintaining classes in painting, lecturing on art, lecturing on philosophy and world economics. At the Scottish Rite Auditorium, in 1917, he horrified his audience by announcing, "California will eventually secede from the Union." The audience sat and shivered, and Hartmann grinned and pulled the few black hairs in his chin beard. Hartmann often grinned but he rarely smiled.

It was in the same week that he perpetrated his most amazing stunt. Up on Russian Hill, at the edge of the hill, was the old Hanford Mansion. It was called a haunted house and the house of mystery. Hanford had built it for his bride, and tragedy had ended the marriage before the house could be occupied. It had stood there for years, looking out over San Francisco and the Bay, a gray box of a house in a lovely garden.

Hartmann rented the house. He collected a group of poets, painters, actors, parlor philosophers, and aesthetic dancers; his salon was called the "lair of the intelligentsia." And then he announced that he would produce a drama and chose Ibsen's *Ghosts*. At the first reading of the play he selected amateur actresses to essay the feminine roles, and he read all the masculine roles. But that was just the prologue. He next announced that he would play the role of the pathological neurotic, Oswald, the boy who craved the sun. It was a fine production, and Sadakichi Hartmann as the demented boy was brilliant.

Now, you recall that when the climax of the drama is reached at the end of the second act, the orphanage catches fire and the flames are seen through the window of Oswald's home. The climax was reached, and the garden house of the Hanford Mansion actually burst into flames. Some more kindly than I am insist that it was a strange and accidental coincidence. But Hartmann was ever a stickler for realism; he had ordered the fire kindled, and it spread beyond control, endangering the lives of the audience. However, the flames were subdued and the performance of *Ghosts* went on to its tragic last curtain. And that was literally the last curtain, for the police stepped in, Hartmann was arrested, and released with an order to give no further performances. His career as a San Francisco theatrical producer was ended.

His next adventure—and Hartmann found adventure where others would find the drab routine of life—was on San Francisco Bay. With a companion he rented a small boat and went rowing. He had seen the Bay and its beauties from the San Francisco hills, now he wanted to see the beauties of the hills from the Bay. But Hartmann was not an athlete; his physical body had given way to the aesthetic soul. The result was that the small boat carried the two men out through the Golden Gate and into the open sea. A million square miles of water, and the poet and his friend were adrift in the midst of it; it was a situation to shake the soul of any man, poet or materialist. They drifted and there are no records to show how long they drifted. They were beaten by blistering sun and chilling fog. Hartmann claimed that they drifted and starved for thirty days, but he was a poet and a man of rich imagination; some say he was absent from San Francisco for only thirty hours. Be that as it may, he was at sea in a rowboat and in peril. And then, without brass bands playing, a United States battleship spotted the tiny speck on the vast ocean, lowered a boat, took Hartmann and his companion on board, and that adventure was ended.

And there you have the picture of Hartmann the adventurous, Hartmann the poet and painter and critic. But it must not be assumed that he did not live a domestic life. His common-law wife and three daughters were a constant problem to the police because Sadakichi would not support them. "Would not" is a strong phrase; he claimed that, being a poet, he could not support them. But he was a familiar figure on the streets of San Francisco, and later, down the Peninsula in San Mateo, marching along, his opera cape flapping, his black hat crushed about his ears, his portfolio under his arm. And behind him trailed Mrs. Hartmann carrying packages of food. Sadakichi, being a poet, would never carry packages.

Then the first World War burst into his world of poetry. Hartmann would not enlist because he did not believe in war; he could not be drafted because he had four dependents and a fifth soon to arrive; he would not labor in war industries because he was a man who labored with his brain and not his hands.

Down in the county seat at Redwood City old Judge Buck had other ideas. Sadakichi was thrust before him, accused of not supporting his family. The Judge painted a glowing picture of the fortune to be made in the shipyards; why, shipyard riveters were making sixty dollars a day! He ordered the poet to the Potrero yards of Bethlehem Steel. Sadakichi went and sat down on a coil of rope and gazed out into the Bay. Now, that was a thing that was not being done during the first World War! One might beat the iron side of a hull with a hammer and pretend one was toiling, but one never sat down in the shipyards.

In desperation the yard straw bosses ordered Sadakichi back to Judge Buck. Buck shouted at him and, adamant, Hartmann shook his head and said, "You cannot make me work with my hands. You may throw me into prison, but still I am a poet, not a laborer." Judge Buck was not one to argue, or to be argued with. He said Hartmann would either find a way to support his family or go to jail. Hartmann compromised by agreeing to give a series of lectures on art and world economy.

It was in January of 1919 that he gave, not a lecture, but his most remarkable concert. It was a symphony of odors, a concert of perfumes. The setting was the Paul Elder Gallery on Post Street, and to this day people tell of the sweet, strange cadences that drifted into the busy street to blend with carbon monoxide gas.

For four more years Sadakichi Hartmann and his opera cape and portfolio drifted around San Francisco and San

236

Mateo. Then, one day, the artistic world of Hollywood called him. Douglas Fairbanks was producing a great spectacle, *The Thief of Bagdad*. He wanted Sadakichi Hartmann to play an important role.

So, Sadakichi went to Hollywood. They dressed him in brilliant colors. They bowed to him and wined him and banqueted him—and led him before the camera. But Hartmann could not act that day; he had a toothache. Even poets may have toothaches. The next day he could not act because the studio shoes hurt his feet. For a series of days and weeks he drove the inmates of the picture world mad; first it was his teeth, then his feet, then it was both together. He did not like Hollywood; he did not like motion pictures. What if they were willing to pay him a thousand dollars a day? Money meant nothing to him; he was a poet. So, limping away on his aching feet, pressing his fist to his aching mouth, he left Hollywood high and dry. His career as a movie actor was ended, and Hollywood sighed with relief. The directors acknowledged that the Hartmann experiment had cost them sixty thousand dollars in salaries and wasted time, but they sighed with relief.

That was his last great adventure, the last fling of a man who combined the deportment of a madman and a circus clown. But, underneath the fantastic veneer, Sadakichi Hartmann was a great artist in all the fields of art, with an honest and sincere critical mind. There has been very little printed about his life and few things more expressive than this quotation found in an old magazine: "Sadakichi Hartmann was born out of his age. He was a man who belonged in Cellini's gang or with the rowdy geniuses of the Mermaid Tavern."

He left Hollywood and found a shanty high in the mountains behind Banning, California, and for many years lived the life of a hermit there. And yet he was not altogether a hermit, for he had found one sympathetic companion in Hollywood, a man who could drink with him, sing with him, play the clown with him, and love beauty with him. To the shack in the hills behind Banning came, now and then, that other poet with the veneer of a clown——John Barrymore.

Several years ago the following line appeared in the *San Francisco Examiner*: "Sadakichi Hartmann, artist, died suddenly, November 22, 1944, in Florida at the age of 78."

XXX

"The Cool, Grey City"

The secret of San Francisco is captured in an exquisite phrase of poetry by George Sterling——"The cool, grey city . . ."

That is San Francisco. Its glamour and its beauty and its excitement and its charm are all heightened by contrast with the cool gray. We think of cities that are beautiful in themselves, of Los Angeles, New York, and Washington, and Portland in Oregon. But the bright colors and the excitement of Los Angeles lose their full value because they blend rather than contrast with the rich, orange sun hues of the south. The aliveness and the glamour of New York are part of the exciting skyline. The trees, the river, the hot sun in summer and deep snows of winter are not counterpoint but in tune with the pulse of Washington. And the mellow hills, deep-wooded, and the broad rivers are a part of the heart of Portland. But San Francisco is exciting, warm, glamorous and impulsive, painted on its canvas of contrasting cool grays. The Artist has worked with cunning in painting the calm background for the city of contrasting lights and shades. . . .

At first there was a great serenity there, a cold, almost austere serenity. That was in the days of the first inhabitants —the Indians. The site was empty, rolling hills of sand dunes then, shifting with the winds that came in from the Pacific, dunes unbound by grass, unsheltered by trees. The dunes lay in the dark nights and in the lighted nights of the moon, things of silver, shapes without form. Great birds waded at night in the river that ran from what is now the Presidio, across what is now Sixth and Market streets, and out into South Channel. Bears roamed the salty dunes, and theirs were the only sounds at night.

And then the white man came, and the night stirred with the mellow chiming bells of Mission Dolores. San Francisco has always been most beautiful at night.

In the 1850's it was noisiest at night, and the later the hours the greater was the noise. Above the pools and puddles on Montgomery Street, and around about the Plaza, oil lamps swung from iron bars and hooks in front of saloons and palaces of chance and dance halls and melodeons, and dripping oil from the lamps spluttered and flared and sizzled into quiescence in the mud-splashed streets. The noise was the noise of the roulette wheel, of the dice cage, and the wheel of fortune. The noise was the drunken laughter of roistering miners and the furious shouts of fights as unpremeditated as spontaneous combustion. The noise was the music of small upright pianos, of accordions and guitars and banjos and mandolins, and of the singing voices of groups in harmony that was neither close nor harmonious. Shadows, like grotesque shadow dancers, moved up and down the roads, with lanterns or lighted candles in tin cans dangling from iron chains. The trundling noise was the sound of wheelbarrows full of personal possessions, pushed by the owners from newly docked ships to the lodginghouses. Drunks stood in doorways and shouted, and at the corner of Clay and Dupont a nomad evangelist shouted his version of the gospel with vivid promise of eternal damnation.

240

But out in the wild, unexplored lands beyond what is now downtown Powell Street, the sand dunes still were silent at night, brooding, resenting the invaders at the border, but secure in the knowledge that the borders would never be crossed.

That was in the 1850's. In the 'eighties and to the turn of the century, the Barbary Coast shed its glare upon the city. The Barbary Coast was tough—and evil. Night after night there, year after year, men were robbed of their gold dust and later of their payrolls, and murdered, and their bodies tossed into the Bay. Drab women stood in doorways and picked their prey; sharpers and sharks and pimps and derelicts slunk along the pavements. The corner of Jackson and Kearny streets was called Murderers' Corner. It was there that the notorious Opera Comique melodeon offered its salacious entertainment to the throngs that milled up the hill to Pacific Street—Pacific, where the lamps swayed in front of the Hippodrome, the Thalia, Negro Purcell's, and the dozens of other music halls of evil repute.

It was along these streets at night that the men of all nations fought and laughed and spent their gold and were drunk—Scandinavian sailors, Dutch sailors, "Sydney Ducks," lascars, Chinese, Limehouse bruisers, huge black Algerians, turbaned Arabs, Eurasians. The Barbary Coast at night had the color and the excitement and the noise and the cacophony of voices that were like the fascinating, insidious evil of a market place in Bagdad.

Evil? Of course, it was evil. But the Barbary Coast at night was a part of the romance of San Francisco, and when it became a synthetic paradise for tourists, the city at night became a more moral place, but much of its color was dimmed.

Then, there were the nights after the turn of the century and through the years that preceded the first World War, nights bright with a new sophistication, when dapper young men promenaded, twisting their waxed mustaches and swinging their bamboo canes and tilting their derby hats, nights when ladies wore feather boas and Merry Widow and peach-basket hats. Carriages rolled down the cobblestoned hills, rattling on their iron wheels, and the first horseless carriage wheezed up the hills. And, as darkness settled on the city, the proud owners of horseless carriages made a great business of lighting the acetylene gas lamps or oil lamps in front of their vehicles, a difficult and important task at all times, but most difficult and impractical when the rain fell in torrents or the wind danced a wild bacchanal around corners. Then, as the night grew gray, the rattle of carriages gave way to the rattle of milk-wagon wheels on the cobblestones.

There were oil or acetylene lamps on the horseless carriages, but the nighttime city was becoming a place of brighter lights, of dazzling and mysterious electric lights that beckoned the entertainment-loving city to the Alhambra Theatre, the Columbia Theatre, the Wigwam, the Alcazar, the Princess, the Tivoli, the Orpheum—all legitimate houses. (Only the Orpheum offered an added feature, the new novelty, the animatoscope with its pictures in motion. Of course, it was only a novelty, one that could never be popular. Pictures in motion flickered and hurt one's eyes. They were an impractical novelty and couldn't last.)

And then, one night Market Street blazed from end to end with tall, golden standards bearing brilliant clusters of light; the street was renamed the "Path of Gold" and San Francisco had become a metropolis. . . .

"The cool, grey city" I love! Night on the hills of San Francisco. . . .

In my memory there was the time when Telegraph Hill was topped with scrub eucalyptus trees and goat trails. There was no Coit Memorial Tower then; there were no paved roads, no well-trimmed shrubbery, and no artists' studios with wide, glass windows—studios renting for two hundred dollars a month. No, in those days Telegraph Hill was a rough place, beautiful in its raggle-taggle, topsy-turvy madness. The shacks that were called houses leaned at crazy angles and teetered on the edge of cliffs like small boys climbing fences and shouting, "Watch me fall off!" There were beautiful smells on Telegraph Hill, especially at night and the dinner hour, smells of garlic and red wine and strong cheese and huge loaves of bread baking in roaring ovens of brick. There were beautiful sounds at night, of babies crying and children laughing and stout and thin and tall and short mamas collecting their progeny, screaming as they collected them. There were whispered voices among the eucalyptus trees where boys and girls made love. There were sounds of wheezing accordions and tin harmonicas, and thin-voiced pianos in the houses that were shacks.

But, then as now when the hill has become a dignified dowager with important apartments replacing the shacks, you could stand up there at night, and the full beauty of the city was spread at your feet. Down there were the wharves and docks, most mysterious at night of all the beautiful things of the city. The wharves and docks with great hulks of shadows that were the ships with the fascinating names on their prows—ships that called at Surabaya, at Canton and Bombay and Bali and Rio and Glasgow and a thousand other ports of fascination. And their red and green

243

lights, to port and to starboard, danced in the waters of the Bay—"pretty colors," the children on the hill called them, those red and green lights of the ships at anchor.

Then, to the immediate south there were the flamboyant lights of the dives and the palaces of the Barbary Coast, and silhouetted against the sky, rubbing shoulders with the sinks of iniquity, were the great steeples of the new Cathedral. And far to the south and far to the west, as though a child had taken a piece of cardboard and pierced it with a thousand pinholes and then held it to the sun, there was the dancing, endless pattern of lights of the homes of the city, with a bright Milky Way cutting diagonally across it—the Milky Way that was Market Street.

The boys and girls still whisper up there on Telegraph Hill in the shadow of the Coit Memorial Tower or in parked automobiles; there still is the smell of garlic and baking bread and red wine. But the accordions and the tin harmonicas and the asthmatic pianos have made way for radios that fill the night with the music of singing commercials, and juke boxes that run the gamut from Lithuanian folk dances to crooning baritones and boogie-woogie.

South of Market Street at night! "South of the slot" they used to call it; Third Street, Mission Street, Howard Street, and out Bryant—Skid Row. These are the streets of the riffraff, the down-at-heels, and the man who has done eight hours hard labor; for these the sidewalks are living room, night club, and parlor. There is not much beauty here, not to the eye. But there are dreams and ambitions and frustrations—the things of which drama is made.

Here are the Greek restaurants and the Armenian restaurants and the Turkish coffeehouses with men at small tables, drinking coffee thick as chocolate and playing dominoes.

244

Here is the alley of the panhandlers, where every man is either blind or pretends blindness, or is without arms or legs or pretends he is without limbs; here are creatures who display horrible scabs and sores; here are boys who paint to look like old men and then assume the physical disabilities of old age with an art that would have delighted the heart of Stanislavski. And because all this is color-contrast with the cool gray of the city, there is a beauty in the misery of Skid Row.

Chinatown at night! The most fascinating part of Chinatown's night is the sight of hundreds of Chinese children milling through the streets, home from night school—Chinese children and Chinese babies eating licorice strings and ice-cream cornucopias, and singing jive and cheering Frank Sinatra. Yesterday they trotted along, wearing the wide, silk-brocade pants and the beautiful, silk-brocade blouses of their ancestors, and clinging to the hands of stout, shapeless Chinese mothers. Today the phonograph shops in Chinatown blare boogie-woogie; yesterday, at night, the weird quarter-tone music of Chinese instruments sang raucous emotion to the stars. But yesterday or today, Chinatown was and is most mysterious and most beautiful in the very late hours of the night and the early hours of morning, when the shadows are long.

When the before-dawn fogs pour through its byways and the street-light lanterns are dark, strange shapes and forms move on silent feet along the alleys. You seldom hear laughter; you seldom hear a raised voice. And yet, there is an intense design of business in the moving forms; there is no night or day in the business of Chinatown. And it takes but little imagination to smell the sweet, cloying vapors of opium drifting from places below sidewalk level, or to hear, com-

245

ing from behind closed doors, the rattle and clatter of fan-tan chips and mah-jongg tiles.

If I were to show the city to a newcomer, wanting him to capture in his impressions all the romance and fascination and beauty of San Francisco, I would bring him into the city at night. I would drive him across Nineteenth Avenue, up through St. Francis Wood. And, if he was a perceptive visitor, he would surely say, "This is very nice, but I've seen lovely homes like these in almost every city I've visited." So then I would drive him out of St. Francis Wood and into the darkness up the Corbett Road, and we would wind away from the homes into a reach of comparatively colorless empty space. Then, suddenly we would top the hill and round the hill and there, below us, would stretch that most beautiful wonderland of magic lights.

There are lights stretching to the east and the north, mile upon sparkling mile of them, an endless carpet of dancing jewels. Beyond are the lights of the Bay Bridge, golden amber, reaching into darkness and coming out of darkness in a new pattern, a diamond lavaliere along the eastern shores of the Bay. And there in the East Bay, high above, the single light flashing red at intervals marks the broad highway of the air lanes.

There is no sound, no human form, but just the millions of lights, and every one marking the life and mingled emotions and excitement and glamour and color and hopes and dreams of the men and women of——"the cool, grey city" I love.

246

Appreciations and Acknowledgments

In March of 1943 the San Francisco store of W. & J. Sloane was interested in a series of narratives about San Francisco life and traditions to be embodied in a radio program called "This Is Your Home." In a round-table discussion I was asked how long I could reasonably sustain a schedule of San Francisco narratives, and with some misgivings I answered: at least thirteen weeks.

The program is now in its fifth year. So many requests for copies of the weekly scripts were received that this volume, *San Francisco Is Your Home,* was conceived, partly to satisfy the requests, partly to preserve a more tangible form of radio programs that, once broadcast, would be lost.

The co-operation and good will of the firm of W. & J. Sloane, and the encouragement of its vice-president and general manager of the San Francisco store, Ruskin B. Hamlin, has made the task a happy one. These chapters, selected from more than two hundred fifty episodes, are printed with the kind encouragement of W. & J. Sloane.

A stimulating influence has been the constant and friendly interest and the encouragement I have received from John W. Elwood, general manager of National Broadcasting Company, Station KNBC, in San Francisco.

Much of the success of the radio program has been due to the sympathetic, fine presentation by the narrator, Budd Heyde.

The material has been gathered from my personal memories, recollections of friends who love San Francisco as I do,

247

and from a comprehensive search of printed San Francisciana. I am indebted to my friend, Joseph Henry Jackson, literary editor of the *San Francisco Chronicle,* for permission to quote from his books on California, particularly his fine study of Black Bart, a source that discards most of the foolish legends and reveals the true picture. I have found valuable source material in the Bancroft Library; the Stanford Hoover Library on War, Revolution, and Peace; the San Francisco and San Mateo Public Libraries; the open stacks of the Mechanics Library of San Francisco; private libraries of friends; and in the co-operation of Western book dealers, particularly my good friend Jack Newbegin who is never too busy to dig under his shelves to find a valuable bit of San Francisco lore for my typewriter.

The following partial bibliography includes books on San Francisco that are readily available to interested readers but it does not pretend to be an exhaustive list of my sources.

SELECTIVE BIBLIOGRAPHY

Asbury, Herbert. *The Barbary Coast.* New York: Garden City Publishing Company, 1933.

Dana, Julian. *The Man Who Built San Francisco.* New York: The Macmillan Company, 1936.

Davis, William Heath. *Seventy-five Years in California.* San Francisco: John Howell, 1929.

Dobie, Charles Caldwell. *San Francisco's Chinatown.* New York: D. Appleton-Century Company, Inc., 1936.

Hart, Jerome Alfred. *In Our Second Century.* San Francisco: Pioneer Press, 1931.

Jacobson, Pauline. *City of the Golden 'Fifties.* Berkeley: University of California Press, 1941.

Jackson, Joseph Henry. *Anybody's Gold: The Story of California's Mining Towns*. New York: D. Appleton-Century Company, Inc., 1941.

Lewis, Oscar. *The Big Four*. New York: Alfred A. Knopf, 1938.

Lewis, Oscar, and Hall, C. D. *Bonanza Inn*. New York: Alfred A. Knopf, 1939.

Lyman, George D. *Ralston's Ring*. New York: Charles Scribner's Sons, 1937.

MacMinn, George R. *Theater of the Golden Era in California*. Caldwell, Idaho: The Caxton Printers, 1941.

Mighels, Ella Starling (Clark). *Story of the Files*. San Francisco: Co-operative Printing Company, 1893.

Neville, Amelia (Ransome). *Fantastic City*. Boston and New York: Houghton Mifflin Company, 1932.

Soulé, Frank, Gihon, John H., and Nisbet, James. *Annals of San Francisco*. New York and San Francisco: D. Appleton, 1855.

Underhill, Reuben L. *From Cowhides to Golden Fleece*. Stanford: Stanford University Press, 1939.

Walker, Franklin. *San Francisco's Literary Frontier*. New York: Alfred A. Knopf, 1939.

BOOK TWO

SAN FRANCISCO KALEIDOSCOPE

For My Daughters

BARBARA
CATHERINE
HELEN

Prologue

This is the San Francisco kaleidoscope! Our stage setting is magnificent. Breathtaking hills with the bay, the ocean, and the Golden Gate spread before them, and more hills beyond. The music for our pageant is old Spanish-California melodies strummed on a guitar; it's the voice of opera singers, and it's the full-throated voice of a great symphony; it's sentimental ballads, and the cacophony of Chinese instruments, and accordions playing Italian street songs. It's the Grizzly Bear and the Turkey Trot played on honky-tonk pianos. And it's colored with the song of the foghorns and the clang of fire bells and the mellow intoning of church bells. Music is a very important part of the pageant of San Francisco.

Our cast of characters are first a handful of men, then a hundred, then thousands, then hundreds of thousands, and each man marching in the direction his vagabond spirit guided him. There you have the stage setting, the music, and the cast of characters for our kaleidoscopic pageant of San Francisco.

Oh, yes, and lights! There are lights that are dim on foggy nights, and a million dancing lights that are a part of the carnival of San Francisco when the night is clear beneath a billion stars.

The cavalcade of men commences—poets, dreamers, beggars and millionaires, vagabonds and scholars, thieves and saints, cowards and men of courage, adventurers, and poor benighted souls who never knew an adventure. They're Iowans and they're Nebraskans, and they're Swedes and Danes and Frenchmen and Germans and Italians and Spaniards and Chinese and Japanese; they're Christians and Jews and Mohammedans, and some who have no god. They're a colorful lot and that's why their story is a pageant. It commenced on the day in 1769 when Sergeant José Ortega, a scout in the party of Don Gaspar de Portolá, stood somewhere in a clearing in the San Mateo hills and saw San Francisco Bay. That was the beginning.

Six years later, the fog rising above the ocean showed an opening between the hills, and between threatening rocks and sheer cliffs a sailing ship came tacking before the wind. She passed through the Golden Gate with canvas flapping, and dropped anchor—the first ship in San Francisco Bay. She was the *San Carlos,* piloted by her good master, Lieutenant Juan Manuel de Ayala.

Another year was to pass, and colonists came from Mexico under the leadership of Juan Bautista de Anza. They selected a thousand acres of sand dunes, created a military post, and called it the Presidio. After having first given thought to the welfare of the fighting men, on the following day de Anza gave thought to God and chose the site for Mission San Francisco de Asís, called Mission Dolores.

At first came a few stragglers, arriving by threes and fours. There was William Antonio Richardson, who settled as far from the Presidio and the Mission as he could, along the sandy beach of the bay in the area called Yerba Buena. He built the first dwelling place in San Francisco, a large tent made of a ship's sail. Then, not long later, came Jacob Leese. He was a merchant, and he set up shop and sold silk shawls to the ladies of the haciendas, and coffee, rum, and tobacco to the dons. Mr. Leese built the first substantial home, a wooden frame house that he completed on July 4, 1836. Richardson and Leese thought that this called for a celebration. They invited folks from many miles around to the festivities marking the Fourth of July of the United States of America, which was a place somewhere beyond the mountains to the east. So the dons and the duennas, their children, and the various sailors from the sailing ships that came into the bay, had a fiesta and danced, sang songs, drank rum, fought, and loved. Everyone had a wonderful time!

And now the stragglers became more numerous. There was Mr. W. D. S. Howard who was a shrewd merchant himself, and he sent for a home and had it carried on a sailing ship around the Horn; and there was his relative by marriage, Mr. William Heath Davis, whom men called Kanaka Davis because he ran sailing ships between the Golden Gate and the Sandwich Islands, and traded in various commodities, some approved and some contraband.

Then a ship came sailing in with a group of Mormons led by a highly adventurous gentleman named Brannan, Mr. Sam Brannan. As soon as he landed, he became a renegade from his Mormon followers for various reasons, but he adopted San Francisco and everybody in it. He formed a social club so that the men could have celebrations. He started a newspaper so the men could read the news of the world. He encouraged a public school so that the children of the men could learn to count and be good merchants. And later, when the village became disorderly and there were no police to keep order, he banded a group of vigilantes together and they took the law into their own hands.

These men were the first to come. They were like the mounted police that lead a parade. Now the cavalcade began to build up. James Lick landed with thirty thousand dollars, bought most of the sand lots on Montgomery Street, and made more millions than he could count. The Swiss captain, Jean Jacques Vioget, landed. Jean Jacques could play a pretty

255

tune on a violin, and whenever he brought out his fiddle there was pretty sure to be a fiesta. But he had other accomplishments, this Monsieur Jean Jacques Vioget. He could handle a slide rule and a compass and a plumb line, and so he was put to work laying out the sand lots in the squares which became the pattern for the village that was to become the city.

Then Johnnie Stevenson came along. He had the dignified title of Colonel Jonathan D. Stevenson, and with him he brought several hundred volunteers from New York to put down any uprisings that might occur. There didn't happen to be any uprisings at the time, so Colonel Stevenson and his men stayed, and between Sam Brannan's Mormons and Stevenson's New York Volunteers the forty or fifty men who made up the population had grown to several hundred.

Then, one day, Sam Brannan threw a bombshell into the village! He came tearing down Montgomery Street shouting for all to hear, and when anyone on Montgomery shouted, all of Yerba Buena knew about it. He came down the street shouting that gold had been discovered in John Sutter's millrace up at Coloma and that everybody was going to be a millionaire. Within a year of the day that he did his shouting, the village of Yerba Buena, with a population of about six hundred, had become the city of San Francisco with a population of thirty thousand.

Now the fiesta was in full swing. Montgomery Street was lined with dance halls and pretty girls, beautifully painted. Pianos, concertinas, and guitars made music all day and all' night. There was the music of the rattle of dice, and the music of the clinking of many glasses. There were the creaking of booms and capstans and blocks and tackles along the water front of Sansome and Battery Streets, and the bay was an army of the masts of seven hundred ships.

These were the days when the German watchmaker, Russ, came; an Englishman named Joshua Norton and thousands of others came too. Suddenly, just as fast as they came, they emptied out of the city and headed for the hills and the treasures of gold. As suddenly as the village became a city, so it became a deserted city overnight. Everyone—almost everyone—had gone to the hills to become millionaires, and the few who stayed behind were men like Lick and Norton, and a young fellow named Baldwin whom men called "Lucky," and a blind man who played a concertina on Jackson Street and made his own lonely little San Francisco fiesta.

All is not gold that glitters in the red earth of the Sierra. So, little by little, the cavalcade came straggling back from the hills, some with sacks of gold on their backs, some with small pokes of gold in their pockets, and plenty of them starving, and looking for trouble. Now the carnival became pretty much of a bedlam. A small portion of the community was looking for a decent home to raise families, a great portion looking for trouble, and all of them looking for entertainment. And the entertainment came!

Stephen Massett came to put on a one-man show, writing and singing his own songs, and also selling the tickets and receiving them at the door. Biscaccianti came to sing melodies of Mozart. Annie Bishop came to sing "Home Sweet Home." Edwin Booth played tunes on his guitar and played *Hamlet*. Lola Montez danced her sensational Spider Dance. Johnnie Stevenson's New York Volunteers put on minstrel shows. Tom Maguire opened his Jenny Lind Opera House. Parepa-Rosa, huge and fat, sang opera. Theaters opened one after the other: the Metropolitan, the Bella Union, and all the others.

For every theater there were a hundred saloons, dance halls, and gambling palaces. Gentlemen and scholars and riffraff poured into the city. With the riffraff came some several hundred prisoners from the penal colonies of Australia and New Zealand. The Sydney Ducks, they were called, and they were asking for trouble, and found it. One day a gambler named Mr. Cora shot and killed a gentleman named Richardson who had insulted the highly colored lady who called herself Mrs. Cora. And that, added to the fact that the Sydney Ducks and other troublemakers had burned the city to the ground five—or was it six—times, so infuriated the good citizens that with Mr. Brannan as their inspiration, and Mr. William Coleman as their leader, they formed themselves into Vigilance Committees. Quite suddenly the village that had become a city settled down and became a staid and respectable place. In fact, it almost threatened to become dull. But San Francisco wasn't born with a dull bone in her body. In good times and bad she had to have excitement, and she found it.

First it came when a nondescript individual named Comstock stumbled across a treasure of gold and silver in the hills of western Nevada. Comstock never benefited by his discovery, but out of San Francisco came four sons of Erin, Flood, O'Brien, Mackay, and Fair, to develop the big bonanza in the Comstock Hill, and into San Francisco poured the flood of gold and silver and a new generation of millionaires.

Meanwhile, four other shrewd individuals, Mr. Stanford and Mr. Crocker, Mr. Huntington and Mr. Hopkins, had built a railroad that spanned the nation, and when a golden spike was driven and more millionaires had been created, the city by the bay celebrated again. Brass bands played, speeches were made, and everybody had a wonderful time. However, most sensible San Franciscans said no steam car could possibly cross the Rocky Mountains and they weren't going to risk their necks on any new-fangled contraptions.

They stayed at home, and the new millionaires built mansions on Nob Hill all covered with turrets and bay windows, balconies and towers. A gentleman named Andrew Hallidie, who was in the business of making wire rope and wire cables, decided that the city was going to move to the top of the hills, and there would have to be a way to get to the hilltops. So he built a cable car, the first in the world, some say it was. It ran up the Clay Street hill, and when it had completed its first trip the city held a celebration.

Well, all of that was more than eighty years ago, and only twenty years of the pageant had been acted. Characters now moved more swiftly across the scene. Bill Ralston built his fabulous Palace Hotel. Joshua Norton lost his fortune, went quietly mad, and thought he was an emperor. Oofty Goofty made a living by letting gentlemen kick him in the seat of his trousers. Denis Kearney objected to the foreign labor the railroad builders had imported, and started a series of mild riots. Mr. Kalloch, a preacher and a politician and a silver-tongued orator, was shot for denouncing the policies of an unfriendly newspaper publisher from a platform in front of his church on Fifth Street.

Millionaires and prize fighters, sundry famous poets and writers of stories and painters of pictures had become, along with an endless parade of actors and singers, drunken sailors and scoundrels, bums and dreamers, the men of the city of three hundred thousand. Then one day somebody discovered gold in Alaska, and that was thousands of miles from San Francisco, but the city at the Golden Gate became a center of the new gold rush. The next year, which was 1898, some-

259

body discovered oil in Kern County which was hundreds of miles from San Francisco, but the city on the bay became a center of the rush for liquid gold. Four times in fifty years fortunes had been found in the earth; 1848 and the discovery of California gold, the 1860's and the discovery of Virginia City gold, 1897 and the discovery of Alaska gold, and 1898 with the finding of oil. Each time San Francisco had been the hub of the excitement, the clearing house of the millions, and the playground where the millionaires built their turreted castles, spent their millions, and made their fiesta. And that year of 1898 the California boys came marching home from the Philippines and the city had another celebration.

Then the century ended and the city quieted down. It said, "We're grown up now and we'll go sedately along in dignity." Sedate dignity in San Francisco! Not a chance! While the city rested, nature took things into her own hands and shook the living daylights out of San Francisco! It was grim and terrible, that earthquake and fire of 1906, but San Francisco made a celebration out of it. They sang, did those mad San Franciscans, sang on the hills and on the Presidio slopes while the city burned. When the ashes were cool— no, before the ashes were cool—they started building again. What was a fire that it should stop the carnival of San Francisco! Hadn't it burned five times before, or was it six, and risen each time from the ashes? So they built a new city. It was to be a dignified city, a city of skyscrapers and solid walls. Gone were the towers and turrets, the gingerbread carvings and bay windows. No more nonsense! No more nonsense in San Francisco? They loved it when Smiling Jim Rolph, his honor the mayor, sent motor cops screaming their sirens up and down the streets welcoming visiting firemen, and doling out, with the greatest of liberality, keys to the city and the

Golden Gate. They strung the city with lights and made a carnival when the Gaspar de Portolá of 1909 came riding.

They filled marsh lands and made a great and beautiful exposition at the foot of Fillmore Street in 1915, and bands played and singers sang, and thousands paid ten cents to see the painting of Stella. It was a merry carnival. They threw a great bridge across the bay and strung it with golden lights, and the bridge opened and the city marched across it and made carnival. They threw a great bridge across the Golden Gate where wise men had said a bridge could never be, and they opened it and made a fiesta. They built an island in the bay and built another exposition, built it in a time of world war when wise men said no exposition could be built. They made of it a pageant of color. Meanwhile, through the years of the new century, new characters, new millionaires, and new vagabonds joined the parade, along with new poets and dreamers. Tetrazzini sang and the city stood still. White Hat McCarthy paraded and the city loved him. A grower of flowers became his honor the mayor, and instead of golden keys for visiting firemen, everyone wore gardenias. Biscaccianti and Annie Bishop were long since gone, but out of their memories the city built the second greatest opera company in the land. A sedate and dignified city now—no more nonsense! But they wept sentimental tears when their cable cars' lives were threatened. They wept sentimental tears when an Italian restaurant owner died, and they wept tears when their flower stands were threatened. But no more carnival! No more fiesta! No more pageant! They had grown up!

Grown up? San Francisco will never grow up. It's a very Peter Pan kind of city that always stays young. They must have a fiesta, a fiesta to remember the day one hundred and seventy-nine years ago when Don Gaspar de Portolá traveled for one hundred and eight tortuous days up across the hills to San Francisco Bay. They must have another Don Gaspar! But, on second thought, a single Don Gaspar would never be able to express the love of carnival and fiesta and pageant that is inherent in every life-loving San Franciscan. It was quite simple! They had to have *four* Don Gaspar de Portolás, and everyone had a wonderful time!

PART ONE
GOLDEN DAYS OF YOUTH

I

Henry Meiggs

There are few things on earth more sad than the spectacle of a man exiled from the land he loves, and forbidden ever to return. To those of us who love San Francisco, what could be more tragic than to be exiled from its lovely hills and colorful valleys? That is the story we have to tell you, the tale of a man who truly loved San Francisco and was driven from it, never to return. The fact that he was a thief and something of a scoundrel doesn't soothe the pain. To those who love the city there is the need for it which is similar, I am told, to the need of those habitual slaves of narcotics, who are cut off from the drug they crave. This is the story of Henry Meiggs, popularly called "Good old Harry Meiggs," a man of vision and dreams and schemes.

Henry Meiggs—good old Harry—landed in San Francisco in July of 1849. Born in New York State, he had spent his early years there, buying and selling lumber. But when the cry of gold swept across the world, Harry lost his interest in

263

lumber; after all, the buying and selling of lumber had been his vocation, but by avocation he was a promoter, one of the most spectacular promoters the West had ever known. What possible Utopia could be conceived that would lend itself better to promoting than the fabulous gold fields of the Sierra and the gold mine that was the village of San Francisco in 1849.

Harry Meiggs loved San Francisco and everything about it, and what made the picture more pleasant was the fact that the city loved him. From the day of his arrival he won wide popularity. He was an exceedingly good-looking man. According to early chronicles, he had charming manners, great tact, a sound business head, and a great capacity for work. He was a promoter, but hard labor went into his promotions, and while the mining-camp town was busy day and night finding entertainment in dance halls, gambling palaces, and gilded saloons, Harry Meiggs was industriously planning the future of the city. He was charitable, and his purse was always open to the needy. By 1850 disgruntled men were drifting back from the mines, discouraged and often hungry, and it became something of a tradition on Montgomery Street and in the Plaza that if you were down and out you could always go to good old Harry Meiggs and be rewarded for your efforts with a gold coin.

He would walk down the street and everyone who was a San Franciscan knew him and greeted him cordially. And for the unknown stranger whom he passed, he had an equally gracious greeting. In every sense of the word, Harry Meiggs was a charming, cultured, and distinguished gentleman.

In San Francisco, as in New York, his principal occupation was the buying and selling of lumber, and lumber was a vital commodity in the swiftly growing city, a city that had a habit of burning down once a year. He went out to North Beach and built a small sawmill and a small wharf. He organized a company and built the largest sawmill in California up in the redwoods of Mendocino County. In 1850, in recognition of his efforts for the community, he was made an alderman. But he spent most of his time strolling along the edge of the bay out at North Beach, making great plans for the future. North Beach was far removed from the city in those days. Telegraph Hill lay between it and the city, and all the plans were for letting the new community spread southward from the hill and all the way to the cowpath that was Market Street.

Harry Meiggs had other ideas. He said the logical place for the city to grow was along the shore of North Beach. There was more flat land there and it lay close to the Golden Gate, through which the treasure-laden sailing ships came. It was absurd for the ships to have to furl canvas and be towed by small boats all the way around Telegraph Hill before they could drop anchor. The logical thing to do was to build a great wharf right there at the foot of Powell Street, a wharf to which the sailing ships could come without being menaced by the mud flats of the lower bay.

He loved the city, but his plans were not entirely altruistic. By building the wharf and charging for space along it he could clear a fortune. And by buying the inexpensive land along the northern shores of the city, he could make more millions than the most successful operators had made by speculating in the less desirable property along Dupont, Kearny, Montgomery, and Sansome Streets. He had another great scheme, but it was so absurd that even the good citizens who had nothing but respect for his business acumen told him it was a fantastic impossibility.

Harry Meiggs had looked at the lands at the further end, the southern end, of Powell Street and Stockton Street. There was a great valley out there, with fields of stubble grass and sand dunes, but flat land nevertheless. He figured that he could strike a tunnel through the mountain that separated North Beach from the cowpath of Market Street, a tunnel that would run right under Stockton Street! The city fathers told him that his idea was absurd, that it could never be done, and that he had better stick to his sawmill and his alderman's chair, and make what money he could developing the district of North Beach.

But day after day, night after night, Harry Meiggs tramped the cowpaths and mud-mired roadways of the city, always planning for the great future he knew was to be the destiny of the city that he had learned so swiftly to love.

His walks took him far afield. A pleasant and cultured Englishman had come to San Francisco; he was called Lord George or Sir George Gordon, although there was some question as to whether he was qualified by royal decree to the title before his name. Lord George was something of a promoter himself, interested in lands that could be developed with an eye to a profit. Harry Meiggs showed Sir George North Beach and the lands that lay at the other end of Stockton Street, out through Happy Valley and Hayes Valley, but Sir George wanted something a little bit more remote. He wanted land that could repel the invasion of the riffraff that infested the mining camp, so Harry Meiggs took him up Rincon Hill. At the foot of the hill was a small hollow, the ideal place he was looking for. The two men began to plan, to figure, and to draw maps. While Meiggs had very little to do with the ultimate completion of the plan, out of their figures and maps emerged a select small square, modeled exactly on the plan of Berkeley Square in London, a small and select piece of land with dwellings to be built around an oval garden surrounded by an iron grille fence. In the center of the garden was a small windmill that would pump water to irrigate the flowers that grew therein. That was the beginning of San Francisco's first haven for elegant and select society, South Park.

The interests of Harry Meiggs were unlimited. While he was planning South Park, while he was busy year after year as alderman, while he was finding charities that needed his attention and festivities that demanded his presence, he never lost sight of his ultimate ambition—to build his great wharf at North Beach and make North Beach the center of the new city. His interests were unlimited, and as varied as were San Francisco men.

A concert pianist came to town as accompanist to the beloved Kate Hayes. His name was Rudolph Herold. He saw San Francisco, fell in love with it, met a charming San Francisco girl, fell in love with her, and married the girl and the city. Herold was a true artist. He had been a pupil and devotee of Felix Mendelssohn and he lived for music. The mining camp was starved for the fine things of life, particularly music. Herold was there to supply it, but he was first and last an artist with few of the attributes that make a successful promoter. On the other hand, Harry Meiggs was rapidly building a reputation as the greatest promoter the city had known. So, in 1854, Harry Meiggs and Rudolph Herold founded the Philharmonic Society of San Francisco, the first vocal and orchestral group in the city. In January of 1854, the Philharmonic, directed by Rudolph Herold, presented a great oratorio to an enthusiastic audience of miners and dance hall girls, and Harry Meiggs sat in the audience and wept. Culture had come to the city that he loved.

In *The Annals of San Francisco* we read, "A large Music Hall has been erected in Bush Street, near the corner of Montgomery, by Mr. Henry Meiggs, and here quiet folk are entertained with concerts, oratorios, lectures, fairs, and the like."

That was all very fine, and good old Harry—Honest Harry, as he was now being called—had won the love and respect of the city. But he wasn't for a minute forgetting the fortune he was going to make when his dream for North Beach had become a reality. His lumber interests were bringing him profits, and every dollar he made he was investing in North Beach land that he could buy at one-quarter the price asked for property along Montgomery Street. But Montgomery Street could not be entirely forgotten, so to increase the value of his property he built a dirt road from Montgomery around the foot of Telegraph Hill to the beach. The earth removed in the cutting of that road he used to fill in tidelands along North Beach to create new city lots for himself. Then he built his wharf.

It jutted straight out from Powell Street into the bay a distance of two thousand feet—a third of a mile. At the corner near the entrance to the wharf he induced a friend to build what became one of the most famous resorts in the city, Warner's Cobweb Palace. Many years have passed since Meiggs' Wharf disappeared from the San Francisco scene, and the place where it jutted out into the bay has become, to a great degree, filled land. But for those who are newcomers, unfamiliar with the past of the city, it might be well to explain at this point that the site of Honest Harry Meiggs' Wharf is now the world-famed Fishermen's Wharf, with its lobster pots.

There was a cemetery in the block bounded by Powell,

Stockton, Lombard, and Chestnut Streets. Meiggs saw in it a detriment to the growth of the community he was planning, so he had the bones removed to a new burial ground and converted the land into building property. He graded Stockton Street; he inspired the grading of Powell Street and many other byways that would make egress to North Beach easy.

But now he was becoming land poor. He owned so much property, he was spending so much money on its development, his taxes and street assessments were so high, that he was hard put to find cash for his simplest needs. Then, in 1854, San Francisco suffered one of its first business depressions, and the value of city property crashed. Speculators became apathetic. What excuse could there be for investing in a remote land scheme when business was on the toboggan? In a word, while he kept the matter a deep personal secret, Honest Harry Meiggs was bankrupt.

He guarded his secret well. The city fathers had confidence in him, and, in his capacity as alderman and respected businessman, he had access to city papers and affairs. When the city incurred debts and obligations it would issue warrants, or promissory notes, signed by the mayor and controller. Frequently the holder of a San Francisco promissory note would sell it at fifty percent discount for quick cash. Meiggs was always welcome and free to come and go in the municipal offices at his own pleasure, and he obtained a quantity of blank promissory notes. Whenever one of his creditors would make demand on him for money owed, Honest Harry forged the signature of the mayor or the controller, or both, and paid his debt. It was later believed that in addition to the notes that he forged he had obtained a book of blank warrants that the mayor and controller had already signed for use as the occasion arose. Local politics was a happy-go-lucky business in 1854, and the mayor and controller had more important things to think about than the demands of their political offices. So, by the use of signed notes, and by forging others, Harry Meiggs flooded the city with warrants.

The notes carried no interest, so they drifted around the city month after month and the forgeries were not discovered, and Honest Harry was still Honest Harry to the city that loved him. Over a period of months he had accumulated fraudulent debts amounting to eight hundred thousand dollars.

His career of crime embarked upon, he went beyond the forging of municipal notes. He forged notes of private corporations and San Francisco merchants. He made a fraudulent overissue of three hundred thousand dollars of stock in his lumber company and sold the stock for seventy-five thousand dollars. He borrowed money wherever he could and was willing to pay exorbitant rates of interest. This, more than any other one thing, tended to turn the city against him. The men who respected him began to look on him with suspicion. It was a mild suspicion with no vestige of thought given to the possibility of his actual operations. But they were no longer enthusiastic about his activities. They lost interest in his North Beach development. His property sales fell off to minimum, and a breath of scandal was circulated that he had an improper interest in some city contracts for street grading. Oh, these were all minor details, the kind of municipal scandal that all cities enjoyed; there was nothing really wrong in it, from a criminal point of view. They just didn't feel that Harry Meiggs was entitled to the respect he had enjoyed in the past, and they certainly weren't going to lend him any more money.

Slowly the net was closing, and Harry Meiggs knew it. His days in San Francisco were numbered. The important thing now was to make his escape before the final debacle. He bought, or charted, a small brig, the *American*. He filled its larders with a store of fine provisions—canned meats, wines, and luxuries—and told his friends that he was going out for a pleasure cruise of the bay. The day was October 6, 1854. On board was his brother and his family. Out through the Golden Gate the brig turned its nose, and disappeared on the horizon.

That very day the news broke. Harry Meiggs, forger and manipulator, had failed for eight hundred thousand dollars.

That's the story of the life of Harry Meiggs in the city of San Francisco. But, amazing as it is, it was nothing as compared with the subsequent events in the life of Honest Harry.

He sailed to Tahiti, and then to Chile, where he found work overseeing a small crew of men working on a railroad. He learned about railroads, and men worked well for him. He became a contractor; he built a road from Valparaiso to Santiago. He had landed in Chile with a fortune of eight thousand dollars. That went, and once he had to pawn his watch to buy a meal. But success liked Harry Meiggs, and his reputation as a railroad contractor spread. The country of Peru was undertaking the building of a system of railroads and they sent for Mr. Henry Meiggs to do the contracting of the work. He built eight hundred miles of railroad through almost insurmountable obstacles in Peru, and the contracts amounted to more than.one hundred million dollars.

Harry Meiggs became one of the most highly respected men in South America. He became a multi-millionaire. And that, save for one minor detail, is the end of his story.

The minor detail? Well, success had come to him and

wiped out the taint of his evil days. But not all the success in the world could make up for the loss to him of San Francisco, the city he loved above all others. Twenty years later, in 1873, his friends applied to the legislature of California for a pardon exempting him from trial for his crimes. The legislature unconstitutionally passed the bill exonerating him, but the governor vetoed the bill. Of course, old-timers were of two minds about the affair. Some, remembering all he had done for the city, thought he should be permitted to return. But William Ralston summed it up this way: "My favorite novelist is Thackeray and my favorite dramatist is Shakespeare. I also understand by the late papers that Mr. Meiggs' tastes are similar. But, I hardly think Mr. Meiggs has earned our consideration as an honest man because he is a kind father and reads good books."

Harry Meiggs remained in Peru, a tremendously wealthy, unhappy man, longing, until the day of his death in 1877, for the sight of the Golden Gate and the city from which he had been exiled.

II

Lord George Gordon

This is the story of Lord George Gordon, as varied and as tragic a story as may be found in all the annals of San Francisco history. It's the story of a man who brought color, warmth, and beauty to the city; it's also the story of a man who suffered vile degradation almost unfit to be told, and saw his dreams crumble.

He called himself Lord George Gordon. He spoke with a broad English accent. He dressed with impeccable taste; he fancied himself the Beau Brummell of the Western world. But he was not a lord; there was even question about his British birth. Some unkind gossips claimed that he had been born in New York's Bowery. But more of that later.

Lord George's first big American adventure was to sell passage around the Horn to San Francisco. He was a born promoter. He chartered a ship, formed a company which he called the California Association, and charged each member of the association (and there were two hundred of them) one hundred and sixty dollars to sail in luxury from New York to California. He promised such luxury that the passage money would leave him no profit. His profit was to be made in another way. (I sometimes wonder if Lord George had his tongue in his cheek when he made the contract.) He was to have twenty percent of all the gold the two hundred voyagers took out of the California hills.

The ship set sail, but Lord George Gordon was not on board. He traveled overland with the more than thirty thousand dollars' worth of gold he had collected from the association travelers. The two hundred members of the California Association traveled on a wreck of a ship that had no sleeping accommodations and almost no food. I personally have been unable to find any record of the unhappy bark ever making the California coast.

The next chapter of the adventures of Lord George began the day he sat in the office of the San Francisco banker, Harry Meiggs. Lord George had a fine and noble plan to submit to Mr. Meiggs. Mr. Meiggs and other public-spirited citizens of the young metropolis were to entrust funds to him. With the funds he would terrace Telegraph Hill and turn it into a beauty spot to rival the famed Italian Riviera. He would have trees, shaded walks, monuments, and fountains. It would be a thing of enduring loveliness. But Mr. Meiggs was something of a promoter himself. He said that at the present moment he didn't give a continental darn about beautifying the city; he was only interested in making money. So Lord George changed his song. Very well, he would show Harry Meiggs how to make money. He visualized a great wharf at the point where the waters of the Pacific flowed through the Golden Gate and joined the waters of the bay, a wharf to which every sea-borne visitor to San Francisco would have to come. The wharf should be named—in the words of Lord George Gordon—after San Francisco's most distinguished citizen; it should be called Meiggs' Wharf. Meiggs' Wharf! It did have a pleasant ring. It would be the first name the traveler heard upon putting foot on Western soil. So Banker Harry Meiggs put up the money. Lord George Gordon called in builders and let contracts. And, with a pretty profit for himself, Meiggs' Wharf was built. It was the second big San Francisco adventure of Lord George.

History, when it was written, called Harry Meiggs a thief who had absconded with funds belonging to widows and orphans. Well, if good intentions could be measured, and if Meiggs had succeeded instead of failing in his early promotion schemes, history would have glorified him.

And history said Lord George Gordon was not a lord, which was doubtless a true statement of fact. But when it suggested that he had been born in the Bowery and that his English accent was assumed, history was dealing in fiction. According to all dependable accounts, George Gordon was the son of a self-respecting, highly reputable country gentleman of Yorkshire, England.

Life in the English countryside in the 1840's was staid, polite, and rather smug; and, on the surface at least, it was very virtuous. After all, the good Queen Victoria was just beginning to sow her Victorian oats that were to bear a flourishing crop of Victorian virtue.

The best friend of young George Gordon was Branwell Brontë, the brother of the three Brontë girls. They hunted together, they rode together, they went to church together. They were held in high esteem, although the sisters may well have admonished Branwell at times that young Mr. Gordon was the wild member of the Gordon family, and that Branwell surely didn't want people to say that he, too, was wild. Branwell probably didn't care what people said, for he was frequently to be found in roadside taverns with George Gordon, the two of them sadly under the influence of intoxicating liquors. The good Brontë sisters shook their heads and sighed; the good wives of the countryside shook their heads and sighed. But some of the more sophisticated countryfolk smiled and said that boys would be boys.

There is no disputing that aphorism, but sometimes boys can carry their propensities to tragic lengths. One day George Gordon awoke from one of his drinking bouts to find himself married to a rather attractive but not very Victorian barmaid of his favorite Yorkshire inn. She certainly had none of the cultural attainments of the Brontë sisters. In the cold dawn of grim reality, Gordon realized that he had made a mess of his life. But he was a gentleman and he would stand by his bad bargain. After all, the girl said that she loved him. She was young, and she was pretty; and they *were* married; that was indisputable. On the other hand, he couldn't face the scorn of the smug Victorian Yorkshire countryside. He couldn't take her home to his family or introduce her to his friends. The Brontë sisters would never understand.

So Mr. and Mrs. George Gordon sailed for America, the land of promise. In America everyone made fortunes; everyone wore diamonds and satins, and the young Mrs. Gordon liked diamonds and satins. But it wasn't so easy when they reached New York. It was a big, noisy, unfriendly city, even in the 1840's. They floundered like babes in the dark forest until, after some years of unpleasant poverty, George conceived the idea of chartering a boat and taking a company of gentlemen to the gold fields of California, where, according to all accounts, everyone was a millionaire. Gordon shipped his company by sea, and then traveled overland with his bride. Mrs. Gordon didn't like the journey. Traveling to California by covered wagon train was no life of luxury. They arrived in San Francisco with more than thirty thousand dollars in their pockets, but life in San Francisco was no life of luxury either. San Francisco consisted of muddy streets overrun with rats, gambling halls, and saloons with dancing girls. That was the life Mrs. Gordon thought she had left behind in the Yorkshire tavern. The witch's broth of tragedy was beginning to stew.

Then there were the ladies of San Francisco! It's true that there weren't many of them, but those there were turned up their refined noses and were careful that their skirts did not trail in the dust where Mrs. Gordon walked. She hated everything about them, and everything about life in the West.

She wanted to go home; wanted to go back to Yorkshire where life was simple and pleasant and where she was queen of the tavern. Patiently, at first, Gordon explained that it wasn't practical to return. Of course, being a gentleman of reasonable tact, he couldn't tell her that the real reason for not returning was that the ladies of Yorkshire would be even less reasonable than were the ladies of San Francisco. Arguments, nagging, tears, and rage got her no place.

Then her true character came to the fore. She bluntly told George that she had planned their marriage—had gotten him intoxicated so that the wedding could be contrived. Gordon took the statement without flinching. He'd made a bad bargain and he was still determined to abide by it. Then his wife played her trump card. She told him that she was a habitual alcoholic, that she couldn't live without strong liquor, and that from now on she'd make no effort to control herself. The good ladies of San Francisco could look down their long noses as much as they pleased. She was going to live her own life in her own way. The witch's broth was boiling, but worse was yet to come—depths of depravity beyond the imagination of writers of horror fiction.

Despondent over an unbearable home life, George Gordon plunged into a hectic round of social activity and business enterprise. His days as a promoter of enterprises were not yet ended, and his one big promotion scheme was as yet unthought of. Meanwhile, he became involved in the importing and refining of sugar. He built the first sugar refinery in the northern stretches of California and made a considerable fortune. That industry finally became the nucleus of the vast Spreckels interest and was absorbed by it. In the social world he was equally a success. He had charm, personality, good looks, and a keen interest in life, and the newly sprouting San Francisco society was not at all averse to entertaining a British lord, even if there was question about the authenticity of the title.

Under the inspiration of Bill Ralston and other financial leaders, society was turning its eyes to the vast acres of the Peninsula where, among others, William D. S. Howard had acquired great land grants from Mexico. The Peninsula was to be the Mayfair, the fashion center of the new West, and Gordon went down there and purchased a fine tract of land. Probably inspired by his memories of London Mayfair society, he called his land Mayfield Grange. He built a fine imposing home, which he later sold. It became the residence of Senator and Mrs. Leland Stanford, and the great acres of Mayfield Grange are today the site of Stanford University.

There was, however, the terrible burden of his wife always in the background. She was almost constantly in an intoxicated state. He put a trusted butler in charge of her with strict orders that the miserable secret should be concealed as far as was humanly possible. A baby girl was born to George Gordon and his wife, and she was named Nellie. Nellie Gordon! There are still San Franciscans living who

278

remember her as she grew into a lovely and popular young girl, and they remember her unspeakable tragedy. George adored the baby girl, and his love for her fanned the jealousy of his wife to maniacal lengths. Plotting and scheming with the fiendish cunning of the mentally unbalanced, she commenced to put drops of whiskey into the infant's food. The drops increased little by little until the baby would eat nothing that lacked the flavor of alcohol. And by the time Nellie Gordon was seventeen years old and ready to make her debut in San Francisco society, she was a habitual alcoholic. Crushed by the tragedy, George Gordon sent Nellie away to boarding school. The mother, not to be circumvented, smuggled bottles of liquor to the girl in the bundles of laundry that were forwarded to the school.

Well, it seems futile to write more about that miserable affair of the last century. If, from a psychological point of view or from plain curiosity, you are interested in reading more about it, you will find it told in fictional form in Gertrude Atherton's first novel, *Daughter of the Vine*.

Nellie Gordon married a ship's surgeon who was also an alcoholic, and lived a few short tragic years with him. She died in her early twenties. Brokenhearted, George Gordon died a few years later, and his story was ended. Although his wife did live a few years after him, her story isn't worth telling, further than to say that Mayfield Grange fell into the hands of an equally besotted brother of hers and his wife, who had been the cook at the Grange. But back now to the last big promotion scheme of Lord George Gordon.

He had built the wharf for Harry Meiggs. Then, in one of the dramatic pages of San Francisco's story, Meiggs had disappeared with funds, he had gone to South America. Gordon hadn't forgotten his original suggestion to Meiggs that they beautify Telegraph Hill. Now, with the funds he had accumulated from the wharf contracts, he sought an architect, not with the idea of building on Telegraph Hill—the city had spread since that scheme had been formulated—but to follow his new idea. He walked across the city with the architect, beyond Market Street and beyond the city's outskirts into the sand dunes. They came to a hill of sand, that same hill that, years later, was to be leveled to become the western base for the towers of the Bay Bridge. Rincon Hill! At the foot of the hill were sand lots, and at the edge of the lots rolled the waters of the bay. It was a dismal, wind-swept barren waste of sand!

Lord George Gordon stood there with his architect, and with tears in his eyes said, "Isn't it beautiful?"

Beautiful? The architect couldn't believe his ears. There was no beauty in this wind-swept, sand-piled, dismal waste.

"But yes," said Lord George Gordon, "it's beautiful! I see there the beauty spot of the Western world—a gentleman's paradise! And we're going to build it."

The architect said that San Francisco wasn't interested in building a gentleman's paradise. It was interested in finding a place for mud-begrimed miners to hang their hats.

"But," said George Gordon, "mud-begrimed miners become rich men. And rich men demand a paradise."

That was a reasonable premise, and the architect asked Mr. Gordon to enlarge upon his idea.

This, then, was George Gordon's dream. He would build a park at the base of Rincon Hill, a park such as might grace fashionable Mayfair in London. There would be an oval garden surrounded by a high grille fence such as was built around London's residential parks. There would be an artistic iron gate at each corner of the park. The park was to

280

be surrounded by fashionable, London-style houses, houses with marble steps; houses with brass knockers on the doors; houses furnished with rugs from China and the Near East; houses furnished with the finest art of eighteenth-century English furniture designers, Sheraton in particular; houses with fine parlors lit with the candles of sparkling crystal chandeliers. And in the rear of each house there would be an English rose garden. In short, George Gordon planned to create a replica of London's Berkeley Square in the barren sand lots.

That was the dream, and it became a reality. Lord George Gordon bought the sand dunes for a handful of dollars and built South Park. The lawns were planted, the iron grille fences erected, and the houses styled after the homes of fashionable London. Clipper ships came around the Horn with eighteenth-century English furniture and carpets to furnish them. And the men who made fortunes in gold or in Montgomery Street property, and there were many, swarmed to South Park. It became the fashionable heart of San Francisco. The Hearsts, the Hall McAllisters, and scores of others lived there. Men with flowing moustaches, big black hats, and with heavy gold chains across their flowered vests, tramped the mud of the streets across Oriental rugs. Horses, silver-bridled, cantered around South Park lawns, their riders in tail coats and high black boots. Fashionable ladies and painted ladies drove their carriages around the foot of Rincon Hill and promenaded on the city's first paved sidewalks that edged the lawns. The dream of Lord George Gordon had become a reality, but George Gordon of Yorkshire, England, found his dreams crumbling around him in the dismal, terrible tragedy of his family life. So he died, men said, of a broken heart.

And as his triumphs faded, so the glory of South Park tarnished. Today it's still there, a small piece of land off Third Street between Bryant and Brannan. Warehouses and old wooden frame houses stand there with the paint chipped off and turned gray. Freight trains rattle past it, and above it rise the stone piers of the great Bay Bridge. The lawns are yellow and the few trees are hungry and bare. All that remains is a memory of the glamor of the days when the city was young and the West was the land of opportunity.

III

William Leidesdorff

More than one man has achieved strength and broad stature when tragedy stalked across his path, and even power and nobility have been born of suffering. That's the kind of theme playwrights like; it's a plot made to order for a Shakespeare. But one doesn't look for Shakespearean plots in San Francisco; San Francisco is a happy, lighthearted place—or so we've been told. And yet, out of tragedy and suffering, strength and power came to one of the finest men San Francisco has ever known. He was a city builder and an empire builder. He had vision, courage, integrity, and the respect of all his fellow men. When he died the city went into deep mourning. As though by a mocking prank of destiny, his name is all but forgotten in San Francisco, although there is an alleyway named after him. His father was a Dane and his mother was a West Indian Negress. His name was Leidesdorff, William Alexander Leidesdorff.

I have frequently spoken about Leidesdorff; I have told of episodes in his life, but only in passing, devoting a page or two to him at most. And yet, I don't recall any San Franciscan who has fascinated me more. The only trouble is that there has been so little written about him. He died more than a hundred years ago, so even the legends that have been

handed down by word of mouth from generation to generation are disappearing. Finally, a week or so ago, I made up
my mind to go through every book in my library and all that
I could find in circulating libraries about San Francisco, and
to correlate as much of Leidesdorff's story as I could. When
I had completed my task, I found the next thing was to
delete the bulk of the material and cut down the remainder
to fit into the space allotted to me.

The facts that I found were rather disconnected. A single
line in the book told me that he owned thirty-five thousand
acres of land, by Mexican land grant, in the valley of the
Sacramento, east of Sutter's Fort. Another line says that he
owned great stretches of land at the foot of Mt. Diablo, where
the town of Lafayette now lies, and that he owned sand lots
scattered across the map of San Francisco. But he died in
1848, before San Francisco sand lots had any value beyond
being the shifting homes of millions of fleas, and before California had come into its heritage of gold.

So I turned to the real beginning of his story, which was
in a small village in the Danish West Indies. His mother was
a native girl. His father was a drifting, happy-go-lucky Dane
who had wandered around the world shipping before the
mast and trading in commodities, many of them contraband,
in the ports where he touched. Finally his wandering feet
came to rest in the Indies, and he fell in love with a black-
eyed native girl. Their son was named William Alexander.

Now, just as casually as his Danish father and his West
Indian mother drifted into his story, so they drifted out of it
and, incidentally, out of his life. That is, they drifted out of
his life until after his death, when the shrewd executors of
his estate bought off the West Indian heirs for an amount in
the neighborhood of seventy thousand dollars which was a

twentieth of its true value, but which was a fortune vastly beyond the conception of those he had left behind.

His parents drifted out of the picture, but a new influence came into his life. For reasons unexplained, an English plantation owner in the Indies became interested in the boy while he was still an infant. He raised him as a son and gave him the thorough classical education accorded sons of old English families. Young William Alexander was a well-built youngster, strong, attractive, and with flashing black eyes that were doubtless a heritage from his mother. He was popular, with a winning personality and a zest for life and adventure. This might well have been all that he inherited from his Danish father. The parents were forgotten and the boy was accepted as the son of the British planter.

As he approached young-manhood the Englishman sent him to New Orleans to work for his—the Englishman's—brother in the offices of a large cotton enterprise. But before William Alexander departed for New Orleans, his British benefactor told him that he was destined to be a man of importance, and that under no circumstances was he to reveal the fact of his mixed blood.

So the boy entered the business and social life of New Orleans. Just as the plantation owner had adopted him, so the cotton merchant, a man of equally great wealth, accepted the lad as a member of his family, showering luxury upon him. Young Leidesdorff was gay and popular. New Orleans was, even in those days, a romantic place, a place of color and glamor. Life was rich and society was brilliant. The young daughters of the old Louisiana families were raised in cotton wool, sheltered from realities, yet eager for the song of adventure and equally eager, eventually, for marriage.

William Alexander fell in love. The girl was beautiful

285

and sensitive and, according to legend, as delicate and fragile as a fine bit of Dresden. Her name was Hortense. She had melting blue eyes and golden hair that hung in beautiful curls about her slender shoulders, and she carried her head proudly. She was of a distinguished old family, descended from a nobleman of the court of Louis XIV of France. They made a pretty picture, the delicate, blue-eyed, golden-haired girl and the straight-shouldered, black-eyed, black-haired adventurous lad. Even his complexion, obviously burned to a deep tan by the hot sun of the West Indies, made an attractive contrast to the pink loveliness of Hortense. William fell in love with her and Hortense fell in love with him, and the good and select society of New Orleans beamed and nodded and said it would be a lovely match. Of course, they would have to wait; Leidesdorff was young, with his future before him, and he was in no position to propose marriage until he had made his fortune.

Then fate intervened. Both the British planter and his brother of New Orleans, the cotton merchant, died and left their considerable fortunes to William Alexander Leidesdorff. Now there was no reason to wait until he had made his own mark in the world. But on the other hand—and here the boy's conscience, his innate integrity, and his sense of fairness awoke—there was the secret of his birth. He had carefully kept his word to the planter; no one in New Orleans knew of his Danish father and his West Indian mother. But his love for Hortense was too great to let him go through life with her with a secret between them. So he would have to tell her. On the other hand, if he told her, she never would be allowed to marry him even if she were willing. He argued with himself, and lay awake long hours, torn between love and what he knew was the course he had to pursue. One moment his honor was uppermost and the next his love for the girl overweighed everything else. It was in one such moment that he asked her to marry him. We weren't there to report exactly what happened but we can assume that, as was fitting in a young and lovely girl of that time, she blushed and perhaps wiped a happy tear from her blue eyes, nodded and said, "Yes." Her father was approached. He liked the boy, and gave his consent to the engagement. And William bought Hortense a beautiful diamond ring and their engagement was announced to the delighted social elite of New Orleans.

It was all very lovely, all very romantic, and the world would have been a thrilling and delightful place were it not that Leidesdorff's conscience tormented him night and day. You may say that this is all much ado about nothing, but it must be remembered that this was a romance of the first half of the nineteenth century in the deep South. William couldn't sleep and couldn't eat. He grew thin, gaunt, and hollow-eyed. Then one night, shortly before the day set for their wedding, he told Hortense the truth. And again, not having been there, we can only depend on the details as they have been handed down over a hundred years. Even they may not be accurate, for there is no reason to assume that any other person was present when the boy made his confession. But, as the story is told, Hortense wept, and hiding her blue eyes against the velvet coat of her betrothed she said that her father would never permit the marriage if he knew, that she could not deceive him, and could never disobey him; but, though their dreams were ended, she would love William Leidesdorff as long as she lived, and have love for no other. She probably kissed him good night and sobbed as he walked away under the iron-grilled balconies.

287

The next day he received a package containing the engagement ring and all the other gifts he had given Hortense with a letter in the handwriting of her father forbidding him ever to see her again.

He sold all his possessions, closed the house where he lived, and went away. Through his contact with cotton merchants he found and bought a small schooner, the *Julia Ann*, of some one hundred tons. He equipped her and prepared to sail around the Horn and up the Pacific Coast on a voyage of trade, putting as many miles as the ocean would provide between him and his dream of love. His preparations concluded, he walked heavy-hearted through the streets of New Orleans the day before he planned to sail. As he walked along Canal Street a funeral procession passed him. He stood in the doorway of a store until the procession passed. He saw Hortense's father, mother, and small sister in the first carriage. And, a moment later, the storekeeper told him that this was the funeral of a young daughter of New Orleans' society. She had fallen in love with a mulatto. Her name was Hortense. She had died, people said, of a broken heart.

That night, the priest who had been with Hortense at the end brought William Leidesdorff the small gold crucifix she had worn, and said that her last words were a demand that the priest go to Leidesdorff and tell him she had loved him until death.

There is, in the graveyard of old Mission Dolores, a stone inscribed with the name of William Alexander Leidesdorff. There is an alley off California Street in San Francisco called Leidesdorff. These are the city's monuments to the boy, dark-skinned, swarthy, and strong, who had come wandering in from the sea to become the most distinguished leader of the new colony. But, by a strange quirk of destiny, the date on

288

the gravestone in Mission Dolores shows 1848 as the date of his death—1848, the year of the discovery of gold! William Leidesdorff had lived in San Francisco for seven years preceding his death. Death took him before gold brought fame to the city he had inherited. In the years between his leaving New Orleans and his sailing through the Golden Gate, he had roved the seas as a lonely trader, ever and again returning to the home port of St. Thomas in the Virgin Islands. And always, before he came to the West Coast, men marked him as a lone and tragic man, a man with a secret of sorrow locked in his breast.

San Francisco was a new adventure. San Francisco, even before the discovery of gold, was a place of excitement, the excitement born of primitive frontiers. In the busy activity of the little village, throwing himself eagerly into every event that was shaping the village, he won the friendship of men, drawing a veil of silence, like the fog of the hills, over his agony. Frémont and his men were marching north. General Vallejo, in his peaceful valley of Sonoma, was to be shaken out of his routine of days of sunny dreams. Leidesdorff took an active part in the Sonoma Bear Flag Revolt. These were the days when California was drawing away from Mexican rule.

Thomas Larkin, pioneering the path that would make the state a part of the Union, appointed Leidesdorff American vice-consul in Yerba Buena. Then, a couple of years later, when Yerba Buena changed its name to San Francisco, the ex-sea captain, son of a full-blooded Negress of the Indies and a Danish father, became the new city's first elected American alcalde.

He loved the city with a vision given to few men. Long before the news of the gold discovery he announced unequivocally that the little village sprawled along the shores of the bay was destined to become one of the greatest ports in the world. He built a large hotel, later called the City Hotel; men laughed at first and said the village could never support so large a hotel. But the laughter of men couldn't shake his confidence in the destiny of the city. He foresaw the day that fire would lay the wooden frame buildings of the city in ashes, so he built his hotel of adobe. He opened a general store stocked by the sailing ships that came at rare intervals through the Golden Gate. And, being a shrewd businessman, he opened a ship chandlery to equip departing ships.

Then, always looking into the future of the harbor, a harbor that would demand ships with the name of San Francisco on their helm, he became a shipbuilder. Facilities for shipbuilding were negligible, and he built a lumberyard to expedite his work. The handicaps in the Western outpost were still countless; progress was slow. So he went far afield to purchase his first steamer, a thirty-seven-foot side-wheeler which he planned to put on a regular run between San Francisco and General Sutter's fort at Sacramento. The ship was anchored at the northern port of Sitka. Leidesdorff bought it from its Russian owners, and, packed aboard a bark of the Russian American Fur Company, it was brought into San Francisco Bay.

The day was set for its first scheduled run between the bay and Sacramento. The entire community gathered at the wharf to celebrate. Some unkindly wit in the crowd bet that the tub would never be able to make Sacramento and said he would wager a side of bacon that he could walk the eighty-odd miles faster than Mr. Leidesdorff's steamer could make it. Bets were posted. The small ship tooted her whistle and backed from the wharf, and the walker started to walk. He walked the distance in three days. The sailing time of the steamer was six days and seven hours. But it took more than this to shake the pioneer spirit of William Leidesdorff, or to shake the confidence the citizens had in him, and the walker got his side of bacon.

On September 6, 1846, the local press made the statement that the people of Yerba Buena, though still few in number, and particularly deficient in the fair sex, seemed determined to enjoy life while they might. So on the evening of the sixth, a grand ball was given at the home of William Leidersdorff by the officers and men in the service of the United States, and by the citizens of the town. According to the press, upward of one hundred Californian and American ladies, and a large number of gentlemen were present to do honor to San Francisco's foremost citizen, William Alexander Leidesdorff. The dancing was very spirited and kept up until daylight. The grand ball was also given to honor Commodore Stockton of the United States Navy, and almost all the gentleman guests were newcomers, members of the Mormon Church who had arrived recently under the leadership of Mr. Sam Brannan.

The days of Leidesdorff, still a young man, were drawing to a close. The days of San Francisco's most sensational promoter, San Brannan, were dawning. The village was fast approaching the turn of the tide; overnight it would become the roaring bedlam of a metropolis. Leidesdorff was not to live to see the turn in the fortune of the city that he loved. He died in 1848. He was thirty-eight years old. He left no will, and his estate was involved. It was believed he was in debt to the sum of some sixty or seventy thousand dollars. But when the estate was probated, and his lands and holdings valued, he was found to have left more than a million dollars, almost all of which he had accumulated during his seven years in San Francisco.

He had lived a lonely life and he died a lonely man, even though surrounded by friends. His death was an occasion of deep sorrow. All business in the city closed its doors; all flags flew at half mast; all saloons, dance halls, and gambling halls were closed; guns in the Presidio were fired throughout the day at minute intervals; every man in San Francisco walked in the long funeral cortege, following the mulatto sea captain to his last resting place in the gardens of Mission Dolores. The day after his burial men walked sadly through the streets of the city he had helped build, shook their heads, and said a great man had gone from their midst. And then, as was ever the way, they entered their favorite grogshop and talked about the first whisperings of the discovery of gold, and William Alexander Leidesdorff was forgotten.

IV

Tom Maguire

This is the story of a man who came to San Francisco in 1849, unable to read or to write. He died in 1896, and as far as I know, he went to his grave still unable to read or to write. He personally presented twenty great productions of Shakespeare's *Hamlet* in San Francisco. He was the man who built the fame of the theater in San Francisco. He couldn't play a note of music nor carry a tune, and the one thing in the world that he loved more than drama was grand opera, and he was the first man to produce grand opera in San Francisco. He made a personal tour to Italy to visit Giuseppe Verdi— but he couldn't read or write. This is the story of Tom Maguire. To grant him dignity that he never desired and was seldom accorded, his name was Thomas Maguire, but Thomas was simply a formal title. His name was Tom Maguire and as Tom Maguire he was always known, even when he was a hack driver in New York City, and had only commenced to discover Shakespeare.

Yes, it was at his hack stand in Park Row in New York that Tom Maguire first became known. Actually nothing was or is known of him prior to the hack-driving days, not even the date of his birth. Not even he knew the date of his birth, but it is generally assumed that he was born about the

293

year 1820 of pure Irish parentage. The Park Row hack stand was close to the old Park Theatre.

When business was bad, or when the streets were heavy with snowdrifts or sleet, young Tom would climb to the gallery of the Park Theatre. There he was exposed to drama that ran the gamut from the popular society melodrama Fashion to Shakespeare. It didn't make much difference what the play was; he was as incurable a lover of the footlights as are some of us foolish mortals today. Just the smell of grease paint, the tarnished gold leaf on the proscenium arch, the tense moment before the first curtain parts (or in his day creaked to the bridge) were and are excitements unequaled by the adventure of real life.

There was infinitely more life and reality behind the candle footlights than was to be found driving a hack over the snow-covered cobblestones of New York, so Tom Maguire sold his horse and hack and became bartender in the gallery saloon of the Park Theatre. He tended bar there for a year, and then took over the ownership of one of the most famous saloons in New York's City Hall Place. Maguire's saloon became the meeting place of Tammany Hall politicians and the people of the theater. Then, when prosperity came his way and he was on the road to being a rich man, he sold his saloon, got married, and followed the cavalcade of gold-seeking adventurers to San Francisco.

Not much is known about Mrs. Maguire's early days; less is known than about Tom's beginning. Little Em—that was what she was called—was well known in the saloons and night life of New York's lower East Side. She was not beautiful. In fact, she was fairly ugly, but she had a rare asset, brains. She was shrewd, able, and wise, and the men who loved her loved her for her intelligence.

She was the very good friend, for a period, of a rough, undesirable East Side individual named Dick Donnell. One night in a Bowery saloon Dick and Tom Maguire fought over her. It was a beautiful fight, the kind of fight we are occasionally treated to in gangster movies, in which the contestants leap over tables, smash chairs, use their fists and their feet and their heads as battering rams. According to fragmentary history, the saloon was completely wrecked before the battle was ended and Tom Maguire emerged victor. He took Little Em to a friendly downtown New York priest and they were married. Mr. and Mrs. Maguire moved to San Francisco, where they lived in complete happiness until the death of Little Em some years later, but before she died she had helped Tom far on his road to fame, success, and fortune.

After Little Em had gone to her San Francisco grave Tom Maguire married again, and what his second wife may have lacked in Little Em's shrewd common sense, she made up in beauty. She was called one of the most beautiful, elegant, and graceful ladies in San Francisco.

The Maguires found the San Francisco of 1849 a place of mad confusion, a village of shacks and wooden frames and tents. Rents were exorbitant and vacancies rare. But a large, rambling frame building was located on Kearny Street near Washington, just about where the Hall of Justice now stands, and there Tom Maguire opened a large saloon and gambling hall. From the beginning he was successful, but there was something lacking, something that took the flavor out of the excitement of the mining camp. Tom missed the footlights, the grease paint, and the curtain. He was lonely for the old Park Theatre. Now, fortunately, there was a large, empty loft above Maguire's saloon and gambling hall, and it took a very short time for him to realize that the heterogeneous population of the village craved entertainment, craved theater just as much as he did. So in a short time he had converted the Kearny Street loft into an auditorium and hung out his first shingle—The Jenny Lind Theatre.

No, Jenny Lind never sang there. Jenny Lind, notwithstanding frequent legends to the contrary, never appeared in San Francisco nor in California. But hers was the most popular name in the show business, thanks to the genius of her press agent, P. T. Barnum, so Tom Maguire's hall became the Jenny Lind Theatre. From the day of its first opening it was successful financially, but fate had doomed it to tragedy. It played to full houses for a period, and then it burned to the ground.

The ashes were hardly cool before Maguire had begun to build a new theater on the site, the second Jenny Lind Theatre. This one was more imposing, more handsome, and more elegant than the first, but nine days after it was completed and the first gala performance had been given, it, too, burned to the ground. In all, the theaters that Tom Maguire built passed through five conflagrations. The third Jenny Lind was an imposing affair. In the middle of 1851 the *Herald* announced, "Mr. Thomas Maguire, so often burnt out and as often rising with energies unsubdued by misfortune, is now engaged in constructing a building which will be an ornament to the city." Three stories high, a skyscraper in the mining town, it was built of thick walls of brick with a façade of handsome white sandstone brought for the purpose from Sydney in the Antipodes.

The opening night was history-making. More than two thousand distinguished forty-niners crowded, stamping and cheering, into this, the most imposing theater in the West or, according to some historians, in the land. Mrs. Woodward, a favored thespian, appeared before the curtain and welcomed the audience in a long and handsome poem of greeting. The candlelights along the edge of the apron were lit, the curtain rose, and the third Jenny Lind made its debut to a hysterical and thrilled audience.

But fate continued to throw obstacles in the path of Tom Maguire's theatrical success. The year 1852 was a bad year in San Francisco. The Sydney Ducks had inspired the forming of Vigilance Societies. There were murders and arson and hangings, and nice people found it wise to keep off the streets after dark. The Jenny Lind suffered. It wasn't paying. Tom Maguire was financially embarrassed, so he sold his brick and sandstone to the city of San Francisco for two hundred thousand dollars to be used as the City Hall.

His next venture was perhaps his most famous. It was called San Francisco Hall, and the first San Francisco Minstrels appeared there. Later it became famous as Maguire's Opera House. And in Maguire's Opera House, managed by Junius Brutus Booth Jr., appeared the greatest name in all the hundred years of San Francisco theater history. On its boards Edwin Booth, a boy of twenty, played *Hamlet. Hamlet!* It was strange, the liking that the rough miners had for Shakespeare! And it was strange, the appreciation that Tom Maguire, who couldn't read or write, had for the plays of Shakespeare!

By 1858 Tom Maguire owned theaters in every town of the Mother Lode, all the important theaters in San Francisco, and in Sacramento, Stockton, and Marysville as well. The great names that played his boards are unfamiliar to most of the present generation, but to a few their magic is recalled. Edwin Forrest! John McCullough! Charles Kean! Dion Boucicault! Edwin Booth! Lawrence Barrett! Joseph

Jefferson in *Rip Van Winkle!* The great Madame Ristori, and years later the just as great Madame Modjeska! And, most sensational of all, Adah Isaacs Menken in her scandalous success *Mazeppa*.

Now Tom Maguire's great ambition was to bring grand opera to San Francisco, so in 1863 he built the Academy of Music at the corner of Pine and Montgomery Streets. Sometimes he gave grand opera on its stage, and sometimes it was used for prize fights or minstrel shows. He paid top performers as high as one hundred dollars a night, a fabulous amount in the sixties. He presented the city's darling, Lotta Crabtree. He scandalized the churches and the nice people by producing Dumas' wicked play *Camille*.

He produced every play of Shakespeare's, including the bad ones. He brought the shocking *Black Crook* to San Francisco, and because polite actresses would not appear in tights, he made up his chorus from denizens of the Barbary Coast. He had no office. What need was there for an office—he couldn't read or write. But every morning at eleven he stood on the sidewalk in front of his Opera House and transacted business. His hair was prematurely white. He was a tall, large man with snapping eyes, and he dressed in the extreme of fashion, his hair pomaded, his moustache beautifully waxed, his fingernails highly polished, and his fingers and shirt bosom sparkling with diamonds. He might have been something out of a side show, but everyone respected him and liked him. He was the city's great figure. In 1878 he went to Italy to hear opera in its native home. He had already imported Madame Parepa-Rosa, and critics said of her in later years that her voice was greater than that of Patti or Melba. She didn't walk across the stage. She was so huge, so fat, such a monstrosity of a woman, that she waddled. They said of her that she looked like a bean sack tied in the middle,

298

but her voice was glorious, and the audience forgot her appearance when she sang.

In Italy he achieved the great moment of his life when he met Verdi. Verdi spoke almost no English; Tom Maguire spoke no Italian or French, but in their love of music the two men made themselves understood.

Two years before he had gone to Italy, he went into partnership with Lucky Baldwin. Maguire owned the land at Market and Powell Streets where the Flood Building now stands. He induced Baldwin to build the Baldwin Hotel and Theatre on it, and they opened with the young lad, David Belasco, as stage manager.

Maguire had been in San Francisco for a quarter of a century. He had done more for the theater than any other man. His life was the theater. But now times were no longer so easy, competition was becoming great, the entertainment-starved miners had given way to a fashionable and sophisticated audience somewhat satiated by an endless parade of great talent, and the tide began to turn against Tom Maguire.

He was, however, to engage in one last great and spectacular undertaking, and it ended in disaster. On March 3, 1879, he opened the Grand Opera House on Mission Street with *The Passion Play* written by Salmi Morse. The spectacle was done in such solemn grandeur and with such sacred perfection that (and this I was told by an old radio actress who appeared as a child in that history-making production) the audience, impressed by the sacred perfection, dropped to their knees and prayed with the actors during some of the scenes. The Saviour was depicted by James O'Neill, father of Eugene. Then a committee called on Tom Maguire and told him he was doomed to eternal punishment for the blasphemy of having permitted the Saviour to be depicted on the stage. Death was one thing Tom Maguire would never allow to be

299

mentioned before him. He had an abiding fear of it. He closed the Opera House. Another committee of ministers of all denominations called on the Board of Supervisors and condemned the production as sacrilege. The supervisors passed an ordinance forbidding the presentation of any scriptural character on the stage of any theater. But, notwithstanding the threats, Tom Maguire had not fallen dead. The huge audiences were demanding that *The Passion Play* be continued. He reopened the Opera House on April 15 during Easter Week and at the final curtain of the re-opening performance the police marched in, arrested James O'Neill, released him on bail, and at a later date he and other members of the cast were tried and found guilty. They paid their fines and *The Passion Play* closed, ending Tom Maguire's most ambitious production.

That spelled final financial disaster for the great man of San Francisco's greatest theatrical days. For a time he approached small and unsuccessful ventures. For a time he managed the California Theatre, and on its boards trod some of the great actors who had appeared years before at his Maguire Opera House. Once more his superstitious fear of death rose to haunt him, for word came from New York that Salmi Morse, the author of *The Passion Play,* had gone there brokenhearted and taken his own life.

Disconsolate and discouraged, Tom Maguire trotted from office to office and angel to angel seeking some sympathetic soul, some man with imagination and love of the theater, who would help him recoup his fortunes, and let him once more be a part of that fascinating life of reality that was called "backstage." But angels were few and times were not as prosperous as they had been, and men forgot the good he had done and remembered the bad. His reputation as a great theatrical producer was discarded. His career as bartender, saloonkeeper, and gambling-hall promoter was recalled. He was reminded of the *Passion Play* fiasco. Lucky Baldwin broke partnership with him. The actors who had saluted him turned from him. He was an old man, still tall and handsome with his snow-white hair and his sparkling eyes, but he was old—a has-been!

Sometime in the early eighties Tom Maguire drifted back to New York, to that New York of the forties where he had driven his hack through snow and sleet, where he had climbed to the gallery of the Park Theatre first to see the dramas of Shakespeare, where he had established his famous saloon, and where he had met and fallen in love with his first wife, Little Em. Little Em was long since dead, and his friends of Park Row were gone. New York was a strange land, and the white-haired old man was a derelict, without anchor.

In 1886 a paragraph appeared in the *San Francisco Morning Call*. It read, "Mr. Tom Maguire has just moved into a magnificently furnished house on Thirty-third Street, New York. The California ex-manager is said to be the best-dressed man in the city." It was whispered that the paragraph had been sent to the *Morning Call* by Tom Maguire.

The true picture was far more dismal. Tom Maguire was down and out. He drifted along the streets of New York, a nuisance, an old pest, buttonholing any who would listen to him, telling of his days of glory and begging for financial backing so that he could again embark on a new career as a theatrical producer. He haunted theatrical clubs, haunted booking agencies, and finally, destitute, he was supported in his last years by the Actor's Fund. San Francisco has been called the greatest theatrical town in the land. Tom Maguire was its inspiration. He died friendless and forgotten in New York City in 1896.

301

V

Stephen J. Field

It was a paragraph in a book that first made me want to know more about the man. The paragraph reads:

First experiences in San Francisco. Upon landing from the steamer, my baggage consisted of two trunks, and I had only the sum of ten dollars in my pocket. I might, perhaps, have carried one trunk, but I could not manage two; so I was compelled to pay out seven of my ten dollars to have them taken to a room in an old adobe building on the west side of what is now known as Portsmouth Square. This room was about ten feet long by eight feet wide, and had a bed in it. For its occupation, the sum of thirty-five dollars a week was charged. Two of my fellow passengers and myself engaged it. They took the bed, and I took the floor. I do not think they had much the advantage on the score of comfort.

That paragraph was written by a man who was destined to become one of the greatest national figures California has ever produced; he landed in San Francisco on December 28, 1849; he died fifty years later, in 1899, and those fifty years brought him fame and honor accorded few men. His name was Stephen J. Field. Field? Stephen Field? That name seemed vaguely familiar. And then I remembered. I had read about him in a book called *All This and Heaven Too.*

302

He was one of the brothers of Cyrus W. Field, who laid the Atlantic cable.

All of the sons of the Connecticut Congregational minister, David Dudley Field, achieved fame in their own individual walks of life. There was Cyrus, who had labored for years with the fantastic notion that he could lay a cable under the water of the Atlantic Ocean, and by so doing bring about friendship and better understanding between Great Britain and the United States. He labored, and he succeeded. There was Henry, who, following in his father's footsteps, became a minister of the church. There was David Dudley Junior, who became one of America's most distinguished lawyers. And there was Stephen.

Stephen, at thirty-three, was at loose ends. He had been admitted to the bar; he had practiced law with his brother, David; he had gone to Europe, restless, always with the need of being on the go. On his return, the news of the discovery of gold flashed—flashed slowly, it's true, but flashed—across the world. That meant a new land, a new frontier to grow up with, the opportunity of being in on the development and building of a new world. That appealed to thirty-three-year-old Stephen. He sailed for San Francisco and arrived, as we have quoted from his memoirs, with ten dollars in his pocket. But that mattered little; the village was the doorway to the gold fields.

The early pages of his book read like a fairy tale. He tells his story simply, and with a nice sense of humor and of the ridiculous. He started out the day after his arrival with three dollars in his pocket. He went into a restaurant and ordered the cheapest breakfast he could get. It cost two dollars.

And so he faced a new life in an infant city with one

dollar and unbounded enthusiasm. He walked along the dusty streets of the village. It was a beautiful day—midwinter, but like an Indian-summer day in the East, only finer —blue skies above and the bay beyond.

There was something exhilarating and exciting in the atmosphere that made everybody cheerful and buoyant. The people he met all seemed to be in the highest spirits. Everyone who greeted him said, "It's a glorious country," or "Isn't it a glorious country?" or "Did you ever see a more glorious country?" In every case, Stephen says, the word "glorious" was sure to come out. The infection got into his blood, and before the morning was ended, with one dollar in his pocket and no employment, he found himself saying to everybody he met, "It is a glorious country."

He walked out to Happy Valley, between Mission and Howard Streets. The streets, he says, were filled with people from every nation under heaven, all wearing their peculiar costumes. Everybody was friendly; everybody was interesting; everything was exciting! But all he had in the world was one dollar; one dollar and some chamois skins he had purchased in New York at a dollar apiece, in which he had wrapped his stationery; rather expensive wrapping, but it was suggested that he might sell the skins when he reached California. Chamois skins were in demand to make bags for gold dust.

A dozen chamois skins! They had cost him ten dollars for the lot, and a short time after his arrival in California he sold them for an ounce of gold apiece. An ounce of gold was worth from sixteen to twenty dollars—a nice profit in any man's business. But that was to come later. He had to have immediate cash. All the West was hungry for news of the Eastern coast and Stephen had a bundle of sixty-four New

York newspapers. An acquaintance sold them for a dollar apiece, and Field received one-half of the proceeds. He had thirty-two dollars with which to conquer the West. He had been an attorney in the East; logically, he turned to the courthouse. He saw acquaintances with whom he had traveled west summoned for jury duty at a premium of eight dollars for their services. He took up a position close to the sheriff and smiled in a friendly way. The sheriff was a personage; he had no time for the smiles of youthful strangers. Field nodded to him with a "haven't we met somewhere" expression. The sheriff frowned and ignored the nod. Apparently there was no justice for a hungry man in a court of justice. Field slunk out of the courtroom and walked down the street. He saw a sign hanging in front of a shack—"Jonathan D. Stevenson, Gold Dust Bought and Sold Here." Jonathan D. Stevenson!

Colonel J. D. Stevenson had come West at the head of the famous New York Volunteers to put down Indian uprisings. He had made money in San Francisco and had become a comparatively rich man, but some years earlier he had borrowed between three and four hundred dollars from Stephen's brother, David Dudley. Stephen had the note, signed by Stevenson, in his pocket. He entered the shack. Colonel Stevenson recognized him and greeted him cordially and he told young Field that California was a glorious country. "A very glorious country," he said, "for I have made two hundred thousand dollars." Field gasped.

Frankly, it was more than I could stand. I had already shaken hands with Stevenson but now I shook hands with him a second time. I shook his hand vigorously. I shook it a third time and we talked about the glorious country. And then I pulled out the note and handed it to him.

305

The Colonel turned pale; his face was a mixture of surprise and disgust. He examined the note and acknowledged that it bore his signature. Then, with a sigh, he counted out the full value of the note with accrued interest and handed Stephen Field four hundred and forty dollars in Spanish doubloons.

With cash in his pocket, Field went out to establish himself in the business of law. He found a room in a building at the corner of Clay and Montgomery Streets, paid one month's rent in advance—three hundred dollars—and sat down and waited for business. In the first two weeks one client appeared, a gentleman who wanted a deed drawn. Field asked sixteen dollars for his services, but the client objected that that was too much, so they compromised on eight dollars.

Of course, he could sit and wait for more business, but he was too impatient. San Francisco was too exciting with the streets, the gambling palaces, the saloons, and the noisy hallways of the lodging houses teeming with miners returning from the hills, their pockets stuffed with gold dust. He wandered the streets night and day. One day, in the business office of a mercantile firm by the name of Simmons, Hutchinson and Company, one of the partners told him of a new town they were developing at the junction of the Sacramento and Feather Rivers. They offered to sell Field lots in the new town. He said he had no money. They said that didn't matter; they would be glad to trust him; they wanted to sell lots to boom the town and they were positive Field would soon be a rich man. As a matter of fact, their own steamer was leaving for Sacramento the next day. They would give Mr. Field free passage to Sacramento which, they said, was quite close to the new town of Vernon.

The next morning Stephen Field set out for Sacramento. He arrived there on January 13, 1850. Great floods had overflowed the banks of the river, and the town of Sacramento was under water. Field obtained a rowboat and rowed from the steamer to the hotel. There he met a great crowd of people all enthusiastic about California. They all agreed that it was a glorious country. The next day, with a boatload of cheering, excited men, he started out on another overcrowded steamer for Vernon. They steamed along, and suddenly the boat jolted to a stop. There, in the middle of the vast lake of flood waters, stood a house. "That," said the captain of the steamer, "is Vernon."

It didn't look like a good place to establish a law office, so Field stayed on the steamer until they reached a landing called Nye's Ranch. Close to a thousand men were gathered at Nye's Ranch, studying the map of another new town to be called Yubaville. A man stood behind the map, shouting, "Gentlemen, put your names down, all of you who want lots."

Stephen Field had twenty dollars remaining from the money paid him by Colonel Stevenson. He signed up for sixty-five lots, agreeing to pay $16,250 for them. He caused a sensation. The crowd was sure he was a young Eastern millionaire, and they fought to buy lots adjoining his. The town of Yubaville was born.

A few days later, on January 18, 1850, the town government was established, and it was decided to elect a town council and an alcalde. Field said, "I modestly whispered to different people at the meeting that my name had been mentioned by friends. for the office of alcalde." He was nominated, and found an opponent with odds in his favor, for Field had only been there three days, and the opponent had been a resident for six days. The fight was a stiff one, but Field won by nine votes.

That night the population met in the Adobe House in Yubaville. That was not its name at the time; it had none. Naturally, the newly organized town had to have a name, and the matter was thrown open to discussion. The district was called Yubanville, so Yubaville was suggested as the name of the new city; someone else suggested Yubafield, both names being inspired by the Yuba River that ran past its door. But finally an elderly gentleman arose. "There is," he said, "an American lady in the community. She is Mrs. Covillaud, a survivor of the tragic Donner Party. Her first name is Mary; let us name our new city in her honor, and call it Marysville."

So young Stephen J. Field took up his duties as the first alcalde of the newly born city of Marysville. That day marked the beginning of the career of one of America's truly great men. He had been in California exactly three weeks to the day. He was to live for another fifty years, and his duties would take him back and forth across the nation; he was to establish residence in Eastern cities, but to the end of his life he called California home and loved San Francisco and the towns of Northern California more than any of the other places in the world.

The office of alcalde combined the duties of mayor, counsel, and judge, and in the very beginning Field won a reputation as a fearless and wise judge and as a shrewd businessman. Within ninety days after his arrival in Marysville, the lots for which he had signed had increased in value tenfold. He was a rich man.

Stephen J. Field was a fearless man, an upright and unshakable man. It was an enviable reputation, but fearless men make enemies, and Field made enemies. A district judge came to Marysville, and while under the influence of liquor he reviled Field. When the young lawyer-alcalde turned on the judge, that worthy gentleman ordered Field disbarred. Field took his case to the state Supreme Court, and was exonerated. Men began to talk, up and down the state, about this fearless young son of a minister who was dispensing justice and running the town of Marysville with a strong hand. He won a seat in the state legislature. Still practicing law, he pleaded sixty cases before the California Supreme Court and won forty-one of them. He had enemies, but every man trusted him. His judgment was unshakable. Even his enemies respected him, and their respect was seasoned with fear for the hard-headed, stubborn, clear-thinking alcalde. Alcalde! And then, in 1857, eight years after his arrival in California, he was elected to the bench of the Supreme Court of California. His private practice had brought him forty-two thousand dollars a year, and he gave it up to be a judge on the Supreme Court bench at a salary of six thousand dollars. Then his name became nationally known; the fame of the cases on which he had rendered decisions made history. He became a fighter, a leading fighter to save California for the Union during the Civil War. And on a day in December of 1863, Stephen Field was called to the bench of the Supreme Court of the United States by Abraham Lincoln.

Old photographs are interesting things, and I have had in my hands this past week two photographs of Stephen J. Field, Supreme Court Justice. The first one was made the day he became a member of the Supreme Court. He is a strong-faced, black-haired, black-eyed young man, standing very straight, and his black beard and black moustache cannot hide the strength of his jaw. That picture was made in 1863. The second photograph was made in the late eighties. Stephen J. Field is now a regal old man with full white beard, long white hair, a handsome, strong face, and he is still a Justice of the Supreme Court of the United States. He held that position until 1897 when, under President William McKinley, he resigned. He had been a member of the Supreme Court for thirty-four years—longer than any other man in history.

Those thirty-four years had seen great and fearless fights, and unshakable, unswervable Stephen Field gave his decisions and would not reverse them. Men said he was honest; yes, he was honest to a fault. He was honest with himself too, and there was only one right and one wrong. He could see no middle of the road.

He became old, a very old man. He would sit on the bench, his eyes closed, and sometimes the distinguished gentlemen of the court wondered if he were asleep during the reading of a lengthy appeal. Judge Field gave no sign of having heard, and he sat with his eyes closed, his head foreward on his chest, his chin pressed to his breast. The colleague would read slowly and falteringly, and Judge Field gave no sign of hearing. But suddenly, in the middle of the reading, he would raise his hand. "Read that again," he would command in a ringing voice. The passage was read again. "That is not good law," would cry Stephen Field. And with his eyes glaring, he delivered a forceful and lengthy argument that swept his colleagues to their feet in excited approval. When he finished his argument, he closed his eyes, and his chin settled again to his breast.

Judge Stephen J. Field of San Francisco died on April 9, 1899. He was a great Californian—a great American.

VI

Catharine Hayes

Recently I went up to Columbia, in the Mother Lode Country, to witness the celebration that made that fascinating town of the Southern Mines a part of the California State Park System.

There were parades; there were ceremonies and speeches; there was an old-time dance to the music of hoe-down fiddles; there was a barbecue under the trees at the very spot where the first gold in Columbia was found ninety-five years ago. And there was a restaurant in near-by Sonora where the only items on the menu were T-bone steak, rib steak, lamb chops, veal porterhouse, and roast pork.

But to me, the real fascination of Columbia was late at night, the night before the festivities commenced. The town was a quiet, sleepy street of brick buildings, buildings that had stood for more than ninety years. Old-timers were sitting on benches in front of the buildings, just sitting there, living in the past—living in the days of '49 and '50! They weren't dressed up for a celebration. The women wore the simple cotton and gingham dresses they might have worn in the days when Columbia was the second biggest city in California. The men wore beards and moustaches. The sheriff wore a gun at his hip. The only lights in the buildings were those in saloons, and one in the church up on the hill. We had erased almost a century and were living in yesterday.

I sat at a small table, a glass of refreshment in my hand, and a Columbian joined me. He was an elderly gentleman with a twinkle in his eye. He wore trousers tucked in his boots, a flannel shirt, flowing moustache and chin whiskers, and the longest eyebrows I've ever seen. He told me his name but I'm not going to tell it to you. It might have been Murphy, or O'Flaherty, or Casey. He told me stories of Columbia; he sang songs of the mining days.

"Oh, yes," he said, "I've listened to that radio show of yours Sunday mornings. Radio's a wonderful thing. I listen to it and I don't believe I'm hearing what I'm hearing. It's a great age we're living in. Now, I remember that one morning you told the story of that Italian opera singer—Biscuit-somebody or other."

"Biscaccianti," I said.

"That's the one," he said. "Well, I've heard about her and like as not she was a fine singer, but not as fine as Kitty."

Sensing a story, I asked, "Who is Kitty?"

He replied, "Are you telling me you've never heard of Kitty? Kitty Hayes, the greatest singer I've ever heard in all my life, and I've heard almost all of them right down to the time I went down to San Francisco to hear Tetrazzini. But none of them could hold a feather to the 'Swan of Erin.'"

The Swan of Erin! What a magic name! I settled down, afraid to break the spell. The old-timer filled his pipe and stuffed the tobacco down with his thumb. I offered him a cigarette lighter, and he scorned it. He made a twist of paper and reached over and lit it at the oil lamp. Then he lit his pipe and puffed, and this was his story:

Kate Hayes was the prettiest, the daintiest, the sweetest

312

bit of an Irish colleen I've ever had the good fortune to see. When she sang in Columbia, there wasn't a man in the town who wouldn't have lain down in the roadway and let her walk on him. But she wouldn't have done it—not Kitty! She was too gentle and fine.

It was on the twentieth of November in 1850 that the steamer *Oregon* docked at San Francisco. As always on steamer day, the entire population was at the water front to see the ship come in, and to get letters from home and news of the outside world. And the *Oregon* brought important news this trip. The great statesman, Daniel Webster, had died. His loss was a tragedy, and because he was so great a man, San Francisco could talk about nothing else. The San Francisco newspapers rushed to press with long eulogies of the great man, quotations from his speeches, and sketches of his life.

It was all so very important that nobody had time to pay any attention to the beautiful Irish girl standing at the rail, thrilled, and terribly frightened by the scene of the wild city that sprawled at her feet.

Rain was pouring in torrents. The wind howled down from Telegraph Hill. Horses and men splashed in the mud down there below. With the rain whipping her face she stared aghast, at the mighty city. There were no lights save the dripping oil lamps on the dock, reflecting their glare in the faces of the massed humanity, the strangest humanity she'd ever seen. There was not a face that she knew, not a friend in the excited crowd. What was worse, there was not a man who had ever heard of her, Catharine Hayes, the tall, beautiful, blonde girl with the voice that trilled like a bird. Later they'd call her the Swan of Erin! And they'd call her the Irish Linnet! But now, with no reputation of importance

313

as a singer when she had sung in the East, here she was in the wildest, wettest, maddest town on earth, and no one had ever heard of her. She turned to her manager, Mr. Bushnell. The tears in her eyes mingled with the rain that had splashed her face, and Bushnell laughed.

He was a disciple of P. T. Barnum who, just a couple of years before, had brought Jenny Lind to America. What Barnum could do for Jenny Lind, he, W. A. Bushnell, could do for Kate Hayes—and more. He'd have these gamblers and miners and adventurers and yokels at her feet before you could say "General Tom Thumb." Just give him time!

The next day Catharine sat in the window of the wooden hotel on Dupont Street and watched the torrents of rain make a lake of mud below her. The Oriental Hotel wasn't much of a hotel; the best that could be said of it was that it gave shelter from the rain and the mud. San Francisco was the most dismal city in the world. She turned to Bushnell for sympathy, and he growled. That was the trouble with W. A. Bushnell. He always growled at her. He never seemed to realize that she was a woman, that she was a beautiful tall blonde girl with a lovely complexion and blue eyes that were like the sky on a spring day. No, all he cared about was her bird-like voice; all he thought about was the day she'd be acclaimed as a great singer. And Kate was willing never to sing another note if only he'd at least give some sign that he knew she was alive. But no! Bushnell growled and smoked his large cigar, crossed the room and stood next to her and looked out of the window. She held out her hand to him; he ignored it. He just looked, and suddenly he began to laugh; he had a great, infectious laugh.

He laughed, and looked across the street to the engine house of the volunteer fire company, California Four. They

314

were gathered around the engine, laughing, unaware that they were being watched. Bushnell clapped his high, tan felt hat on his head, filled his pockets with cigars, and strode from the room.

A few minutes later he was leaning against the engine, laughing with them. He pointed to the window where Kate sat. They looked up, swept off their fire helmets, and bowed low. Then W. A. Bushnell, the disciple of P. T. Barnum, went to work.

It was a tradition that whenever an important artist came to town a box would be raffled to the highest bidder. He told the firemen about the forthcoming concert and told them, strictly on the quiet, that their rivals, the Empire Engine Company Number One, had sworn to have the box at any price. Having planted the seed of rivalry, he went to the Empire Engine Company Number One and told them the same story, swearing that the California Four were vowed they'd have the box at any price, and the Empire Engine Company saw red.

It took about an hour for the story to spread around San Francisco! The rivalry of the fire companies was the most important sport in the city. Everyone came to the auction. The bidding started at a hundred dollars, went up by fifties and then by hundreds until the box was knocked down to Captain George W. Green of the Empire Company for $1,125. And to this he added the purchase of dress-circle seats at three hundred dollars apiece. Well a singer who could demand such prices must be great indeed. The rush was on for tickets. Nothing else was talked about! The whole community was on its toes, waiting for the first appearance of Miss Catharine Hayes, billed as the famous Irish soprano. In the Oriental Hotel, W. A. Bushnell sat and laughed, and Kitty Hayes sat, the most frightened young girl in the world.

The night of the concert arrived, and I'll never forget that night as long as I live. At half past seven the Empire Engine Company in full uniform marched to the theater led by a brass band. They marched down the aisle and led their invited guests to the box they had won. Among their guests were the governor of California, and the chief of the Volunteer Fire Department. Then the company filed into the dress-circle seats for which they had paid three hundred dollars apiece. The curtain went up and Kate appeared. She was so much more beautiful than they had expected that instead of the cheers they had planned, they sat in awed silence. There wasn't a whisper in the theater, which was crowded to the doors. Then Kate began to sing. She sang a simple Irish song, and there wasn't a dry eye in the house. But it was when she sang "The Irish Immigrant's Lament" that the storm broke. The audience climbed on their seats and cheered—threw their hats in the air and cheered. Masses of bouquets of flowers were heaped on the stage around the girl's feet. She sang and sang. She sang a Gaelic song called "Savourneen Deelish." She sang "Comin' Through the Rye" and the audience sang with her. She sang a brand-new song they'd never heard called "Kathleen Mavourneen"—and they went mad. They wouldn't let her stop. The moment she came to the end of a song, up they sprang, roaring for more. And all the time, good-looking Mr. W. A. Bushnell stood in the rear of the theater, puffed on his large cigar, and grinned.

The curtain never fell on that performance of Catharine Hayes. When she was so unnerved with the emotion of her ovation that she could sing no more, the men lifted her off the stage and carried her to her carriage. The parade started

316

to the Oriental Hotel, with the men of the Empire Engine Company Number One marching before and behind the carriage. Torches flamed, flags waved, and the brass band play.ed. They mobbed before the hotel and cheered and cheered until Mr. Bushnell appeared and told them they'd really have to let Miss Kitty sleep if they wanted her to sing for them again.

That night was the beginning. Kate Hayes became the adopted daughter of the city. Everyone went to her concerts. The ladies stripped the stores of satins and laces and finery for the concerts. Men who had never before worn anything but flannel shirts and jeans appeared in shirts with ruffles and fancy waistcoats, and with diamonds in their shirts. Night by night the enthusiasm increased. She would sing, and with the bouquets flung to her would be tossed fifty-dollar gold slugs. One night, down from the parquet to the stage was thrown a huge bouquet, and attached to it was a jewel of great worth. A voice shouted: "This is for you, Kate, from Calaveras County."

Gifts came from fraternal organizations. She gave a benefit concert for the Fireman's Charity Fund, and started a fund that eventually, when the volunteer fire companies disbanded, amounted to more than a hundred thousand dollars.

Kate Hayes had arrived—and she was happy. She had triumphed beyond her wildest dreams. She was famous, and she was adored. The only fly in the ointment, to her, was that everybody adored her—she had scores of proposals of marriage—everybody worshipped her, everybody but her manager, W. A. Bushnell, and he was just the growling businessman, refusing to see the girl behind the singer.

Bushnell was not one to rest on his laurels. He had put over Kate Hayes; she was a sensation as a concert singer. But now she had to go further. He announced that she would appear in scenes from operas, costumed for the parts she played. There had been no operas in the mining camp city. This was the high spot of her triumphs. The city literally went mad, to such an extent that indignant opera lovers wrote indignant letters saying the noise and the cheering were so constant that they couldn't hear the songs.

But when San Francisco wants to cheer, it cheers; it's a good or bad habit it has never gotten over. So they cheered and continued to cheer. A grand ball was given in her honor. She went into the Southern Mines and from town to town singing, and triumph heaped on triumph. She returned to the city and could spend no money; everything was free to her. When the time came for her to sail away to South America, the steamship company handed her free passage.

The time for sailing came. Kate Hayes gave her one last concert, and sang as she had never sung before; and as they had done at her first concert, the adoring mob carried her to her hotel, led by flaming torches and a brass band and all the fire companies. The throngs stood below her window and shouted and cheered. She sang "Kathleen Mavourneen," and then made a speech of thanks that they never forgot. When she sailed away all the city gathered at the dock and wept to see her go.

"And," said my old friend in Columbia, "I'll never forget her to my dying day."

That's the story. But I began thinking about my friend in Columbia. Kate Hayes sang in 1855. If he had heard her when he was one year old he'd have to be ninety-two years old! It's doubtful if he heard her at the age of one or would have remembered her if he had! As a matter of fact, he had never heard her or seen her; I don't think he was more than seventy years old. But Kate Hayes was so much a beloved tradition in San Francisco, with her name on everyone's lips for so many years after she had sung here, that eventually almost everyone believed he had heard and known her. Everything else he told me about her was true, and I honestly believe he thought he was telling the truth when he said he'd never forget her or her singing as long as he lived.

There's just one more brief detail in the story of Kate Hayes, and this my friend in Columbia didn't tell me; I found it in an old San Francisco record. It was dated September 1857, and it said: "Some time this month Miss Catharine Hayes married her manager, Mr. W. A. Bushnell."

VII

Charles and Bella Cora

Good men and bad men made the early history of San Francisco, and the standards of the mining-camp days were so confused that it was a matter of personal opinion as to which man was bad and which was good. A man could be a professional gambler and be highly regarded as a leading citizen. But if a man could not hold his liquor, then he was probably labeled bad. A man could draw a six-shooter and put a bullet through an enemy's head and win the approval of the community. But a man who stole a horse was the lowest order of creature, and when caught was hanged without trial. Of course, when it came to women, the problem was much simpler. In those days a woman was either good or bad, and there was no middle path.

This is the story of the man who was responsible for the most dramatic episode in San Francisco's early history, and even to this day men are in disagreement as to whether he was good or bad. He was a professional gambler, but an honest gambler. He murdered a man, but many will tell you the murdered man invited and deserved his fate. He, the murderer, was popular and he had a host of friends. In short, he had most of the virtues of a good man, and few of the faults of a bad man, according to the standards of the fifties.

320

So much for the man. As for the woman in the story, according to the standards of that day, there was no question of doubt; she was bad. The man was Charles Cora and the woman, Bella Cora.

On the night of Thursday, November 15, 1855, all of San Francisco society able to obtain tickets was at the New American Theatre. The edifice itself was the first imposing palace of dramatic art to be built in the West; it was a place of white pillars and gold. It had an ornate and exciting oval dome with a revolving golden sun; it had crystal chandeliers with hundreds of pendants that caught the light of scores of oil lamps; it had great velvet draperies falling from the top of the proscenium boxes, held in place by the beaks of golden eagles. It had a large orchestra pit, holding the lower-priced seats. The expensive and fashionable seats were in the first balcony. At the rear of the orchestra were boxes draped in velvet and reserved for women not considered ladies. Society flocked to the balcony.

The night of November 15, 1855, was a special occasion at the New American Theatre. The amazing Ravels, called the greatest artists of pantomime in the world, were producing a new drama without words—*Nicodemus, or The Unfortunate Fisherman.* Every seat was taken. In the front of the first balcony, with his wife and a lady friend, sat United States Marshal General William H. Richardson. Now, during the intermission, Mrs. Richardson and her friend were annoyed by the persistent rudeness of a man in the orchestra pit who was apparently staring at them. General Richardson promptly investigated and found that the staring was not directed at his party, but at the woman seated behind them—Bella Cora.

Marshal Richardson was enraged. How dared the management permit that woman to sit in the first balcony in the presence of the respected women of the community. The boxes behind the orchestra pit were reserved for such people. He left his seat and stormed downstairs to the box office to demand that the Cora woman be ejected. He argued loud and argued long and the audience paid more attention to the argument than to the pantomime of the Ravels. But the argument availed him nothing. Bella Cora had paid for her seat in the first balcony, and the management would not put her out. Furious, William Richardson returned to his place at the side of his wife, and the audience chuckled. Charles and Bella Cora, seated immediately behind him, chuckled quietly.

The next day Cora, walking down Montgomery Street, passed Marshal Richardson. Cora was a quiet man at heart, disliking an argument, but Richardson's insult rankled. After all, Bella Cora was the daughter of a Southern clergyman, and socially, in their estimation—and in fact in every way—as good as Mrs. Richardson. So, as Charles Cora passed Richardson, he chuckled and flung a stinging phrase at the Marshal.

Fate, or more probably circumstance, brought the two men together again that night, the circumstance being that most San Franciscans of the fifties sought relaxation at the same places. Cora was sitting in the Cosmopolitan Saloon playing backgammon with his friend, Dr. Mills. Richardson entered, went to the bar, and ordered a bottle of champagne. Mills, Cora's friend, hoping to patch up an ugly situation, introduced Cora to Richardson. The two men shook hands, and the Marshal invited Cora to have a drink with him. Having disposed of the bottle the two walked to the street, apparently good friends. But as they reached the sidewalk Richardson, under the influence of liquor, made a disparaging remark, and Cora retorted with the same stinging phrase he had flung that afternoon. Whereupon Richardson announced that he was going to slap Cora's face. Turning from him, Cora reentered the saloon, and the Marshal, following him, announced to all present, "I promised to slap this man's face and I had better do it now." Friends intervened, the two men were led apart, and went their separate ways.

But the following morning William Richardson, rankling under Cora's insult and realizing that even his own friends were laughing at him, walked down Montgomery in search of Cora. His quest led him from gambling hall to gambling hall and from saloon to saloon. By four o'clock in the afternoon, heavily under the influence of alcohol, he told all who would listen to him that he was going to have revenge, and that Charles Cora would pay for his folly. Then the Marshal went along Kearney Street, turned down Clay Street, and met Cora walking with a friend named Ragsdale. Before Richardson could speak, Cora thrust out his hand in greeting. They shook hands; they were reconciled. Enmity was put aside, revenge forgotten, and Cora, Richardson, and Ragsdale entered the Hayes' Saloon to seal their friendship at the bar. Later the three men went to the Cosmopolitan for further libations. An hour or so later, between the hours of six and seven, Charles Cora was standing in the Blue Wing Saloon when an acquaintance brought him word that a friend was waiting to speak to him outside. Cora went out and did not return. Later, some friends went to investigate his absence and found a milling mob of San Franciscans surging along the street. United States Marshal General William Richardson had been shot. He was dead, and Charles Cora was under arrest for his murder.

That night the famous fire bell of the Big Six Engine

House rang out a message that had not been heard in San Francisco since the march of the first Vigilantes in 1851. Out into the street poured the population to gather, shouting and shrieking, in front of the Oriental Hotel. Before them appeared the firebrand, Sam Brannan, the most famous man in the city. He flung an impassioned speech at the crowd, demanding that lynch law should take over to make up for the failure of the law of order. Civic authorities arrested Brannan. He immediately posted bail and was released, to return to the crowd before the hotel to make another fiery speech. A guard of fifty men was thrown around the jail where Cora was held.

A seething, revenge-mad crowd moved like a restless wave, flooding the street from the jail to the Marshal's office in the Merchant's Exchange Building where Richardson's body lay.

A coroner's jury hurriedly found that William H. Richardson came to his death by a pistol shot "fired by the hand of one Charles Cora." Later, evidence was produced to show that the jury rendered the verdict fearing the wrath of the Vigilantes, that Richardson had actually attacked Cora, leveling two guns at him, and that Cora had knocked both weapons from Richardson's hands and fired in self-defense. But no living man knows which story was true.

Then Bella Cora came into the picture. She went to the city's foremost criminal lawyer and great orator, Colonel D. D. Baker. Baker demanded thirty thousand dollars to handle the case. Bella handed him fifteen thousand dollars in gold as a down payment. Then the rage of the city turned against Baker. He tried to return the money to Bella Cora, but she refused to accept it, and finally talked the attorney into defending the man she loved. Cora was tried, and the jury could not agree. After four ballots the vote stood eight for murder, four for manslaughter. The jury was dismissed and a new trial was set for May of 1856. But by now public opinion had swerved, and it was generally assumed that Charles Cora would be acquitted.

Then a strange new element came into the story of Cora and the story of San Francisco. The agitation over California's seceding with the South or remaining with the Union flared to fever heat. Followers of Judge Terry favored the South, and among Terry's followers was a young firebrand editor, James Casey. On the other side, fearlessly editing the *Daily Evening Bulletin,* was James King of William. Casey had a jail record, had been an inmate of Sing Sing for eighteen months. King condemned Casey in an editorial, and that same afternoon, May 14, 1856, as James Casey walked up to him, he flung aside a short cloak that hung from his shoulders, pressed a pistol at King's heart, and fired.

The shot that felled James King of William was the signal. The city went mad. Tens of thousands of infuriated San Franciscans marched the streets, shouting for justice, and shrieking for lynch law. A battalion of cavalry rode through the streets vainly trying to break up the mobs. The mayor, Van Ness, appeared before the jail to plead that San Francisco let the law mete out justice, and the crowd roared him down. The Vigilance Committee seized the council chambers of the City Hall, and citizens who refused to join the Vigilantes were threatened with boycott.

Sheriff David Scannell issued an appeal for citizens to help him enforce the law, and he found few supporters. The blood-mad San Franciscans were roaring for the murderers, Cora and Casey. In forty-eight hours, twenty-six hundred citizens had joined the Vigilantes. They were organized into companies of one hundred, and armed with shotguns, knives, pistols, muskets, and brass cannon. San Francisco was an armed camp at war. For two days and two nights the uproar maintained, and then an ominous silence closed about the city streets, for James King of William lay dying. On Sunday the eighteenth, the headquarters issued a command for all Vigilantes to stand by for orders. At ten o'clock in the morning a hundred armed men moved toward the jail. And an hour later the brass cannon was dragged along Sansome Street and planted defiantly before the jail door.

For three solid hours, troop after troop of a hundred men marched, marched silently. There was the dull reverberation of marching feet and not a word was uttered. Along Broadway the companies stood in triple line, solidly packing the street from Kearny to Montgomery, and then the leaders demanded that first Casey, then Cora be surrendered to them. David Scannell and his officers of the law, powerless, obeyed.

James King of William died early Tuesday afternoon, and the city went into deep mourning. All stores were heavily draped in black. All saloons, all gambling halls, all public places were closed. Every building flew a flag at half-mast. Men moved through the streets with mourning bands on their arms. Throughout the silent, terrible afternoon, bells constantly tolled the death knell.

Charles Cora and James Casey were taken to a building bounded by California, Sacramento, Front, and Davis Streets. Along the main front, on Sacramento Street, gunny bags filled with sand were piled to a height of five feet. At each end of the barricade of sandbags stood a brass cannon. This was Fort Gunnybags! The word went out that as James King's funeral cortege left the Unitarian Church on Stockton Street for its long journey, Cora and Casey would die.

326

The day was Thursday. The silent, constantly shifting throngs moved before the church. The only sound heard was that of carpenters' hammers building an ominous framework. And just as the funeral cortege began to form, a hack came racing at breakneck speed down Sacramento Street and stopped short in front of Fort Gunnybags. Out of it, head held high, her face heavily veiled, stepped Bella Cora. She brushed past the guards at the door as though they were not there. Past the leveled bayonets and muskets and into the crowded star chamber she rushed, where she demanded to be taken to Cora's cell. Dead silence greeted her—dead silence save for the sound of the hammers building the scaffolds. Then someone did speak and asked her what she wanted. She answered that if Charles Cora, whom she loved, was to die branded as a murderer, then she would go through life wearing the murderer's name. They took her to Cora's cell. Father Accolti was seated with the condemned man, and the two were praying. Father Accolti arose and greeted her, and she repeated her demand. At twelve-thirty, with their hands joined, the priest made Charles and Bella Cora man and wife.

That was twelve-thirty. Charles and Bella Cora stood together silently and waited. Twelve forty-five! Two platforms were thrust through the windows of Fort Gunnybags. One o'clock! Then the silence was broken by the solemn and fearsome tolling of bells. The funeral services for James King of William were ended. Pallbearers carried his body to the waiting hearse. Then men came to lead Cora away. Bella clung to him, sobbing, and then stood aside, her eyes closed. And at twenty-one minutes past one, Charles Cora and James Casey were dead.

Bella Cora returned to that ornate mansion in Pike Street —that Charles Cora had built for her. Then the good ladies of the community arose in righteous wrath. They demanded that she be driven out of San Francisco. They wrote impassioned letters to the leaders of the Vigilantes demanding that the work of the committee would not be finished until she had been driven from the city. But, strangely enough, the Vigilantes of 1856 felt their task was ended.

To the end of her days Bella Cora remained in that house. She lived alone, save for her servants, and saw no one. She always dressed in deep and heavy mourning, and she spoke of herself only as the widow of Charles Cora.

She appeared in public only to attend the services regularly at St. Francis' Church. And little by little over the years, the good ladies who had scorned and reviled her began to respect her. Charles Cora had been a rich man, so his widow was wealthy. And she spent her wealth, all of it, giving generously to charities and worthy causes. Oh, there were skeptics; there were those who said, "She's giving now to assure her own forgiveness and salvation." But other stories began to circulate. They said that Bella Cora had always lived for others, and that she had always shared her wealth in her happier days more generously than any other good woman of San Francisco. Legends spread about her with the passing of a brief few years. San Franciscans, men and women, now spoke of her as that poor, gentle, kind soul—the widow of Charles Cora. If her years had been longer, she might have become one of the great women of the city, for San Francisco created great men and women out of all kinds of material.

Bella Cora died just six years after the funeral procession of James King of William had traveled its long journey to Lone Mountain. She was laid in Calvary Cemetery at the side of her husband, Charles Cora.

VIII

Madame Anna Bishop

On February 11, 1854, an event of major importance occurred in San Francisco, an event that brought the populace thronging into the streets to exclaim, "Ah!" and "Oh, how beautiful!" It was on that night that the city was first lighted with coal gas. Now the bringing of light to San Francisco is only incidental to our story, but having mentioned it, let us spend a minute thinking what that meant before we go on to our major theme. Gas lighting was a new thing, a daring innovation. Eastern cities had experimented with it, but the fathers and grandfathers of the average American had used candles and coal-oil lamps, and what was good enough for grandpa was good enough for them. Of course, it was rather hazardous to be abroad on the streets of San Francisco after dark. It was more than a possibility, it was a probability that you would be hit over the head and relieved of your bag of gold dust before you'd walked a hundred yards. So gaslamps brought a feeling of security to the night traveler. But, to say the least, it was a stunt—one of those modern innovations destined to be a fad for a few months. Then everybody would go back to candles and lamps, and stay off the streets at night. At a banquet that night tendered by the San Francisco Gas Company, its president, J. Mora Moss, said, "Considering that

329

the interest rate of money is thirty-six percent per annum and that coal gas is only fifteen dollars a thousand feet, San Francisco is being given a bargain."

One of the first places in the city to be lighted with coal gas was the new and beautiful Metropolitan Theatre, and that brings us to our major theme. San Francisco's love of the theater is a tradition. Even to this day we, of San Francisco, aggravate the populations of other communities by stating that San Francisco has always been the greatest theater town in the land. After all, why shouldn't we tell the truth? But in 1854, or the dawn of 1854, with a citizenry hungry, frankly starving for entertainment, the few fly-by-night theaters were inadequate to care for the city's needs. So the Metropolitan opened, a beautiful, modern house with a resplendent foyer, deep plush seats, gilded pillars, a handsome and genteel curtain, and—gaslight!

Shortly after the Metropolitan opened, an announcement of major importance was made. On a night late in February, the theater would present to the West its first performances of six great operas, operas never heard west of the Mississippi. There would be specially painted scenery, an augmented orchestra, beautiful effects in lighting achieved by the new and sensational coal gaslights, and as an outstanding and sensational feature, the toast of Europe, the woman whom all the world was talking of. It was to be an event that would, for all time, place San Francisco in the gallery of the world's greatest cities.

In February the season opened! The audience gasped at the beauty of the Metropolitan! They arose as a man to cheer the great prima donna. They loved to give ovations, and this was one of the greatest ovations the city had accorded an artist. Night after night the great prima donna thrilled the miners, the gamblers, the saloon keepers, and the business-men. Finally she appeared as Agatha in *Der Freischutz.*" It was a beautiful scene, softly lighted by gaslight. Agatha stood at the window awaiting the return of her lover, the hunts-man. A gaslight moon and gaslight stars shone in the heav-ens. With folded hands, Agatha looked up to the gaslight heaven and prayed for her lover's safe return. She sang her prayer, and the audience trembled with the beauty of the scene. As she sang, the San Francisco Gas Company's light failed. The gas was turned off. The moon, the stars, and all the Metropolitan Theatre were plunged into darkness. There was nervous whispering in the audience, then exclamations, and then angry shouts. And finally, in what might have be-come a serious riot, the audience poured out of the theater, and the prima donna sat down in the middle of the stage and sobbed, and mixed her sobs with a few well-chosen exple-tives. The prima donna was Madame Anna Bishop.

Anna Bishop was the daughter of a French drawing mas-ter in Soho, Monsieur Rivière. He taught drawing and had twelve children. Also, he was devoted to music, so he and his good wife, when she wasn't busy having babies, taught Anna to play the piano. Anna played well, but the piano bored her. So, to relieve her boredom, she sang as she played and discovered, to the amazement of Mama and Papa Rivière and herself, that there was more music in her voice than in her ten fingers. She sang very loudly with her full, rich soprano voice, so loudly that the neighbors heard, and the word got around that the little Rivière girl was a potential sensation. Well, that was no overstatement. Anna proved to be a sen-sation often in her busy life, and not only by singing!

Word about her unusual voice reached a professor at Ox-ford University. The professor was a musician, a composer, and a teacher of voice. He came to hear Anna, fell in love with her untrained voice, and with the girl, and offered to teach her. Papa Rivière couldn't afford so fine a master, and Anna would take no gift without paying for it. The professor was twenty-three years older than she was, but he was a kind old gentleman, and lonely. So she married him. He was Sir Henry Bishop, the composer of "Home Sweet Home."

Anna made home sweet for Sir Henry for a reasonable number of years, and then made her debut in London, where she was acclaimed. Anna then went on tour, and in an orchestra met the man who was called the revolutionary artist of the harp, the world's greatest harpist of the day, Signor Boscha.

She sang for Boscha; Boscha played for her, and as he played he fixed his hypnotic eyes on her and she sang as she had never sung before. So wonderfully did Anna sing when Boscha was at the harp that a story began to circulate that Boscha mesmerized her, and made her sing. That widespread story reached the ears of the author, George Du Maurier, and years later he created his character of Svengali based on Boscha, and his Trilby based on Anna Bishop. Anna was the first Trilby. So completely did Boscha hypnotize her that finally she packed her portmanteau and ran away with him. The artistic world was scandalized, and delighted. Boscha and Anna toured the world, and were lionized and adored. He was an ugly old man; he looked like Svengali. Anna was a lovely young woman with an exquisite voice, and looked like Trilby. They traveled around the world, and when they were in San Francisco word came that Sir Henry Bishop had died, and Anna was free. So, she married her Svengali, and Svengali, old and tired, died within the year.

Anna was forty-five years old and twice widowed, but her voice was still one of the great voices of all time, and she was still beautiful. She sang in Australia and she sang in Chile, Argentina, and Peru. She sang in London, in Vienna, in Berlin, and in St. Petersburg. She went to New York and caused a sensation by singing the role of one of the witches in *Macbeth* at the Academy of Music, with Edwin Booth playing Macbeth. And one night, after she had brewed her witch's broth and sung her song, she sat in her dressing room and there came a discreet knock at the door. It opened and a young man entered. He explained that he was a diamond merchant (Anna was very fond of diamonds) and that he had never heard a more beautiful voice or seen a more beautiful woman than Anna, and if she would forgive him, he would like to introduce himself. His name was Martin Schultz. So Anna fell in love with Martin Schultz and his diamonds, and was no longer lonely.

I don't know just where or when Martin faded out of the picture, but a few years later Anna was to have her greatest experience. This was in 1866, twelve years after she had first sung in San Francisco. She had returned to the Golden Gate in 1864 for a season of concert. She was fifty-four years old, and beautiful. The city had grown sophisticated and was proud of its culture, its refinement, its elegance, and the ease with which its millionaires spent their millions. Anna sang for the city, and the city adored her. The Comstock millionaires dined her and wined her. She was a guest at the great estate of Bill Ralston in Belmont. She drove through the city streets in Ralston's coach and four, and out to the ocean beach. There, near the site of the Cliff House, she looked out to the west and the setting sun, and said the west was the land of romance—she would sing for the Orient. She reminded her companions of the first time she had sung in San Francisco, of the night the gas had gone out at the Metropolitan Theatre, and how people had said, gaslights were only a passing phase, a fad. But how wrong they had been proved! Now, with the developments of science, it was obvious mankind would use gas for lighting as long as mankind endured. Then she reminded them of the night she had sung *Linda de Chamounix* at the Metropolitan—the San Francisco Metropolitan. And how, as an added attraction, the management had offered a curtain raiser called *Why Did You Send Your Wife to San Jose?* Oh, it was all very fascinating and lovely turning back the pages to those dear, funny, nostalgic memories of yesterday, but now Anna wanted to go on, to go west, to sing for the great, undiscovered Orient. And so her great experience came.

She sailed through the Golden Gate and out across the Pacific. In the Sandwich Islands she sang to an audience of Polynesians and missionaries. The King of the Sandwich Islands, plump and swarthy, pompous and good natured, came each time she sang, applauded heartily, and showered her with gifts. She was the honored guest of the royal family. She called the village of Honolulu the paradise of the Pacific. But the audience was small in Paradise, and at the age of fifty-six Anna hungered for the acclamation of the crowd. So on February 18 she sailed out of the bay of Honolulu on the sailing ship *Libelle,* bound for Hong Kong. The Pacific was calm and beautiful. The ship was a good ship, and Anna Bishop thoroughly enjoyed the long voyage. She showed her appreciation by singing for the passengers and crew at any and every opportunity. The Pacific was calm, but the calm Pacific is a treacherous sea, and twenty-five hundred miles out of Honolulu a great storm came up. The ship fought bravely, the frightened passengers huddled together and prayed, and Anna Bishop sang for them to keep their courage up. Anna's singing kept the courage of the passengers up, but she couldn't keep the *Libelle* afloat. The brave ship floundered on a small island, an atoll called Wake Island.

Wake Island was a deserted strip of land in the lonely thousands of uncharted miles of the Pacific, and Wake was without fresh water. The crew of the *Libelle* managed to float ashore a few kegs of Angelica wine and a two-hundred gallon keg of water, and that was all. For five days the passengers and crew, in torn and tattered wardrobes, wet, cold, and hungry, rationed their few provisions and the keg of water. But death from starvation and thirst lay ahead; their plight on Wake Island was hopeless. The only slim finger of hope was in their taking to the two small boats they had beached from the *Libelle* and heading out into the Pacific in quest of salvation. The captain and eight men took the smaller of the boats and their share of the water and set sail. That was in 1866, seventy-eight years ago, and from that day to this no word has ever been heard or trace found of the eight men and the captain.

Anna Bishop and the remainder of the castaways filled the other boat and started out. Her wardrobe, her precious library of music, and her jewels—gifts of rulers, statesmen, and artists—were gone. All she had in the world were the tattered clothes upon her back, her voice, and her unquenchable love of adventure! They sailed into the west, a hapless crew. Their water ration was small, and their food not enough to satisfy their needs for more than a few days. The storm-swept Pacific had returned to its accustomed calm. Now the blazing sun of the tropics beat down on the little boat, no more than a microscopic speck in the thousands of miles of ocean. The men were hopeless, and some went mad. Others sat and brooded, and waited for death. And Anna Bishop, perhaps with her tongue in her cheek, sang the song her deserted husband had written—"Home Sweet Home." Perhaps she sang with her tongue in her cheek, but she kept up the courage of the crew. For thirteen days and nights they sailed west, blazing sun by day, star-showered sky by night, and the sun and the stars were their only compass. And Anna Bishop sang.

Thirteen days and thirteen nights they wandered, and on the thirteenth day one of the men, in his delirium, cried out that land was ahead. But this was no delirium. Out of the Pacific rose the hills of the island of Guam, fifteen hundred miles from Wake. The journey was ended. The poor, tortured pilgrims of the sea tumbled ashore to food, to water, to the kind ministrations of the natives, and Anna Bishop sang for them.

Now, by all odds, Madame Anna Bishop had earned a long rest, but Anna was not one to rest while there was still song in her heart and power in her lungs. She journeyed on to Manila to sing there. She sang in Hong Kong and in Calcutta. From India she sailed to England to sing in London, and from England back to New York and to Boston—in Boston to sing her husband's music, "Home Sweet Home," at a benefit for the writer of the lyrics, John Howard Payne.

On and on she traveled—more concerts, more miles of travel. Then in 1873 Anna Bishop came back to San Francisco. She had sung here in 1854 when the village was in the throes of excitement over its first gaslights. She returned to find it a blasé city, a city to whose footlights had flocked all the world's great artists. Anna Bishop was sixty-three years old, an old lady in the standards of that day, but she was still beautiful, and her voice was still powerful and rich even if she had to stop now and then for breath, and the blasé city forgot its sophistication and wept tears of nostalgic memory. When she sang "Home Sweet Home" the audience stood up and shrieked and stamped and shouted—and wept. Madame Bishop stood there on the stage, smiling happily, and tears poured down her cheeks.

Bummer and Lazarus

This is the sentimental story of three nondescript waifs of the San Francisco streets, waifs who came out of obscurity to win fame and the love of the whole sentimental city. They were only waifs, and they were all simple-minded. The first of the three was a short-legged creature, heavily bearded. He was a strange combination. He had keen eyes and a strong, square jaw; he held his head proudly as he walked, but his walk was a slovenly amble. He slunk along the wooden pavements of the city with a rolling motion like that of a drunken sailor. He begged his food, going from restaurant to restaurant and receiving an occasional handout from a sympathetic waiter, but more often receiving a kick. They called him a bum, and the name clung to him; throughout the city he was known as Bummer. He was only a dog. One of his parents, or perhaps his grandparents, had been a Newfoundland. Of the remainder of his forebears, nothing is known.

Now I have said he begged for food, and that is not entirely accurate. In spite of his undignified carriage and his habit of slinking along Montgomery Street, usually from Washington to Sacramento, Bummer was proud; he would not beg. He knew every restaurant owner, chef, and waiter on Montgomery Street, and they were all his friends, even those who kicked him. Bummer, a dog of epicurean taste, varied his diet by varying his eating places. Having chosen the cafe that appealed to his appetite of the moment, he would station himself before the door and sit patiently, eyeing the patrons that entered. And when, guided by his dog wisdom, he saw a patron enter who had a sympathetic feeling for hungry canines, Bummer would follow him through the door, sit or stretch quietly under the table at the patron's feet and render grateful thanks for the bits of food that fell to the floor. So, while dogs of higher social rank might dine on scrapings from mundane and prosaic dishes, Bummer made his meal of bits of frog legs, wild duck, roast pork, bear meat, steak, or venison. Nor did Bummer, as is the wont of most dogs, carry away bones and scraps of food to bury for a rainy day. He let each day take care of itself, knowing that as many people were hungry and would enter restaurants to eat on rainy days as on days of mellow sunshine. So Bummer, the part Newfoundland, was a familiar character on Montgomery Street for many weeks and months, well known to all the other distinguished characters of Montgomery Street, and holding himself as good as any of them. They respected and liked him, and he achieved a certain small notoriety as a San Francisco character, even in the early days of his story.

However, an event of major importance in his canine life was to occur in the year 1861. Close by the Blue Wing Saloon workmen were excavating, preparatory to building another structure in the fast-growing city. The street had been torn open by the laborers, uncovering a huge nest of rats. Rats had been the bane of the city ever since the great fleet of sailing ships had crowded the harbor in 1849. Rats were hated by San Franciscans, and now a small army of them overran the sidewalk, scattering pedestrians in all directions. Suddenly, singlehanded, and armed only with a savage growl and fierce teeth, out sprang Bummer. Historians say the charge of the light brigade was no more dramatic than was the assault of that lone warrior. To the right and left he swung, the aimless amble forgotten, and rats fell by the score—some say by the hundred. The slaughter was unparalleled in rat history, and when the dust of battle had cleared away, Bummer was the hero of San Francisco.

Now, please understand that I do not use that word lightly. Bummer was, in very fact, the hero of the city. The press extolled his virtues. Headlines in the city papers proclaimed his masterful assault. The rats of Hamelin Town had no more valiant foe than did the rodents of Montgomery Street. Drawings of him appeared in the newspapers made by the famous cartoonist of the Montgomery Block, Ed Jump. And in the social gathering places, where distinguished gentlemen of the city gathered to enjoy their evening cocktails, they vied with each other in boasting of their personal friendship with Bummer. Bummer was everybody's friend. Quite unconcerned, Bummer went about his dog business, trotting the length of the street, and deciding which restaurant he would favor with his patronage for breakfast, lunch, or dinner that day. Differing from dogs of less honored reputation, Bummer ate three square meals a day; even on that score Bummer was more like a human being than the average dog.

So much, for the present, for the first of the three non-

340

descript waifs who came out of obscurity to win undying fame. The second was of lesser nobility, a creature of ignoble habits and depraved tastes. He, too, was a dog. One day, while Bummer was lying in the shade of the Parrot Building scratching fleas—Bummer, being a true San Franciscan, was, like all other San Franciscans, an enemy of fleas—he was aroused from his preoccupation by a great din in the middle of the street. A poor, mangy creature of a dog was being viciously attacked by a large and ferocious member of his race. Now, I'd like to be able to say that the small, mangy creature was putting up a valiant fight, but such is not the case. Running around in circles, his tail between his legs, he was taking an unmerciful beating from his assailant. It was more than Bummer could stand. The archenemy of rats plunged into the fray with a roar that shook the windows in the neighborhood. There was no advancing and retreating, no sparring, and no feinting as is the etiquette of the professional prize ring. Bummer came at the bully as though he had been catapulted out of a gun. His short legs seemed to take on length, his noble head became majestic, his eyes blazed with all the fires of the underworld, and his vicious fangs were like fifty swords of tempered steel. He landed with all his noble weight on the bully's back; he tore, he slashed, and he roared his mightiest roar. The craven aggressor fled swiftly around the corner and out of sight, his tail at half-mast.

The little mangy mongrel looked up at Bummer with tears of gratitude in his eyes as if to say "Whither thou goest, I Will go; whither thou leadest, there will I follow." It was a beautiful moment, and the sentiments were the finest ever expressed by that mangy mongrel. And he was just that. Bummer could at least boast of a Newfoundland as one of his forebears, but the mongrel had never known any of his people. His only claim to distinction was the completely cosmopolitan strain that ran in his blood; he was a son of every race, from Great Dane to Black and Tan. He was just plain cur. He had long legs, smooth fur, the face and throat of a fish, a slanting jaw, and a weak chin. There the vignette ends. He was a cur without even the instincts of a gentleman. His was a miserable character; he knew no loyalty, and after his first flash of gratitude when Bummer saved his life, he lived an utterly selfish life. But Bummer had saved his life, and the cur intimated "Whither thou goest, I will go."

At midnight that night the dogs were discovered in the doorway that Bummer used for a bed in clement weather. The cur was lying on the inside protected from the night air, and Bummer was licking the mongrel's leg which had been all but bitten through by his bully assailant. Through the night the mongrel whined in pain and, as gently as a woman, Bummer nursed him. At dawn, when the lamp-lighter made his rounds putting out the gaslights on Montgomery Street, he found the two dogs sleeping. The mongrel was stretched comfortably at full length, and Bummer was crowded to the edge of the doorway, his jaw resting on the ear of the cur of no family.

That day Bummer made his usual rounds from restaurant to restaurant, selecting a favorable place at which to dine. And, having selected, he entered and took his place under a table and bits of food were dropped to him. But, Bummer didn't eat them; safely hidden in his great jaw he carried them away. That happened throughout that day, the next day, and the next, and tycoons and reprobates of Montgomery Street became curious; they became so curious that they followed him. Bummer led them into a vacant lot and there, under a pile of empty boxes, was the mongrel cur. The creature was still suffering from his wounds, and with

342

whines and mutterings that could be understood even by mere humans, Bummer, the good Samaritan, induced the wounded animal to make a great effort to eat. After all, it stood to reason that if his tortured body were not nourished it would never grow strong. So the mongrel ate, and Bummer sat and watched him with a pleased light in his tender eyes. The mongrel took on strength, and one day he crawled out of his pile of packing cases, and trotted briskly down Montgomery Street after Bummer, completely cured. That was how he came by his name, for San Franciscans, seeing how Bummer had all but raised him from the grave, called him Lazarus, and by that name he was known thereafter. Bummer and Lazarus became two of the most famous characters in the life of San Francisco of the sixties.

And now it is time to speak of the third nondescript waif. Bummer was ugly and misshapen; Lazarus was misshapen and just as ugly. But neither was as odd a sight as the little man they met one day. He wore a frock coat and gray trousers at that time, although later he affected the uniforms of the army and the navy. He wore a high hat with three ostrich feathers on it and he carried a gnarled and twisted and massive cane. He was bowlegged, but he walked with his head held proudly and high. He bowed with courtly grace as he passed acquaintances on the street. He was a creature of the gutter with the bearing of a king, and men called him Emperor Norton.

Now you have often read the story of Emperor Norton, and this is not the time nor the place to repeat, further than to enlighten the few unfamiliar with the tradition and lore of San Francisco that Emperor Norton had been Joshua Norton, a prosperous operator in Montgomery Street real estate during the days of gold. He had been so successful in everyting he undertook that men called him emperor. But failure

343

and disaster caught up with him when he tried to corner the rice market of the world. Having failed in the undertaking, and losing not only his entire fortune but the gold of those he had induced to join him in the project, he went quietly mad. It was a madness seasoned with remarkable vision, judgment, and philosophy. He took the name men had given him seriously; he proclaimed himself Norton, the First, Emperor of the United States, Mexico, and China. And San Franciscans were pleased to be his loyal subjects.

This creature of pomp and circumstance, this tragic joke of the city streets, was walking regally along Clay Street one day when he met Bummer and Lazarus. History does not record what words were spoken, but a complete understanding was arrived at between the two dogs and the emperor, and from that day until the passing of the canines, Bummer and Lazarus and Emperor Norton were inseparable.

On every first night of the theater three seats in the front row of the balcony were reserved, free of charge, for the emperor and his dogs. On Saturday morning the dogs and Norton attended Jewish services in the synagogue. On Sunday Norton and his faithful animals went to mass at Old St. Mary's. The three slept in the small room Norton occupied, and when the Emperor had business of state or economic problems to discuss with civic leaders or politicians in the city hall, he was always accompanied by the faithful pair.

Faithful? Yes! They were always with him, but as I have said, Lazarus lacked the instincts of a gentleman. For no reason that I have been able to discover, a vicious individual fired a shot at Bummer, wounding him in the leg. When Lazarus had lain suffering, Bummer had nursed him to health, but when Bummer fell, wounded, Lazarus deserted him. The city was furious; such ingratitude was intolerable.

344

Again the city newspapers gave columns to the two dogs, glorifying the nobility of Bummer, and condemning the perfidy of Lazarus. The War of Rebellion with its tragic headlines was forgotten for a day, and the topic on every San Francisco tongue was Bummer and Lazarus. But Bummer recovered, his wound healed, and back came Lazarus, with a hypocritical smile on his canine jowl and an enthusiastic wag of his ignominious tail as though to say, "You see, I was only pretending; I really love you very much." And, in the greatness of his heart, Bummer took him back.

But a new threat to the peaceful harmony of their days occurred. San Francisco was a city of dogs, and the streets were overrun with dogs. They became a nuisance; their noise, their ill behavior, and the vicious tendencies of some of them became an actual menace. So the city fathers passed an ordinance to the effect that any dog roaming the streets without a muzzle was to be put in the pound, and if unclaimed within twenty-four hours, was to be shot. This was before the day that Bummer and Lazarus had adopted Emperor Norton. The ordinance was passed and then people said, "But how about Bummer and Lazarus? The whole city owns them, and yet nobody owns them." A huge petition was drawn up and signed by every important businessman in the city, demanding that the Board of Supervisors make an exception of Bummer and Lazarus. Again the newspapers carried headlines; again Bummer and his fickle henchman were the favorite topic of conversation. The gentlemen supervisors met in executive session. Outside the door of the municipal chambers, the two dogs sat and awaited the verdict. How they happened to be there has never been explained; they couldn't read the newspapers, but loyal citizens insisted that a superior canine instinct had impelled the dogs to go to the city hall. A less imaginative few claimed that Bummer and Lazarus had been placed there by a newspaperman to tug at the heartstrings of the supervisors. Be that as it may, the results were electrifying. The august body, in executive session, issued an order under the official seal of the city that Bummer and Lazarus were wards of the city, and as such were authorized to roam the city streets at will, unmuzzled, and unfettered by any of the laws and edicts that controlled the actions of less distinguished dogs.

In October of 1863 a fire raged in the city. Through the streets came roaring the brave men of the Volunteer Fire companies, the St. Francis Hook and Ladder, the Columbia Eleven, the Knickerbocker Five, and the Washington Hose. One of the trucks ran over and killed Lazarus; it was not known which truck it was, although each company sorrowfully claimed the credit. The body of Lazarus was stuffed, and although the supervisors claimed it, the remains went to a purveyor of hard liquor named Martin. He paid the taxidermist fifty dollars, and put the mortal remains of Lazarus on public display. The city didn't mourn very much. After all, Lazarus had won the contempt of the citizens for his ungallant behavior.

Bummer, the victim of his bad manners, mourned. For days on end he would touch no food. He hid in dark corners listlessly, with his head between his paws. He came out at night and walked slowly and disconsolately along Montgomery Street with a haunted expression in his bleary eyes. He walked close to the buildings in the shadows with his tail drooping and his short legs shuffling aimlessly. And when a hand would reach out to give him the friendly pat to which he was accustomed from all men, Bummer would growl; a man had killed Lazarus, and men were his enemies. He grew skeleton thin. His jowls drooped and his eyes were haggard. But man—and dog—must eat to live, and that instinctive

346

struggle for self-preservation that is the heritage of all mankind and all dogdom finally won out. Bummer ate. But he was no longer the proud aristocrat of Montgomery Street who selected his eating place with careful dignity. No, Bummer had lost character; he whined, he pleaded, he begged, and was fed. And as he let his mantle of nobility slip from him, so the men of the city lost interest and slipped out of his life. Now, in truth, Bummer had become a guttersnipe and a derelict, friendless and unsung. San Francisco forgot him. It forgot him, until the day that the city papers announced that Bummer had met with disaster. A drunk had kicked him down a stairway on Montgomery Street and Bummer was dying. Then the city remembered how it had loved the nondescript waif. Men gathered before the bulletin board of the paper every day and read the reports of his condition. Bummer was suffering mortal wounds. Bummer was failing fast. Bummer was slipping away. And finally, one fateful morning, Bummer was dead.

Four quatrains of elegy were printed in the press. Mark Twain wrote a long eulogy, and it appeared in the columns of the *Enterprise*. The city went into mourning, but a strange thing had come to pass. Lazarus, the mongrel, condemned for ingratitude and behavior unbecoming a dog of proud traditions, had died and had lain in state. Thousands of San Franciscans had walked in his funeral procession before he was placed, stuffed, on his perch in Martin's saloon. When Bummer died—the good Samaritan, the dog who proudly boasted of a Newfoundland sire—the papers printed his eulogy and his elegy, and he was stuffed and forgotten.

However, he didn't pass completely out of the picture. His stuffed frame was mounted and placed next to the stuffed frame of Lazarus, the mongrel he had raised from the gutter. The two of them, Bummer and Lazarus, favorite wards of the city of San Francisco, were born to the museum in Golden Gate Park, there to stand for a time until museum addicts of the new generation sniffed and said, "What dirty old mongrel dogs; people *do* save the darnedest things!"

X

Ralston
and the Subtreasury

The story I am going to tell you now is, in my opinion, the most fantastic story in the history of San Francisco. It's a story I've often heard, a story about which I have read many thousand words in various sources, and I have never been able to understand it. I haven't been able to understand how it could have happened, how the machinery of it was accomplished, and how it happened that, right or wrong, it was condoned. Now, facing the possibility of an anticlimax, I am going to tell you at once that it is the story of the man who robbed the United States Subtreasury to save the city. To be perfectly fair, it should be explained that the robbers did give value received for every gold coin they took from the bank; no one was the loser.

To commence at the approximate beginning, out of the merger of various banks, the Bank of California was incorporated on June 15, 1864. D. O. Mills was the president of the new bank. Mills was a shrewd, cold, and calculating man, conservative and grim. He was not a colorful individual to draw friendly patronage to the new enterprise. The power behind the bank, the vision and the high spirit of adventure, the color and the glamor, and the dynamic force that was to make it one of the greatest banking institutions in the land, was vested in Bill Ralston—William Chapman Ralston.

Mills moved slowly; Ralston moved swiftly. Mills was conservative; Ralston was daring. Mills was president, but Bill Ralston was the friend of every depositor and knew almost all of them by name. Of all the men who loved San Francisco and grew with it, and who swore by the city's future and typified its irresistible glamorous charm, none was more popular than Bill Ralston.

The bank opened in offices at the corner of Battery and Washington Streets with a capital of two and a half million dollars. D. O. Mills was president, William Ralston treasurer, and Stephen Franklin secretary. Mr. Franklin was a quiet and distinguished gentleman, constantly busy with his routine duties as secretary. Mr. Mills was seldom in the picture; his interests divided his time between New York and the Nevada Comstock. The bank was Bill Ralston.

In a year's time the capital had doubled. In two years the bank moved to new and elaborate quarters at the corner of California and Sansome Streets, a location that it has occupied to this day. According to the colorful description painted by San Francisco's brilliant writer, Oscar Lewis, the banking room itself had no grilles or cages to separate the tellers and their gold from the public. The tellers and cashiers stood at the center of a rectangular mahogany counter with stacks of gold heaped close at hand, and the customers lined up at the counter just as customers do today to purchase food and household necessities.

Ralston was like a child with a new toy. He loved to work, loved excitement, loved people. The days that saw the opening of the bank were the days when gold and silver flooded out of the Comstock in inconceivable quantities. In a word, business was good. A branch bank was opened in Virginia City to handle the Comstock accounts; millionaires were being made over night. The Comstock bonanza was a bonanza for Wall Street in New York, California Street in San Francisco, and most of the territory in between. The city by the Golden Gate was going through almost the same excitement it had enjoyed fifteen years earlier with the California Gold Rush.

But there was one tangible difference. In 1849 and 1850 the city was a wild, chaotic maelstrom of rough individuals, high boots, pistols, dirt, and dripping oil lamps. In 1865 the dirt had given way to silks and satins, diamonds and champagne, and the oil lamps had been replaced by brilliant, dazzling gaslights. The mining camp had become a cosmopolitan city, the Paris of America, and the denizens of saloons and dance halls had made way for fashionable society. Mansions were being built where hovels had stood, and life moved with ostentatious elegance beneath the shade trees of South Park. Prosperity had come to stay!

Of course, economists and students of history would have told you that prosperity moves in cycles and that after the harvest there must be the lean days. But not even the student and economists could have foreseen how swiftly the top of the circle was to be reached and how breathtaking would be the avalanche when the slide commenced. The Comstock began to go through bad times. Warring factions and thinning veins of ore were causing stocks to fluctuate. Then the paternal government in Washington issued a large offer of United States Government bonds that paid princely interest. Hundreds of thousands of dollars, some say millions, were withdrawn from San Francisco banks to be invested in profitable government bonds. The Bank of California, with all the other banks in the city, felt the pressure.

Of course, that in itself wasn't very serious. But nature, up to one of her perennial diabolical tricks, took a hand in destiny, and sometime in the year 1868 San Francisco enjoyed one of its finest earthquakes. Men can understand tremblings in the stock market and cope with them under normal conditions, but tremblings of the earth are another matter. It makes men who love security realize how insecure everything is in life. Depositors in banks withdrew their gold, stuffed it in stockings and boots and leather trunks, and departed for the hills, the plains, or anyplace where the earth was better behaved. And the banks suffered.

But jovial Bill Ralston went happily on his prosperous way. Down the Peninsula in Belmont he was host to all the famous people who visited California. The stories of his great mansion with its elegant furnishings, of his lavish entertainments, of his coach and six horses that carried guests down the country road with a flourish of whips and the sound of his coach trumpet—all these stories were traveling around the world. Of course, there were whispers of impending trouble. People said the Comstock couldn't last forever; they said he was putting his eggs into too many baskets; they said he was inviting trouble by competing with the Vanderbilt interests in building steamship lines for trade between California and South America; and they said that fighting Adolph Sutro and the tunnel he was trying to build into the Comstock would shake the strength of Ralston, Sharon, Flood, O'Brien, and Mackay—all the great names that were taking millions out of the Nevada hills.

And Bill Ralston continued on his prosperous way. People might shake their heads and say he was inviting disaster, but

352

everybody liked him, everybody admired him. He was daring and spectacular, and the name they gave him in those days has remained a tradition. They called him the man who built San Francisco. Every morning he appeared behind his large desk, with the favorite pictures of Yosemite and the redwoods hanging behind it. Every day his office door in the bank stood open, and the little men and big men were greeted by the smiling welcome of genial Bill Ralston.

Then things in the banking world began to get worse. The Bank of California had loaned several million dollars to the men undertaking the building of a great railroad connecting the Atlantic and the Pacific, and thoughtful men shook their heads and said the railroad would never be built; it would be impossible to cross the Rockies. The bank had sunk millions into the South American activities which were to include a steamship line on Lake Nicaragua in Central America. Not only the Bank of California but all San Francisco banks were feeling the pinch.

It was an amazing situation. Here the strongbox of the California gold mines and the new bountiful mines of Nevada was suffering from a shortage of gold. Oh, of course there were great stores of gold bullion in the vaults of the bank, but a perverseness of circumstances had closed the San Francisco branch of the United States Mint. No gold coin was being minted. There was plenty of gold coin in the United States Subtreasury in San Francisco, but due to stringency across the nation, explicit instructions had been sent from Washington that no coin was to be exchanged for gold bullion. And gold bullion wasn't legal tender. When a depositor came to a bank to withdraw his money, it wasn't practical or possible to honor his demand by handing him a pound or more of gold bullion. Again and again the bankers

353

of San Francisco appealed to Washington and were turned down. Again and again Bill Ralston appealed directly to President Ulysses S. Grant, and the answer was always "No!" Gold coin would not be released.

It really was a rather amusing state of affairs when you stopped to think of it—a new angle on "water, water everywhere, nor any drop to drink." Gold! Vast storehouses of gold! Tons, literally tons, of gold, and yet no gold coin to keep bank depositors satisfied. Very amusing! But laughing Bill Ralston didn't find it amusing. He fully appreciated the seriousness of the matter. This could go on and mean disaster for San Francisco, and there was nothing in all the world Ralston loved as much as he did San Francisco.

Now all that was needed was a whispered rumor that a bank was unable to meet the demands of the depositors, and a run on the bank would result. A run on any one bank could precipitate a run on all banks.

The largest and most vulnerable bank in the city was Bill Ralston's Bank of California. Bill Ralston knew that the Bank of California could fall with the avalanche, or it could be the instrument to save the situation and save the city.

San Francisco after midnight was then, as it is today, a place of bright lights, of noise and night life. But walk down Montgomery Street today, or California Street, down through the canyons of the financial district, and a great and solemn silence pervades the district—silence and shadows, after midnight. The district was even more spectral in the sixties. It was a graveyard of towering mausoleums, a place of silence where every footstep rang out like the shot of a gun.

The Bank of California, as I have said, was at California and Sansome Streets. The gaslights were few, the night was dark, and the streets were in deep shadow. Slowly, quietly, the doors of the bank opened, and from the shadows emerged three men, coats buttoned to the neck and hats drawn down over their eyes. They walked swiftly and silently up California Street to Montgomery and a half block up Montgomery to a point between Sacramento and California, to the doors of the United States Subtreasury. The men were William Ralston, Maurice Dore, and Asbury Harpending. Harpending had been a partner of Ralston in many of his enterprises. It was he who had inspired Ralston to press the fight to cut Montgomery Street through to the south. But never before or since had Harpending engaged in so dramatic an adventure as he did that night with Dore and Ralston.

They reached the doors of the Subtreasury. A dim light was burning inside. But, strange to say, there were no guards in sight, no uniformed men with loaded guns to protect the vast fortune in gold coin buried in the vaults. And more strange to relate, the great doors were not locked. Someone some place has written that a man did stand by with folded arms and a smile on his face, watching what then transpired. I have a vague recollection that he wore the title of a high officer in the United States Army, that same army in which General Grant, the president had fought.

Ralston posted Harpending and Dore at the entrance, and then entered the dim, ghostly halls of the Subtreasury. Harpending and Dore stood silently in the gray night. Then the portals swung open again, and Ralston emerged. There was an excited twinkle in his eyes, but his face was without a smile. He spoke crisply and quietly. "Take these to the bank," he said, "The gentleman at the door will give you something to bring back." Over to California Street, down to Battery, the two men hurried, heavy bags on their shoulders. At the door of the Bank of California they were greeted by a fourth man; I believe he was the secretary, Stephen Franklin. Without a word he took the bags handed to him, and disappeared into the bank. He checked the contents of the bag, stacks of gold coin of the United States. He tallied them, stacked them away, and then returned to the entrance with a heavy burden. "Take these back to the Subtreasury," he ordered. And for the amount of the gold coins counted he handed Harpending and Dore blocks of gold bullion.

That was the first trip—the first of many, many trips. Throughout that gray and endless night the men made their journeys to and from the bank and the Subtreasury. Five tons of gold coins were taken from the Subtreasury and deposited in the vaults of the bank. Five tons of gold bullion were taken from the bank and deposited in the Subtreasury. When the dawn crept up over the Berkeley hills, the three exhausted men staggered home, their amazing night's work finished.

But the drama wasn't ended. The conspirators were tired to exhaustion, but there was more work to be done. As the sun crept up the canyons of the financial district, men began to gather in California Street, at first with sheepish expressions on their faces. Then, as the gathering became a crowd, the sheepish looks gave way to determination and, what was more apparent, fear. Mob fear! Crowd hysteria!

There were men with drawn faces, men who had spent sleepless nights, and men with despair in their eyes! By that mysterious grapevine that reaches its tentacles out with insidious force, the word had spread that all the banks in the city were in a serious plight and that the powerful Bank of California was on the verge of disaster. Behind those doors was what was left of their lifetime savings. No one knew how much was there or how much could be saved. But they were all wise enough to fear the growing of the crowd. No matter how sound the bank might be, a run on it under present conditions would become a debacle. Nervous hands fumbled at large watch chains and fingers nervously drew huge Waltham and P. S.. Bartlett watches from waistcoat pockets. Seven o'clock! Eight o'clock! Nine o'clock! Nine-thirty, nine-forty-five, nine-fifty—what would happen when the watches said ten o'clock and banking hours?

On the stroke of ten, the doors of the Bank of California opened. The crowd drew back for a moment and then began to surge forward. The pressure became a tidal wave of humanity, pushing, trampling, shoving, and overflowing through the great doors. It was a terrible but silently ominous mob, each man for himself, each determined to get what he could for himself out of the wreckage. Up to the huge mahogany counters the avalanche crashed its way—and then stopped! Eyes popped in amazement, mouths hung open, lips trembled and could speak no words. For there behind the counters stood the gentlemen of the bank, the tellers and the cashiers, smiles of pleasant greeting on their lips. And before them in huge stacks, stacks two and three feet high, were a million dollars in gold coins, shining, yellow gold, fresh from the ovens of the mint.

Outside the door, the bulk of the crowd, unable to fight their way in, had no way of knowing what was happening. But they swiftly learned. One of the men inside the door leaped to a box and shouted the news to those who were outside. The bank was full of gold, enough gold to take care of every depositor in full and have plenty left over. The Bank of California was solvent. Why, of course, it was solvent. They had always known it was solvent. A cheer broke from the crowd, a cheer that became a roar that was heard throughout the city and echoed three thousand miles away in Wall Street.

Mingled with the cheers again and again was heard the name of Billy Ralston. In the doorway of his office, William Chapman Ralston stood and smiled, and nodded to friends, and shook hands with those who forced their way through the cheering crowd determined to shake his mighty hand. The Bank of California was saved, and San Francisco was saved, and that cycle of prosperity that had reached a low ebb started the upward climb again. Oh, there were to be more alarms and excursions. New panics were to come. There were to be new lows in the Comstock, new threats of disaster. And during one of them Bill Ralston died. But that is another story.

The story of the raid on the United States Subtreasury was ended. The details of how the building was entered were buried when Ralston went to his grave. And the Bank of California went on, growing with the city Ralston loved, to become one of the greatest and strongest banking institutions in the United States.

But I still would like to know who unlocked the doors of the Subtreasury that September night in 1869.

XI

Asbury Harpending

San Franciscans are funny people! They have so many human peculiarities. For instance, they are exceedingly proud of the great men, the fantastic men, the honorable men, the bandits, the crooks, the adventurers, the great scholars, and the crazy men who made the city's amazing history. Talk to any old-timer and he is pretty sure to say that he knew Emperor Norton, Ambrose Bierce, Bill Ralston, Jack London, Lucky Baldwin, or a hundred others. And half the time he has never even seen the man about whom he speaks. He's not really lying; it's simply that he has become so accustomed to hearing those famous or notorious names that they become a part of his life; he really believes he has seen and known them.

But there is one name in San Francisco history that doesn't fit into the picture. I have mentioned him a score of times in connection with twenty different events in the story of the city. I have found his name mentioned at least once in practically every book ever written about San Francisco, but I have never been able to find anybody who knew him, or, for that matter, knew very much about him. Then suddenly only last week I realized that I, personally, had seen him often. He had lived in Fruitvale when I lived there as a boy. He was a white-haired old man who seldom spoke to anyone. I remember—and considering the circumstances, this is very remarkable—that he constantly had the stars and stripes flying from the flagpole in front of his home. And yet he had been one of the most consummate rebels in the West, and had done everything he could to induce California to secede from the Union and join the South in the War of the Rebellion. His name was Asbury Harpending.

My father came to San Francisco in the middle sixties and has lived here ever since. "Harpending," he said, "Harpending. I never heard of him." Then he reconsidered. "Oh, yes," he said, "you mean Asbury Harpending. There's a building on Market Street named after him, but he never was very important. A dull sort of a person. Never amounted to much!"

A dull sort of a person! But I have managed to put the pieces of the jigsaw puzzle together, and Asbury Harpending emerges as one of the most remarkable, unbelievable characters ever to come to this city of amazing characters. He was the man who helped William Ralston remove five tons of gold from the United States Treasury. And he was the man who initiated the scheme that resulted in cutting Montgomery Street south. But these were only two events in a life of mad adventures.

Asbury Harpending was born in Hopkinsville, Kentucky, in 1839. As a boy he was a mental prodigy; he entered college when he was fifteen years old. He was a mental prodigy, but mental exercise was not enough for his adventurous spirit. His college career lasted less than a year. He was still fifteen years old when he ran away from home to join that other amazing Californian, Filibuster Walker, who had gone to Nicaragua to foment revolution there and have himself appointed king, or emperor, or president. Walker's expedition ended in disaster. The filibustering chieftain was captured, and a firing squad ended his career at the base of a stone wall. Young Harpending was arrested, but managed to escape. With whatever facilities there were for hitch-hiking in those days, he made his way home to Hopkinsville.

He was restless; he had to have action, and Hopkinsville, Kentucky, had none to offer. When Asbury was sixteen he left home again. This time he didn't run away; he was given permission by his astute father to set sail for California. A steamship ticket and necessary paraphernalia of travel were purchased, and sixteen-year-old Asbury Harpending set sail for San Francisco, via New Orleans, with five dollars in one pocket and a pistol in another.

The journey was a long one. Of course, there was little opportunity on shipboard to spend money, and five dollars was less than nothing. So when the steamer docked at New Orleans, the boy invested his five dollars in oranges and bananas. You could buy a great many oranges and bananas in New Orleans for five dollars in 1856. Not that Asbury had a penchant for bananas and oranges. Oh, no, already he was mapping the course of his future career. He took his fresh fruit on board, and on the long voyage to the Golden Gate, he retailed his purchases to hungry passengers on the cruise. He started that cruise with five dollars in his pocket, and a pistol. He reached San Francisco with the gun and four hundred dollars. He was just turning seventeen.

Now in the years between the gold rush of 1849 and Harpending's arrival at the foot of Telegraph Hill in 1856, bad times had come to the city. The Sydney Ducks had burned it down several times. The Vigilance Societies had come into being. Gold-hungry miners were returning from the Mother

Lode without gold. Hundreds of men were out of work, hundreds hungry. Asbury Harpending, seeking adventure and his fortune, could find neither in San Francisco. With four hundred dollars, and his pistol in his pocket, he started for Mexico.

Very little is known about his adventures in Mexico. As a matter of fact, I personally know nothing of his Mexican interlude; I know only the results. He returned from Mexico four years later. He was twenty years old. One quarter of a million dollars was credited to his account in the bank, and he owned a gold mine in Mexico worth at least one million dollars more. He was twenty years old and a millionaire!

That first fortune of Asbury Harpending lasted exactly three years. He returned to San Francisco to find the city divided into two camps; more than twenty-five percent of its population rabidly sympathized with the Southern rebellion, and were making every effort to induce California to secede from the Union.

Militantly, Harpending plunged into the verbal battle. Against Thomas Starr King and other loyal Northerners, young Harpending mounted soap boxes and platforms and roared his rebellion. He organized a San Francisco chapter of the Knights of the Golden Circle. The duties and activities of the Knights were simple; each of the thirty members was sworn to enlist the support of one hundred men, to equip and arm them, ready to fight for the South. In short, three thousand men were to seize the arsenal at Benicia, overthrow the state government, and form a new republic to be called the Republic of the Pacific, an ally of the rebelling Southern states.

The Knights of the Golden Circle was a secret society.

362

The members were sworn under penalty of death to keep the actions of the society secret, even from their wives. But one of the more garrulous knights was indiscreet; the plans to seize the state reached the ears of Albert Sidney Johnston, in command of the army on the Pacific. Johnston was a Texan, and during the War of the Rebellion was an honored Southern general. But until war was declared he was a loyal American. He sent for young Harpending and commanded him to disband the Knights or be attacked by the United States Army. The Knights disbanded.

A few months later the Civil War broke out. Harpending traveled by devious roads to Mexico again, and then turning in his tracks, ran the blockade, and fought his way to Jefferson Davis. The President of the Confederacy recommended a commission for him in the Southern navy.

Out of uniform, he again ran the blockade, returning to San Francisco on a Pacific Mail liner. In his pocket he carried explosive letters that would have sealed his fate if they had been discovered, letters from southern leaders to southern sympathizers in San Francisco. On the steamer he met one of the most charming of the city's society women, Lady Fairfax, wife of the fabulous Lord Charlie Fairfax. Lord Charlie was San Francisco's favorite playboy, but Lady Fairfax was a serious-minded Victorian lady. She spent many quiet hours on deck with young Harpending. Harpending was a Southern radical; Lady Fairfax was from Virginia.

The steamer sailed through the Golden Gate and tied up at the docks. Army officers came on board and searched Harpending for anything of a seditious nature. Nothing was found on him, and he was released. The incriminating letters were sewed to Lady Fairfax's Victorian undergarments. Harpending delivered the letters to prominent Southern sym-

363

pathizers in San Francisco. His plan was to travel up and down the Pacific Coast as a privateer, seizing Pacific Mail steamers and shipping the gold they carried in their holds to leaders in the South.

He enlisted the aid of a group of men, raised a quarter of a million dollars, and purchased a ship to be used as a privateer. Before going on, I should explain that Harpending's original fortune had been seized by the United States Government when he became an officer in the navy of the South.

A ship was purchased, manned, and prepared to sail, but before the anchor could be weighed, United States officials boarded her; Harpending's plans had been revealed by one of his men, and he and others were placed under arrest, tried for treason, and convicted. Two of his companions were sentenced to ten years in the United States Disciplinary Barracks on Alcatraz Island, and Asbury Harpending was sentenced to ten years in the San Francisco County Jail.

Four months later, for no good reason further than that the United States Government had more serious matters on its mind, the conspirators were pardoned.

Harpending left San Francisco, traveled by foot through the California hills and found a hideout in the mountains of Tulare County. And within a few months' time he had discovered a rich gold mine—the Kernville gold field. He piled up a fortune, and was instrumental in dividing Tulare County and creating the new county of Kern. In 1865, when the war had ended, he returned to San Francisco, a millionaire again. He was twenty-five years old.

Then he plunged with mad enthusiasm into San Francisco real estate speculation. He met William Ralston, and sold him the idea of cutting Montgomery Street south to the bay.

364

At the corner of Market and New Montgomery was property owned by the Catholic church, and property owned by Selim Woodworth, son of the author of "The Old Oaken Bucket." Woodworth valued his property at half a million dollars. In 1868 San Francisco experienced its most terrible earthquake up to that time. The day of the shake Harpending met Woodworth at the site of his property. Woodworth was frightened. Harpending said things looked bad; probably the whole city would be shaken into the bay eventually. Woodworth trembled and perspired. Harpending said utter destruction was its inevitable fate. Woodworth groaned and wiped his brow. Harpending offered him one hundred and fifty thousand dollars for the property worth half a million. Woodworth clinched the deal there and then, and left San Francisco.

On that lot facing the Palace Hotel—that lot where the Bank of America now stands—Asbury Harpending built the Grand Hotel.

The young genius went real-estate mad, but he was looking in other directions, too. His association with William Ralston gave him opportunities to add to his fortune in the Comstock. Harpending was weaving, weaving like an untiring, persistent spider, active in every enterprise in the booming city. He built the San Francisco and Humboldt Railroad connecting Sausalito and Eureka, a forerunner of the Northwestern Pacific.

Meanwhile, Harpending's real-estate operations had widened. On Market Street, between First and Second, he built what was, at that time, probably the most impressive office building in the city. It was a square, solid structure, costing close to half a million dollars. A block further up on Market he owned the Grand Hotel. He was twenty-nine years old, one of the richest men in San Francisco, owner of the two most imposing structures on Market Street.

Then, for the second time in his career, the tide turned for Asbury Harpending. In 1871 the Harpending Building burned to the ground, a total loss. Then, on the property owned by the Catholic church across New Montgomery from his Grand Hotel, Bill Ralston built the world's greatest hotel, the Palace. True, it was connected with the Grand by a glass Bridge of Sighs, but the Grand became second rate. And finally Leland Stanford, building the Central Pacific Railroad, resented Harpending's building of the little San Francisco and Humboldt Railroad. He pulled financial and political strings, and Harpending was forced to sell out at a terrible sacrifice. He had built a great financial structure on the shifting sands of San Francisco, and the sands were being swept away beneath his foundations.

His morale was crumbling. San Franciscans remembered his espousal of the Southern cause and condemned him for it. San Franciscans remembered his innocent participation in the great hoax, and condemned him for it. San Francisco had lost its flavor for him. He sold his holdings in Montgomery Street real estate to the Ralston interests at a loss. He auctioned off all his city property at a loss, but still he realized more than a million dollars in the liquidation. And he went back to Hopkinsville, Kentucky, the little town where he had been born, to retire and live a quiet life at the age of thirty. Retire? A quiet life? No, that wasn't in Asbury Harpending's scheme. He had married, he had three daughters, and he had wealth—not as great as in the height of his bonanza, but still sufficient to let him live the sedentary, comfortable life of a rich family man.

He began to dabble in mines again. He speculated in

Wall Street. The mines failed him. Wall Street drained him. Mexico had been one of the first fields of success for him; he speculated in Mexico and Central American silver mines and lost another fortune. Then he fairly faced the cold, unpleasant facts—his days as a great operator were over. Out of the wreckage he salvaged enough to really retire and live in modest comfort with his family. And the one place in the world that he loved, the one place that had meant excitement and success for him, was San Francisco. So, back to California he came. The days of the Ralston hierachy were ended. The old days were forgotten, and the name of Asbury Harpending was unknown to the new generation.

He built a modest home in Fruitvale. He planted roses and fruit trees and walked in the sunshine along the old county road or East 14th Street. People liked the quiet, taciturn, white-haired old man. The fact that he had been a rabid rebel, fighting to separate California from the Union, was forgotten. Now he was a patriot, proudly raising the stars and stripes to the top of the white flag pole in his front garden. A good man, a good American citizen, that's what they called him. He didn't appear in public very often. He was very busy, people said, busy writing a book—a story of California—a story of a great hoax.

Asbury Harpending left Fruitvale in 1918. One of his daughters had moved to New York with her husband; old man Harpending, lonely and forgotten, went to New York to spend his last days, perhaps years, with her. Life was rather empty. But his memories were crowded with more dramatic and thrilling adventures than any man is justified in expecting in a span of eighty-four years. He died in his daughter's home in New York in 1923.

XII

The Great Diamond Hoax

It was 1906—the autumn of the earthquake year. I was learning a trade in a temporary, post-earthquake office on Fillmore Street. One afternoon the office door opened and a very old man hobbled in. He had a long white tobacco-stained moustache, and a flowing white beard. He was toothless, and his eyes were watery and without expression. His garments were ragged. He looked like a gentle madman. He hobbled up to the roll-top desk and pulled a chamois bag from his trouser pocket. His trembling fingers unwound the leather thong that bound it, and on the desk he poured a dozen or more dirty-looking natural uncut crystals, ranging from the size of a sewing thimble to a golf ball. I asked him what they were, and in a spectral voice he whispered, "Diamonds! A fortune in diamonds! A million dollars worth of diamonds! I want to sell them!"

After I had gotten rid of the poor old madman, I asked questions around the city and learned that he was a familiar figure in jewelry stores, always trying to sell his million dollars worth of diamonds. It seems that once he had been a very rich man, but he had been swindled by crooks, induced to invest his fortune in a worthless, salted diamond mine. When he realized that he was ruined, he had gone quietly mad. And then, having acquired a bagfull of worthless crystals, he had spent thirty-five years wandering the streets of San Francisco, trying to sell them.

Thirty-five years! Why, then he must have been swindled in 1871.

In December of 1871, two roughly garbed miners entered Bill Ralston's Bank of California. They were ill at ease, and looked and acted as though they were uncomfortable in so handsome an edifice as the great bank. They were just simple, inarticulate miners. They didn't want to talk to anybody. All they wanted was the privilege of depositing in the vaults of the bank several large bags that they carried. They were very shy, very timid, and really didn't want to explain to the polite young bank teller who greeted them what the bags contained. But the employee of the bank politely explained that the bank could not assume the responsibility of placing bags in the vaults unless the contents were revealed. After all, although the bank teller did not say as much, the bags might have contained bombs to blow up the edifice. The two shy, simple, and poorly dressed prospectors were impressed. They said their names were Arnold and Slack, Phillip Arnold and John Slack, and they hoped the polite young gentleman would not reveal their secret. The bags contained a monstrous fortune in diamonds—rough, uncut diamonds—that they had discovered when they were prospecting for gold. The bank clerk accepted the bags, deposited them in the vault, gave the two simple prospectors a receipt for them, and Arnold and Slack hurried away as though happy to be out of so imposing a structure.

In some way or other word of the diamonds in the vault

came to the ears of Bill Ralston. After all, Ralston knew almost everything that was going on, in and out of the bank. It was exciting, intriguing news that in the bank were bags containing a huge fortune in diamonds. California had thrived on such news. First there had been the rumors of coal mines on the slopes of the Mother Lode, and then the gold and silver fortunes in the Virginia City Comstock. First coal, then gold, then gold and silver, and now diamonds! There was no limit to the bounty of Mother Nature in California! Ralston sent for the two miners, Arnold and Slack.

At first they didn't want to talk about their astounding fortune. They seemed dazed, confused, and overwhelmed by it. No, they were not disposed to sell shares or an interest in their diamond mines. Ralston casually asked where the mines were. Arnold and Slack were vague; the mines were someplace—out there. They were not educated men. They didn't know much about geography. All they knew was that they had been prospecting for gold and had stumbled onto the fortune in diamonds. The mines were someplace east of Ralston's office, maybe in Wyoming—or Colorado—Arizona —Nevada—they weren't sure. Yes, they knew how to reach them again. Finally, after considerable stalling, they agreed that it might be wise to sell a half-interest in their discovery to someone who knew more about developing the property than they did. A figure was discussed, a very large figure. Yes, they would be willing to sell a half-interest in their diamond mine for that amount. "Well, then," said Bill Ralston, "before we close the deal, we will have to inspect the mines."

At first Arnold and Slack were dubious about letting anyone know where the property lay. They didn't realize business was transacted that way and, as a matter of fact, they didn't see why Mr. Ralston didn't trust them. They hadn't sought him out. They hadn't asked to do business with him. But Bill Ralston patiently explained that bankers were not in the habit of buying pigs in pokes. He had entire confidence in Mr. Slack and Mr. Arnold, but he would have to send experts to appraise the property before a deal could be closed. Finally the prospectors agreed, with the stipulation that when the expert selected by Mr. Ralston had accompanied them to the edge of the desert country where they had made their strike, he was to be blindfolded. He was to accompany them blindfolded over the remaining miles to and from their claim, so that if the final deal was not consummated, they themselves would still be the only persons knowing the location of the mines. Ralston agreeed that that was a sound business proposition.

He selected General David S. Colton, Southern Pacific magnate and a distinguished San Franciscan, as his emissary. One morning General Colton departed for the mines—someplace out there—with Arnold and Slack. He returned in a few days. He entered Ralston's office, closed the door, and sat at the banker's desk, trembling with excitement. Then he opened bags and poured out onto the desk the gems that he, with his own hands, had taken from the mine—a fortune in gems! There were perhaps a million dollars worth of gems, and he had not even hunted for them. All he had had to do was reach down and pick them up. And there were probably a billion dollars more waiting to be taken. The most amazing part of it all was that there were not only diamonds but he had also found rubies, sapphires, and emeralds!

Now anyone ought to know that diamonds, rubies, sapphires, and emeralds are not found in any one mine or any one locality. But General Colton, and later Ralston and all the others who went into the deal, were so carried away by the discovery that if the prospectors had produced pearls of oysters in that inland desert, they would probably have found an explanation to satisfy themselves. After all, the diamonds *were* genuine. One of those brought back by General Colton was offered to a prominent San Francisco jeweler. It weighed one hundred and three carats, and the jeweler offered ninety-six thousand dollars for it. The gems were submitted to other experts; all of them were established as being genuine, and of fabulous worth.

Now Asbury Harpending, partner of Bill Ralston in the deal that cut New Montgomery Street through to the south, the deal that developed into the Montgomery Street Realty Company, was on a trip to London, and one morning he received a cable from William Ralston. It was the most remarkable cable he had ever read and the most costly cable he had ever received. It cost eleven hundred dollars to send. It told the story of the diamond mines and stated that Ralston was organizing the San Francisco and New York Mining and Commercial Company, with a capital stock of ten million dollars. Stockholders would only become multi-millionaires when the gem mines were properly developed, and Ralston demanded that Harpending return immediately from London to become a partner and stockholder in the enterprise. Harpending cabled that he was leaving at once. His cable cost much less than eleven hundred dollars.

Meanwhile, Ralston was investigating the antecedents of Arnold and Slack, learning that they were just well-liked old-time prospectors, real, honest-to-goodness forty-niners, but he wanted some proof of their integrity. The prospectors agreed to supply the proof themselves. They would go to the mines and bring back at least two million dollars worth of precious gems before the deal was consummated.

They started out on their journey. Harpending, having arrived from London, was sent to meet them at Lathrop on their return. He did meet them, and then came back to San Francisco with them. That night Asbury Harpending called a meeting of the prospective officers of the new corporation. They met in his mansion on Rincon Hill. He told an amazing story of the misadventures suffered by Slack and Arnold. They had taken two million dollars worth of gems from the mines and started their return journey. They had been overtaken by a terrible storm and cloudburst and had tried to ford a swollen river on a raft. They had suffered terrible hardships and had almost lost their lives. And while making the crossing on the raft, they had lost one of the bags with a million dollars worth of diamonds. But they had saved the other; Harpending had it in his hand. He stood at his billiard table, the stockholders clustered breathlessly about him, and across the green baize of the billiard table he spilled a million dollars in precious diamonds.

Well, that was enough to convince anybody, but the deal was so gigantic that no chances could be taken. So a committee was delegated to travel to New York with a bag of the jewels. A meeting was held before Horace Greeley and other distinguished Easterners. The head of a Fifth Avenue jewelry house examined the diamonds and appraised them— about one-tenth of the quantity already in the hands of Ralston—at more than one hundred and fifty thousand dollars. And, like the explosion of a bomb, the news of American diamonds burst upon the nation.

Ralston's next step in representing the syndicate was to select an engineer who would expert the mines and make arrangements for ultimate operations. Henry Janin, the man selected, had the reputation for being the foremost mining engineer living. Great things were told about him. He was never known to speculate or take any kind of a chance. The worst thing said about him was that he was overcareful. He had experted hundreds of mines and never made a mistake. Janin accepted the assignment at a large fee. He went to the mines. He made a thorough examination, and he returned, enthusiastic. The diamond fields were the most amazing harvest he had ever seen. Why, according to his calculations, a million dollars' worth of diamonds a month could be mined. He figured the potential value of the mines at sixty-five million dollars. How Henry Janin, America's foremost mining engineer, could have overlooked—as all the others had overlooked—the fact that diamonds, rubies, sapphires, and emeralds were never to be found in the same area, remains one of the strange mysteries of the great diamond hoax. He made his report to Ralston, and that was all the reassurance Bill Ralston required. He paid three hundred thousand dollars to Messrs. Arnold and Slack, a first installment of the cash to be paid them for half their interest in the North American Diamond Mines. Then he opened handsome offices to carry on the business, and secretaries were hired. An additional three hundred thousand dollars was paid to Slack and Arnold, David Colton resigned his executive position with the Southern Pacific Railroad to become general manager, and the North American Diamond Company was functioning.

There is nothing more curious in human nature than curiosity. It leads little men into experiments that become great inventions; it guides science, and shapes the course of medicine. The imagination and curiosity of the nation, of the world, for that matter, was kindled by the fabulous stories of the diamond mines. To satisfy that curiosity Clarence King made a journey to the mines. King was a scientist, a distinguished scholar, a leader of American scientists. He took assistants with him and made a thorough survey of the area. Everything he found was amazing. For instance, he found little ant hills. There would be one powdered with emerald dust, and in that hill there would be an uncut emerald; there were hills powdered with ruby dust, sapphire dust, diamond dust, and each contained uncut stones. But he found more than that. He found that the gems were not imbedded in rock but lay in loose sand. Oh, that was only the beginning. He found diamonds in forks of trees. And finally—and here somebody had obviously made the ultimate error—he found a diamond partially cut by the lapidary's art. That settled it. He sent a wire to William Ralston:

The alleged diamond mines are fraudulent. Plainly they are salted. The discovery is a gigantic fraud. The company has been pitifully duped.

Clarence King

Then the storm broke! Search was made for the conspirators. Slack was never heard of again. Arnold had gone to Kentucky, and he merely laughed at the demands of the Californians. As a matter of fact, the whole state of Kentucky laughed at the Californians, who had stood out against the South during the Civil War. The law could not, or at any rate did not, touch him. But Arnold did return one hundred thousand dollars with the understanding that all charges be dropped against him. Then he became a banker of Elizabethtown, Kentucky, a vocation that he followed until a blast from a double-barreled shotgun put an end to his scheming life.

Little by little the explanation of the Slack-Arnold operations became clear. Before they had embarked on the diamond hoax they had purchased in London some fifty thousand dollars' worth of worthless uncut diamonds—discards. These were the specimens used to salt the mines. Rough uncut diamonds are not familiar to large jewelers, and they and others had fallen for the hoax.

Now William Ralston took command of the situation. He had paid Slack and Arnold three hundred thousand dollars out of his own pocket; that was a total loss that he assumed. But he returned all the money put up by the investors in the North American Company. He received receipts in full, and framed them and hung them on his office wall. The story of the great diamond hoax was ended.

The story is ended, but I still remember that old toothless bearded man who came to our office on Fillmore Street in 1906. All the money invested in the North American Company had been returned to the investors, so the old man could not have lost his fortune that way. Something else must have driven him mad and made him believe the handful of worthless crystals in his chamois bag were diamonds of fabulous worth. Sometimes I wonder if he were Slack, returned to haunt the scene of his crime. But no, that could hardly have been possible. He was just a strange old unbalanced character, one of the many who haunted the streets of San Francisco, living in the memory of its past tragedies and adventures and triumphs.

XIII

The Cable Cars

This is the story of a fight—a fight between practical common sense and sentimentality, a fight between realistic foresightedness and old dreams, a fight between good business and poetry. It's the same fight that said we ought to level all of the San Francisco hills and make the city a nice practical level plain like any other clear-thinking city. It's the same fight that said we ought to order all the flower stands off the streets with their ever changing pageant of color, and make the city look like a city and not an Oriental bazaar. And today it's saying, "Get rid of the cable cars." Just like you'd say "The horse is too old to run a mile, we might as well shoot it," so they're saying the old cable car is a relic of the gay nineties and we might as well turn it into scrap iron. Of course, if you're softhearted you'll not shoot the old horse; you'll turn him out in green pastures. But you can't very well turn the cable cars out to pasture. Again, just because your sons and daughters are modern sophisticates and like speed you don't shoot your grandmother; you're even disposed sometimes to let her live just as a matter of sentiment. And the cable cars are the very active and quite noisy grandmothers of the electric cars that sway like scenic railways, and the buses into which we struggle through fighting mobs, and having found scant standing room in them, struggle for breath in their lethal chambers.

Of course we, being practical people, can't think of any valid reason why the cable cars should be preserved, unless that reason be sentiment and romance. And there's no place for romance and sentiment in our world since we've coined our most popular, new, and current phrase, "realistic thought." Oh, of course there may be minor arguments. We may say it colors life to hear the conductor on the Jackson-Washington line shout, "Hold tight going 'round the curve!" That might be an argument. And we may say that an electric car couldn't possibly make the grade going up the Powell Street hill, and motor buses of today couldn't make the grade. But this is an age of science; science can do anything, including the wiping out of civilization with split atoms.

Of course, science will eventually build a bus or an electric car that not only will mount the Powell Street hill, but may even be equipped with a snack bar and a cocktail lounge. Science *is* wonderful! But, on the other hand, a world without romance and sentiment and tradition would be about as interesting as the love life of a Columbia River salmon. And the thing that year after year, for almost a hundred years, has made San Francisco a lovable, intimate, warm, and human city in contrast to most of the industrial cities built on plains, is its romance and sentiment and tradition.

The story of the beginning of the cable cars was a sentimental episode in itself. It started in San Francisco; the first cable car in the world was developed in San Francisco. People called it a fantastic, impossible idea, and in other cities the San Francisco cable cars were called absurd nonsense. That was in the beginning. But within a few short years almost every metropolitan city in the world was using cable cars

378

without apology. There was no sentiment about them; they were just useful. But, as we said, the beginning was a sentimental episode.

There was a gentleman named Hallidie—Mr. Andrew S. Hallidie. However, to be accurate, that was not really his name to start out with. He was born Andrew Smith, but later he adopted the name of his godfather and uncle, Sir Andrew Hallidie, who was court physician to Queen Victoria. Andrew Smith Hallidie was born in London in 1836. His mother and father were Scottish. The boy, Andrew, found work at the age of thirteen in a machine shop under the supervision of his older brother, and his interests throughout life were influenced by his knowledge and skill in mechanical invention.

It happened that the boy's father had certain interest in lands owned by General Frémont out in the wilds of California, and when California became the focal center of world interest and everybody who could find the way started for the gold fields, Smith Senior joined the cavalcade. With him he brought young Andrew, making the journey after the Gold Rush had reached its peak.

They arrived in the port of San Francisco in 1852. The boy, Andrew, was sixteen years old. The father and son parted company in the seaport village, and the senior Smith drops out of the story. Andrew went to the gold mines. He dug for gold and panned gold and experimented in inventing sluices and rockers. He surveyed claims, he worked at road building and bridge building, and after three years in the gold fields he constructed a cable-suspended viaduct over the American River. A cable-suspended viaduct! From that day Andrew Hallidie's life work was the building of cables. He came back to San Francisco. He developed powerful cables of twisted steel wire capable of hauling heavy loads. He built a steel cable company and grew wealthy.

Now, one day or one evening, according to the legends that are told, he went for a walk up a San Francisco hill. It was in the winter of 1869, a cold, dismal, wet winter. As he walked, head bent to wind and driving rain, he saw a horse-car approaching. (Horsecars were the only means of commercial locomotion in the city.) The car was being hauled by four horses—a car crowded to the platform with San Franciscans evading the storm. The horses wheezed and panted and labored, dragging the unwieldy burden up the hill, and their iron shoes slipped on the wet cobblestones and progress was almost out of the question. Finally, halfway up the hill, one of the horses slipped and fell. The driver of the car threw on his brake so quickly that the chain holding the brake snapped in two, and the car commenced to slide swiftly backwards down the hill dragging the four horses after it. When the car reached the foot of the hill, the four tortured beasts were piled up in a heap, bruised, bleeding, with bones broken and their flesh pounded by the cobblestones.

Andrew Hallidie went home and sat and stared out into the mist and rain that drenched the city, and pictured the suffering beasts. He remembered the stories that had come out of his native England—that five thousand horses a year were destroyed or made useless by their task of dragging the trams through the streets of London town. It was impractical, cruel, and inhumane. So, Andrew Hallidie, master builder of cables, combined his trade with his humanitarian instincts, and built a car that could be pulled up hill and down at will by cables driven by steam power.

He raised funds and incorporated a railroad company. He was granted franchises to operate his trick car on Clay

Street from Kearny to Leavenworth. The city laughed. They called it "Hallidie's folly." They said no cable and no power on earth could drag a car up the Clay Street hill. And no citizen would be mad enough to risk his life riding on the car if the trip were attempted, not up the hill, nor down the hill! What was to prevent the contraption from rushing at breakneck speed down the hill, killing everything and everyone in its way. Why, a man might as well risk his life trying to fly through space in a flying machine!

But Andy Hallidie went ahead with his job. He had perfected cables that would withstand strain. He had invented a grip that would seize the traveling cable and travel with it, and release it at will. He had his franchise, and now he had to run a cable car up and down the Clay Street hill on August 1, 1873, or lose all he had ventured. At midnight of July 31 a small group of nervous men gathered at the steam powerhouse at Leavenworth and Clay. Mr. Edgar M. Kahn tells of that night in his fascinating book, *Cable Car Days in San Francisco,* and Mr. Henry C. Collins, the architect, tells of it in the brilliant papers he has written based on his study and research on the San Francisco cable cars. They gathered, tired and nervous, and inspected the preparations.

They tested the cables, measured the steam power, tested the grip and the brakes, and as dawn broke, they were ready to make the first journey. Fog poured in through the Golden Gate and over the hills. The foot of the Clay Street hill was lost in the fog. The chosen workman took his place, grasped the handle of the grip, and Hallidie shouted, "Jimmie, are you ready?" Jimmie looked down again into the billowing fog below and shook his head. It was a mad, impossible adventure. No man would dare go plunging down that hill submerged in fog. He turned pale and climbed off the car.

381

Andrew Hallidie, taking his place, released the brakes, seized the cable with the grip, and slowly the car rolled down the hill and came to its destined stop at the turntable at Kearny Street.

Well, that was one thing! It was natural that a body heavier than air would roll down a hill. But could the cable drag the cumbersome thing up the hill again? Hallidie shoved the turntable around, and the little car pointed its nose up the hill. Hallidie released the brakes, the grip seized the cable, and up Clay Street block after block rolled the gallant little car. Exciting? Yes! It was a breathtaking adventure; a new era was born. But there were no cheers, no blaring bands. Hallidie and his friends stood solemnly at Leavenworth Street after the run had been made and quietly shook hands. That was all. No, not all, for among the legends of that night it is told that an excited Frenchman thrust his head out of a window as the little car rolled by and threw a bouquet of flowers on it. That was the night of July 31, and the dawn of August 1, 1873. On the afternoon of August 1 civic dignitaries, firemen, policemen, and citizens gathered to see the first official and public journey of the Clay Street cable car. There were mishaps. The enthusiastic crowd mobbed the little turntable and broke a bolt shoving it around. The bolt was replaced. Then the mob crowded on the car. It was built to carry not more than twenty-six people, and was overburdened with ninety enthusiasts. On the steepest hill between Powell and Mason the car balked, the grip skidded. Another delay was suffered while the grip pulley was sanded. But the journey ended triumphantly. Cable cars had come to San Francisco.

That was the beginning. The Clay Street cable car served the public well, and brought wealth to the company stock-

382

holders. People began to say that maybe there was something in these funny little cable cars after all.

Even Governor Stanford said it. He was building a great mansion at the southwest corner of Powell and California. Stanford had always loved horses, and his fine horses pulled Mrs. Stanford's carriage up and down the steep hills. But it was not only hard on the horses, it just wasn't practical. There were prize horses, race horses, in the Stanford stables, but the grumbling little cable cars could beat them up the hills, and do it without zigzagging. So Stanford discussed the matter with his railroad friends, Charlie Crocker and Mark Hopkins, and other owners of Nob Hill mansions, Lloyd Tevis and David Colton. They all agreed that a cable car on California Street would be a blessing for Nob Hill residents. But on the other hand, as an investment—well, you just couldn't grow rich on an investment that cost the consumer five cents. So they grumbled and shook their heads, and Leland Stanford went ahead with his plans. He absorbed the major part of the stock, and on April 10, 1878, five years after Andrew Hallidie's Clay Street cars were running, the California Street line commenced operations. It was the first attempt to give adequate transportation to Western Addition residents. The California Street line turned the sandlots west of Van Ness Avenue into a city of homes, and year in and year out brought wealth to its stockholders.

That was in 1878. In the ten years following Hallidie's first cable on Clay Street, cable cars were rolling along Sutter, Geary, Market, California, Ellis, O'Farrell, Post, Powell, Sacramento, Washington, Jackson, and Union Streets, to name only a part of them. And in every case the gallant little cars were climbing the hills that horses balked at, climbing hills that were making pedestrian San Franciscans breathless. Oh, they were still treated with kindly and amused patronage by some. It was said that they had a habit of swooping around curves and assaulting you when you least expected them. It was said that hanging on them as they mounted the hills was as thrilling and spectacular an adventure as a ride in a captive balloon. Little boys would lie flat on their stomachs in the middle of the tracks and look down into the slot to see what made the wheels go around. Little boys would lie on the tracks with their ears to the slot and listen to the magic humming. But, on the other hand, they became the affectionate property of the city. People would gather at the turntables and grunt and push with the gripman to turn the car around. And people would hang on —as they still hang on—to posts that ran from the car steps, and watch the city unroll before them as they mounted the hills. It was as good as a ride on a scenic railway or a ferris wheel, and San Francisco always loved scenic railways and ferris wheels.

Funny? Yes, of course they were funny contraptions in those days. And they're funny contraptions today, as they climb the Powell Street hill, and climb the California Street hill and roll out the other street to the Western Addition that they helped build. They're just as funny as the little flower stands that display their pageants of color along Grant Avenue and Stockton Street. Of course, they've lost some of their charm. They no longer stop in the middle of the block so you can step from the car to your front door. They no longer carry livestock! I'm thinking of the day when the Pacific Avenue cable car used to pick up little Tom William's Shetland pony at the stables at Pacific near Polk and take him up the hill to Pacific and Divisadero. There young Tom would be waiting, and the gripman would lift the pony off the dummy of the car and Tom would climb into the saddle and head west for his daily ride. They no longer strain at their leash carrying the thousands and tens of thousands down the Fillmore Street hill to the dream world that was the exposition of 1915. They no longer rattle out Fulton Street as they did in the days when the gripman would throw on the brakes and then climb off the car and go to the entrance of the ball park to find out, for the information of the passengers, what the score was. But they're still a part of the tradition and the romance and the color and the fascination of San Francisco. And they're still dragging San Franciscans up the hills that electric cars and busses have not as yet mastered.

When San Francisco hills are leveled, when the flower stands are gone, when there's no more red wine and garlic on Telegraph Hill, no more hungry artists on Montgomery Street, no more Chinese children laughing in Portsmouth Square, and no more cable cars rattling up Powell Street and California Street and Jones Street and Hyde, then San Francisco will take its place as a good, realistic, modern city of industry, and the color and the romance will be gone. There'll be nothing left but memories, and as new generations are born, even the memories will disappear.

385

XIV

Shanghai Kelly

This is a story of adventure, with little romance and no nostalgia. It's a cruel, bestial story. It is customary in telling stories of adventure to overglamorize, to heighten the color and intensity of the affair. It shall be my task to understate the true story here and spare your sensitivities. This is the story of Shanghai Kelly and his coworkers and competitors.

To begin at the approximate beginning, there were seven hundred deserted ships lying in San Francisco Bay in 1849, and six hundred in 1850. The numbers dwindled as the years passed. The story of those ships has been told often by me and others—the ships that brought thousands of adventurers through the Golden Gate in quest of gold. No sooner had the ships dropped anchor than the passengers and crew would desert and head for the gold-laden hills. Ships had to be manned so that they could sail around the world collecting more and more gold seekers, and there were no robot ships in those days; the decks had to be manned.

One of the longest voyages San Francisco bottoms were called upon to make was from the Golden Gate to Shanghai. There was no direct passage; passengers bound for Shanghai had to travel around the world. In the natural course of events, any ship destined to make an unnaturally long voy-

386

age was said to be embarking on a Shanghai voyage. And when it became necessary to find sailors to man the ships by foul means, the conscripted sailor was, in the popular idiom of the day, "sent to Shanghai." Later, for brevity, the term became "shanghaied." The fine, nefarious art of shanghaiing commenced about 1852, and for almost forty years, up to the days of the Klondike in the late nineties, the term "shanghai" was as freely used in San Francisco as "two-bit piece." The masters of the fine art, bearing the unsavory name of "crimps," were many, and the greatest and most brutal of them all was Shanghai Kelly.

Now, before I turn to his story, and in case any of my gentle readers are looking for a new enterprise and feel they might be interested in shanghaiing as a profession, I might perhaps explain how the art was practiced. The crimp was the mastermind. His assistants and aides-de-camp and lieutenants were a heterogeneous conglomeration of water-front and Barbary Coast habitues. They wore the polite title of "runners"; they were runners for boardinghouses and less elegant establishments.

When a ship sailed through the Golden Gate and dropped anchor off Telegraph Hill, the waters of San Francisco Bay would be busy with scores of little boats darting between the wharves and the landing ladders. In the little boats would be the runners. They would climb on board. One of their favorite opening gambits was to enter the galley and pour a jar of liquid soap into the soup. That encouraged the sailors on board in their willingness to leave the ship. They were gentlemen of nice imaginations, were the runners. Then they would circulate among the sailors. They plied them with free liquor. They gave them cordial invitations to be guests at the boardinghouses they represented. They promised them all the free liquor they could drink. They promised them sundry other inducements that time and the occasion does not permit my discussing here. They even promised them full pockets of money, so that they could indulge themselves as their fancy dictated. And to cap the fascinating climax, they promised to introduce them to kind-hearted, humanity-loving skippers who were shortly prepared to sail on pleasure cruises to the bewitching islands of the South Seas, skippers in quest of adventure-loving, honorable sailors of the sea. What more could a poor sailor ask, especially after a lunch of soup spiked with liquid soap? Down over the sides, down the landing ladders to the small boats, poured the crew. They were encouraged with more liquor. If they had a sudden change of mind they were hit over the head with brass knuckles or a blackjack. If more convincing argument was needed, a knife was used. And if by careless misfortune the resisting sailor died, then it was a simple matter to drop him over the side of the small boat into the arms of friendly San Francisco Bay. We are sorry to have to confess that a newspaper of San Francisco warned visiting skippers that if they interfered with the industry of the crimps, the officials of San Francisco politics would see to it that they procured no crews for their own ships.

So the runners brought their victims to the lodginghouses. Lovely ladies plied them with liquor. Their possessions were taken away from them and locked up. The runner's work was finished. For his industry he was paid three to five dollars a victim. Now the crimp took over. He kept the sailor well saturated with doped liquor, and then a skipper arrived, prepared to hire a crew. The crimp and skipper discussed details while the object of their attention sat or sprawled, all but dead to the world. Papers were drawn up; a pen was put in the sailor's hand, and guided as he signed his name agreeing to sail that very day. One clause of the pretty document stated that for services rendered the sailor agreed to have his first two months' salary paid to the crimp. Then he was searched. All valuables on him were removed and they became the property of the crimp. Penniless and dead to the world, the sailor was shanghaiied on board the new ship, all set for a long voyage of brutality, filth, and misery. He was usually carried to the dock, hoisted over the side, and dumped into the hold. Then the last transaction was completed. The skipper paid the crimp a bonus ranging from fifty to three hundred dollars, depending on the exigencies of the occasion. And that money was later deducted from the sailor's wages. It was a profitable business. Runners banked as much as five hundred dollars a week. Crimps showed an annual profit individually of from fifty to seventy-five thousand dollars; it was a prosperous profession.

In passing, and before coming to the story of our hero, I should mention one other whimsical practice of the crimps. So often were the shanghaiied men stripped of their possessions and most of their clothing, that it was a common occurrence to have them carried on board rolled in blankets, so saturated with liquor that they appeared more dead than alive. When by unfortunate circumstance a crimp or a runner killed a sailor, or even if a San Franciscan was killed in the everyday run of events, it was a simple matter to wrap the body in a blanket, carry it on board a ship requiring a crew, and collect a few hundred dollars. Of course, the discovery by the skipper of a dead body at a later date was very annoying; it was decidedly a dishonest practice. Some of the crimps were so dishonest that they didn't even go to the trouble of finding dead bodies; they simply took a suit of clothes, stuffed it with straw, rolled it up in a blanket, and delivered it to the poor innocent skipper and collected the fees.

That was a favorite game of a lady crimp named Miss Piggott. Miss Piggott was a wicked old lady who ran a boardinghouse on Davis Street. She was six feet tall and tough as iron. She was also a lady of imagination. The crimp would bring in a sailor. Miss Piggott would stand behind the bar and serve him a doped drink. Then she would lean politely over the bar and tap him on the top of the head with a beer-barrel bung-starter. And as he crumpled, she would pull a lever behind the bar, a trap door would open under his feet, and he would land in the cellar. But Miss Piggott was a kindly old soul. She had thoughtfully placed a mattress in the celler on which the sailor would fall. After all, a sailor with broken bones was of less value to a sea captain than one in reasonably good repair. But after all, crimping was hardly a business for ladies, and men resented them. The masculine crimps were many. The greatest of them was Shanghai Kelly, and we will come to him in a moment.

First a story about one of his contemporaries, Calico Jim. This story has been told a thousand times, and denied a thousand times, especially by the San Francisco Police Department. Whether or not it actually happened, we don't know. But, according to the legend, six policemen were sent, at different times, to arrest Calico Jim. Jim received them cordially, plied them with drinks, and shanghaiied each of the six of them. Some time later Calico Jim left San Francisco for his home in Callao, Chile. Still some time later, the six policemen returned to San Francisco from their enforced voyages. They pooled their resources, and by drawing lots selected one of their number to go after Calico Jim. He traveled to South America, found Calico Jim walking the streets of Callao, and pumped six bullets into his body, one for each of the police-men. So justice was served—if the story can be believed.

Shanghai Kelly was a dumpy little man. He had a mass of riotous red hair, and a huge red beard. He had fury written all over his ugly face. He was so terribly ugly that San Fran-cisco mothers used to frighten their recalcitrant offspring by saying, "You be a good boy or I'll give you to Shanghai Kelly." He ran a boardinghouse on Pacific Street between Drumm and Davis. If you care to go and look at the location some time, it was Number 33. Kelly played the game in two ways. He not only would supply skippers with crews, but if respected San Franciscans had enemies they wished disposed of, they would contact Kelly, and he would go after the un-popular individual and shanghai him, and everybody but the victim was happy.

Miss Piggott—Mother Piggott—had a trap door in front of her bar. Shanghai Kelly had three trap doors. He would serve the victims poisoned and doped liquor, and add to the charm by treating them to opium-doped cigars. Then, in the vulgar language of our own time, he would konk them on the head with a blackjack, the trap door would open, and down they would go!

Normally, Kelly didn't need to hire runners; his saloon and boardinghouse was always full of sailors. They gravi-tated to him as rats seek poisoned meat. No one will ever know how many men Shanghai Kelly murdered. But with all his brutality, all his ruthless monstrosities of behavior, Shanghai Kelly had an imaginative sense of humor, and that led to one of the most amazing episodes in the history of San Francisco's shanghai trade.

It happened about the year 1875. San Francisco was a thriving, busy metropolis in those years. The mining-camp days were gone; the railroad had come; the city fathers wore silk stovepipe hats; millionaires were as plentiful as five-story skyscrapers. On a day in 1875 three ships passed the Farallones and dropped anchor outside the Heads. They sent word in through the Golden Gate, probably by the pilot boat, that they each required a complete crew immediately. One of the ships was the *Reefer*. To this day sailors will tell you of the odious reputation of the *Reefer*. Its captain was a brutality-mad monster. Its decks were overrun with vermin. It was a floating palace of filth and obscenity. Crew after crew had deserted to escape the insane cruelty of the skipper. Its reputation had traveled all the seas ahead of it, and it was all but impossible to sign a crew for its nefarious voyages. Well, that was Shanghai Kelly's pretty assignment, to supply crews for the *Reefer* and its two companions. A wholesale order! But, by a strange perversity of fate, Kelly's boardinghouse was almost empty when the call came, and Kelly was not one to pass up an opportunity to make money in wholesale figures. There was no time to send runners up and down the docks seeking stray sailors. That would be a costly undertaking and would take too long. No, this was wholesale business, and Shanghai Kelly handled it on a wholesale basis.

He chartered the *Goliah,* which was an ancient paddle-wheel steamer that had drifted around the bay for years. Everybody in San Francisco knew the *Goliah*. He announced that his birthday was imminent, and because he had so many friends who had been kind to him in the past, he would celebrate his birthday by giving a great picnic. There would be all the food they could eat, all the liquor they could drink, all the tobacco they could smoke or chew. There would be music, and less refined attractions. The invitation was broadcast up and down the Barbary Coast. All were welcome,

392

riffraff, bums, degenerates, and cutthroats. Shanghai Kelly drew no social line! It was his picnic, and he wanted everybody to have a good time. They came by droves. They clambered and they staggered up the gangplank. When ninety guests stood clustered on the deck he pulled in the gangplank. The *Goliah* tooted its asthmatic whistle and put into the stream. It chugged out past Black Point, Fort Point, Mile Rock, through the Golden Gate and the Heads and out into the open sea. Everybody had a good time! As Kelly had promised, there was all the food they could eat and all the liquor they could drink. The ninety gathered on deck and sang, and drank toast after toast to Shanghai Kelly, and wished him many happy returns of the day. And then, one by one, they crumpled on the deck in drunken stupors. It was a fine job! Kelly was well pleased. He steamed out to where the three ships lay at anchor, and crews were hoisted over the sides of the *Reefer* and its two companions. Of course, none of the shanghaiied men were sailors, but that didn't matter. They would work, or they wouldn't eat.

Having collected his thousands of dollars in fees and bonus, Kelly gave orders to the skipper of the lumbering old *Goliah* and she turned her stumpy nose back to the Golden Gate. Then Kelly faced a problem. He had no perceptible conscience in the matter, or in fact in any other matter. But he had steamed out of San Francisco with ninety men. He might have some difficulty explaining their absence when he returned. So, he steamed down the California coast waiting for providence to take a hand in his affairs, and kindly providence smiled and said, "Be of brave heart—here's the answer to your problem." Off Point Concepcion, the ship *Yankee Blade* had been wrecked on a rock. It was a well-manned ship, and Shanghai Kelly nobly saved every man on board. He carried the survivors to the deck of the *Goliah,* and back to San Francisco it wheezed and tooted—a victory ship. It tooted triumphantly up to the dock. And down to the dock came San Francisco, cheering with wild excitement the contingent of sea-soaked, weather-worn men. Shanghai Kelly was a hero! Everybody forgot about the ninety men with which he had sailed away. After all, they were only riffraff.

Shanghaiing was only one of the arts practiced at Kelly's boardinghouse. It was a hotbed of thieves, pickpockets, and men who murdered for a silver dollar. His runners were as ruthless as he was.

The most famous of them, a New York boy named Johnny Devine and known as Shanghai Chicken, had committed every crime on the calendar, including a dozen killings. The climax was reached in 1868 when Devine went on a killing spree with his chum, Johnny Nyland, one of Kelly's milder runners. They headed down Pacific Street to Battery and over Battery to the saloon of Billy Lewis, where they knifed and shot several men without provocation. They traveled along Front Street to Vallejo. In the Maitland boardinghouse, they slashed their way through men gathered there, wounding several. They shot out the lights and fired at the bartender. Finally they came to grips with huge Billy Maitland in person. To tell of that fight, our own weak fiber pales. It is enough to say that Devine left with his hand severed at the wrist. Devine left the hospital with an iron hook instead of a hand. It proved a handy weapon, but Shanghai Kelly was very angry and discharged Johnny Devine, and the runner went downgrade swiftly. After all, Shanghai Kelly had a reputation to live up to.

Many years ago, at the time of its publication, I read Jack London's *Sea Wolf,* and I remember the controversy the book aroused. People said, "It's a great book, but the author has too much imagination; there could not be so much brutality concentrated in one man as London has concentrated in the skipper of the *Sea Wolf."* There was the same controversy some years earlier when Frank Norris wrote his masterpiece, *McTeague.* People said, "It's a work of art, but only in fiction could you find a monstrosity to compare with McTeague." But year after year the Kellys, the Devines, the runners, the crimps, and the boardinghouse ladies were a part of the San Francisco picture, surpassing in vile brutality any character of fiction from the days of the tragic Greeks to the days of Norris and London. It's an ugly picture—not a picture to be proud of. But it was a significant chapter in the story of San Francisco, side by side with its stories of high adventure and nostalgic romance. It was a time of terror when it all was happening. Today it savours of legend, something to be remembered with amused disdain, for time and the gentle fogs that drift across our hills have a way of seasoning horror and tragedy.

XV

E Clampus Vitus

This story of E Clampus Vitus came to me from various sources. The story of Downieville at Christmas came to me from friends in Downieville, and from Mr. H. S. Furlong, a member of the Lord Sholto Douglas Chapter Number 3, Ancient and Honorable Order of E Clampus Vitus, through whose inspiration and labors the Downieville Christmas party was made possible. From Auburn, the home of the Lord Sholto Douglas Chapter, went forth the call of peace on earth and kindness to little children. Men of good will have kept the traditions of Christmas alive for two thousand years. And this is a story of men of good will.

Downieville is on the north fork of the Yuba River way up in Sierra County. Its location on the river gave it its original name; in the days of '49 it was called The Forks. It might have gone on through years of western history as The Forks if it hadn't been for the visit of Major Charles Downie.

The Major, with a working crew, was covering a large area in the Yuba and Feather River countries, looking for gold. He came to the town of The Forks, liked the looks of it, and decided that there were probably rich deposits of gold in its vicinity. Some people say that this part of the story is true, and some say that it is just a legend. Some tell us that their fathers lived thereabouts in 1849 and that the story is absolutely true, and others tell us that they had an uncle who had a claim right on the edge of Downieville in 1849 and 1850 and there's not a grain of truth in it. But the story is that Major Downie, having seen The Forks and having liked its looks, paid the local authorities twenty dollars to change its name to Downieville in his honor.

Just a few miles to the east of Downieville there was a camp called Sierra City. In the fifties, local citizens were convinced that either Downieville, if you lived in Downieville, or Sierra City, if you lived in Sierra City, was destined to become the largest, most metropolitan, and wealthiest city in California.

Sierra City was a wild and woolly town, an exciting place at the height of the gold fever. The men fought for gold, and sometimes they had to fight for beans and bacon. When they weren't fighting they were working hard at the business of finding entertainment. So one night in 1857, when the greater excitement of the Gold Rush had faded away and the citizens of Sierra City had settled down to the steady routine of gold digging, a group of Sierra City gentlemen, looking for entertainment, said, "Let's have a lodge."

So they formed a lodge and called it E Clampus Vitus, and what that means, I, a Clamper, have never been able to discover. But E Clampus Vitus was the most remarkable lodge, brotherhood, or secret society ever founded in the West. The brethren, in secret session that night in 1857, first decided that they had to have a master for their lodge. There was some argument as to whether he was to be called Exalted High Master, Worshipful Pasha, or a number of other names that would frankly have no place here, but they finally agreed to call him First Noble Grand Humbug. Sam Hartley of Sierra

397

City was elected to that exalted position. That night Sam and the brethren laid down the rules and regulations that would govern the activities of the Ancient and Honorable Order of E Clampus Vitus.

The first and practically the last, and by far the most important rule agreed upon was that any traveling man, drummer, or commercial salesman who came to town would be ineligible to sell merchandise in the town until he had become a Clamper. The cost of initiation was every bit of gold he had on him. The sky was the limit!

As to the motivating objective of the order—there was none! The members simply met to initiate new members and increase their treasury. The results were inevitable. Word of the Sierra City organization reached the outside world, and traveling men began to give the town a wide berth. Every merchant in the town was a Clamper, and by mutual agreement the business of the town was closed to all non-Clampers.

Now traveling men were willing to spend a couple of dollars to encourage a joke, but when it came to sums that ran into many hundreds of dollars, the joke became an expensive tragedy. So traveling men passed Sierra City by and sold their wares in Downieville, Goodyear Bar, Moore's Flat, and Randy Doodler. Whereupon the merchants of Downieville, Randy Doodler, Goodyear Bar, and Moore's Flat were given charters by the mother lodge, and in no time at all E Clampus Vitus had spread through every town, city, and mining camp from the Northern Mines down through the Mother Lode to the Southern Mines.

That settled it! California was the traveling man's paradise. Any amount of merchandise of any quality at any fantastic price could be sold to the miners. So the traveling men fell in line. They came to town, to Sierra City and all the other towns, and the first thing they did was to seek out E Clampus Vitus and either establish the fact that they were already members, or join then and there. Of course, word of the unlimited initiation cost had become generally known, and the traveling men were careful not to have too much gold on their person when they came to town. A hundred dollars was considered a reasonable initiation fee, and it was a simple matter to add a hundred dollars to the price of the merchandise sold. The result was that E Clampus Vitus, with no regular activities or justification for being, and even without regular meetings or a meeting place, became a tremendously wealthy organization, and the most distinguished thing about it was its treasury.

Then new stories began to circulate; stories that the Clampers were an organization of rowdies, meeting to invent what later became known as "traveling-men stories"; that they spent their time playing practical jokes on members and non-members, and that the jokes were not the kind generally discussed either in polite society or in the less select society of mining camps. All in all, the joke that had commenced in Sierra City was developing into a disreputable and far-reaching organization with great potential power, and all that power was apparently being put to bad use.

One day a story came to one of the Northern Mines of a family of grubstakers who were in desperate want. They could find no gold; the father of the family was tubercular; the mother was trying to care for a dozen or more children; the daughters were being tempted by the gay lights of the mining camps. You may add to or vary the story as much as your imagination pleases, but the fact remains that there was a family in desperate want. The miners were hard men, according to all standards, but at the same time they were sentimental and easily moved by suffering. So they decided a fund must be raised to put the family on its feet; whereupon one member of the round-table or saloon-bar discussion demanded, "Why raise a fund? The Clampers are rich! We're all Clampers! Why not use some of the organization's gold?"

Then there was an argument. Someone suggested that instead of digging into the treasury they tax every Clamper within sound of a ram's horn. Thereupon a ram's horn, a sheep's horn, or perhaps a horn of an ox, became the symbol of E Clampus Vitus. The station or office of Grand Noble Musician was created. The horn was dignified by the name of Hew-gag, and at the sound of the Hew-gag all Clampers would drop what they were doing and come to a meeting. The immediate wants of the tubercular miner were alleviated. And from that day on, at the sound of the Hew-gag in the hills, or in any town of the hills, every miner, merchant, blacksmith, and card-dealing gambler would drop what he was doing at the moment, and rush posthaste to the designated meeting place to give help.

Overnight the Ancient and Honorable Order of E Clampus Vitus became one of the most powerful charitable organizations in America.

For instance, there was the night that fire wiped out almost all of Sierra City. The Hew-gag was sounded in every camp over a radius of fifty miles. The Noble Grand Humbug, the Clamps Peetrix, the Clamps Veetrix, and the Grand Royal Treasurer of every chapter passed the hat. One chapter reported a collection of one thousand dollars that had been left over from funds raised for a Fourth of July celebration. That went into the hat. Thousands of dollars poured into the treasury of Baalam, the mother chapter of E Clampus Vitus, to relieve the brethren of Sierra City. That was only one instance; there were dozens, perhaps hundreds, of them. Nice ladies whispered that they heard that the men did the most awful things at the Clamper meetings. But the good that was being done far outweighed the evil, and E Clampus Vitus had become a proud, honored, and powerful organization. Then gradually, just as it had started, it died out.

Now all of that was eighty and ninety years ago, and for a good part of those years E Clampus Vitus was only a tradition and something of a joke among the new generation of traveling salesmen.

Then one day, it must have been about 1930, three prominent San Franciscans whose grandfathers or fathers had been Clampers met in San Francisco. Each of them was vitally interested in the history and legend of San Francisco, and they agreed that E Clampus Vitus should be revived. Those three men were Leon Whitsell, George Dane, and Carl Wheat. They sent messengers into the hills. They sounded the Hew-gag, and old-timers who had not heard that sound for more than half a century dropped what they were doing and came to the meeting. E Clampus Vitus was functioning again.

In the beginning I promised you a Christmas story about men of good will, and it's time to come to the story.

It happened that a number of years ago great floods swept the Sierras, storms such as had not been seen within the memory of old-timers for many years. The rivers rose and overflowed their banks; small camps were completely wiped out, and the thriving town of Downieville lay in the full path of the storm. The bridge over the north fork of the Yuba River at Downieville was piled high with the flood tide. Then suddenly the bridge gave way, the dam made by the piled-up debris burst, and Downieville was submerged below the rushing waters.

They still tell stories up there of that strange cargo that came rushing with the tide; a goat, a turkey, a pig, a crate of onions, an old shed, a part of Barton's store, and the Ponta House came sailing by like an ark with smoke pouring from its chimney. The whole town was floating. All telephone and telegraph wires were down, roads were impassable, and it was impossible to send to Nevada City and other towns for help.

In the middle of that raging flood, perched on a slight rise of land, was the Downieville School crowded with children all clustered around their teacher, Marian Billings. She stood there with the youngsters huddled around her while their world flooded by them; she led them in song, from one song to another, and she wouldn't let them stop singing long enough to think about the disaster. Finally somehow men made their way in rowboats to the school door, and all the youngsters were rowed home. Eventually, of course, the storm subsided and the waters rolled away.

Now all of that was very exciting, and all was well that ended well. But it wasn't ending well for the school children of Downieville. The town had been struck a staggering blow; everybody was hard up; Christmas was just two weeks away; and it was one of those strange conditions that seemed to happen so often: Santa Claus was threatening to pass Downieville by, just because Downieville was financially embarrassed. In short, it was mutually agreed that there would be no Christmas in Downieville in 1937.

Then suddenly one day in Auburn the sound of the Hew-gag was heard. At the sound of the Hew-gag, the soda jerkers, the gas-station man, the pin-ball enthusiast, and the banker dropped what they were doing and rushed to the meeting place, and the Grand Noble Humbug of Auburn proclaimed, "The children of Downieville need you. What say the Brethren?"

And from the assembled brethren came the traditional shout, "Satisfactory!"

The Hew-gag sounded in Nevada City, and the brethren of Nevada City shouted, "Satisfactory!"

The Hew-gag sounded in Marysville, and the brethren of Marysville shouted, "Satisfactory!"

In Grass Valley, in Colfax, in Yuba City, up and down the valley and the hills, the Hew-gag sounded, and the brethren shouted, "Satisfactory!"

Finally, the Hew-gag was sounded louder than it had ever been sounded before, and the Royal Musician shouted, "California, the children of Downieville need you. What say the brethren?"

And as if with one voice, the brethren answered, "Satisfactory!"

So it was that on Christmas Eve in the year of Our Lord 1937, a caravan of one hundred automobiles came winding up the Yuba Canyon, up the north fork to Downieville. Into the main street of Downieville they roared, and then they stopped. The Hew-gag was sounded in the main street of Downieville, and out of the houses came the Downieville children as the children of Hamelin Town had come at the call of the piper. In a few of the automobiles forty men, forty Clampers, sang Christmas carols. Out of other automobiles were poured huge bags of every kind of toy that ever delighted the heart of a child. And out of another, fat and ruddy, but with tears pouring down his cheeks, stepped Santa Claus.

With songs E Clampus Vitus had come back to Downieville in its hour of trouble, and the children of Downieville joined in and sang the Christmas carols with the Clampers. The Royal Musician blasted and blasted on the Hew-gag to proclaim to all the world that flood and storm couldn't stop men from being brothers when there were little children concerned.

XVI

Don Alfredo Robinson

For many years an old man lived in a gray house up on Rincon Hill, close to the spot where the western piles of the Bay Bridge rest on the hill today.

He was a very old man. Old-timers who remember him say that he was always an old man, at least in the years that they had known him. He died just before the turn of the century, and at the time of his death he was the oldest California pioneer. He had come to California in 1829, and in the days of which I speak, he was nearly ninety years old. A few years before his death he was to be seen on sunny mornings, walking the trails of Rincon Hill—walking very slowly. Yet even in the slowness of his gait there was virility and dignity; he was very erect, straight-shouldered, and strong. But he walked very slowly, and people who saw him and did not know him seldom realized that he walked slowly because he was almost blind. Then as the darkness closed in upon him more and more, he forsook the paths and trails of the hill, and sat in the window of his house, with his head held erect, wearing a small black skullcap. He sat there in the darkness of the room and saw the people passing by—saw them in shadow. He liked to send one of his grandchildren out into the bright sunshine of the roadway so that he could see him

405

in shadow. He was a stubborn, proud old man. He had seen the city born, had seen the city grow, and now as the shadows of his days grew longer, he clung to the living shadows that were the pulse of the new city he had never seen.

His name was Mr. Robinson—blind old Mr. Robinson. People talked about him, and said, "Poor old man. He's been very lonely for so many years."

Now that was absurd because he had many children, grandchildren, and even great-grandchildren, and they didn't neglect him; they were good to him, thoughtful of him, and considerate of his age, and had for him the natural love that the younger generations have for the very old.

But even before his blindness had closed in upon him, Mr. Robinson seemed to live apart from people, even when he was with them, as though he lived in a secret world of his own; and as though, perhaps, a part of him had died many years before and what was left was only the shell of the Mr. Robinson who had come to California in 1829. On the other hand, for many years, until his blindness had closed off the streets that went down to the city, he had been an important part of the business life of San Francisco. He had a host of friends and countless acquaintances in the business world. He was respected, admired, and held up as an example of all that was fine, dignified, and honorable in business through the sixties, seventies, and eighties of the last century.

In short, Mr. Robinson was one of the builders of San Francisco. He was wealthy and handsome in middle age, and the desirable young Victorian ladies of San Francisco set their Victorian caps for him, and papas of Victorian young ladies were willing to settle nice plump dowries on their gentle daughters, but Mr. Robinson had no thought for marriage. He had been married once, long years before, and sadness had come to him and he never would marry again. So for forty years he had lived his lonely life in San Francisco, and people shook their heads and said, "What a pity." But, there were others, older people, who knew his story, and they said, "No! Mr. Robinson would never marry again. You see, you mustn't forget that he is Don Alfredo Robinson."

Now there is an odd mingling of names that will be explained presently. The California story of Don Alfredo commences in 1829, when at the age of twenty-two he landed in Santa Barbara as supercargo, or assistant supercargo of the ship *Brookline* out of Boston. His name then, of course, was Alfred Robinson. He was an attractive, eager, straight-shouldered, strong young man, and the good Spanish Californians delighted in welcoming and entertaining desirable young men from the Eastern seaboard of the United States of America.

One family in particular was especially charmed by young Mr. Robinson—the family of Don José de la Guerra. I visited the De la Guerra house in Santa Barbara just last month. It was rather tragic. If you have visited Santa Barbara and are as fond of it as are my wife and I, you are surely familiar with the De la Guerra house. You know its courtyards, fountains, arched passageways, and iron-grilled balconies in the Spanish tradition. You know its shops, its bookshops, children's shops, shops where antique jewelry is sold, shops selling old porcelains, pewter, brass, and copper; its shops with beautifully woven textiles, and all the others. Of course, you know El Paseo, the Spanish-California restaurant that occupies a portion of the beautiful adobe buildings that are offshoots of the original Hacienda de la Guerra. We remembered rare epicurean feasts there, and authentic Spanish-American music played and sung by costumed musicians and singers who, at

407

least to all outward appearance, were authentic Spanish-California relics of the days of the dons. That was as we remember it. But, as I have said, when we visited there a month ago it was rather tragic. It was off season. The shops were not busy. In fact, we found most of the shopkeepers walking in the gardens, visiting with each other—possibly looking for potential customers in one another. And El Paseo restaurant was closed; it had gone out of business. There was, however, a sign on one of the windows of the cafe announcing that an application for a liquor license had been filed. When, and if, El Paseo becomes a cocktail bar, then indeed you can write off the days of romance as legends that are dead.

In 1829 young Alfred Robinson, having come around the Horn in the ship *Brookline,* sailed up the coast, put into Monterey Bay and, I believe, into the San Francisco Bay. Then he sailed south again and dropped anchor off Santa Barbara. He went ashore with the skipper of the *Brookline,* Captain William Gale—"Four Eyes" and "Four-Eye Gale" they called him, because he wore Yankee spectacles. They landed on the beach, commandeered a couple of mules, mounted them, and rode through the sand and shrubbery. On their saddles they carried gifts that "Four Eyes" was bringing to the De la Guerra family. Everyone who came to Santa Barbara visited the De la Guerras. That was a social custom as strictly established as an audience with the Pope in Rome, or with the President, or one of his secretaries, in Washington. They came to the hacienda and found it a beautiful, sprawling adobe with great courtyards (where today the shops stand), with fountains that played in the sunshine, and with flowers everywhere. They were made welcome and were led through the stately halls that Don José de la Guerra had furnished with rare pieces from the treasure houses of Mexico and Cathay, and even from that same Boston whence had come the good ship *Brookline*.

The travelers, "Four-Eye Gale" and young Robinson, were welcomed by Don José and his wife, Dona María Antonia of the Carrillo family, who was called the most beautiful woman in all of California. They delivered their gifts, they drank the sweet and rich chocolate that had been prepared for them, and they marveled at the luxury that surrounded them. Don José was one of the wealthiest men in Spanish California; his lands covered miles, and his cattle grazed on his more than three hundred thousand acres. It was said that a ladder led to secret rooms under the red-tiled roof where the floor was covered with huge baskets heaped to brimming with gold doubloons. Now, I frankly don't know the monetary value of a doubloon, but it is sufficient to say that these baskets, huge as barrels, overflowed with gold.

There is always an inclination to romanticize about events that happened more than a hundred years ago, and to color them because there is no one living who can dispute the facts. But the scenes I am going to describe for you now are in no way colored by my imagination. They are taken from the memoirs of Alfred Robinson as he put them down in *Life in California*, a book he wrote in the 1850's, and that classic of American literature, *Two Years Before the Mast*, written by young Richard Henry Dana after he had visited the Hacienda de la Guerra.

Alfred Robinson was welcomed and accepted, in the tradition of California hospitality, as a member of the household. Festivities and entertainments were planned for him. One day a *merienda*, a dancing picnic, was held at Laguna Blanca, the White Lake. The guests came in scores, all in ox-drawn carts, sheltered from the hot sun by unbleached cloth

409

that was stretched above them. Behind the cart that carried Dona María Antonia with her sister and young Robinson came the carts with dozens of singing, laughing, shouting youngsters. Their oxen were driven by Indians. Then came carts carrying great baskets and platters of chicken, turkey, tamales, and sweets. Next came the riders on horseback, singing as they rode through the trees. They reached the pavilion at the side of the lake, and there musicians were waiting to play for them, and singers to sing for them, and there were dancers in lovely bright colors. It was an unforgettable fiesta. But in that gay and colorful gathering there was one for whom Alfred Robinson had no eye; she was Dona María Antonia's small daughter, Ana. She was a pretty little thing, but she was only a child, far too young to interest so fine a gentleman as Mr. Robinson from Boston. But small Ana never took her huge black eyes from Mr. Robinson. When he smiled, she smiled; when he frowned, she frowned; when he sighed, she sighed. She was like a parrot or a little monkey mimicking a human being.

Well, that was in 1829, and Ana was seven years old. Alfred Robinson stayed in Santa Barbara as a guest of the De la Guerras for seven years. He was baptized and became Don Alfredo Robinson—baptized José Maria Alfredo. His Yankee days were forgotten; he was a Spanish Californian.

He set himself up in business as agent for the Bryant-Sturgis Company of New England, the first United States agency to be established in California. Up and down the coast of California he sailed, trading in tallow, hides, and otter skins. Whenever he returned to Santa Barbara, small Ana was waiting for him, her great eyes following him, smiling when he smiled, frowning when he frowned. And quite suddenly Alfred Robinson, Don Alfredo, woke up and realized that he had never seen Ana before, and here she was, a beautiful woman. He fell in love, and was unreasonably astounded to find that the woman, Ana, loved him. Not that she was really a woman—she was only fourteen years old—but a girl of those tender years was a woman in the warm sunny days of old California. So, they were married. Ana was not yet fifteen years old, and Alfredo was twice her age, and that was as it should be; Dona María felt toward Alfred as though he were her own son, and it was well that her daughter should marry young, and marry a man old enough to be wise and strong.

No wedding in all the history of California was more wonderful. It was the first wedding in California history of a California girl and a man from the United States of America. Richard Henry Dana and the captain of the *Alert* were among the wedding guests. The steward of the *Alert* spent three days at the hacienda, making pastry and cake for the wedding festivities. Dressed in deep black, the bride went into the mission to the confessional with her sister at ten o'clock in the morning. Nearly an hour later the mission bells rang out, the great doors swung open, and the bride came out. She was now dressed in white, and was accompanied by the bridegroom and followed by a long procession. As she stepped from the church door, the *Alert,* lying in the bay, fired a salute of twenty-four guns, and instantly was dressed from stem to stern in flags and pennants. At sunset another salute of twenty-four guns was fired, and the flags were run down. At dusk the crew of the *Alert* went ashore and joined the wedding party, a strange and gay and colorful company.

In the courtyard of the hacienda a great tent, capable of accommodating several hundred guests, had been raised. No invitations had been sent out; all the townspeople and their children were welcome at the festivities.

Violins and guitars played, and dancers whirled in and out of the crowd. The dancers were, for the most part, young girls. The old women sat in rows, clapping their hands to the time of the Spanish music. The dancers stood upright with their hands down at their sides, their eyes fixed on the ground before them, and glided about without any perceptible means of motion; their feet were invisible, the hems of their dresses forming a circle about them reaching to the ground. They looked as grave as if they were going through some religious ceremony. The men did better. They danced with grace and spirit; they moved in circles around their nearly stationary partners, showing their figures to advantage.

The great amusement of the evening, owing to its being the carnival, was the breaking of eggs filled with cologne or other essences upon the heads of the company. Another custom was for a young lady to sneak up behind a gentleman and knock off his hat, whereupon the two would join in the dance. Or a gentleman would creep up behind a lady and plunge his hat on her head and down over her eyes, and then, without knowing to whom the hat belonged, it was the girl's privilege to say whether or not she would dance with the owner. If she decided to dance, then the gentleman was to be her partner the rest of the evening and was to escort her home.

For three days and three nights the dancing and the carnival continued, and the gay Spanish costumes of the Californians and the dress uniforms of the sailors and officers from the *Alert* made an unforgettable scene.

So Ana and Don Alfredo were married, and when Ana was just turning fifteen her daughter was born. Then her

412

husband, Alfredo, horrified her by telling her she must now go to Boston with him and to go to school to be educated as young New England girls were educated. Ana was horrified, but she was a dutiful wife, and Alfred Robinson and his bride set sail for Boston, via Honolulu, leaving the infant to be raised by Dona María Antonia.

Then commenced long and sad years for the young wife. Business took her husband back to California; he was away for two years at a time. And each time he did return he found Ana confused by American ways, confused by American schoolgirls who giggled and whispered about the black-eyed Spanish girl who had a baby in far-off California. Thirteen years passed, and the years meant long separations from Alfredo and eager hours when he did return.

The family increased. There had been the baby girl in Santa Barbara, then a son in Boston, then another baby and another until the family of Don Alfredo Robinson numbered eight children. Children, heartache, loneliness, the cold snows of Boston winters, and the cold humor of Boston matrons—all these took their toll, and Ana faded. On one trip to Boston Robinson was shocked by the white, pale face and deep, hollow eyes of Ana, and the thin flesh that hung loose on her bones. All boded no good, so he took her back to Santa Barbara. There were festivities when she arrived, fiesta and carnival and dancing, and great tables heaped with cakes and wine. But Dona Ana Robinson had lost her grip on life. She stayed there in the Hacienda de la Guerra with her children and her mother, Dona María Antonia, and awaited the infrequent returns of Don Alfredo from his business trips. Slowly, too tired to struggle longer, she died. She was still a girl, less than thirty years old.

They buried her under the altar of the Santa Barbara Mis-

413

sion. And Don Alfredo—Alfred Robinson—went away to San Francisco. This was in 1855 when the first fever of the Gold Rush had ended, and San Francisco was the Western metropolis. For more than forty years he lived there, a sad and lonely old man. He walked through the business life of the city, distinguished, straight-shouldered, and esteemed by all—one of the builders of San Francisco. When passers-by saw the old man walking slowly along the trails of Rincon Hill with his hands clasped behind him, he would nod his head courteously and perhaps smile, but as though he didn't really see them, as though he were living in the past. Then the darkness of blindness closed about him, and all that was left was the old man in the skullcap sitting at his window in his darkened room, watching the shadows pass in the sunshine outside.

XVII

The Crocker Spite Fence

To commence at the beginning, a few weeks ago a very old man came into my garden and asked for work. He said he was a good gardener and could make things grow. He was straight-shouldered and keen-eyed, but he looked much too old to do garden work. I didn't like to tell him that, although as all who enjoy their gardens know, gardeners were at a premium during the war—and still are. So I simply said that garden work was pretty hard work, especially when the ground was baked by the sun and had too much adobe in it, but he persisted. Of course, he couldn't do a lot of spading, but at least he could come around late evenings and water the flowers and shrubs.

I agreed to have him come and water during the two weeks I would be north on vacation, and then we talked for a while. I asked him if he had always been a gardener, and he said with dignity, "Sir, I have been almost everything. I've been a stevedore. I've been a pipe fitter. I've been a church janitor and I've been a bartender." Then he returned the courtesy and asked me what I did, and I said, "I write for radio, a Sunday show called 'This Is Your Home.'" "Oh, yes," he said, "I've heard it. I could tell you some stories about San Francisco. I was born here eighty-five years ago."

"Did you ever tell the story," he asked me, "about Charlie Crocker and his spite fence?" I said that I had told it briefly in passing, but I didn't know much about it—only what I had read. "I can tell you more about it," he said, "I was there."

Now, it's very interesting to delve through shelves of volumes of books and suddenly light on bits of unknown or unfamiliar history or romance or adventure, but far more fascinating is the privilege of meeting a relic of old times who can say, "I was there," as calmly as you might say "Please pass the salt." Of course, the memories of the rare old-timers one meets are not always reliable, and my old gardener was very vague on certain points and I know he was inaccurate in others. But to the story of Charlie Crocker and his spite fence, as I know it briefly, the old man added so many details that it came alive for me, and as a matter of fact became much more than a comedy drama of San Francisco comic opera days. So here is the story.

Charles Crocker, as all who have been exposed to Western history know, made a great fortune when he, with Mark Hopkins, Collis P. Huntington, and Leland Stanford, built the Central Pacific Railroad, which united with the Union Pacific to connect the Atlantic and the Pacific. Having made his fortune, Crocker, like the other three—in fact, like all the millionaires created by the railroads, the Comstock bonanzas, and the earlier gold fever in the Mother Lode—started out to spend as much money as quickly as he could in a way that would be in keeping with the development of that section of the city. But behind all the lavish spending, there was a streak of shrewd business. Crocker was willing to pay for the show he bought, but for every dollar he spent he wanted a dollar value, and would prefer, when possible, to get a dollar and a half.

416

So up Nob Hill went the railroad and bonanza millionaires, the Tevises, the Floods, the Townes, the Crockers, the
Stanfords, the Huntingtons, and the Hopkins. If I have repeated this part of the story too often during the years I have
been telling stories of San Francisco, it is simply because it
fascinates me every time I go up the California Street hill and
see those names perpetuated in the great hotels and apartment houses, the Stanford Court, the Huntington, the Fairmont, the Mark Hopkins.

Mrs. Hopkins was the best, or the worst, of all the spend-
ers. The huge mass of ornamentation she created at the
corner of Mason and California Streets looked like one of
those ornate wedding cakes fabricated by a baker whose
sugar and flour has turned from white to gray. Next door, in
simpler and better taste, Leland Stanford and his gentle wife
built a huge mansion. Huntington selected his site, and then
Charlie Crocker came down from Sacramento, climbed the
hill, and determined to build the most imposing of all the
San Francisco mansions. He selected the square bounded by
California, Sacramento, Taylor, and Jones Streets, the site
now occupied by Grace Cathedral. To acquire the property,
he had to buy it piecemeal from its numerous owners and,
driving a shrewd bargain, Crocker bought to right and left
as reasonably as he could until he had acquired all but one
small piece of ground owned by a gentleman named Yung.

It's a funny thing about that gentleman named Yung. My
old gardener, telling about it, said "Oh, yes, it was owned by
a man named Yung—Y-U-N-G." And, in all the various
accounts I have read in books and papers, it was always a
gentleman named Yung. He never used a first name, or even
initials. He was just a gentleman named Yung who was an
undertaker. Mr. Yung was a little man; Charlie Crocker

weighed two hundred and thirty pounds. Huge Mr. Crocker went to small Mr. Yung and offered to buy. Mr. Yung said he would consider selling if Mr. Crocker would pay his price. Mr. Crocker replied that he was always willing to pay value for value received, and as a matter of fact had to have Mr. Yung's property at any price. I am uncertain as to the actual historical sequence of events, but Mr. Yung, either at that time or at a slightly later date, demanded thirty thousand dollars for his little Nob Hill lot. Mr. Yung wanted thirty thousand dollars! That was probably thirty times what the property was worth. Mr. Crocker said he wouldn't pay the price. "Very well," said Mr. Yung, "Then I won't sell." So, owning all but one little chunk of that great square block, Charles Crocker ordered his architect, Arthur Brown, to build an imposing, magnificent mansion, the tallest mansion in the metropolis of San Francisco.

I have a vague memory of the mansion of Charles Crocker in the days preceding the fire of 1906, and the one feature that is most distinct in my memory is the tower on the California street front. Its top was seventy-six feet above the sidewalk. Mr. Crocker not only wanted the highest structure in San Francisco, but he loved a view. He took particular delight, after the mansion was completed, in wheezing ahead of his guests up those flights upon flights of stairs—two hundred and thirty pounds being transported in the operation—just to show his guests the view. The importance of a view is very significant, in the light of subsequent events.

When the mansion was completed, Mr. Brown, the architect, called it early Renaissance. Mr. Willis Polk, a distinguished architect of a later day, called it "a delirium of the wood carver." Be that as it may, the mansion was completed. It cost a fortune, and it was not only the highest but the fanciest and most imposing affair in the city. Charlie Crocker was delighted.

There was only one fly in the ointment of his delight, that little piece of ground on the Sacramento Street side owned by the gentleman named Yung. Again and again he called on the undertaker, demanding that he sell, and again and again the gentleman named Yung refused, or rather raised his price still more.

Mr. Yung had built himself a modest little house on the small piece of land he owned. To the north he looked out to the Golden Gate; to the east, the Bay and the Berkeley hills; to the south the new city sprawled below. And all around was a great flood of light and fresh air. Mr. Yung had selected his ground with wisdom.

"All right," said Charlie Crocker, "you won't sell. I can't do anything about your view to the north; you can look at the Golden Gate until the mountains close in again." But, around the three remaining sides of Mr. Yung's house and tiny garden, Crocker built a fence forty feet high. To all intents, the Yung home might have been at the bottom of a well.

The news spread through the city. All through the days that the carpenters were at work building the spite fence, throngs climbed the Taylor and California Street hills to watch the progress of the work, and to cheer. Charlie Crocker had many friends, and as many enemies, and the enemies cheered as well as the friends. The fence was completed, Mr. Yung was hidden from view on three sides, and still the crowds came. It became a pastime in San Francisco, when there was no fire or circus or other things to do, for the good citizens to say, "Let's go up Nob Hill and look at Charlie Crocker's fence." Mr. Crocker's archenemy, the railroad attorney A. A. Cohen, said, "If Charlie had the brains we all believed he had, he could have charged the spectators a bit apiece and bought the lot a dozen times over with the profits."

Then a new element came into the affair. The element, rather than absurd comic opera, was grim tragedy. Twenty years earlier a young boy had run away from his home in Ireland and shipped before the mast as cabin boy. He was a hotheaded adventurous youngster. As a matter of fact, he was only eleven when he ran away to sea. His name was Denis Kearney. For twenty years Denis knocked around from port to port and from pillar to post, and by devious paths eventually found himself in the most adventurous of all ports, San Francisco. He was thirty years old. He had developed a wild, fighting spirit and a vitriolic tongue, combined with the smooth Irish persuasive speech sometimes called blarney. He was ready for any adventure, ready to align himself with any crusade that called for fighting and oratory. He came to San Francisco and found the city seething under the domination of William Coleman, the pioneer who had headed the Vigilance Committees of 1851 and 1855.

Kearney embarked on a new crusade. He demanded that the port of San Francisco be closed to Chinese immigration; he claimed that Chinese laundrymen were driving business away from all other laundries; he proclaimed that cheap coolie labor was ruining the chance of American labor to make a living wage; he cried out in the phrase that San Francisco has tried to live down for seventy years and now has all but forgotten, "The Chinese must go!" That cry was the clarion call of a new Vigilante.

Fundamentally it was far more serious than that. The Bank of California had failed, resulting in financial and commercial disturbances approaching panic. Thousands of un-employed marched the city streets. Churches and charitable organizations were feeding thousands of people each day. Bread lines formed. This was all new and incomprehensible to a population who had lived in wealth and extravagance since the discovery of gold a few years earlier. It was, in addition, a time of unrest across the nation. In the Eastern states and cities strikes, especially railroad strikes, had cul-minated in riots and bloodshed. The melting pot of labor was at a boiling point. It required but a leader to blow the top off; a leader, and a place to put the blame. Well, that was easy.

The wealthy industrialists, the railroad builders in par-ticularly, were responsible. They had imported the cheap Chi-nese labor. They were the men who had taken the bread out of the mouths of the American workers. The Stanfords, the Hopkins, the Huntingtons, and the Crockers were re-sponsible; and against the Big Four of the railroad hierarchy most of the hatred was directed. A great mass meeting was called. The designated place of meeting was the vacant sand lot adjoining the city hall. The entire police force and the National Guard were called out to preserve order. And to the sand lots marched most of the population of San Fran-cisco.

James F. D'Arcy, a national labor organizer, presided. He spoke with strength, lamenting the introduction of cheap labor into a community that had known prosperity for a generation. The crowds, close enough to hear his words, listened with tense silence. But on the outskirts of the vast gathering, hoodlums, trouble-seekers, and trouble-makers started spontaneous riots. The riots lasted for three days and three nights. Chinese laundries throughout the city were wrecked. Several persons were killed. Mobs marched on the docks of the Pacific Mail Steamship Company, and holding that company responsible for the transporting of Chinese labor from the Orient, tried to burn the ships lying alongside the wharves. Unsuccessful in that, they burned lumberyards and warehouses. Against the rioting, plundering mob, four thousand good citizens banded together to put the disorder down. Neither laboring man nor industrialist had use or respect for the unlawful marauders.

But that week the laboring men of San Francisco learned that they had strength. It was time they organized! And that was the signal for a young adventurous opportunist to emerge and take his place as a leader. He was Denis Kearney. Kearney took a leading part in the organization of the first, the San Francisco chapter of the Workingmen's Party of California. Its charter demanded reduction in the hours of labor, abolition of national banks, all property to be assessed at its full value, and a closed door to China. Its battle cry was, "The Chinese must go!"

There was much that was right and much that was wrong in the platform of that first Western labor union, and it is not for me to argue the points. But after that first meeting, Denis Kearney held forth every Sunday on his sand lot and the sand-lot meetings became history. The climax was reached when, at one of the meetings, a state senator and editor of a San Francisco paper preached tolerance and compromise. Kearney answered him by demanding that every workingman buy a gun to enforce his demands, and that every capitalist be hanged. The crowd cheered and laughed, and State Senator Roach retired in confusion. Denis Kearney had become, if not a hero, at least a figure to be reckoned with, and the crowd was with him. But Mr. Kearney, a demagogue of demagogues, began to confuse issues; he shouted and ranted and railed and didn't care very much what the subject of his attack was so long as the sensation-loving San Franciscans would listen to him. He berated the Chinese population, and then almost forgot about the Chinese in his attack on the railroad kings, the Comstock tycoons, the steamship magnates, the bank presidents, and even the little grocery-store owners who, according to him, were dragging mankind in the dust. In a word, Denis Kearney was wholeheartedly against almost everything.

Meanwhile, up on Nob Hill, fat, huge, genial Charlie Crocker enjoyed taking the sun on sunny days on the sidewalk in front of his California Street mansion. He would walk slowly, with his hands clasped behind him, and smile benignly on the monstrous palace he had created, and the lark was on the wing and all was right with the world. He would stroll serenely around the corner and there would be the forty-foot fence behind which, like a man at the bottom of a well, Mr. Yung, the undertaker, crouched in his castle that was a shack. Oh, unquestionably Charlie had won a victory; unquestionably the people of San Francisco delighted in his victory. But there was gall in his cup of happiness. He still didn't own that little piece of land that Mr. Yung called home.

Then suddenly, on October 29, 1877, Denis Kearney changed the picture. No longer would he preach from sand lots; no, he would storm the strongholds of the masters. He marched an audience of thousands up Taylor and Mason and Jones Street hills to the crest of Nob Hill. He made a wild and impassioned speech, crying that he would "destroy all the rich hell-hounds in California." He led three hundred of his followers to the edge of the Crocker-Yung spite fence and said, "This is the symbol. This is the way the overlords crush the little men—one a ruthless builder of railroads, the other a poor defenseless little undertaker. Tear down the fence!" he shouted.

But by this time the temper of the crowd had changed. They were determined to have their rights, but they'd destroy no property. It's true they pressed and milled against the fence and it shook on its foundations, but they wouldn't tear it down. Meanwhile, in his mansion with the high tower, stout Charlie Crocker perspired and trembled, and in his little dwelling at the bottom of the great well, Mr. Yung trembled and shivered. My old gardener was in that mob that day, a gangling youngster seeking excitement, and when the excitement subsided, for him that was the end of the story.

According to the records, some time later Mr. Yung did sell the small bit of land to the Crocker estate at a much more reasonable but still exorbitant figure, and the fence came down. And eventually that land that had seen strife and rioting and bitterness was presented to the Church and today, high above the city on the ground where Charlie Crocker's mansion and Mr. Yung's shack stood, rise the beautiful walls and buttresses and spires of Grace Cathederal.

Isadora Duncan

The San Francisco part of this story came to me in bits, like the insignificant pieces of a jigsaw puzzle that have no particular import in themselves, but which, when placed in their proper positions in the over-all design, make a fascinating picture.

I found the first small piece in a book on old San Francisco. The year was 1878, and the item tells of the home of Joseph Duncan, a suave and cultured gentleman who was a cashier of the Bank of California and whose fortune crashed with William Ralston's. He was known as a connoisseur of the arts, and was often asked to select paintings and marbles for the palaces of his friends who knew little about them. His own home at Geary and Taylor Streets held many treasures. At one corner now stands a drugstore, at another a grocery and fruit store, at another the Bellevue Hotel, and the Clift Hotel on the fourth. In 1878 Joseph Duncan's home of art treasures occupied one of those corners. I am under the im-

425

pression that it stood at the northwest corner where the drugstore now stands. But it was shortly after 1878 that the home was broken up and scandal and divorce resulted. Mrs. Duncan was a virtuous, high-principled Victorian lady. Joseph, the poet—a very good poet, too—the dreamer, the connoisseur of arts, had lost his heart to a spinster lady on Russian Hill, and Mrs. Duncan divorced him.

The Duncans had several children and very little money, and that made the scandal more tragic. Joseph Duncan had been a brute and a scoundrel, and Mrs. Duncan virtuously spent many years telling the children what a scoundrel their father was. However, one of the children met Papa some years later and found him a charming, cultured gentleman of appealing personality. But that all came later.

The second small piece in the jigsaw puzzle was a personal experience of mine that happened a few months less than fifty years after the scandal at the corner of Geary and Taylor Streets. It was the summer of 1927. I had been invited to a soiree—no other word describes the function—in a home out on Pacific Avenue. There were long-haired artists; there were hungry musicians; there were starving poets; and I, who belonged to none of those classes, joined the shrilling throng. It was the hour between sunset and darkness. Most of the guests congregated around a grand piano while a lady of mature years with a page-boy bob explained that she had never studied music or learned to play the piano, but in a dream had been inspired to go to the keyboard and play. She now sat at the keyboard and played the most amazing music I had ever heard, while most of the guests congregated around her and sighed and clasped their hands. I sat on a small stool at Ina Coolbrith's feet.

Ina Coolbrith, the poet laureate of California, was very

old. That was the last year of her long life. She was a gentle, sweet-faced old lady, as old-fashioned and old-world as a miniature painted on ivory. She wore a simple, black silk dress, an old brooch at her throat, and her mantilla falling over her thin white hair. She told me of the men and women she had known when San Francisco was young. Her friends had been legion. Many of them had achieved greatness and died, and only Ina Coolbrith remained, a link between the Golden Dawn and the San Francisco of 1927.

Her friends had been Mark Twain, Bret Harte, Charles Warren Stoddard, Robert Louis Stevenson, Joaquin Miller, Harr Wagner, and Jack London, and they all had loved her. She told me about them quite simply as though their love was her rightful heritage. And there was one other. He was a poet, a dreamer, a musician, and a connoisseur of the arts! She had been the one great love of his life. His name was Joseph Duncan. Joseph Duncan was long since dead and she, the poet laureate, went on, dreaming in the memories of the departed years. Joseph Duncan! He had been so gentle, so great an idealist, and so fine a poet! What if he was a cashier in a bank; even a bank cashier could dream of sonnets. But he was dead and the pages of his story were closed. Yet it was not really ended, for he lived on in his children. There were four of them, and Ina Coolbrith had learned to know and love one of them well. Her name was Isadora Duncan.

As I stated before, that is the second bit in the pattern of the jigsaw puzzle. Now, before we come to the story of Isadora Duncan—for after all, this is her story—there is one more small piece in the puzzle pattern. It happened only a year or so ago. I went to see *The Lute Song*, one of the Theatre Guild productions at the Curran Theatre, and in that lovely pageantry one of the characters was an old blind father.

427

He was led across the stage, his steps faltering, as the blind should be led. But this wasn't acting; this was type-casting. He was in fact blind. He was Raymond, one of the four children of Joseph Duncan.

There are the bits in the pattern. It was in Oakland, a few years after the scandal at Geary and Taylor Streets, that Ina Coolbrith met the child, Isadora. She came to the Oakland Public Library, as a few years later Jack London was to come, to ask the library lady, Miss Coolbrith, for a book to read. Just as Ina Coolbrith was to guide Jack London's reading some time later, so she guided and shaped the mind of the small daughter of Joseph Duncan.

Isadora was a quaint child, a strange mixture of practical common sense and worldly sophistication, and she was a dreamer like her father. The child loved poetry, beauty, and rhythm, and she hated reality. She was, in fact, a rebel. Her childhood had been an unhappy one. There was strife and divorce, with her mother's insistence that her father, Joseph, was a demon in human garb. Then there was her mother's disavowal of the religion in which she had been raised, and her espousal of the atheism of Robert Ingersoll. These were the unhealthy shapers of Isadora's childhood. Of course, when she eventually met her father, she found him a charming, lovable poet, and that heightened the confusion in her mind. Passing years tend to soften the intolerance of childhood, but Isadora Duncan never lost her contempt for the institution of marriage as she had seen it. When she was twelve years old she made a solemn vow that she would welcome love when it came, but she would never marry.

After the divorce, Mrs. Duncan found a small, drab home in Oakland for her brood of four children. The constant poverty in which they lived was softened by the wealth of poetry and music that Mrs. Duncan brought into the home, molding the lives of her small offspring. The four of them loved to sing, loved to play-act, and above all, loved to dance.

Somewhere I have read that Isadora Duncan gave no thought to becoming a dancer until she had gone to Europe. This was an absurd distortion of fact. Isadora Duncan danced as soon as she could walk. The children read every book, good or bad, that chance flung in their path, and when chance was busy with other people's problems, Isadora went to the Public Library. There she met Ina Coolbrith. Ina possessed a rare talent. She not only created beauty, but she had the gift, as well, of inspiring the creative instinct in others. Isadora was an eager pupil. Her reading carried her back to the classical culture of ancient Greece, and the natural, unaffected, spontaneous Grecian art became her inspiration and dream. Toe-dancing, social gymnastics, was to be scorned. She demanded, from the very beginning, self-expression unrestrained by rule and custom.

When she was fourteen years old, pupils, children of neighbors, came to her to be taught to dance. The Oakland classes grew and then there were classes across the bay in San Francisco. Every day Isadora and her sister, Elizabeth, took the ferryboat to San Francisco and then walked from the Ferry building to Sutter and Van Ness Avenue. There, in the old home they had rented—the Castle mansion—they taught the young hopefuls of San Francisco society forms of the dance that were fifty years ahead of their time. Charles Caldwell Dobie, speaking of those days, said that he visited the old Castle mansion after the school had seen its last days, and found the hardwood mantels chopped away. Possibly surmises Dobie, it was used for kindling wood to keep the Duncan sisters and their pupils warm during their days of poverty.

But Isadora didn't like poverty and she didn't like restrictions. She didn't like boundaries to life or to the place in which she lived. There were distant horizons awaiting her. She read about them in her books, the faraway places that call to all imbued with the creative instinct. Any place would do as long as it was "away." She induced her mother to take her to Chicago. What matter that the family purse was, as always, almost empty? Funds were found and, armed with a wealth of enthusiasm, mother and daughter started out.

The Eastern theatrical managers saw the girl dance, praised her, told her it was all very lovely. But, after all, that wasn't the accepted way to dance; it wasn't the way of the theater. No, it would never do. She'd better go home to San Francisco and be a schoolteacher! Their funds were gone, so they pawned their jewelry. They ripped a bit of old Irish lace from Isadora's dress and sold it. Finally, starvation, not a threat but an actuality, faced them, and then Isadora received an engagement. At last, she was to dance—to dance in a music hall. In a fogged atmosphere of stale beer and tobacco smoke the girl appeared, a breath of ancient Greece. Her audience chewed on its cigars. They found it all a little uncomfortable. This certainly wasn't what they'd come to see! In short, they wished she'd get through so the next act could appear.

But in the audience one night sat a dreamer like herself. He was Augustin Daly, the theatrical producer. He saw what none of the others had seen—the vision, the ideal, and the dream behind the dancing of the girl. He cast her as one of Titania's dancing fairies in his production of *A Midsummer Night's Dream*. He gave her small parts in pantomimes. Perhaps she couldn't force her audience to understand the

430

beauty of simplicity, but at least this gave her the opportunity to dance, and to eat.

Her brothers and sisters were sent for, and the family settled to New York. One night Isadora danced to the music of Ethelbert Nevin; Nevin was in the audience, entranced. He arranged for concerts for her, and suddenly blasé New York hailed a new star, a child with the wisdom of the ages and the simple innocence of the sheep that grazed on the Athenian hills. Society accepted her. She danced for the four hundred in Newport's exclusive salons. They made much of her, but just as swiftly they dropped her. And again the family purse was empty.

Once again the lodestone of distant horizons beckoned. What did it matter that the family had no money? They would go to London. After Isadora had borrowed right and left from her former friends of Newport society, the Duncans sailed.

In London, a few engagements brought a few dollars, but the few dollars weren't enough to fill the young hungry stomachs. Then one night Isadora and one of her brothers were dancing in their Grecian veils in the small garden of a tiny house in Kensington Gardens. They danced by the light of the stars and their only audience was their own shadows. Quite unexpectedly, a beautiful lady came and stood watching them and was amazed. When they had finished their dance she swooped down upon them and took them to her own home. She was Mrs. Patrick Campbell, the idol of the London stage. She played for them and they danced for her; she sobbed dramatic tears, and introduced them to London society.

The meeting with Mrs. Pat Campbell was the turning point in the story of Isadora Duncan. Mrs. Campbell intro-

431

duced them to London society and London acclaimed them, and British royalty honored them. Life became busy, hectic, and full to overflowing with triumphs—and setbacks. Duncan, the dancer, had arrived, but the girl, Isadora, was still a rebel against customs and traditions—and marriage.

She danced in Paris and was cheered. She danced in Berlin, and the art-loving Germans went mad with enthusiasm. The artists and students of Munich idolized her. The story is told of the night that, unharnessing her horses, they dragged her carriage through the streets of Munich in a rain of flowers. They carried her into their cafe, lifted her onto a table, and she danced for them. Life was gorgeous. But always at the back of her persistent mind was her dream. Some day she would dance in the land of ancient culture where the Athenian maidens had made the dance a religion. Some day she would bring back the beauty of classical simplicity to the people of the nineteenth century. What if she did dance in scant veils that showed the honest beauty of her form? There could be no evil in honest beauty. Europe cheered her and virtuous old wives condemned her. Isadora went to Athens and took her mother, brothers, and sister with her. And on a green hill that faced the Acropolis, she made a solemn vow that here she would build a temple to art.

In the Athenian hills Isadora gathered a class of small Grecian boys about her. She taught them the dances of ancient Byzantium, as well as Greek choruses and songs. Bare-legged, with sandaled feet and flowing draperies, the Duncans danced from village to village, and the world called them mad. A year passed, and their purse was empty. Bidding a tearful farewell to the peasants who had learned to love the lady on Kopanos Hill, Isadora and her kin returned to modern civilization and Vienna.

Vienna took her to its gay heart, and success and wealth returned. But now Isadora Duncan learned that life without the fullness of love was incomplete. Then, in Berlin, in 1905, she met Gordon Craig, the colorful, handsome, glamorous son of Ellen Terry. This was the great love; this was life at its highest. The world sighed, and giggled, and was delighted. Isadora was perfectly happy. A baby was born, and they named her Deirdre. Isadora adored her.

New friends came to join the strange household. Eleanor Duse, her life shattered by the tragedy of her romance with D'Annunzio, took them to Italy to aid her in the production of an Ibsen drama. Isadora danced her dances of the Athenian hills in Rome. But now a new ambition and dream was born. She would train choruses, and build her greatest ballet around the music of Beethoven's immortal *Ninth Symphony*.

She came to the United States and danced to the music of Walter Damrosch's orchestra. America was shocked, and delighted. Of course, everyone had a body, but one didn't acknowledge the fact. Even modest ankles weren't to be exposed. That nonsense was ended by an edict from no less a wielder of strong opinion than Teddy Roosevelt. "Isadora Duncan," he proclaimed, "seems to me as innocent as a child dancing through the garden in the morning sunshine and picking the beautiful flowers of her fantasy." So the master politician became poet, and Isadora danced and was forgiven her sins.

She built a school where she taught young girls the beauty of the dance. She was the priestess of the dance, and in that role did more to return it to its ancient glory than has any other single man or woman in the world's history of terpsichore.

433

Then, one night in Paris, Isadora Duncan danced to the haunting melody of Chopin's "Funeral March," and a vision of tragedy came to her. She danced with eyes closed and saw her two children threatened by evil. She danced as though in a trance, and her audience sat, thrilled, chilled, and breathless. It was terrible and it was beautiful. A few days passed and the father of her son stood before her. His lips were dry and his eyes were haggard. He told of the death of her two children.

Life was dead; dreams were dead; the world was empty. Isadora Duncan, the rebel, had won her rebellion and lost all that was worth the fight. She felt she would never dance again. But she did dance. In her tragedy she had become a giantess, and life does not or cannot stand still. She won new triumphs, found new loves, and achieved new furors. She faced new tragedy in 1914 when, under the shadow of the dawn of the first World War, another baby was born—dead. Still she danced, and still she continued to teach her girls. She danced her *Ninth Symphony* to an audience that sat as though in the presence of a creature divine. Her greatest creative dream had become a reality.

Isadora Duncan, the little girl of Geary and Taylor Streets in San Francisco, died in 1927. A veil caught in the wheel of her automobile. There was the grinding of brakes—and then darkness. She died tragically, horribly, and the world was upset for a few hours and then went about its business. But those who had loved her and who knew her dream of beauty mourned the passing of a human creature who had been an honest builder of dreams. She had done more for the art of the dance than any other man or woman in history. And above all else, she had been the honest daughter of her poet father.

434

XIX

Memories

Here, in this time of stress, are bits of San Francisco and incidents and people that almost everyone has forgotten; many of them things today's generation has never heard of; many that the old-timers have forgotten all about.

For instance, the old Tivoli Opera House was one of the city's dearest memories. But do you remember the days when the Tivoli moved from Sutter Street between Powell and Stockton to its new and ornate home on Eddy Street? It was a white building, an overdecorated villa; it had lattices and trailing vines; it was pretty in the rococo prettiness of the Victorian era. Yes, many of you have heard of it, if you don't remember it. But do you know of the wide doors that led from the balcony to an outside gallery where refreshments were served?

Best of all, do you remember Gracie Plaisted? Gracie had more San Francisco dowagers worried than peace of mind permitted, and Gracie had more gay blades wearing carnations in their buttonholes and a little extra wax on their moustaches than any other soubrette who sang in San Francisco. Gracie was a heartbreaker, and night after night, week after week, season after season, the handsome San Francisco lotharios went to the Tivoli to see Gracie in *Don Caeser, The*

435

Wizard of the Nile, The Idol's Eye, The Queen's Lace Handkerchief and the other musical comedies of musical-comedy days. Gracie was tiny and cute; she had the butterfly waist of the soubrettes of the nineties; she was so adorable that countless fond San Francisco mothers watched their eager sons with misgivings. All the girls of the original Floradora Sextette had married millionaires; anything could happen.

But the passing of time took Gracie from the San Francisco scene, and a new menace, a new soubrette, came to threaten the equanimity of the feminine elite. She was Christine Nielsen, who didn't sing very well and didn't dance very well, but she was pretty as a blond valentine. She had blond hair; she had a baby-doll face; she had an irresistible smile and soulful eyes. That was her most dangerous threat—her soulful eyes. Young men would crowd the Princess Theatre to ogle her. They crowded every corner of the Princess except the front row, and that was invariably filled with stout, bald-headed, middle-aged gentlemen who came to listen to the music. Christine had such soulful eyes that the word got around that she had a soul. Then, one night, during the performance of *The Isle of Spice,* Christine sang in the middle of the front row of the chorus. That is, the chorus sang and Christine stood there, apparently oblivious to the audience, picking her teeth with a celluloid toothpick. Whereupon a lady in the audience said, so audibly to her husband that all the orchestra audience could hear her, "Christine is digging for her soul."

Do you remember when Lunt's Dancing School was on Polk Street? Now, don't treat that question lightly, for Lunt's Dancing School was a significant, important part of San Francisco life. In the eighties and the nineties all of the nice little boys and girls of the nice families went to Lunt's. They were taught the schottische, the polka, the circular waltz, and a dance long forgotten—the *varsovienne*. Professor Lunt was a huge, square, solid man, and he danced as lightly as a bubble. He was always very formal. He always led the dancing-school cotillion garbed in a Prince Albert coat and striped trousers and a high collar that could hardly find parking space under his heavy jowls. And while he strode through his gyrations, followed by his flock of the children of the first families, his assistant, Mr. Reynolds, would recite in a tired voice, "One-two-three-one-two-three-turn out them little toes—twos-threes!"

One afternoon, in the middle of the schottische, Professor Lunt stopped suddenly and clapped his hands briskly together. Mr. Reynolds stopped counting his "Toes—twos-threes." The children stopped, open-mouthed, still holding their poses, as though playing "Still water, no more moving." Professor Lunt, with sad resignation in his voice, said, "Frank, I shall never be able to make a dancer of you; you are incapable of paying attention; you have not the brains to make a dancer. That is all, children. Continue, Mr. Reynolds. One-two-three." Frank was Frank Norris, perhaps the greatest of California novelists.

Do you remember, forty and more years ago, a very beautiful San Francisco woman with silver-white hair and dark, flashing eyes? Hers was a familiar face in the city of the seventies, the eighties, and the nineties. But people looked at her with not exactly distrust, not exactly disapproval, but as though she were threatening the sanctity of feminine traditions. For this handsome woman had presumed to invade the masculine world, and had become a physician and surgeon. It wasn't quite good taste, when you stop to think of it. Certainly, it was not practical. No sane-minded person

437

would trust their fate in the hands of a woman physician! But the lady persisted. She had first come to California with her parents in 1850, when she was a small child. The family had moved away. She grew up, went to an Eastern university, married, and had three children. After her children were born, she decided to take up the study of medicine. It was really scandalous. Woman's place was in the home, and this woman had three children and certainly plenty to do without assuming masculine prerogatives. But she persisted, went East to a medical school, graduated, and came back to San Francisco to practice medicine. With the exception of a chosen few, her name is forgotten. She was one of the great women of San Francisco—Dr. Charlotte Blake Brown, the founder of the Children's Hospital.

Do you remember when Adeline Patti came to San Francisco in the eighties? That must have been in 1884. The city went hysterical over her. The shop windows on Kearny Street advertised Patti opera glasses, Patti reticules, Patti lace fans. The fashionable dressmakers were busy for weeks building impressive gowns for the ladies of "The 500." The florists' shelves were literally emptied the week of her arrival. She arrived, she sang and the city adored her. Her carriage drove through the streets and to Van Ness Avenue on the outskirts of the city; and wherever the carriage went, cheering crowds followed it.

One afternoon a formal reception was given for Madame Patti at the Van Ness Avenue mansion of General and Mrs. Walter Turnbull. As a compliment to the great singer, Mrs. Turnbull had engaged three child prodigies, the Joran children, to give a musical recital during the reception. Madame Patti beamed, patted the children on the head, wiped a sentimental tear from her eyes, and turning to Walter Jr., the small son of the Turnbulls, she asked, "And what

438

do you play on, my little man?" Young Walter drew himself up proudly and answered, "I play on the sidewalk."

Do you remember General W. H. L. Barnes? The General was a man of many interests, but his most beloved project was the Mercantile Library, that Mercantile Library that was later to combine with and lose its identity in the Mechanics Library of today. The Mercantile Library was heavily burdened with debt, under which it staggered year after year. Finally the debt was lifted when General Barnes conceived and consummated a huge lottery—but that's another story.

Before the conception of the lottery, General Barnes promoted an amateur theatrical benefit at the California Theatre, the proceeds to go to the indigent library. But General Barnes never did things on a small scale, so he enlisted the services of two of the greatest actors of the day, Barrett and McCullough. The play, if my memory does not fail me, was called *Rosedale*. Every seat in the California Theatre was sold for five dollars. Society turned out in a fashionable array that, we are told, has never been equaled in the city's gala nights. Bush Street, from Market to Grant Avenue, was solidly packed with carriages and coupes and victorias. Members of "The 500" played all the roles, and McCullough—poor John McCullough, who later went completely mad—stood in the wings, tears pouring down his cheeks, and recited, "All the world's a stage, and these are the greatest actors I've ever seen on it." At the end of the first act of *Rosedale,* fifteen hundred bouquets of flowers were heaped on the stage. And in his box General Barnes grinned and grinned. The Mercantile Library was saved! I wonder if there is anyone reading this who remembers that night of *Rosedale.*

And I wonder if they remember a major who came to California to live in the late sixties or the early seventies.

439

Yes, there was one great San Franciscan who remembered Major Rathbone. Gertrude Atherton remembered him, although she must have been a small child at that time, for the Major married a Miss Atherton, who was either an aunt or a sister of Gertrude Atherton's husband. And I can hear Gertrude Atherton say, "It really doesn't make much difference."

At any rate, the Major built a beautiful home for his bride in Menlo Park close to the Atherton home. Great homes were being built down the Peninsula in those days, and the new California millionaires, vying with each other, put everything into their homes. There were the great estates of Edward Barron, Senator Latham, Bill Ralston, and many others. Well, Major Rathbone saw them all and determined to surpass them all. He personally supervised the purchase of furnishings, draperies, and fixtures. And the crowning glory of the mansion was a huge and beautiful crystal chandelier he ordered for his reception hall. The salesman beamed approval. "Senator Latham," he said, "ordered one exactly like that for his home." "Where did he hang it?" the Major demanded, and the salesman answered, "In the stable, sir."

Do you remember when the dean of California painters, Virgil Williams, found a sponsor who subsidized him to go to Italy and make copies of the world's masterpieces for his Mission Street home? Williams went to Rome, and spent several years there copying the paintings of Titian, Tintoretto, Leonardo da Vinci, Botticelli, and many others. In all, he copied more than one hundred great masterpieces. These copies were shipped to San Francisco to hang in the gallery of the home of the sponsor. They caused so much excited comment that finally the sponsor had to open the galleries to the public. Mission Street became the haven of culture-minded San Franciscans, and a steady parade of eager art lovers and many who knew nothing about art streamed into the great hall of the Mission Street mansion. The name of the sponsor was R. B. Woodward, and his art gallery became so famous and his visitors so many that finally he opened the gardens of his estate to the public, and Woodward's Gardens became a feature of San Francisco life. With shrewd perception, Woodward realized that many of the sightseers cared nothing about art. For their benefit he added a music stand, artificial lakes where children could play, fountains that danced in the sunshine of Mission Street, and finally, as an attraction that completely overshadowed the popularity of the art galleries, live seals and sea lions were established in a huge tank, a zoo was added, and Woodward's Gardens became an unforgettable San Francisco tradition. But not many remember the copied masterpieces of Virgil Williams.

Do you remember when the miles of sand dunes that lay beyond Stanyan Street were just sand dunes, later to be turned into Golden Gate Park? In the days of the sand dunes, Point Lobos road ran through them out to the beach, and the road was gay, day and night, with smart carriages, teams and tandems of horses, phaetons, surreys, and victorias. Out at the beach there was a highly respected resort, a fashionable and refined resort, called the Ocean Side House. It was there that the leaders of San Francisco, the Hall McAllisters, gave a brilliant dance, a cotillion that was attended by "The 500." Polite waltzes and polkas were played by the orchestra, and the fame of the Ocean Side House spread. But it reached its peak and waned, and eventually became a dilapidated and disreputable beer hall. Meanwhile, fashionable San Francisco was driving a little further up the beach to the original Cliff House. There were many attractions at the Cliff House; its cuisine was compared with the offerings of the most famous restaurateurs of Paris. One ate delicacies and watched through opera glasses the patriarch of the sea lions, Ben Butler, on the Seal Rocks. Old Ben died eventually, and his stuffed carcass was mounted in Sutro Baths. The Cliff House had one strict rule—fine wines and liquors were served to its masculine clientele, but nothing stronger than a glass of sherry was ever served to a lady.

Do you remember when Bret Harte lectured on modern literature at the University of California, and his wife, who had the misfortune of being the wife of a great man, delighted her guests with her beautiful contralto voice?

Do you remember when the warship *Zealous* steamed into San Francisco Bay with Admiral Farquhar in command, and the Admiral invited a select group to divine services on deck Sunday morning? It was a radiant day of brilliant sunshine, and in the quiet calm of the morning four hundred sailors stood on deck and chanted The Litany, and the voices, like a heavenly choir, rang out across the waters.

Do you remember when thirty thousand San Franciscans marched down Post Street, down Market Street, all to converge on Montgomery Street? And there, on an improvised platform, a young clergyman, speaking softly and slowly at first, finally lifted the huge assemblage to a frenzy of enthusiasm with his impassioned plea that California remain a state of the Union and not secede. When he was through, the state was saved for the Union. That young clergyman was Thomas Starr King.

Do you remember all these things, big and small? No, you can hardly remember them, for San Francisco is a new world today and these were the things that happened—important and unimportant—when the Golden Dawn was still golden.

442

XX

Toby Rosenthal

People who sit, hour after hour, before one painting in an art gallery have always aroused suspicion in me. They're probably perfectly sincere, enraptured and fascinated by the painting that has crystallized their attention. And yet I invariably feel that they are either sitting with a soulful expression in their eyes to impress other people in the gallery, or else their feet hurt. Still, without guile, I went time and time again to look at a picture. I stood before it—well, not hour after hour, but for interminable minutes. I was too young to have guile; I was nine years old. I was too young to be bothered with aching feet. I went to see that picture again and again and again because it thrilled me. I fell in love with it, fell in love with the girl in the picture. I dreamed about her. Her name was Constance. Her last name was Beverley. Constance de Beverley. I loved to say the name out loud. There was as much music in her name as there was romance in the picture of Constance.

As I recall her, and almost fifty years have passed since I have seen her, she stood, in a crimson suit, a boy's suit, in a dismal, somber inquisition chamber of gray stone, being tried by a group of terrifying and solemn priests in brown robes. In later years, especially when I saw Katharine Cornell as St.

443

Joan, the picture of Constance de Beverley always made me think of the trial of Jeanne d'Arc.   ,

"Constance de Beverley" was painted by Toby Rosenthal, and Toby Rosenthal was to have a temporary although unhappy effect on my boyhood. I wanted to be an artist. Mozart was writing symphonies when he was eight years old. I was drawing pictures when I was nine years old. There the parallel ends. But my parents were impressed with the drawings I made. A couple of generations ahead of me, a granduncle had been a fairly famous artist in Germany. Perhaps I was destined to be great. So I was sent to the Mark Hopkins Institute every Saturday morning, and when classes were over at noon, I always went to the top of the hill, into the Mark Hopkins Gallery, to look at Constance de Beverley.

For newcomers unfamiliar with the traditions of San Francisco, I should explain that the erstwhile Mark Hopkins Institute is now the California School of Fine Arts and a portion of the University of California. But in the days of my love for Constance de Beverley it was the Mark Hopkins Institute, with classes held in the Mark Hopkins family stables at the corner of Pine and Mason Streets. Above the stables, at the corner of California and Mason, stood the Mark Hopkins mansion on the ground now occupied by the Mark Hopkins Hotel. The mansion was the gaudiest affair in San Francisco, a mass of cupolas, turrets, and flying buttresses, and I suppose there must have been gargoyles, too. There were balconies and bay windows, and the whole thing was somewhat like one of those sugar confections of a castle seen in bakery windows, only instead of being sugar-white it was a somber gray-black.

Mark Hopkins never lived in the mansion. After he and his companions of the Big Four had completed the Overland

444

Railroad and made millions of dollars, Hopkins, whose tastes were simple, found a modest home downtown. However, his young wife had other ideas. She intended to live in the grandest and most expensive house in San Francisco. Well, she was young, and Mark Hopkins loved her, so he said, "Go right ahead. I have all the money in the world. You can build a combination of Buckingham Palace and the Petit Trianon as long as you are happy." So Mrs. Hopkins went right ahead. If she had stopped at the combination of Buckingham and the Trianon it would not have been so bad, but with her young architect, she combined every type of architecture from the ruins of Cambodia to New York brownstone fronts. Mark Hopkins never lived in it. He died, mercifully, just about the time it was completed, and Mrs. Hopkins moved to New York, married her young architect, and built several more mansions. The Mark Hopkins mansion on Nob Hill was opened to the public so that they might enjoy the art galleries that were a part of it. The stables became the Mark Hopkins Institute. Amazing stories were told about it. It was said that the entire hill was a catacomb of underground secret passages. It was not only said, but we, the small pupils, did actually penetrate tunnels dug in the hill as far as our courage would let us go, and each neophyte, each newcomer to the school, was initiated by being thrown into one of the dark tunnels for a few minutes, and the door locked behind him—a grim experience, as grim as the trial of Constance de Beverley.

And now let us return to Constance, or rather to Toby Rosenthal, or, if you will, to the effect he had on my youth. My career as an embryonic artist was a failure. I revolted against supervision and resented having the teachers tell me how to draw the things I saw. I was doing the seeing and knew how I saw them. Complaints went home to my father,

445

and his invariable attack was, "How do you expect to be as great as Toby Rosenthal if you don't do what you're told?" It was like having the virtues of a cousin or elder brother held up for example. I loved Constance de Beverley, but I hated the name of Toby Rosenthal, and my father didn't hesitate to pour salt on my wounds. The story of Toby Rosenthal was like the traditional story of log cabin to president.

Toby Rosenthal had been born in Prussia in 1848. That was the year that gold was discovered in California. The name of California was on the lips of every man every place in the civilized world. Thousands and thousands came to California, but tens upon tens of thousands started an emigration to America. There was gold in California, so all of America must be a land of wealth, prosperity, and milk and honey. The Rosenthals joined the cavalcade, spending some time between New Haven, Connecticut, and New York City, but the milk and honey was elusive, and wealth and prosperity were not on speaking terms with the Rosenthal clan. So, late in the fifties, Father Rosenthal and his family came to San Francisco in the shadow of the gold fields. Rosenthal was a tailor by trade. He had a sorry little tailor shop in Stockton Street. There was a Chinese laundry on one side of his tailor shop, and a fruit stand on the other. The family was very poor and the going was hard. Somehow or other, when the boy, Toby, at the age of fourteen showed definite skill in drawing pictures, his father, Jacob, managed to scrape together enough money to send him to an art school up on Telegraph Hill.

There was no question about the boy's talent. Of course, at the age of fourteen he was doing little creative work, and his favorite pastime was the copying of cartoons and pictures from magazines, copies which, according to his father, were

446

better than the original. Into one history-making effort he crowded one hundred heads, each done with a nicety of detail, a perfection of care, and a purity of line that was nothing short of genius. According to Papa Rosenthal it was a work of art that could not be withheld from the public, so he placed it on display in the window of the small Stockton Street tailor shop. Passers-by stopped to gaze and admire. Groups gathered at the tailor-shop window and, cross-legged on his bench, Jacob Rosenthal worked at his trade with dreams in his patriarchal heart that his son might some day win world fame.

Then one evening, in the passing crowd, a wealthy San Francisco baker, Mr. Hess, stopped to admire the hundred heads of the cartoon. He entered the shop, demanded to know who the artist was, and the stitching of cloth was swiftly forgotten as the tailor told proudly of his son. Mr. Hess was a baker by vocation, a good Samaritan by instinct. With his aid, Toby became the pupil of the outstanding art teacher of San Francisco, Fortunato Arriola. Arriola was enthusiastic. Yes, unquestionably there was the spark of genius in young Toby Rosenthal and he, Arriola, would proudly assume the responsibility of making an artist of the boy. Anybody could copy pictures. He, Arriola, would inspire the boy to create. Why, some day Toby might even be as fine an artist as he, Arriola, was himself.

That was when Toby was fourteen. A year and a half later Fortunato Arriola sent for Jacob Rosenthal, the tailor of Stockton Street.

"Your son," he said, "is an artist. I have taught him all I know and he has gone steadily forward and left me behind. If he is to learn more, it must be from greater instructors than I, and you will not find such a one in San Francisco or the American continent, for that matter. Toby must go to Europe."

Go to Europe? Why that was even a greater, a more difficult project than had been the emigration of the Rosenthal family from Europe to New Haven, Connecticut. But art must be served. Dollars were scraped together and into the purse went the savings of the little Stockton Street tailor. Philanthropic San Franciscans added to the purse, and Toby Rosenthal went to Munich to be a pupil at the Royal Academy. And in his tailor shop, Jacob Rosenthal sat cross-legged on his tailor bench and sewed far into the night, and waited for word from his artist son.

It was September 1868. Throngs crowded the pavilion of the Mechanics' Industrial Fair to see the latest wonders of science, to see the prize products of California fields, to listen to promenade music, and to savor culture in the art gallery. Before one large canvas San Franciscans stood six deep—stood, stared and stared, and brushed sentimental tears from their eyes. They stared, walked away, and returned to gaze again. The subject was a dead child lying as though asleep on a bier heaped with flowers, and up a somber winding stairway are grouped the childhood friends of the dead child and the sad-eyed, somber old school teacher. The brightest, the happiest bit of color in the picture is that of the dead child in its cradle of flowers. The painting was called, "Affection's Last Offering." The artist was Toby Rosenthal. He had sent his first great canvas to San Francisco.

Other paintings followed in rapid succession and, as in the case of "Affection's Last Offering," each painting told a story. There was "The Artist Model," a young priest at his easel while his model, the cardinal in crimson robes, falls asleep. There was my old boyhood love "Constance de Beverley," and a year later, again at the Mechanics' Industrial Fair, were exhibited two Toby Rosenthal masterpieces, "Return of the Exile" and "Orphan Children at Their Mother's Grave."

Toby Rosenthal became San Francisco's favorite son. Those were the years of the railroad and Comstock millionaires, and men of wealth were building pretentious mansions to display their wealth. Nob Hill was becoming the show place of the West. Every mansion had an art gallery, and in line with the taste of the day, paintings that told stories, paintings that excited the imagination, paintings that brought tears of emotion to sentimental eyes were in constant demand. Toby Rosenthal was a sensational success. But his greatest work was yet to be seen. Rumors of it had traveled from Munich. This was the crowning glory of the artist's life. He had painted an immortal masterpiece based on Tennyson's *Idylls of the King,* and people who had forgotten their Tennyson rushed to libraries to reread the sugar-sweet lyrics. Breathless, San Francisco awaited the western journey of the masterpiece.

The painting was called "Elaine." I have seen it and I don't remember where, but I have a vague memory of the fair Elaine stretched on a bed of garlands of roses on the deck of a golden ship floating down a silver river. It had been painted at the order of Mr. Tiburcio Parrott of San Francisco, but Rosenthal had gone far beyond the idea offered by Mr. Parrott, and when the painting was completed he sold it to Mrs. R. C. Johnson of San Francisco for three thousand dollars. Oh, it was worth far more than that. All San Francisco was agreed that ten times three thousand would not have been too much and when, in 1875, Mrs. Johnson brought the painting to San Francisco to exhibit it, the city became hysterical. Probably no painting in the history of the West

449

drawn such an audience, with the possible exception of "Stella" at the expositions of 1915 and 1939-40.

"Elaine" was hung in the galleries of Snow and May on Kearny Street at the corner of what is now Maiden Lane— a street which, in 1875, had a less colorful name and a far less respectable reputation. The city thronged to the galleries of Snow and May. The fame of "Elaine" had traveled before her. Songs had been written, and society was dancing to the Elaine Waltzes. Young lovers wrote jingles to their lady loves and called them "Fair Maidens of Astolat," rhyming Astolat with Camelot. And now the picture that had been the sensation of Berlin and the sensation of Boston was actually hanging in an art gallery on Kearny Street! If the murals of the Sistine Chapel had been hung in the San Francisco City Hall, they would have caused no greater sensation. After all, a San Francisco boy had painted what in 1875 was called the greatest painting in the world, and the city came to acclaim him.

Thousands gathered on Kearny Street, seeking admission to the galleries. More than five thousand San Franciscans passed through the portals of Snow and May on the Wednesday and Thursday of the exhibit. I have read in various books about the thrills of that day, and I have been given firsthand information about the event from old San Franciscans who actually were there, but I have found no one who could tell me if, in that great crowd, little Jacob Rosenthal came to enjoy the triumph of his son.

Wednesday! Thursday! In silent, solemn procession San Franciscans filed past the canvas, awed and moved to tears by the beauty of the painting. The crowds were so great that many could not gain admittance, but there was always another day. Those who could not be admitted Wednesday or

450

Thursday would be permitted to pay homage to "Elaine" on Friday.

Friday morning San Francisco was shaken by a spiritual earthquake more terrible than any that nature had visited upon the city. When the doors of Snow and May were opened at seven o'clock in the morning "Elaine" was gone! She had been ruthlessly torn from her golden frame, and she was gone! Again San Francisco massed to Kearny street and Maiden Lane to stand in solemn silence before the doors of Snow and May, but now they stood in mourning. They filed, as in a funeral procession, before the empty frame, and they spoke in whispers. While the city mourned, the police department was at work. A network of detectives was flung around the city. Clues were discovered and discarded. Theories as to the reason for the theft were offered. Some said it was the work of a maniac who had fallen in love with "Elaine" and could not live without her. But far more reasonable was the opinion that the value of the painting had tempted thieves. True, it had been sold to Mrs. Johnson for three thousand dollars, but just after she had purchased it, Crown Prince Friedrich Wilhelm of Prussia had offered Rosenthal twenty-five thousand dollars for it.

As swiftly as the tragedy had brought grief to the heart of San Francisco, just as swiftly the mystery was solved. Into the office of San Francisco's Chief of Police walked an unidentified stranger. He had been in the vicinity of the Snow and May galleries on the night of the crime, and he had seen four suspicious-looking individuals eyeing the galleries and whispering together. He could describe the four to Police Captain Lees. One of them had a large scar on his face, and that was all the astute Captain Lees needed. Unquestionably, the criminals were four men well-known to the police—"Cut-face" Donohoe, James Curran, Tommy Wallace, and James E. Allen. Three of the men were located in a rooming house on Third Street. Accused of the crime and believing that the police had proof of their complicity in it, the culprits led the police posse to a shack in the rear of a vacant lot on Langton Street near Folsom. There, hidden in the bed clothes, rolled and sealed, and marked "Custom House Official Maps," lay the fair "Elaine." The men made a complete confession. They had made two attempts to steal the painting. The first had failed, but the second was simple. James Allen had entered the galleries, neatly cut "Elaine" from her frame, rolled and tucked it under his arm, and walked nonchalantly down Kearny Street. The entire operation had taken fifteen minutes. The confession revealed that the painting had been taken to be held for ransom—a cut-and-dried case of kidnaping. The culprits went to San Quentin for a long term.

Today, property of the University of Illinois, "Elaine" hangs in the galleries in Urbana, Illinois, and sophisticated art lovers pass her by with a glance and probably say, "Pretty, isn't it, but I prefer paintings that don't tell stories." Well, every man to his taste. Paintings that tell stories haven't a great deal of charm for me, either. But there was Constance de Beverley in her crimson trousers, her golden hair hanging about her lovely slender shoulders, her fearless, youthful courage shining as she stood boldly before her inquisitors in that somber, solemn dungeon. Yes, Toby Rosenthal's "Constance de Beverley" has all the thrill for me, even to this day, that I found in the drama of Jeanne D'Arc. Finally, when all the sentiment is forgotten, Toby Rosenthal, son of the Stockton Street tailor, was probably the most popular artist ever created by San Francisco, a city that loves its artists, even if she doesn't always support them.

XXI

Night Life

San Francisco, with all its beauty, is a gray city by day; but at night it's a city of flamboyant color—color of lights, color of shadows, and color of human life and emotions. It was only ninety years ago that a few streets were first lit with gas lights, and even in those days the custom was to travel through the muddy streets at night swinging lanterns or, in many cases, glass chimneys protecting fluttering candles. It was in the middle fifties that venturesome citizens abroad at night found it expedient to put out their lamps and candles and walk in darkness, thus escaping the attention of the Sidney Ducks, marauding gangsters who would kill a man for his purse, or if he had no purse, just for the lust of killing. So the venturesome citizen would walk in darkness, plodding his way through streets deep with mud, and likely at any moment to plunge headlong into deep pools of water. Added to the mud and the prowling Sidney Ducks were the tribes of wharf rats that infested the streets, huge evil beasts that scurried between the walker's legs, snapping at his boots as they ran. Life at night in the San Francisco streets ninety years ago was a colorful, but not a pleasant, adventure.

Of course, this was not the case on the main thoroughfares—Sansome, Montgomery, Dupont, and along Clay and

Sacramento Streets and the roads surrounding the Plaza. Here lights blazed and the clock stood still. At an early hour of the morning there was as much activity and noise at the corner of Clay and Montgomery as there was at noonday.

Gentlewomen did not appear on the streets at night. The ladies who did appear were not gentlewomen. It was unfortunate, too, because after all gentlewomen craved entertainment. San Francisco was rapidly importing actors, singers, and musicians for the entertainment of the menfolk, but no gentlewoman would go to the theater. They couldn't even visit their sister gentlewomen, because the streets were unsafe at night, so they sat at home and, at best, read the latest installment of the latest novel by that fascinating and sensational young London author, Charles Dickens. And the menfolk went to the show!

Then along came Miss Annette Ince. Miss Ince was an actress, and a crusader. She devoted herself, to quote her own words, to "raising the drama in its moral purity so that the wives and daughters of California might safely patronize the temple of Thespis." Miss Ince toured in a series of pure plays. She even appeared in the shockingly wicked *Camille*. But the Lady of the Camellias, instead of wearing the passionate flower Monsieur Dumas had ordained for her, wore lilies of the valley instead.

Little by little the joy unconfined and unrefined that had brought audiences of shouting miners and gamblers and merchants to the Bella Union and Maguire's Opera House and the American Theatre became seasoned with gentility and Annette Ince and Shakespeare. Of course, the miners had always liked Shakespeare, and the louder the lines were read, the better they liked it. When Shakespeare became too much for them, there was always Dr. Robinson.

454

Dr. Robinson! He was the city's first impressario. He loved the theater and would rather lose money angeling a theatrical performance than make money with his pills and nostrums. So every time a Shakespearean performance came to town, Dr. Robinson would follow it with his own version. Perhaps his greatest success was the drama called *Antony and Cleopatra, Married and Settled*. He produced *Romeo and Juliet* with the male roles all played by women and the feminine roles all played by men. He was angel, stage manager, actor, and box-office attendant. It was probably because of the influence of Annette Ince that he would not produce the lively, salacious Falstaff plays, *The Merry Wives of Windsor* and *Henry IV*.

However, in 1860, the first Falstaff did come to town. By now the streets were well lighted at night; the temple of Thespis had taken on new dignity, and gentlewomen were regular attendants at the theater. Falstaff came to town in the person of Mr. James H. Hackett. He gave great performances and hundreds were turned away—so many, in fact, that he had to give special readings of Shakespeare at the Academy of Music to satisfy the demands of the people who could not get into the theater. The story of Hackett's appearance is interesting today only because of a letter he received while in San Francisco, a letter that appeared in the *Daily Californian*, I believe it was, on October 14, 1863:

To James H. Hackett, Esq.
My dear sir:
    Months ago I should have acknowledged the receipt of your book and accompanying kind note, and I now have to beg your pardon for not having done so.
    For one of my age I have seen very little of the drama. The first presentation of Falstaff I ever saw was yours last winter or spring.

Perhaps the best compliment I can pay is to say, as I truly can, I am very anxious to see it again. Some of Shakespeare's plays I have never read, whilst others I have gone over perhaps as frequently as any professional reader. Among the latter are Lear, Richard the Third, Henry the Eighth, Hamlet, and especially Macbeth. I think none equals Macbeth. It is wonderful. Unlike you gentlemen of the profession, I think the soliloquy in Hamlet commencing, "O my offense is rank", surpasses that commencing "To be or not to be." But pardon this small attempt at criticism. I should like to hear you pronounce the opening speech of Richard the Third.

Will you not soon visit Washington again? If you do, please call and let me make your personal acquaintance.

Yours truly,
A. Lincoln

James Hackett came and went and Shakespeare dropped in from time to time. San Francisco became a theater town, a town of night life.

Nature had destined our city to be a port of ships, and with the ships came thousands of sailors, roving men, men of sailing vessels, men who often did not see a human face save those of their shipmates for months at a time. Along the Embarcadero the ships dumped their human cargoes, and up into the city went sailors of every land in quest of night life. Those were the real beginnings of the days of the Barbary Coast. Pacific Street was a street of noise, music, raucous laughter, and murder. And the tentacles of the Barbary Coast reached out, down through Chinatown all the way to Ellis and O'Farrell, and from Powell Street west to Mason and Taylor. This was the Tenderloin. Here the night life of the city was at its brightest; arc lights, Welsbach lights, and finally strings of electric lights proclaimed joy unconfined. Here were the theaters, the Alhambra, the Tivoli, the Alcazar, and the Baldwin. Here Madame Modjeska played *Le Sorcière,* Sothern and Marlowe were Romeo and

456

Juliet, and Nance O'Niel was a noisy Camille. Here was Marchand's Restaurant where the terrapin and nectar and the wine were cold. Here the epicure delighted in *pompano en papillote*. Of course, you're not old enough to remember *pompano en papillote,* a delicious small fish that finally disappeared from this Western epicurean world and was replaced by the more democratic sand dab. Here, at Pratt and Tierneys and at Pratt and Beckers, the pianist played "Up in a Balloon Boys, Up in a Balloon." And they were still thriving when the pianist was playing "In My Merry Oldsmobile."

The Tenderloin was gay and wicked and the Barbary Coast was sordid and wicked, but in between the two were the depths of depravity, the alleys that cut through the blocks where the White House and Sherman Clay & Company now stand. Of all the evil sinks of iniquity in the city's night life, none were worse than the place called Morton Street. Sinners often become virtuous as old age creeps upon them, and as age came to Morton Street it took on a gentle dignity. It drove out vice and changed its name to Maiden Lane. Yes, Maiden Lane, running from Union Square to Kearny Street between Geary and Post was once called Morton Street, the road to perdition. So evil had the night life of the city become in the late years of the nineteenth century, that crusaders and evangelists flocked to the Golden Gate to cry out against sin. The flickering motion pictures were coming into being. The evangelists condemned them. The trolley cars that bounced along Kearny Street were denounced and called dance halls on wheels. Poor dears, they're still being denounced! Roller rinks were condemned because they were dangerous to the spiritual welfare and moral strength of the San Franciscan and, furthermore, were dangerous to his body. The police were called on to dim the city lights and drive out vice.

457

There's another story to be told some day about the gentleman called Chief of Police; his name was Jesse B. Cook. Chief of Police Cook functioned in a pleasant sort of way when the Schmitz-Ruef scandals were shaking the city. Chief Cook had come to his chieftainhood by devious routes. Before becoming a policeman, he had been an acrobat on the vaudeville circuit with a considerable reputation as a tumbler. And, before his vaudeville days—that was far back in 1875— he had been a member of the original Black Crook Companies.

It was in the years that followed the earthquake that Oscar Wilde's *Salome* achieved its greatest popularity and the "Dance of the Seven Veils" became a popular scandal. So it was quite reasonable that a city which did every unreasonable thing with the greatest of reason should confuse Salome's dance and the dance of Little Egypt, brought from the Chicago World's Fair to the Midwinter Fair in Golden Gate Park, and a little bit of the Polynesian hula. At the corner of Kearny and Pacific, up a flight of stairs, each night the Oriental dancer did her international muscle dance. But the dance was not the most unique detail of the evening. The thing for which polite San Franciscans claimed they went to the Little Egypt Cafe was to drink Turkish coffee. Of course, the statement in itself was inaccurate. The coffee was made of a minimum of coffee, a certain amount of chicory, and a large amount of ground chocolate. One did not drink it—one ate it with a spoon!

Did you ever watch a puppy dog looking for trouble? He will tear to pieces the most precious flower bush in the garden. He will drag the laundry from the line. He will chew the furniture and refuse to eat his dinner. He will ruin the carpet and sleep on the hardwood floor. Well, San Francisco night life in its younger days was very much like a puppy dog looking for trouble, and having a sublimely good time being wicked. The more wicked it was, the louder it barked, boasting of its iniquities. But puppy dogs grow up to forget their youthful follies; San Francisco grew up and discarded its folly, but couldn't forget it. In fact, it still likes to boast naïvely; to say, "You have no idea how wicked I was when I was young." Why it's not so long ago that it was a simple matter to infuriate a San Franciscan by saying Marseilles or Pago Pago were the wickedest spots on earth. San Francisco insisted on being the wickedest! But struggle as she would to live up to her boast, the night life of the city, although it didn't disappear, changed its color. And so, just a few years ago, before the war and the embarkation of thousands of troops blurred the picture, you might walk at night up Kearny Street and climb Telegraph Hill. Little boys and little girls would bounce at your heels begging for dimes. An old man would sit in the window of a house that hung precariously on the edge of the hill and play "Santa Lucia" on an accordion. A priest would stand on the steps of Old St. Mary's and scratch his ear while he watched two Chinese youngsters walking like Charlie Chaplin.

You might walk up Russian Hill at night and find gardens riotous with geraniums, nasturtiums, heliotrope, and rich-smelling lemon verbena. The silence up there would be serene, and the night perfume-laden. You'd see the strange house built on an eight-sided floor plan, surrounded by windows that looked to every point of the compass and has lately been torn down. You would see the house in Bush Street where Robert Louis Stevenson wrote, and the little shack in the alley where Sadakichi Hartmann wrote and painted and went pleasantly mad.

You might walk up Nob Hill at night and see giggling debutantes and callow embryonic bachelors racing along

California Street in formals and dinner coats. You might come to the bench in the park that lies in the shade of Grace Cathedral—that particular bench where daring sub-debutantes, who are forbidden to smoke, puff their surreptitious cigarettes.

You might have walked at night up the blocks that were there before they cut away Rincon Hill, and smell coffee roasting, and seen the ferryboats ply the bay and hear the fog horns. Night after night up there on Rincon Hill you'd find an aged seafaring man who would tell you of the days when the last clipper ship came to San Francisco. He was second mate, an odd old character. He was there only a few years ago. He only came out at night, and strangest of all his strangeness was his hair, hair that was long and fell far below his shoulders. He wore it braided, tied with a shoestring, and tucked inside his leather cap.

Some day the night life of San Francisco will return. It will be a saner night life. Perhaps even the fascination of wicked traditions will be forgotten, but there'll not be an end to the traditions of James H. Hackett. Marchand's is gone, but it'll again be a city of amazing foods. Perhaps the old-time Welsh rarebit in the chafing dish will not come back, but there'll be Fishermen's Wharf with the burning coal embers beneath the lobster pots.

Men come and men go and fashions change, but the San Franciscan, loving his theater, loving the perfume of his flower gardens at night, loving the millions of lights that reach to the edge of the bay and to the hills beyond, loving the fog that rolls through the Golden Gate at night, loving the silhouette of Tamalpais rising above the fog, will always tell you that there's nothing in the world to compare with night life in San Francisco.

460

XXII

Tivoli Opera House

Unless you're an old San Franciscan, you've probably never heard of the man called Doc Leahy, and even if you are an old San Franciscan you may have forgotten who Doc Leahy was. Fame is short-lived and, for that matter, popularity and friendship are often easily forgotten. Doc never achieved a very wide fame, but he was one of the most popular men in San Francisco, and his friends numbered thousands. Doc liked music; he was a good judge of fine music and a stickler for perfection. He explained his virtues quite simply. "You see," he said, "when I was a kid I worked in a furniture store. One of my duties was to dust the keys of the pianos, and that gave me an appreciation for and knowledge of music." From 1893 to the days that it passed out of local history, William H. Leahy was the manager of the institution that was perhaps the most beloved of all San Francisco traditions, the Tivoli Opera House. Doc Leahy was its spark plug, its driving power, and its anchor of stability.

Now this is not to be the story of Doc Leahy, although in telling the story he will, of course, come into it. It's the story, as it has come to me from many and various sources, of the rise and decline of the old Tivoli, first as the Tivoli Gardens and then as the Tivoli Opera House, a paradise garden

461

of unforgettable music that brought more joy into the lives of San Franciscans than perhaps any other one thing. Joy unlimited—and the price was twenty-five cents.

The Tivoli Gardens opened in 1875 on Sutter Street between Powell and Stockton, on the land where the Temple Emanu-El later stood, and where now stands the doctors and dentists building, 450 Sutter. It opened in the home of Joe Kreling. From the front it looked like any old-time, high-chested San Francisco residence. Inside, it was a beer garden where the guests sat at tables, drank their beer, and listened to music. The fame of its good beer spread, but no faster than did the fame of its ten-piece orchestra and the group of Tyrolean singers who entertained between orchestral numbers.

In 1879 it burned to the ground, and Joe Kreling and his brother and wife built a new house and called it the Tivoli Opera House. It ran for twenty-six years, and in those twenty-six years of comic opera and grand opera the house was closed only one night. That was the night Mrs. Kreling died.

But let's begin with 1875 and the nature of the times, 1875, when San Francisco was ripe for entertainment. Of course, that's an absurd phrase. There has never been a time since its name was changed from Yerba Buena to San Francisco—that was in 1847—that the city has not been ripe for entertainment. The Palace Hotel was nearing completion; it was to open on the second day of October. The two great Comstock bonanzas had poured millions of dollars into the city; there had been a national financial crisis that the city had weathered, and money was free. The coast-to-coast Railroad had been completed, and the city had become cosmopolitan. Gentlemen were wearing silk hats and frock coats; ladies were wearing satins and taffetas, and diamonds on every finger of their hands; 1875 was a mad, exciting time of great fortunes and wild extravagences. Of course, there were some poor people in the city, even some who didn't have enough to eat, but they had no place in history. The city was born of gold—a city of gold—and the spending of gold became a race. French restaurants were opening. Billy Ralston was dead, but his California Theatre on Bush Street was flourishing. Opera singers, great actors, great musicians, and great clowns were traveling in luxury by steamcars, where a few short years before the long journey had been made in covered wagons. The time was ripe for something new in entertainment, and Joe Kreling opened his Tivoli Gardens.

From the opening day, the gardens were successful. It was very pleasant to leave one's wife at home of an evening— after all, a wife's place was in the home where she could do the mending and watch over the children—and to go, with convivial friends, down Sutter Street, which wasn't much of a street in 1875. It seemed that the finer homes were being built either below it on Geary and O'Farrell or along Jones and Taylor and right up the Mason Street hill to the summit. But we are digressing. It was pleasant to sit with friends in that wooden home in the four-hundred block of Sutter Street while the ten-piece band played, the Tyrolean singers sang and the waiters bustled from table to table with huge trays heaped with stemmed goblets of beer.

Joe Kreling wandered from table to table with a pleasant greeting for his patrons, and meanwhile he, too, was enjoying the music of the ten-piece band. Now Kreling was a rather shrewd businessman, and it didn't take him long to realize that the most popular music was the music of the comic operas. The music of von Suppe, Offenbach, and Mozart,

463

melodies from the *Chimes of Normandy,* and tunes from *La Belle Helene* always delighted his guests. And an idea was born. Some day he'd build a finer Tivoli Gardens, a garden that would be a palace of musical comedy, and he'd give the audience what they wanted. That day was to come sooner than he expected.

In 1879 the Tivoli Gardens burned to the ground, and Kreling built the Tivoli Opera House. It opened on July 3, 1879. For the opening, Kreling selected a new and very gay musical comedy written by two young British lads named Gilbert and Sullivan. It was called *H.M.S. Pinafore.* It ran for sixty-three nights.

Of course, the new opera house had retained the charm of the Tivoli Gardens. The guests sat at tables—for parties of four, six, or eight—in the pit, in the balconies that ran along the side a couple of feet above the pit, or in the galleries still higher up that also ran along the side from the stage to the rear of the house. Beautiful circles of gaslights hung from the ceiling, and a great chandelier of gaslights hung in the center of the stage. Noble statues stood in niches on either side of the stage, garlands and festoons of flowers were draped above the stage, and all in all, the sight was an impressive one. And in this most satisfying setting, the waiters circulated, poured glasses of beer, and served cheese sandwiches while a young man on the stage sang of the days when he "polished up the handles of the big front door," and the dumpy little lady sang that she was "called Little Buttercup" —all for twenty-five cents.

After *Pinafore* came *Trial By Jury,* and then a parody on Gilbert and Sullivan called *The Wreck of the Pinafore.* And then, during the first seventeen years, something new came into the story of American theaters—a musical comedy stock company of outstanding singers and comedians who learned a new role every one or two weeks.

You will recognize few of the names of the comic operas today—*Girofle-Girofla, Fatinitza, The Light Cavalry, Maritana, Fra Diavolo, The Pretty Galatea, The Bohemian Girl, The Daughter of Madam Angot, Boccaccio, The Mikado,* and all the rest of the Gilbert and Sullivan repertoire, *Lily of Killarney,* and *The Gypsy Baron.* The list goes on and on, and in 1882 new names were added—the names of grand operas, particularly the Italian operas of Verdi.

Behind the gaslights, and later behind the very modern electric footlights, appeared an endless array of the boys and girls who made up the stock company. I have before me a list of more than one hundred who appeared before 1895. Some of those names have never been forgotten, such as Emilie Melville, the most adorable of singing ingenues, pretty as an old-fashioned bouquet, tiny, graceful, with a lovely light voice, and a will as strong as tempered steel, a dainty and enchanting young wisp of a girl.

Emilie Melville was only one of them in those first days of the Tivoli. There was Tillie Salinger; there was Caro Roma; there was Max Figman, later famous for his role in *The Man on the Box;* there were Frances Powers, Arthur Messmer, Phil Branson, and Ferris Hartmann. And year after year, season after season, night after night, while the others came and went, there was one girl who was always there, always singing, always dancing, always laughing. Of course, you've never heard of her. But ask your grandfather and watch his eyes light up, and then perhaps an innocent look come into them as though he might say, just offhand, "Oh, yes, I've got a recollection of her. A vague recollection." Why, there wasn't a gay lad or a two-fisted man in San Fran-

465

cisco who wasn't in love with Gracie Plaisted. Gracie Plaisted! They wrote a song about her; one of the lines was, "She broke a thousand hearts with the greatest of ease." After all, music and the theater were the heart of romance.

There were real-life dramas and real-life romances at the old Tivoli. There was the little girl, pretty as a picture, who stood in the second row of the chorus night after night after night. One night, a stage-door Johnny, standing in the wings with a bunch of American Beauty roses in his arms, heard a lovely lilting soprano voice coming from the chorus dressing room. He demanded to know the name of the singer from the call boy, and the boy said, "Oh, a cute kid named Alice Nielsen." Alice Nielsen! She was "discovered" that night, and left the second row of the chorus. She sang soprano leads in comic operas, was promoted to grand opera, left the Tivoli, became one of the greatest grand opera sopranos of the day, and all the world acclaimed her. That was real-life drama.

By a strange chance, I stumbled on a real-life romance of the Tivoli only last week. My very good friend, Bill Torello, was in my office, and he asked me what I was writing. I told him, "Memories of the Old Tivoli."

"Yes?" he said. "You know my mother was *première danseuse* in the Tivoli ballet."

And then he told me the story.

Her name was Leonida Ortori. She was a great dancer and a famous beauty. One night a young medical student fell in love with her, went backstage, took her out of the Tivoli, and married her. That ended her dancing career sixty-three years ago, but it also ended the medical career of the young student. At best, marriage is a responsibility, and sixty-three years ago young men didn't rush into it unless they could sup-

466

port their wives. So it meant no more study of medicine, but a job. The young lad, Emil Torello, went to Alaska for the Alaska Commercial Company and put in many years for them. When he was thirty-seven years old and the father of three children, he came back, not to get another job, but to complete his career as a medical student. It's pretty tough going picking up the threads of a complicated profession after years have elapsed. But Leonida had given up her career as a *première danseuse* and she saw no reason why both members of the family should forsake their chosen vocations. So, with her encouragement, her husband took his degree and became a distinguished member of the medical profession. The home of Dr. Emil Torello became a strange mixture of surgical instruments and the songs of musical comedy and the grand opera stage.

From Sutter Street the Tivoli Gardens and the Tivoli Opera House had moved down to the Tenderloin and the theater district—the heart of San Francisco night life. Theaters came and theaters went, making fortunes, losing fortunes, flashing bright lights for a period, then standing idle with the three-sheets flapping in tatters on the billboards. But year after year the Tivoli played to full houses. It was a part of San Francisco, one of the city's most beloved possessions.

And in 1893 Doc Leahy, the boy who had learned to appreciate music by dusting piano keys in a furniture store, became the manager. Mrs. Ernestine Kreling was now the proprietor; Doc was the spark plug, always with an eye for a lovely face, an ear for a lovely voice. The next ten years were perhaps the most brilliant, the most exciting Tivoli years.

So we came to the turn of the century. I now have some programs before me. Monday, February 9, 1903—Gilbert and

Sullivan's *Patience*. Caro Roma was one of the ladies in waiting. Ferris Hartmann and Teddy Webb were the two poets. And Arthur Cunningham, who was with us up until a couple of years ago, and had a chest like a barrel and a voice that could fill even the Civic Auditorium, was Colonel Calverly. The costumes were made by Goldstein and Company, and the wigs by Goldstein and Cohn. When I last saw Louis Goldstein a few weeks ago, he became mellow-eyed with his memories of Tivoli days. Ferris Hartmann was stage manager, and Paul Steindorff, one of the most beloved orchestra leaders the city has ever called its own, was in the pit.

The program of the Tivoli for May 1905 was *The Burgo-master*. And the program carries a polite note: "The audience is requested not to worry about historical inaccuracies, anachronisms, lapses from logical sequence, and common sense in this piece. It is dangerous to worry. Just keep cool."

My own most vivid and unforgettable memory of the Tivoli was the night my father took me there to hear grand opera. He was a good friend of Doc Leahy's, and Doc had warned him that he had discovered a mighty good soprano, someone not to be missed. By that time Doc Leahy's reputation as a talent scout was well established, and when he told his friends that something good was scheduled for the Tivoli, his words were taken at face value. Of course, the days of twenty-five cent operas were gone; the Tivoli had become fashionable; seats in the orchestra were two dollars. The opera that night was *Rigoletto*. The first act passed with no sign of any unusual offering, but when it came to Gilda's entrance and her aria, "Caro Nome," it was as though an electric shock ran through the house. Gilda sang "Caro Nome" and the audience sat in tense silence until the last lovely, perfect note, and then hysteria broke loose. They stood up and

468

cheered. They showered the stage with flowers. They roared. In the excitement my father went out to the box office and bought seats for the family for every Friday night of the seven weeks of the engagement. I don't know what prompted him, but he handed me my seven tickets and I put them in my pocket. After the next act I went out to the box office and exchanged my orchestra tickets for twenty-eight standing-room tickets at fifty cents apiece. And in the next seven weeks I heard Tetrazzini twenty-eight times. That's reason enough for loving the Tivoli.

Of course, there'll never be another Tivoli. There'll never be another stock company singing week after week, year after year, the tunes and melodies that have made life so rich and fine for so many tens of thousands of people. Life isn't designed that way today. Musical comedy isn't sensational enough. Of course, there's always an *Oklahoma,* a *Carousel,* or a *Showboat,* but who wants to sit through *Giofle-Girofla,* or go week after week and sit in the same seat and see the same faces in the chorus and the same principals before the footlights. As a matter of fact, who wants traditions today? But what a pity it is! Just think how much our youngsters would have to talk about to their children and grandchildren a couple of generations from now, and how bored their grandchildren would be listening to stories of Teddy Webb, Ferris Hartmann, Arthur Cunningham, Emilie Melville, and Gracie Plaisted of the old Tivoli!

XXIII

The Seven Ages of Man

Most things are so pleasant in retrospect that sometimes I wonder if perhaps we overemphasize the nostalgic charm of the San Francisco of our memories. We are even disposed, when the pain is gone, to speak proudly of the toothache we had a week ago, to speak of it with boastful affection; it was the best toothache we'd ever had. The truth of the cliché was forcefully brought home to me a year or so ago when I took my children to see the modern version of the *Merry Widow*.

I remember when I first heard the music of the *Merry Widow*. I was sitting in the Louvre Restaurant on Fillmore Street a few months after the earthquake and fire of 1906. A Viennese orchestra was playing old Vienna waltzes, music for which they had a certain renown. Young Meyerfeldt, whose father and uncle had founded the Orpheum, came to our table and sat down to talk. He was the manager of the Louvre. In the course of conversation, he said that a friend had sent him some music of a new comic opera that had just opened in Vienna. He thought the melodies had a chance of becoming very popular, and on the spur of the moment he took the music to his orchestra leader and asked, "Can you play this?" So the orchestra played the *Merry Widow* waltzes. That was the first time the lovely melodies were heard in the West. They made such an immediate impression on me, as well as on the other guests drinking Pilsener in tall glasses and dark Munchener in heavy, fat glasses, that I anticipated the coming of the *Merry Widow* as eagerly as some of us more recently looked forward to seeing the production of *Oklahoma*.

Finally, after two or three years, the *Merry Widow* arrived, and it came up to all of my hopes and expectations. It was a wonderful show! I saw it at least four or five times in those years preceding the first World War. Then for twenty-five years afterwards I talked about it. I told of it as the most brilliantly entertaining and irresistible musical comedy I'd ever seen. I'd hear the melodies played and I'd ask, "Do you remember the first time Mabel Wilbur sang it at the Columbia Theatre?"

In more recent years I'd go to a current musical comedy and say, "Oh, it's all right, but you should have seen Mabel Wilbur in the *Merry Widow*." I said it so often that it got to a point where my daughters would say to me, "Just what was Mabel Wilbur to you?" Well, she was only a name— but a glamorous name.

Finally, a few years ago, the modern version of the *Merry Widow* was announced. I got tickets for the family far in advance. I built it up to the family to such a degree that they were as excited about the forthcoming production as I was. What a tragic letdown it was! I sat in my seat and squirmed and suffered through the dated comedy and the artificial scenery, but I said, "It's going to be all right. Just wait until the next act when they dance the 'Merry Widow Waltz.'" When it came time for the exciting routine that had been twenty minutes of sheer beauty a generation ago, the scene was cut to about half a minute, and instead of dancing to the

471

"Merry Widow Waltz," the Prince and the Merry Widow danced to waltzes from *Die Fledermaus.*

Later, when we were sitting sucking our chocolate ice cream sodas through straws, I took my courage in hand and asked, "Well, what did you think?" My daughters politely and charitably said, "Oh, it was very nice, but sort of dull. Life must have been very dull when you were young, Daddy."

Now I insist that life was *not* dull when I was young, nor has life ever been dull in San Francisco. It's true that the recent production of the *Merry Widow* was a flimsy, badly staged, stupid imitation. But, on the other hand, it's just possible that the original *Merry Widow* was more pleasant in retrospect than it actually had been; just like the toothache, it became pleasant when the pain was done.

No, life wasn't dull thirty and forty years ago, but I wonder how many people today would find pleasure in the things we did in those days. For instance, on Sundays we went to Muir Woods and Tamalpais. We went dancing Saturday night, went to a debutante's ball at the Palace or the St. Francis or the Fairmont or even perhaps the ballroom of the California Club. We danced until three or four o'clock in the morning. There were cotillions with favors that we cherished. No stag line cut in on our dances; we stuck faithfully to the letter of the dance card, and scribbled our name ten out of the twelve times on our favorite girl's card. And, being sentimental, the girl was sure to take the dance card home and hang it by its silk string from a knob on her dressing table. Supper was served at midnight, and the next day we boasted about the number of glasses of Cliquot we had absorbed. Of course, no one ever heard of California champagne in those days. At three or four in the morning the orchestra would play "Home Sweet Home," and we'd be on our way. In the beginning there'd be a carriage waiting for us from Kelly's Stable on California Street or the Pacific Avenue stables. But, as years progressed, we'd have a hired limousine waiting. Incidentally, it was an expensive business to take your girl to a ball in those days—and complicated! Etiquette demanded that we call at the girl's house a week before the ball. We sent orchids to the debutante's mother, to the debutante, and to the girl we were escorting, and that wasn't always a wholehearted pleasure, because often our invitation read, "Please escort Miss So-and-So," and frequently little Miss So-and-So was a sour, lanky creature at whom we wouldn't look twice under normal conditions. At any rate, there were the orchids to buy and the carriage or limousine to hire; and, all in all, the gay social whirl was a serious financial problem for boys in their late teens.

We'd reach our own home at about the time that the milkman was arriving. And two or three hours later, say at eight o'clock Sunday morning, we'd call for our girl and head for the Ferry Building. There would be a seething mass of humanity, noisy, exuberant humanity. There were boys in corduroys, girls in short hobble skirts and sweaters, old men with rucksacks hanging from straps over their shoulders, and old ladies in sweaters and skirts and high leather boots. We'd crowd noisily aboard the ferryboat, and I use the word "crowd" advisedly. It was nothing to see between thirty and forty thousand San Franciscans head for Muir Woods on Sunday. We'd reach Mill Valley, head for the little store across from the Mt. Tamalpais Railroad depot, and buy dill pickles and Saratoga chips and chocolate bars. And we'd start out, scornfully ignoring the few dozen staid, antiquated beings who planned to go up the mountain on the little one-lung train. We'd start walking, perhaps just my girl and I, or perhaps a party of a dozen. We'd skirt the old mill, cross the stream, and then the argument would begin. Should we go by way of the Steep Trail, the Pipe Line, or the Throckmorton Trail? The answer depended pretty much on the girl. If the situation was romantic we took the Throckmorton Trail, with its ferns and dense shrubbery. Even the name Throckmorton had romance in it. If the girl was the rugged, athletic, and no-nonsense-my-man type, we'd take the Steep Trail. And if she was just the average, everyday girl who liked to saunter along eating Saratoga chips, we'd take the Pipe Line. At the fork of the road we might go down into Muir Woods and walk in the serene shade of the redwoods. We might even keep on going over the hogback and down to Dipsea and the ocean beach. But the road up the mountain was more favored. I neglected to say that there was always one girl in every group who insisted on having her knapsack and her sweater carried; the rest of them took off their sweaters and wound them around their waists when climbing became a business. We paused on the way at West Point, and finally came to the cradle at the summit of Tamalpais. There the world stretched out at our feet—the bay, the city, and the ocean beyond. Then we ate more pickles and chocolate, and started down the mountain again. We came down the mountain, crowded into the train at Mill Valley, crowded on the ferryboat, and landed in the city at nightfall in time to go to Sanginetti's or Papa Coppa's or Buon Gusto for an Italian dinner with spaghetti, red wine, and fried cream. There were no juke boxes in those days to spoil our pleasure. We pounded on the tables with knives and spoons, and sang while we ate. A favorite song was the "Dollar Princess."

Before I leave these memories of Tamalpais, one more

474

comes back to me and that's the best of all. The Saturday nights that we forswore debutante balls, a group of eight or ten boys and girls would go up Tamalpais at sunset, well and duly chaperoned, of course. The destination was West Point, a little tavern hanging on the side of the mountain at the fork of the road. The proprietors were a genial, moustached Swiss mountaineer and his friendly wife. There'd be a huge log fire roaring in the open fireplace and the meal, served in front of the fire, would be ample and good. After supper, mellowed by the fire and the good Swiss wine, we'd sit or stand on the edge of the hill and see the million lights of the city glimmering across the bay, and the lights of the villages flickering at the foot of Tamalpais. We'd look at the lights and philosophize about life and the why and wherefore of things, and then turn in. There were three small cabins, little more than lean-tos open on one side, tucked into the hill. The boys would all crowd into one cabin, the girls into another, and we'd lie there on hard bunks and see the lights across the bay and perhaps an inconstant moon of shimmering silver overhead, and below would be the deep shadows of the redwoods. Yes, after all, life was very good when we were young.

But then, almost all of my memories of San Francisco are good memories. There is one memory of my school days that remains vivid. It was the annual visit of the Shakespearian thespians, Louis James and Frederick Warde. They would play their season at the Columbia Theatre, and on the days when there was no matinee, they would visit the public schools. They would read the argument scene from *Julius Caesar*. James would do a scene from *King Lear,* and Warde would do a scene from the *The Merry Wives of Windsor—* which was way over our innocent heads—and James would

475

do a *Hamlet* soliloquy. Then Frederick Warde would do the "Seven Ages of Man" from *As You Like It*. That speech always excited our youthful imaginations. We heard it done at the Grant School on Pacific Avenue; we heard it done at the Pacific Heights School on Jackson Street; we heard it done across the bay at the Fruitvale Grammar School. We always waited eagerly for that startling line:

"The infant, mewling and puking in the nurse's arms."

Mr. Warde always paused after that line to give us opportunity to vent our enthusiasm. We laughed; we roared; we cheered; we whistled. Then Mr. Warde would smile benignly, with a self-satisfied expression, as though he had been author of the line, and would continue with the speech—and we were silent.

All the world's a stage, and all the men and women merely players.

But we San Franciscans played our roles more enthusiastically than the players on other stages.

One man in his time plays many parts, his acts being seven ages. At first the infant, mewling and puking in the nurse's arms.

Well, frankly, and to my relief, my memory does not go back to that stage. But I have a mental picture of our home in a row of flats on O'Farrell Street just below Van Ness Avenue. That was in 1890. We had no telephone, and our house was lighted by ornate crystal gas fixtures. There was the sound of music in the house; it was from a music box some three feet long and a foot square. It had a large metal roll under its glass, and upon winding a crank tinkling music came

476

forth. The melodies were "Boccaccio," "The Poet and Peasant Overture," and the marching song from *Faust*. It was the forerunner of the more elegant Regina Music Box. Our nursemaid used to wheel us, in a high-wheeled baby carriage, up and down and down and up O'Farrell Street. The only memory I have of that street (I must have been a couple of years old) was of a gentleman who always stopped to lift the hood of my carriage and say, "Well, well, well," as though he had discovered some unusual manifestation of nature therein. Now, the strange thing is that I remember only three things about that gentleman—his "well, well, well," his very black waxed moustache, and his black, gold-handled cane. Long afterwards I learned that he owned property at that corner, and that he was Michael de Young, founder of the *San Francisco Chronicle*.

The second stage was the whining schoolboy with his satchel and shining morning face, creeping unwillingly to school like a snail. That stage belonged to the Pacific Heights School. Miss Kincaid was the principal, and undoubtedly a fine, sensible, and friendly lady of erudition. But she frightened us worse than the witches in Hans Christian Andersen's stories, and after two weeks in Pacific Heights I ran away from school, and away from home. I wandered all day, and when darkness closed on Alta Plaza Park I gave up the idea of running away to sea for the time being, and went home to supper.

I say I gave up the idea for the time being. It returned, however, to be with me constantly, even to this day. But I transferred to the Grant School, and in the second grade my teacher, Miss Burnell, read my composition called, "I Have a Dog." She read it aloud to the class and said, "This young man will probably be a writer when he grows up." I have never quite forgiven Miss Burnell for planting that seed in my impressionable mind.

The third stage was

the lover, sighing like furnace, with a woful ballad made to his mistress' eyebrow.

Now of course, I wrote no ballads, but the picture grows much more clear. I climbed Russian Hill at night, in the good days before Russian Hill was paved and terraced, and respectable. I sat out on the edge of the rock at Taylor and Green Streets and quoted Browning, Robert Service and—forgive us our sins—the passionate love lyrics of Laurence Hope. I saw the bay sprawled at my feet, its green and red lights glimmering in their aura of fog. I discussed the philosophy of life, whether or not there was a hereafter, and the validity of the Darwin theory. Then I went down to Polk Street and had an ice cream soda—there were no milk shakes in those days.

Well, that was the third stage. The fourth and fifth stages I by-pass, and now to the sixth stage, which is today.

We travel in crowded busses. We grumble about the behavior of the crowds in the streets; we grumble about the passing of the days of the old French restaurants; we grumble about the death of romance; we grumble about the fog and the rain and the sunshine. We even grumble because we have no snow. But we still go up Russian Hill and marvel at the city's loveliness, and when foreigners come to our town we still boast to them that, of course, no other city lives so richly or has so fine a sense of the joy of life.

And that brings us to the seventh stage. There, of course, Shakespeare is dated, for in our time men and women never grow as old as the picture that Shakespeare paints:

478

. . . mere oblivion, sans teeth, sans eyes, sans taste, sans everything.

Especially in San Francisco, men and women in their eighties and even their nineties are comparatively young. Senility has gone out of fashion!

So I look forward to that old age—quite a few years away still—when I can say I have reached a better seventh age of man than Shakespeare ever dreamed of. Then, if I'm too feeble to perambulate, I want to spend my last days sitting by a window, high on a San Francisco hill, looking out at the eager, throbbing, grumbling, joyous life of the loveliest city I have ever known.

XXIV

Frank Norris

It must have been in 1890 or 1891 that a large part of the student body of the University of California crossed the bay to attend a performance at the Tivoli Opera House. The major portion of the audience had been seated when the student body arrived. On the way to the opera house they had marched up Market Street, and near the corner of Market and Taylor they had found the old man who nightly stood on the corner with a large telescope mounted on a tripod, permitting the passing crowd to look through the telescope at the moon, Venus, Jupiter, or Mars for a dime. The students borrowed or rented the telescope, shouldered it, and marched to the Tivoli and down the aisle. They set it up in the middle of the aisle after the performance had commenced, and then took turns eyeing the chorus girls through it. An exceptionally good time was had by all, although the students of the university almost ran riot when the ladies of the chorus appeared in one song and dance number clad in gowns and mortar boards. That's all there is to that particular story, except that the ring leader and instigator of the stunt was one of the most popular and most misunderstood students at the university. His name was Frank Norris.

Now, in telling of Frank Norris I realize full well that to

many of the present generation the name means little more than would the name Tom Smith or Bill Brown. Frank Norris—a good plain American name! And yet, of the great number of writers and artists who called San Francisco their home, three names stand out: Jack London, Ambrose Bierce, and Frank Norris. I would not presume to say which of the three was the greatest, but my personal choice would be Norris. So he was a writer! What did he write? *McTeague!* Oh yes, you probably remember *McTeague,* that remarkable moving picture made by Eric Von Stroheim, the story of a brutal Polk Street dentist. Frank Norris is forgotten and *McTeague* lives in the fame of a moving picture. But *McTeague* was only one of the half-dozen or more novels of Frank Norris, and certainly not the finest. Before we go on with our story, we'll name just a few, books that were entered on the honor roll of great American novels. There was *Vandover and The Brute.* There was *The Octopus,* a tremendous story of the California wheat fields, and an indictment of the political racketeers of the day. There was *The Pit,* a dramatic story of the Chicago wheat exchange. There was *Moran of the Lady Letty.* There was *Blix,* and there was *McTeague.* Frank Norris, a San Francisco immortal, was born in the south side of Chicago on the fifth of March, 1870. He died on October 25, 1902. He was thirty-two years old, and in thirty-two years he had achieved immortality.

If you talk to old San Franciscans, they'll tell you about the tragedy of his life. It was such a sad tragedy, they'll tell you, a young man, only thirty-two years old, hardly having reached the prime of life, to be taken away! It was so needless, such futile waste! He had never really lived; he'd only reached the threshold of life.

Well, of course that's utter nonsense! Frank Norris lived

more in his thirty-two years than a dozen men live in their lifetimes. Because life was exciting and fascinating and colorful, even in its more somber and sordid aspects, he loved San Francisco. He found in the city every phase and color of life, and as he brought glory to the city, so the city brought inspiration to him. I have no intention of writing a critical analysis of his writings, or do anything further than to sum up his life work in a few words.

With Emile Zola as his inspiration, Frank Norris became the first great American realist. People who know more about it than I state that there are only two kinds of writers, romantic and realist. The romantic author writes of life, coloring it to make it romantically entertaining. The realist writes of life as it is. Frank Norris was a realist in love with romance, and in the San Francisco of the eighties and the nineties rough realism walked hand in hand with high romance. The result was that, irrespective of all literary virtues, no writer has ever written of San Francisco more realistically or with greater love and understanding of the city than did the boy, Frank Norris.

He was born in Chicago in 1870. His mother, Gertrude Doggett, had been a schoolteacher, and with the advent of the Civil War she gave up teaching and turned to the stage. She was talented and she was well received. She played Shakespeare, and plays of the grand manner popular at the time. She was a bundle of energy, and an indefatigable worker in love with her business, the business of being an actress. Then she met a young jewelry salesman and fell in love with him. He had started as a jewelry peddler and had saved a little money. He, like Gertrude, was a bundle of energy, an indefatigable worker, and in love with all business, not necessarily only his own. He was a dyed-in-the-wool businessman, and the probabilities are that he never forgave any of his

482

three sons for refusing to follow in his footsteps. He did very well without the assistance of his sons, and the small jewelry concern started by young Norris when he married Gertrude Doggett grew to be perhaps the largest wholesale jewelry concern in the United States, the firm known as Norris Allister Ball.

Frank was their first son. He spent a contented early childhood in Chicago. When he was eight years old he wrote in his diary, "The time of departure has arrived! Is this a dream, said I." The family, on the wave of prosperity, was going to Europe. They saw the galleries and the museums. They returned to America, and Gertrude Norris became the mother of another son, Charles Gilman Norris, affectionately known to all San Franciscans as C.G.

Gertrude Norris put the stage out of her mind. A third son had been born, and two daughters. The little girls had died in early childhood, but the business of bringing five children into the world left little room for dreams of the theater. Mrs. Norris had other problems—not of material things, for her husband was rapidly becoming a wealthy man—mainly young Frank. There was a situation to deal with. He was constantly making believe. He peopled the house with imaginary personalities, particularly medieval knights and ladies! And he didn't tell the truth; he told small white lies that worried the virtuous mother. For instance, just as she was about to sit in a chair, small Frank might say, "Don't sit in that chair, Mama. Sir Arthur of the Golden Feather is sitting in it." It was hard to know just what to do with such a child. He had too much imagination. Too much imagination was a bad thing; it might lead to a bad end.

Of course, the parents did the worst possible thing parents of an overimaginative child could do. When the boy was fourteen years old they were established in Oakland, and from Oakland soon moved with him to San Francisco. They stayed for a short time at the old Palace Hotel, and then Norris purchased the Henry Scott residence on Sacramento Street near Octavia. Life became a living story for the boy. In fact, it was only a very few years later that he was to be one of the first to say, "There are just three cities in the United States that are 'story cities'—New York, New Orleans, and best of all, San Francisco."

Best of all the "story cities"—San Francisco! The Sacramento Street home stood at the top of a hill. Cable cars rattled past the door. In the neighbor's back yard lived a family of hens and two roosters. Across the street in a vacant lot cows were pastured. This was on Sacramento Street three blocks west of Van Ness Avenue in 1884. Along Van Ness Avenue wild Western cowboys drove their cattle to the stockyards. Along the avenue from Black Point and the Presidio marched the Army and the state militia. A block below Van Ness was Polk Street. Even to the imaginative Gertrude Norris with her background of the theatre, Polk Street was dull and drab—a street of small shops and small people. But not so to her son Frank. Polk Street to him was the street of fascinating odors of bakery and delicatessen shops, and the music of small pianos drifting under the swinging doors of saloons; it was a street of windows with fascinating arrays of colors. Polk Street was an Egyptian bazaar, a Persian market place. And that early impression was to last long after the flavor of the bazaar had dimmed. Polk Street and the people of Polk Street were to be the color of his short stories and his book *McTeague*. But that was to come later.

He was sent to Boy's High School to learn to be a businessman, eventually to sell jewelry. He didn't like it any more than he had liked his earlier schooling at the establishment opened by Dr. Reed on Bill Ralston's place down the Peninsula. He didn't like grammar, he couldn't spell, he hated arithmetic, and he abominated wholesale jewelry. Something had to be done with the boy. His father stormed, "Well, very well, what do you want to do?" And, clutching at straws, Frank said he wanted to be an artist, wanted to paint pictures.

His dreams of making a business tycoon of his son shattered, Norris Senior sent the boy to the San Francisco Art Association, later to become the Mark Hopkins Institute. Frank drew and painted, and revolted against assignments, and made friends who were to endure throughout his short life. There were two in particular, Virgil Williams, who had been the boon companion of Robert Louis Stevenson, and Ernest Peixotto, artist, dreamer, and a man who was to devote his life to San Francisco in art, culture, and civic progress.

New horizons beckoned. He loved San Francisco, but to be a great artist, tradition demanded that a novitiate go to the Latin Quarter of Paris. He was sent to Paris. He went to the Atelier Julien. He painted, he drew, he walked the alleys and boulevards of Paris, thrilling to the constantly changing colors of life, fascinated by the wickedness of Paris, and frightened by it. In all his life and in all his writings, Frank Norris combined the excitable imagination of the creative mind with a stilted prudishness. In Paris that prudish streak, a mild priggishness, was jolted by the writings of the man who was the sensation of the day, not only in Paris but throughout the world, Emile Zola, who had discarded the romantic leanings of the nineteenth-century writers and was writing of life as it was, crude, fierce, and primitive. He was called the first of the realist school of writers. This was the inspiration of the boy still in his teens, and so Frank Norris, painting, drawing, and dreaming, turned from his paints and

485

brushes to write an article, a discussion of armor and costumes of the days when knighthood was in glory. He sent the article to his mother and it was published, unsigned, in the *San Francisco Chronicle* of March 31, 1889—his first published work.

Now he was nineteen years old. Thirteen years of life remained to him, and almost as with a foreboding of the shortness of his days, he crowded a lifetime into those few short years. Paris was exciting, but no place in all the world warmed his blood or fired his imagination as did San Francisco. So he came home. Art was forgotten; he had found his medium; he would write. But he had to hurry; there was so much to write and life was so short. He went to the University of California. He didn't want to go, but he had to do something; his father still dreamed of making a jewelry salesman of him, and even an education was better than that. So he went to college, spent four years there without graduating, and received uniformly poor grades. Later he went to Harvard for more intensive study of literature and convinced the distinguished professors that he was never intended to be a student. After all, what inducement could there be in studying books when one could study life? He studied life, not consciously, but at a high pitch. Those were the days of the caricatured "rah rah" college boys, the sophomoric, rambunctious college boys. Frank Norris was the ring leader in stunts and undergraduate clownery, and fitted the picture about as well as a derby hat would have fitted a knight in armor. Yet during the four years at Berkeley and the months at Harvard, driving his professors desperate with inattention and poor grades, he was working on a book that was to be the story of a Polk Street dentist, a book called *McTeague*.

All this was the prologue. Of the book of his life itself, all must be told in a few words. San Francisco was fascinating, but to be a writer he knew he would have to see other phases of the world's life. He went to South Africa, arriving there in time to take part in the disastrous Jameson Raid; he came back from Africa brimming with stories, and with his health undermined by fever. He fell in love. The girl was young—only seventeen—lovely, and had his own zest for life. She was a sub-debutante. They saw the city together; they flirted; they had a wonderful time; and one night Jeannette (her name was Jeannette Black) said point-blank, "Do you love me?" Just as bluntly Frank said, "No." Jeannette said, "There! And I don't love you. Let's stop flirting and enjoy life."

They were married four years later, and they had two years of rich happiness. A baby girl was born to them, and then the pages of Frank Norris' life were closed. Meanwhile they had traveled, dreamed together, and seen life together. There had been the Spanish-American War. With his zest for adventure, Norris went as correspondent to Cuba. He hated war, hated its principle, and hated the unimaginative way in which it was waged. It was not at all like his beloved legends of the knights of old. He came back from the war disgruntled and with new fever in his blood weakening his physical stamina.

The hours became a mad race with life. There was so much to be done. *McTeague* was published and the polite world was horrified. A few rare minds said that this was the beginning of a new era. Frank Norris had discarded the romantic, saccharine, puerile novels of the eighteenth century. Such books as *When Knighthood Was in Flower* and *Dorothy Vernon of Haddon Hall* were things of the past.

With the coming of Frank Norris, the school of American realism was born. He had seen the world, and again and again he had turned from Paris, New York, and far places to find the life he loved in San Francisco. All the inspiration he needed was the smell of California sunshine. California sunshine! Now there was a theme! The fever of his blood became a fever of enthusiasm in his brain. California sunshine meant California wheat fields. He'd write a great epic, the epic of wheat. It would be a trilogy. First there would be the battle of the wheat fields and the political machinations of the railroad. He'd call it *The Octopus*—tentacles of the railroad reaching out to choke the fields. Then he'd tell of the wheat market of Chicago, the pit into which men were flung, buried by the avalanche of wheat. Finally, he'd tell about the world, the people of the little and big lands of Europe, absorbing the harvest. The first two books were written and fame came to Frank Norris, fame that made his name ring around the world. When the time came to write the third novel of the trilogy, nature interfered. He awoke one day—it was in 1902—suffering miserable pains, pains that he laughed off. When they took him to the hospital and an appendectomy was ordered, it was too late. He died on Saturday, the twenty-fifth of October, 1902, at the age of thirty-two.

A tragedy? Yes, of course it was a tragedy. It's always a tragedy when a young man is taken by death in the prime of his youth. Frank Norris loved San Francisco; it was his inspiration. He loved life; it was his inspiration. The men and women who knew him loved him for his simplicity, his modesty, his charm, his zest for life, and the rich fullness of his dreams. He was the first great realist of American literature—Frank Norris of San Francisco.

488

XXV

Portrait Album

You probably have an album, such as mine, gathering dust on a forgotten shelf. My album, bound in black leather with polished brass clasps, is ninety-five years old, dating back to the real beginnings of San Francisco in 1850. Some of the portraits are quaint daguerreotypes, such as the one of Great-Aunt Fanny in her black alpaca dress with the white collar, a chatelaine watch pinned to her bosom, and a black parasol with black lace edging in her hand. But the portraits in it are not all old; some are quite modern.

For example, there is a portrait made not more than fifteen or twenty years ago. It is of a small lady with a lovely face. She is not young, yet there is youth in the face; her skin is so unwrinkled, so pretty a pink and white that you would not want to guess her age to be much more than fifty. But actually, she is in her eighties. The rest of the picture— well, the setting is the weekly meeting of the drama section of the Commonwealth Club of California. There are fifteen or twenty dignified San Francisco businessmen seated at the lunch table, and the one little old lady. She is Emilie Melville. Going back in memory, she was to be the speaker of the day. The chairman introduced her. The guests all rose and applauded, but she didn't stand up to make her speech.

She said, "My goodness, I can't make a speech; I never made a speech in my life." So someone said, "Well, just talk to us, Miss Melville." And she replied, "What can I talk about? I'm not interesting. I've just always read the lines that other people wrote."

The lines that other people wrote! She had been raised in Oakland, she had gone away, traveled around the world, and had come back to play the lead at the Metropolitan Theatre on—she wasn't quite sure—was it Sansome Street or Montgomery? That was quite a long time ago, in 1875. Then Bill Ralston had built the California Theatre on Bush Street for those two great actors, Barrett and McCullough. Old Tom Maguire had brought Barrett and McCullough west, and when Tom was up against it, Bill Ralston had built the California Theatre for them.

Little old Emilie Melville stopped and looked up quickly like a canary bird cocking its head. "Bill isn't here at the lunch today, is he?" she asked. And then she shook her head and whispered, "No, he couldn't be here; he's been dead for fifty years."

(I wasn't sure if Emilie Melville had really forgotten the passing of time, or had just seized the opportunity to do what she loved to do more than anything in the world, be an actress.)

She talked about those dear, wonderful days when she had starred at the Metropolitan Theatre, and when she had been a member of that first company of McCullough and Lawrence Barrett to open the old California Theatre on Bush Street. And suddenly a spark came into her eyes and she did stand up. She stood very straight, her little shoulders back, and her eyes dancing. "Gentlemen," she said, "I didn't come here to make a speech because I don't know how to make

490

speeches. But, I came here to ask you a favor. On that spot where San Francisco theatre history was made—the California Theatre on Bush Street—there's a large building now. The gas company has a large building there. I'm an old woman, more than eighty years old, and before I die I want to see a bronze plaque on the front of that building with the names of all those dear people who started the California Theatre in 1869."

Well, the luncheon came to an end and I walked to the street with Emilie Melville. It was a stormy day, with rain falling in torrents. I signaled a cab. She asked, "What are you doing?" "I'm going to take you home," I said. (She lived high up on Russian Hill.) She turned on me with a merry laugh. "Indeed you're not," she said, "I'm not an old woman. And furthermore I'm not riding in one of those contraptions!" With a gesture like E. H. Sothern sweeping his sword from his scabbard, she swept her umbrella open, cocked it down over her little black bonnet, said, "Good-bye, young man," and trotted off up Sutter Street.

Before I turn to the next portrait in my old album, I do want to add that Emilie Melville did live to see her precious bronze plaque of memories placed on the front of the Pacific Telephone and Telegraph Company Building on Bush Street.

My next portrait is of a plump little man at the piano. The scene was the Barbary Coast, and the plump little man was not the regular pianist at the Thalia and the Old Hippodrome. No, the regular musicians on Pacific Street were men of recognized talent, but this little man was just an "extra" called in to play when the regular was sick, or perhaps drunk.

So this plump little man sat at his piano and little by little the crowd became aware of him. They stopped their dancing and their drinking to listen to him. You see, those were the days when the Barbary Coast was giving the world the "Turkey Trot," "The Grizzly Bear," and the "Bunny Hug." They gathered around the piano, cigarettes trailing from the corners of their mouths, and the little man played the familiar jazz or ragtime melodies. Sometimes he ragged a bit of unfamiliar melody, and they asked, "What's that tune, brother?" And he answered, "Oh, just something I made up." So they rocked their shoulders to the little thing he'd made up, and little by little he became famous—oh, not in the world of music, nor in any part of the world except that small select bit of the world called the Barbary Coast. But he was capturing a flavor of American life, a flavor that was reflected in the Negro dance tunes and sea chanties of the Barbary Coast. He found in those tunes a thing that Ludwig von Beethoven had discovered almost a century before, the irresistible urge of syncopation.

The name of this plump young man who was an "extra" piano player on the Barbary Coast was Ferde Grofe. Of course, all of this was long before Grofe thought of writing his *Grand Canyon Suite* or his *Knute Rockne Suite,* but the seed of his great music was germinating. Finally his reputation as a master of ragtime jazz drifted down from Pacific Street to the select elite of the St. Francis Hotel, and Ferde went from the Thalia to play in the St. Francis Hotel orchestra of one of the most beloved band leaders San Francisco has ever known, Art Hickman. Hickman, under the influence of Grofe's very American syncopation, began to develop his own style, and the Rose Room of the St. Francis Hotel became a tradition.

There was another young band leader in San Francisco at that time who was fascinated by the Barbary Coast honky-tonk pianist, just as Hickman had been. Ferde drifted to the new young man's band, and there his influence was felt as it had never been felt before. That young man was Paul Whiteman.

My portrait of Ferde Grofe leads me directly to another portrait of the Barbary Coast of the same era. Down Pacific Street from the Hippodrome and the Thalia was the Olympia, a dive of iniquity on a level with the others. In those days "slumming" was a popular pastime, and from Nob Hill and the Pacific Heights the "five hundred" and some five thousand imitators drifted to the Barbary Coast for vicarious thrills. You know, quite recently I heard a San Francisco matron say, "I've taken to riding in the streetcars; it's a new experience and very fascinating to see the way the other half lives." Well, it was the same thing in those Barbary Coast days; the elite wandered to Pacific Street to see the way the other half lived.

Of course, there was more to it than that. The fame of the ragtime jazz of Ferde Grofe and other musicians of the Barbary Coast had spread, and there was nothing vicarious in this music; the thrill was real. One night, into the Olympia drifted a lady and a gentleman. The doorman offered to show them to one of the discreet boxes where "slummers" could watch the wicked revelry unseen. But the lady declined and said that they would join the dancers on the floor. The smoke was thick, the din terrific, and the crowd dense. There were sailors of every color and nationality. There were the regular Barbary Coast denizens, bleary-eyed men, dope fiends, and drunks. There were staid businessmen on clandestine frolics, and there were the drab, painted women, circling through the crowd inviting the customers to buy a bottle of beer, at a dollar a bottle. The music blared, the saxophones brayed, and the percussion virtuoso rocked his shoulders and

493

tossed his drumsticks into the air between beats. Into the crowd pressed the lady and gentleman, and they began to dance.

At first no one noticed them. It was not unusual to see a well-dressed couple dancing among the nondescript crowd. But little by little these two newcomers made their presence felt. First one couple and then another danced to the sidelines and stood there to watch the well-dressed lady and gentleman. Soon all of the throng had moved to the sidelines and stood there silently while the man and the woman danced. The band continued its exciting, pulsing, primitive syncopation, playing better than they had ever played before. With a final burst and a crash of the timpani the tune came to its end. There was a moment's tense silence, and then the storm broke. The crowd cheered, yelled, and screamed. Hats were thrown into the air. Into the uproar came a measured rhythmic chorus of shouts, "More! More!" until all the Olympia was rocking. The gentleman stood, quietly dignified, in the middle of the dance floor, and his lady stood at his side, tears of happy emotion pouring down her cheeks. The gentleman was San Francisco's favorite photographer, Dr. Arnold Genthe. The lady was the great Russian ballerina, Anna Pavlova.

Years later, telling of the experience, Pavlova said, "The appreciation of my Barbary Coast audience meant more to me than the tribute of royalty."

That brings me to another portrait in my album. Today the world knows Dr. Arnold Genthe as one of the great artists of photography—one of the greatest the world has known. But in those days Arnold Genthe was unknown beyond San Francisco. He was the city's pet; he photographed the debutantes and the society matrons, and to ap-

494

pear before his camera was a privilege almost equal to appearing at court in the days of Queen Victoria.

Of course, there had been other photographers before the days of Arnold Genthe, and each of you old San Franciscans had a favorite photographer for your family. If you will turn to your own family album you'll probably find stiff, amusing studies made of Great-Aunt Elizabeth or Uncle Ben by the Bradley and Rulofson Galleries of 429 Montgomery Street, and on the back of each you will find the modest statement that Bradley and Rulofson have the "only elevator connected with photography in the world." But of the early photographers, the most popular was Taber. Taber's gallery was at Number 8 Montgomery Street, and ignoring the boast of Bradley and Rulofson, each Taber photograph states, "8 Montgomery Street, ELEVATOR, opposite the Palace and Grand Hotels."

These were commercial photographers in a day when photography was young, but Dr. Arnold Genthe was an artist. He approached his camera as the painter approached his canvas. You looked at a Taber photograph and said, "It looks like Aunt Elizabeth, doesn't it?" You looked at a Genthe photograph and said, "It's beautiful."

One of the most beautiful and most dramatic of Arnold Genthe's early photographs was called "The End of Old Chinatown." He made the picture on April 23, 1906. It's in somber tones; the smoke of the burning city lies on it like a blanket of fog; there is a brick chimney, all that remains of a dwelling; there are crumbling brick walls; there are disorderly piles of bricks; there is a fire hydrant and a flag pole. To the left of the scene of destruction an aged Chinaman stands, his face turned from the camera. He wears the traditional black Oriental dress that all Chinese still wore in 1906. Even

495

though his face is turned from the camera, his whole being expresses misery and sorrow and hopelessness. Old Chinatown was gone, and with its passing an era was ended.

Out of all Dr. Genthe's beautiful photographs made in the ten years preceding the disaster, only the pictures of Chinatown were saved; all the rest were lost in the fire. In the small hours of the night he was to be seen, camera in hand, slowly pacing up Dupont Street or into Commercial Alley and down the steps that led to Hell's Half Acre. In those days the Chinese citizens resented the intrusion of the white men, and called the white man's camera the "devil machine" and protected their children from its lens. But when Dr. Genthe appeared they would smile and pose for him and order the children to pose, and proudly boast, "Him belong me."

And that brings me to one last portrait. It is a Genthe photograph, the picture of an aged Chinaman, very tall, very thin, and very old. He wore a beard of a few straggling black hairs, and his eyes were those of a mystic. Some of us still remember him, the poor, mad "Emperor of the Universe." That's what he called himself, and that's what he believed he was. Hour after hour he'd wander through the paths of Portsmouth Square, or sit on a bench with his hands in his sleeves and gaze into miles of space. He smoked a long, curved pipe. He would walk, puffing on his pipe, and smile with a kindly, patronizing smile upon passing men and women; he smiled patronizingly, for they were all his subjects and he was their emperor. Across from Portsmouth Square in the Hall of Justice was the Central Police Station. Each afternoon at four o'clock the downtown squad of police would stand at attention before being dismissed for the day. And each afternoon the "Emperor of the Universe" would march down the line, with the manner of a general reviewing his troops. At the end of the line he would salute formally, the troop of policemen would salute, the "Emperor" would trot away up Jackson Street, and the squad would disband.

That was yesterday and these are photographs of yesterday, photographs that could not happen in this all-too-busy world we live in today. They are the San Francisco of serene memories.

XXVI

Secundino
and María Robles

This is the story of an unimportant man. Or, on second thought, inasmuch as no man is unimportant in the scheme of things, it is the story of a man about whom no history books will be written. Even that is not a fair evaluation, because millions of important people are overlooked by history. So we might say it is the story of a Californian whose life was uneventful. That will be the most inaccurate statement of all, because any man who is the father of twenty-nine children must have lived an eventful life.

I never knew him, but I did know his widow forty years ago. It came about in this way. In the nineties, before the coming of horseless carriages in any perceptible number, the roads that led south out of San Francisco and Oakland were the highways of bicyclists. On weekends, Saturdays and especially on Sundays, the dusty roads were a whirling marathon of speeding bicycles—single bicycles, tandems, and even contraptions built to carry entire families (not of twenty-nine children, but of three or four). They sped along the road at a breathless pace, endangering the lives of pedestrians, and they were a source of constant irritation and worry to the drivers of skittish horses. It was the beginning of the age of speed.

Now in those years, when I was eight or nine years old, my father, who might have been called a bicycle addict or even a speed maniac, went by bicycle almost every Sunday from East Oakland down the east side of the bay, usually through Niles Canyon, to San Jose, and Alum Rock Park. Then he came back in the late afternoon up the west side of the bay to San Francisco, concluding the day with a French dinner at The Pup or The Poodle Dog or Marchand's.

In the beginning he was accompanied by my mother, but she finally concluded that bicycle-riding was unrefined, that skirts bound to ankles by bicycle skirt-clips were a vulgar sight, and that one met such vulgar people bicycle riding, to say nothing of the fact that a round trip of one hundred miles or more in one day, pumping pedals, was a strenuous undertaking to say the least. So she finally revolted and my father, looking for new companionship, lit on me. My mother was shocked; she said a boy of nine was too young to undergo such rugged exercise; to which my father replied, "It will make a man of him." When the weather was clement, we went each Sunday, accompanied by sundry convivial businessmen of Oakland and San Francisco.

We'd get an early start in the morning. We'd reach San Jose about noon; we'd toil up the dusty hill to Alum Rock Park, pushing our bicycles before us; we'd arrive in time for a swim—that is, a swim for me; my father and his adult companions would take a steam bath and then a swim. Then we would go into the tavern where a very stout lady chef would serve us the wonderful broiled steaks for which Alum Rock Park was famous. The sophisticated men would refresh themselves with bottles of California red wine, and I would have a long glass of Seltzer water, colored with a soupçon of red wine and flavored with sugar. Then we'd all go to sleep. About an hour later we'd start home up the west side of the bay to San Francisco. Halfway along we'd stop at an old adobe where a genial, smiling, good-natured old woman would greet us.

My father would say, "María, we're dry and thirsty."

And María would reply, "Little wonder, with your tearing along the highroad on those contraptions. Your worse than my husband used to be with his horses."

She'd grunt and serve wine to the men, and to me a foaming glass of milk usually accompanied by a thin dry cake, something like a sweet tortilla. I've never forgotten the wonderful taste of those cakes and that fresh foaming milk, probably still warm from the cow. Nor have I ever forgotten the adobe, which stood not far from where Dinah's Shack now stands below Mayfield. In fact, it was on the very same land. Neither have I forgotten María, who was the mother of the twenty-nine children.

María Antonio García was born in Santa Cruz. In 1835 she married Secundino Robles, who was also born in Santa Cruz, and who was a daring and remarkably handsome young Castilian lad, twenty-two or twenty-three years old. It was very much of a love match. A great gathering of friends, relatives, and neighbors came to the celebration of the wedding, danced all day and all night, and sang happy songs. They said that there never was a lovelier young girl, a prettier black-eyed young girl, than María, and that surely from the City of Mexico to Sonoma there was not a more handsome *muchacho* than the more than six-foot-tall, blue-eyed Castilian lad Secundino Robles. Father Picos married them at the Mission Santa Clara. He beamed upon the great

500

crowd gathered and said, in so many words, that in very truth, here were two young people who would build a fine tribe of Californians, a credit to their worthy parents and an honor to Spain. And it is rumored that he warned María, with a twinkle in his eye, that Secundino was a spirited and adventurous and hot-blooded young man and that, like a fine and spirited and hot-blooded horse—Secundino was a great lover of fine horse flesh—a tight rein must be kept on him at times. María winked demurely and did not answer, because she knew that her beauty would be a well-woven rope to keep the spirits of her young husband in bond.

Of course, this is all pure imagination on my part. I wasn't there in 1835, nor have any written works recorded the actual words spoken by Father Picos or the thoughts registered by Secundino and María. But by all reports handed down from decade to decade by word of mouth, I have not far escaped the truth.

Added to bits of their story pieced together from sundry sources, I have the story of the Rancho Rincon de San Francisquito, which was the land of Secundino Robles, as related in *Historic Spots in California*. Secundino was, as I have said, born in Santa Cruz, California, just about the time one Napoleon Bonaparte rode to his Waterloo across the seas. Before his marriage, when he was in fact still in his late teens, Secundino, in search of adventure, had traveled into the foothills that lay between Mission Santa Clara and the ocean, and there had made an amazing discovery. In the stream bed of Almaden Creek in the Santa Cruz Mountains he had found a vivid red clay, an outcropping of the stuff the native Indians valued highly as a paint with which to decorate their bodies. Men called the deposit cinnabar, and agreed that it had a commercial value beyond its importance as a desired pigment for Indians. In fact, not long after Secundino found and laid claim to the outcropping, it was discovered that the cinnabar was rich in quicksilver, and that became the basis for the fortune of Secundino Robles. He sold his claim to a company formed to extract the precious flowing mineral, and he and his brother, Teodoro, were paid thirteen thousand dollars for it, which was a considerable fortune in those days; but not only that, Secundino and Teodoro retained a small interest in the quicksilver company. Now Secundino was a rich man, and the dignity of his position demanded that he build a family. He fell in love and wooed and won María Antonio García. They were wed, as I have told, at the Santa Clara Mission in 1835.

Secundino found various things to occupy his time, most important of which was the training and riding of spirited horses across the broad fields of the Santa Clara Valley. In 1841 he became major-domo of the Mission Santa Clara. Children were born to him and María, and he settled down to the staid and dignified life of a family man.

But the serene peacefulness of life was not to last. Newcomers came tramping the miles of California lands, and there were wars and much fighting, and much more parading and drilling in fine uniforms, and Secundino became a commander of troops under General Sanchez. He was a bold and fearless soldier, handsome and distinguished, and María was proud of him. Disaster, however, overcame his troops, and in 1846 Commandante Secundino Robles was taken prisoner by the invading enemy. History tells little of that capture, but one incident remains to be told proudly by María to their four children, and by the four to their children, and so handed down from generation to generation as an epic of glory of the family Robles. Secundino was marched, a prisoner, before his foe. His blue eyes snapped fire. He stood head erect and proud. As was the tradition, he drew his

502

sword from his scabbard to hand it to his captors. But he paused in the act, and lifting a knee, he bent the tempered steel across it and broke it into two pieces. Then he flung it upon the ground and was marched away, a prisoner, but with his spirit undefeated. And as all things do end in this life, so his imprisonment ended, and he returned to María and his children and their home at Mission Santa Clara.

But now, as he became the head of a family, more impos-ing residence was in order, and he looked around for lands that would do credit to his tribe, which still consisted of four fine youngsters. He found it in the land called Rancho Rin-con de San Francisquito, or Rancho Santa Rita. The land belonged to one José Pena. José was an artilleryman at the Presidio in San Francisco, and had been a teacher of the children of the Presidio in the early 'twenties. For his serv-ices to the Spanish rulers, he had been granted permission to occupy two square leagues of land—actually most of the land that lay between the Mission Santa Clara and Palo Alto. Twenty years later, when he was teaching at Santa Clara, he was given a deed to the land, and proceeded to build a pleasant small adobe home on it. That was in 1841, the year that Secundino Robles was major-domo at Santa Clara. The wars being over, Secundino, seeking a home for his family, went to José Pena and asked him to sell him the rancho. José was growing old, and the vast acres were becoming a burden. He agreed to sell, accepting the interest that Secun-dino Robles and his brother Teodoro held in the quicksilver mines of New Almaden as payment for the lands, fruit trees, and improvements. He moved out, the Robles family moved in, and at once Secundino began improving the land and the adobe on it. The adobe was too small for him, Maria, and the four children. He hired two Mexican workmen to add to it. One named Mena was the carpenter, and Jesus Ramos was

503

to do the adobe work. For this labor, Secundino and Teodoro gave the workmen the thirteen thousand dollars they had originally received in the sale of the cinnabar and quicksilver mines.

Secundino was a man who loved life. He loved happiness, laughter, song, dancing, and all the things that went with fiesta. So his first command to the workmen, Mena and Ramos, was that on the roof of the adobe, open to the sky, they should lay a fine and spacious dance floor. The order was obeyed, and on any moonlit night that you might be riding down through the Santa Clara Valley on your horse, or in your ox-drawn conveyance, you would be pretty sure to hear the music of guitars and mandolins floating from the roof of the adobe of Senor Secundino and his good wife María. In the moonlight there would be shadows moving to the rhythm of the music, sometimes slowly and regally, other times swiftly and firily in the tempo of the tarantella or jota or passionate bolero, and then the dignified tread of the *paso dobles*. From far and wide in the valley of Santa Clara, night after night and year after year, neighbors and friends and relatives came to dance on the roof of the adobe of Secundino Robles and María. It became a halfway point between the pueblo of San Jose and San Francisco, which with the fever of gold had become a thriving community. No one who was in good repute failed to break their journey and enjoy the hospitality of María and Secundino Robles.

María was not always on hand to receive and entertain her guests. After all, she was the duenna of the hacienda, with the preparation of food to be supervised, candles to be made, wool to be woven on the looms, to say nothing of the raising and educating of a family. For, as I have told you, when María and Secundino moved into the adobe they had four children. But with the passing of the years, kind providence smiled on them and twenty-five more children were born, twenty-nine in all.

Then the housing question became something of a problem. Of course, there was plenty of room for the adobe to spread out, on and on if need be until it reached from San Diego to the Oregon Territory. However, that would not have been practical, so Secundino built a roof over his dance floor, shingled it, and divided the space into three rooms. Now there were three rooms upstairs and three rooms downstairs to take care of the mama, the papa, and the twenty-nine children. No room for dancing now!

But the music and the singing kept on, and Secundino found a new way to entertain the host of friends who stopped to enjoy his refreshments, liquid and otherwise. He built an arena in front of the adobe where he held bear fights and bullfights to thrill his guests. In the miles of acres that surrounded the adobe and in the foothills, vast quantities of wild life abounded—bear, mountain lions, deer, wild fowl— and the Robles adobe became a haven for sportsmen. They all stopped at the adobe for a drink, a hearty welcome from Secundino, and a smile from María, when she wasn't busy having another baby.

And there Secundino Robles, the unimportant man, lived his uneventful life! He drove his spirited, high-blooded horses up and down the highroads that lay between San Jose and San Francisco. Of course, driving wasn't as good as it used to be, for now men had laid steel rails, and the monster steamcars came belching their smoke and frightening the horses. He loved to make pilgrimages to San Francisco to see the sights of the great city, sometimes with María, but more often alone. One thing above all else he loved. He would have one of his children or one of his grandchildren read him the newspaper that came from the city. Whenever

505

it told that the circus was coming to town, Secundino could hardly contain himself until the big day when he would have a ringside seat. He loved a traveling circus. He loved them so much that once when the circus was scheduled to play in San Jose, he found himself short of cash and had to borrow money to go to it. Why he needed the amount the records say he required, I have been unable to figure. But the circus was coming and he couldn't miss the circus and he had to have seventy-five dollars to go to it. He borrowed the money, repaying it by giving the lender fifty and a half acres of his fine Santa Clara land in payment.

Then Secundino Robles began to grow old. He spent many years sitting in the sun or in the shade of the grape arbor that was the shelter for the friends who came riding down the highway in fine horse-carriages from the mansions of Nob Hill and Pacific Heights. Some people said he had more friends than any other man in California. Of course, his money was gone, much of his land had been sold to pay debts, and other pieces of the land had gone as dowry to his daughters and even to his grandchildren. But he was still able to offer a cup of wine to a thirsty traveler on the highway.

The uneventful life of Secundino Robles ended on January 10, 1890. María, his widow, lived on for several years after he died, a little old white-haired, black-eyed lady, living on memories of her handsome Castilian husband, her twenty-nine children, and goodness knows how many grandchildren. She never got over liking children. You could tell it in her smile when we stopped at the adobe and stacked our bicycles against the grape arbor; you could see it in her eyes when she poured the glasses of red wine for the gentleman speeders, and the foaming glass of fresh warm milk for me.

XXVII

2409 Scott Street

It is our indomitable sentimentality that gives us our deep affection for the past. Events and places that may have been even ugly in fact become mellow and lovely in retrospect.

For instance, there was Miss Fisher's kindergarten. I went there more than fifty years ago. It must have been on Steiner or Pierce Streets between Clay and Sacramento. I hated Miss Fisher's kindergarten in those days, yet it broke my heart—to a certain extent—when I had to leave. There was a very exciting feature of Miss Fisher's kindergarten. On the wooden floor in the classroom there was a gigantic painted circle. The children would stand facing the center of the circle, with their toes touching the circle, and they would sing songs at the tops of their lungs. I have done no singing since those days, due to pressure from without, but I've never forgotten that circle painted on the floor. After I graduated to the dignity of the primary grades, I had my hide well tanned because I spilled a bucket of paint while trying to paint a circle on my own bedroom floor, and the paint leaked through the ceiling.

I think the most cherished memory of those primary-grade years was a vacant lot on Jackson Street—the north side of Jackson Street between Scott and Divisadero. The bottom of the lot was several feet higher than Jackson Street, and it was surrounded by a high fence. How we ever managed to get into it when we were in the first and second grade, I can neither remember nor imagine, but we called it the football lot. We played football, baseball, and mumblety-peg there, and I smoked my first cigarette and got sick there. I passed there the other day and wondered what had happened to the names that used to people the lot—the Elinwoods, the Van Fleets, Ned Cutter, Dick Turner, the Monteagles, and the Tum Sudens. There was also a red-faced stout boy named Kingsbury Parker, and there was Benny Baird who knocked me down and broke my front tooth off right at the root. There was Dudley Gunn, too. I had to fight Dudley Gunn one day because the other kids told us we had to. We were both six years old. Neither of us wanted to fight and neither of us knew how to fight. For the life of me I can't remember how we managed it, but we both went home with bloody noses.

One day a terrible adventure occurred right around the corner from the football lot. The Talbot boys lived there on the corner, and their property ran the full block from Jackson Street to Pacific Avenue. On this particular day, policemen arrived and there was much coming and going of people, rushing in and out of the Talbot home. All the neighbors, including my own parents, looked solemn and said, "Isn't it too bad? The Talbot boys have disappeared."

It seemed to me that they were gone for months and months. It was probably only a day, but so many stories piled up, stories of kidnapping or of their having run away to sea. I remember particularly the Talbot cook standing in the middle of Scott Street with her apron over her head, sobbing her eyes out. The mysterious policemen in their bowler hats scurried up and down the block, and it was a beautifully exciting adventure. Finally the Talbot boys were found. The gardener remembered that he had seen them doing something or other with a spade out in the lot in back of the garden. Then the policemen, the gardener, and millions of other people, as I seem to remember it, went searching over every inch of that lot, and finally found them. They had dug a deep hole, like a foxhole with a lid over it, and had disguised it with brush and branches. They had made a hideaway down there and stocked it with food—and probably some copies of Nick Carter!

About that time it was decided that I was to be musical. My musical education began with a Regina Music Box, then an Edison Gramophone, and subsequently an upright piano. Then there was a procession of music teachers, who labored and wept and told me glamorous stories about the operas and the life of the boy Mozart. I learned to play "Für Elise," the Mozart "Minuet," and the "Scarf Dance," although I wouldn't practice much. I didn't play well but I played loud. So it was decided that none but the finest master of music could make a musician of me, and into the house came Professor William McCoy. I wonder how many today remember Professor McCoy. Of course, he's well remembered at the Bohemian Club. His Bohemian Grove Jinks made history. As a matter of fact, he was a great musician. He wore an imperial moustache something like Kaiser Wilhelm. He would make me do Czerny exercises, and all the time I was pounding the keyboard he'd stand behind me and chew apples in rhythm. After school, when I was so hungry, the odor of those apples drove me frantic. But I had my revenge. One day when the professor arrived he found a large apple carefully cut in half and placed on a plate, with a large live worm—garden variety—crawling across the plate. That ended not only that lesson, but my musical career.

Card games and card parties were nostalgic affairs when I was young. Bridge whist had not arrived from London, and the fashionable game was euchre. How euchre is played I have no idea today, but the euchre parties in our home were characteristic of countless euchre parties in the nineties. In the attic there was a large room with a wooden floor and game tables. Today it would be called a rumpus room. On party nights, sand was sprinkled on the floor to make it look like a saloon. Each card table was equipped with four large German beer steins, and on a wooden stand in the corner of the room was an eight-gallon keg of beer. The men smoked long German pipes or strong Havana cigars, never a cigarette. The ladies smoked not at all. The high spot of the euchre parties was the food. It came from Grossman's delicatessen on Divisadero Street. There were cartons and cartons of potato and chicken salad, and sliced cold meats of every variety. There were dill pickles, sweet pickles, green olives, chicken-liver paste, smoked salmon, and a delicacy called sturgeon—smoked sturgeon which we never see any more. There was also a delicious macaroon torte from Lechten's bakery.

The gentlemen all wore long graceful moustaches and large ascot ties, and their white collars were so high that they cut their chins. The ladies all wore dresses that trailed in the sand, and their small-waisted blouses had collars as high as those worn by the men. About that time the pompadour became the fashionable ladies' hair style, but the nice ladies would not wear them for obvious reasons aptly expressed by a lady at one of our euchre parties.

"My husband," she said, "would never speak to me again

510

if I wore a hairdress named after that vile French creature, Madame Pompadour."

We, being a very modern family, had further entertainment for our guests. It was quite an innovation—a stereopticon machine. After the prizes had been awarded to the euchre winners (of course, one would not play for money when there were ladies present), my father would stretch a sheet across the end of the rumpus room and somebody would turn out all the gaslights. People would giggle and make jokes that were over my young head, and then Papa would project a series of stereopticon slides of Niagara Falls, the Swiss Alps, and huge colored pictures of single red roses, calla lilies, and bunches of forget-me-nots. And the evening would usually end with Papa playing his guitar, somebody else playing the piano, and everybody singing "Lo! Here the Gentle Lark" and "Ach Du Lieber Augustin." Yes, life was very gay at parties when we were young.

Of course, the best day of the week was Saturday, because there was no school. There was no school on Sunday either except Sunday School, but we wore our best clothes and were circumspect. But Saturdays—they were days of routine joy. On Saturday mornings, for more years than I can remember, I would beg large Irish potatoes, a small package of pepper and salt, and a huge hunk of butter from the Chinese cook. With a couple of friends who spoke my language, I would go to a vacant lot and build a bonfire. We'd cook the potatoes in the embers and they'd come out hard inside, and black and brittle as coal outside. Dripping with butter, they were ambrosia. Those Saturday-morning revels ended when the son of one of the city's most distinguished attorneys stole ten cents from his father and bought a pack of cigarettes. (There was a cigarette picture of Anna Held in the packet.) We smoked the whole pack and went home sick. I remember that we chewed the bitter leaves of calla lilies to take the smell of tobacco from our lips. The leaves were horrible to taste, and in spite of them the smell of tobacco remained, and our potato revels ended.

But there were still Saturday afternoons. My weekly allowance was twenty-five cents, and every Saturday afternoon —I don't think I missed a Saturday from the time I was six years old until I was ten—I would walk all the way downtown because, of course, my allowance wouldn't cover carfare. I'd walk all the way from Scott and Jackson Streets to the Grand Opera House on Mission Street near Third. Twenty-five cents admitted me to the gallery. I started with such innocent entertainment as *Aladdin and His Wonderful Lamp, Sinbad the Sailor,* and *Snow White and the Seven Dwarfs.* Then the fare became more substantial, and I still have vivid memories of *East Lynne, Thelma, In Old Kentucky, The Swanee River,* and the best of all melodramas, *The Two Orphans.* There was one rugged melodrama called *The Cherry Pickers,* in which the hero was chained to a wall in a huge stone tower. A master cannon was trained on him and the fuse lighted. At the psychological moment the heroine arrived, cut the fuse, beat off the hero's chains, and everybody lived happily ever after. There were other melodramas I saw in those days—*Michael Strogoff, Shore Acres,* and *May Blossom.* Finally, I saw *Sappho.* My mother cried when I told her the name of the play and I, being eight years old, had no idea why it should have led to such a heated argument between Mama and Papa.

Of course, that was all in the amazing nineties. A few years later we became a very modern and sophisticated family. (You will appreciate the fact that though I speak person-

512

ally, I am also thinking of San Franciscans in general.) We began to take the decoration of the modern home very seriously. We have a photograph which was made as a Christmas gift exactly forty years ago. It's a photograph of our family of six assembled in one corner of our living room. It's the most amazing display of bad taste we've seen outside a museum. The room is crowded, and it's as dark as a crypt. The wallpaper of heavy gold and brown is mixed up with the huge dark mahogony bookcases, the dark mahogany piano, the large dark mahogany reading table, mahogany cabinets, and a black ebony mantel with black ormolu clock and sidepieces. The clock is supported by two bronze elephants. A huge chandelier dangles, one half of it devoted to electric lights and one half to gas. There are huge oil paintings covering the walls—cows at pasture and angels eating sponge cake. There are Chinese and Japanese brocades flung around with abandon; there are scarves on the table, on the piano, and on the mantel. There are Satsuma vases, bronze bowls, copper trays, and brass boxes. You look at the picture and know that if anybody took a step in the wrong direction there'd be a catastrophe. The years of the nineties may have been amusing, even funny, but the first ten years of the twentieth century were overstuffed to the point of indigestion.

Well, that's my own intimate city of yesterday. The outward city was much as it is today. You walked in those days down the Powell Street hill from California to Sutter as you do today, and you took little mincing steps for fear of landing on your ear. You stood in the afternoon at your window on Pacific Heights and saw steamers sailing out through the Golden Gate to the world of fascination that was the Orient. You may stand today at windows on Telegraph or Russian

Hill, Presidio Heights or Sea Cliff, and see the steamers sailing out. You know, through a lesson bitterly learned, that there's more romance right here than there is in the Orient, and more joy of life on San Francisco hills than there is in any distant Nineveh or Shangri-La.

You read fascinating stories of David Garrick starving in an inn in the village of Bath, and you walk along Montgomery Street in the shadow of McCullough and Barrett and Edwin Booth and Lotta Crabtree and Emilie Melville.

You read Alfred Noyes' poem about the barrel organ and the lilacs that bloom in Kew Gardens. You are sentimental with the beauty of it, and all the time you are walking along Pacific Avenue or an avenue in St. Francis Wood, seeing gardens of flowers in a pageant of colorful bloom while winter snows whiten the rest of the world. The only time you are really annoyed is when you have to pay thirty-five cents for California violets, those same tender little violets that used to cost five cents a fragrant bunch before the days of war.

You long for foreign lands and faraway places of mysterious charm, and up and down San Francisco hills run the streets of Chinatown, Little Italy, Little Russia, the Spanish Quarter, the French Quarter, and the streets of the antique dealers. In the windows of food stores you see Italian chocolates, Mexican frijoles, Jewish matzos, Russian caviar, and Chinese clams; and up from below the sidewalk drifts the exquisite perfume of shish kebab.

And at night, as I did forty and fifty years ago, you stand on the summit of a hill, any hill, but preferably Telegraph Hill or Twin Peaks, and there is the pattern of humanity spread out before you in a map of myriad lights. There are the lights of the city, lights of the wonderful bay, and lights of the other cities scattered along the further edges of the bay.

514

The only difference between the city of today and yesterday is that into the galaxy of lights there is a newcomer. Lights are in the sky overhead as great ships of the air travel their far-flung courses. They complete the cycle—the naïve, hectic, beautiful city of yesterday; the hectic, fascinating city of today; and the city of tomorrow.

XXVIII

St. Mary's Square

In all my wanderings around San Francisco, no other piece of ground has the fascination for me that I find in St. Mary's Square across from Old St. Mary's Church at the corner of California and Grant Avenue. Now I realize that generalities are ill-advised, and that you may find little fascination in that small sloping hill of green grass hemmed in on all sides by oddly assorted buildings. But after all the political speeches we have heard recently, I am convinced that a man is at least entitled to his opinion and, in my opinion, St. Mary's Square has more exotic flavor, more beauty, and more changing moods than any other place in the city. If you are a stranger to the West, you will identify the square by the stone and stainless-steel statue of Dr. Sun Yat-sen that stands at the upper side of it. Again, in my opinion, that statue of Dr. Sun Yat-sen is the most beautiful man-made thing in the city, and I have no intention of arguing with the thousands who know so much more than I do about art, and who find in it a rather clumsy stunt, an unnecessary mixture of the classic and ultra-modern. I'll not argue, either, with those who say it reminds them of a hardware-store window. Beniamino Bufano, who didn't care very much about other people's opinions either, created it as he pleased, and it pleased him to clothe the

516

twelve-foot-tall figure in a robe of stainless steel, surmounted by a head of rose granite. It stands at the top of the lawn, facing the east.

Perhaps a part of the pleasure I find in the statue is sentimental, for I remember meeting Dr. Sun Yat-sen in Chinatown many years ago, and the impression he gave me of great strength and majesty and, above all, great serenity, has never left me. These I find reflected in the Bufano statue. I have stood before it at night with the moon shining on the silver of its stainless steel, and it is so serene, so utterly peaceful, and removed from the petty turmoils of life, that I believe a person, unnerved, neurotic, or unbalanced by problems, would find tranquility simply by sitting on a bench in front of it for a little while. It is the most peaceful thing in all the city, and yet amazingly alive for all its robe of stainless steel and its head and hands of rose-hued granite.

So I've seen it time and time again at night, under the stars and under the full moon, and most strangely fascinating of all, in a night of heavy fogs. I've seen it when the rain poured down on it, and I've walked by it in the full glare of the noonday sun, and, no matter what the mood of the elements, the great doctor stands there with that patient, wise, and immutable strength with a hint of a smile of humanity on his lips. It is a thing so dependable, so far above the material things of life, that I do believe if ever a great disaster was to come to the city, a mighty earthquake, or a falling bomb that would lay all the rest of the city in wreckage, Dr. Sun Yat-sen would still stand there, unshaken, in his robe of stainless steel.

The statue of Sun Yat-sen, however, occupies only a few feet of St. Mary's Square and is only one detail of the charm of the square. The buildings on which the Doctor turns his

517

back are separated from him by a narrow alley, the kind of an alley I would expect to find in Shanghai or in the old portion of Hong Kong. The buildings are the rear elevations of Chinese stores, with balconies and paper lanterns. They are the more intimate side of Chinatown life; their windows are the windows of the homes of Chinese families. The window sills have Chinese bowls with white Chinese lilies, and the clotheslines that periodically appear are dressed with Oriental trousers, mandarin coats, and Hollywood sports shirts.

And in the square, day or night, there are sure to be innumerable Chinese children, boys, girls, and babies of indefinite sex. Most Chinese babies look like boy babies, which is as it should be, because everyone knows that in the past, if not today, the only baby worth having was a boy baby. Girl babies were useless things sent by angry gods to either be peremptorily disposed of, or to clutter needlessly the lives of their unfortunate parents. I think that Dr. Sun Yat-sen was one of the few noble Chinese who liked all babies, boys or girls. Dr. Sun was of the new order and he, more than any other person in modern times, revolutionized the thinking of his people. There are sure to be children in St. Mary's Square any time you go there, and you will find one very significant thing about Chinese children. They laugh all the time. I have never heard a Chinese baby cry. But, by the same token, I have never heard a Chinese parent shriek at his or her children. They're strange people, the Chinese.

The other people, Oriental and Occidental, who frequent the square are as oddly assorted as you are likely to find anywhere in this or any other city. There are old men sleeping in the sun; there are girls with inviting eyes eating their lunch on the benches behind the statue or under the trees;

there are men with shifty eyes who look as if they might be medicine-show spielers, pitchmen, or shills from side shows, or from even more nefarious professions. And likely as not there will be clerks from Montgomery Street money mills, a few tourists who drift down from Grant Avenue, or Paulist Fathers who walk there in the sun. On the morning of Easter Sunday the square is a crowded mass of humanity attending open-air overflow services from Old St. Mary's. During the week of Chinese New Year the square is a bedlam of shouting youngsters and exploding firecrackers. Over all the strange, shifting, and yet usually serene pageant of heterogeneous life, Dr. Sun Yat-sen stands in his stainless-steel dignity and smiles his ineffable smile of benign charity. But there was one aspect of St. Mary's Square that the statue of Dr. Sun never saw.

It was more than fifty years ago, in the early nineties. Grant Avenue, or Dupont Street, as it was then called, was the highway to the Barbary Coast, and the buildings that lined the street were houses of evil fame. Dupont Street was the promenade of their inmates. Then the good and virtuous ladies of San Francisco took action; Dupont Street had to be an avenue of virtue. The nefarious houses were doomed, and all the inmates were moved to the shacks that lined St. Mary's Square. Tattoo artists and proprietors of shooting galleries opened shops. The sickly sweet odor of opium smoke drifted through the square. It became a tradition for visiting British and American sailors to choose the center of the square to settle their international arguments with fights that were as frequent and bloody as any to be found in the most exciting of Hollywood B pictures.

There was no statue of Dr. Sun to look down on the sore spot of the city, but right across the street was Old St. Mary's

Church and the good Paulist Fathers were having a bad time. In 1898 they organized the St. Mary's Association and raised money to buy the land and use a part of it for the city's good. But city fathers move slowly, and city grafters did away with funds. It took the earthquake and fire to do what human effort couldn't do; the flames swept the area clean, and with the rebuilding of the city, St. Mary's Square of today became a reality.

That was only the first of the transformations that turned the little plot of grass-grown ground into a restful haven, a sort of Sleepy Hollow in the center of turmoil. All kinds of trees grow in San Francisco. There are not enough of them, but at least in the parks you will find cypress and yews and all types of evergreens and deciduous foliage. But it's hard to fathom the imaginative stroke of genius that inspired the city fathers or some of their sons-in-law to plant a row of beautifully dignified and utterly serene poplars, tall, slender, and graceful, reaching to the stars. They were planted the full width of the square along the top of the plaza, separating the rear elevations of the buildings from the statue of Dr. Sun.

There you have the square, poplar trees at its top, then the narrow park of sloping green grass less than a third the width of a city block, and at the base of the slope an entirely different world—little St. Anne Street, with its rear elevations of industrial houses. But even that doesn't give the true picture, for next to a brick wall dressed with conventional glass windows will be a brick wall dressed with iron grille balconies, reminiscent of the balconies of old New Orleans.

Now the colors of the square began to take form; tall green trees and green lawns, stainless steel and rose granite, blue sky and gray fog. But more was to come.

Some years ago—it must have been twenty years ago—a school of design took up residence in St. Anne Street. The name, School of Design, hardly gave a true picture of the worthy enterprise. Color was almost a religion with its founder. On the premise that the drab colors of cities should be a thing of the past, and that there was no limitation to the colors that could be used, in good taste, to decorate a city, the School of Design blossomed in bricks that were painted several colors of the spectrum. Each floor of the building had a façade of bricks in a different color. I believe the building is all yellow today, but the seed of color had been planted, and the bricks of neighboring buildings took on amazing hues. At first there was an outcry of horror from the staid citizens who had always done things just as their grandfathers had done them. Bricks were supposed to be red, so they should always be red. But the dissension died, or was forgotten, and today the buildings that line St. Anne Street are a bright and happy array in a city that needs color to accentuate the beauty of its fogs and blend with its moods of sunshine and star-emblazoned nights.

Well, there is your picture of St. Mary's Square, and I suppose there will be some of you who will say I have written at length about a little corner of the city and said nothing. Some day, when you're not too far from California Street, you will wander into the square just to see what inspired all these words, and you'll look and say, "Oh, is that all?" or you may even deal in the vernacular and say, "So what?" if you are so disposed.

But you must remember that the physical aspects of St. Mary's Square, like the physical aspects of every corner of every city, are only a small part of the picture. One must not forget the ghosts—the ghosts of dead dreams, the ghosts of

521

long-forgotten men, and the ghosts of strange romances that inhabit the turning of almost every corner.

For instance, when you stand in the square, turn and look to the north. You see buildings and more buildings below Old St. Mary's Church. But right there, on the north side of California Street above Kearny facing St. Anne Street, was the home of Dr. Jones. You've probably never heard of Dr. Jones. I don't suppose any man living today could possibly have known him, for Dr. Jones built his house in 1849, and he was not so very young in those days. I have turned pages upon pages of San Francisco lore and found nothing about Dr. Jones. Yet I know that he built his two-story wooden house in 1849, and from here and there, bit by bit, I have gathered a vague framework on which you may hang your own story.

I don't know when Dr. Jones came to San Francisco, or what his first name was, or even if he had a first name, but I do know that, during his residence in the wooden house on California Street, he was a gentleman who imbibed freely, copiously, and with great dignity. If you had lived here a hundred years ago, you might have seen him walking along Montgomery Street, turning up California, and climbing the dirt road with the grand manner and noble histrionics of an Edwin Booth or a Henry Irving. With haughty mien he would at times bow to passing acquaintances, but more often he would pass them by, his thoughts to all appearance a thousand miles away, probably preserved in alcohol. He wore, above his high boots and gaiters, a stiff white shirt, a high white collar, and a small black string tie. Over his shoulders he wore a black broadcloth cloak, velvet lined, a cloak that hung to the top of his boots. The dignity of his gait, the proud way in which he held his head, and the impressive fullness and length of his velvet-lined cloak, gave to his small frame the impression of a Wotan, a man of the gods.

There were times when Dr. Jones was not all dignity; times when, surrounded by convivial friends at a friendly mahogany bar, he regaled them with tales of his adventures, and he would pound the mahogany at regular intervals, ordering more and more libations for all who cared to join him. Then he'd throw a huge and overstuffed bag of gold dust onto the bar and command the proprietor to help himself.

There lay the core of the fascination of Dr. Jones' story. He loved gold and was said to have more gold dust than any other individual in San Francisco, not excepting Sam Brannan, William Howard, and Kanaka Davis. Whether he had dug the dust himself, tramping the Sierra and uncovering pockets with the instinct of an oracle, whether he had earned it in traffic with clients, or whether he had come by it by nefarious means, no one seemed to know. Nor in my search have I been able to ascertain whether his title of doctor was that of medicine, philosophy, or simply an honorary title assumed for the pleasure of its sound. After all, it was his gold and his gold dust that mattered, and in his two-story wooden house on California Street, facing what is now St. Anne Street and St. Mary's Square, Dr. Jones reveled in his gold. This is not a general statement, loosely used. Dr. Jones' house overflowed with gold dust, even escaping into the night air on California Street through his open window. Time and time again he was seen with white sheets spread on the wooden floor of his bedroom—white sheets on which he would pour hills and mounds of gold dust. Then he would tramp barefooted through it, letting the fine dust stream between his toes; he would reach down and take great handfuls of gold dust and pour them over his head and shoulders. His plodding would become a wild dance in dust of gold, culminating when he would fall to the floor and heap the gold about his body and roll in it. The next day, sedate and dignified, clad in his long, black, velvet-lined broadcloth cloak, Dr. Jones of California Street would make his noble progress along Dupont, Kearny, and Montgomery Streets, bowing with haughty mien to casual friends, or walking past them as though his thoughts were a thousand miles away.

Dr. Jones of California Street was another bit of mosaic in the pattern that made up the color and the fascination of a hundred years, a century in which the life of the square has been the story of saints and painted women; of derelicts who sleep in the sun on the green grass; of laughing Chinese children and placid-faced, shapeless old Chinese women; of tall poplar trees and strange music; and the serene and beautifully peaceful figure of Dr. Sun Yat-sen who stands in his coat of stainless steel, with his rose-granite hands clasped in utter repose, immutable to changing days and changing ways.

Appreciations and Acknowledgments

There is a very tangible satisfaction in typing, as I have just typed, the last period after the last word in the last sentence of a book. Then you may sit back, as I am sitting back, and say: "There! It's finished. I hope it's good."

Of course the story of the kaleidoscope of San Francisco will never be finished, and, as a matter of fact, my work will never be finished until I have tried, inadequately, to thank all of the people who have helped me. An impossible task! Many have phoned to me and given me stories, and I have not met them personally, nor do I know their names. I have found source material in literally scores of books; to name them all would require a book in itself; they are a cross section of any comprehensive bibliography of Californiana. Private and public libraries have been of inestimable help. Old-timers have stopped me on the street and asked, "Do you know the story of ———?" It is impossible to begin to name all of them, so I can only say: "Thanks. I am appreciative."

But there are certain very tangible sources of help, and the most valuable of all help is, I believe, encouragement. John W. Elwood, general manager of KNBC-NBC in San Francisco, has been a constant inspiration with his friendship, encouragement, enthusiasm, and guidance; I sometimes wonder whether I have sold him, or he has sold me San Francisco.

San Francisco Kaleidoscope, like its predecessor, *San Fran-*

cisco Is Your Home, has been based on the KNBC radio program, "This Is Your Home," sponsored for more than seven years by W. & J. Sloane. Ruskin B. Hamlin, general manager of Sloane in San Francisco, and vice-president of W. & J. Sloane, has been highly generous in his enthusiasm and encouragement; and, most unusual in this tortuous business of radio-writing, he has given me a free hand to tell the stories I wanted to tell, as I wanted to tell them. This should make me the envy of all sponsored radio writers.

Budd Heyde, long-suffering, has read with fine restraint and sympathetic understanding the Sloane shows since their beginning, and has constantly had to explain that he is not senile, nor approaching senility, and that the lines he reads are the memories of Mr. Dickson, and not his own.

My knowledge of spelling is atrocious, and I dangle prepositions and split infinitives. My admiration and thanks to Florence Crowell and Claire Patrick for the careful editing of this manuscript.

And finally, to my wife, who has heard me tell all these stories a hundred times, and patiently sits and listens to them again and again, my thanks and my devotion.

BOOK THREE

THE STREETS OF SAN FRANCISCO

For ROSE *and* LEONARD DICKSON

"The streets of San Francisco are free"

<small>LUISA TETRAZZINI</small>

"At the end of our streets is sunrise;
at the end of our streets are spars;
at the end of our streets is sunset;
at the end of our streets are stars."

<small>GEORGE STERLING</small>

Prologue

Luisa Tetrazzini said, "The streets of San Francisco are free." In those half dozen words is all the inspiration a man could ask to write a book, all the inspiration I want to challenge me to capture in words my favorite memories and stories, and the sounds and impressions and colors and odors of the San Francisco that I love.

They will be pages beaten out on my typewriter, not for their literary merit or lack of it. Nor will they be included because they have wide popular appeal. There will be no chronological sequence in the telling of the stories, nor will they be related one to the other in any way, save for the fact that they were born in the streets of San Francisco. And there, by the most obvious of clichés, I discover the secret of the city. Its fascination, its glamour, its perfume and its beauty, its impish air of devil-may-care, its joys and its tragic sorrows, and its eternal youth lie in its drab, gray streets.

The names of the streets have very little bearing on the case. Sutter Street was named for John August Sutter, and, so far as I know, John August Sutter on whose land gold was discovered, may never have walked the muddy trail of his days that later was to be labeled "Sutter Street." Pacific Street, sink of iniquity in its prime, was anything but pacific. Dupont Street, named after I know not whom, became Grant Avenue, although General Grant achieved his greatest distinction in San Francisco by losing his false teeth over the rail while steaming through the Golden Gate, and by dining and wining at the Palace Hotel. And Front Street lay far below the waters of the bay when the city was in its youthful prime.

529

Minna Street! Annie Street! Jessie Street! And Clementina! Now there's a happy company of street names! Good, wholesome, old-fashioned, characteristic American names! Named after, I am told, "and of course this may only be gossip," named after the very popular girls who lived in the alleys that bear their names.

No, I do not hunt for glamour in the names of the city streets. But in the perfume of the streets, in the shadows of the streets, and in the sunrise and sunset at the end of the streets, are the myriad ghosts whose stories are woven into the fabric that is the beauty of San Francisco. These I love, and of these I write.

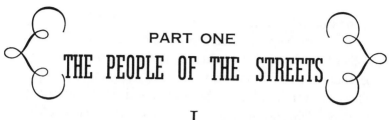

PART ONE
THE PEOPLE OF THE STREETS

I

Tetrazzini

She said, "The streets of San Francisco are free." San Francisco loved her, and I, being a San Franciscan, loved her, and, above all, she loved San Francisco. She was not a very profound person, nor was she given to an expression of her emotions and reactions in esoteric philosophizing. She simply said, "The streets of San Francisco are free," and you would be wasting your time if you were to seek for hidden subtleties in the words when she said them.

Any city's streets are controlled by traffic laws, belong to the community through which they run, and are governed by rules and regulations and taxes. Yet, with that zest for life that inspired her, Luisa Tetrazzini knew that in the streets of San Francisco was to be found a freedom of life, a freedom of breathing, a free and easy joy of living to be found in few other places. Perhaps unwittingly, she had discovered the secret of San Francisco. Hold a mirror before the story of Luisa Tetrazzini, and you will have the essence of San

Francisco.

The story began for me one morning in 1905. The hills of San Francisco point downtown, and it was the habit then of countless San Franciscans to walk downtown to their offices and various places of business morning after morning, smoking rich Havana cigars, and swinging malacca sticks. It was on a morning in 1905 that my father, walking to his office, met Fred Belasco, the brother of David Belasco. With him was George Davis. Belasco and Davis, with Fred Mayer, were the managers and proprietors of the old Alcazar, called at that time the most popular repertoire stock theater in all the world. My father had been an "angel" of the Alcazar some years earlier. Standing at the curb with Belasco and Davis was "Doc" Leahy. Leahy was and for twelve years had been the manager of the Tivoli, where week after week and year in and year out the finest musical comedy was being presented, with a change in the bill almost every week in the year. Leahy was a perfectionist, with an abiding love in his work. His eyes danced when he talked of the Tivoli and its shows: shows that ranged from Donizetti and Verdi and Rossini to Gilbert and Sullivan and Reginald De Koven. One week it might be *Lucia di Lammermoor,* the next *The Prince of Pilsen* or *Giroflé-Girofla.*

So they stood, the three of them, at the curb, and Fred Belasco, with a charitable smile on his lips, tapped his forehead as though to imply that Doc Leahy was, to put it mildly, living in a San Francisco fog.

But Doc Leahy's eyes were dancing. "Don't miss Friday night," he said.

The annual season of grand opera was about to open at the Tivoli, and Leahy had made a find. She was a young woman he had discovered while on a visit to Mexico City, and in his humble estimation she was the greatest coloratura soprano he had ever heard. Young? Well, actually she was not so very young; at least she wasn't a schoolgirl; she was thirty-three at the time. But Leahy, who worshiped great art, could not, for the kindly life of him, understand why she had not been acclaimed as one of the greatest singers of the day. In short, she had made her debut in Italy nine years before, she had sung in Mexico City and other places, but for some inexplicable reason, she was simply accepted as another good singer. A good utility singer! Doc Leahy was leaving it to the city he loved to discover her and to place her at the top of the ladder of fame and glory.

Belasco smiled a charitable smile and lit a fresh cigar, and my father, who loved all music from Wagner to "Climbing Up the Golden Stairs," purchased tickets for the family for Friday night far up front in the orchestra, at two dollars apiece. The opera was *Rigoletto*.

You of course know that in *Rigoletto* Gilda does not appear until the opera is well under way. So the orchestra played the overture and the first curtain came up, the music played and the singers sang, and the audience was well pleased. In those days, discriminating as they were, San Francisco audiences loved all opera. The gallery and most of the balcony was crowded with humanity from North Beach. They clapped and cheered and the perfume of garlic was everywhere. Downstairs, in the orchestra seats, the audience was more restrained, just pleasantly enjoying itself.

Then Gilda made her entrance at the top of a flight of stairs. Now this is not imagination on my part. Some fifty years have passed since that night, and yet I can still feel, as though it were yesterday, the cold thrill of anticipation as she stood there, even before she had sung her first note. That was a part of the intangible fascination of Tetrazzini; even when she was not singing, exuberance and a spellbinding excitement flowed from her. I can only remember one other night that I felt that same anticipatory thrill; that was the night, the first time I heard her, that Flagstad appeared out of the papier-mâché clouds to sing "Ho-yo-to-ho," in *Die Walküre*.

Gilda stood there, at the top of the flight of stairs. She was lovely and she was slender; yes, at that time Tetrazzini was as slender as a girl. And I can remember that she looked frightened. Then she smiled and commenced to sing her "Caro Nome," and, at the very first notes, that San Francisco audience knew! This was it; this was a moment never to be forgotten. She sang, and the audience held its breath.

Oh, you'll say I'm oversentimentalizing something that happened half a century ago. But I was there, and I was too young to know the difference between good singing and great art. But I knew that night.

She sang "Caro Nome" and at the end the audience did not, as it so often did, burst into applause before the last note was ended. The last note faded into absolute silence, there was a breath-taking pause, and then they went mad.

They shouted and stamped and stood up; all the audience stood up and cheered, and the orchestra men stood up and cheered. Men stood on the seats of their chairs and threw their hats in the air; women tore flowers from their dresses and threw them on the stage. And when that mad pandemonium had finally stilled—in those days arias were repeated when the audience demanded an encore—Tetrazzini sang the "Caro Nome" again.

And that is all I can remember of the singing that night;

the rest of the opera is a complete blank to me. At the end of the second act, my father went out to the box office and reserved seats for the family for every Friday night of the engagement. The next day I asked him for my tickets and took them down to the box office and changed the seven orchestra tickets for twenty-eight "standing room's" at fifty cents apiece. I went to the Tivoli twenty-eight times in those seven weeks. For a long time I believed that I had heard Tetrazzini twenty-eight times, but that does not now seem possible. I know that I did hear her in *Rigoletto* and *La Traviata*, *Lucia* and *Il Trovatore*, *Faust* and *Linda di Chamounix*, and *Dinorah*, in which, slender and tiny, she danced the dance of the mad girl to the shadow of her goat. I heard her in *The Masked Ball*—but the list seems endless, and there is nothing to be gained by naming them all, especially as someone with a more accurate memory than mine will write to tell me that my imagination is again playing tricks and that Luisa Tetrazzini never did sing that role. The important thing is that, on that night in 1905, San Francisco discovered Luisa Tetrazzini and told of its discovery to the world. When the call came for her to go to New York and sing, she refused at first; she was afraid of New York and wanted to stay in San Francisco always; she loved the city and the city loved her; she had become as much a part of the streets of San Francisco as the wind and the fog and the sunrise and the sunset.

That was in 1905, but those nights are only part of my memories of Tetrazzini. Other memories are more intimate. On Saturday night of that first week, I had dinner with my grandmother at the Marie Antoinette apartments on Van Ness Avenue between Pine and Bush streets. Before dinner, while we were sitting, silently, my grandmother rubbing the rheumatic joints of her fingers, each finger one hundred times, and I staring out the window; while we sat there, we suddenly heard an exquisite voice coming through the wall. It sounded like Tetrazzini, but of course it couldn't possibly be Tetrazzini. The soprano was singing harmony, singing an Italian street song with an equally beautiful tenor voice. It couldn't be, but it was Tetrazzini. Her room was next to my grandmother's and she was singing duets with gramophone records of Caruso.

Every day during that wonderful season I went to my grandmother's. She wasn't misled, she didn't for a moment believe it was a newly developed devotion for her on my part: I came to hear Tetrazzini and Grandma knew it. Luisa sang all the time, from unaccompanied arias to duets with Caruso, Scotti, and Jean de Reszke, from grand opera to gay folk melodies. Day after day I lay on the floor, as close to the wall as I could get, my ear pressed to the wall, and listened. As thrilling as her singing was her laughter. She would sing and go into long peals of the happiest laughter. She would chatter to herself in Italian very fast and begin laughing or singing again. Sometimes Grandma would shake her head. People who talked to themselves were not quite right in their mind.

When it was time to go downstairs to dinner, I waited till I heard Tetrazzini's door open and close, and then I ran to get to the elevator at the same time as she did. We rode down together night after night, while she grinned at my grandmother and me, but we never spoke a word. After all, she spoke only Italian, and even if I could have made myself understood, I would not have had the courage.

In the dining room, she sat at the next table. I have since learned that most opera singers eat lightly before singing.

But not Tetrazzini! Her dinner was always the same: a huge turkey-platter of *tagliarini* and a full quart of red wine. She wound the tagliarini around her fork with great plunges, and shoveled it into her broad, laughing mouth. She gulped the red wine by glassfuls. Dinner over, she would unpin the large linen napkin that was spread over her, leave the table, and go to the Tivoli and sing her bell-toned arias.

It is foolish to try to find metaphors to describe the quality of that voice when she reached for her E flat and E above high C. It was something more than human. I have heard Galli-Curci sing those beautiful notes, and they left me cold because the notes flowed with such colorless ease from her lips. But they came dancing from the lips of Tetrazzini, with the ease of a high note lightly touched on a celeste, and yet you knew that each one of them was delighting Luisa Tetrazzini; she played with them as a child might play with the bubbles that dance from a clay soap-pipe. Those high notes were so beautiful that people forgot to listen to the beauty of her middle register. She sang like a bird, high in the sky.

The grand opera season of the Tivoli ended, and San Francisco rubbed its eyes and came out of its beautiful dream. Still Tetrazzini stayed on, singing silver notes, eating huge meals, growing stout, and loving every corner of the city that adored her. She became a familiar figure in the streets of San Francisco, and people like me, who love to drop names, would tell of hearing her sing at unexpected moments in the most unexpected places.

It was in that same year, 1905, that I went on Christmas Eve to the old Palace Hotel to hear the choir boys singing Christmas carols at midnight. I stood on the seventh-floor balcony, leaning against the rail between the marble pillars and looking down to the Palm Court so far below. As the

537

bells tolled midnight, the boys, in white surplices, entered from what is now the Rose Room and slowly circled the Palm Court, singing their lovely carols. And as they sang, a woman came and stood next to me. She was garbed in black and had a black and purple veil that fell to below her waist; in her hands she clasped a bunch of purple California violets. The choir boys sang, and as they sang her voice joined with theirs. The choirmaster looked up to where we stood, then with a slow motion of his hand made a signal for the boys to sing more softly. Their voices faded while the woman in black sang on. It was more beautiful than any singing I have ever heard.

Of course it was Luisa Tetrazzini, making one of those unscheduled, unheralded appearances that she so loved to make. I had heard her through the walls and in the hallways of the Marie Antoinette, I had heard her in the choir loft of the little French church on Pine Street, and now those crystal-pure notes went dancing and tumbling from the seventh-floor balcony of the old Palace Hotel. This, I know, was a great part of the charm and great art of Tetrazzini: not only was the voice lovely, but she loved to sing.

With the passing of the week after that Christmas Eve, the year 1905 ended, and with it a complete chapter in the story of San Francisco. The city had grown through fifty-six years, from its golden dawn and through its champagne days; the muddy roadways of the mining camp had become broad streets that ran from east to west and from north to south in a nice, orderly, uninspired geometrical pattern, as neat and orderly as a picket fence. Then came 1906, and with it the fire and earthquake, and the picket fence fell down. There was little time now in the city that had been leveled for re-membering nights of song. But, with amazing speed, the

538

dust, ashes, fallen bricks, and broken glass were swept away, and San Franciscans commenced to ask, "Where is Tetrazzini?"

The stories and rumors came tumbling in. Tetrazzini had fallen in love with a young man several years younger than herself. Tetrazzini was being sued for bills unpaid. Tetrazzini was growing stout. There were whispers and there was gossip and there was scandal, but it was all part of the happy, careless, carefree road that Tetrazzini was traveling to fame. She did outrageous things, and people chuckled and said, "It's just Tetrazzini." She was making large sums of money now. She was always in debt, and people said, "It's just Tetrazzini." She became a tradition. She went to New York and had triumphs beyond her dreams, probably beyond the dreams of old Doc Leahy. She became one of the great names in American opera during the era that has since been called the Golden Age, the era of Melba and Sembrich, Gadski and Homer, Caruso, Scotti, and De Reszke and all the others. For a few years the name of Luisa Tetrazzini was on every music lover's lips.

Of course the critics disagreed. Some shook their critical heads and said her middle register was not good; others grumbled in their beards that her high notes were tricks. But when those high notes tumbled like a waterfall of dancing bits of sunshine, each perfect in itself, then you didn't care very much what the critics said or thought.

Meanwhile, in San Francisco, the city that loved her was clamoring for Tetrazzini to come back. She had been singing in New York under contract to Oscar Hammerstein. They had had troubles; she was temperamental and Hammerstein, a little bit temperamental himself, had no patience with temperamental artists; they were constantly in dispute

539

and she was constantly having legal difficulties. Hammerstein wanted her to sing in New York. She wanted to sing in San Francisco. She said her manager was Doc Leahy and she was going to sing for him in San Francisco. She held a press conference and told the newspapermen, "I will sing in San Francisco if I have to sing there in the streets, for I KNOW THE STREETS OF SAN FRANCISCO ARE FREE."

She won her case, and Doc Leahy won, and it was announced that Tetrazzini would return to the city she loved above all others, to sing in the streets on Christmas Eve.

Christmas Eve was radiant. I was there that night, and I remember the gathering of the crowd. All the streets of San Francisco pointed to the corners of Market and Kearny, and Lotta's Fountain, where a concert platform had been erected. I stood in that solidly packed mass of humanity, two blocks away from the platform. Out Kearny Street, over Third Street, up and down Market Street, and west on Geary Street, the throng stretched for blocks—some say it numbered three hundred thousand.

Paul Steindorff, the beloved orchestra leader of the Tivoli, stood on the platform, conducting a symphony orchestra, and a huge choir sang Christmas carols. A green light flashed on top the Monadnock Building across the street and, leaning on the arm of Mayor McCarthy, Tetrazzini mounted the platform. I was blocks away, but I could see that dazzling white form; I say "dazzling," for she wore a white gown covered with thousands of diamond-flashing spangles. I have a huge old photograph in my pigskin chest of memory treasures, a full-page photograph of her standing there that night, dazzling, her plump arms stretched out to the crowd and to the city she adored.

It seemed, at first, that the ovation would never end.

540

San Francisco had come to hear her sing but now that was forgotten in the joy of seeing her again. But the ovation did end, and she sang. She sang "I Would Linger in This Dream." I stood two blocks away, and every note was crystal clear, and every word distinct. Silence, save for her voice, spread over the city, like the silence of night in the desert. Streetcars were stopped, horses and wagons and the few automobiles stood still. The clanging of the cable car bells was stilled. Not a sound came from that vast audience.

She sang again, and if you had closed your eyes you would have thought yourself alone in the world with that beautiful voice. She sang "The Last Rose of Summer." When she finished, there was another tumultuous ovation. She held out her arms to her people, asking for quiet, and commenced to sing once more. This time, all San Francisco sang with her. Up and down the streets and alleys and from the windows of buildings high above the streets came the song from the hundreds of thousands, and Luisa Tetrazzini sang with them: "Auld Lang Syne."

Then silently, as though they had stood in a divine presence, the people of San Francisco went home, with joy in their hearts. It was San Francisco's most wonderful Christmas Eve.

I was to hear Tetrazzini one more time. I know that we of San Francisco had talked Tetrazzini and dreamed of Tetrazzini, and made nuisances of ourselves by telling newcomers who had neither seen nor heard her, that there had never been another like her. We built a reputation for her that was almost too much for a mortal to carry, and the newcomers smiled indulgently, mentally tapped their foreheads, and said, "San Franciscans! Nice, but slightly mad!" But there was an insistent, constant demand that Tetrazzini come again, and finally the glad tidings appeared in the press: Luisa Tetrazzini would sing at the Civic Auditorium on such and such a night so many weeks or months hence. The Civic Auditorium is a huge barn of a place, cold and severe, and notable chiefly for its large size, huge seating capacity, and bad acoustics. But long before the night of Tetrazzini's return, every seat had been sold.

The excitement of anticipation hung over the city for days before the concert; I am not using the words idly, for even to those San Franciscans who were not at all interested in music the love for the tradition of Tetrazzini was enough to make them behave like—well, like schoolboys looking forward to the first day of vacation.

We were in our seats long before the hour for the concert to commence. An excited sound, like the busy buzzing of twenty thousand bees, hummed around the walls of the auditorium. There were spontaneous stamping of feet and rhythmic, measured clapping of hands, like the noise from the audience at a prize fight clamoring for the show to get started. But this was no prize-fight audience. These were the garlic-fragrant Italians from Telegraph Hill; the theater crowd from O'Farrell Street; the warm-blooded crowds from South of the Slot; the nobs from Nob Hill and the refined elegants from Pacific Heights, the ladies in their finest silks and satins and diamond tiaras and flowers, the menfolk in their swallowtails and silk hats.

The waiting seemed interminable. The clamor swelled. At last a stagehand crossed the high, improvised stage that ran the full width of the auditorium and opened the top of the concert grand piano, stage center. The audience applauded and cheered. The stagehand made his exit and the accompanist, a well-known and distinguished pianist, came on stage. He sat quietly at the keyboard and commenced to play his solo. At first the audience was polite, but they had not come to hear or see a distinguished pianist. Halfway through his solo, the shuffling commenced, then the stamping of feet and clapping of hands; the noise became an uproar. With a kind and entirely understanding smile, the pianist stopped playing, his solo unfinished. He rose, laughed, and waved to the audience. Then he turned and gestured to the back of the stage, where on either side winding stairways led high up. The audience roared, and cheered, and waited. Finally, at the top of the stairway at stage right appeared the collosal form of Luisa Tetrazzini, clad in a gown of black sequins. And into the sequins was woven or sewed, in whatever manner is usual with sequins, an immense peacock. The head of the peacock was on Tetrazzini's shoulder, the neck and body, across her broad bosom; and the beautifully colored tail of the peacock spread itself across the broad expanse of Tetrazzini's rear.

She stood there, while the audience rose, and shouted and cheered and screamed. As they had done years before at the Tivoli, men stood on their seats and threw their silk hats into the air, and women flung their flowers at the stage. Tetrazzini commenced her descent of the steps. She didn't walk down or run down, she tottered down, clumsily. She reached the stage floor and teetered across it, tottered across it, arms stretched out. She came to the footlights, and tears were pouring down her cheeks. She sank to the stage, on the broad tail of the peacock, and bowed her head and sobbed. After a little, she clambered to her knees, lifted herself to her feet, and waited for the pandemonium to fade.

It did fade, but when the accompaniment started and she had sung a half dozen notes, she sobbed again, and the pandemonium recommenced. Finally, sanity returned to that San Francisco audience, calm returned to Luisa Tetrazzini, and she sang her opening aria.

I have forgotten what the song was, I have forgotten all the numbers on the program. I know only that Tetrazzini's voice had matured with the years, that every note, from the breath-taking notes high above high C to the critic's "middle register," were perfect. I know that we had justified ourselves with the newcomers who had tapped their foreheads and politely murmured that all San Franciscans were slightly mad. There was only one, there had only been one Tetrazzini.

It seems only a few years ago, hardly more than yesterday, that I wrote to a musician friend of mine at the "Met" in New York and asked what had happened to Tetrazzini. My friend answered the letter, saying that Tetrazzini was in Italy, living in poverty in a pension, a poor, tenement sort of pension, giving singing lessons to poor children and receiving hardly enough pay to buy the dishes of spaghetti and tagliarini, and the bottles of red wine, that were barely keeping her alive.

Soon after the arrival of the letter—this was in 1940—a few brief lines appeared in the newspapers of San Francisco, the city that had adored her and the city she had loved, saying simply that the old-time coloratura soprano, Luisa Tetrazzini, had died in a garret in Florence.

II

Giovanni, Friedman, and Jim Lee

Many years have passed since I read *Asmodeus, or The Devil on Two Sticks,* by Alain René Le Sage, and I have forgotten everything about the book except the underlying theme; that theme fired my imagination when I was in my youth, and, because of it, kindled my excitement in the streets of San Francisco. The story, as I remember it after almost fifty years, was of Zambullo, a young student of Madrid. Zambullo was lonely, disgruntled, and hungry, hungry for food to feed his body and hungry for life to feed his soul. Through his attic window came the Devil, Asmodeus, and, in the way of Mephistopheles with Faust, Asmodeus agreed to show Zambullo life in exchange for his soul. The bargain was made. The Devil broke a stick in two, gave one piece to Zambullo, and then the two adventurers mounted their sticks and flew through the window and out over the roofs of Madrid. As they flew, Asmodeus waved his hand above the city and each roof, rising, showed the drama, romance, and high adventure in the life of every man and woman in the city.

That is the story as my faulty memory recalls it. But I do

know that in my youth, having read *Asmodeus*, I walked the streets of San Francisco and discovered or imagined high adventure in the life of each passer-by, found it in the lives of the thousands turning from the city streets into the revolving doors of the stone office buildings on Montgomery Street, found it in the vendors at flower stands that colored the city streets, found it in the policeman who swung his arms like semaphores, directing traffic at the intersection of the streets (he was a Napoleon leading his army, that policeman), found it in the beautifully and smartly dressed ladies of fashion parading Grant Avenue.

Some of them, of course, were empire builders; some were great names of the American stage, some were poets and painters and writers of fine prose, some were scientists who one day would discover the secrets of the atom. But there were others, too, little men and women who never would achieve fame nor even passing comment, yet in whose drab and commonplace lives was the seed of high drama. Of three such men, three whom I knew well, I want to tell you now: three men in the streets of San Francisco.

There was Giovanni Campisciano. Giovanni came to California from Sicily in the late 'eighties to make his fortune. Not that money in itself meant a great deal to Giovanni, but he had a wife he dearly loved, and two fine small children, and opportunity was elusive in the old world. Giovanni left his family in Sicily, promising them that he would send for them when he had made his fortune in California, the land of gold and milk and honey. He wandered the streets of San Francisco for a month, jobless, lonely, and confused; but walking far south one day, he found himself in open fields beyond the fog bank on the outskirts of the city, a stretch of fields and rolling hills that later would be called Daly City. He found work there as a truck gardener, earning a dollar a day in the vegetable gardens, and very soon people were saying, "Giovanni has a green thumb. Everything he touches grows." He did so well that in a few months he had leased a small piece of ground and had his own truck garden, which was so successful that after a very few years Giovanni Campisciano had opened his own produce depot down near Clay and Front streets and had a dozen men working for him.

Of course, almost as soon as Giovanni reached San Francisco he discarded his brown velvet pants and the red handkerchief around his throat, and took to wearing "Boss of the Road" overalls and a blue shirt, the way San Francisco truck gardeners dressed. Soon he went to Prager's Red Front up on Market Street and bought a sedate brown suit, a white shirt and a celluloid collar, and a ready-made bow tie. Later he went to fashionable Roos Brothers on Kearny Street and bought a single-breasted suit with cuffs on the trousers, a dignified checked black and white vest, and a brown derby hat; he discarded the celluloid collars and wore high linen collars that cut his chin, and instead of the bow tie he wore a handsome gray ascot. He carried a cane when he paraded Columbus Avenue on Saturday night, and when he went to Mass at SS. Peter and Paul he carried a cane and wore yellow kid gloves. He boarded in a house that hung precariously on the edge of Telegraph Hill, and his Italian neighbors on Green Street said he was the handsomest Sicilian in San Francisco, much more handsome than he had been when he arrived. Rosalie, the seventeen-year-old daughter of his landlady, thought he was the most handsome gentleman she had ever seen, and she didn't hesitate, with invitation in her eyes, to

547

let him know it. But Johnnie—he no longer called himself Giovanni—Johnnie had no eye for Rosalie, nor, for that matter, for any other pretty San Francisco girl. All he thought about was his lovely Marianne in Sicily.

Some day soon he would buy a bank check and send it to Marianne, and she would take the steamer and come to California with his two children, and then he would say to his friends at the Bocci Ball, "Now you see why I do not look at San Francisco girls. There is not a girl in San Francisco as beautiful as my Marianne." Oh, of course Johnnie had plenty of friends now. He would play bocci ball with them, or listen to Italian opera in the gallery of the Tivoli Opera House, or sit with them in the Buon Gusto or the Fior d'Italia in the evening, drinking red wine and eating spaghetti heaped with mushrooms, and they'd sing Neapolitan songs, "Funiculi" and "Torna a Sorrento," and grow mildly mellow. But when the hour was growing late, and the friends would say, "Well, shall we go down to Columbus Square and make eyes at the girls, or go down to Pacific Street to see the women?" then Johnnie would say, "No. You go ahead. I go home to my room up on the hill and write my letter to Marianne." He talked so much about Marianne that he became something of a nuisance. His friends would laugh, and pull their noses, and tell him that Marianne had forgotten him long ago. Johnnie would growl, then chuckle and shake his head with all the confidence in the world.

Well, quite a few years passed, ten years, to be exact, and then one day John Campisciano took stock and realized that he was a rich man, rich enough to build a fine house high on Telegraph Hill for Marianne and the *bambini*. He built the house, painted it white, with a green railed balcony looking out over San Francisco Bay, and he furnished it with Welsbach gas lamps, lace curtains, and feather beds, and then sent money to Marianne to come to the land of gold.

The two months that he awaited her arrival were almost unendurable. He became more of a nuisance on Clay Street, telling all the produce merchants about his beautiful Marianne and the bambini, and the merchants would laugh and go ahead weighing carrots and onions.

Finally the great day came. Johnnie, dressed up in his best suit, wearing his derby hat, and smoking a fine Havana cigar, went down to the pier to see the steamer come in. It came down the bay, its two stacks belching smoke, and Johnnie had tears in his eyes. It docked, and the crowd came ashore; first the officers with bags of mail, and then the passengers. But no Marianne. Johnnie didn't understand. He squinted at the milling crowd, and then he saw her, or thought he saw her, although she didn't recognize him. She was standing on the deck, straining against the rail. She was huge and fat, and she wore a gray flannel petticoat and had a black shawl around her shoulders. Her hair was thin and lifeless, and there was a large black, unsightly mole on her chin. Marianne was ten years older, and she hadn't grown old in San Francisco.

Johnnie couldn't face it. He had grown into a new life. He couldn't say to his friends at the Buon Gusto, "Look, this is the beautiful Marianne I told you about." So he ran away. For a month he hid at the home of a friend who had a vineyard in the Napa Valley near Sonoma. He drank much red wine, because he was so miserably unhappy. Then one day he went back to San Francisco, not to find Marianne, but just because he couldn't stay away from Telegraph Hill. He sat on a rock, up on the top of Union Street, all day, looking out at the bay and thinking how strange life was. Strange and all wrong! Just a bad dream! And then he saw Marianne. But this, too, must be just part of the dream. She was coming toward him. It was the old Marianne, the Marianne as he remembered her when he had left Sicily. She was young and lovely, with black, dancing eyes and shining black hair.

He called, "Marianne!" And she looked at him, surprised, and came to him and said, "I am not Marianne. My name is Giovanna. My mother is called Marianne." And Johnnie Campisciana knew then that this was no dream. He took his daughter's hand, and they walked across the hill to the house he had built for Marianne, the house to which kindly friends had taken her. The girl, Giovanna, opened the door, and Marianne, big and fat and smiling, stood there, an apron tied around her middle. She smiled and blinked and said, "Come, Giovanni, come in. You have been a long time coming. There is Chianti on the table, and the spaghetti is hot on the stove."

Then there was Ben Rab Friedman. Ben was an exceptionally ugly man. He had no hair at all on his head, but that did not matter, because he always wore his black skullcap. He had a scraggly red chin beard that ran from ear to ear, and no moustache. He had been beaten almost to death in a pogrom in Kiev during the days of Imperial Russia, and his nose was crushed to an ugly pulp and spread across his face. A deep, red, ugly scar ran from the corner of his right eye to the place where his right nostril should have been. The stage door man at the Orpheum told me that Ben was ugly enough to be a comedian in vaudeville. He was horribly ugly, but he worshiped beauty.

Of course he had never married; he knew how ugly he was and he would not presume to ask anyone, no, not even a schatchen, a marriage broker, to find a bride for him. When he would find courage at times to smile at the young girls who strolled along McAllister Street, they would giggle and talk very fast to each other and not stop.

Ben had an antique shop on McAllister Street, and there he could indulge his love of beauty. All sorts of objects were crowded high, and buried beneath dust. There were seven-branch candlesticks of old brass, copper pots, and bronze bowls. There were stacks of old and mildewed books, including a large Old Testament in a binding of mother-of-pearl. There were crystal chandeliers and silver coffeepots and a samovar in a covering of delicate needlepoint. There were old lithographs and copper etchings of Jewish patriarchs; there was a highboy of shining mahogany. There were German beer steins and pewter mugs. There were cracked porcelain washbasins and a broken-down baby carriage and a stack of *Harpers* magazines of 1894 and 1895. Everything was buried beneath dirt and dust and mildew and rust, but Ben Friedman loved all the articles in the shop. They were the only friends he had.

When customers came they usually found the shop empty, and they would have to cough and sometimes call out before Ben emerged from behind the stack of confusion at the rear of the store. He never let anyone go back there, for there, hidden behind the pyramid of junk, Ben Friedman sat hour upon hour before an easel, painting pictures he never would try to sell, never would show to anyone. Ben loved beautiful things.

One December morning Ben sat at his easel, painting, and there was a great coughing in the front of the store, and, rubbing his hands together, he went out to see what was wanted. A red-faced Catholic priest stood there, wheezing for breath, and said he was looking for a Turkish coffeepot for a friend. Ben Friedman said he had no Turkish coffeepot. The priest, Father Moran, said, "Well, then we'll have to do without." He looked at Friedman a moment, measuring him, and said, "I'll tell you the truth. I came in because I was curious. I passed here last night and I saw three candles burning in your window." "Yes," said Ben, "those were Chanukah Lights." "Ah, yes," said Father Moran. "It is a beautiful ceremony that you observe during your Chanukah Festival. Each night of the week, you add, or the oldest son in the family adds, one lighted candle in the window until there are seven. When an ancient enemy came to destroy your people, they burned the candles to make the enemy believe they were at prayer and, being at prayer, would not battle. But when the enemy attacked, your men came out in righteous cause and vanquished them."

"That is the story," said Ben, "and now on Chanukah we give gifts to our children, just as next week on Christmas you will give gifts to yours." "It's a pretty story," said Father Moran. Then the two men sat down and talked, talked about their ancient religions and folklore, and about mysterious and esoteric philosophies hidden in the pages of the Talmud and the writings of Josephus. That was the first of many talks, talks that lasted for more than twenty years. Father Moran became Ben Friedman's friend. They sat in the rear of the little antique shop, drank sacramental wine and ate kosher sausage and strong cheese, and talked of many things, and the priest admired the paintings of Ben Rab Friedman.

Then, one day, during the Chanukah Festival in the year 1905, Father Moran, a very old man, came to Ben with a package wrapped in newspaper. Proudly he opened it, and said, "You see! I, too, love to paint in my rare leisure moments. And for a Chanukah present, I've painted this for you." With tears in his scarred eyes, Ben Friedman looked at a very bad painting of the Angel of God giving the Tablets of Stone that were the Ten Commandments to Moses on Mount Sinai. He took the picture and bowed his head; he could not speak. When the priest had walked away, Ben swore that he would make a gift for Father Moran, and into it he would pour all his love of beauty.

He labored at the painting he was making for long hours of the day and night, always with a fear in his heart that old age would take Father Moran away before the painting was finished, yet it was work that could not be hurried. Friedman knew that his friend was slowly dying. Week upon week he labored, and when the painting was almost finished, he even painted on a Sabbath, knowing that he would be forgiven. Finally, on the Tuesday night after that Sabbath, the work was done.

Ben Friedman went to his bed in the back of the shop, happy, and before dawn of Wednesday morning a great earthquake shook down the walls of San Francisco and, with the dawn, fire raged. Up and down McAllister Street Ben Friedman paced, watching the crumbling of the city he loved. But he would not move far from the shop that held all his beloved possessions. On Thursday afternoon, April nineteenth, the fire raged up Hayes Valley, up Golden Gate Avenue, and up McAllister Street, and flames licked their way into Ben Friedman's shop. Past soldiers who shouted at him and tried to stop him and threatened to shoot him, Ben dashed into the shop. He didn't see his seven-branch candlesticks or his copper bowls, or the Bible bound in mother-of-pearl. He labored to the rear of the shop and out through the flames, clutching the canvas in his arms.

Up McAllister Street he trudged, out Fillmore and over Pine Street, to the home and bedside of old Father Moran, and into the Father's hands he placed the painting he had made for him: a tender, lovely picture of the Christ-child in the Manger.

Then there was Jim Lee. His name was probably Lee Fong or Lee-something-else when he came to San Francisco from Pekin, but we always knew him as Jim Lee. He was our Chinese cook when we lived on Scott Street, in the days when Scott Street was on the edge of the sand dunes, and people said my father had been mad to build so far west, because the city could never grow out that far. But that's another story. Jim Lee had been in San Francisco forty years when he came to work for us; he was an old man, his head was as smooth as an ivory billiard ball, and his only hirsute adornment was a half dozen long black hairs that sprouted from his chin. We had had another Chinese cook before Jim Lee, but he came to the family one day and said, "Goodbye. I go back China. I send my cousin." The next day Jim Lee arrived.

He was my best friend when I was five years old. Although he sometimes would disappear at night, he reappeared the next morning with paper bags of lichee nuts and candied cocoanut for us. On Chinese New Year he brought my mother a China lily, and every Fourth of July he brought me huge and wonderful boxes of firecrackers, wrapped up in beautiful red paper powdered with gold dust. The package had a wonderful, strange smell, a mysterious haunting smell that was a combination of Chinatown and gunpowder and incense and dry rot. It smelled like Jim Lee's room, an odor that was fascinating to a five-year-old.

554

That was one of the family problems with Jim Lee. My mother was constantly saying, "His room smells terrible. He smokes in it all the time and never airs it, and I am convinced it's not tobacco he's smoking."

Of course there were other problems. I heard them discussed at the dinner table. Some of them my father and mother discussed in German or French to protect our innocent ears. But about one problem they were quite open and blunt. Jim Lee gambled! Now, in San Francisco gambling had never been considered a crime. My grandfather had died gambling in the Comstock. My father loved poker and euchre and horse races and even cigar-store slot machines. And I have been a born gambler all my life. But the gambling of Jim Lee was a more pernicious thing. It possessed him like the smoking of an opium pipe. The moment he got his monthly wages of thirty dollars, which was high salary in 1895, he'd trot down to Chinatown and gamble it all away.

But the most delightful of Jim Lee's sins was that he swore, constantly and impressively; most of the profanity and blasphemy I knew I learned from him. He would make wonderful apple pie, with crusts so short that they crinkled, and he would curse them. He cursed the flies in the kitchen, the California sulphur matches on the stove, and the tinsmith who came in his little wagon to mend our pots and pans. He cursed the fresh-fish man and the fresh-vegetable man, the coal-and-wood furnace and the hot-water boiler behind the stove. He cursed my parents to their face. I believe I was the only person or thing in the world that he didn't swear at. He liked children.

When my parents went to the theater at night, and to Zinkand's after the theater, Jim would sit up in the kitchen to guard the children, and he wouldn't shuffle off to bed in his flapping slippers until he heard my father's latchkey in the front door. Time and again, after they had gone out, I would sneak down to the kitchen and Jim would tell me about the fan-tan games, about all his cousins in Chinatown, and about how, some day, he would go back to China to die. That was the most important thing in his life: to save enough money to go back to China to die. But that, it appeared, was a difficult undertaking, because every time he saved a silver dollar or a ten-dollar gold piece, the fan-tan game or the Chinese lottery would get it.

Jim stayed with us for seven years, and then my mother said she couldn't stand the smell anymore. She couldn't stand his constant habit of scratching his nose when he got angry; there was a chronic, unpleasant looking sore on the bridge of his nose. And he was growing blind; he had cataracts. He broke the dishes in our Wedgewood set, and he bumped into doors, and there was always the danger of his setting the house on fire with his interminable cigarettes. So my father pensioned him, and he went away to Chinatown and said he would send his cousin to cook for us.

The day he went away he gave my mother a great bowl of China lilies, and to me he gave my most cherished possession, a set of hand-carved ivory chessmen. After that, on every Chinese New Year he hobbled out Jackson Street to Scott to bring my mother China lilies, and on every Fourth of July he brought me amazingly long strings of firecrackers. We sat on the kitchen steps and he would tell me about the money he was saving to go back to China to die, because everyone knows that if a Chinese is not buried in his land of China, his immortal soul will not be able to rejoin its ancestors. So he would tell me about the money he had saved, and then he would go back to Chinatown and gamble it away.

When I grew older and went to Polytechnic High School at Bush and Stockton streets, I used to go over to Chinatown periodically on my lunch hour and see Jim. He would be sitting in his smelly room in an alley off Dupont Street, and though he was so blind that he could hardly see me, he knew my footsteps and would say, "Oh, hullo, missy Sam. You like pipe?"

Then he'd laugh and curse, and tell me about the big ship on which he was going to sail to China.

One night I went to Jim Lee's room, and he wasn't there, but one of his thousand cousins told me where he had gone. He had begun to die. He wasn't sick, he was just very old, so he had begun to die. Knowing it, he went down to the fan-tan game to win enough money to take him back to China. And the Chinese goddess of chance smiled on Jim and he couldn't lose. When he left the fan-tan table at dawn, he had five hundred dollars. He went down Montgomery Street to Market, and stood in front of the steamship office and waited for it to open, and when it opened he bought a ticket to China.

He went back to Chinatown and bought new silk brocade coats and black silk trousers and a black silk cap with a little red button on it. He bought a huge twenty-four-carat-gold ring to wear on his finger, and a huge gold watch and chain.

Then he went, feeling his blind way, along Dupont Street—that was of course before it had become Grant Avenue, and walked slowly to the crest of Telegraph Hill. He sat up there for hours, looking at the city with his almost sightless eyes. Then he spoke. He said, "One damn fine city!"

557

He took the steamer ticket out of his pocket and tore it into bits, and the wind carried the bits away. Then he clambered to his feet, went back to his room in the alley off Dupont Street, and died that night. After his body had lain in state, and his cousins had brought gifts of fruit and nuts, flowers and bits of designs cut out of colored paper, and raw pig to feed his departed soul, other cousins packed him in a box and shipped him back to China to be buried in the soil of his ancestors.

III

David Josephi

Among the characters that walk the city streets, some become familiar because fame has smiled upon them, some because scandal has made them famous, some because of their personal idiosyncrasies. There was one man who year after year walked down Post Street every morning, and all I ever knew about him was that, day in and day out, he always wore a white carnation in his buttonhole. There was a grim, scowling individual who walked toward you stiffly and then suddenly, just as you approached, would crook his arm and, seemingly by accident, jolt you with a jab in the ribs. And there was the white-haired old man who, every morning for many years, walked downtown, some three miles, and walked home every night; he wore a black derby hat and a sedate black overcoat, and winter and summer, in sunshine and in fog and in rain, he carried a neatly rolled black umbrella. When I last saw him walking those three miles, he was a straight, keen-eyed, handsome old man is his late eighties.

This is his story, the story of an unimportant man, unimportant if any man, in your philosophy, can be unimportant in the greater blueprint of life. He was a San Franciscan, but most San Franciscans knew little about him; his name was not known in public places, nor does it appear in the printed pages of the history of the city. But he had a few friends, and they were staunch friends throughout his long life. A strange impulse has moved me to write his story, if it can be called a story. He lived a life quite remote from the realities as we know them. The impulse is simply this: though he was a modest, remote person, quite unimportant in his own estimation, seeking no honors, and no fame, and yet, if a kindly fortune so disposes, his unimportant story may now be read by others, and thus it may confer some slight distinction upon him, many years after his death.

I hardly know how to begin the story. On the surface, it lacks the drama and the suspense and the high emotion that are the ingredients of a story, but probably you will agree that every man who has lived has known, in his time, drama and suspense and high emotion.

I remember him, David Josephi, as a handsome, heavy, white-haired gentleman with kind, wise eyes, a gentle, pleasantly cultured voice, and an innate dignity. I knew him for many years, and I never knew him when his hair was not white. The kind eyes, the white, curly hair and the full white moustache, and the black suit and black umbrella are the physical things I remember about him. He always wore a black suit, and whether he owned more than one is open to question. But that black suit was always immaculate; he moved so quietly and serenely through life that the black cloth never even seemed to take on a silken sheen.

David Josephi came to work for my grandfather when he and my grandfather were very young men, hardly in their twenties. That must have been all of eighty-five years ago. David was a bookkeeper, meticulous in his work, a neat penman, a perfect accountant. But he wanted something more.

560

He had to earn his way early in life, and his limited education was a constant grief to him; he wanted much more than the elementary schooling that life had afforded him. He seemed to have a strange instinct that made him aware of the treasures hidden in the scholastic life. Other than that, I know nothing of his early days. And of his years in the employment of my grandfather I know little more. The story, as I know it, commenced many years after my grandfather's death, when, one day, David Josephi resigned from the firm that my father had inherited. I was five years old at the time.

Even then, Josephi was white haired and, to me, a very old man, although I was to know him for another thirty-five years; and to me, in all those years, he never seemed to change or grow older.

He had saved a few thousand dollars. But the nation had just enjoyed the financial panic of 1894, and business enterprise was a hazardous thing, so Mr. Josephi decided to retire from business and seek other fields of activity. The hazard of business was one reason. Another was that, now that he had reached middle-aged maturity, he wanted to spend some of the time left to him in studying the arts and sciences that had been closed books in his youth. The third reason was that his wife was an invalid, confined to a wheel chair. She was a lovely person, gentle, quiet, and fine, and very patient in her suffering. She was, in short, the most desirable picture of a Victorian lady. Mr. Josephi wanted to have more time to devote to her and their young daughter. So he retired from business, and that was the real beginning of his story.

There had always been the urge to study. Now, in his late forties or early fifties, he was going to indulge his dream. But he had to be practical; after all, he had only a few thousand dollars. So he went into a field comparatively rare at that time: he determined to become a gentleman farmer. He enrolled in the University of California and took courses in husbandry, in the propagation of fruit trees and the growth of grain. He had the strange idea that he could grow citrus fruits in Southern California. But that mad idea was squashed by his advisers: lemons and oranges and other citrus fruits would never grow in California. So he centered on the development of grain, and that led him to a strange enterprise.

In those days, much more than today, when perhaps more than half the world lives in apartment houses, almost every family owned a canary. Canary birds ate canary seed and all the canary seed was imported from Germany at a high price. David Josephi decided to grow canary seed in California. First he had to find a farm. Kern County was making a reputation at that time: it was said that every crop in the world would grow there, from tobacco and cotton to alfalfa and fruit trees, and why not canary seed? Josephi purchased a farm of some twenty-five acres, with a small, adequate farmhouse, about ten miles from Bakersfield. He called it Greenfield Ranch. He and his family went there in the spring, when the land was lush and the sun was warm. The invalid wife thrived in her wheel chair; and Mr. Josephi, with the knowledge he had culled from books, commenced to till the soil. Then neighbors came, and leaned on his rail fence, and asked him what he was planting. He told them it was canary seed, and they laughed and winked, and made circular motions with an index finger to imply that he was slightly mad, just another mad San Franciscan. Oh, they could see the virtue of growing canary seed in California, if it could be grown.

But it wouldn't grow there; they knew it wouldn't grow

there. Canary seed was indigenous to Germany. But Mr. Josephi persisted, and planted his canary seed, and proved the neighbors wrong. A fine crop came up, but before he could harvest it the blackbirds came by the thousands, beautiful red-winged blackbirds, and they ate his entire crop.

The canary-seed crop was a failure, but by now the Josephis had learned to love the land. To supply the family needs, David planted a few fruit trees and a kitchen garden, and a few acres of alfalfa. He had to have an income, too, so he took a part-time position as bookkeeper and accountant on the adjoining huge tract of land, the Butterfield Ranch, owned by the California land barons, Miller and Lux. Between supervising his twenty-five acres and driving once a week in the buckboard to the Miller and Lux ranch to post the books, seeing his daughter blossom and his invalid wife thrive under the sunshine of farm life, and with the books he was able to have sent from time to time from San Francisco, books in which he could find the knowledge he had missed in his youth, David Josephi entered a serene and happy period of life.

It was in 1898, just a month or two before the outbreak of the Spanish-American War, that my father decided that farm life would be good for me, would put flesh on my bones and muscles on my spindly legs. I was nine years old. So I was sent to the little farm outside Bakersfield, and to one of the most amazing adventures of my life.

I loved the farm. Raised on Scott Street at the edge of the sand dunes, in those days the frontier on the western border of urban San Francisco, I was thrilled by the land where apples and cherries could be picked from the trees in the kitchen garden. I liked fishing for catfish in the irrigation stream that ran along the edge of Greenfield Ranch.

I also liked Mr. Josephi's friends, although not till long after did I realize what a strange group they were. A small company of retired English army officers and their wives had established a little colony a mile or two from the ranch. They had built typical English-countryside cottages, with hedgerows and rosebushes. It was a bit of England transplanted. They lived a quiet, sedately retired life. I remember the names of only one or two of the families. There was Colonel Mason and his family. The Colonel, a dignified gentleman with a broad British accent, had his walls stacked with books, more books than I had even seen in a private home. And the bookshelves were open to me, at the age of nine. I was left alone to discover the Restoration dramatists, Smollett and Fielding, and the new English writer, Rudyard Kipling, and any number of others whom I could not understand. But understanding was not necessary to my enjoyment. I had stumbled into a magic world, although much of the magic would never have passed the censorship of my Victorian mother.

The other gentleman I remember was a Mr. Beebee. He was the kind of a very small and jumpy little gentleman who should have had the name of Beebee. There was considerable gossip in the British colony about Mr. Beebee and Mr. Josephi's daughter. The matchmakers were busy, and the two were carelessly thrown together, by careful design, at every opportunity. But I think Mr. Beebee was frightened; nothing ever came of it, neither ever married.

Just at this time the battleship *Maine* was sunk, the Spanish-American War began, and Dewey was the hero of the day. The weekly paper brought headline stories of the achievements of the American forces and the heroes: Hobson, who kissed all the girls; Colonel Teddy Roosevelt at

San Juan Hill; General Shafter, Colonel McKittrick, and Commodore Schley. But almost as swiftly as the war had commenced, it came to an end. Then my amazing adventure happened.

My father had made a business trip to New York and a side trip to Menlo Park to visit the electrical wizard, Thomas Edison. At the end of the visit Mr. Edison gave my father a wonderful gift: two models of his new invention, the gramophone, which was able to capture music and the human voice on wax cylinders and release them through a large horn or through small receivers held to the ears. My father brought the two gramophones home, and later he told me, although I have never been able to substantiate this, that they were the first talking machines to be heard in the West. He kept one of them for our home in San Francisco, and the other he sent as a gift to the Josephi family on the Kern County farm.

On Saturday morning, David Josephi bundled me onto the seat of the buckboard next to him, and we started out to visit all his neighbors for miles around. We stopped at all the farmhouses and invited the farmers and their families to come to Greenfield the following night to listen to the wonderful new invention.

Sunday night, the county road was lined with buckboards and surreys and phaetons and hay wagons, all heading for the Josephi home. There seemed to be at least a hundred farmers and their wives and children crowded into the parlor, or "best room" as it was called, at the Greenfield Ranch. The Edison gramophone was set up on a wooden table in the center of the room. A wax cylinder was put on the revolving steel cylinder. The winding arm was cranked. The needle was lowered into place. And out of the horn a voice as clear as life, or almost as clear, announced, "The Edison Phonograph Company of New York and Paris. John Philip Sousa's 'El Capitan March'!"

Then came the music of Sousa and his band!

Pandemonium broke loose. Those Kern County people simply couldn't believe it. Here was the human voice coming out of a piece of machinery! Josephi's Chinese cook let out a scream, crying that the devil was in the box, and fled from the farm and never was seen again. More wax cylinders were played, and then the climax was reached. A blank cylinder was put on the machine and a few of the guests were induced to talk into it. They shuffled their feet and cleared their throats, looked questioningly at their wives or husbands, and then spoke. Then their voices came back. "This is Farmer Allen from Crossroads and this is the greatest thing I've ever seen." Speeches like that.

I still haven't come to my adventure, but now I do. At the moment when the excitement was at its highest pitch, the front door of the farmhouse burst open. Two wild-eyed men stood there, filthy, black with grime, their fists clenched against their thighs, perspiration streaming down their cheeks; their eyes were red and their hair was tousled. David Josephi greeted them and said something about this being the wonderful new invention of Thomas Edison. One of the two intruders strode to the table and shouted, "The hell with Mr. Edison and his invention!" With a sweep of his hand he swept the gramophone from the table, and it smashed to the floor, beyond repair. Then, while crowds stood back, mouths open and eyes popping, the intruder shouted, "We've got more important things than toy inventions. We've just struck oil on McKittrick's land!"

The two men were General Shafter, the speaker, and

566

Colonel McKittrick, and that was the first oil struck in Kern County, the first important find of oil in California.

As you can well imagine, Thomas Edison and his gramophone were swiftly forgotten. The rush was on. Prospectors poured into Kern County. Everybody was digging for oil. David Josephi took the few thousand dollars he had saved and sank it into the ground and struck water! And I came home to San Francisco.

It was a few years later, just four months before the 1906 earthquake and fire, that my father, who rarely discussed business matters with or in the presence of his family, this being the custom of the times, relaxed his rule and told us that he had to find a reliable bookkeeper for the business he was maintaining. The current bookkeeper had falsified the books and defrauded him, and he had to find someone who could be depended upon. But he doubted if there was an honest man in the world. I said, "How about Mr. Josephi?"

My father looked at me as though I were some strange species of life he had never observed before. Then his expression brightened, as though he were mentally saying, "That's the first intelligent idea ever to come out of your head."

That night he sat down and wrote a letter, and a couple of weeks later David Josephi arrived. He went to work for the firm for one hundred and twenty-five dollars a month, which was good pay in those days. When the earthquake and fire wiped out the business, my father commenced a new enterprise and I went to work for him, or rather, I was installed as an apprentice without pay. David Josephi continued to be the bookkeeper.

It was then that I really began to know the wonderful old man. Yes, he was growing old, and he was as set in his ways as the heavenly bodies were set in their courses. He had no use for newfangled contraptions, so we could not have a typewriter in the office. He wrote every business letter for the firm in meticulous longhand and put the letters, moistened with a sponge, into the letter press to make tissue paper copies. He insisted on writing the letters himself. The thought of an office helper was out of the question. The thought of a feminine helper was shocking to him; females had no place in business. And as for acquiring an adding machine! In desperation, one day, I purchased one, a small affair that could be carried under the arm, and I trotted it into the office. For the only time I ever saw him infuriated, Mr. Josephi arose in his wrath and commanded me to trot it back to the place from which it had come. My father agreed with him. They had kept books accurately without the help of machinery for lo, these many years, probably with greater accuracy than a machine could accomplish. "It'll be a sad day," said David Josephi, "when man has to have a machine to think for him."

But that was the bookkeeper Josephi. The real David Josephi, the man that I learned to know so well, was a very different person. At last he had come into his heritage, or at least had begun to see the fulfillment of his dreams. For a dozen years he had been studying all the things that had escaped him in his youth, and he had accumulated a fund of knowledge given to few men, knowledge ranging from Socrates to the new science of electronics. In that he never did anything with the treasures he accumulated, you may argue as you please as to whether his studies were worth while. He died and they were buried with him, leaving the world, to all appearance, no better than it had been before. But for him it had meant fulfillment of life.

Of the subjects he studied, I remember passing incidents. There was the day that I told him about a beautiful Persian rug I had seen; it had a strange shade of peacock blue in it. He told me, without seeing the rug, that it was not Persian; that particular shade of blue was characteristic of the rug weavers of Samarkand. I checked on his information and found that the rug was, indeed, of Samarkand origin.

Mr. Josephi could discuss the architecture of Flanders or that of Byzantium. He could discuss eighteenth-century English furniture and furniture makers, and the stone utensils of the cave dwellers. He had read and studied the philosophers, from Socrates and Plato down through Descartes and Emanuel Kant to Schopenhauer and Nietzsche. He was familiar with the music of Palestrina and through the years to Stravinsky. He knew Shakespeare from cover to cover, and the German and French philosophical novelists and dramatists. He could discuss the science of Newton and of the new man, Einstein. He had mastered Euclid and high mathematics. He knew the work of the great painters from the early Italian school, down through the Renaissance, and into the Impressionists and neo-Impressionists of France. Hand in hand with all this, he knew how to take stains out of ivory, how to polish a diamond, what acids to use to bleach wood, how to use a slide rule, and how to chart the movements of the stars.

About 1915 or 1916 he gave up his work as bookkeeper and retired from the business world. For several years he could be seen each morning, walking from his home out in the neighborhood of Sacramento and Divisadero streets. Straight-shouldered, handsome, white-haired, in his immaculate black suit, clutching a black umbrella, he walked all the way downtown to the Mechanics Library on Post Street near

Kearny. He would sit there all day reading, studying, accumulating more and more knowledge; now he studied with almost a frenzy, like a miser accumulating as much gold as possible in his few remaining years. When the library closed at night, he would walk slowly home, a lonely, very old gentleman, with a brain that had become a treasure house of knowledge.

I said in the beginning that few San Franciscans knew him. But I went to his funeral and sat in the chapel, and every seat was taken, and people were standing at the door and along the wall; others clustered on the sidewalk. Most of the gathering were men, and most of them were old.

There were doctors, lawyers, scientists, authors, college professors, and businessmen and civic leaders. I remember that the Catholic archbishop was there, and a distinguished rabbi, and the dean of the Episcopal Church. A famous Jewish vaudeville comedian was there, and the librarian of the Bancroft Library, and a Negro window washer. There were men of all walks of life, men who had come to say *ave atque vale* to an unimportant man whose name has left little impression on the pages of the story of San Francisco.

IV

Mad San Franciscans

A great author once wrote, "San Francisco is a mad city, inhabited for the most part by perfectly insane people whose women are of a remarkable beauty." He said other things about San Francisco that many San Franciscans didn't like. They ignored his praise and resented the slander. But, when he left, he wrote, "San Francisco has only one drawback. 'Tis hard to leave."

He walked the streets of San Francisco, fascinated by the mad people he passed. He climbed the city hills, and grumbled into his moustache and shook his head at the madness of a people who would build their city on hills so steep that even goats disdained to climb straight up them but ascended by cutting their own winding trails. He wandered the city streets, by night and by day, a stranger recognized by no one, a friendless man, ignored by the strangely mad populace, and yet loving the irresponsible, crazy, devil-may-care children of the city, children who never seemed to grow up. Unaware, he had discovered the fascination of the streets of San Francisco more aptly than had those who have, since his day, tried with well-rounded phrases to describe the beauty and the charm that is San Francisco. More of this man in a few moments; let's look at some of the people that he found mad.

They unquestionably did insane things, these irresponsible San Franciscans. There was the night that the great Russian Chaliapin sang in the Civic Auditorium to an audience of ten thousand. Many years ago San Franciscans had introduced an innovation in concert behavior. When they liked a great artist, they would rush down the aisles at the end of the scheduled program and, mobbing before the stage, would roar for encores.

Chaliapin concluded his program. Down the center and side aisles, from the gallery and the balcony and the orchestra floor, down to the orchestra pit came the mad San Franciscans, pushing and shouting and crowding, a veritable mob. Chaliapin was a man built on heroic lines, a giant of a man with a giant's voice, but he knew what the frenzy of mobs meant in Imperial and revolutionary Russia. He looked and saw the charging avalanche, he blanched, clenched his fists at his sides, and convinced that they were coming to murder him, or at the very least, beat him and drive him out of town, he fled. Yes, he fled, trembling and perspiring, into the wings, and in the wings he heard the cheers grow to screams. White, trembling, he hid behind draperies, and finally dashed out of the Auditorium, swearing he would never return to the city of madmen. He did, however, come back in his last years, a very old man but still a giant of a man with a powerful voice. He sang again for the madmen, and even then he wasn't sure that his life was safe when the enthusiasts flooded down the center and side aisles and mobbed the stage.

Yes, they were mad San Franciscans, and they were sentimental in their madness. They built an exposition in the marshlands at the foot of the Fillmore Street hill, as precipitous and ill-conceived a street-and-hill as could be found in a city of absurd hills. They turned the marsh called Cow Hollow into the most beautiful exposition the world had seen.

That was, of course, in 1915. The world said they were mad. Most of the world was at war; it was impossible to make a success of an international exposition with the world at war. But they built a dream city that will never be forgotten and they did make it succeed.

On the opening day, the streets that led down the plunging hills were packed with milling humanity. They gathered by the thousands at the top of the hills, and at a signal they flooded down the hills with the rush of a bursting dam. They took over the city of lights and flowers and trees and travertine marble, and 1915 became a year of fiesta.

Finally came the closing night. The last night of the Court of the Seasons! The last night of the Tower of Jewels! The last night of the Brangwyn murals! The last night of Stella, the painting of the naked lady on the "Zone"; millions of "art lovers" had paid a dime to see her! The last night of the Marimba Band in the California Building! The last night of the lush Court of Flowers, of the statues of the Rising and the Setting Sun!

That last night of the Panama-Pacific International Exposition the lights blazed, the crowds cheered, the spielers and pitchmen on the Zone shouted their chants, and the fountains played, and the hot jelly scones sold by the thousands; and, on the stroke of midnight, a bugle sounded. The noise stopped. The wheels stopped turning. The only sound was the water feebly trickling in the fountains. A half million men and women stood still. Tears poured from their eyes. And the lights went out.

Then, so silently that hardly a footfall was heard, the half

573

million started slowly climbing the hills back into reality. The madness of San Franciscans took strange forms.

Mad? Why, of course they were mad. There was Emperor Norton, the wisest and shrewdest of madmen. The city knew he was mad, chuckled when he had printed and issued his own currency, and cashed it, worthless as it was, when he presented it. The city knew he was mad, and yet the city accepted him as its favorite son. When his mongrel dog, Lazarus, died, ten thousand San Franciscans followed the funeral cortege. Where, except in a city of madmen, would ten thousand turn out to bury a dog?

In the beginning I mentioned the great author who wrote, "San Francisco is a mad city, inhabited for the most part by perfectly insane people whose women are of a remarkable beauty."

He had many reasons to love and some good reasons to hate San Francisco. Not the least was his physical hunger. He finished a thick manuscript, which in his estimation was quite a story, and took it to the editorial offices of the San Francisco *Examiner*. He wanted to see the managing editor and sole proprietor, George Hearst, but Sam, the Negro doorboy, said that Mr. Hearst could not be disturbed, he was in conference. What could he, Sam, do for the gentleman? The gentleman handed Sam the stout manuscript and asked him to put it on Mr. Hearst's desk, and said that he would come back. He went away, and when he returned a few days later he was again greeted by Sam. Sam was very unhappy. Mr. Hearst had read or had had his literary staff read the manuscript, and they were not interested in it. But he, Sam, had read it, and he thought it was a fine, wonderful story.

He handed it back to the gentleman, with tears in his eyes.

The gentleman was Rudyard Kipling, and the rejected manuscript was *The Light That Failed*.

But Rudyard Kipling stayed on in San Francisco. He climbed the hills and walked the streets; and writing of his walks, he said, "A cable car without any visible means of support slid stealthily behind me and nearly struck me in the back." The cable cars fascinated him. He wrote, "They turn corners almost at right angles; cross other lines, and for aught I know, may run up the sides of houses." He also said, "These strange people speak a language that is vaguely related to English."

The fact is that San Franciscans found Rudyard Kipling peculiar and he found them completely mad. But, as he said, "San Francisco has only one drawback. 'Tis hard to leave."

Some of the madness of the mad San Franciscans wasn't so amusing. There had been a fiddle-playing mayor of the city, and his henchman who really was, through strange and unethical machinations, his guiding light and superior brain. They were accused, with their lieutenants, of many and various peculations and sins against the city government, including vicious graft. On city lands that they controlled they maintained nefarious establishments of ill fame. They granted city contracts to their friends and pocketed huge profits.

At the end of his term, the mayor, Eugene Schmitz, who had fiddled while the city burned with indignation, ran again for office. Notwithstanding the indictments against him, he was re-elected—not on his merits, but through the strength of the diminutive man who was his manager and his inspiration, Abe Ruef.

575

Election night the city went completely mad. And when the returns had been counted, and Eugene Schmitz had been conceded the victory, then tens of thousands of San Franciscans mobbed the campaign headquarters at a corner of Market Street. The campaign offices were on the second floor at the point of a triangular-shaped, "flatiron" building, and the mob formed a pyramid, standing on each other's shoulders, till they reached the second-story windows. The windows opened, and the pyramid lifted out, not the elected mayor, but his little campaign manager, Abe Ruef. Singing and dancing, the cheering mob carried him the length of Market Street in triumph.

And the fact that Schmitz and Ruef were later held on graft charges and convicted, and that Abe Ruef served his prison term, in no way detracted from the triumph of that night.

But then the city had always been mad. There was the occasion in 1850 when James Savage, the first white man to establish a trading post for the Indians of the San Joaquin Valley, came into the city leading a band of Yosemite Indians. They marched in a wild parade along Montgomery Street, and the leaders carried a barrel of gold dust. Most of the gold was deposited as credit against goods to be delivered as needed, but Savage and his Indians, including two who were his wives, kept enough for a period of fabulous gambling and reckless spending. They were the sensation of San Francisco during their stay. Then, scorning the smoke-belching steamers that plied the bay, they started their two-hundred-mile walk back to their bailiwick in the Sierra.

For many months Californians sent posses into the hills

to capture the West's most notorious and desperate bandit, Joaquin Murietta, Murietta the man of a thousand legends, Murietta who had as many hiding places for his bandit crew as Yorick had skulls. Murietta was, at long last, trapped and killed. And thousands of San Franciscans paid a silver dollar to enter a Montgomery Street store and look at a head claimed to be the head of the bandit. It didn't matter that some said he had been buried, with his head, in the Pacheco Pass, or that others said that it was not Murietta but one of his lieutenants who had been killed. And an old man who claimed to be the nephew of Murietta later told me, personally, that Murietta had returned to his native Sonora in Mexico and had reformed and spent his last years in virtue, propagating a mighty family. None of this mattered. The mad San Franciscans, whether it was the head of Murietta or not, poured their dollars into the Montgomery Street shop of horrors.

1906. The city had been felled by earthquake. The water mains burst. Fire swept the alleys and canyons of the city streets, left the home-covered hills in ashes. But up on Telegraph Hill, where most of the homes were crazy shacks that clung to the goat trails, the Italian-American families formed a fire-fighting brigade. The raging fire raced up the hill, and there was no water to fight it. After all, water was not the most cherished of possessions to those Italians of Telegraph Hill. But out into the streets they rolled their precious barrels of red wine. And with buckets and with sacks soaked in red wine, the brigade fought flame with wine. Many homes were saved, the only homes in an area that reached from Polk Street to the Bay. The fragrance of red wine blessed the hill for many months after the smell of smoke and fire had blown away. Yes, it was a mad city.

The maddest of all San Francisco nights in my memory was a night in November when the scourge of influenza was sweeping the civilized world. Throughout the world, in that November of 1918, hundreds of thousands were dying; the disease struck swiftly and the end often came within twenty-four hours. Tens of thousands were dead or dying in America, and there weren't doctors or nurses to care for more than a small fraction of the sick. A law was passed, making it compulsory for every man, woman, and child to wear a "flu" mask, a piece of gauze tied across the mouth and nose, at all times. Men sweating in the shipyards wore them while they toiled with riveting guns and welding flames. Fashionably dressed women wore them in the theaters and at such social gatherings as the few were willing to grace during the crisis. No man dared nor wanted to appear in public without a mask.

Then, in the small hours of the morning of the maddest of mad nights, a cannon was fired. Bells rang out. Windows and doors were flung open, and the half a million San Franciscans poured into the city streets. The Armistice was signed! The Kaiser had abdicated! The doughboys were coming home! Oh, they celebrated that armistice everywhere, celebrated it in New York and in London and in the villages across the world. But not as they celebrated it in San Francisco.

Down the hills, down the streets of the city, in those dark hours before dawn, and down to Market Street gravitated the shouting, singing, cheering throngs. At the corner of Powell and Market, in the middle of the streetcar tracks in front of the Emporium Department Store, a huge fire was built, a fire fed with "flu" masks. It was like an Indian war dance, and each newcomer threw his mask into the flames.

What if germs were released! What if fever and disease were in the blood of that hilarious throng! The Kaiser was overthrown, the Armistice was signed, and a fever didn't amount to a row of dressmaker's pins as long as the guns were stilled.

A mad city! A lovable, exciting, irresponsible city! A city that loved life, and lived every minute of it! A city that loved the theater, and made a high drama of life, seasoned with tragedy and comedy! Perhaps, after all, Rudyard Kipling was right.

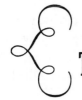
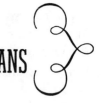

PART TWO
TYCOONS AND BOHEMIANS

V

Robert Dollar

One of the noblest lines in all the literature of American history was written by John Adams in 1779: "All men are born free and equal."

To indulge for a moment in hackneyed profundity, or as a friend of mine was wont to say, "To coin a cliché," there is no question in my mind but that all men are born free. But equal? I wonder. If all men are born equal, with the same basic, fundamental qualities, instincts, and potentialities, then how can one account for the fact that of two men born in the same depths of poverty or even degradation, although their opportunities are equal one will never leave his low level, while the other, a blood brother, perhaps, will rise to triumphant heights. I'm not willing to credit that to chance, luck, fate, or destiny. I believe that there must be some quality, inherent or otherwise, that refutes the premise of equality, and permits one man to rise and the other to fall by the way.

580

There was a man who, for many years, was a familiar figure in the streets of San Francisco. I met him when I was young; I knew him slightly, but I knew his face well. The years have passed and my memory may play me tricks, but the impression that lingers, speaking only of the physical man, is of a combination of Abraham Lincoln and Ichabod Crane.

This, in brief and inadequate sketch, is his story, the story of a boy who was born in a small Scottish town on March 20, 1844.

The village of Falkirk lies some three or four miles from the Firth of Forth, and not many miles from Edinburgh. I think that anybody born in that corner of the British Isles, with its names rich in history, on the shores of that arm of the sea, must by nature have been born with a love of the sea and imbued with its high adventure. There, for you, is an environment to stimulate the imagination, to plant, deep in the fiber of youth, a love of adventure and an irrepressible urge to go places and to accomplish much. Add to this one other attribute. The Scotch Presbyterian, especially of a century ago, was a man of tough fiber, of a strict design of living; the life of the family was one of frugal thrift, and there was little time or excuse for nonsense. Into such a family Robert Dollar was born in the year 1844.

Robert's granduncle owned a small lumberyard. Robert's father managed the yard, and in the beginning the family lived in a room over the yard office. Later they moved to a cottage in a small garden, in Falkirk, and there the boy spent his early years. He went to school and learned the simple fundamentals under a one-armed master who taught with a cane in his one hand. That, Robert Dollar said in later years, was one big feature of the education of those days: a good sound thrashing several times a week. But the students thanked Providence that the master had only one hand.

That was his schooling. But life at home was as strict, life dominated by the stern Scotch Presbyterian tenets, the Scotch thrift, and the frugal living that circumstances made mandatory.

Young Robert Dollar went to work. His first week in a machine shop earned sixty cents for him, the first money he had ever owned. Falkirk meant lumber, the sea, and the Bible, and now it meant wealth, wealth counted in sixty copper pennies. And strangely, although there had been a minimum of happiness in the austere home life of his childhood, the memories of Falkirk remained a dominating influence throughout his long life; time and again the paths that took him around the earth led him back on nostalgic visits to the village on the Firth of Forth.

When Robert's mother died, his father turned to whisky to forget his sorrow, and the home life fell to pieces. There and then young Dollar make a vow never to touch intoxicating liquor as long as he lived, a vow that he never broke. Then the father married again and his father and stepmother took him and his brother across the seas to start a new life in the western world; they traveled under the broad canvas of a wooden sailing ship. The dreams of the small boy were becoming a reality.

We find young Robert Dollar next in Ottawa City, working in a stave factory. The working day was twelve hours long; he earned six dollars a month. After a few years of that routine mill labor, he plunged into a grimmer reality. Though still in his middle teens, he became chore boy to the cook in a lumber camp. The French-Canadian lumberjacks were huge, red-blooded, two-fisted men of the forest. Their ways were rough, their life almost primitive. Their speech, in their patois of French and a little English, was a colorful rhapsody of finely phrased filth. They sweated, they labored. They fought the hazards of the Canadian rivers and forests; they fought the elements and they fought each other. They trapped deer and moose; they fished. They drank lustily and when, with embers of the fire burning low, they slept, it was a sleep as sound as death itself. This was the backdrop against which the cook's chore boy, Bible clenched in fist, struggled his way to manhood.

The winter came, with freezing days and short rations. For months, Dollar wrote, their only food was salt pork and bread, with, now and then, pea soup and beans. Malnutrition resulted in disease and tormented bodies. The killing cold of the Canadian winter wasted flesh until the boy, like the men with whom he worked, had a frame of bone and thin hard muscle. But he was making progress. He was earning ten dollars a month and saving almost every cent to buy a farm for his parents. The saving was the least of his virtues, for there was little opportunity to spend.

Meanwhile the schooling that had been interrupted when he was a boy of twelve in Falkirk was resumed. But now it was schooling self-taught. On Sundays, and after work, between readings of his Bible, he found time to labor, ploddingly, at reading and writing and simple arithmetic; figures were important in a lumber camp if a man wanted to make a future of lumbering.

One Sunday the owner of the camp, passing through, found him plugging away at his lessons. Hiram Robinson recognized good material when he saw it, and the following year he sent Dollar up the Gatineau River to take over the camp accounts. This camp of Frenchmen was even more rugged than the one in which he had started his work as cook's helper.

During the day he worked in the clearing at the labors of a lumberjack; at night, by the flickering light of the fire, he worked at the bookkeeping. For three years Robert Dollar kept on at this double job, while eyestrain, nightblindneess, and physical fatigue were taking their toll. But he was learning the lumber trade, from the practical end of the laborer and from the commercial point of view. Thin, angular, his muscle and his nerve hardening, he was growing out of his youth. Men liked and respected him. Looking back at the time-faded picture one may be disposed to see a prig, something of a stilted youngster, too big for his trousers, too good for the men with whom he worked. Robert Dollar was anything but that. He was, and he continued to be throughout his long life, a shrewd, tough, decent specimen of determined humanity, with a driving ambition that motivated everything he did. Yes, men liked him, and photographs of the time bear out the often-repeated impression: he looked like a young Abraham Lincoln.

He was twenty years old. Life had been tough, hard, and brutal. Now the tempo was beginning to accelerate. At twenty-two he was made foreman of a camp. His pay went up to twenty-six and later to forty dollars a month. He saved most of it, enough to purchase, with his brother, a five-hundred-acre farm for the parents. That was the first tangible dream realized in the life he had planned for himself. Now, again saving, again working by day and by night, he cut his personal needs to the minimum; he didn't drink; he didn't smoke. He didn't see his thrift as a virtue; he was simply Scotch to the core, and saving money was second nature.

When he was twenty-eight, he had saved enough to go into partnership with Johnson, his former employer. They bought timberland and commenced their operations. They worked hard and felt they were headed for success.

Then came that day remembered in the history of the United States as "Black Friday," perhaps the most disastrous financial panic in the life of the nation. On the crash of the market all commodities fell, and Robert Dollar was wiped out. His savings were gone and he had neither money to pay his men nor money to carry on. The men took his notes for the $2,500 which was his share of the debt. He took a job as manager of several lumber camps, at a salary of a hundred dollars a month, and paid his debts in three years. Meanwhile, he married a young Scottish girl living in Ottawa, Margaret Proudfoot. It was a new partnership, a partnership that was to endure, in business, in the building of dreams, in his endless travels round the world, to the day of his death.

That's the story of Robert Dollar's youth. And, as the tempo of his life moved faster and faster, so must our narrative, crowding into a few pages the rest of the drama of eighty-eight years that built Robert Dollar into one of the greatest giants of the West, in a day when the West, and San Francisco in particular, was a world of giants. That, in itself, is an understatement, for Robert Dollar became one of the great giants of world industry and commerce. He became known as a master of ships, a builder of ships, and that was only logical, the natural heritage of his Falkirk youth. He was even called captain, Captain Robert Dollar, although he would tell you with a dry chuckle that it was an honorary title, never earned. He had never served as master of a ship. Ships were only a means to an end. He was born a lumberman, he lived and died a lumberman, and the world was his market.

He cut his own trees and shipped the lumber up and down the coasts of the continent, and then reached out. There was a market for huge pine timbers in England. By cutting out the middleman exporter and thereby incurring plenty of animosity, by chartering a sailing ship, he shipped his cargo of timber, then sailed ahead of the chartered ship on a faster vessel, and sold at a saving to the buyers in Manchester and Liverpool, with increased profits for himself. Men began to take note of this gangling young man, noted him with a dubious shake of the head, seasoned ultimately with approval. He was perhaps too shrewd—well, he was simply characteristic of the giants of his day, and you could measure him as you saw fit. But in the final analysis, men agreed that he was a bit of Abraham Lincoln and a bit of the popular conception of Uncle Sam, this clear-eyed young man who drove a hard, shrewd bargain, but a bargain of implicit honesty. Shrewd thrift and his Bible were his compass and his steering wheel.

Again he traveled to England, and up the coast and into the Firth of Forth, and to Falkirk, his wife accompanying him; it was a home-coming. The Falkirk boy, still young, was, in a modest way, a rich man. Falkirk was proud of him, but Dollar's memory went back to the day when he had craved learning and education. He crystallized his longings and the memory in a gift to Falkirk of a library of books, for which Andrew Carnegie later donated a building, then sailed back to America for new ventures.

The late 1880's found him heading for California. San Francisco, keen, alive, vibrating with the lust of its young years, was magic to him. The great harbor, with its passageway leading out through the cliffs that were the Golden Gate, a passageway leading to the Orient, this was Utopia to a mind that knew no limits of horizon. It was wonderland to him: the wooden ships mast to mast in the bay; the steam-driven iron ships that were driving the beautiful canvas-heavy sailing ships off the sea, the confusion and excitement of the growing city, and the constant coming and going, as the tides came and went in the waters of the bay.

In the long years that followed, Robert Dollar and his wife traveled countless miles, to the corners of the earth, but San Francisco and its bay would always be the home port. Across the Golden Gate, beneath the blue shadows of Mount Tamalpais, he bought land in the village of San Rafael and built his family home; it was to be his home thereafter. With two partners, he bought the largest remaining tract of redwood in Sonoma County; part of that great stand of ageless trees later became the grove of the Bohemian Club.

It is impossible to touch on, or even mention, all the ventures and enterprises that now filled the days and years of Captain Robert Dollar. But there at the gateway of the Pacific was born his greatest dream and his greatest work. The Orient had been opened to the Occident by diplomatic treaty. The next step was to open it to trade and commerce and, if possible, mutual understanding and friendship.

For this, the dream of Robert Dollar demanded a great American merchant marine. He pleaded for the merchant marine, fought for it, and marched up and down the land and into the sacrosanct chambers of diplomatic Washington, preaching (in his quiet voice) the creed of the American merchant marine.

And that, to leave the narrative for a moment, showed one of the amazing personal developments of the man. He had been poorly educated, according to the popular conception, but he was a master of words. Rarely has greater extemporaneous oratory been displayed than when Robert Dollar stood before a customer, or an industrial group, or a parliament of men to make his demands.

The merchants of the Orient, Chinese and Japanese, were suspicious of American business methods. But they trusted Robert Dollar and accepted him as one of them, and the ordinary people of the East idolized him. On one of his innumerable trips to the Orient, for three hours a procession of thousands of men and women and children paraded past his hotel to honor him. A power in his own land, he was all but a god in the Orient.

New fields were opening to him. Gold was discovered on the Klondike, a gold rush was on, and the gateways to Alaska and the Klondike were San Francisco and Seattle. Dollar chartered more and more ships to carry the human cargoes and cargoes of goods into the Far North. His fortune pyramided.

The century ended and his ships were now reaching both East and West, and a new field of trade was opening on the Pacific slopes of Siberia. Into the field went the man who laughed at miles. He carried cargoes at his own price, a price from which he never deviated; he was a shrewd businessman but never open to bargaining. When he could not find cargoes to carry at his price, then he would buy cargoes, at his price, on either side of the Pacific. He developed the copra trade of the Philippines, only one of many industries in which his was the steering hand.

Out of the ships he chartered and the ships he built, the Dollar Steamship Line was developed. It had been a long journey for the boy of the Falkirk lumberyard. But that was all business.

There was another Robert Dollar, the old man of San Rafael, the town across the Golden Gate from San Francisco, with his children and his fifteen grandchildren. There was the gaunt, tall, strong-fisted replica of Uncle Sam, marching along Montgomery Street, new dreams of world conquest still in his eyes, his Bible in his pocket.

I have held the Bible of Robert Dollar in my hands. Slips of white paper mark many pages. He had said, without unction, but simply as a statement of practical reasoning, "When I have found myself faced with a problem, spiritual or material, I have opened my Bible at random and found the answer."

There was the old-young master of the seas who had become the respected and intimate friend of Theodore Roosevelt, Woodrow Wilson, Herbert Hoover, and Sun Yat Sen. A simple, plain-spoken, old-young man, Robert Dollar, who fought congressmen and senators and powers, in America and out, in his dream to bring the United States glory on the seas, master of the greatest merchant marine.

There was the boy of Falkirk who had earned sixty priceless pennies in his first week of labor, who had from that time gone through life true to his beliefs, faithful to the laws he had made for himself. There was the lank old man, who in his eighties was still traveling round the world, always with his girl from Scotland.

And there was the man who sat in his garden with his grandchildren around him in San Rafael, and said, "God has been good. His guidance has made my life rich . . . and my business successful."

One day in 1932, the United States Navy dirigible *Akron*, stationed near San Francisco, flew over the gardens of the home in San Rafael and dropped flowers that drifted from the great airship to the graveled paths. Robert Dollar had died the day before. The United States Navy was paying its last respects to the man who had built the American merchant marine.

VI

"Tad"

In all my peregrinations through the streets of San Francisco there was one adventure that was little more than an incident, and yet it meant more to me than events of far greater significance. I walked down Jackson Street to Polk Street, where twelve square blocks of dynamiting had keep the fire of 1906 from spreading into the residential blocks of the Western Division. And from Polk Street I climbed the hills, through the fallen bricks and broken glass and ashes, to the pile of debris at the corner of Bush and Stockton streets that was the ruins of Polytechnic High School. I had been a pupil there till the earthquake shook the city, and now I was a businessman of seventeen, my school days ended forever.

I walked up there, through the grim, tragedy-beaten streets, to see if I could find my most cherished possessions: my mechanical drawing set and some sketches of cartoons by "Tad."

I've always wanted to tell the story of Tad. He was a boyhood idol of mine, a hero to me, something of a god. I can well imagine the cynical amusement on his gaunt, thin face if he were alive today and could hear anyone speak of him as a god. I have wanted to tell his story for many years, and have procrastinated consistently because, actually, I knew, and know, so little about him. I have spoken, time and again, to men who knew him well, and invariably they have said: "Oh, he was a wonderful guy. He was the kindest, most lovable, most lonely, saddest guy. . . ." Then they would stop; that was all they could tell me about him.

I went to my friend Norman Green, at the Mechanics Library, and he went through the files of books and magazines and found scores of items. But they told me nothing about the man. My friend Dwight Newton, newspaperman, critic, journalist, and connoisseur of the good things of life, took me down to the library of the San Francisco *Examiner*, and the files were put at my disposal. I found beautiful obituaries in finely rounded phrases, and little more. But they all said the same thing. "He was a wonderful guy! A great man! A kind, lovable, life-loving, lonely man."

When he died, all the flags in San Francisco flew at half-mast. And then the streets of San Francisco forgot him. His name was Thomas Aloysius—Thomas Aloysius Dorgan. He signed his name: TAD.

My own slight acquaintance with Tad came about in this way. I had just entered Polytechnic High School, up there in the dismal brick building at Bush and Stockton streets. I was a notoriously bad student. I didn't dislike school but I hated study. I was bad in English, fairly good in composition. The rest of the academic courses left me cold; I flunked out of Latin. But then, some day I hoped to be a writer and I could not figure that Latin would do me any good; even at that early age I had an intuition that there was more to be learned in the city streets. Polytechnic was primarily a school of mechanical training in those days. I was reasonably good at cabinet making; I made bookcases and chests and things, but my carpentry joints never quite met.

I filled the cracks with a mixture of sawdust and glue and after it had hardened I sandpapered the result; to all but a discerning eye, the joints were not bad. I liked blacksmithing, or, as we called it, "forge," but drove our forge master, Mr. Carnelia, desperate by overheating and crystallizing my wrought iron. And I was reasonably good in "art." I say "reasonably" because I had a nice sense of color and a good sense of composition, but I couldn't draw.

My art teacher, the beloved Rosey Murdock, would stand over me, struggling with my creative soul, and when she saw that it was hopeless she used to say, "Oh, if you could only draw one thousandth as well as Tom Dorgan." Everybody else called him Tad; she called him Tom Dorgan. He became the bane not only of my life but of most of the boys in the art class. Every time we did something badly or incorrectly, Tom Dorgan was held up to us as a shining example. At first I think most of us hated him.

Then, little by little, it began to dawn on our feeble consciousness that there was something remarkable, not about Tom Dorgan, about the art classes at Polytechnic. Rosey Murdock never took any of the credit for it. That belonged to her senior, Maria Van Vleck, or, as we knew her and called her, Nanny Van Vleck. And Nanny took no credit; she was simply, as was Rosey Murdock, an art teacher. But in the days of Nanny Van Vleck and Rosey Murdock at Polytechnic, there had been three boys who were to rank among the world's great cartoonists. Herb Roth, with his biting humor! Rube Goldberg, the inventor of amazing contraptions! And Tom Dorgan, or Tad! And of the three, great as all were, Tad stood out head and shoulders above his fellows.

San Francisco liked cartoonists. San Francisco gave their start to the three Polytechnic boys. And to the great political cartoonist, Homer Davenport. To Jimmie Swinnerton, creator of "Little Jimmie" and distinguished painter of the Southwest. And to Bud Fisher, the creator of "Mutt and Jeff." They were all familiar figures in the streets of San Francisco, but it was Goldberg, Roth, and Tad who found their inspiration in the cold brick dungeons of Polytechnic.

Of course Tad was much more than a cartoonist. He was an artist-draftsman. Critics have said that in his pencil drawings he approached in perfection, as no other artist has approached, the great art of the immortal eighteenth-century Hogarth. I was vaguely aware of all of this when I was a quasi-student in Polytechnic, but not till I finally met Tad did I realize, with horrifying impact, the marvel of his drawing, for Tad, Tom Dorgan, had only two fingers on his right hand. The accident that caused the disaster happened when he was ten years old, after he had learned to write and draw with his right hand. But, then, all of his life Tad was a person to rise above obstacles that would have defeated a smaller man.

My meeting with him must have been in about 1901. Rosey Murdock, like a mother hen with a wild brood of geese, was constantly clucking about us, the chosen few from whom she hoped some day to develop an artist, a cartoonist, or a draftsman who might travel in the company of the three great ones who had been Nanny Van Vleck boys. Not that she wanted fame or glory or even a vicarious joy in having created an artist; Rosey Murdock wasn't like that. She simply could not help fanning a flame when she saw a spark of creative ability. So she showed me Tad sketches and Tad drawings and Tad cartoons. She had stacks of originals treasured in cupboard drawers.

One day, while she was sadly shaking her head, convinced that I would never achieve anything as an artist, Tad walked in. There was my hero, in the living flesh, a hollow-eyed, skinny, hungry-looking person. He was about twenty-four years old at the time. Rosey Murdock positively turned white. Just behind Tad stood Nanny Van Vleck with a smile on her broad, kind face.

She said, "Well, Rosey, here's the boy!"

And Tad, the great Tad, said, "Yes, we have no bananas!" Just that: "Yes, we have no bananas!"

Long after, I learned the origin of that weird statement. An uncle, cousin, or some friend of Tad's had been in the Philippines, during or after the Spanish-American War, and over there he had heard some native say, "Yes, we have no bananas." He repeated it carelessly to Tad and the sentence stuck. Tad used it in greetings and used it constantly in his cartoons. It emerged with regularity in the balloons that came from the mouths of his comic-strip characters, and finally it became the inspiration for one of Tin-Pan Alley's most famous, if not distinguished, songs.

So Tad said "Yes, we have no bananas," and Rosey Murdock said "Oh, you!"

She introduced us, and told Tad that I wanted to be an artist. Tad said, "Do you?" I shivered and said "Uh-huh," and he said "You're crazy." We talked no more of art, but discussed the Polytechnic football squad and its two giants, Garibaldi and Harry Mackenzie.

That was practically all that happened, but now Tad was more of a hero to me than ever. Then, a few years later, San Francisco shook and burned, and in the last days of April 1906, when the ashes had more or less cooled, and one could walk through the debris of the ruins without being

595

shot for looting, I made my sentimental journey through the streets of San Francisco to the crumbled pile of red bricks and broken glass that had been Polytechnic, now a shamble of charred books, twisted blacksmith forges and desks, and charred and water-soaked examination papers. I knew what I was looking for, and somehow I found it: my desk in the English class. There in the rubble I found my mechanical drawing set, rusted and half melted, and the three original Tad cartoons Rosey Murdock gave me the day Tad told me I was crazy.

The cartoons were blackened and water-stained, but I carried them home as though they were the Golden Fleece. They reposed, treasured in my desk in the corner of my den until one day my mother, on her periodic pilgrimage of cleaning out the house, threw them out with the rubbish.

Four or five years later I was working in New York City, not an artist, but a clerk in G. P. Putnam's 23d Street bookstore, earning sixty fat dollars a month. One day Tad came in. He recognized me before I recognized him. After all, I had not changed very much at that time, but Tad, now about thirty-four, seemed to have grown old and tired and thin; he looked as though his flesh was wasting away. He glared at me, then laughed and said, "You wanted to be an artist. Well, you're smart, you didn't become one. But look at me! I wanted to be a prize fighter."

He fingered some of the books, turning the pages and looking at them, as though he didn't see them. He said, "Rosey Murdock! Good girl! And Nanny Van Vleck! I'd like to see her, too." Then he walked out of the store, like a man without a destination. It was my last meeting with him. And now, from bits gleaned here and there, a story of Tad emerges.

Thomas Aloysius Dorgan was born to Tom and Annie Dorgan in 1877. He was a Hayes Valley kid; in San Francisco, that is as significant as being called a South of Market boy, or a Cow Hollow kid, or a kid from the Sand Dunes. Long afterward Tad was also spoken of as one of the Hayes Valley boys. His father kept a little stationery and cigar store. He was a tough little guy, was Tad, and very popular; everybody liked him, just as they liked Tom, senior.

Someone asked Tad what he wanted to be when he grew up, and he answered that he wanted to be a scientific boxer like Gentleman Jim Corbett. He rigged up a home-made punching bag, and imitated the stance of boxers in newspaper pictures. He boasted, kidlike, that he knocked the living daylight out of the punching bag. He did succeed in demolishing it with his small fists, when he was seven years old, and when he wasn't pounding the punching bag or shadowboxing, he was drawing pictures of fighters. The prize ring was the backdrop for all his childhood drawings, and, for being from the hands of a small child, the drawings were remarkably realistic, well-drawn achievements.

Realistic? There was no limit to his realism. He liked plenty of blood in his fights, so he was constantly borrowing or begging bits of red crayon to splatter his drawings with blood. He covered the walls of neighborhood livery stables and warehouses with bloody prize-ring pictures, and anyone could recognize the faces he drew.

John L. Sullivan! Jake Kilrain! And the pride and joy of San Francisco, the man that small Tad followed through the streets of San Francisco, not daring to speak to him: Jim Corbett. Gentleman Jim was the shining, living manifestation of the goal young Tom Aloysius Dorgan hoped to achieve, dreamed of achieving, swore he would achieve.

597

Tragedy smashed the dreams of Tad when he was ten years old. A would-be boxer, a would-be artist, all his talent for either was in his fists. A house was being moved out in the Mission district. Tad and a crowd of South of the Slot youngsters marched behind the slowly rolling structure. The windlass winding the rope that dragged the house in its snail-like pace fascinated Tad. He ran his hand along the cable, and the machinery closed on his fingers. There was a piercing scream, a gathering crowd, the clanging bell of the horse-drawn ambulance, and when Tom Dorgan left the hospital, the potential prize fighter and artist had only the thumb and first knuckle of his right hand to carry him into the tough world of competition.

Well, tough young Tom Dorgan could beat the handicap when it came to drawing. There was still his left hand to train. But fighting, the prize ring, was out! For the rest of his life Tad was an avid fan, an onlooker, and from his ringside seat in the early years, and from his bedside in his last years, when radio brought the prize ring to him, Tad never missed an important fight. Out of his love of the ring his fight pictures became world famous, and he became the world's greatest cartoonist and sports artist.

He witnessed one of the most famous fights, if not the greatest, in all the history of the ring. Gentleman Jim Corbett was matched against Joe Choynski. The fight had been set originally for Fairfax. The crowd had gathered, and the bout began, but in the fourth round the police stopped it. A week later, under cover of secrecy that was no secret, Jim Corbett and Joe Choynski met on a barge in San Francisco Bay. It was one of the fiercest, most grueling fights of all times. It was bare-fist fighting. Corbett broke his left hand, and in the twenty-eighth round Choynski took a fierce left hook to the jaw and fell to the deck of the barge. The spectators were there by the hundreds, aboard row boats, rafts, tugboats, and on or in anything that would float. The roars and frenzy of the mob rocked the craft surrounding the prize-ring barge, and when Jim Corbett connected with that left hook, scores of spectators fell into the bay. With them was twelve-year-old Tad. He was hauled out of the water, spanked, and shipped home, to draw his first fine picture of a prize-ring event.

It was not long before Dorgan senior decided it was time for the boy to begin making a living. He needed a book-keeper, and young Tom was marked for the job. A good enough beginning for a fourteen-year-old, but Tad had other ideas. No lifetime of laboring, bent-shouldered, over a book-keeper's desk for him! He got a job for himself as office boy in the art department of the San Francisco *Bulletin*. His salary, for a year, was three dollars a week. But he got himself into trouble and lost his job. He had made a practice of surreptitiously slipping some of his own drawings into the dummy, and they were, unfortunately, so much better than the work of his superior that there wasn't room for both of them on one daily sheet. So Tad lost his job. But, for once, good work did not go unappreciated. In 1897 Tad was hired as the regular artist on the *Bulletin* at eighteen dollars a week. That was a fortune! His duties called for cartoons, but to assure his earning his salary he was also made boxing editor. It was like finding gold at the end of the rainbow.

The royal command came six years later. William Randolph Hearst had his eye on the amazing young cartoonist. Moreover, Hearst was commencing a campaign to run for mayor of New York City. He wanted someone who could do stinging cartoons that would make his opponent ride the rail of public derision. Nobody could do that better than young Tom Dorgan of San Francisco; the boy was young but unquestionably a genius. He sent for Tad, ordering him to report to the New York office. The year was 1903.

"Well," demanded Mr. Hearst, "do you think you can do the job?"

"Would you have sent for me if *you* didn't think so?" demanded Tad.

"You're very young," said Hearst.

"Applesauce!" said Tad. It was one of the phrases he had coined.

The campaign of 1905, one of the toughest, most bitterly contested in all New York City history, resulted in Hearst's defeat. But all New York was talking about the wonderful Tad cartoons, and doing a lot of talking about Tom Dorgan, the man. They said he was gentle and kind, and tough; a wonderful lad to have around, and a drinker. He lived hard, he never seemed to sleep, he liked people, liked a good time, liked hard liquor, and liked the sporting world. He was welcome wherever he went. But his friends didn't like his appearance. He was too thin, too pale, too young to have such heavy lines in his face. They said he ought to slow down. Slow down? Those were words Tad couldn't understand.

His fame was spreading. He was standing on his own two feet, afraid of no one, sure of himself, and a complete cynic when it came to the nonsense of the day. When the question of a new contract with Hearst arose, Tad didn't like the terms. Hearst held his ground. Tad simply stopped work.

Hearst sent for him and demanded, "Just who do you think you are? The President of the United States?"

"No," said Tad, "but I'm a damned sight more popular."

The new contract was signed on his terms. Hearst's fair-haired boy, Arthur Brisbane, made Tad his own fair-haired boy. Money was pouring in. The eighteen-dollars-a-week days were far behind. Tad fell in love, he was married, blissfully married to a girl who adored him and understood him and tried to keep a tight rein on him for his own sake. But you might as well have tried to put a halter on the sun and moon; Tad simply could not stand still. There was nothing he was afraid of, life, death, or his superiors. He was one of the few men in the Hearst hierarchy to tell Arthur Brisbane where to head in. And Brisbane liked it, most of the time.

There was the day that Tad, returning from a protracted spree, and up against a deadline, picked one of his old cartoons out of his file and scratched the date on it. Just then Brisbane stopped at the desk.

"Hasn't that cartoon been used before?"

"Yes," Tad answered, "but just like a lot of your editorials, it's going to be repeated by request."

Brisbane roared in fury, growled and shook his leonine head, and then walked away, no doubt grinning when the door was closed behind him. The cartoon was used. You simply could not stop Tad.

You couldn't stop Tad! But nature stepped in and made him mark time. It was at the Dempsey-Miske fight in New York in 1920. At the crucial punch in the fight, Tad rose from his seat, and collapsed, victim of a heart attack. They carried him home to his wife at Great Neck, Long Island. He never saw another fight. He hardly left his room again in the ten years remaining to him.

"My ticker gave out," he would say.

That was only one of the slang expressions Tad coined. My ticker gave out! Yes, we have no bananas! Applesauce!

What, no spinach? As busy as a one-armed paper-hanger with the hives! Twenty-three, skidoo! The cat's pajamas! Dumbbell! Cake eater! Officer, call a cop! Flatfoot! For crying out loud! Drugstore cowboy! All these were Tad's expressions, coined by his irrepressible genius, his contribution to America's lexicon of slang. There were many more, and they all made America laugh. But Tad, Thomas Aloysius Dorgan, was not laughing very much any more. He lay in his bed, his drawing board propped up before him, and worked, worked, worked. He knew there wasn't a great deal of time left. He became bitter, caustic, and miserably lonely. Once in a long while he went on a lonely ride in his car. But it was an effort. So he lay in bed, and said "Applesauce," and looked back over the few full years. He had traveled far from the days of Nanny Van Vleck and Rosey Murdock and the old Polytechnic High School at Bush and Stockton streets in San Francisco.

He lay in bed, and when he wasn't drawing his immortal cartoons, he was listening to his radio, hour upon hour, listening to fights and sports events.

They missed him on Broadway, missed him in the night spots, missed him at the city desk of the *Journal*. He plugged away, in constant physical pain, body sick, soul sick. But strangely enough, the bitterness in his heart never crept into his cartoons. He was still the world's greatest cartoonist.

They found him one day, his pencil in his hand, dead at his drawing board. He had just completed a cartoon for the *Journal*. He was two weeks ahead of the deadline.

VII

William O'Brien

It was in the early 1930's that a strange incident of no great importance was given space for a day or so in the local press. You remember the early 1930's, the days when erstwhile gentlemen of wealth were selling apples on street corners, when banks were tottering and incomes were crashing. The highways that led to the cities were the highroad of bums and blanket-stiffs and just plain tramps; wayside fires glowed in a thousand hobo jungles along the railroad tracks, and thirteen million men were unemployed.

It was during that period that a gentleman, walking just for the sake of walking, through the streets of San Francisco, found himself in the neighborhood of the hill called Lone Mountain. That small and unimpressive hill had been devoted to the prosperous pursuit of cemeteries, four of the city's most distinguished boasting acres on Lone Mountain.

The gentleman came to the gates of Calvary Cemetery and paused, perhaps to admire, perhaps to contemplate with stoic philosophy the several ages of man, all of which inevitably ended in acres such as these. He paused, and looked upon the marble and granite slabs and monuments, and his unbelieving eyes saw smoke emerging from a vault. The word "vault" is an injustice; it was a mausoleum, an imposing structure of stone, with stained-glass windows and bronze doors. It was a tomb that proclaimed, "This is the last resting place of a graveyard aristocrat," a structure proclaiming in flamboyant elegance the snobbery of the graveyard. It was an ugly mass of misguided architecture, as ugly as one could find in a long search through the graveyards and the avenues and streets of a city long famous for its architectural abortions.

And there it sat, in the serene quiet of Calvary Cemetery, and a stained-glass window had been removed, and through the aperture projected a black stovepipe out of which smoke drifted, fragrant with the aroma of fried bacon and burned beans.

Now one must expect to find almost anything in the streets of San Francisco. The city has always been famed for its eccentric characters and strange events, and much might go unnoticed here that would cause alarums and excursions in a city of more prosaic traditions. But smoke flavored with the aroma of fried bacon emerging from a stovepipe thrust through the window of a graveyard architectural monstrosity was more than even dyed-in-the-wool San Franciscans could accept with equanimity. The walking gentleman called the police. The police investigated, found the bronze door of the mausoleum had been crashed or pried open, and the interior been made the pleasant, if perhaps cheerless, home of a group of itinerants. They had set up housekeeping there, and had lived there, in comparative comfort and rent free, for several months. The unsentimental police drove them forth, and whether they were given new lodgings as vagrants in the Hall of Justice, I have never learned.

The mausoleum returned to its former undisturbed serenity, a silent home of the dead. Which, from any point of view that you may approach the situation, seems a pity. For if there was ever a man who would have enjoyed the company of those down-and-out, poverty-stricken bums of the 1930's, it was the man whose remains lay beneath the stones of that architectural abomination.

His name was William O'Brien, and, having lived a simple and modest life without pomp or circumstance, his only claim to elegant ostentation was the tomb he had commissioned to be built a few months before his death.

As long as I can remember, and that is more than fifty years, the name of William O'Brien has been a familiar one to me. Yet all that I knew about him was vague save for the association of his name with other San Franciscans, a name that was a part of the story of San Francisco.

Then, one Sunday afternoon, several years ago, I was sitting on the lawn of the Family Club at Woodside with Mr. J. B. Levison. Mr. Levison, a leader in the musical and artistic endeavors of the city, and the distinguished head of a large insurance company, was a man whose story, too, ought to be told some day; he was a great philanthropist, a fine citizen with an abiding appreciation of fine things, and a San Franciscan with a deep pleasure in the traditions and romance and quirks of the city.

It was a warm and mellow afternoon, and Mr. Levison was telling me about old-time San Franciscans he had known. He said to me, "Some day you must write the story of William O'Brien." I said that I would like to, that there was no time like the present, at least to start collecting material. What could he, Mr. Levison, tell me about O'Brien? He laughed and said, "Frankly, nothing. There really isn't much to tell about him as an individual."

O'Brien, he explained, was just a simple, kindly, unassuming Irishman from Dublin. He didn't have an overabundance of brains; he was strangely lacking in ambition; he asked very little of life, but enjoyed all of it. His story was really the story of the men he was associated with. "Of course," concluded Mr. Levison, "I was a young man when he died. But I did know him, and I knew that there were few men in San Francisco with more friends than he had; they loved him for his generosity and his good nature. They called him 'the jolly millionaire.' He was a good, kind, generous, and happy man."

On that slender thread, the few facts about his life that Mr. Levison told me, and from incidents and bits of color gleaned from other writers of San Franciscana, my story of William O'Brien must be woven. I did find, in everything I have been told about him and in everything I have read about him, a consistent agreement: he was good, kind, and generous, and a happy man.

William O'Brien, William Shoney O'Brien if you prefer, arrived in San Francisco from New York City on July 6, 1849. He was twenty-three years old, and he didn't have a dollar in his pocket. Born in Dublin, he had come to New York with the constant stream of Irish emigrants that turned to America as the land of promise. He worked as a grocery clerk in New York, one of thousands of Irish lads all waiting for opportunity or Lady Luck to beckon. But the lady was too busy in other places, and young Bill O'Brien pulled the shelves of the grocery store down around his ears, and sailed away to California to hunt for gold.

He arrived in July of 1849 and found San Francisco an all but deserted village; overnight, the village had become a city, and as quickly it had emptied itself into the hills. Oh, there was activity of course. Ships were daily casting anchor off Clarke's Point at the foot of Telegraph Hill and dropping their human cargoes on Clarke's Wharf. And up Clay Street and up Pacific Street toiled the wide-eyed, never-ending parade of gold-frenzied men. This was San Francisco, the place they'd heard the fabulous stories about; San Francisco, where unschooled farm boys and road bums were becoming millionaires overnight. But a glance at the dance halls, saloons, and gambling hells lining the roadways was enough. It wasn't for this that they'd traveled six months around the Cape, or over the Isthmus, or across the prairies and the Rockies. They had come for gold, gold that could be picked up on the trails, that glistened in the crotches of pine trees, that leaped at you, yellow and shining as the sun, every time you swung your ax or pick.

One glance at the sprawling village of San Francisco and the bay with its deserted ships, and they were off to the hills. By river boat, by burro or horseback, or on shanks' mare, they headed for the Mother Lode.

But not Bill O'Brien. Gold meant little to him, either then or later. Of course he'd come West to find gold because it was the thing to do, but he didn't care whether or not he found it, or whether it found him. He landed penniless, his only worldly possession being the tattered homespun suit on his back.

He got a job, unloading ships in the bay. It was a rough, tough job, unloading the heterogeneous army of ships that dropped anchor off Clarke's Point. The cargoes of rubber boots, calico, coffee, sugar, tobacco, and rum had to be carried on strong shoulders up the beach and through roadways deep in dust in summer, deep in mud in winter and spring. One day a chance acquaintance stopped the tall, good-looking Irish lad and remonstrated with him for the ragged appearance of his dress and the tatters of his shoes. But there was nothing much Bill O'Brien could do about it; boots and shoes cost from twenty to fifty dollars a pair in San Francisco. So the friend presented him with a pair of shoes that, although they had already done service, were still better than nothing. O'Brien put them on and found the going easier. Years later he made a persistent effort to find the Samaritan who had come to his aid, but without success. After all, it was no small matter to have a pair of reasonably serviceable boots shoved on feet that were torn and bleeding from the hazards of the roadway.

The fact is, William O'Brien found men friendly creatures. There were men of all kinds who had made the journey from New York with him on the brig *Tarolinta*. Rich men, poor men, adventurers, and scholars, they had all been well disposed to the young Irishman. He liked to remember that in later years; friendships won when a lad was penniless were friendships worth having. How he remembered those friends is another part of his story.

Without ambition, Bill O'Brien drifted through the years of the gold rush, making friends, enjoying life in its simplest form. But the ships that massed the bay were now ghost ships; fewer cargoes were coming into the harbor, fewer men were heading for the diggings, and more and more men were drifting back, broke. O'Brien hunted for a job more likely to supply him with three meals a day. He clerked in a tobacco and newspaper shop owned by William C. Hoff, and eventually became Hoff's partner. He saved a little money. Then he bought an interest in W. J. Rosner's ship chandlery. That was a business designed to kindle the imagination of any young lad; through the doors of the chandlery came an endless string of skippers and mates and pursers from ships that had spoken every port of the seas. There were few pursuits more glamorous.

More than that, the business of ship chandlering was vaguely related to horse trading; sharp deals were made, close corners were cut, and any deal was a legitimate transaction as long as it didn't make a barefaced practice of breaking the laws. It planted in O'Brien a degree of shrewdness he hadn't possessed before, and it increased his knowledge of men, a knowledge that had, at no time, been absent in him. And during these early days he became fast friends with another young Irishman, a store clerk named Jim Flood.

I have a small book on my shelves, written in 1873 by T. A. Barry and B. A. Patten; they called it *Men and Memories of San Francisco in the Spring of '50.* In a few lines they note that "J. C. Flood and W. S. O'Brien were living on the corner of Pacific and Mason Streets in 1849–1850, boarding at Mr. Parker's house. . . . we found them unassuming, amiable men, always prompt, shrewd and correct in business."

That is the only printed record I have been able to find of the early days of Flood and O'Brien; after all, they were then quite unimportant young fellows, in a day when getting by was becoming more and more of a struggle.

Hard times were closing in on San Francisco. The harvest of the gold fields had thinned out; banks were failing. Five or six fires had left the city in ashes. The streets were overrun with hoodlums and escaped convicts from the penal colonies of Australia and New Zealand. The self-appointed Vigilantes were making their own rules of order, and death by common causes were hardly more frequent than were murders and hangings. The city was enjoying its bleakest, blackest days. Ship chandleries didn't do much business; merchants didn't do much business, but saloons were always full. So, pooling their resources, both having saved reasonably comfortable nest eggs, Bill O'Brien and Jim Flood opened a saloon.

The year was 1857. Their establishment for the dispensing of hard liquor stood at the corner of Pacific and Stockton streets. This was not a very good location. With the growth of the city, business was moving south toward Market Street. So they found a new location at 509 Washington Street, just west of Sansome. They called their saloon the Auction Lunch; the clientele was largely drawn from the auction and commission houses in the neighborhood. The Auction Lunch! A feature of the Flood and O'Brien saloon was the high quality of their free lunch. A merchant, an auctioneer, a banker, or a bum could come in and buy a glass of beer for a nickel, or a shot of whisky for little more, and eat to his heart's and stomach's content. It took very little time for the Auction Lunch to become the most popular gathering place of big and little men in the city.

With the coming of success the difference in the natures of the two partners evinced itself. Jim Flood, innately a gentleman, dressed like a gentleman and preferred to mingle with his patrons on the floor of his establishment as one of them. Not Bill O'Brien! He was a bartender. He wore his white apron, he stood behind the bar, and he made change for the gold coins that were flung on the bar; because that was his job, he was proud of it and happy in it. He liked people and people liked him, and where could you meet more and different kinds of men than when you were dispensing hard liquor across the mahogany of the Flood and O'Brien saloon?

Years later, when he was a multimillionaire, a man so

wealthy that he had no idea what his material wealth amounted to, then his favorite haunt was in a deep chair on a white-sanded floor of a Montgomery Street saloon. There was no pretense, no affectation about William O'Brien; he was a plain, earthy man, who liked people as long as they met him on his own ground, which was, incidentally, a ground premised on honest decency.

Five O Nine Washington Street was a busy place, and that block on Washington Street was to become increasingly important. Next to the Flood and O'Brien establishment was the Washington Market, the most important and most heavily patronized produce market in the city; all the important people went there, and many a gentleman of importance in the city combined his duties at the market with his pleasures at the friendly place next door. But even more important than the market was the coming, in 1862, of the San Francisco Mining Exchange to a location just a few doors west. Now, even more distinguished patrons found their way into Flood and O'Brien's, and the two proprietors spruced up their garb in a manner fitting the new clientele. O'Brien wore broadcloth and a high silk hat; the very picture of a man of distinction, he liked to stand on the sidewalk and greet his friends.

Flood, more sedate, wore well-tailored suits of fashionable gray; he was less boisterous in his greeting of friends; he was always willing to listen when they talked. And listening, he learned much about the trend of the mines, especially the fabulous gold and silver mines recently developed in a hillside above Virginia City in the territory of Nevada. Tips on mining shares were generously given, and with the shrewd perception and vision that characterized all of his activities, James Flood played the tips that were sound and rejected the

611

unstable ones. Good-natured Bill O'Brien played along with him, not very much concerned with which way the wind blew.

The result was that, ten years after they had become partners, James Flood and William O'Brien, through playing the tips on the Mining Exchange, were reasonably wealthy men. The next and obvious step was the sale of the Auction Lunch. Flood and O'Brien moved out and opened offices in a loft on Montgomery Street as brokers of mining stocks. One day to their office came two other Irishmen, who had started like themselves with nothing. But these two men were practical miners, experts in their field. They were John Mackay and James Fair.

Mackay was a shrewd businessman and a mining wizard. Fair was a hard, vindictive, cold individual, climbing the heights no matter the necks he trod on. Flood was a wise businessman with the untested instincts of a financier. And O'Brien? Well, Bill O'Brien made no pretense. He wasn't much of a businessman, he didn't pretend to be, he didn't especially care to be. He simply, as he liked to tell, grabbed hold of the tale of a kite and was "histed up" into the air. It was a swift and a dazzling ascent. Within four years after they had sold the Auction Lunch, James Flood and William O'Brien were, according to various and reliable authorities, enjoying an income of more than half a million dollars a month.

It was probably the most difficult task William O'Brien ever tackled. How, in the name of all that was honest, could one man enjoy a half million dollars a month, especially if, as in the case of O'Brien, his tastes were simple, his needs few, and money had no glamour for him? He never married. He bought himself a rather pretentious home at 517 Sutter Street

612

just above Powell. Not that he wanted to make a splurge with his millions, but the house was large, and he could bring his various brothers and sisters and nieces and nephews to it and lavish comforts and luxuries upon them.

Now he was an important member of the society of San Francisco financial leaders, but he refused to accept the honor or the responsibility. It wasn't his fault that he had made millions that he had never particularly wanted. He went along in his easy, happy way, just as unassuming, just as matter-of-fact an everyday individual as he had been when, years before, a Good Samaritan has given him a pair of serviceable boots in his stevedoring days.

Not that O'Brien was shiftless or an easy mark; he liked to drive a shrewd bargain, just for the game of it. He had far more money than he could spend, but there was that innate horse-trading instinct that had made him, even in the early days, a useful partner for Jim Flood. He drove so hard a bargain that at times people called him an old skinflint, but there was affection in their voice, and he had friends from all walks of life.

He particularly liked to remember the friends of his early days in San Francisco, when the going had been hard. He liked to gather them around him and give parties and banquets for the friends he had known on the *Tarolinta*, the brig that had brought him to San Francisco. For several years he gave parties to celebrate the anniversary of their arrival, and in 1877 he chartered a tug and invited his friends of the *Tarolinta* on a tour of the bay; he was able to locate fifty of them. It was, in the most glorious sense, a gala Irish picnic. A brass band played; gentlemen in frock coats and silk hats made speeches with forensic might and with tears in their eyes. The banquet was copious, the liquid refreshments sufficient and various enough to satisfy any appetite. His friends slapped his back and pumped his arm and told him he was a wonderful lad; everybody sang "O Susanna." And Bill O'Brien was a happy man.

He died the following year. He had never wanted very much of life; just good friends, and good food, and time to relax and take things easy. But when he died, he left a fortune stated to have ranged from six to fifteen million dollars. The huge estate was left to friends and immediate relatives and to his favorite charities.

His only gesture of ostentation was the mausoleum he ordered built in Calvary Cemetery, the one with bronze doors and the stained-glass window through which the hoboes of 1930 thrust a stovepipe to let out the smoke of the bacon they were frying.

Bill O'Brien would have enjoyed that.

VIII

Arnold Genthe

San Francisco Society was very formal fifty and sixty years ago. The "500" took themselves very seriously, and it was a difficult, an almost impossible undertaking to become number five hundred and one.

The debut, the coming-out party, was an occasion as auspicious as presentation to Queen Victoria.

For months prior to the event, Mme. Baer or Mme. Chevalier or Mme. Labourdette worked on the debutante's gown—unless her parents were in the very top echelon of the five hundred, in which case her gown was imported from Paquin's in Paris. After all, it was an important event; so much depended on the debut. You appeared at the ball, and stood in the receiving line, and were extra-particularly polite and demure before all the dowagers. After all, any one of them might prove to be your future mother-in-law, for they were there to look you over and decide if you were suitable material for marriage to their eligible sons.

And debuts were no small problem to the sons. You might be the scion of a millionaire family, but at the age of nineteen or twenty you were not likely to be overburdened with pocket money. In "the season" there were two or three debuts each week, and on popular nights you might be expected to travel between three or four coming-out parties. Your first expense was a carriage from Kelly's Stable. That cost about $2.50. You called for the girl you were to escort, and in many cases she was accompanied by her chaperon, perhaps an aunt or an old family nurse. You of course sent her an orchid; you also sent an orchid to the debutante, and if you were schooled to really do things properly you sent an orchid or a box of flowers to the debutante's mother.

Naturally, before each debut, you, being a proper young man, had your nails manicured and highly polished, and all these things cost a lot of money, to say nothing of your masculine attire: tails and white tie, white gloves, and silk hat. I have sometimes wondered what would happen to a nineteen-year-old San Francisco boy today if he walked down Powell Street wearing a silk hat.

The stage setting for the debut ranged from the California Club to the St. Francis or Fairmont or Palace hotels. I particularly recall the functions at the Palace because, in the years immediately following the earthquake, it was considered a very daring and sophisticated thing to take a shy and modest young thing into the bar after midnight. Not for a drink! No lady ever drank in a bar! But to show the shy thing the Maxfield Parrish painting of the Pied Piper that hung above the mahogany. That post-midnight adventure was called "slumming for art's sake."

Mama, the brains behind the debut, had one especially important duty to perform. She notified the society editors of the local press, describing the floral decorations, the cotillion favors, giving the list of invited guests, and, most important, she supplied the press with pictures of the modest maiden.

Well, photographers came and went, and suddenly a new

616

name dawned on the horizon. Not much was known about this one, other than that he was poor, very good looking, and terribly radical in his approach to photography. Radical? He was a revolutionist! He produced pictures that made dumpy, squint-eyed, chinless products of the best finishing schools look like ethereal creatures. He went further than that; he took pictures out of focus! They had a vague, foggy beauty. He went still further. He didn't insist on his victims glaring straight into the camera; he even let them assume a faraway, dreamy expression, as though having their picture taken was the last thing in the world they had in their mind. He had a charming habit, too, of draping a figure that weighed more than one hundred and fifty pounds in a piece of tulle or a chiffon scarf, and sometimes, instead of having his subjects stare into the light, he attacked them with light reflected from the rear, especially when their features were good and their complexion was bad.

But the most amazing thing about this amazing young man was his disreputable and inadequate studio, or perhaps it was not disreputable but it certainly was inadequate. It was on Sutter Street opposite the old University Club, one room, lighted by a gas jet, walls covered in burlap, yet San Francisco society flocked to it. They flocked and they crowded. The one room couldn't possibly accommodate more than one patron at a time, so while the handsome young man was busy making his ethereal shots, other clients waited their turn in their carriages, great ladies and dignified dowagers, or sat and waited on the narrow stairs outside the studio door. Waited? Why, they considered it a privilege to wait, for this young man was Arnold Genthe.

His debut was sheer luck. Mrs. William Crocker brought her three children to be photographed, and she was so pleased with the result that a few days later she brought her sister, Princess Poniatowski, for a sitting. They found the handsome young man remarkable. He didn't bother to pose his subjects; he actually snapped them when they didn't know they were being photographed. The results were not only flattering, but gratifying and very artistic. In not much longer than it takes to make a time exposure, Arnold Genthe had become the vogue of polite society.

San Francisco society lionized him. You couldn't help being boastful, in a modest way of course, when you said, "Oh, yes, I am going to be busy this afternoon. I am sitting for Arnold Genthe." In time he became one of the greatest and most famous of photographers, but his fame began with the debutante studies printed on very "arty" paper, which did not look at all like a photograph print, but looked, in some cases, as though the work had been done on a piece of vellum, or on old leather, or on a piece of damask or Irish linen. And people found him charming and began to wonder about his background.

He was born in Germany in 1868. His father was professor of Latin and Greek at the Gray Monastery in Berlin, and Arnold's boyhood was spent in an environment of dignified culture. The boy liked to draw and wanted to be an artist. With sacrifice on the part of his parents he was sent to the University of Jena. His professor of science was the great scholar, Ernst Haeckel. Haeckel had a strange theory: to fully understand people and things, he said, the student should draw what he saw; that would teach him to see more clearly. So, with pencil and paper, Arnold Genthe began sketching the life of his undergraduate days.

In Hamburg he met Baron Heinrich von Schroeder, who had married the daughter of Mervyn Donahue of the Donahue-Kelly bank of San Francisco. The baron wanted to take a German tutor back to San Francisco with him for his son. He offered the position to Genthe for one year. It was an opportunity to travel; at the end of the year he would return to the Continent. A year in that remote and fantastic world called California and the colorful city of San Francisco! He eagerly accepted the offer.

He reached San Francisco in 1895. The Von Schroeders lived on Sutter Street near fashionable Van Ness Avenue. As soon as Genthe had unpacked his possessions, he went for a walk, up hill and down hill through the city streets.

Here, he wrote, was a city with a flavor all its own: the approach through vestibules of cliffs and mountainsides; the golden stretches of the dunes; the bay, misted by the silver fog, or captured by the softly incandescent blue of a clear sky; the full-rigged barkentines and the many little ships always coming and going, their sails bellying in the stiff breeze; the long curve of the waterfront with its rows of sailing ships from all ports of the world; the spicy tang of the sea and of cargoes piled high on the wharves; Fisherman's Wharf and its rainbow fleet; the songs of the Italian fishermen as they mended their nets; Telegraph Hill, where the fishermen's shacks clung like swallows' nests to the sides of the cliff. This was a backdrop to delight the soul of any creative artist.

There was one small corner of San Francisco, eight square blocks in all, that was to change the course of Genthe's life. He had been warned not to go through Chinatown without a guide. That was just the kind of warning the adventurous spirit liked. He went to Chinatown without a guide, and his destiny was decided.

He said: The painted balconies were hung with wind bells and flowered lanterns. Brocades and embroideries, bronzes and porcelains, carvings of jade and ivory, of coral and rose crystal, decorated the shop windows. Shuffling along in single file were the dark-clad silent figures of the men, their faces strange, inscrutable. Children in gay silken costume thronged the sidewalks and doorways. From the windows in the "Street of the Sing-song Girls" bright eyes peered out from under brighter headdresses.

It was a scene that had to be captured. Genthe wanted pictures to send home with his letters from this strange new land, but no pictures were available. Genthe had never used a camera and knew nothing about photography. He did know that the Chinese were deeply superstitious about having their pictures taken. All the evils of the dark places were bottled up in that small square black box. But he had to have pictures. He bought a small pocket camera with a good lens and started out to win the confidence of the old-country Chinese, and to capture the romance and color and exotic fascination of San Francisco's Chinatown.

Hour upon hour Genthe haunted the streets and alleys of Chinatown. He would stand, immobile, leaning against a wall or a telegraph pole, waiting for the light and shadows to favor him, apparently unaware of the figures in the passing scene.

At first the softly trotting Chinese ignored him, then were suspicious of him, then found him harmless and accepted him. It was a step in the right direction, but they still, even the children, feared and resented the little black box that he carried. In later years, clients of Arnold Genthe never knew just when he was snapping the shutter to take a picture; that explained the natural charm of his portraiture, and so, in Chinatown, his finger barely moved as it released the shutter. Of course he could not use a tripod, and at times the camera had to be tucked under his arm or was held peeking out from his greatcoat when the picture was being made. But the pictures *were* made, and became a record of pre-earthquake Chinatown, a priceless record of San Francisco.

Through opium dens, gambling dens, dens of the long since extinct tong men and highbinders, and into the more beautiful and exotic corners of the Orient in the new world, the temples and joss houses and family gardens and wonderful shops where exquisite jades and porcelains were framed in gilded carvings; through all the walks of Chinese life went Arnold Genthe and his camera.

Out of that pageant of color and age-old beauty Genthe assembled a collection of Chinese photographs that were later to illustrate a book that has become a collector's item; one of the most fascinating and precious books built around San Francisco. Here was something new in bookmaking, too, for instead of the author writing his pages and having them illustrated by an artist of his choice, this was a volume of illustrations, with the writer selected to describe the pictures. The book was *Pictures of Old Chinatown*. The artist was Dr. Arnold Genthe. The writer was San Francisco's beloved Will Irwin.

In a letter to the artist, Will Irwin wrote, "My dear Dr. Genthe: Long before I knew who you were, I used to mark you in shadows and recesses of Chinatown, your little camera half-hidden under your coat, you, the only man who had the patience to photograph the Chinese, you who found art in the snap-shot, you were making yourself, unconsciously all that time, the sole recorder of Old Chinatown. I but write as a frame for your pictures; I am illustrating you."

So that was the beginning. But San Francisco had other fascination for Arnold Genthe: the amazing hills, the shadows, and the fog that drifted through the canyons of the streets.

Gray chiffon veils of fog! Now there was a subject made to delight the artist's hand, or the artist's camera. Pictures seen through the drifting fog! Why, with the camera, the chiffon veils could be created where no fog existed! Created by a lens slightly out of focus! Created by deeply matted paper that dimmed the picture's outline! Created, and this was the most mechanical of tricks but the results were there, created by printing the negative through a screen, or even through fine Irish linen, or for that matter, a chiffon veil! Tricks? Yes, they all were tricks, but they were the first step in the adventure of divorcing photography from the stilted, unimaginative mechanics of the past.

Genthe joined the Camera Club, and people came to the club to see his photographs. That was truly something new; before that, people had their pictures taken for the record; now they came to see photographs as they went to see paintings in an art gallery. A few men posed for him, but not for professional pictures; there was no thought of turning his newly discovered toy into a business.

One day a young girl came to pose for him, or perhaps that is not the correct word. Genthe never permitted a pose, the picture was always snapped when the subject was unaware of it. So the young girl came—well, to have her picture taken. She was fifteen years old, and Genthe made a very lovely picture of her. He gave it to her and she showed it to her friends. That was probably the real beginning of Arnold Genthe's career as a world-famous portrait photographer. The young girl was Alma de Bretteville, who later married Adolph Spreckels, the same Alma de Bretteville Spreckels who was to so large a degree responsible for San

622

Francisco's beautiful Legion of Honor and its great art collection.

Meanwhile young Von Schroeder had finished his tutelage and was ready to go to Germany for his examinations; Genthe's job was finished. Of course he, too, would return to Germany, would perhaps become a professor in a German university and carry on the teaching traditions of his family. But did he want to go back? Here are his own words:

"It is a habit of mine, when troubled in thought, to go for a long walk. One late afternoon I found myself at the top of Russian Hill. Around me ran the full circle of what I would be giving up if I were to leave San Francisco, a city I had grown to love. I began to see clearly that teaching would never bring me the happiness I wanted. It was here I belonged, in this new country which has broadened my horizons, opened my eyes to a new conception of life, and shown me a way to satisfy my desire for beauty. So I took the first step in my career as a portrait photographer. I started in search of a studio."

He found the studio opposite the old University Club on Sutter Street; the rent was twenty-five dollars a month. To it flocked the turn-of-the-century society of San Francisco, and Arnold Genthe had become the new lion of the city. His first patrons were from the social elite, old San Franciscans of the "500": Mrs. William Crocker, Mrs. Rudolph Spreckels, Mrs. Will Tevis, Mrs. Philip Lilienthal, Mrs. Kenneth Kingsbury, Genevieve Goad . . .

Then, one day, Nance O'Neil found her way to the crowded little studio. That name doesn't mean very much to the present generation, but in the late 'nineties and the early years of the twentieth century, Nance O'Neil was one of the great tragediennes of the American stage. Genthe took her

623

picture. Her husband and manager had it blown up to a three-sheet for poster purposes. It was the most expensive poster he had ever made, Genthe liked to boast. It was so stunning that people would soak it off the billboards and keep it for a souvenir.

That was the beginning of Genthe's fame as a theatrical photographer. Henry Miller, one of the beloved names in the story of the American stage, the man who year after year played San Francisco and called it his city: Henry Miller came to Genthe to be photographed. Margaret Anglin came, garbed in the flowing robes of her Greek tragedies. Maxine Elliot and Julia Marlowe, two of the most beautiful women and actresses of all times, sat for him. The fame of the young photographer traveled far beyond San Francisco Bay.

A new group came, the first a shy, very distinguished young man. He was Frank Norris, San Francisco's favorite author, and after him came the writers and poets: Jack London, Will and Wallace Irwin, Jimmie Hopper, handsome, white-haired Ambrose Bierce, Edwin Markham of "The Man with the Hoe," and many musicians, among them Paderewski. And Genthe, who had passed up the starving career of a German university professor, one day opened the chest in which he had stored the gold pieces paid him for his labor. He had amassed three thousand dollars.

That was not a great deal of gold, but it was a fortune to the young tutor. Now he could indulge himself in the things that made life beautiful for him. He could buy a bit of dark jade in the Chinatown that he loved. He could go to Papa Coppa's for an Italian dinner with red wine. He could see the glamorous city with the friends who had become his circle, the Irwins, Gelett Burgess, and George Sterling, the writers, the poets, the dreamers.

Life was gay in San Francisco, and such a fine life tended to interfere with the art to which the San Francisco bohemians were dedicated. A retreat was needed, and Arnold Genthe found the retreat along the Monterey coast in a wilderness of pine trees and cypress that bent in strangely fantastic beauty before the wind at the ocean's edge. There was no town, no village, just a couple of cabins in the pines, one of which belonged to the poet, George Sterling. That was the beginning of the artist colony that was to become Carmel, and in their pine-covered hillside retreat, George Sterling, Jack London, and Arnold Genthe became an inseparable trio, such a trio as Du Maurier's three bohemians in *Trilby*. They were later joined by Harry Leon Wilson, and still later Sinclair Lewis, and then Theodore Dreiser and Lincoln Steffens. There was much drinking of red wine, much singing of songs, and a reasonable amount of carefree love, but there was quiet when quiet was desired, and perhaps no place in the world could have lent itself any more perfectly to the artist's brush than did the hills and rocks and cypress and pines of Carmel to the camera of Arnold Genthe; here was beauty and here was serenity.

He never married, though many women loved him. He liked to talk about his art, never about his loves. His friends ranged from a little Chinese girl with slant eyes and a missing front tooth to the great people of the world. Sarah Bernhardt cherished his friendship. The great opera singers came to his studio, Melba, Emma Eames, Gadski, Scotti, and many others, to sit for their pictures. Scotti, gay, handsome, a bohemian of the bohemians, loved to come to San Francisco, to go with Genthe at night to his favorite Italian restaurants; and then the two men would wander the streets of Chinatown, stopping to watch a fan-tan game, or to walk through the alleys into opium dens and dens of iniquity that were rich with color for those who saw with the eyes of artists.

Genthe had become a wealthy man. But far more precious than gold were the art treasures he had accumulated: rare oriental brocades, ivory and jade and precious stones, rare paintings and books, exquisite castings in bronze. He became something of a miser, hoarding his possessions, collecting till he confessed it had become something more than a delight in beautiful things; he fell in love with possessions until he reached the point where the possessions were possessing him.

One April night he went to the opera on Mission Street, the old Grand Opera House, where Caruso and Fremstad were singing *Carmen*. After that wonderful performance he walked slowly home with friends, had a "goodnight" drink, and went to bed. He later said: "The music of Carmen was still singing in my ears. It seemed as if I had scarcely been asleep when I was awakened by a terrifying sound; the Chinese porcelains that I had been collecting in the past year had crashed to the ground." It was the morning of the earthquake of 1906. And, said Genthe, "My interest in Chinese porcelains ever since then has been purely platonic."

He found his cameras ruined by falling plaster. He walked downtown to the store of his friend George Kahn, on Montgomery Street, to borrow a camera. "Take anything you please," said Kahn, "the place is going to burn down anyway." With a small 3A Kodak Genthe went into the streets and made pictures of the disaster that are, to this day, things of terrible and breath-taking beauty.

His studio was in ruins and his cherished collections gone; even his own file of the photographs he had made over the years was destroyed, though by a lucky chance the pre-earthquake pictures of Chinatown were saved. He vowed he would never again collect treasures, or at any rate nothing but small treasures precious for their beauty and their legend, a bit of jade or a Milan-carved cameo. He'd never again let himself love possessions and become their slave.

He found a new studio out on Clay Street, and there pioneered in a new expression of photographic art: processed color pictures. Society flocked to the new studio, and new friends of the stage and concert world came to him. David Belasco! Otis Skinner! Walter Hampden! Minnie Maddern Fiske! And one day, the imperious lady of the London stage, Mrs. Pat Campbell, came to be photographed in the role associated later and so affectionately with Gertrude Lawrence: the street girl of Bernard Shaw's *Pygmalion*.

But now the wide world began to demand the artist. He traveled, first to the scenic places of America; he went to the Grand Canyon of the Colorado, where he made pictures of indescribable beauty. He went to Italy, Egypt, India, to the Orient. In Greece he became the devoted friend and photographer of Isadora Duncan. Toscanini sat for him, and three presidents, Teddy Roosevelt, William Taft, Woodrow Wilson. He was acclaimed wherever he went; in those years of travel Arnold Genthe photographed almost every great or near-great personage in the world.

He had lived in San Francisco and been a part of the picture, a familiar face in the streets of San Francisco for fifteen years. Now, on his travels, he found many of his old friends of San Francisco; in particular, he found his companion of San Francisco's Chinatown, Will Irwin, established in New York. With Irwin and others a new circle was formed and a new life of fame began. The young tutor from Germany had become a world figure.

One brief incident, and his reaction to it, summed up his life. Again and again he returned to San Francisco. On one such visit he went slumming one night with two new visitors, a man and a woman, and took them to see the new Barbary Coast, built after the earthquake in imitation of the old one that had been the nefarious and exciting sink of San Francisco iniquity.

The three went into the most notorious of the Barbary Coast dance halls, the Olympia. The dance floor was crowded with sailors, drifters, rowdies, painted women, dancing to the rhythm of the Grizzly Bear, but the crowd ignored Genthe and his companions. Slumming parties were a familiar sight on the Barbary Coast.

The man and the woman with Genthe whispered together for a moment, then joined the crowd on the floor and began to dance. That was a less familiar move, since the slummers usually kept themselves superciliously aloof.

But these two danced, and little by little, as they danced, the crowd on the floor became silent, and drifted to the sidelines and watched. When the honky-tonk music stopped and the two dancers stood still, the crowd broke into a roar of cheers; they demanded more and more and more. The dancers were Pavlova and Mordkin. The heterogeneous mob in the Olympia had witnessed a spectacle that, in all reason, could happen in San Francisco and in no other place in the world.

Looking back on that night, Arnold Genthe wrote: "Of this I am sure. I have never been bored, and I dare say I have had as much out of life as is coming to any man."

IX

The Dusty 'Nineties

When I close my eyes and try to capture a picture of the streets of San Francisco, the camera of my subconscious mind inevitably shows me a picture of the city of the eighteen-nineties. Today my most vivid impressions are of the city of that decade, probably because that was the most characteristic. I can see block after block and row after row of narrow houses, all of them of wood, all of them with bay windows, all of them painted gray. It's a drab, gray picture, but the drab gray is a neutral background for the golden sunshine and silver fog, for the blue of the bay, and for the gardens. I think every house in the city had its front and back garden of red geraniums and purple heliotrope and yellow marguerites. To this rich, garden-variety of color, add the habits and customs of the day, and you have a reasonable picture of the eighteen-nineties in San Francisco, perhaps a picture of the English-speaking world at the end of the Victorian era, but I prefer to think it a picture of the streets of San Francisco.

I have at my disposal the complete files of a daily San Francisco paper for those ten years, and in its pages is a more faithful photograph of the times than I can leave to my flighty memory. For instance, if you are interested in home furnishings, the advertisement of a Murphy Bed should appeal to you. I suppose there are still some Murphy Beds in unpopular use, but for those of this generation who never saw nor heard of one, I should explain that the Murphy Bed was a folding bed that, when it was upright and closed, looked like a huge wardrobe. When you wanted to retire you leaped into the air, seized the upper handle of the wardrobe, pulled it to the floor, and you had a bed. You climbed in, shut your eyes and clenched your fists, and prayed that the monster wouldn't close on you, like an envelope, leaving you asleep standing on your head. Murphy Beds that closed at the wrong time were a favorite topic of hilarious humor in *Puck* and *Judge* of the 'nineties.

Next to the advertisement for Solid Mahogany Murphy Beds in the San Francisco *Chronicle* of January 22, 1890, I find this headline, "Nelly Bly arrives on the Steamship *Oceanic*." Nelly Bly, it goes on to say, sailed through the Golden Gate on the lap of her voyage that brought her from Hong Kong to San Francisco. Ten thousand San Franciscans greeted the great vessel as it approached the dock.

My father, who was one of the ten thousand, told me more about the event. Nelly strode down the gangplank to the cheering of the multitude. Nice people thought she was vulgar; nice ladies did not stride. Nelly's voice boomed. Gentlemen of the 'nineties did not like ladies with booming voices. They asked Nelly what she was going to do, and she said:

"I'm going to complete my journey. I'm going to make the complete circle of the world in *less* than eighty days. And then I'm going to Paris, and I'm going to call on Jules Verne. And I'm going to say to him, 'Mr. Verne, you wrote a wonderful book about a trip around the world in eighty days. Well, I've been around the world in seventy-five days, and I prophesy that in a hundred years from now we'll be going around the world, not in seventy-five days, but in forty days.' That's what I'm going to tell Mr. Verne, even if he thinks I'm crazy. And if he does not like what I have to say, he can go way back and sit down."

That was the beginning of the gay and hectic 'nineties! The days when nice ladies didn't go trotting around the world at breakneck speed, but diligently applied themselves to the making of leather sofa-cushions with designs burned on them, and apropos mottoes; for example, a leather-covered cushion might be stuffed with balsam and pine, in which case the inscription would surely read, "I bawl-some and pine for you."

The humor of the 'nineties was amazing!

The popular phrase became The Gay 'Nineties. A famous author called it The Mauve Decade. Others called it The Hectic 'Nineties. I prefer my mother's words; she called it The Dusty 'Nineties. Our home, like most San Francisco homes, was furnished with every dust-catcher ever conceived by man. Our favorite was, of course, the curtain of eucalyptus acorns, characteristic of San Francisco, or the curtain of large glass beads or small sea shells that separated room from room. Because we were a city built on the sea, with fishing boats and fishermen, a popular expression of the designer's art was a fish net draped in the corner of a room, with champagne corks and playing cards pinned to it; dust found a happy home in the fish nets. Then, in my own room in the attic, I had a nice, grimy corner called The Turkish Alcove. I had crossed drapes hanging above a divan and full of dust; the drapes were caught together with crossed Turkish swords, and on an ivory-inlaid tabouret I had a Turkish water pipe that I smoked once, and only once.

In the basement of the four-story house papa had his workshop. His equipment consisted of a scroll saw that worked with a foot pedal like the old-time sewing machines. Papa was a past master of the scroll-saw art. He made fascinating cabinets and boxes and even a carved table that was a mass of intricate scroll-saw design, and so full of corners and crannies that dust simply moved in and took over as though it had been planned for it. For years the house was littered with scroll-saw objects of art, but the only practical thing papa made was an inlaid chess board. He never learned to play chess.

Returning to my lair or den, I had college pennants on the wall and a pin-up of Lillian Russell and another of Della Fox; on a shelf I had a South Sea skull full of tobacco, and a bulldog pipe; that was at the beginning of the tradition of the "rah rah" boy. The pennants, incidentally, were of the University of California and Stanford University, and in a glass-covered picture frame was a newspaper clipping stating that the University of California at Berkeley would meet students of the new Stanford University at Palo Alto in a football match at Haight and Stanyan streets. That was the first Big Game.

The manager of the Stanford squad was a young student named Herbert Hoover. The teams gathered at the Palace Hotel for a pre-game lunch. Coaches drawn by six horses each carried the rival teams the seven or eight miles from the hotel to the Haight and Stanyan Street sand dunes. A huge crowd was gathered, at least twelve thousand. The excitement was tense. The moustached teams trotted out onto the playing field in their overpadded suits, and the crowd became hectic. The teams lined up. And then it was discovered that, in the pre-game excitement the vice-president-in-charge, or whoever was responsible for such duties, had forgotten to provide a football. A man volunteered, mounted one of the horses that had drawn one of the stagecoaches, and started the long journey downtown to find a football or a sporting-goods house that would provide one. The crowd sat and waited for two hours. Then the intrepid horseman reappeared, an inflated football under his arm, and the game went on. I forget who won.

To return to our house: next to the bathroom on the third floor, with its shining red granite or red marble washstand always supplied with a dish containing a cake of Pear's Soap, was the sewing room, where, year after year, stood my mother's dress form. It was a wire contraption, built to my mother's figure. Each season the dressmaker came in and made a dress of a different material according to the fashion of the season, but always on the same line, the same figure, the same style, varying only to make allowance for the increasing plumpness that was the fruit of passing years.

Then, in 1893, we had a new innovation in the house. On January 10, 1893, the *Chronicle* stated, "The United States Congress demands government assume protectorate of Hawaiian Islands." A few days later, on February 1, the startling announcement appeared, "Stars and Stripes fly over Capitol building in Honolulu." That was the inspiration for the new vogue. No wall decoration was complete without a dust-catching grass skirt. This led to a certain confusion, for on January 1, 1894, the Midwinter Fair was opened in Golden Gate Park, and the most sensational, if not the most popular single feature of the Fair was Little Egypt and the hootchy-kootchy dancers of the Streets of Cairo. People confused the hootchy-kootchy and the hula hula, and the resulting terpsichorean efforts were neither convincing nor attractive. Meanwhile, on January 29, 1894, the *Chronicle* announced, "The first exhibition of electrical illumination in the West was seen when the great tower of the central court of the Midwinter Fair was festooned with amazing electric lights." Next to that announcement was this advertisement: "Get your cigarette picture of Lottie Gilman with your next package of Sweet Caporal Cigarettes."

An advertisement in an issue of July 1896 intrigues me: "Davis, Haber and Company, auctioneers and commission merchants offer, at auction, a consignment of moustache cups, German Beer Steins, paintings by foremost German painters, and ten thousand Panama hats from Haiti." I have reason to remember, in particular, the "paintings by foremost German artists," because we acquired six of them. They were very large: pastoral scenes of cows grazing in pastures, they were framed in very heavy, deeply carved gold frames, and they hung on the walls of our living room throughout my youth, masterpieces that nobody wanted, masterpieces large enough to fill the walls of an art gallery, and completely overpowering in our modest living room. Three of them still repose, wrapped in newspapers in my basement, awaiting the amazement of future generations. We also acquired a music box; a long, oblong, coffin-like affair with a long steel cylinder that revolved; the cylinder was covered with tiny pinlike steel points that did something or other resulting in "Sweet Rosie O'Grady," "My Gal's a Coal Black Lady," "Elsie from Chelsea," and a song popular at the time of which I have never been able to find a copy; the lyrics ran, "Sweet Tillie Taylor, she loved a sailor."

Turning to the newspaper of March 12, 1895, there is this naïve headline: "Dudes paralyzed by bloomers as ladies ride bicycles in the park." Now that revives a pertinent memory.

634

There was a lady, every inch a lady, but a lady with ideas fifty years ahead of her time, who lived in the corner room of the second floor of the Palace Hotel; this was in the quite late 'nineties. She was my grandmother's chum, and my grandmother looked like, was built like, and to an ineffective degree thought like Queen Victoria. Grandma would, with a tsk tsk of her false teeth, take me to visit the lady; I was fed macaroons and tiny silver-coated mints from Italy. And the lady, who also looked like Queen Victoria, but did not think at all like her, would sit in her window, in plain view of Market Street, sit there hour upon hour, a small table at her hand, on the table a large soup plate, and the plate heaped with a pyramid of cigarette ashes; she chain-smoked cigarettes throughout the day in plain view of passers-by; crowds would gather at the corner of Market and New Montgomery streets to see a lady smoking.

The lady had a daughter, a very pretty daughter, even less Victorian in behavior than her mother. Daughter rode a bicycle, rode it clad in bloomers, and one day she rode down Market Street with her feet on the handle bars, showing her legs up to her knees, and wheeled right on into the Palm Court of the Palace Hotel. The police were called, and they put an end to the shocking exhibition. It was a scandal of major proportion in a city that dearly loved a healthy scandal.

The truth is, the city was becoming worried about bicycles; they were a traffic hazard, and they made life difficult for pedestrians. Then, to cap the climax, in April of 1899 the newspaper announced, "Perils of Market Street Pedestrians! Constant Danger! The Octopus has too many tracks! Menace increases!" That bit of yellow-journal melodrama had been inspired by the fact that four car-tracks had been laid on Market Street and the hazard was terrible, to say nothing of the fact that the din made by the bells of the horse-cars was deafening. In contrast to the turmoil appears this genteel advertisement: "William Carr, Parisian artist, will instruct refined ladies in the fine art of painting on china."

Meanwhile, San Francisco had built a great reputation as a theater town; for almost fifty years every great star, every great singer, every great virtuoso who played New York, wanted to play, and played, San Francisco. The 1890's were the heyday of the theater in San Francisco; more houses played to larger audiences, offering more varied bills than any time before or since. Here, then, is the list offered in the Sunday paper of May 16, 1897: Daniel Frawley in *The Fatal Card*; Joseph Cawthorne in *Excelsior Jr.*; Denis O'Sullivan in *Shamus O'Brien* at the Tivoli; *East Lynne* at Morosco's Grand Opera House; Nat Goodwin and Maxine Elliott at the Baldwin in *The Rivals*; *The First Born* at the Alcazar; and "The World's Greatest Vaudeville" at the Orpheum.

Seven productions to choose from every night; that was San Francisco in 1897. That was the year, I believe, that my father took my mother to see Olga Nethersole in a play about which there had been much whispering. All I knew about it in my immaturity was that in one scene a gentleman carried a lady up a flight of stairs. The play was *Sapho*. The city was scandalized and it was months before my mother forgave my father for subjecting her to such a disgraceful experience. However, my father was never one to learn. The following week he took her to the Alcazar. The play was *Zaza*. The star was Mrs. Leslie Carter. Now, you could not possibly know the plot of *Zaza* today, nor, for that matter, do I. But I do know there is one scene played in a basement saloon in Paris in which all the characters become drunk. At any rate, Mrs. Carter, with an eye for realism, succeeded in getting all the cast including herself royally intoxicated before the performance started; the result was a raid by the police during the first act; Mrs. Carter and the cast were taken to jail, and my mother never did learn what wickedness she missed that night.

As for fashions that year of 1897, the newest vogue in fashionable gentlemen's neckwear was high, white or colored stocks that took the place of collar and tie. They were suffocating affairs, but more comfortable than the stand-up collars averaging four inches in height. That was 1897, the year that the San Francisco Board of Supervisors voted that every hotel lobby and every hotel room must be equipped with cuspidors.

That, still on the subject of fashion, was the period of the white and gold parlor. We had one; I was admitted to it only on the second and fourth Thursday in each month; that was mama's day-at-home, and I was brought in during the afternoon in a Lord Fauntleroy suit to say how do you do and I am very well, thank you, and to be given a ladyfinger and a glass of lemonade. The white and gold parlor was all done in Louis Fourteenth white and gold furniture; there was a white and gold cabinet filled with filigree silver miniatures, carved ivory treasures from China, and inevitably a mother-of-pearl and lace fan; there was, too, a silver snuffbox filled with miniature candies. Our white and gold parlor was of particular distinction because it was one of the first rooms in San Francisco to be lighted with Welsbach gas mantles.

That was 1897, but surely 1898 was the great year of the 'nineties; the newspapers were happy in a plethora of sensational headlines.

On April 2, 1898, the paper announced, "Gold is discovered in great quantity in the Klondike. Thousands of San Franciscans fighting for passage to the Yukon."

Market Street stores advertised miners' boots, picks, pans, red-flannel shirts, and chewing tobacco. The streets of San Francisco were like a Hollywood movie set: the sidewalks milled with every type and order of humanity, pushing, shoving, and dressed in what they presumed to be suitable garb for ice-bound gold fields, as odd an assortment as frenzied imaginations could conceive.

But overnight the prospector's and miner's garb gave way to a new order of dress; the headlines announced: "The United States warns Spain."

Then, "The battleship Maine is blown up."

"United States warships sail for the Philippines."

"The battleship Oregon, built on San Francisco Bay, is rushed to southern waters, putting in at Rio de Janeiro."

April 22, 1898, "The first gun of the war with Spain is fired."

May 1, 1898, "Admiral George Dewey attacks and captures the Spanish fleet in Manila Bay." Dewey is a hero, Admiral Schley is a hero, Admiral Sampson is a hero, Hobson is a hero kissing all the girls.

And out of the Presidio and down Clay Street to the Embarcadero marched the California regiment and soldiers from every other state; and girls lined the sidewalks cheering and crying and the marching men sang the song that became a San Francisco tradition, the song San Francisco claimed as its own, "There'll Be a Hot Time in the Old Town Tonight!"

Five days after the battle of Manila, ten thousand spectators crowded a San Francisco arena to see James J. Jeffries, the Pride of Los Angeles, meet Tom Sharkey, the Pride of the Navy, in a twenty-round fight. At the height of the battle

638

the grandstand collapsed, endangering the lives of thousands. Jeffries won the fight on a technical knockout and kept the world's heavyweight championship.

And on June 10, 1898, self-respecting citizens of San Francisco held a mass meeting to protest against the nefarious practice on shanghaiing sailors and civilians for service on Alaska-bound steamers.

But the headlines of the year 1898 were not ended. July 1898, the California Boys landed in the Philippines, and in August 1898, Colonel McKittrick raised the Stars and Stripes at Santiago, Cuba. Then McKittrick and General Shafter returned with the California Boys, marched out Clay Street to the Presidio, and went ranching in Kern County, where they made the first major oil strike in California.

In November, the horse-drawn fire engines went clanging and plunging through the streets of San Francisco to fight the most disastrous fire the city had known since the 'fifties. The Baldwin Theater, built by Lucky Baldwin for David Belasco, burned to the ground with, according to newspaper accounts, the loss of hundreds of lives. The following Sunday morning a minister of the gospel stood in his pulpit and shook his fist at the congregation and cried out, "You are a people of evil inconsistencies. The loss of a traditional landmark means more to you than the loss of human life; human life is sacred, the theater is a place of evil."

That was 1898. The year 1899 was prophetic, a year that was the herald of things to come. On Van Ness Avenue the first horseless carriage panted down the street, and the crowds booed and laughed, while horses ran away. At the Mechanics Institute Fair the first motion picture was exhibited, and the crowds laughed and booed and wouldn't believe it.

In the Western Addition, out on Pacific Heights, the first

installation of home electric lights was made. Downtown, on Montgomery Street, an insurance firm hired a woman stenographer; she was discharged after a short tenure because she, like all women, was not strong enough to manipulate the letter press. And in the Palm Court of the Palace Hotel the guests were shocked at the sight of a lady, at least a woman who called herself a lady, wearing a hobble skirt, with its hem six inches off the ground.

The Gay 'Nineties! The Mauve Decade! The Purple 'Nineties! The Hectic 'Nineties! The Dusty 'Nineties! The end of the Victorian Era! The years when gentlemen blustered, and ladies were gentle and artificial to a fault, and the sanctimonious had a Roman holiday rolling scandal around their tongue. Perhaps it was the new-fangled electric light that made the artificial pettiness glare; maybe it was the fume-belching horseless carriage that took the city, and the world, out of the sequestered shades of dark-hallwayed homes into the full glare of normal sunshine. Perhaps it was the boredom of Victorian traditions and Victorian amenities! But it was on January 1, 1900, that San Francisco became a city.

Yet, looking back at that picture developed from a faint negative, it is pleasant to be sentimental about it: to remember the days when handle-bar mustaches draped over lips that crooned "Silver Threads Among the Gold" and "Listen to the Mocking Bird"; to remember the dear ladies who had nothing to do but paint dinky little violets and marguerites on porcelain. After all, the housewife of reasonable means could not have much else to do, at least about the house. A cook, who would do the upstairs work and take care of the children and mend the family clothes and do the laundry by hand, was paid fifteen dollars a month in San Francisco. It is pleasant to remember the fathers of families who, with their chests out and their shoulders well padded, walked with their progeny along Van Ness Avenue enjoying the Sunday morning promenade, walked wearing their frock coats and silk top hats, and swinging their malacca sticks. It is even pleasant to remember the wicked fathers of families, and their numbers were legion, who sought entertainment in a *cabinet particulier* of the Poodle Dog or out at the Trocadero; pleasant to remember the docile wives who joined Browning Societies, and were at home on the second and fourth Thursday of each month; pleasant to remember the pungent odor of the dust-catching eucalyptus drapes, and later the heavy drapes that became the vogue; they were made of red or green velvet with appliqued leaves of gold cloth; pleasant to remember the fashionable evenings at home when the room that later was to be called "the rumpus room" had sand sprinkled on the floor, the liquid refreshment was beer drawn from eight-gallon barrels and served in German steins, the food was a mouth-watering array of delicatessen from Grossman's on Fillmore Street, and the guests played euchre; pleasant to remember the Regina Music Box tinkling "Chimes of Normandy"; pleasant to remember the rattling wagon and the street cry of the merchant, "Any rags, any bottles, any sacks today?"

Yes, it's all very pleasant to remember, for those were the dear, hectic, dusty 'nineties.

X

Oliver Morosco

It is a futile thing to try to crowd into a dozen pages the story of the life of a man, any man. The least important of the men who wandered the streets of San Francisco yesterday, or today for that matter, surely has had enough of adventure and tragedy and romance in his life for a shelf of stout books. I am frankly faced with such futility now, for this cannot be the story but rather a dim mirror held to the life of a man who played a leading role in the glamorous days of San Francisco.

His family name was Mitchell, but no one knew him by that name; he found a foster father when he was a small boy, and his foster father's name became his. He lived the life of a poor boy in San Francisco; then he achieved triumphs and fortune; he lost fortunes and made others; he was swept like the tides of the ocean, lifting to great heights and plunging to great depths, then lifting and plunging again. He was a dramatic figure, melodramatic for that matter, but then I have always liked melodrama, that is if it was of the old school and was presented behind the footlights.

I was seven or eight years old when I first began trotting downtown Saturday afternoons, all the way from Scott and Jackson streets to Mission Street near Third, to the Morosco

Grand Opera House. I walked the long distance because my weekly allowance would just about pay my admission to the "top heaven." It was a wonderful old theater, and there is nothing like in it the West today; I doubt if a theater like it can be found any place. It was dark and rather somber, with a musty odor, born no doubt of age, but to me it was the odor of theater and the footlights. It had many balconies; there must have been at least six or seven balconies and galleries up to the top heaven, where admission was twenty-five cents. From that dramatic vantage point, miles, it seemed to me, above the heads of the stylish carriage-trade audience in the orchestra pit, I saw *The Two Orphans*, and *Thelma*, and *Bertha, the Sewing Machine Girl*, and *Shore Acres*, and *East Lynne*, and *May Blossom*, and *The Old Homestead*, and *The Cherry Pickers*, and countless others, and it was from there, on the night of April 17, 1906, that I heard Caruso sing Don José in *Carmen*.

That, in fact, was the last night of the Grand Opera House, or Morosco's Grand Opera House, on Mission Street near Third, the night of the earthquake that terminated in THE FIRE.

Much later, seeing the silent movie *The Phantom of the Opera*, all I could think of was the ghosts that haunted that block on Mission Street, back to the days when James O'Neill, the father of Eugene O'Neill, was arrested with his cast during the production of the *Passion Play*; the days when Emma Calvé sang there, and Adelina Patti, too, although she refused to appear until the management had paid the huge fee she demanded; the days of Melba and Sembrich and Scotti and Nordica and De Reszke; the days when it was Tom Maguire's Grand Opera House, and Tom Maguire was starving; the days when Sigmund and Charles Ackerman were

643

the managing proprietors, and in their office was one of the finest theatrical libraries in all the world—David Garrick prompt books and other priceless treasures—all crumbled to ashes in that holocaust of 1906.

But best of all were the ghosts of the old melodramas, *Shore Acres*, *The Two Orphans*, and the others of the days when it was Morosco's Grand Opera House. That name was given to it, not by Oliver Morosco, but by his foster father, Walter Morosco.

Oliver Morosco was born in 1875 in Logan, Utah. When he was still an infant, his mother, Esmah Mitchell, separated from her husband, Sir John Leslie Mitchell, and moved to California with her sons, Oliver and Leslie, junior. There was a brief interlude in Bakersfield, where Esmah married a railroad engineer. His name, I believe, was Joe St. Mary. A child was born to them in Bakersfield. Esmah's husband is of little importance in the story, and I have no idea what happened to him. There is some record of Esmah Mitchell St. Mary having purchased and operated a hotel in Bakersfield, but the story of young Oliver comes into clearer perspective when he was about five years old, and the family, in modest if not straitened circumstances, moved to San Francisco.

They found quarters in a low-priced house called the Turk Street Hotel. Downtown Turk Street was the playground of Oliver and Leslie. Directly across the street from the hotel, in about 1880 or 1881, there was one of the many German basement beer halls and restaurants, so popular then and later: the German Grotto. The Grotto was to pay an important role in the shaping of the life of Oliver Morosco.

An iron rail enclosed the steps leading down to the basement café. One day one of the boys swung on the crossbar of the railing, hanging from his knees, then whirled his small body around it as on a trapeze bar. It was quite a performance, put on for their own amazement, but it had possibilities. Day after day the two boys practiced on their iron railing when the street was empty, and finally their act was ready for popular acclaim. When a reasonable number of passers-by had stopped to watch, Leslie performed his tour de force, swinging around the bar twenty times without stopping. The crowd applauded, and Oliver, aged six, stepped out onto the sidewalk and passed his cap. The result was a net take of forty-five cents, not bad business for the nine-year-old Leslie and the six-year-old Oliver. Every day thereafter, at high noon, they appeared on the rail in front of the German Grotto and did their act. Oliver collected the purse, while Leslie swung on the bar.

This might have gone on indefinitely, and led to fame and fortune, if Mrs. Esmah Mitchell St. Mary, all unaware of the business enterprise of her two sons, had not decided that the streets of San Francisco were no place for them to run wild. She enrolled them in the historic old Lincoln Grammar School on Fifth Street, between Mission and Market.

There was one great advantage in being enrolled in Lincoln Grammar School; it was situated only a short distance from the most glamorous, the most exciting place in all the exciting city of San Francisco: Woodward's Gardens on Valencia Street at Fourteenth. Right in the heart of the famous gardens there was a huge canvas pavilion, and from it flew banners proclaiming Walter Morosco's Royal Russian Circus. Back of the circus and the skating rink there was a rehearsal room where the stars of the Russian Circus practiced their tumbling and acrobatic feats. There, when the place was otherwise empty, Leslie and Oliver practiced their

645

tricks and became acrobats. Then their great chance came; they were offered a billing with the Star Minstrel Company. They earned all of two dollars and fifty cents a week; two dollars went to their mother, the fifty cents was their spending money. But the money didn't matter, the important thing was that they were in show business.

Then, just as suddenly as it had commenced, their show career ended; things were bad at home. So Oliver went into business. His inspiration was the rags-bottle-sacks man with his plaintive street cry, a familiar figure in the streets of San Francisco. Begging old rags from door to door, retrieving discarded sacks from the city dump, Oliver accumulated a stock in trade and sold it to the rags-bottle-sacks man for eighty cents.

His next step had the earmark of business wizardry. With his eighty cents he went to a manufacturer of matches, and bought ten dollars worth of matches, paying eighty cents deposit, the balance to be paid when he had sold his stock. He carried them home and wrapped them up in bundles of fifty which he sold on the streets for a penny a bundle. When his stock was gone he found that he had a profit of more than six dollars. But it was bitter, hard labor, and it lacked the fascination of show business. That was where Walter Morosco came into the picture.

Walter Morosco was, as I have said, the proprietor of Morosco's Royal Russian Circus in Woodward's Gardens. He discovered the two boy acrobats at practice, liked the youngsters, and offered them jobs as tumblers in the circus. One night he called at the Mitchell home. He told Esmah Mitchell that he planned a future for her boys, and offered to make an important place for them in his show. They would travel around the world with him; he would make

646

them famous; and, what was more important, he would not only raise them as his own sons but would pave the way for them by giving them his own name. They would be the young Moroscos.

Of course there might have been some question as to whether it was more important to be the sons of Morosco, the circus man, or of the British titled gentleman, Sir John Leslie Mitchell. But with the best interests of her boys at heart, Esmah agreed, and they became Oliver and Leslie Morosco, juvenile tumblers at Woodward's Gardens.

It all began under the most glowing of rosy hues, but it ended in grief when Oliver refused to do a triple somersault and quit, not only his job, but Walter Morosco, too, for the time being. Once again he walked the streets of San Francisco hunting work. He found employment washing crockery in the establishment of the Great American Tea Importing Company. Then he became a messenger for Western Union.

Finally Walter Morosco sought him again. He had a new enterprise, managing a theater on Howard Street, over the carbarn. It was called the Amphitheatre, and was a house of glorified melodrama. The repertoire company played *Ten Thousand Leagues Under the Sea*, played *Monte Cristo*, and played a melodrama that made a lasting impression on me: *Michael Strogoff*, the terrible story of the blind man. Now, to his San Francisco enterprise, Morosco added the Auditorium in San Jose, and Oliver, still in his teens, was made manager of the two houses at the munificent salary of fifty dollars a week. That was wealth beyond his most optimistic dreams, wealth and success.

Meanwhile Walter Morosco established himself in a beautiful home across the bay in Fruitvale, and it was there I

647

first became aware of the Moroscos as a family rather than as a name in the theater. Fruitvale became the home of the two boys, and Oliver entered the Fruitvale Grammar School in 1891, that same school from which I graduated only a dozen years later.

I remember my thrill when Miss Scheuk, our principal and English teacher, told us that Oliver Morosco had been a pupil in that very room. That, and the associations of the name and the melodramas of Morosco's Grand Opera House on Mission Street, brought me into the world of the gods. Morosco's Grand Opera House had known vicissitude and triumphs for many years but none of its triumphs, not even the golden days of the Grau and Conreid Grand Opera, compared in my youthful mind with the melodramas of Morosco.

The very odor of the place was rich with drama. From the ceiling of the auditorium hung a great crystal chandelier, twenty or more feet in diameter. The great lobby was, according to some accounts, one hundred feet wide; above the lobby was a great promenade and a resplendent restaurant and bar. The stage was huge, and lighted with the latest innovations in gaslight. The plays ranged from Dion Boucicault to Shakespeare, and from *Richelieu* to *Hazel Kirke*. Somewhere I have read that there have been more performances of *Hazel Kirke* in San Francisco than of any other play, but that's beside the point. The important thing was that now Oliver Morosco was a theater man, marked for the rest of his life with grease paint and words that were spoken trippingly on the tongue.

There was, however, one fly in the ointment. Oliver was young, and in the springtime of life—well, anyway, Oliver fell in love. His foster father, Walter, disappointed in love in *his* youth, did everything he could to break up the affair.

648

He pleaded, shouted, stormed, and finally there was a bitter fight, another split in their friendship. Oliver Morosco married the girl. This, however, is not to be the story of Oliver and Annie Morosco, with its pattern of gay young love and tragedy in the end. Oliver, separated from Walter Morosco, went out to harvest new fields, and the only ones he knew were the aisles of the theater. So, in 1899, he traveled to the small, sleepy, pleasant village of Los Angeles. People said he was mad, Walter Morosco said he was mad. There was no future in Los Angeles. It could never be a show town; in fact it could never grow to be a city.

That was 1899. Los Angeles, in all fairness, was only a good-sized village in 1899, the kind of California village that might some day grow to be a very pleasant little place. When Lucky Baldwin put an absurdly high price on his land down there, he said that he was not selling land, he was selling climate. But it did have potential possibilities, it was the kind of village young men liked to go to, a frontier town, so to speak, where pleasant little fortunes could be made. So Oliver Morosco went to Los Angeles, and by cutting every corner and by pawning everything but his histrionic soul he opened a theater.

It was an imposing theater, a fine theater, the first good theater in Los Angeles. It had been called The Burbank and it had gone through failure after failure; it was called a jinx house, a haunted house. It was dilapidated, the oak seats were stained and dirty, the red drapes were filthy and hideous. Morosco agreed to lease the house and open with the best of legitimate plays, if the owner would stain the seats mahogany; for his part, Morosco would buy new green drapes and green carpets.

The house opened on September 3, 1899. The advance

publicity announced the presentation of Daniel Frawley in *Madame Sans-Gêne*. Every seat was sold. There was an ovation at the end of the first act, for Frawley, for the leading lady, for the play, and for the progressive young man who had opened the house.

At the final curtain the enthusiastic audience milled up the aisles and into the foyer, and Morosco, hiding in the box office, watching his patrons walk out, faced a horrible situation, a grim spectacle. It had been a stylish audience, stylishly gowned, and every lady of fashion paraded past the box office with the seat of her gown stained red mahogany. The owner of the house had used red paint instead of mahogany stain, and had not given it a chance to dry.

Of course it was very funny, under other circumstances it might have been high comedy, but Morosco faced disaster. He was penniless, his whole future in the balance. What if all the ladies with mahogany-stained *derrières* sued him? But he had been capable of opening a theater when he had only a few hundred dollars; he had to be capable of meeting this new dilemma.

He met it. He went to a dyeing and cleaning establishment on Fifth Street, and convinced the proprietor that here was a way for him to acquire a fine new clientele. He would send every complaining lady to him, and guarantee to them that their dresses would be returned to them as good as new. The proprietor of the cleaning establishment, in return for all the new patronage, was to give Morosco unlimited credit and sufficient time to pay every bill. Meanwhile, all the seats in the theater would be covered with white cloth; white cloth in hot Los Angeles would be cool and inviting.

The proprietor agreed, the complaining ladies came and were assured that their garments would be returned to them in perfect condition. They were satisfied. They went again to the theater, now dressed in its seats of cool white cloth, and they liked it. The house immediately became a success. In the first ten weeks, Morosco had made close to ten thousand dollars net profit for himself.

That was the real beginning of the career of Oliver Morosco, born Oliver Mitchell, son of Esmah and Sir John Leslie Mitchell; Oliver Morosco, who was responsible for the discovery and early successes of Charlotte Greenwood, Leo Carrillo, Charles Ruggles, Lewis Stone, Warner Baxter, Eddie Cantor, and countless others.

Those Los Angeles days, with all their success, were days of grim enough melodrama; Morosco had come to Los Angeles with his few dollars in his pocket, his young and not very happy wife, and the baby who squalled through the long nights when he was trying to figure ways and means to start his enterprise and to maintain it after it was well started. But with the tragicomedy of the mahogany-stained ladies, and all the rest, it was the real beginning of the career of the San Francisco boy who was to stand shoulder to shoulder with the Schuberts, the Frohmans, and David Belasco as one of the great discoverers and builders of the men and women who traveled to fame behind the footlights of the American stage.

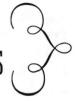

PART THREE

DREAMERS AND REALISTS

XI

Jack London

He was born in San Francisco. He knew the streets of San Francisco and the streets of San Francisco knew him well. But he no more belonged to San Francisco than to Samarkand. He was Jack London of the restless feet.

I remember, with sentimental and nostalgic memory, the days when Miss Scheuk, our English teacher at the Fruitvale Grammar School, told us of the stuff that went into the making of London as a writer. When we wrote a poor composition she would say, "*He* wouldn't have been satisfied with that." When we stared at blank pages she would say, "*He* found inspiration in everything." When we wrote and were pleased with what we had written, she would say, "*He* was never satisfied with anything he wrote." He became something of a god to us, a god to be venerated, and to be hated, too, because he was held up to us as an example of everything we were not and should aspire to be. We thought of him as a legend, but Miss Scheuk said, "No, when he was here in

Fruitvale Grammar School he was anything but a legend; he was a tough reality." Finally, I met him.

The meeting was one of those rare perfect hours that can happen in the life of a boy and stay with him all his life. I had played hookey from school and hiked to the yacht club on the north bank of the Oakland Estuary; on week days the yachting members were few, and I could climb into one of the small boats moored there and lie on my stomach and look at the ships. So I lay on my stomach and looked at the ships, and a voice said, "If you look hard enough you can see all the way to China."

I rolled over on my back and sat up. There he was, a chunky, small, laughing-faced man with laughing eyes and a mass of brown curly hair. He said, "What's your name, Skipper?" I told him and asked, "What's your name?" And he said, "Jack London."

It was a wonderful beautiful day for a boy of eleven. He sat down and told me how to see all the way to China, and of things he had seen in the Orient and up the Klondike. I went home, my head in the clouds.

I met him again two or three years later, when I was playing football on the scrub team of the Oakland High School. It was the day before our annual Big Game, the game between Oakland High and Berkeley High. The student body had assembled for the football rally in a room almost on a level with the lawns on East Tenth Street. Our principal, Jimmie Pond, announced that the speaker would be a former Oakland High School boy, Jack London. We cheered, and Jack stood up and grinned.

"Boys," he said, "you must not take too seriously the lot of nonsense the school teachers hand out to you. They don't believe half of it themselves, but they're paid to say it. It's the system and they can't fight it."

At this point, Jimmie Pond interrupted. He said, "That's very interesting, Jack. And now, boys, let's escort Mr. London to the lawn."

He looked at the window as he spoke, and we, the members of the scrub football team, jumped to our feet, picked Jack London up, and threw him out the window.

London was born in San Francisco on January 12, 1876, the illegitimate son of Flora Wellman and Professor W. H. Chaney, a traveling lecturer with a forceful, strong intelligence. Deserted by Chaney, Flora married John London when the child was eight months old, and London proved himself a good husband and a kind foster father to little Jack.

The family was very poor. Jack's early childhood was spent on various farms, with little of ordinary companionship, guidance, or education. He taught himself to read and was reading adult novels when he was eight. The family drifted around the San Francisco Bay area, and eventually found a home in Oakland. Jack was ten years old. He delivered newspapers during the week, and on week ends he set pins in a waterfront bowling alley. He wandered into the Oakland Public Library, and found that the librarian was interested in seeing that he got books to read, any books, an endless succession of books. She was Ina Coolbrith, later to be poet laureate of California by an act of the legislature.

Jack's foster father was an invalid and money was badly needed. Jack found work in a cannery, working up to sixteen hours a day, often at ten cents an hour. It was bitter training, and the seed of socialism was planted in him. He wandered at night along the Estuary and the waterfront, and there was born a love of the sea that would never leave him.

654

He managed to save six dollars, and bought a small, unseaworthy skiff.

Into the Estuary in the end of the 'eighties and the beginning 'nineties came sailing ships from all over the world: spice ships, whaling ships, ships manned by men of all nations and all kinds, good men and evil. They milled along the waterfront: common seamen, stevedores, opium smugglers, and the oyster pirates who plied their trade from the mud flats of the East Bay down to the hatcheries below the San Mateo shore line.

Among the varied crew, Jack London made strange friends. There was French Frank, Whiskey Bob, Spider, Big George, Nicky the Greek, men who scorned the life of the white-collar weaklings in the city and told the boy tall tales of the glory of the smuggler's life. An oyster pirate who owned his own boat made as much as two hundred dollars a night, a pirate's helper made twenty-five. Jack London, who had known hunger, and had worked for ten cents an hour, saw a world of easy wealth opening before him; not only wealth, but adventure, too, and the excitement of danger.

One day French Frank said he was willing to sell his boat, the *Razzle Dazzle*, for three hundred dollars. To own the craft became the most important thing in Jack's life, but three hundred dollars was as remote for the fifteen-year-old boy as thirty thousand, unless—yes, there was one source always to be depended on. His old Negro nurse, Mammy Jennie, would give him anything she had, and Mammy usually had a stocking pretty well filled with gold.

He went to Mammy Jennie, and the next day the *Razzle Dazzle* was his. In a few weeks he became an adept oyster pirate. Time and again his craft was boarded by revenue officers; brazenly he treated them to raw oysters and beer, and won them with his irrepressible personality and his chatter; and time and again the officers left the *Razzle Dazzle* without imposing on him the penalties reserved for older and more hardened men in the traffic. In a reasonably short time Jack returned the money borrowed from Mammy Jennie, and relieved the want of his parents without revealing to them the source of his wealth.

He was a successful racketeer, and at the same time he was spending hours at the desk of Ina Coolbrith in the library. He was also studying with his good friends, the padres and brothers of the parochial school down the Peninsula in Belmont; he was their pupil. They recognized in him the potential stuff of a writer; they liked him, encouraged him, trained him, and doubtless were never aware that he stole out of the school window at night to ply his pirate trade. Nor, with all their faith in him, could they have foreseen that his writings would earn him, throughout his life, over a million dollars.

Meanwhile his success as a pirate had antagonized his erstwhile friends. French Frank became an enemy, and Jack's right-hand man and crew, Spider, deserted the *Razzle Dazzle* one night; then French Frank and his gang boarded, scuttled, and sank her.

London went to another friend, Johnny Heinhold, owner of the First and Last Chance Saloon, borrowed money from him, and bought a half interest in the craft *Reindeer* from its owner, young Scratch Nelson. The two boys, joining forces, returned to the oyster beds and prosperity. Then one night they were boarded by a state officer. He could understand their love of adventure and excitement, so he offered to show them how they could find as much excitement and adventure within the law. He induced them to join the fish patrol as

656

guardians instead of enemies of the law; their monetary reward would be one half of the fines collected. For almost a year, Jack London was an officer of the law, still in his middle teens.

Out of such a background came the genius who was to be acclaimed in the Sorbonne as the "Dante of America," the genius called by Imperial Russia the most vital writer of the end of the nineteenth century. By some strange alchemy was born the poet and dreamer who wrote, in his closing days: "I retain my belief in the nobility and excellence of the human. I believe that spiritual sweetness and unselfishness will conquer the gross gluttony of today."

At the end of Jack London's term as an officer of the law, his restless urge sent him to the high seas on a cruise that was later to be the inspiration for perhaps his most sensational novel, *The Sea Wolf*. He signed on as an able-bodied seaman on the *Sophie Sutherland*, a sealer, which hunted all the way from the shores of Japan to the Aleutians. He knew nothing of the duties of an able-bodied seaman, knew only that the pay was more than that of a sailor, so he became an able-bodied seaman. He was seventeen years old, a cub, and the older men resented his rating. The resentment quickly changed to respect when, having given the youngster a bad time when the sea was calm, they saw him stand his trick at the wheel during a hurricane.

They made the Bonin Islands, and during the ten days that the schooner lay at anchor, Jack London met whalers and traders and other characters of the far Pacific who stored his brain with stories that would emerge long later as prose masterpieces.

They sailed out of the Bonins, and headed north toward

the coast of Siberia. It was London's job to row the seal-hunters out from the schooner in pursuit of a herd of seal and back at the end of each hunt, then to skin the seals, salt the precious pelts, and toss the carcasses to the sharks that darted alongside. It was a life to harden, to brutalize a man, to make him forget his dreams. London, plunging from adventure to adventure, had his goal before him always: he would be a writer of books, and his books would be made of his dreams.

When the cruise ended, Jack London sailed back through the Golden Gate, passed Old Fort Point and the wooden docks that skirted the old small Ferry Building, and wandered into the streets of San Francisco. It was 1893. The nation had just gone through a severe financial panic. In the aftermath was a great army of unemployed; there was hunger and fear; and desperate men begging for work would take any job for a pittance. Jack London went to his home, poured into his parents' laps the money he had earned on the cruise, and went hunting a job. He found one in a jute mill, at ten cents an hour. In the hours between hard labor he wrote a story of that typhoon off the coast of Japan. He entered the story in a contest sponsored by the San Francisco *Call*, and won first prize.

The second and third prizes went to university students at California and Stanford. That made him take stock. He had no formal education, and yet he had won a literary contest over university students. Then, surely, he could go far with education; that should be his next adventure. He would go to college.

But first there was the business of suffering, hungry humanity. General Coxey was marching on Washington, demanding work for the unemployed, and in Oakland, General

Kelly had organized a unit to join Coxey. So Jack London traveled out of Oakland on a freight train, to catch up with Kelly's army. Bumming his way, sometimes begging, sometimes working for food, he eventually caught up with the Kelly contingent, but he never reached Washington. He left the army in Illinois, and rode the rails to New York City. He wandered the streets of New York, fascinated by the metropolis of 1894, and in the parks, on the Bowery, on the docks, and in the avenues he found a treasury of stories to be stored away in his hungry brain for future use.

The life of a panhandler in New York palled. He took the hobo trail again, north to Niagara Falls, and was arrested for vagrancy and sentenced to thirty days in the Erie County jail. He won the good will of the prison's trusties, was made a trusty himself, and so was at liberty to wander somewhat freely through the prison. He saw the brutality of prison life, saw inmates maddened by it, and saw men beaten to death. A philosophy not born of books was germinating in the eighteen-year-old boy.

On his release he hopped a freight into Canada. His hobo progress westward across Canada took several months. Reaching Vancouver, he shipped on the *Umatilla* as a sailor, bound for San Francisco. Again he sailed through the Golden Gate: he had traveled ten thousand miles since his determination to find education. Now the time was ripe. He entered Oakland High School at the age of nineteen. After a couple of semesters he left, disgruntled. He put in seventeen weeks of study and passed examinations admitting him to the University of California, two years ahead of his high school class.

College was disillusioning. He had traveled more and had seen more of life than any of the students and probably any of the professors he met. He had lived a mature life;

college was immature. At the end of one semester, he quit and turned to another great adventure.

The discovery of gold was reported from Alaska. In a week San Francisco returned to the gold-rush fever of 1849; it became the point of departure for the gold fields. London, wanting gold, but above all wanting adventure, wanting fuel for the stories and books he was determined to write, began to look for ways and means to reach the North. You couldn't ride rails to Alaska, nor, in the beginning, could you ship as sailor or able-bodied seaman on the few ships bound for the Alaska coast.

Through the years there had been one friend to whom Jack could turn in any emergency, his sister Eliza. He adored her; she idolized him and was his champion even during his days as an oyster pirate. She found money for him to buy passage north on the same *Umatilla* on which he had worked his way from Vancouver. The ship, loaded to the gunwales, arrived at Skagway and dumped its human cargo of gold seekers, gamblers, adventurers, and quasi-merchants on Dyea Beach.

The goal of the cavalcade was the dread Chilkoot Pass. The Alaskan Indians were charging forty and fifty cents a pound for portage over the pass. The Northwest Mounted Police were demanding that each prospector carry five hundred dollars in cash as well as one thousand pounds of food. Jack London landed in Skagway in April; the journey across the pass to Dawson had to be made before the northern winter set in. He bought a small boat and, with three newly made friends, made several trips to transport eight thousand pounds of supplies up the Dyea River. Adventure? Yes, here was adventure, adventure that was to inspire London's two great books of the north: *White Fang* and his immortal *The Call of the Wild*.

Rugged, cruel at times, *The Call of the Wild* is withal a work of art of sensitive beauty. London loved words, and in realism or in phantasy the beauty of his words is unforgettable. This book lives in its realism and its beauty of words and its tender humanity.

They reached the Chilkoot Pass. It rose before them, six miles of sheer rock, cliffs rising almost perpendicularly. Jack, leading the group, started the climb, one hundred and fifty pounds of provisions on his back, a climb so difficult that at times it was necessary to crawl on hands and knees; the passage of six miles took a full day. It took the group three months to move their supplies to the top of the pass.

They came to Lake Linderman and built two boats for the crossing, which London christened *Yukon Belle* and *Belle of the Yukon*. They reached the headwaters of the Yukon and found thousands of frightened men, afraid to attempt the passage of the White Horse Rapids, in whose treacherous waters so many had lost their lives. London decided to travel with the current rather than invite being crashed on the rocks by fighting it; they shot the rapids in one boat, returned overland and successfully brought the second boat through. The word of his success spread, and in the passing of a few days, he had earned three thousand dollars taking boat after boat through the White Horse. Winter closed in when they were still seventy-two miles from Dawson, so Jack and his companions dug in to await the coming of spring.

During that winter, snow- and icebound in a small cabin, Jack London met men who were to appear later in his books, all kind and manner of men, all with the love and the fever of gold in their veins. Into the cabin drifted Burning Daylight, Del Bishop, Malemute Kid, and other characters he was to immortalize.

When the long white winter ended, the logs from an old

cabin were lashed together to make a raft, and the four partners floated down river to Dawson. In June, Jack and two
companions embarked in a small boat and traveled nineteen
hundred miles down the Yukon and along the Bering Sea
to St. Michael's. From there, he worked his way as a coal
stoker to British Columbia, then by steerage to Seattle, and
riding the freights down the coast, he came back to Oakland.

He brought no gold, but his harvest had been rich and
rewarding: adventure, and the stories of adventure of the
men he had lived with, rough individuals like himself, some
dreamers, some scoundrels, some poets; he had learned to
know them and understand them.

While Jack had been north, John London, the foster
father, had died. Jack had loved the quiet, patient man
deeply, and felt his loss keenly. Meanwhile, the backwash
of the panic of 1893 had left the country in an apathy of
depression. Work was hard to find. He passed an examination for the United States Postal Service, and while he was
waiting for a call to work he found justification in living by
writing stories based on his experiences in the Yukon. He
wrote quantities, wrote swiftly, and mailed reams of manuscript to publishers.

Short of funds, at times short of food, and with the spark
of incentive dimming, he sent a story to the *Overland
Monthly*, the magazine that had been a San Francisco tradition for many years. They liked his story, "To the Man on
the Trail." They wanted to publish it, and they offered him
five dollars for the five thousand words. It was, of course, an
honor to appear in the magazine of which, in earlier years,
Bret Harte had been editor. It was, and I suppose still is,
assumed that creative artists can live on honor and glory.
Jack London mentally scratched his head.

662

That was in the morning. In the afternoon mail came a letter from *The Black Cat*, at that time one of the most popular and interesting small magazines on the American newsstands. The editors of *The Black Cat* liked Mr. London's story, "A Thousand Deaths," and were enclosing a check for forty dollars. Forty dollars for a two-thousand-word story! That was glory and honor and wealth. With forty dollars in his pocket he was an established writer.

In 1900 London married an Oakland school teacher, Bessie Maddern. A daughter was born. In 1902, at a time when he was deep in debt and Bessie was again pregnant, the American Press commissioned him to cover the Boer War. New adventure was tossed into his lap. He set sail, but on reaching England found that the assignment had been canceled. The British publishers, however, were pleased to lionize the young writer, but with his characteristic independence he spent the major part of three months in London slums. He lived in workhouses, stood in bread lines, slept in the parks and the streets; he came closer to abject, downtrodden humanity than before, and the misery of the slums kindled a new fire in him. Out of that dire experience he wrote his first major book, *The People of the Abyss*.

Then he set sail for San Francisco again, and on the journey home sold the manuscript to a New York publisher. He was twenty-seven years old. He had known sorrow and deep tragedy, excitement, adventure, and ecstasy; he had lived more in his twenty-seven years than a dozen men would live in a lifetime. He had seen and known hunger, had lived with the underdog and sorrowed for him, had known knaves and charlatans and leeches. It was a dismal broth out of which to brew a philosophy of life, a philosophy that he crystallized, with compassion and beauty and a rich love of life and a tolerant understanding of man's frailty, in a new masterpiece.

663

This was the story of the dog, Buck, in *The Call of the Wild*, the good and bad men he had known from the day he left the Santa Clara Valley and, in his dog's life, followed the trail Jack London had followed up the Brea River to the Klondike, and on to the night he answered the howling of the wolves in the country of the Yeehat tribe. For this novel London received a check for two thousand dollars.

During the summer of 1903, London became infatuated with Charmian Kittredge, somewhat surprisingly, since he had known her for several years. But now his feeling for her had suddenly become so intense that he separated from his wife, and the next year his wife divorced him on grounds of desertion.

Then came the year 1904 and the Russo-Japanese War. London sailed for Tokyo as war correspondent. He broke the rules governing the activities of correspondents, and antagonized the Japanese by going into restricted territories. Time and again he was jailed in Korea. Determined to reach Chemulpho, where the Japanese landed their troops, he bought a junk, hired three Koreans as crew, and set sail across the Yellow Sea.

There was hazard, and disaster threatened every minute. The thermometer read fourteen below. He reached Chemulpho with frozen hands, frozen feet, frozen ears, his body wasted to a shadow, but he wrote, "The wildest and most gorgeous thing ever!"

He pressed on to Pingyang, the most northerly point reached by any correspondent. There, at the instigation of correspondents who had been unable to keep up with him, he was jailed again. Then he was given permission to observe the war, forty miles behind the front. Court-martialed by a Japanese general for knocking down a Korean who had cheated him, London was threatened with execution. Richard Harding Davis cabled President Roosevelt, and Teddy, with the emphasis of the Big Stick, ordered the Japanese to release him. London turned his back on the Korean scene and returned to California.

He was now twenty-eight. Now he would settle down to a quiet life, live his remaining years peacefully, writing his books, letting the world find vicarious satisfaction in the reading of them. No more adventure for him. After all, he was a reasonable, peaceful man, and he knew when he had enough! The next year he bought a farm in Sonoma County. After all, there could be no more peaceful and humdrum existence than life on a farm. The Hill Ranch was one hundred thirty acres, later to grow to almost fifteen hundred, in the beautiful Valley of the Moon.

In November of 1905 he married Charmian Kittredge. They were ideally happy together. They adored each other and found perfect companionship in each other, for Charmian loved adventure with Jack's fearless zest.

A few years later Jack and Charmian London started out on what was to be their great adventure, a journey around the world that they intended to last for seven years.

Jack designed a forty-five-foot ketch, the *Snark*, the building of which cost thirty thousand dollars. He sailed out of the Golden Gate with Charmian and a crew on April 22, 1907, a year after the earthquake and fire. The ketch was captained by one Roscoe Eames, but it soon became apparent that Captain Eames knew nothing of navigation. It had a cook named Mr. Johnson, who knew nothing about cooking. "Mr. Johnson," incidentally, was Martin Johnson, later to become the famed African explorer. A Stanford University student was engineer, and a young Japanese was cabin boy. They sailed into the Pacific, no word came back from them and eventually the *Snark* was rumored lost. Jack London and his wife were mourned. People sadly shook their heads and said, "They were a great couple, but they were just too full of mad adventure."

Then, twenty-seven days after leaving San Francisco, the *Snark* rounded Diamond Head and into Honolulu. Jack had dug out navigation books, spent four hours of intensive study, and he and Charmian had navigated the ketch across the Pacific. They spent a week in the leper colony on Molokai, in daily contact with the victims of the disease. They sailed south to the Marquesas. Experienced navigators said it couldn't be done, that the equatorial currents and trade winds couldn't be weathered by a small boat.

For sixty days they saw no land and spoke no passing ship. They lost half their drinking water overboard, and were saved by a sudden rain. They reached Nuka-hiva in the Marquesas and pressed on to Tahiti, where London learned of circumstances at home that made it necessary to return to California.

They took passage to San Francisco on the steamship *Mariposa*, and after straightening out his affairs there, Jack and Charmian returned to Tahiti and the cruise of the *Snark* was resumed. It was a lazy-adventurous voyage. They sailed down through the Polynesians to Bora Bora, to Pago Pago, and to Suva in the Fijis. The services of the inefficient captain had long since been dispensed with and a more capable man signed on in his place, but at Suva the new captain deserted, and for the balance of the voyage Jack London was skipper of the *Snark*.

Thrown into frequent contact with disease, the diseases not only of the islanders but of his own crew, for whom he had to act as doctor, London contracted an unfamiliar ailment that no one could diagnose. He suffered excruciating pain, and at Charmian's insistence abandoned the cruise and boarded a steamer bound for Sydney, Australia, where adequate medical care could be provided. He entered a hospital in Sydney for five weeks of tests that left the doctors baffled. He remained there five months, fighting to regain his health, and finally and reluctantly returned to California. The cruise of the *Snark*, planned as a seven-year adventure, had ended when two years were passed. It was to be Jack London's last great adventure.

The last eight years of his life were spent largely in feverish writing, to try to write out all the wealth of thought and feeling that was in him, as well as to maintain a small army of dependents and workmen on his ranch. At the end, worn out with work, and in almost constant pain from uremic infection, he succumbed to an overdose of morphine sulphate, on November 22, 1916.

I am indebted to Charmian London, who has been a good friend to me, and to Mrs. Oliver Remick Grant for immeasurable help in correlating this outline of Jack London's adventures. He was a great adventurer, a lover of adventure. He was a writer, a great writer. Far beyond all of that, Jack London was a great friend of humanity: a fighter, rugged and fearless, for the rights of man and the decencies of life that were meant for men to enjoy. He was human, utterly human, and it was that fine sensitive humanity of his, and his compassion, that made his hand strong when he wrote of men and their affairs. He was a dreamer, of course he was a dreamer, all big men are dreamers. But he was a fighting and a realistic dreamer, a visionary who worked with strong tools to make realities of his visions. He had faith to the end, that faith that put into his lips in his closing days, the words: *I retain my belief in the nobility and excellence of the human. I believe that spiritual sweetness and unselfishness will conquer the gross gluttony of today. Always before my eyes everburning and blazing the Holy Grail, Christ's own Grail.*

XII

Arthur Putnam

It is reported that George Inness, the American landscape artist, once said, "I am the greatest artist in America, and the second greatest is William Keith of San Francisco." And William Keith of San Francisco said, "I am the greatest artist in America and the second greatest is George Inness of New York State."

This is worthy of note only because it shows that, while it is quite obvious that art should demand respect in New York, New York was also willing to recognize that there was art in San Francisco. New Yorkers visiting San Francisco could not escape the fact; at least, if art was not flamboyantly apparent, the presence of artists was. The downtown streets of San Francisco were colored with them; you saw them, you still see them, striding intently along Montgomery Street in the neighborhood of the city's longest enduring building, the Montgomery Block, affectionately called "The Monkey Block." You saw them going along, with canvases under their arms, wearing corduroy jackets, paint smeared; saw them hurrying along swinging a demijohn of red wine in one hand, a hunk of unwrapped salami or a loaf of French bread in the other. You saw them at tables at the Tour Eiffel in the old days, and at Steve Sanguinetti's, and Bigin's; you saw them earning the price of a dinner by painting pictures on the walls of Papa Coppa's. You found them perched on goat trails on Telegraph Hill, easel set up, a little tin of paints on their knee, and a canvas splashed with the blue of San Francisco Bay.

I knew them in the rat-ridden rooms of the Montgomery Block: Ralph Stackpole, the sculptor; Sid Bagshaw, who specialized in linoleum cuts; Kenneth Callahan, later the curator of the Seattle Museum of Art—in those days he owned one canvas; he would paint a portrait a day on it and at night cover the portrait with white paint so that it would be ready for another portrait the next day. There was Jimmy Swinnerton of "Little Jimmy" fame, and Maynard Dixon, both to win fame later as painters of the southwest desert. I have mentioned only half a dozen, they were there, and they still are there, by the hundreds, ever since the day in the early 1850's when one of them sat in the shadow of a Montgomery Street brick building and made uncomplimentary pencil likenesses of the passers-by. There were many who struggled to create an atmosphere of Paris bohemia; there were far more who scorned *la vie de Bohème* and honestly starved at their art. There was one, I remember him well, who graduated from Stanford University and who, upon being asked by a doting mother and an adoring grandmother what he wanted to be, said he wanted to be an artist. So they paid the rent of a room in the Montgomery Block, they gave him a modest ration of pocket money, and he took up residence. He had a fine easel and nicely primed canvases; he had a beautiful assortment of brushes and an enviable stock of good paints. He had a fine palette that he spread with a mess of gobs of many-colored paints. And he had a studio couch.

He bought a good phonograph and albums of good music; he bought a glass case some three feet long and a foot square. He filled the case with a variety of live snakes, and he spent his days lying on the studio couch, listening to good music, and watching his snakes. Once a month his doting mother and adoring grandmother visited him. The day before the visit, any one of the artists from down the hall would come in and sketch a portrait on the canvas that stood on the easel; then, on the day of the visit, the snake-fancying artist would sit before the easel adding meaningless gobs of good paint to the sketch; mother and grandmother lived happily from month to month in the joy of their artist. Yes, there was comedy as well as tragedy in the world of the artists that roamed the streets of San Francisco.

The story of Arthur Putnam is a San Francisco story of tragedy and of cruel comedy, a strange, unreasonable tragedy of a man who loved life and loved laughter, and whose laughter was great and boisterous and infectious. The tragic artist is a theme so commonplace, of course, that it hardly kindles sympathy or imagination. Painters, sculptors, even writers comprise that minority who, being too lazy to labor like normal mortals, must eat their bread without jam. Of course, bread can be palatable without jam, but when there's not even bread on which to put the nonexistent jam, then the situation becomes tragic.

Arthur Putnam was a sculptor, born by chance in Mississippi, in 1873. I say "by chance" advisedly; the Putnams were traveling in a westerly journey, and stopped in the small town of Waveland, Mississippi, so that their second son, Arthur, might be born into the grim struggle that was to be his life. Continuing the western passage by slow stages, the family finally arrived in San Francisco in 1880.

Before continuing with the story, I feel the need of explaining that I am not telling the saga of Arthur Putnam because it was tragedy, or comedy, or high drama, but because in my opinion, and in the opinion of some other people, Arthur Putnam was the greatest of all San Francisco artists, one of the greatest sculptors of our times; some have called him one of the greatest of all times. San Francisco has boasted many great artists, but few worthy of being called genius. Arthur Putnam, beyond question of a doubt, was a genius.

The Putnams were an old and a distinguished family. An ancestor had been in Salem, Massachusetts, in the middle of the seventeenth century. A Putnam fought in the French and Indian War, and another in the American Revolution. Arthur's father had been a lieutenant in the War Between the States. His mother was descended from John Hancock, a signer of the Declaration of Independence.

Mary Putnam was a strong, handsome woman, proud, regal, and of vital determination and unlimited courage. Her husband, no less a personality in his own right, a clear-thinking, high-principled man, died when Arthur was seven years old. The building of the strong character of the three children became the mother's task.

Looking back over the facts I have been able to gather about Arthur Putnam's life, I find, as I found the couple of times I met him when I was young, that same strength of character and purpose always dominant. It is freely assumed that artists, from San Francisco or any other place, should be gay bohemians, mixing art with artless pleasure, dining on French bread, salami, red wine, and enjoying careless love, and a colorful life while starving. There was nothing of the bohemian in Arthur Putnam; Putnam, the genius, was a laborer. That made the man no less interesting, no less wonderful. His life was devoted to his few friends, his family, and his art.

The first time I met him I was a juvenile pupil in the Mark Hopkins Institute of Art up on Nob Hill, in the galleries that had been the home, or rather the huge and rococo mansion, built by the wife of the railroad magnate Mark Hopkins. I was modeling the head of a lion in clay, using a plaster cast as model, when Putnam came into the classroom. He made the round of the class, passing from one modeling table to another, and stopped at mine, stopped, not because my work was good, but because I was doing the head of a lion.

"Hmm," he said. "Why are you doing a lion?"

I answered something to the effect that I liked lions because they were strong and everything. He said yes, I was right, but that he preferred modeling pumas. The lion was handsome, it was true, and was called the King of Beasts, but the other cats had more character and were also human in their attributes.

That was the gist of it. Years later, I saw his bronze pumas, sleek, wise, terrible, with their wonderfully co-ordinated muscles and their great and terrible power, and I understood. But that Saturday morning all I saw was a remarkably handsome man, in his twenties, just a teacher who liked to model animals, too.

He took my wooden knife. With a few swift slices, he made my lion come alive, and I took it home and cast it in plaster. It hung on my den wall all through my youth, then it went to the junk pile. But I would trade my most valuable material possession today to have that lion that Arthur Putnam had, with a few swift movements of his wonderful hands, imbued with life.

As a small child, he was fascinated by insects and field animals, and by the skeletons and bones of animals he found in the fields. With ruthless realism he cut up small creatures to see how they were made. There was no sense of cruelty in the act, at least not in the consciousness of the small boy; he had to know what made the creatures move, how their muscles and their joints functioned. Throughout his life, the things he learned were reflected in the beautiful perfection of the animals he cut from clay and stone. Everything he did led to something else; without awareness, he was always shaping his life to achieve ultimate perfection.

As though it were a grim mockery of fate, an incident occurred that probably was to shape his destiny. Before he had reached his teens, he fell out of a tree, striking his head on the pavement some forty feet below. The result was a severe concussion of the brain; he was unconscious for days, and his convalescence was long and miserable. Before the accident he had been a poor student, little interested in routine lessons; after it, he lost all interest in his studies; he was, bluntly, a problem child. And, no model of virtue, at the age of nine he smoked, chewed tobacco, and helped drive his teachers to an early grave. In desperation, his mother at great sacrifice entered him in a military academy, but in less than a year the head of the school requested that he be removed. The only bright hope in the letter of dismissal was the comment, "There is one thing Arthur is very fond of and in which he has a real interest; that is natural science. He takes to it instinctively; I sometimes think that by means of his love of nature he may be led to other and higher things."

There, then, is the rather bleak picture of the schoolboy, out of which we have to build a hero. It must be realized that he was not the demon the picture suggests; he was a lovable, highly imaginative youngster, affectionate, considerate, and happy, and he was adored by his friends, the boys and girls of his own age, and by adults. Even as an adolescent boy, he was exceedingly handsome, with great, bright eyes, a strong face, dense black hair, and an irresistible smile that would break into guffaws of laughter at a small provocation. Actually, in his boyhood Arthur Putnam was a problem to everybody but himself.

In her struggle to support her three children, Mrs. Putnam moved from place to place. There was a period when Arthur worked in a photoengraving shop; another, when he had a job in an iron foundry in New Orleans; and at eighteen he joined his mother on a ranch near San Diego, where she was trying to manage a lemon grove. When he was twenty, the gangling boy walked into the classroom of Miss Julie Heyneman, a San Francisco artist and teacher and a founding member of the Art Students' League; the school was on Columbus Avenue, a few doors from Montgomery Street in San Francisco. Arthur Putnam said that he wanted to take drawing lessons. Miss Heyneman asked if he had had lessons; he said no, he had been working on a ranch, but he did a lot of drawing. He produced some rough sketches in pen and ink of bucking, galloping rodeo horses. They were crude, and yet they were good, exceedingly good. There was motion in them. Miss Heyneman led him to a drawing board, handed him a piece of charcoal, which he had never used before, and told him to draw the plaster-cast model before him; then she walked away. Two minutes later he shouted across the classroom, "Say, I've done it!"

Miss Heyneman was a little annoyed; the lad had too much assurance. She returned to his drawing board, and knew then, according to her own statement, that she was in

675

the presence of genius. With rough swift strokes he had produced a charcoal sketch that lived. She studied the drawing and demanded, "How long do you expect to stay in San Francisco?" He answered, "As long as my money holds out; I've saved thirty dollars."

Thus Arthur Putnam became an art student. He moved into the quarters of the Art Students' League, sleeping on a couch in the studio and paying for his lodging by sweeping the place. It was 1894, the year of the Midwinter Fair in Golden Gate Park; the city was active, perhaps he could find work to support his drawing and his modeling, for it soon became evident to Putnam, as to his friends, that he excelled as a sculptor. Well, he could find clay for modeling, even stone for chiseling. But money? No! So he went to work in a slaughterhouse in Butchertown, out in the Potrero.

He was apparently happy in his art, and satisfied to work in the slaughterhouse. But he was eating scant meals, growing gaunt, emaciated, hollow-eyed, so he drifted back to the ranch in San Diego. He found an opportunity to do some teaching in a San Diego art school, and there he fell in love.

Grace Storey was a girl whose life had, in a manner, paralleled his own. She loved art and loved to paint. She was born of a wealthy, distinguished family. They had become land poor, and Grace had to earn her own living.

They adored each other, and worked together with a mutual and wonderful understanding. They were married in 1899 and moved to Lincoln, a small town in central California near Sacramento, where Gladding McBean and Company had a terra cotta works. Arthur Putnam found work, mechanical work, fashioning molds for the factory products, but it was only mechanical work, and he was always driven by the urge to find work that would let him exercise his

676

creative genius. A short tenure in the terra cotta factory, and they drifted back to San Francisco; or rather, he left Grace with an aunt across the bay in Berkeley while he sought lodgings in San Francisco.

He found them in a small French hotel on Columbus Avenue, the same hotel where Robert Louis Stevenson had lived before he went to Samoa. Then Putnam crossed the bay and returned with his wife. They carried all their worldly possessions in bundles on their backs. Standing at the rail of the ferryboat, watching the beautiful hills of San Francisco rising before them, they dug their hands into their pockets to find out how much cash they had with which to commence their new life. Grace had nothing; Arthur had a five-cent piece. That wouldn't take them far, so he tossed it into the air as an offering to the gods of luck, and watched a sea gull swoop down as the coin hit the water.

Looking back at those years, one realizes that much of their suffering was needless. Arthur Putnam's great art was quickly recognized by a few, and he sold some small figures and figurines; but he was never willing to turn his art into a business, nor would he accept financial help, at least not without giving value received.

He was proud and stubborn, and he and his wife starved. Not that it mattered a great deal to them; their love was so fine, so wonderful, so nearly complete in itself that such mundane things as food and decent clothing became relatively unimportant. Meanwhile his friends pleaded to let them help him, and he growled, and cursed vociferously; he loved to curse loud and long and beautifully, in anger or simply in an exuberance of the joy of living. He'd take no help from any man.

His friends pleaded, and shook their heads. There was

677

the beloved San Franciscan, Bruce Porter; there was the most popular of San Francisco artists and art teachers, little Signor Piazzoni; there was the society matron, Mrs. William Crocker, one of the kindest of benefactors; and in San Diego there was the man who did help him keep alive during this early period by giving him constant assignments, the millionaire newspaperman, E. W. Scripps.

To satisfy his creative urge, Putnam modeled wonderful groups of wild animals. To earn his bread-without-jam he designed bronze door knockers, mortuary sculpture for graveyards, and architectural decorations for many San Francisco buildings, thanks to the commissions of the architect Willis Polk. He loved San Francisco, loved to wander the streets of the city, and abominated the atrocious taste that inspired so many of the overstuffed, overdecorated, overcarved, and overturreted buildings, particularly the homes that had been raised by the gold and silver of the Comstock and by the millionaires of the 'seventies, 'eighties, and 'nineties. He loved San Francisco and the streets of the city, but he was becoming restive.

Finally, at the insistence of his friends, he accepted one hundred dollars a month from Mrs. William Crocker, for which he insisted he would complete a series of bronze figures for her. Then he would go to Europe.

He went to Rome and Paris with his wife, Grace, and with Signor and Signora Piazzoni. All artists sooner or later went to Paris, some for the flavor of bohemia, some to learn the new trends and tendencies in art.

He discovered Paris with delight, and slightly to his own amazement, slightly, I say, because at no time was Arthur Putnam uncertain about the quality of his own work, Paris discovered him, lionized him, acclaimed him as a master, but

678

he found himself in a strange and an artificial world; he was restless and physically ill. Even with Paris at his feet, he craved the hills of San Francisco and missed the friends he loved in California. Too, there was the constant urge to drive himself, always pressing, pressing, as though a premonition of impending evil was warning him that he would have to hurry if he was to have time to create the things he had to create.

Grace and Arthur Putnam returned to Columbus Avenue in the shade of Telegraph Hill. They had been in Europe a year and a half, and during that period Arthur Putnam achieved the full flowering of his creative power. He was a giant in art, acclaimed by the aesthetic world, but he was a sick and confused man. They came back to San Francisco, and the turning point.

He was sitting at his modeling block, pressing life into the wet clay that was a snarling, hunch-backed puma. He worked swiftly, surely; his fingers and his modeling knife worked with the clean, sure precision of a master surgeon. Then he frowned and stopped. The tool fell from his fingers and cut a gash in the haunch of the puma. His left thumb was numb; he rubbed it to bring warmth, but it was cold and numb. Another day, and his left hand refused to function. It was like a paralysis. Then the paralysis disappeared for a time. The cold and the numbness were gone, but some of the sureness and magnificent power had gone out of his creative hands. Oh, it was probably only a passing phase, but somewhere in his consciousness was a vague memory of a bad fall when he was a child, a fall that had resulted in brain concussion. It was probably only a passing phase, but his fine hands had grown clumsy.

Finally the seriousness of his condition could no longer

be shrugged aside; the paralysis was no longer intermittent, but permanent. A brain operation, in October 1911, disclosed a tumor, which required such extensive cutting that his left arm and leg were almost useless afterward, and he suffered severe seizures. He could never again sketch or model the magnificent animals that had brought him fame. He was, indeed, not the same man. The operation, though necessary, had permanently changed the Jekyll of the artist into a Mr. Hyde.

Uncontrolled bitterness drove a wedge into his fiber and his soul. He turned against his friends. The only one left, always faithful, always ready to laugh with him, weep with him, triumph with him, and starve with him, was his wife. He developed a persecution complex; strangers, friends, even his wife were included in the nightmare world of ghosts conspiring to ruin him.

He became unkempt in his person. His eyes became hollow, like the eyes of a madman. He flung himself into blind, horrible rages. He shrieked, thundered at the world; then shrieked and thundered at Grace. Afterward, abject, he would come crawling for forgiveness, and a ghost of the old Arthur Putnam would reappear, reappear until he tried to model a crouching puma or a leaping cat, only to find the power gone, the physical and mental paralysis still upon him. Finally, to protect her own life from his blind, frenzied, brutal rages, Grace was compelled at the determined instance of Putnam's closest friends, to get a divorce. His world now had utterly crashed about him.

Oh, it wasn't the end, yet. He was to live for another nineteen years, the last nine of them in Paris. He married again, and he knew periods of prosperity from sales of his past works. He became an alcoholic; he lost his fastidious instincts; there was nothing left but the wasted shell. At times he sat before his modeling board, and cut great hunks of clay and saw a semblance of the beautifully real, life-breathing wild animals emerge. Then the truth would crash upon him: this was no art, this was a feeble imitation of the art that had been his; and in another blind rage he dumped the clay upon the floor, and trampled upon it. A madman, yes, in all but the final judgment he had become a madman, but there was still the wisdom to tell him that his art was dead.

Meanwhile the fame of the earlier Arthur Putnam spread through the world of art. Here, in San Francisco, his wonderful bronzes were to be seen in the Palace of the Legion of Honor, in the Bohemian Club, and in the architectural decoration of the city's more imposing buildings. His bronzes were exhibited in more than one Paris Salon, in London, and in many of the important galleries of Europe. They were purchased by the New York Metropolitan Museum of Art, and from the heights of glory to the depths of absurdity, his work was found, in plaster, decorating the front of a dance-hall on the old Barbary Coast.

A beautiful, bronze drinking fountain, an animal group, was placed inside the Geary Street entrance of the St. Francis Hotel. In the Bank of California, two of his superb pumas still frame the clock above the vault. Several pieces decorate the Crocker First National Bank, and even the electric-light standards on Market Street carry the magic touch of his hand. In the lobby of the Bohemian Club stands his wonderful "Primitive Man." These are only a scant few of the countless masterpieces that brought him world fame.

I remember walking through the galleries and courts of the Panama-Pacific International Exposition in 1915 and coming on his "Puma and Snake." I believed I could see the pulsing of the flesh of the puma. And though the signs said PLEASE DO NOT TOUCH THE EXHIBITS, I laid my fingers on the puma's shoulder, and seemed to feel the pulsing of living flesh.

Arthur Putnam died in Paris on May 27, 1930. There had been a brief period when he had felt his strength returning; perhaps there was to be a rebirth of the power he loved. He made great plans, he flexed his fingers to show the strength that still was in them. Now that bread-with-jam meant little to him, his bronzes were selling, and financial prosperity had arrived. But that meant nothing. Just let him get his hands into the clay again and out of that crude, wet earth create beauty that would, perhaps, even please the God in His Heavens. He reached for his modeling knife, and died, the greatest of San Francisco's artists.

XIII

Sol Bloom

Through the many years that I have been interested in San Francisco personalities, I have heard many fabulous stories about Sol Bloom. I heard my parents speak of him often, usually as just another of the men who lived, or had lived, in San Francisco; they knew him personally, and one does not as a general thing overrate or even give full credit to a person whom one knows in the everyday routine of life. Later, seeing him from a remote point of vantage, I knew him to be a great man, and as is always the case with great and powerful men, I heard many stories of his vision and his power and his usefulness in the world, and I heard his enemies malign and disparage and anathematize him. I was to discover, with the passing of time, that his most vitriolic critic was himself.

I remember one of the more feeble of my father's favorite jokes. He liked to say to me, "You know, you were born in 1889, and that year Sol Bloom left San Francisco." I wasn't sure what the inference was supposed to be, but I later decided that if my birth was responsible for Sol Bloom's leaving, then I had made my contribution to humanity, for the day he left San Francisco he started on his road to greatnesss.

I never saw him when I was young, but because he was a

powerful man and a great man, I had pictured him as a physical giant. Then, I met him one afternoon in May of 1945, in my official capacity as a producer in the studios of KNBC, the "owned and operated" radio station of the National Broadcasting Company in San Francisco. The occasion was a round-table forum of United States members of the committee to prepare a charter for the United Nations.

It was a distinguished group gathered before the microphones that afternoon, and what they had to say as a group made no impression on me; they were simply a gathering of statesmen, or politicians if you will. There was Stettinius, large, handsome, and white-haired but youthful; there was Tom Connally, huge and portly, the perfect picture of a traditional United States senator; there was Harold Stassen, dynamic, aggressive, and very positive. But the man who made the lasting impression on me was the little, wiry, dapper man with the large mouth, the keen, wide-spaced eyes, and the high, bald forehead. He sat in a corner of the studio, twiddling the nose glasses that dangled from the black silk ribbon around his neck.

That was a thrilling, unforgettable few weeks in San Francisco; those weeks that saw the shaping of the United Nations and the ending of the Second World War. The streets of San Francisco were a pageant of dignitaries, and of nonentities trying to look dignified; there was the traditional dress of China, of Egypt, of Arabia and Persia. There were statesmen from London and Paris and Moscow. There was Mr. Molotov, very benign, and courteous and amenable to suggestion; there was the fabulous General Smuts from South Africa. There were men of all colors and creeds and beliefs, to all intent come together with one purpose; and while they mapped their campaigns they wandered the streets of the city, crowded the hotel lobbies, and wined and dined in the city's colorful restaurants. Cosmopolitan San Francisco had never been so cosmopolitan.

In the studio I sat down by Sol Bloom for a moment, and said, "It's thrilling, isn't it?"

He sighed, almost with a catch of his breath, and answered, "San Francisco is always thrilling."

I hurried to say, "I don't mean San Francisco. I mean the way things are working out."

He nodded, and said, "Yes, I hope so. But now I'm thinking about San Francisco."

His precise words have not remained with me, but the gist of what he said was that he had traveled all round the world; he had been almost everywhere and seen almost everything. He hadn't visited San Francisco for fifty years, but coming back to it meant coming home; no place in the world had the warmth and the thrill for him that he found when he climbed up and down the hills of San Francisco.

It reads like a Horatio Alger story, this story of the congressman from New York, the man who fought to put over the United Nations Relief and Rehabilitation Administration, the UNRRA; the man who was the chosen friend of presidents and foreign rulers; the man who had infinite compassion for the suffering of underdog humanity. It's a story to fill a book, and my telling of it is only a brief outline.

Sol Bloom was the son of orthodox Jewish parents, and that may account for that compassion, that sympathy and understanding of the tragedy of humanity, born of a people that has suffered. It's perhaps best summed up in his own words during the conference in San Francisco.

"Here I was," he wrote in his autobiography, "about to sit

in conference with foreign ministers and ambassadors speaking a score of tongues. Here I was, preparing to add my voice to those of men like Halifax of Great Britain, Koo of China, Smuts of South Africa, Molotov of the Soviet Union, Paul Boncour of France, Mackenzie King of Canada, Loudon of the Netherlands, and Masaryk of Czechoslovakia. Yes, here I was, commissioned to help write a charter for the United Nations. No! It couldn't be! Why, I was nothing but the child of penniless immigrants who had come from Poland. It was preposterous! Why, I was just the ignorant runt who had quit school forever after one day because I lacked money to buy a single book.

"This must all be a dream! I was only the kid who washed windows and swept floors and ran errands in a brush factory down there on Sacramento Street. I was only the little Jewish boy who peddled violets on Market Street near Lotta's Fountain."

I don't think I will ever forget those words. They are very disarming in their simplicity, but they crystallize, far better than a professional writer could do, the meaning of America, both to the immigrant and to the American-born child, no matter what his social or economic status might be. I like to put those words on one side of the ledger, and balance them against the unending propagandizing by people of some other lands against the social and political structure of free countries.

When Sol Bloom, the youngest of six children, was four years old, his parents migrated from Peoria, Illinois, to San Francisco. They arrived, practically destitute, and found a little house available on Brannan Street near Seventh. Mother Bloom swept the place clean, and then set up a "charity box." Into it went pennies, pennies stolen from family needs, to go to the aid of those less fortunate. Sol Bloom said, "We never were so poor that we needed its contents for ourselves."

When he was six years old he started school, but, as he has said, because he didn't have money to buy a required book his schooling lasted one day. It was true that books could be obtained free by those too poor to buy them, but giving charity was one thing, accepting it was another. So the new pupil ran home, and his school days were ended. He went to work, selling newspapers on the San Francisco streets, and at night his mother taught him to write, and to read, and to read with discrimination. The days on the streets as a newsboy lasted for a year.

The next year he found his first real job as a salaried employee. When Bloom, senior, had no steady work, he made a stop-gap living by peddling brushes, chamois, and sponges for the Filger Brothers of 615 Sacramento Street, and young Sol found employment there. He swept floors, washed windows, ran errands, helped pack merchandise, and was handy boy around the place. His day started at six in the morning, and ended at six at night. His pay was one dollar and twenty-five cents a week.

That job itself was a twelve-hour day, but his day wasn't finished. It was a fifteen-block walk home to Brannan Street and supper, and then he headed back to the throbbing heart of the city. There, in the shadow of Lotta's Fountain, he peddled his California violets. Compared with the brush and sponge business, this was an exciting enterprise; it was thrilling to stand there and see the parade of life passing by. The streets of San Francisco were a theatrical pageant to the boy who, though not yet conscious of it, had the instincts of an actor and would find his greatest joy in life in the theater.

There were all kinds of people, fascinating people, tragic

687

people, gay laughing people, misshapen derelicts, and silk-hatted millionaires from the Palace Hotel across the street. It was like having an orchestra seat in the theater; the streets of the city were the stage, and the people who passed were the actors, garbed in every conceivable costume, living every conceivable emotion. Young Sol Bloom had become a San Franciscan, and as all San Franciscans loved the theater, so did the small wiry youngster.

He loved it so much that he would add to the distance in his walk home to Brannan Street, just to turn up Bush Street, past Bill Ralston's California Theater, and the others in the neighborhood; the heart of the theater world was Bush Street. Then, from Bush, he'd swing down to Market Street to go past the irresistible fascination of Lucky Baldwin's theater, on Market near Fifth.

He was walking there, one night, savoring the vicarious thrill of footlights and grease paint, stage silks and satins and of musicians tuning up their instruments. He stood and stared into the lighted wonderland and a voice called to him from the foyer. Did he want a job? There was a part open that night; he would have no lines to speak, he would just appear on the stage twice, once only as a shadow. But the part was his if he wanted it!

He recognized the owner of the voice; he was the son of a poor family who lived near the Bloom home on Brannan Street, and he worked as callboy at the Baldwin Theater. His name was David Belasco.

That was Sol Bloom's debut. For half a dozen years he found jobs at the Baldwin, at the Grand Opera House on Mission Street, the California, the Bush Street theater, and the Standard. He didn't care what the job was, didn't care how little it paid; he couldn't resist the blood-warming call of the footlights. On rare occasions he was given a walk-on part; more often he checked hats, or sold candy in the aisles, or ushered. But it was all a part of the theater, and, not entirely incidentally, he was making money.

He profited, for example, by an episode in the Irish comedy-drama, *Kerry Gow*, which had an Irish blacksmith as hero. There was a scene in the smithy, with blacksmith Joe Murphy beating out a horseshoe on the anvil. The Irish sons of San Francisco loved the scene; loved it so much that one night one of them shouted that he had to have the horseshoe Murphy had just heated to flaming red and beaten into form.

"I'll get it for you," said the young eager-beaver Bloom.

He raced backstage, returned with the horseshoe, and received fifty cents for his trouble. The next night he appeared on the sidewalk when the audience was filing out, the horseshoe of that night clutched in his fist, and it took no time for an enthusiast to offer him fifty cents for it. That was the beginning.

The following day Sol bought a small keg of horseshoes from a smithy, and rolled the keg to the theater, and, night after night thereafter, he would locate sentimental Irishmen who wanted the very shoe that Joe Murphy had beaten out on his anvil, and out of the keg would come another shoe from the boy's private stock. He sold hundreds of "original" Joe Murphy horseshoes before Joe retired.

Then there were theater patrons who had forgotten their handkerchiefs. So Sol Bloom carried a side line of handkerchiefs, shoelaces for gentlemen who had broken a lace, and collar buttons for gentlemen who had lost their collarbuttons.

Sol Bloom laughed when, long later, he told about those years. He had, in his own words, become a walking department store. But there was bigger game in the theater, and the department store became a side line. He sold free programs. He scalped tickets. He supplied claques.

He was busy every minute. Now his day was divided into three sections: twelve hours for the broom factory, the early evening hours for selling violets, and the remainder of the evening for theater business. But there had to be some use made of the hours after the last theater curtain had fallen, so he worked after midnight for two young San Franciscans who owned a newspaper that had started as a theatrical sheet. His job was to fold the papers as they came off the press. The young publishers were Michel and Charles de Young, the paper was the San Francisco *Chronicle*.

When Sol Bloom was fifteen years old he quit his job at the broom factory, with the blessing of the Filger Brothers. He had a new job. Michel de Young was theater struck, too. He built a theater and called it the Alcazar, and the fifteen-year-old Bloom boy was given the job of running the box office, bookkeeping, paying the cast and running costs, and generally doing everything that the immortal Figaro had been called upon to do in his time. De Young was willing to pay for services rendered, and he knew the caliber of the boy he had hired. Sol started at fifty dollars a week, a salary not to be scorned by a boy of fifteen today; in the 1880's it was a fortune.

He stepped out, he became a gentleman of fashion. His barber plastered two spit curls on his forehead, on either side of the part down the middle. He had his nails manicured, his shoes shined for a nickel.

He was respected by his employers, and respected by the men, years older than himself, with whom his work brought him in contact. He was a familiar figure in the theater district, a wiry little fellow, bursting with energy, flushed with enthusiasm. He was still in his teens; he was ambitious, and he was swept along by the joy of life in San Francisco and in the San Francisco theater to a degree that made eating and sleeping only a necessary brief interruption in the daily routine. Opportunities were dumped in his lap, and with amazing acumen he made use of every opportunity; a boy in years, he was developing the stature of a tycoon.

When Sol Bloom was seventeen years old his income was between fifteen and twenty thousand dollars a year. He kept no books, he never was sure just how much he was earning, but he did know that when he was eighteen he had twenty-five thousand dollars in gold. He was constantly on the lookout for new ventures. Again he found a side line: he went on the road selling medicated window screens, guaranteed to keep flies and insects out of the house.

Then the De Young brothers, recognizing the genius of the boy, let him come in on a deal with them. They were buying land in southern California, near the village of Los Angeles. Of course there was no future in Los Angeles real estate. For about ten thousand dollars the partners bought some eighty thousand lots, and, over a brief period, gave away a lot with every ticket purchased for a seat in the Alcazar Theater. Oh, it built up business wonderfully. But the lots had to be recorded, and the partners opened an office where property recording would be handled at two dollars and fifty cents a lot, one half of the amount to go to the Recorder of Deeds, the remainder to be credited to the office: Sol Bloom was in charge. Then when he was nineteen years old Sol went to Michel de Young and told him he was quitting. He had made eighty thousand dollars. He was going to stop work and see the world.

That, to all intents, ended the San Francisco story of Sol Bloom; it was only the beginning of a life of amazing activities. He saw the world. Paris fascinated him, and it was at the Paris International Exposition of 1889 that his imagination was rekindled by the exotic Algerian Village; he was so fascinated that he bought, for about one thousand dollars, the rights to bring the Algerian Village to the United States. Plans were made, the complicated journey was begun, and after some accidents and setbacks and suffering for the group, intrigue with diplomats and immigration officers, and obstacles that, although minor, seemed insurmountable, he finally brought them to the Chicago World's Fair, exhibited them, and made more money.

But one comparatively small project was never enough for Sol Bloom; he managed his Algerian Village, he promoted prize fights, and his bank balance mounted. His activities brought him in contact and good favor with Chicago politicians, and his world widened. The political prize ring was fascinating to him. Its possibilites were tremendous. He loved it, but at the same time his multiple-faceted mind was constantly on the alert. On the Midway he saw Little Egypt dance her famous dance; that, in his lexicon, was good show business. So he wrote a song for Little Egypt, the song that the world has remembered ever since as "The Streets of Cairo."

On the surface, that appears a small and an unimportant thing, the writing of a successful side-show song, but it opened a new field for Sol Bloom, catapulted him into the music business as a song writer, a song plugger, and eventually representative of the important publishers of popular songs, M. Whitmark and Company. The next step was obvious; it worked out as all Sol Bloom's projects worked out. He became the head of the entire Whitmark organization.

By now, Bloom's activities were becoming so ramified that it is impossible to keep up with them. He was a rich man, still in his twenties. And during this Chicago period he fell in love, and was married to the girl who was to be his devoted partner to the day of her death, some thirty-three years later. When she died, the joy went out of life for Sol Bloom, for the inner, the personal man, the man of the home, who adored his family in the traditions of his people.

The other man, the man who loved the world and the theatrical pageant, that man had become a servant of men. A little tired, yes! After all, he was almost eighty years old. But the world that he loved was at war; mankind was suffering and badly hurt. And so Sol Bloom, congressman from New York, threw himself into the work of relief and rehabilitation; he was the inspiration of UNRRA.

He had worked under President Harding, under Coolidge, Hoover, and then Franklin Roosevelt, and they all called him their friend. For he still made friends, even though he had become a little more withdrawn, a little more shy, a little more the introvert than he had been as a young man.

That was the man who sat with me in the radio studio in those hectic days of 1945, delegate to the United Nations Conference; the man who said that coming back to San Francisco meant coming home.

Added to his compassion and his gratitude, a quality of humbleness had come into Sol Bloom's last years. He said, "This must all be a dream! I was only the kid who washed windows and swept floors and ran errands in a brush factory down there on Sacramento Street. I was only the little Jewish boy who peddled violets on Market Street near Lotta's Fountain."

XIV

The Streets of San Francisco

In my infancy, instead of a silver spoon, I was given a god-father. It was, to all intents, a very unimportant event, the acquisition of my godfather. He was a roaring, blustering little man, slender, hard as iron, and, to my young eyes, always very old. I was always afraid of him; I am quite sure I never felt any affection for him, but with the passing of years I have learned to feel gratitude for the only occasion in my memory when I came in close contact with him.

I was probably eight years old. One morning the telephone rang, and my mother took the receiver off its hook on the wall, and shouted into it (everybody seemed to think it was necessary to shout into the telephone in those days), and then paused, and then she said, "Very well!" and hung the receiver back on the hook. She turned to me and said, "Your godfather is going to take you for a walk."

If she had said "Your godfather is going to take you on a space-ship to Mars" I'd have been no more surprised, and no more frightened. I duly reported to my godfather, and we began our walk.

He was a little man but he took huge strides, and I clattered after him with little steps, determined to keep up. We walked over Jackson Street from Scott, and toward the bay. We climbed Russian Hill, and at the top of it he stood and

694

looked at the city, and grunted. We did no talking. We followed a goat trail down the eastern slope of Russian Hill and marched into the Chinatown of the 1890's. My godfather grunted again, ignoring me, and we walked the length of Chinatown to the foot of Telegraph Hill. We climbed Telegraph Hill, and stood on the top, and the city was spread below us and the bay before us. My godfather grunted and I looked at him and there were tears in his eyes. I asked, "What's the matter?" and he said, "It's the wind. It makes my eyes water."

We descended the eastern slope of Telegraph Hill and came to the Embarcadero. Long wharves ran out into the bay, wooden wharves, most of them uncovered. The smell of it has remained with me for almost sixty years: the smell of hemp rope and tar and of bananas. We walked out to the end of a wharf and sat down, and dangled our feet over the edge of the wharf, and he chewed on the rhinoceros horn cane he carried. I still have that cane.

I'd seen many ships before, but always from the hilltops, the Pacific Avenue hill and the Fillmore Street hill, and from our windows on Scott Street, through which we could see the ships sailing or steaming through the Golden Gate. But here they were, close enough to touch: wooden ships, steel ships, sailing ships and steamers and ferry boats, and small red tugs and pilot boats. They creaked, and wheezed, and piped, and there was the screeching of winches and the whining of tackle.

There were roustabouts around, shouting words that I had been warned never to use. I winced, but the words seemed to make no impression on my godfather. He sat, with his hands clasped on the top of his cane and his chin resting on the back of his hands. Finally he spoke.

"There's nothing like it."

I said, "What?"

And he turned on me and roared, "Nothing! I wasn't talking to you."

Then we went home, rode home in a dilapidated water-front carriage, drawn by a dilapidated horse, and driven by a dilapidated cabby who wore a silk stovepipe hat. We drove along Montgomery Street and my godfather volunteered the information that this was where San Francisco had its beginnings; we drove up the California Street hill past the mansions of the Comstock and the railroad millionaires; we came to Polk Street and my godfather pointed with his cane to a wooden building with a dentist sign in the window and said, "A man named Frank Norris wrote a book about that place." He told the cabby to wait, and took me across the street to Lechten's French pastry shop and bought me a bag of macaroons, and we went home. I have had a penchant for macaroons ever since.

That was my introduction to the streets of San Francisco. I don't know if my godfather realized that he was planting a seed in me; I was unaware of it myself, at the time. But the seed was planted, and ever since I have tramped the streets of San Francisco, and have watched the city changing. I have climbed its desolate hills when earthquake and fire had turned it into rubble. I have climbed the hills at night to see the pageant of lights dancing in the gray of the fog. I have, in my maturing youth, wandered alone into Chinatown, in the small hours of the morning, and found vicarious thrill in its odors and sounds and mystery. I have drunk red wine in the Italian restaurants that clustered about the foot of Telegraph Hill, and I have sat in Portsmouth Square on the grass before the small statue of the ship, raised in memory of

696

Robert Louis Stevenson, where he sat on the grass in his hungry days. I have wandered into Gump's, to touch stone carvings brought from Cambodia and Angkor Wat, carvings nine centuries old. I have leaned against the railing of a pier jutting out from Fisherman's Wharf and, at three o'clock in the morning, seen the great fleet of blue-hulled, white-sailed fishing boats put out to sea. I have watched cowboys driving herd in Butchertown, and I have found my way, time and again, past the flophouses of Skid Row, and wandered into the alley called Thieves' Alley, where most of the inmates are one-legged panhandlers. I have haunted the streets that run into Powell Street, the streets of the theaters in the days of John Drew and Otis Skinner and Minnie Maddern Fiske and Sothern and Marlowe and Maude Adams and Richard Mansfield and William Crane and Henry Miller and Nat Goodwin and Sarah Bernhardt and Holbrook Blinn. I have known the streets of the Tenderloin through three wars, and the Barbary Coast in its heyday and in its synthetic revival. I have danced in dives that were sinks of pale iniquity, and I have danced at the Palace Hotel.

I danced, one night at the Palace Hotel, at a debutantes' cotillion. It was in the palmy days when debutantes' cotillions were affairs of important dignity almost approaching solemnity. There was one small girl I had not known before. I danced almost every dance with her, and between dances I talked about my immortal soul, and what was the meaning of life, and where were we going, and why. We ate terrapin and we drank champagne, and I took her home at three o'clock in the morning.

Before leaving her, I asked if she liked to walk, and she said yes, and I asked if she would like to go for a walk that morning; remember, it was now three o'clock. She said yes again. I left then, and called for her at eight o'clock.

I rushed her across the city. I rushed her up hills and down hills. I rushed her across Market Street, and rushed her up Twin Peaks. From the top of Twin Peaks the whole world that was the city was spilled gloriously at our feet. I told her about the streets of San Francisco, and I rushed her down the hill, always two or three steps ahead of her. I rushed her across the city, and rushed her up Pacific Heights, and left her at her front door.

She went into the dining room, where her parents were at dinner. They said, "Did you have a good time?" And she said, "Yes, but I couldn't stand much of that."

We were married for fifty years.

Acknowledgments

It is customary, when writing a book of this kind, to give thanks to those individuals and those sources that have helped in the research and fine-combed the material for inaccuracies, but where to begin?

My publishers asked me how I knew that Tetrazzini said, "The streets of San Francisco are free." Well, I have been writing these stories of San Francisco once a week for the fourteen years that they have been heard over radio KNBC in San Francisco. That means something over two and a half million words about San Francisco and San Franciscans and a properly cross-indexed file of sources would have been a major undertaking. But on second thought, I do know where I found the Tetrazzini quote; it was in the San Francisco *Chronicle*.

I should acknowledge material received from my father; there were some stories he told me when I was a young boy, and he'd repeat them year after year, some of them right up to the year of his death. He'd say, "Did I ever tell you the story of So-and-So?" And I'd say, "Yes." And he'd say, "Well, it'll bear repeating." And he'd tell it again with embellishments. It was the embellishments I was always afraid of; like Tartarin of Tarascon, after a while I believed them.

My friend, Norman Green at the Mechanics Library, has with a bored expression put vast quantities of good material at my disposal. And the public libraries have been gracious in their help. Then there have been the books on California written by the fine California authors who have done a far better work of research than I am capable of; it's impossible to name them all, but to them my thanks and appreciation.

These have been stories of men and women who have been coming to San Francisco over the past hundred years in quest of the gold of adventure and the gold of the earth and the gold of culture. As I have said, they have been selected from the series broadcast over Radio KNBC in San Francisco every Sunday morning, and currently sponsored by the Rickey Restaurants and Hotel.

The pessimist tells us that the day of adventure and the day of opportunity are gone, and John Rickey is only one of the scores who refute that tired platitude: they still come to the Golden Gate, men and women in quest of adventure and culture and opportunity, and tomorrow's historian will include them with the men and women of yesterday who have built the West. In a dozen short years he has made his enterprises famous, and for that we appreciate him. But more than that is his appreciation. He came from the Old World to find opportunity and adventure and culture; he found rich welcome, and peace, and a deep and abiding love for San Francisco.

Finally, my thanks for a life that has permitted me to be a San Franciscan for not far from seventy years; to have learned to love its beauties and its oddities, its sunshine and its fogs, it full-lived men and women, and the irresistible fascination of its streets.

Index

706